Contents

List of colour plates   *page*   vii

Acknowledgments   ix

Glossary   xi

Introduction by ROBERT FOSSIER   1

Part 1 Break-up of the old worlds: 395–700   15

1   Autopsy of the West: the early fifth century   17
    MICHEL ROUCHE

2   Break-up and metamorphosis of the West: fifth to seventh   52
    centuries
    MICHEL ROUCHE

3   Prologue to a history of the East: early fifth century   104
    EVELYNE PATLAGEAN

4   The empire in its glory: mid-fifth to mid-seventh centuries   148
    EVELYNE PATLAGEAN

Part 2 The building of new worlds in the East: seventh to tenth   179
centuries

5   From the Hegiran model to the Arab kingdom: seventh to mid-   181
    eighth centuries
    HENRI BRESC and PIERRE GUICHARD

6   The world of the Abbasids, 'apogee' of Islam   223
    HENRI BRESC and PIERRE GUICHARD

Contents

7 A new Byzantium in the making? Mid-seventh to mid-ninth   281
   centuries
   EVELYNE PATLAGEAN

8 The renaissance in the East: mid-ninth to mid-tenth centuries   336
   EVELYNE PATLAGEAN

Part 3 The first stirrings of Europe: seventh to mid-tenth centuries   379

9 Barbarian kingdoms, Christian empire or independent   381
   principalities?
   MICHEL ROUCHE

10 The Carolingian 'renewal'   416
    MICHEL ROUCHE

11 Europe accumulates its first gains: sixth to ninth centuries 474
    MICHEL ROUCHE

   Bibliography   530
   Index   541

Colour plates

Between pages 72 and 73

Irish metalwork. Bronze plaque of the Crucifixion, tenth century. Clonmacnoise, Co. Offaly.

Roman art in Germania. Footed glass, early fifth century, from the necropolis of Vireux-
Molhain, Belgium.

Imperial art in Gaul. The 'Port' dish from the Kaiseraugst Treasure. Silver with gilt
decoration, mid-fourth century (Augst, Römermuseum).

Lombard art. Frontal plaque of a gilt bronze helmet, *c.* 600, showing King Agilulf
enthroned (Florence, Bargello Museum).

Between pages 136 and 137

Woman with pitcher. Detail from a floor mosaic in the Great Palace, Constantinople, fifth
century.

Man's head. Church of St George, Salonika, detail of dome mosaic, fifth century.

The Empress Theodora. Detail from choir mosaic, San Vitalis, Ravenna, sixth century.

Virgin and Child. Mosaic on a gold ground in the apse of St Sophia, Constantinople, ninth
century.

Between pages 200 and 201

The Dome of the Rock, Jerusalem, the oldest standing Muslim building, built 688–91.

The minaret of the Great Mosque of Cairouan, mid-ninth century.

The famous spiral minaret of the Great Mosque of Abu Dulaf at Samarra, Iraq, 859–61.

Columns in the prayer hall of the Great Mosque of Cordoba, Spain, late eighth to tenth
century.

Between pages 296 and 297

Syria: arcaded main facade of the monastery of St Symeon Stylites the Elder, fifth century.

St Sophia, Constantinople. General view of the central dome, piers and buttresses, sixth
century.

Syria: west facade and single apse of the church of Qalb Lozé, sixth century.

Cave church in Cappadocia (probably ninth or tenth century).

Colour plates

Between pages 392 and 393

Byzantine goldwork. Cross of Justin II, sixth century (Vatican, St Peter's Treasury).

Bulgar necklace in gold, enamel and pearls, ninth or tenth century (Archaeological Museum, Preslav).

First-century Roman chalice of polished semi-precious stone set in a tenth-century Byzantine gold mount with enamel inlay (Venice, St Mark's Treasury).

Gospel cover with enamel inlay depicting St Michael, tenth century (Venice, St Mark's Treasury).

Between pages 456 and 457

Carolingian manuscript, Moutier-Grandval, *c.* 840 (British Library).

Irish manuscripts from the *Gospels of St Willibrord, c.* 690 (Paris, Bibliothèque Nationale).

Initial of the Incarnation, from the *Lindisfarne Gospels, c.* 698 (British Library).

Carolingian manuscript, *Bible of S. Paolo fuori le Mura, c.* 870.

Acknowledgements

Photographic agencies

ANA pp. 192, 234
Atlas Photo pp. 183, 217, 338
Boudot-Lamotte p. 138
Bresc H p. 215
Gerard Degeorge pp. 159, 213, 247, 324, 359
Gerard Dufresne pp. 289, 329
Giraudon pp. 4, 9, 44, 65, 75, 82, 157, 238, 311, 327, 340
Alinari-Giraudon pp. 13, 390
Lauros-Giraudon p. 72
Hassia p. 177
Kirmer Fotoarchiv p. 365
Kutschera Ch. pp. 224, 322, 374
Magnum p. 157
Mas pp. 296, 347, 362
Photothèque Armand-Colin pp. 18, 81, 92, 97, 99, 105, 188, 257, 300, 354, 414, 424,
    451, 484
Jean-Claude Poulain pp. 178, 266
J. Powell pp. 112, 131, 163
Rapho pp. 3, 168, 274, 288, 521
Roger-Viollet p. 114
Yan p. 41
Zodiaque pp. 2, 88, 403, 454, 527

Scholarly institutions

Avignon, Musée Calvet p. 45
Bamberg, Staatsbibliothek p. 459
Berlin, Staatliche Museen Preussicher Kulturbesitz p. 456
Berne, Burgerbibliothek p. 436

Acknowledgements

Bonn, Rheinisches Landesmuseum p. 382
Brescia, Civici Istuti Culturali p. 143
Cologne, Rheinisches Bildarchiv pp. 25, 469
Douai, Bibliotheque municipale p. 49
Dublin, Trinity College Library p. 463
Heidelberg, Universitatsbibliothek p. 435
London, The British Library p. 404
London, The British Museum pp. 6, 60, 480
London, The School of Oriental and African Studies p. 196
Madrid, Biblioteca Nacional pp. 296, 347, 362
Madrid, Museo Archeologico Nacional p. 479
Nantes, Musées départementaux de Loire-Atlantique p. 79
New York, Metropolitan Museum of Arts p. 119
Nuremberg, Germanisches Nationalmuseum p. 456
Oslo, Universitets Oldsaksamling p. 407
Paris, Bibliothèque nationale pp. 162, 204, 208, 269, 311, 320, 327, 343, 489
Paris, collection de l'Ecole de Hautes Etudes en sciences sociales pp. 135, 302, 303, 318
Paris Réunion des Musées nationaux pp. 28, 32, 38, 110, 122, 149, 174, 229, 238, 255, 265, 378
Reims, Bibliothèque municipale p. 524
Rome, Biblioteca Apostolica Vaticana pp. 101, 210, 303, 340, 370, 395, 493
Rome, Musei du Vatican p. 322
Treves, Rheinisches Landesmuseum pp. 23, 517
Troyes, Trésor de la cathédrale p. 300
Utrecht, Bibliothek der Rijksuniversiteit pp. 433, 446, 509
Venice, Biblioteca Nazionale Marciana p. 340
Vienna, Kunsthistorisches Museum p. 105
Vienna, Osterreischiche Nationalbibliothek pp. 499, 501
Zurich, Musée national suisse p. 470

COLOUR PLATES (between pp. 72–73, 136–137, 200–201, 296–297, 392–393 and 456–457)

ANA
Gerard Degeorge
Gerard Dufresne
Giraudon
Lauros-Giraudon
Ch. Kutschera
Photothèque Armand-Colin
Réunion des Musées nationaux
Scala Istituto Fotografico Editoriale S.P.A.

Glossary

This glossary of technical terms is intended to save the reader the trouble of hunting for the place where they are first explained. Words easily found in a dictionary are omitted.

ADAERATIO: payment of taxes in coin, usually gold

ADVOCATUS, VOGT: guardian (*custos*) of a religious establishment who deputised for the ecclesiastics in the handling of military or judicial affairs; usually the office was entrusted or fell to the most powerful local lord

AEDELINGI, AETHELINGS, EDELINGI: members of high-ranking Saxon or Gothic families potentially eligible for kingship

AGER: tilled land, ground tamed by man; generally that part in private hands

AKKER (derived from *ager?*): patch of cleared land, or land tilled for some time, part of whose product went to the owner, the rest to the cultivator

AKRITAÏ: Byzantine warriors who garrisoned the eastern frontiers

ALLOD: personal property on whose owner there were no constraints other than those binding on a free subject of the ruler

AMIL: tax-collector appointed by the caliph

AMMA: the urban mass of craftsmen, shopkeepers, idlers and unemployed in Muslim towns, as opposed to the KHASSA

AMSAR: Islamic new towns, usually with a military garrison as the core

ANNONA: corn ration provided for the army

ANSANGE: plot of land, usually carved from the landowner's DEMESNE (see below), granted either to one of the agents on the estate, or to a 'domiciled' slave (see under CASATUS below), or to a free man in return for household services

ANTRUSTION: free man, of high social standing, bound to the person of the Merovingian king or his representative by an oath of fidelity (see TRUSTIS)

APRISIO: share-cropping lease with promise of ownership after 30 years, offered in particular to Goths from Spain who fled to Septimania

ARATRUM: type of plough used in the Byzantine empire

ARCHONTES COMETES: in Byzantium, heads of the admiralty, or of administrative departments in general

Glossary

ARIMANNI: free Lombard warriors (literally 'Men of the army') granted plots of land and answerable to the king or his agents

ATA: pension paid to retired Muslim warriors living in towns

ATRIUM: area of asylum round a church, sometimes including the cemetery and guest-houses; communal place of assembly, considered to be common land for the free men of a village

BACAUDAE: bands of peasants from the district of Tarragona, the Pyrenees, the Alps and the territory between the Loire and the Seine

BANNUM: right of the sovereign to command and to punish

BARID: courier service of the Persian empire, also taken over by Islam; network which conveyed the ruler's fiscal or military commands

BASILICA: a building (used as a law-court and later for worship) modelled on the audience halls of the Roman or Persian rulers. Another meaning: in post-Justinianic Byzantine legislation, written pronouncement on the law issuing from the emperor

BASTARNAE: convoys supplying Frankish armies on campaign with forage, horses and weapons; usually manned by non-combatants

BEHETRIA: benefit in land or kind granted by a Spanish ruler to a faithful warrior

BENEFICIUM: gift, originally of any type, but later more commonly in return for services rendered; possibly a grant of land in full ownership

BRETWALDA: 'overlord of the British'; title used by several Anglo-Saxon kings to demonstrate their superiority over other local chieftains

BROILUM: area of uncultivated land (forest, warren, heath), usually enclosed, set aside by the landowner or king for hunting and sport

BUCCELARII: literally, 'those who eat army biscuits'; soldiers of inferior social standing forming the bodyguard of a magnate and available for any task

BURH: type of fortified complex found in Wessex during King Alfred's reign

BYRNIE: leather jerkin reinforced with metal plates, worn by Carolingian warriors wealthy enough to afford such heavy armour

CABALLARII: tenants, often of extensive parcels of land, who were required to perform for their lord services involving horses (message-taking, escort duty, sentry duty, cartage, ploughing?); often of servile origin

CAPITULARY: document divided into chapters (*capitula*) which recapitulated the orders given and approved at the assembly of the 'Field of May', prior to the annual departure of the Carolingian army on campaign

CARAT: (from *keratia*, Mesopotamian unit of weight): used in weighing out merchandise and later to assess the fineness of gold (1 unit = 24 carats)

CASATUS: used of a person who was 'domiciled' on a piece of land to bring it into cultivation in order to win his loyalty and services

CENTENA: in Germanic regions, an area where order was maintained by a band of a hundred warriors (CENTENARII); by extension, sub-division of the county. Corresponds to the English 'hundred'

CEORL: Anglo-Saxon free man

CHAMBERLAIN: originally a household servant, later an official, who was responsible at Germanic courts for the royal *camera*, and by extension for the king's personal treasure and wardrobe

CHANCELLOR: official responsible for confirming and authenticating letters and documents issuing from the palace; an ecclesiastic familiar with diplomatic custom

CHRYSOBOULLOÏ: Byzantine imperial edicts authenticated by a gold seal

CODEX: a book, composed as in the modern world of sheets bound at one side, as opposed to the Antique ROTULUS

COLLATIO LUSTRALIS: tax imposed on merchants trading independently

COLLEGIA: craft or trading associations in the urban world of Antiquity, usually controlled by the public authorities

COLONUS: a tenant-farmer, free in principle but subject to fiscal or military obligations; in the Byzantine world the COLONUS lapsed into a state of dependence on a magnate

COLONICA: tenement occupied by a COLONUS; later could be used to denote a holding comprising a number of scattered plots

COMITATENSES: Byzantine field army

COMITATUS: office held by the count; by extension, the count's prerogatives and revenues, and the territory in which he exercised or received them. Another meaning: Byzantine assault troops

CONDAMINA: parcels of arable, usually lying together, directly exploited by the landowner

CONSTABLE: originally a servant, later an official, who was responsible at Germanic courts for the upkeep of the horses (*comes stabuli*); high-ranking military officer

CONVENIENTIA: a reciprocally binding written contract under Roman law; later signified any legally binding agreement in writing (promise of fidelity, leases etc.) to which the two parties subscribed as equals

CURIA: municipal council in the Roman State

CURIALES: town-councillors of late Antiquity; also called decurions

CURSUS PUBLICUS: Roman courier service, used for the rapid communication of military or other orders issued by emperors or provincial governors

CURTIS: group of farm buildings in a DEMESNE

DANEGELD: tribute in silver or gold paid to the Northmen in the ninth century

DANELAW: the north-eastern part of England under 'Danish law' in the tenth century

DAY'A, DIY'A: large estate held in usufruct in the Muslim world

DECURION: see CURIALES

DEMESNE: non-medieval word used by scholarly convention to denote that part of a large estate which remained under the direct control of the landowner and was cultivated by the labour services of tenants or by a servile labour force. Something like the English 'home farm'

DENIER: Western silver coin

DHIMMI: 'bowed-down'; non-Muslim subject in Islamic society

DIHQANS: landed proprietors who volunteered to collect taxes in the Muslim world and kept back part of the proceeds

Glossary

DINAR: Muslim gold coin

DIRHAM (from Greek *drachma*): Muslim silver coin

DIWAN: book, register; by extension, any administrative department in the Muslim world, diwan of the army, diwan of finance etc.

DROMON: Byzantine warship along the lines of the Antique galley

DROMOS: the Byzantine CURSUS PUBLICUS, that is, the courier service; also responsible for policing and even external relations; the LOGOTHETE of the DROMOS played a key role in the imperial palace

DRONGARIOS: commander of a Byzantine naval division; later admiral of the fleet

DUNATOI: the powerful, the rich, the leaders in the Byzantine world of the ninth to tenth centuries

EALDORMAN: member of an Anglo-Saxon family important enough to govern a shire; landowner

EIGENKIRCHE: churches and by extension parishes founded or appropriated by a large landowner who appointed the ministrant, claimed the tithe for himself and exploited any accompanying lands, often with restraint, and for pious purposes

EMPHYTEUSIS: type of Roman lease of not less than eighteen and not more than 99 years, entailing the payment of a ground-rent ('*canon*'), and assignment of the property to the tenant at the end of the contract

EREMOS: the desert, emptiness, solitude

EXARCH: governor in outpost of the Byzantine empire and for that reason enjoying a large measure of independence

EXCUBITORES: regiment of palace guards, composed of Thracians, Illyrians and Isaurians

EXILARCH: representative and protector of Jewish communities in the eastern empires

FADDAN: Arabic term of measurement

FAIDA: clan vengeance in Germanic customary law

FAQIH: man of piety and learning leading a solitary, contemplative existence in accordance with Islam

FARA: subdivision of Lombard clan

FEDERATES: barbarian tribes fighting alongside Roman troops

FEO, FEUM, FEVUM: until the end of the tenth century, gift, generally in full ownership, but by way of recompense for a service rendered; renewable in the same way as the Roman STIPENDIUM; more like a salary than a BENEFICIUM

FEORM (from Latin *firma?*): revenue paid in the form of food in Anglo-Saxon England; by extension, the exaction of food and lodging for the ruler and his entourage

FIQH: Islamic juridical and religious learning

FISC: State-owned property and the departments which administered it; gradually became synonymous with the State-owned lands of the Roman empire and its successors

FODRUM: requisition of forage for Germanic armies

FOLLIS: low-denomination bronze coin in the West and Byzantium. *Fals, fullus*: Islamic copper coins

FOSSATUM: in particular the frontier zone in Spain between Muslims and Christians

FREDA: judicial fines in Germanic countries

FUNDUQ: lock-up markets in Islamic towns where wholesale transactions were allowed under certain conditions; by extension, the market or later the quarter reserved for foreign merchants

FUNDUS: territorial and juridical entity comprising a large landed estate with a centralised living area which often housed all of the estate workers

FUQAHA: specialist in Muslim law

FUTUAWA: association in Islamic towns whose members had to undergo rites of initiation; a political force, it also lent support to religious movements, frequently Shi'ite

FYRD: the army of free men in Anglo-Saxon England and the various obligations which it imposed

GAFFOLAND: arable land subject to tax in Anglo-Saxon England

GARDINGI: sworn retainers of the king in Christian parts of Spain; or retainers of the Gothic king obliged to perform a specific type of military service

GARUM: a thick sauce made from fish, much appreciated in Antiquity as a seasoning for other dishes

GASINDI: Lombard servants of servile origin

GASTALDS: Lombard stewards of royal estates, who could also attain public office

GAU: Germanic district with a certain ethnic or geographical cohesion which was also a unit of public administration; it thus resembled both the PAGUS and the COMITATUS

GEBUR: 'domiciled' slave among the Anglo-Saxons

GENIZA: archives of a synagogue, particularly the one in Cairo

GESITHS: Saxon retainers, like the Lombard GASINDI, but often 'domiciled' and assimilated to the COLONI; the land they cultivated was called *gesithland*

GHILDE: associations of freemen, craftsmen, merchants etc., who swore to give each other aid and mutual support

GNOSIS: philosophical approach adopted in the first centuries A.D. with the aim of integrating pagan thought and Christian teachings into a coherent scheme

GRAFIO: Germanic count charged with defence of a frontier zone

GROD: Slav 'town'; fortified camp which attracted adjacent settlements of merchants and craftsmen

GUALDI PUBLICI: Lombard equivalent of the FISC

GYROVAGUS: monk who had left his community, or had never had one, and who wandered from place to place, preaching and begging

HACKSILVER: fragments of silver or gold ornaments, or even coins, hacked into pieces by the Vikings to obtain a specific weight

HADITH: commands and sayings attributed to Muhammad but not included in the 'recitation', that is, the Koran; also denotes glosses on the latter

HAIA: forest, generally common land; but can also denote a wall of branches erected for defensive purposes

HAJJ: the pilgrimage to Mecca

HANIF: devout man, living in the community and giving an example to the Islamic faithful

HEGIRA: see HIJRA

HENOTIKON: formula of reconciliation between orthodox believers and Monophysites

HERIBANNUM: failure to obey the summons to the Frankish army, punishable by a heavy fine

HERISLIZ: desertion of the army, desertion on campaign; punishable by death

HIDE: see MANSUS

HIJRA: refuge, resting-place; associated above all with the departure of Muhammad for Yathrib, the HEGIRA

HIMAYA: in Islamic lands, protection given by a powerful lord to the weak; to secure their loyalty he sometimes paid their taxes

HONOR: public office rewarded with perquisites and the revenues from property attached to that office; by extension, the property itself

HOSPITALITAS: late Antique custom of billeting soldiers on campaign; later became an obligation on Roman landowners to make over part of their possessions (dwellings, lands, revenues or slaves) to barbarian garrison troops

HOST: (from Latin *hostis*): army of Germanic free men; see FYRD

HULK: Frisian sailing vessel in the shape of a nut-shell

HUFE: see MANSUS

HUNDRED: see CENTENA

IMAM: leader of praise offered to Allah, perhaps only the prayer-leader; by extension, spiritual leader at the time of religious renewal

IMMIXTIO MANUUM: joining of hands by two individuals; more broadly, an act whereby a man placed his hands between those of a superior; symbol of submission

IMMUNITY: legal status of land, very often belonging to the Church, which the agents of central government could neither tax, examine nor requisition without the consent of the authority established there; originally applied only to taxation

INDICTION: period of fifteen years corresponding to the intervals between the updating of the Roman or Byzantine tax register; hence a unit of chronology

INFIELD: ground brought under cultivation, in contrast with the OUTFIELD, left as wilderness. Not necessarily arable

IQTA: grant, in principle for a limited term, of a fiscal property by the ruler to a servant, warrior or large landowner in Islamic territory

IRDABB: Arabic term of measurement

ISMAʾILIAN: from Ismaʾil (Ishmael) son of Abraham, protector of the Arabs and link between the biblical world and Islam; name adopted by oppositionist movements in Islam, Shi'ism in particular; in certain cases the name of the particular religious leader replaced the generic term

JARID: Persian measure for cereals handed over in respect of the JIZIYA

JIHAD: obligation to extend the Islamic faith by all possible means, the holy war in particular, although the use of violence is not necessarily implied by the word

JIZIYA: poll-tax (literally 'neck-tax'), paid by the DHIMMIS

JUGATIO, JUGUM: area of land forming a fiscal unit in late Antiquity and Byzantium, and by extension the taxes due from it; calculated in relation to the surface that could be ploughed in a year by a team of oxen

JUND: tribal contingent, originally of Arabs, employed as mercenaries by the central power; by extension, a military district

KA'BA: the cube, Isma'il's original dwelling-place, centre of pre-Muslim rites, chosen and sanctified by the Prophet as the most favoured destination of the HAJJ

KALAM: reason, freedom of thought, as opposed to the constraints of religious dogma

KARAITE: Jewish dissident, wedded to the most literal reading (*qara* in Hebrew) of the Mosaic Law

KATIB: secretary or scribe, in Islam

KHAN: leader of a federation of Asiatic Turko-Mongolic tribes. Another meaning: centre for money-changing in Islamic countries

KHARAJ: burden, the land-tax in Islamic countries

KHARIJITES: the 'seceders', those who insisted on a rigorous, almost puritanical application of the Muslim Law; fertile ground for Shi'ism

KHASSA: the wealthy and organized sector in Islamic towns, consisting of the aristocracy, court officials and administrators; in contrast to the AMMA

KHITTA: in Muslim towns, quarter set aside for the settlement of a tribe or one of its components

KHUTBA: proclamation of the sanctity of the faith and the name of the leader of the faithful, made during the Muslim Friday prayer

KLASMATA: plots of land left fallow for 30 years and confiscated for redistribution (Byzantium)

KÖNIGSFREI: former COLONUS, 'domiciled' and subjected to taxation by Germanic count

KUFIC (from Kufa, town in Lower Mesopotamia): cursive script somewhat different from the religious hand reserved for Koranic inscriptions

KUTTER (from Latin *cultura?*): in northern Europe, parcel of land allotted to tenants to be brought into cultivation, subject to various obligations of a communitarian nature

LAETI, LETI: mercenaries, usually Germanic (but possibly Iranian or Celtic), enlisted by the Romans and billeted in relatively large contingents in open country

LATIFUNDIA: huge estates, usually devoted to extensive stock-rearing under slave management; the result of the accumulation of landed property in Mediterranean countries

LAVRA, LAURA: a group of men or women religious who lived in solitude following the precepts of orthodoxy, but came together at the end of the week for corporate worship

LAZZI: Saxon or Scandinavian slaves

LEIBEIGNE: peasants with freedom of movement, 'owners of their bodies'

LIBELLUM, LIVELLO (Ital): 29-year lease without onerous dues

LIMITANEI: soldiers who guarded the *limes*, the frontier in Antiquity; regional defence force. The meaning of RIPARIENSES is comparable

LOGOTHETE: head of an administrative department in Byzantium

MACHTIERN: head of a Breton clan who wielded authority in the parish or parishes containing his properties

MAGISTER: commander-in-chief in the Roman army

MAHDI: the 'rightly-guided one', the prophet who would herald a return to purity; the advent and recognition of the MAHDI figured in all oppositionist religious movements in Islam, in Shi'ism in particular

MALLUS: Germanic assembly of free men; by extension, any public tribunal

MANCIPIA: slaves

MANSIO: staging-post of the Roman and Greek CURSUS PUBLICUS

MANSUS: area of ploughland, which might be all of a piece or in dispersed plots, sufficient to sustain one peasant family, and which correspondingly varied in extent; unit of assessment for fiscal and military purposes. Corresponds to the Anglo-Saxon HIDE and Germanic HUFE

MAQSURA: the screened-off portion of a mosque from which the IMAM led the prayer

MARTYRIA: saints' tombs, places of worship

MASSA: in northern Italy, a group of FUNDI, generally spread over a wide area

MATRICULA: list of those entitled to receive the bread dole dispensed in late Antiquity by the civic authorities or later by the bishops; list of people deserving charitable assistance (*matricularii*)

MAWALI: client, armed or otherwise, in Islam (from *mawla*, meaning 'honourable dependence')

MENSA: part of ecclesiastical estate set aside to supply the table of the abbot or of the community, consisting of the lands as such or their revenues

MIHRAB: niche in the QIBLA wall of the mosque indicating the direction in which to pray

MINBAR: in Muhammad's house, the Prophet's seat; in the mosque, pulpit from which the IMAM might preach or recite

MINISTERIUM, MINISTERIALES: office, function or trade, and their practitioners; became a general term for any local official

MISAHA: land measurement used in Eastern Islam as the basis of the KHARAJ

MISSUS: special envoy

MONOPHYSITISM: form of Christian doctrine according to which the human nature and the divine nature of Christ are combined within a single nature, predominantly divine

MONOTHELITISM: Byzantine compromise formula according to which Christ's two natures are distinct, yet inspired by a single action and will, which is essentially divine

MONTANISTS: Christian visionaries who believed in the imminence of a New Jerusalem through the intervention of the saints; millenarian in tendency

MOZARABS: Christians living among Muslims, specifically in Spain

MUDEJARS: Muslims living among Christians, specifically in Spain

MUFTI: professional jurisconsult, adviser to the Islamic ruler

MUHAJIRUN: auxiliary of the faith, fanatical warrior in the JIHAD

MUHTASIB: custodian, for example of the market; by extension, any person responsible for public order

MUKHAHENAH: partnership of Islamic merchants formed by the pooling of movable goods for the launching of a joint enterprise

MUND, MUNDEBURDIUM: magical power, inherent in certain Germanic clans and their leaders because of a divine ancestry; the protection they thus gave to kinsmen and dependants; by extension, a form of defence of the weak by the strong

MUQASAMA: practice in Islam whereby the shares of the harvest due to the ruler and the landlord were determined on the threshing-floor

MUSAQAH: share-cropping in Islamic countries

MUʾTAZILITE: strict form of Muslim belief sustained by expectation of a righteous IMAM who would inaugurate a classless society, where right prevailed

MUWALLAD: in Spain and the Maghrib, a recent native convert to Islam

NESTORIANISM: marginally Christian doctrine, according to which Christ was no more than the provisional 'temple' of the divine Word

NEUM: notation intended to guide the voice in plainchant by marking the stresses and lengths of the notes; has no melodic significance

NOMISMA: the face, and by extension a Greek coin bearing the ruler's effigy

NORIA: bucket-wheel used for irrigation, driven by the current of a river, or, in the case of an underground reservoir, by animal teams or slaves

NOVELS: judicial decisions and the reasons for them in post-Justinianic jurisprudence

OBOLE: coin, half of one DENIER

OBSEQUIUM: respect and obedience due from a freedman to his former master; by extension, moral obligation of the weak towards the powerful

OUTFIELD: wasteland, untamed by man

PAGUS, PAGENSES: region, and its inhabitants; not necessarily rural; circumscription dating from late Antiquity, or possibly earlier, with certain characteristic physical, ethnic, linguistic or other features

PALLIUM: white woollen band decorated with dark crosses, worn by the pope, and granted by him to metropolitan bishops when they came to the gates of Rome (*ad limina*) to receive confirmation of their appointment

PATRIARCH: episcopal title, in principle used only in the case of towns which played an essential role in the development of the Christian faith

PATRONATE: protection by a 'patron' or master: can apply to a church, a man, or a piece of land

PAULICIANS: Christian dissidents, especially in Armenia, hostile to images, the ecclesiastical hierarchy, the sacraments, marriage etc.

PAUPERES: the weak

PENITENTIALS: books prescribing bodily or spiritual punishments, in the form of lists of sins with penances appropriate to the social status of the sinner

PENNY: Anglo-Saxon silver coin

PIEVE: see PLEBS

PLACITUM: assembly of free men at which pleas were heard; used increasingly of the local court

PLEBS, PLOU, PIEVE (Ital.): early medieval parish

PLUM: not clear whether this is the Germanic heavy plough or some other ploughing implement

POLITIKOÏ: loaves distributed to the urban populace by the Byzantine public authorities

POLYPTYCH: literally, assembled leaves of a book; in diplomatics the term is more narrowly applied to the inventories of possessions and dues drawn up by landowners, particularly churches and monasteries, between the sixth and tenth centuries

PORPHYROGENITOS: literally, born in the imperial 'purple chamber' at Byzantium; designation of the legitimate ruler born during the reign of his father

POUND WEIGHT: the Roman *libra* (of about 327g, increased in the West to 406g and later to 491g), used for the weighing of merchandise; more particularly, weight unit for silver and gold, but used only for assessing the quantity of goods worth a certain weight of precious metal

PRAEDIUM: similar in meaning to FUNDUS

PREBEND: combined revenues, whether from land or not, assigned to the upkeep of a cathedral canon; also any gift of victuals or money guaranteeing subsistence – the 'prebendaries' in this case were clients 'with board'

PRECARIA: ecclesiastical property ceded in return for a token rent to a lay proprietor on the 'prayer' of the beneficiary or even of the king (*verbo regis*)

PRESTAMO: grant of fiscal land in Spain to a GARDINGO

PROTONOTARY: Byzantine official responsible for despatches and official correspondence

QADI: urban or rural magistrate in the Islamic world

QARMATIANS: egalitarian Muslim sect, close in inspiration to ISMAʾILISM

QIBLA: the wall of the mosque to which the believer turns; originally indicated the east, later the direction of Mecca; can be a mystic symbol

QUAESTOR: the emperor's spokesman

RACHIMBURGII: free men in the Germanic community responsible for declaring the law at the MALLUS

RAQIQ: literally, 'lacking in honour': denoted the dependent peasantry in Islam

REFERENDARY: public official, usually an ecclesiastic, responsible for verifying the authenticity of letters drawn up in the Germanic Palace

RIGA: literally, 'ridge, furrow'; name for the labour service which consisted of breaking and maintaining a certain number of furrows on the demesne

RIPARIENSES: see LIMITANEI

ROTULUS: parchments sewn end to end and rolled round one or two rods, the 'book' of Antiquity; this form remained in use for accounts and for certain other liturgical or legal documents

SACELLARII: subordinates of the CAMERARIUS who supervised the Treasury's monetary income

SACRAMENTARY: book containing the prayers and forms of words to be used in church services

SAKKA: bill of credit equivalent to a promise to pay on expiry; cheque

SAIONES: among the Visigoths, menials who could be used for any service

SALTUS: virgin land in Roman times – woodland, heaths, clearings; by extension, unappropriated land over which the ruler was normally lord

SAWAFI: property confiscated by Muslims, mostly in Persia, from the aristocracy of a conquered country, or from the Church

SCABINI: permanent professional judges acting as assessors in the PLACITUM or MALLUS, originally in countries with written law, later throughout the West

SCEATTAS: Anglo-Saxon silver coin (*cf.* German *Schatz*, treasure?)

SCHOLAI: Byzantine garrison troops

SCRIPTORIUM: writing-room, lay or ecclesiastical

SCULDHAIS: in Lombard Italy, royal agent charged with administration of an urban district

SENESCHAL (from *Sinisskalk*, eldest household servant): official responsible for the palace commissariat in Germanic kingdoms

SETICI: plots of land around the dwelling, cultivated by tenants for their own use; kitchen gardens, orchards

SHARIKA: commercial partnership with shared capital, formed to finance a single transaction (Islam)

SHI'A: literally 'party', the legitimist sect in Islam; after the ejection of the Alids became identified with the Messianic movement awaiting their return; Shi'ism

SILENTION, SILENTIARIES: advisory council of the Byzantine emperor; its members

SKLAVINIAI: zones with a relatively dense population of Sklavenes, the generic name for the Slavs

SNEKKJA: Scandinavian vessel, at once warship and cargo ship, deckless, ideally propelled by rowing

SOLIDUS: Byzantine gold coin, originally minted to pay soldiers their wages (hence the name). In the West, used to express the monetary value of merchandise or a fine, whatever the actual means of payment – deniers, objects, ingots etc.

STÄMME: Germanic groupings with common ethnic, linguistic and cultural characteristics; only later used to denote territorial units

STÄPL: wooden post implanted in water; by extension riverside or coastal quay

STIPENDIUM: pay or salary; could be in the form of land

STRATIOTE: Byzantine soldier-peasant

STYLITE: ascetic perched on a pillar, who devoted himself to meditation

SUFTADJA: letter of credit for deferred payment, possibly in another place; forerunner of the bill of exchange?

SULH: truce or peace treaty between two Muslim tribes

SUQ: retail market in Muslim town

TABELLIONES: Roman notaries, so called after the tablets on which they recorded contracts, acts of sale and wills

TA'DIL: in Islamic countries, government assessment of personal wealth for tax purposes

TADJIR: sedentary Islamic merchant who sent couriers and agents to do business for him in distant places

TAGMATA: regiments of Byzantine troops forming the central army; see COMITATUS

TALDJIA: moral and political protection provided by a lord to a dependant of good social standing; see HIMAYA

Glossary

TERPS: mounds above sea-level, possibly artificially heightened, along the coast of the Netherlands

THEGN, THANE: Anglo-Saxon noble, landowner

THEME, THEMATA: Byzantine district; the troops stationed there for the defence of its frontiers

THING: Scandinavian assembly of free men

TIRAZ: government stamp on textiles in the Islamic world; by extension, workshops where clothing and other articles were manufactured under government supervision

TIRONIAN NOTES (from Tiro, name of Cicero's freedman–secretary?): the abridgements (not a shorthand) used to speed up correspondence in offices and chanceries

TRACTUS: comparable in meaning to SALTUS

TREMISSES: small gold coins equivalent to a third of a SOLIDUS

TREUWA: truce; judicial settlement

TRIENTES: comparable to TREMISSES

TRUSTIS: oath of fidelity – see ANTRUSTION; can refer to a group bound by such an oath

TSAR (from Caesar): title used by Bulgar rulers

ULAMA: teachers of Muslim law

VASSUS (from Celtic *gwass*, young boy?): dependant of honourable status

VERBUM REGIS: royal command, delivered in particular at the Field of May

VICARIA: jurisdictional and later territorial division of the count's HONOR; the VICARIUS was usually responsible for minor justice, policing of the highways, tax-collection; his military role is not clear

VICECOMITATUS: count's deputy, 'viscount'; capable in principle of exercising the count's authority in his absence but in practice permanent subordinate

VICUS: village; agglomeration of shops and booths around a religious centre or palace; the Scandinavian word *vik* (signifying 'bay') may have acquired the same meaning by transference

VILLA: in principle, a large bipartite estate; soon came to denote any settlement, later a 'village'

VIZIR, WAZIR: 'burden-bearer', helper; by extension, the caliph's chief minister

WAQF: exempt land, generally intended originally for charitable use; in the West would be described as 'mortmain'; a means of rewarding faithful service in the Islamic world

WAZIR: see VIZIR

WERGELD: 'blood-money'; financial compensation which a victim or his kindred was entitled to exact, proportionate to his social rank and status

WESTWORK: massive structure at the west end of Carolingian churches, usually comprising a second transept and two towers as a frontage

WICH: see VICUS

WILAYAT: supervision, particularly of the market; area within which such control was exercised (Islam)

WITENAGEMOT: Anglo-Saxon council of wise men; guided the king

XENIA: gifts in kind exacted from Byzantine COLONI whose rent had reached the permissible ceiling

XENODOCHIA: refuges and hostels for pilgrims, beggars and the sick, often founded by the Irish

ZAKAT, SADAQUA, USH (in Spain): voluntary alms-giving required of the faithful in Islamic lands

ZINDIQS: heretical Muslim sect of dualistic tendency, sceptical in its attitude to the sacred texts and of a freely critical disposition

Introduction

'The Middle Ages began when the antique civilisation of the Mediterranean became extinct.' Bald statements of this kind, drummed for a century or more into children's minds, and enshrined there, inevitably confront us as we set out on this journey. Valéry takes it for granted that all civilisations pass away; Pigagnol exclaims, 'The Roman empire was assassinated!' Such blindness is inexcusable. Civilisations do not die: when they grow old they mutate, become another species. From Peru to the Rio Grande, evidence of the civilisation in the Americas crushed by Spanish gunfire still stares us in the face. Violated, sold into slavery or otherwise corrupted, the civilisations of Black Africa can hardly be said to have vanished from the modern world, whether in Louisiana or on the Zambesi. The same goes for the civilisations of the Near East, the Indies and the Far East, notwithstanding the ravages of conquest, pillage and oppression. Similarly, our own civilisation remains identifiably West European, however surprising its present aspect might appear to men of the Middle Ages or to contemporaries of the French Revolution or the Victorian Age. Seventeenth-century scholars who located Clovis and Charlemagne in Antiquity had a clearer perception of the underlying continuities than did their nineteenth-century successors.

A transition from one world to another?

The problem is to know where to begin. Is there some turning-point, between 350 and 450, which can be taken as marking the transition from one world to another, the point at which we cross the threshold of the Middle Ages? Perhaps we should start by asking whether contemporaries were aware of living in a state of transition. Their writings – and not all these authors were well-to-do – leave us with two over-riding impressions. They betray first a deep-rooted sense of inertia and despondency which causes them to dwell solely on the oppressive aspects of the governmental machine, to deplore the prevalence of flagrant abuses and cruel injustices and to bewail the uncertainty of the future; as a hypothetical remedy for the 'crisis' of their society, they toy with the idea of flight or even revolt. While we need hardly doubt that they remained conscious of the continuing bond which united the wealthiest, from Britain to Syria, in a common culture, community of

Figurine in enamelled bronze from a Norwegian burial at Miklebostad; late eighth century (Bergen, Historical Museum).

Merovingian sarcophagi at Civaux (Vienne, France). The grave furniture (weapons, jewellery, textiles) sheds light on everyday life, craftsmanship, taste, even beliefs. The provenance of objects gives an indication of commercial networks.

interest and common lifestyle, in their letters, be they bishops or orators, they harp continually on the pressing need for a *renovatio*. Second, though this is not their chief complaint, they are conscious of being hemmed in by foreigners, people to whom they give money, house-room and employment, but whose habits and diet they find alien and repugnant: Sidonius, Bishop of Clermont, describes the Goths on his doorstep as over-familiar and intrusive, stinking of onions and rancid butter. Nobody seems very certain when this infliction began – perhaps around the year 250 or at the latest 300 – but there is a tenacious belief that it can and will shortly be terminated. These clearly expressed sentiments come so close to certain twentieth-century attitudes that it is tempting to equate our own situation with that of the 'Romans' at the time of the 'Invasions'; except that nowadays the 'invasions' are from south to north, instead of *vice versa*.

Knowing as we do what lay in store for them, we are perhaps more sensitive than men of the time to two further phenomena they rarely mention or believe to be transitory. To us it is evident that the administrative institutions of Antiquity were losing their grip, that the wheels of State were becoming progressively clogged, that the *res publica* was giving way to another type of authority: evident, that is to say, only if we consider Gaul, Britain or Spain,

A Romanised 'Barbarian': Stilicho, son of a Vandal chieftain, became commander-in-chief of the Roman army under the emperor Theodosius (379–95) and was victorious in Italy against the Visigothic leader, Alaric (Monza cathedral, ivory).

or even Illyricum or Africa, since elsewhere the unseemliness of regional divisions is still concealed beneath the umbrella of 'imperial authority'. What strikes us next is that the traditional objectives of *Romania* have evolved: there is scarcely any talk now of holding the frontier, the *limes*, of protecting civilisations, of citizens taking up arms; voices are even raised in rejoicing over the influx of new blood into the empire, brought by newcomers who move freely back and forth across the Rhine, the Danube, the Euphrates and the Atlas. The people most disposed to turn their back on Rome's old siege mentality are the Christians, for whom all men are brothers, the poorer folk, and the far-sighted intellectuals who expect the

4

renovatio to come about through these men of no pedigree now emerging as soldiers, farmers, smiths or 'domestics'. There are times, of course, when their 'invasions' have the wholesale and violent quality which so struck the chroniclers and still clutters up our textbooks; but infiltration by ones and twos or in small family groups began in the mid-third century and the term *Völkerwanderung* (popular migrations) comes closer to the reality. On the other hand, the third image so often adduced, of a metamorphosis into something quite other, is one I would certainly reject: the notion, that is to say, of a cultural, political – and some even dare to say economic – 'regression' to be laid at the door of these 'foreigners', these 'barbarians', although the designation has yet to acquire its pejorative connotation. Some French fanatics for a Celtic revival still find the fall of Rome cause for rejoicing; the Italians and Spaniards may find it regrettable, but are more aware of the gradual nature of the transition; the Germans naturally approve. Perhaps we should concentrate on simpler matters, so as not to fall into the traps and errors in which moral and value judgements notoriously abound. Facts such as the shared use of cemeteries, the toleration of mixed marriages, the adjustment of legal codes, all speak of a gradual, inescapable osmosis, acquiesced in perhaps rather than desired, but explicable only on the assumption that the inhabitants of both worlds, at every level and in every sphere, were on an equal footing. It will be objected that nothing of the sort is found in the East; but the difference is merely one of timing. A little later, with the irruption of the Slavs, Arabs and Berbers, the picture is the same. And who in any case would argue that the art of the steppes is in any way comparable with Hellenism? Finally, it is pertinent to mention that pockets of resistance, wherever they exist, have nothing elitist about them; whether they know it or not, the people who matter henceforth are the masses, awakening to new life in the Middle Ages.

The problem of choosing a starting-point

Since this problem must somehow be resolved, our most obvious course is to scrutinise all the domains of human activity for signs of a possible hiatus. What is known, for example, about population numbers? The extent of their variation is impossible to gauge exactly. However, on the basis of logic, 'impressions' and climatic probabilities, scholars are increasingly persuaded that the Mediterranean region was afflicted at this period by a prolonged and severe drought which along with the accompanying famines, malaria and epidemic diseases seriously impaired the vigour and productive capacity of peoples and places all along its southern flank; further north, on the other hand, the warming of the climate made peoples of the forest and steppes trek towards the south. The cessation of border raids, which were a source of free labour, and the consequent willingness to recruit immigrant workers from lands east of the Rhine and north of the Danube add up to a justification for the 'invasions' and account for many of their characteristics. But it is less certain, or at all events less obvious, that anything similar occurred in the East. Furthermore, in such matters where is one to draw a line? Let us therefore note the cause and context of the 'invasions' but not attempt to pin them to a precise date.

Let us also leave aside the question of cultural mutation. This is not to ignore the

The Herul Odoacer (*c.* 434–93), head of the imperial troops, deposed Romulus Augustulus in 476 and sent the imperial insignia to Zeno: the empire of the West was at an end (British Museum).

debasement of Latin and the recession of Greek bewailed by the intellectual elite, to which there is ample testimony, or the decline of Hellenistic art and the crassness of contemporary monuments. What has to be borne in mind, however, is that these trends and complaints are not new but go back at least to the second century. In art and literature, value judgements are even less trustworthy than in other spheres; so much depends on taste and viewpoint. In any case, how could one fasten on a date when the stream of writings and ideas is continuous from the time of Ulpian in the third century to the *Lex Gundobada* in the sixth?

The religious domain may give us pause. Is it significant that the two worlds which issue from *Romania*, with Islam later making a third, are monotheistic and have their roots in oriental cults of great antiquity? Yet the Neoplatonists of the third century also had a hand in this evolution, which again extends over a very long period. Suppose we train the spotlight on Christianity. It has a bad reputation among the historians of late Antiquity; its preaching of fraternity and non-violence and its contempt for the city of men could have undermined from within men's sense of citizenship, patriotism and respect for the law, and opened the gates to the barbarians in the name of universal, as opposed to civic, justice. Suppose we accept this line of argument, even if it assumes a great deal in its postulate. Have we not then to decide when the triumph of the new religion, the cementing of a different ideology, was complete? If so, we are immediately plunged, in the East, into a thicket of doctrinal, provincial disputes which are essentially rebellions and through which Islam will in most instances cut a clean path; in the West, the cemeteries bear witness that we must wait a long while, at least until the eighth or ninth century, for the balance to be finally tipped in favour of the official faith. Should we then go back to the beginnings, for example to 325 and the first general council of the Church at Nicaea, held under the official auspices of the emperor Constantine? Perhaps so; yet at that date, having made an astonishing recovery from the grave crisis of the third century, *Romania* appears flourishing and intact; this is not the Middle Ages. It would make just as much sense to go back to the persecutions under Diocletian at the end of the third century.

Political events, to which nowadays we merely give a sideways glance as we concentrate on social structures, greatly preoccupied the scholars of previous generations, who took it for granted that they fixed, and still fix, indefeasible chronological boundaries. The choice is wide, and the fact that such events tend to be symbolic rather than political does not lessen the difficulty. Suppose we decide on the death of Theodosius in 395, on the grounds that it 'marked the end of *Romania* as a single unit', the last occasion when the empire was in the hands of a sole ruler. Yet who could have predicted that this situation would never recur? Furthermore, after he had driven the 'last emperor of the West' out of Rome in 476, the barbarian leader of the day despatched the imperial insignia to the emperor Zeno in Constantinople; rightly speaking, the unity of *Romania* was restored. Is there nevertheless a case for 476 as the key date? No contemporary took note of it, and fifty years later Justinian, the 'Roman' emperor of the East, sent his troops to occupy Rome as a substitute for appearing there in person. Would anything be gained by moving back to the death of Constantine (337) or forward to the reign of Marjorian (457–61), the last emperor to legislate for the West, or by stopping halfway, at 378, the date when the last army with any pretensions to be 'Roman' was crushingly defeated by the Goths at Adrianople, south of the Danube? Unless, of course, one prefers some other landmark: Alaric's sack of Rome (410), which set up waves of panic throughout the empire and drew tears from St Jerome in his remote eastern retreat; or the composition by St Augustine of his *City of God* (425), in which he turns his back on the City of men; or the 'consulship' of Clovis (510), or any other date. It hardly matters, since none of these occurrences was truly new and portentous, or for that matter symbolic of finality. As for the 'invasions', one can only pick events more or less at random from the mass, starting with the settlement of the Franks south of the Rhine by Decius in 270 and ending with the penetration of the Slavs into the Balkans around 600, which includes incidents such as the crossing of the frozen Rhine in 406 and the death of Attila in 453: the choice is wide open.

We are left with the evidently all-important economic and social transformations: slavery in retreat, reinforcement of the rural 'patronate', disconnection between the town and the countryside, disappearance of a 'middle class', changing horizons, reorientation of exchanges, growing imbalance between East and West, mixing up of the State with the ruler's patrimony. These are the things that matter, which shall be the subject of closer study. My original question must therefore remain unanswered: the Middle Ages are the natural sequel to Antiquity; in the mid-fourth century, between 330 and 360, they have not yet begun; after 460 they have definitely arrived.

The features which endure

Through the long series of question marks there at least runs a thread of consistency; in no sphere was change immediate, clear-cut or total. Yet on advancing further into this misty terrain, it becomes possible to distinguish between features which remain in place, features already half-obliterated or about to vanish, and others again which are new and unexpected.

Violence and the continuing cult of violence, which appears the most striking permanent feature, has as much to do with men's moral attitudes as with the means of political control. There has too long been a tendency to exalt the Roman ideal of a public-spirited citizen army of peasants upholding the *pax romana* in contrast with the regime of the warrior band, ignorant of the State and resorting to interminable feuds as the means of settling disputes. Embedded in our collective consciousness, this view is strenuously promoted by adulators of the Antique: it has been quite forgotten that such shining heroes as Scipio, Caesar or Trajan were the authors of horrendous pillages and massacres; we have allowed Seneca's philosophical discourses to blind us to his slaves; we have chosen to ignore the gladiators and the circus 'games', the assassination of embarrassing opponents, the praetorian mutinies, the spectacle of mercenaries placing an illiterate from their own ranks on the throne – just as we ignore the military revolts and sordid intrigues which punctuate the whole of Roman history, or indeed that of the Greeks. The men who in the time of Gregory of Tours fight to the death over trifles or in the days before Herakleios cut one another's throats in the name of religion are not 'barbarians' but 'Romans'. The cult of violence, the exaltation of the warrior do not originate with Wotan or the Nibelungs. One might indeed say that these traits are more excusable and explicable among peoples who had to contend, in the south, with the rigours of the desert, or in the north with land resistant to cultivation; the newcomers were soldiers from necessity. But who can say which is better, to drink horse's blood fresh from a brimming cup or to consign a slave to the galleys, a Christian to the lions?

There is another aspect of this society, linked in part with the preceding one, though not in this instance raising any moral issue, which seems insufficiently stressed: the scope for human mobility. This assertion may come as a surprise. Our picture is of an urban world, of *villae* tied to the soil, and of roads meant to be indestructible; even the law attempted to chain men to their villages, and to their trades, as Marjorian laid down as late as 460. The growing disorder would inevitably lead people, as we know was often the case, to cluster more tightly round the head of a family, a master, or a warlord; the letter of the law classed the men of the time, on both sides of the *limes*, with their clan, their *gens* or their family. On all this there is little room for disagreement. But two factors tend to be ignored. One is conjunctural: the disturbances brought by wars, but equally fiscal oppression and the quite excessive demands of bureaucracy, put men to flight. Having torn up their roots, they fell into the state of outlawry and insecurity which for centuries was to be the fate of the lone individual. To escape the oncoming Alamans, Saxons, Persians or Vandals, men fled from Belgica to Provence, from Wales to Armorica, from Syria as far as Pontus, from Africa to Sicily; the many treasure-hoards from the third or fourth century found buried along the highways are testimony to these precipitate departures from which there was no return. On the other hand, the half-starved marauding bands which scoured the countryside and even terrorised the towns, the *circumcelliones* of Africa and the *bacaudae* in Gaul, seem to have reached the stage of social protest and chronic insubmission. Beneath the surface of what was supposed to be a single *Romania* the forces of decomposition were making headway.

Until quite recently it was usual to contrast a world composed of sedentary peasants and urban merchants with a world beyond the *limes* inhabited by nomad herdsmen and itinerant farmers, who scratched the soil and then moved on. The remarkable achieve-

On this Gallo-Roman 'labours of the months' from
St-Roman-en-Gall, two slaves operate the levers of
an oil-press (St-Germain-en-Laye, Musée des
Antiquités nationales).

ments of agrarian archaeologists have made it necessary to revise this traditional picture. It
is not only in non-Romanised regions, such as Frisia and central Germany, where it would
be natural, but also west of the Rhine and Danube, in England, Gaul and Rhaetia, that the
area of habitation appears to be slight and ill-defined, moving over cultivable clearings
where the plots are indistinct and no set pattern of sowing seems to have been followed.
Naturally we come across certain fixed points: the *villae*, where they survive, cemeteries, if
still in use, the towns, of course, centuriations, wherever the fields have been laid out in this
chessboard fashion; and this phenomenon becomes more noticeable further to the south
and east. For the area actually bordering the Mediterranean we still lack studies in
sufficient quantity and depth, which makes it wiser in this instance to stick to the
traditional picture.

Slavery, the basic mode of production, was still in evidence. As well as being practised
among the Saxons, Goths and Slavs, although this is often denied, it had by no means been
abandoned further south, notwithstanding the difficulties of breeding human cattle. The
Church entered a weak protest, but since it regarded work as alienating had nothing
constructive to offer. The slave economy thus continued, with all its well-known consequences: technical stagnation, absence of specialised skills, non-differentiation of labour,
low yields, risk of revolts and bloodshed. So long as this mode of production remained intact
Antiquity was still in being.

It is easy to seize on the town and its territory, the *civitas* of Antiquity, as typifying
Graeco-Roman society, and to conclude that their disappearance marks the beginning of
the Middle Ages, especially if it is accepted that the very idea of the *civitas*, its ways and its
purposes, was beyond the newcomers' grasp. Reservations on this latter poinr will be
mentioned below, but recent historical scholarship has shown in any case that the death of
towns is not to be presumed. Although often weakened, diminished, robbed in part of their

9

control over the surrounding country, towns managed to survive and remain influential, even in the heart of Gaul and Britain or on the fringe of the Germanic, Arab or Berber worlds. That as regards their functions, their adornment and their political or economic importance these towns, except those in the East, bore little resemblance to their ancestors is not in dispute; but what we witness here is a transformation rather than a deathbed. It should all the same be stressed that the tax system, unable to operate effectively in the countryside, battened on the towns, draining them of vitality, driving away their inhabitants and undermining their authority; yet apart from a belt badly affected by burnings and evacuations, the towns in question would still be on the map in the early Middle Ages.

To describe a Chilperic or a Reccared as not fundamentally different from a Herakleios, a Chosroes or a Valentinian will shock any true devotee of *Romania*. Yet the difference is only one of scale – the nature of their power remains the same. The State had long since ceased to be the property of all; it was now the property of the prince, who indeed might not even possess the advantage of a magic aura to raise him above his barbarian following, as with the Merovingians, or that of an ecclesiastical sacring, as with the Visigoths. Whether the source is the Sun-God, Zoroaster or the God of the Christians, authority depended on the sacred and the divine for its justification and legitimacy. Power was military, charismatic, personal; it was a mingling of the profane and the sacred, and everything pertaining to the prince became his, the public land and the treasury as well as the soldiers and clients. Among the Saxons, untouched by Rome, or the Merovingians, whose reputation stands mid-way between the odious and the grotesque, there was indeed a greater feeling for the *res publica*, for the respect due to the law, than was displayed by Persian potentates or by the soldiers of fortune enthroned at Byzantium. So it seems inappropriate to speak of political anaemia in the West, when the essence of *auctoritas* was not changed. Ine, Dagobert, Theodoric can stand beside a Justinian, not to mention a Maurice, inasmuch as they show the same preoccupation with an effective moral order, the same dependence on their entourage, indeed the same resort to force. And the one fundamental difference, the perpetuation in the East of a ponderous bureaucratic machine of Egyptian proportions, which with its formalistic and tyrannical ways snarled up, delayed or frustrated any attempt at originality, is surely nothing to boast about.

Vanishing landmarks

We therefore have one or two firm footholds from which to advance into the Middle Ages. Meanwhile, other landmarks become conspicuous by their absence. The most obvious – however many nuances and revisions may be called for – is the growing separation between the fragmented halves of the mutilated *Romania*: soon it would not be possible to address letters from Clermont to Nicaea, or to travel from York to Hippo. The idea of a common history undoubtedly persists, and in the West will be appropriated by 'barbarians' convinced that they too are 'Romans'; but the top stratum of society, that of the wealthy and educated, whose estates, like their friendships and disciples, were once scattered all round the Mediterranean, was losing its coherence and was obliged to concentrate on more parochial interests. And since this is virtually the only class to speak to us directly, we sympathise with their laments: Roman universalism was indeed receding into the realm of ideals or lofty memories. It took all the pertinacity of a conquering Church to assert the corporate existence of its believers, extending far beyond Rome itself, and to view as a moral victory what was in fact an intellectually crippling defeat.

Nothing has so far been said about the material aspect of the ever-enlarging wound, the 'haemorrhage of gold', as Marc Bloch termed it; this was perhaps an exaggeration, but there is certainly evidence of a contraction of demand in the West and a narrowing of its trading contacts. Even in those regions where urban centres remain most active – southern Gaul, Spain, Italy – relations with the East were less intense: for their vital food supplies the urban populations were clearly more dependent on the great landowners than on merchants arriving from Syria. And since the aristocracy, whether senatorial or barbarian, remained faithful to the old ways in their fondness for luxury foods and ostentatious living, one might sum up by saying that the tendencies of the trading balance and of the balance of payments were reversed; the West's trading balance was now adverse, and was to remain so for the foreseeable future. One would like to be equally confident about the rural sector, to be sure that open-ended patterns of settlement were henceforth to be the rule, that the untilled waste, the Roman *saltus*, public property or not, was being exploited as the second face of the ecosystem now germinating. But archaeology has yet to furnish proofs: so far it has only demonstrated that the majority of the great estates cultivated in the second century, and even those which were reinstated after the chaos of the third century, were abandoned at some time between 400 and 600. But what took their place? Inflated *vici*? Hamlets of collective cultivators roaming over the soil? Farmsteads (*casae*) dispersed among the vast mass of a landed *plebs*? Or a mixture of all three? And when room has to be made for newcomers, what is the precise nature of the *hospitalitas* which the State forces on the owners of the land: cohabitation? Partition? Fragmentation? On this fundamental subject there is much that remains obscure, but the general drift is for once quite clear: the importance vested in the countryside by the contraction of towns finds reflection in a reordering of the agrarian structure, and perhaps of its social components.

Lastly, on another level, the ground simply disappears, above all in the West, where this served to aggravate the conflicts already touched on. The question of whether land registers and tax schedules were actually drawn up for all the provinces of the Roman empire is largely academic. For what seems to be beyond doubt is that in consequence of the fragmentation of the empire in the West into a number of units under princely rule, often with a substratum of regional lordships, and in the East of difficulties encountered by a theoretically uniform government in imposing its demands on outlying or semi-conquered provinces, the two fundamental supports of a supreme authority were being undermined: the power to enlist citizens in the army, and the power to impose taxes. Recourse to mercenaries was already long-standing and there is no need to dwell here on the contribution of these immigrants, in all parts of *Romania*, to the dilution of civic values; in this connection, the recourse in the West during troubled times to the alternative of enlisting and arming freemen, who then became merged with the professional warriors of the prince's entourage, bears a closer resemblance to the legionary levies of Classical times than was achieved by the army of foreign mercenaries employed by the rulers of Byzantium or Ctesiphon, or by the meagre and reluctant bands of tax-payers conscripted to the army in fulfilment of their obligation. In regard to taxes, the situation seems to have been the other way about: in the East the fiscal system was still theoretically in being, and although there were difficulties over collection, and amounts were apt to diminish en route as a result of theft or corruption, a little of what was levied still found its way – though in what sort of currency? – to the public treasury; attaching the tax-payer to the soil in accordance with well-tried fourth-century methods, or making a neighbour responsible for his quota, merely provoked headlong flight in the face of requisitions, tax demands or the call to arms. In the West, where the authority of the tax bureaux was in tatters, even in Italy and Spain, kings found they could get rid of trouble-makers merely by appointing them to collect taxes, after which they were rarely seen again. The Anglo-Saxons, strangely enough, were an exception, for although never in close contact with Rome, they appear to have been the one people who clung to the idea of a material service being due to the prince.

Pointers to the future

It took five centuries for Western Europe to recover; but for another ten centuries it would dominate the world. We can admit that around the year 500 there was more to Western Europe than a pile of dust and 'remnants'.

Because our sources give the impression that they were exceptional, it has been all too easy to discount signs that the newcomers were positively welcomed, just as it has been easy to condemn the later conversion to Islam of so many ancient centres of Christianity. Such acts are seen as a mark of aberrancy, treason or a perverted ideology, following Cicero or Marcus Aurelius. The question is not posed in relation to the overwhelming mass of the poor; yet the acclamations in fact originate from them, which should remind us that nothing lasts or is possible if nine-tenths of the population are against it, but that everything is possible so long as it accords with their deep-seated and tacit desires. This is how the fifth-century priest Salvian summed up the situation: 'The poor, plundered and beaten, and having lost the honour of being Romans and thereby any right to liberty, sought to rediscover the humanity of the Romans among the barbarians.' It is easy for the more sophisticated to sneer at this as the 'myth of the noble savage', which perhaps it is; yet when the Church subscribes to it, when a number of senators discover that it safeguards their interests, we have arrived unknowingly in 'Merovingian' Gaul. Was it a justified investment, guaranteed to succeed? I believe it was, and similarly with the later investment in Islam. People who had felt themselves betrayed were becoming more insistent in their demand for an uncompromising but uncomplicated religion, for a power that was concrete and visible, for a reduced but secure horizon. Are we to see in all this merely a regression?

Moreover, the movement to the countryside tends to be accompanied by revivals of many kinds, linguistic, mental and familial, which cause cracks to appear in the Graeco-Roman veneer spread across Gaul, Illyricum, Egypt, Africa and Spain. It is hard to see that

Defence of the empire. Roman cavalry and barbarian prisoners. Late Roman porphyry sarcophagus (Rome, Vatican Museum).

the contributions of the newcomers in any way merit the contempt reserved for them by the adepts of *romanitas*. Gaul itself appears to have gained very little from the Roman occupation. After the fifth century there is not a burial which does not disclose the superior industrial skills of the 'barbarian' in comparison with the mediocrity of Mediterranean techniques, as has been demonstrated for tools and weapons with the aid of the electric arc. The arts of building in wood, rearing pigs and dairy cattle, and cavalry warfare, like the abstract or animal art forms which still exert an attraction, can all stand comparison with the Graeco-Roman inheritance. The regulation of family affairs, and agrarian techniques, are by no means inferior to Roman law or the impoverished agricultures of the south. If we   13 also take into the account the demographic vigour which seems to have deserted the old world at this period, then justice will perhaps have been done.

But there is another area of growth which leaves no room for argument, since it is indisputable and easy to measure: the world was becoming larger. This phenomenon, whose importance can scarcely be over-rated, is the only one which might justify placing the break between Antiquity and the Middle Ages precisely where we expect to find one. Before about 300 or 350, 'History' is limited to a band of territories running from Gibraltar to Japan and sandwiched between the Tropic and the 50th degree of latitude north: in this 'civilised zone', then shared by the four great Mediterranean or sub-tropical empires, written records flourished but progress was slow. To the south of it there existed independent cultural zones, such as pre-Islamic Arabia, the federations of black peoples, or Indo-China, which were exploited by the 'empires' as a source of slaves, precious metals and raw materials. But new cultural areas were developing, especially in the north, more of whose riches are being uncovered each year by the archaeologists. The peoples in question, the Dacians, the Sarmatians, the Germans, the Celts and possibly the Turks, remain mute; but their burials, their habitations, the tales of their heroic deeds penetrating to the south, testify to their energy, character and diversity. These two zones, the northern and the southern, henceforth become part of 'History': from now on the Western world stretches from the Baltic to Guinea, from the Urals to Zanzibar. Whatever cause one assigns to it, this was a turning-point in human history, a sudden opening up of possibilities and prospects and a natural prelude to the second great expansion of horizons which occurred in the sixteenth century. A change of this magnitude does not come unannounced. Premonitions of it could be felt in the 'middle' zone well before the 'invasions', with the result that the nerve centres of economic or intellectual activity gradually approached the new worlds, as if going out to meet them, moving from Rome to Milan and thence to Trier, from Athens to Constantinople or Alexandria; soon it was to be Baghdad, Cairo, Kairouan, York or Cologne. Well before Alaric laid hands on it, Rome had ceased to be Rome; the Mediterranean was no longer the locus of Western civilisation but merely an object in contention between riparian powers whose strength lay in remote hinterlands long despised or unknown. Is it then surprising that in face of this desertion of the centre, in contemplation of the death throes of the earthly city, a thinker such as Augustine should seek to turn men's thoughts towards the city of God?

PART 1

Break-up of the old worlds: 395–700

Autopsy of the West: the early fifth century 1

In Western Europe there is a tradition of approaching the medieval domain from the western rather than the eastern side. The reasons are obvious: it makes sense for scholars whose concerns are with France or Iberia, or with England or Germany, to pass directly from the ruins of Rome to the 'barbarian' realm; what was happening in the distant East seems of no relevance or importance. If long-term trends are what matter, the view is not entirely mistaken; the result is that these books, like the rest, would again condemn Byzantium to oblivion. Yet it might make still more sense to reverse the usual procedure, to look first at the *Romania* stretching from Naples to the Nile and from the Adriatic to the Euphrates which remained very much alive. From this standpoint it becomes easier to lay stress on the continuity which typifies the 'early Middle Ages', to expose as false for good and all any notion of a decisive break, and to put a dethroned West back where it belongs, in second place. Our reason for adhering yet again to the traditional order, that is, following the Western developments first, is that to plunge directly into the less familiar world of the East might be confusing to the general reader; and it may be that the Byzantine counter-point, introduced at a later stage, will strike an original, and also a more comprehensible, note. But it should be stressed that the main reason is to suit the reader's convenience.

In 388, Pacatus Drepanius, rhetor of Bordeaux, addressed the following words to the emperor Theodosius: 'We know that no revolution will ever overthrow the State, because the Roman empire is foreordained to remain with you and your descendants.' Yet by 406 the Germans were already crossing the Rhine; in 455 the last scion of the Theodosian dynasty, Valentinian III, was assassinated; and in 476 the last Roman emperor in the West, Romulus Augustulus, was deposed. Julius Nepos, whose throne Romulus had usurped, however, reigned as acknowledged Emperor in exile in Dalmatia until 480. The empire broke up into a multiplicity of Germanic realms.

The admiration, bordering on blind faith, evinced by Pacatus towards Rome can be explained. It was an attempt to exorcise the future, an over-optimistic effort to assert the immutability of Rome's civilisation in the face of all indications to the contrary. Pacatus was but one of many devotees of Graeco-Roman civilisation and culture who, having freely succumbed to the attractions of the *orbis romanus*, the civilised world of Rome, had acquired an emotional attachment to its universality. It is thus important for us to have a good grasp

Survival of Classical art: pagan and Christian themes. Panel of an ivory diptych of Adam and St Paul. Here we see Adam in the earthly Paradise: his carefree posture, the trust reigning between him and the animals, the beauty of the sculpted human and animal forms suggest a wholly pagan enjoyment of life (Northern Italy, late fourth century; Florence, Bargello).

of the essential structures of late Roman Antiquity, bequeathed in due course to the barbarian kingdoms, before moving on to witness the slow, seemingly unending process of Rome's demise, throughout which Rome did not cease to polarise men's affections and generate nostalgia. Next, having seen what were the distinctive features of the Roman and German antagonists, we shall be equipped to confront the crises in the Germanic kingdoms, uneasily poised as they were between the abandonment of old and obsolete solutions and the contrivance of social or economic practices better suited to their needs. For the so-called era of the barbarian kingdoms, after a brief period of stabilisation, in fact witnessed some of the greatest changes in recorded history.

Because of its linguistically pejorative associations, the term Low Empire (*Bas Empire*) will not be used here to describe the Roman civilisation of the fourth and fifth centuries, which it is better to call 'late Antiquity'. In the course of these centuries the empire was indeed profoundly altered, not to say transformed, by emperors of the Constantinian and Valentinian–Theodosian dynasties in their efforts to ward off the Germanic threat. A much greater rigidity was imposed on a political system which had once been accommodating but was now bureaucratic and Christianised. Society came to be dominated by a few important senatorial families whose power was constantly increasing. Lastly, the relative prosperity of an economy less and less dependent on slave labour ensured a measure of stability and sustained Rome's prestige with the mass of peoples inside and outside the empire. This civilisation was thus at once a prize and a bait which could not fail to attract the barbarians, out of a mixture of fear and admiration.

A rigid and voracious state

The year 395 saw the division of the Roman empire between two emperors, the West going to Honorius, whose chief seat was Ravenna, and the East to Arcadius, who ruled it from the capital city, Constantinople, the New Rome. Between them they presided over a great mass of territories – Italy and the islands, North Africa, Spain, Gaul as far as the Rhine, Britain south of Scotland, the lands of Illyricum, Pannonia, Noricum and Raetia reaching to the Danube – which the Romans had welded into a political unit but which were now greatly coveted by the barbarians. It may be true that from 405 there was a growing acknowledgment, at any rate in theory, of the bonds of friendship uniting the two parts of the empire. In reality, the diametrically opposed nature of their respective evolutions drove them increasingly further apart, a fact made plain by the adroitness with which the East got rid of its own barbarians by diverting them to the West.

The hollow majesty of the imperial office

As the quotation from Pacatus implies, the panegyrists, the propagandists of the age, sought at every opportunity to hallow the person of the emperor. The epithet 'sacred' is applied, furthermore, to all that relates to his person, his chief ministers and his palace. But this urge to place the emperor on a pinnacle does not make him a totalitarian monarch; for although such a tendency is plain enough in the East, it is less so in the West, in consequence of the Roman juridical tradition. Officially, the emperor promulgated the laws and remained bound by them. St Ambrose, one of the first to place some limit on the Roman emperor's absolute power, puts it thus: 'The emperor promulgates laws and is the first to respect them.' It was this respect for the law which gave such great authority to the Theodosian Code, promulgated to the Eastern Empire in 438, with effect from 1 January 439, and accepted as authoritative by the West. Thereafter, and for centuries to come, it remained the sole foundation of all Roman legislation in the West. Imperial laws and constitutions, naturally also regarded as sacred, were henceforward unalterable, the more so because the courts, when giving judgment, had to refer to them by the exact date of their promulgation.

This primacy of the written law forms the essential dividing line between civilised man and the barbarian, who depends for his law on oral tradition. By enacting the law, the Roman emperor enabled citizens to invoke the law against him; and Roman citizens enjoyed a further protection stemming from the essential distinction drawn in Roman law between public and private affairs, which resulted in two separate laws under the same name. Public law and private law existed in genuine opposition, the domain of the State (*res publica*) being kept carefully distinct from that of private persons. The logicality of these distinctions, which gave Roman law its flexibility but above all its precision, made the law an essential tool of government. Indeed, to correspond with the contrast between public and private spheres we have another pairing: that of military service (*militia armata*) and civil service (*militia officialis*). All the fundamentals of Roman society were thus brought within the compass of the law; private citizens looked to functionaries of the *militia officialis* for administration and to the *militia armata* for defence. The Roman law of which the emperor was the fount is here seen at its most sublime.

The imperial power could also draw inspiration from the Church. Paganism had been abolished since 392 and Christianity was now the state religion. But if the temples were shut and public worship of the pagan gods forbidden, practices and beliefs associated with the former religion persisted. Offerings of coins to the healing spirits of thermal springs may have disappeared between 400 and 450, at dates varying according to the region, but ignorance of the new religion was widespread, especially in country districts and at the extremities of the Western world – Mauretania, Galicia, Armorica, Britain, by the Channel or the North Sea. To compensate, nearly all the towns were Christianised, each with its resident bishop. It was the duty of Councils, to which every bishop was summoned, to safeguard the orthodoxy of the faith. The emperor presided and took part in the debates, intervening in his capacity of upholder of the divine peace. Depending on the forcefulness of his personality, he went along with the doctrinal decrees or decided to enact them himself, without always consulting the interested parties. But the emperor was not the only one to claim the role of supreme arbiter in religious affairs. For if it fell to him to arrest and punish heretics, the fact of his removal to Ravenna made it easier for another personage, the pope, to assert himself in Rome, where the city of Romulus and Remus showed signs of becoming a new capital, founded for a second time by a pair of 'brothers', Peter and Paul, fellow-martyrs in the faith. The popes of the fourth and fifth centuries entered in full into their Roman inheritance, and by extending their jurisdiction to all the Churches claimed to be their head. The City *par excellence* having been redeemed by the baptised, the popes were able to identify *romanitas* with Christendom and make of Rome a symbol of eternity. Thus through the channel of papal power Christianity reinforced imperial power, while not explicitly deferring to the emperor on the question of moral tutelage over the world. Christians therefore ceased to question the Roman empire. On the contrary, they became its mainstay and took for granted the identification of the new religion with *romanitas*.

We must now descend from these ideological heights to inspect the actual components of imperial power. The dynasty known as the Theodosian held power more or less on sufferance. The old Roman tradition harking back to the beginnings of the empire, that

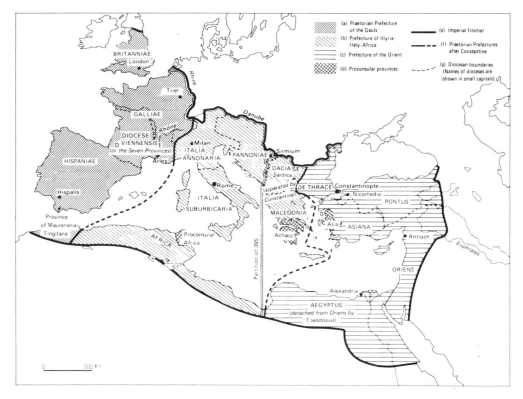

1 The Roman Empire in the fourth century

emperors were made by the army, was still current. The possibility that a general would be proclaimed emperor by his troops was ever-present, especially on one of the threatened frontiers. If he failed, he went the way of oblivion (*damnatio memoriae*) and was execrated by posterity; but if the erstwhile tyrant succeeded he became sacred and worthy of respect. In troubled times the possibility of such usurpations naturally increased; and because the emperor no longer commanded the army in person, the generals in his entourage became all the more dangerous and had their movements carefully watched. The greatest of these potential rivals was always the *magister militum praesentalis* (commander-in-chief), who was frequently adorned with the dignity of consul or *patricius*. Confident of the loyalty of the army at his back, the *magister* was able to play the part of an all-powerful vice-emperor who leaves a semblance of authority to the puppet he has allowed to occupy the throne or directly installed on it. With his distinctive insignia (the gold circlet around his head), he was the man with the last word, the *de facto* ruler, but equally the object of such hatred that he went in constant danger of assassination. Thus, for all its impressive facade and numerous supports, the imperial power contained an intrinsic flaw: the lack of a convincing claim to legitimacy where the emperor was not a war leader.

21

A bureaucracy hungry for men and gold

If the imperial government nevertheless remains impressive it is on account of its bureau-cratic organisation, which was very advanced for the age. From whichever residence they were issued, Ravenna, Milan, Trier, or after 407 Arles, imperial orders were regularly conveyed by the state postal service to top-ranking officials stationed in the regions: the praetorian prefects (of which the West had three), the sub-prefects in charge of each diocese (subdivision of the prefecture), and the provincial governors. Only the *civitates*, the smallest of the subdivisions, continued to be governed by the assembly of local notables or *curiales*, members of the *curia*, a sort of municipal senate which met to discuss implementation of the imperial decrees. At the centre was the *comitatus*, composed of the emperor's chief ministers. Around them buzzed a host of functionaries with high-sounding titles whose salaries were paid in gold. However it is precisely this top tier of officials, comprising the central administration, that we see gradually fading out, to disappear altogether during the course of the fifth century. For this reason it is more important to concentrate on those parts of the administration which survived, that is to say the judicial, financial and military organisation at provincial level.

The important local officials referred to above all had power to hold a court of justice, which meant it was possible for an appeal to go from one to the other, right up to the imperial praetorian prefect and the emperor himself. But because these courts were so quickly encumbered with suits and so slow to decide them, the system had proved inadequate. Accordingly, to protect the interests of the poorest, jurisdiction in minor civil suits was reserved to *defensores*, persons elected by certain citizens from the town, one for each *civitas*. It was also accepted that bishops could hear cases, provided both parties agreed, and their jurisdiction soon became much sought after. But in the absence of professional judges, the officials responsible for the tribunals still found the work almost more than they could cope with, even those who had themselves been lawyers. Finally, in an effort to bring justice within everyone's reach, Valentinian III (or it may have been Marjorian, 457–61) installed a 'count' (*comes*) with judicial functions in the capital of the *civitas*, thus suppressing what remained of urban autonomy. Paradoxically, this final act of centralisation in the West was also one of the most durable. Mention should also be made of the *notarii*, petty officials in the governor's entourage or employed to register the court's decisions. More like stenographers than notaries in our modern sense, they took notes of meetings and of all policy decisions, recording them in 'tironian notes' (shorthand) for subsequent transcription. Although mere functionaries, they were privy to many impor-tant secrets from which they often went on to pursue brilliant careers. Few hopes of this kind could be entertained by the *tabelliones* (the rough equivalents of modern notaries), who were named after the tablets on which they wrote down contracts, acts of sale and wills. Of humble origin, the *tabelliones* were none the less depositaries at the lowest level of Roman legal culture, deriving their knowledge from the formularies which they faithfully copied in their deeds, paying scrupulous attention to each clause. Other than this, all they had to do was to insert the relevant place-names and figures at the places left blank in the

Paying taxes. Third-century bas-relief from Noviomagus (Neumagen, Germany; Landesmuseum, Trier).

formula, along with the names of the contracting parties. *Tabelliones* were to be found in every town and even in the larger rural centres, with the result that Roman law managed to penetrate deep into the countryside.

It was much the same with the financial administration, which, although creaking, managed everywhere to retain its hold over rent and tax-payers. A good part of the State's revenues came from public lands. These included lands confiscated from traitors and from pagan temples, properties lying intestate or unexploited, and areas devastated by war or deserted by their inhabitants. Leased out by bailiffs to peasants, these lands brought in considerable revenue, and there can have been few *civitates* without such properties in their territory. Among other imperial revenues, the taxes on mines, quarries and mints brought in appreciable returns.

The West had only six official mints: Trier, Lyons and Arles in Gaul, Aquileia and Rome in Italy, and Sirmium (Sremska Mitrovica) in Pannonia. Constantine had succeeded in standardising the coinage with the issue of a gold coin, the *solidus*, of 4.55g. The circulation of these coins, which were issued in great quantity, was facilitated by the State's refusal to accept tax payments in any other coin. The circulation of silver coins was on a very small scale. Copper coins were used for all petty transactions and for the pay of common soldiers. The high quality of this Roman coinage, which made its issue profitable to the State and stimulated trade, had done much to promote the development of a monetary economy.

The most obvious proof is the progressive spread during the fifth century of payment of taxes in gold coin, at a time when it was normally reckoned in kind. The Roman bureaucracy had come to excel in the complexity of its fiscal arrangements, which varied from region to region. In theory, two forms of tax existed side by side – a tax on the soil and a tax on heads, the land-tax and the poll-tax. The units used for tax purposes were abstractions, arrived at by grouping together types of land, or by counting a certain number of heads. This required the regular updating of land registers and censuses, which

23

was supposed to happen every fifteen years; this period was known as the indiction. The tax rate per unit was fixed annually by the government prior to the beginning of the financial year (1 September). The municipal councils then appointed collectors from among themselves who consulted the registers kept on tablets in the tax office and informed tax-payers of the amount due. It was collected in three instalments, which prevented congestion on the highways and abrupt falls in the price of produce on the markets. Although the offices employed an army of scribes to keep accounts up to date, the idea of using civil servants to collect taxes seems never to have occurred to the Roman government. The curial or decurion acting in this capacity remained a private individual and was obliged to make good any deficiency from his own resources. As a result these amateur government agents were often overbearing and ruthless in their extraction of taxes and tended to make themselves unpopular. If on the other hand they failed to recover the fixed amount, fear of financial ruin would make them abandon their status and sink out of sight far from their town. When there was a shortfall in the portion of the tax still to be rendered in kind, the government could make up the deficiency by requisitions. And it was of course assiduous in pursuit of arrears.

The system thus gave rise to abuses, if only because land registers and censuses were not systematically revised. These could take the form of misappropriation of funds at the top and extortionate demands upon simple peasants at the bottom. Great landed proprietors often intervened to ensure that their quota was underestimated. Even as things stood, however, the State was able to collect what it needed, although the burden on agriculture was heavy. The one tax levied specifically on craftsmen and merchants, the *collatio lustralis*, brought in only about five per cent of the total from land-tax. The growing volume of complaint against the fiscal system in the fifth century makes it necessary to ask whether this method of taxation was impoverishing the tax-payers. The first thing to note is that the system penalised large families and that, local exceptions apart, it did not discriminate between fertile and less fertile land. Second, to judge from such figures as are available, it seems that in Italy, for example, the total levy on the crop came close to two-thirds, without counting the rent tenants paid for their land. The rates prevailing in the western part of the empire must almost certainly have been higher than in the eastern part, since the taxes raised on lands in Egypt amounted to two-fifths of the crop. Yet we also know that of all the eastern provinces, Egypt produced the most in taxes. In the West, Africa headed the list – yet the total of its fiscal receipts was equivalent only to one-third of those derived from Egypt! There can be little doubt, then, that the West was poorer than the East and would therefore have had greater difficulty in finding the wherewithal for defence, as well as being so heavily taxed.

A crushing and fruitless military burden

Expenditure in connection with the army did indeed represent the main drain on the West's resources. True, there were other items: civil service salaries, the upkeep of the imperial court and the cost of supplying free rations to the heads of 120,000 citizen households in

Cologne was the oldest Roman town in Germania and strategically very important. Divitia (Deutz), the fortress built facing it on the east bank of the Rhine (the illustration represents a reconstruction) was large enough for a garrison of 900 soldiers.

Rome. In the West, however, the number of civil servants never exceeded 15,000, quite a modest figure, while the bread, pork and oil doled out to the Romans could be procured from the emperor's private or public estates or imported by the *navicularii*, the state-controlled corporations of shippers. The tax product was thus very largely devoted to the West's standing army of 250,000 troops. The ferocity of fiscal demands was a consequence of the continual threats pressing against the frontiers.

There are two essential points to be grasped about the Roman army. The first is the way in which military and civilian functions were kept totally separate, so as to leave the superiority in law with officials whose role was wholly administrative and to minimise the opportunities for a *coup d'état*. Second, the units composing the army were of two main types; those which guarded the frontiers (*riparienses, limitanei*), and those in the field army (the *comitatenses*), stationed in the interior and available for deployment by the emperor at the most threatened points on the border. In the West the frontier army had an approximate strength of 135,000, the imperial army of 115,000.

Of the two, the frontier army was the less effectual. Relatively strong in numbers on the Danube and on the Scottish borders, it had dwindled on the Rhine to a force of around 6,000. As a rule, these soldiers were garrisoned in small forts and led a bipartite existence, devoting their time partly to guard duties and drill, and partly to the cultivation of a small plot of land or perhaps to the exercise of a trade. Many of these units had no existence outside the official registers. The regiments in Africa and Spain were made up almost exclusively of troops of this unsatisfactory type.

25

There were only three regions with proper field armies at their disposal: Italy and Gaul, each with 30,000 men, and Britain, with 5,000. If, as is estimated by English demographers, the total population of Western Europe and Africa was in the region of 26 million, Rome was very poorly protected, even by the theoretical figure of 250,000 men, but all the more so in practice by an effective contingent of 65,000.

The chief reason for the shortfall was the poor return from recruitment. Conscription took place annually and in theory affected all citizens of the empire. The number of free peasants each landowner was expected to furnish was related to the number of tax units on which he was assessed. Smaller landowners whose individual holdings did not qualify as a full fiscal unit were grouped into a consortium in order that they might designate one of their number to serve and contribute towards his expenses. All soldiers were exempt from taxes, and clerics were officially exempt from military service. The engagement was a long one, at least 25 years of service having to be completed before a soldier could claim the privileges of a veteran: fiscal immunity, an allotment of land and honorary privileges. In reality, landowners reluctant to weaken their labour force would either rid themselves in this way of the most idle or pay the equivalent of a recruit in cash. Those who did not succeed in evading the draft often deserted. This explains why military service in practice became hereditary, especially among the troops of the frontier armies, the *limitanei*. In such regions, where wars were commonplace, recruitment was relatively easy; but this was not the case in Africa, Spain, southern Gaul and Italy, which remained destitute of effective troops. These peaceful interior parts of the empire were thus more vulnerable than parts lying close to the frontiers.

It was the lack of a large regular army which made Roman commanders turn to the barbarians. Some of those engaged were volunteers who, once they had made their fortune, returned to their homes across the Rhine, where their sumptuous burials have been discovered. Others – Sueves, Sarmatians or Burgundians – originally prisoners of war, had been settled on vacant lands well inside the empire and bound to military service. These were known as *laeti*. Entire contingents of Franks or Goths were sometimes enlisted to form crack regiments of the field army. Their officers frequently became romanised and rose to such high rank that they came into direct contact with the emperor's entourage. The policy of forming alliances with particular barbarian tribes led in many instances to the conclusion of treaties (*foedus*) requiring them to fight alongside Roman troops. It was not long before whole tribes of these *federates* became settled on Roman territory. In the West the most obvious example is provided by the Franks. Since the time of Constantine a contingent of Rhineland Franks had been employed to mount guard on the left bank of the Rhine, the *ripa*, hence their designation as 'Ripuarian Franks'. Meanwhile, a second group, the 'Salian' Franks, had been settled by the emperor Julian (mid-fourth century) in Toxandria, in the north of present-day Belgium, where their settlement zone was defined by a chain of garrisoned forts running from Tongres through Bavay to Odilienberg. In these two instances barbarians were thus already present on imperial territory before the 'invasions' had even started. But their loyalty, their hope of becoming Romanised, and above all the example of the Germanic contingents already successfully incorporated into

Roman units all served to allay suspicions regarding these *federates*, who continued to live under their own laws, differing in this respect from the volunteers who continued to make up a substantial proportion of the regular forces. If statistics derived from excavation of late fourth- and early fifth-century cemeteries annexed to Roman forts in Belgium are to be believed, for every hundred soldiers based around Vermand (near Saint-Quentin), between ten and twenty were of Germanic origin, while at Furfooz in southern Belgium the proportion was as high as 70 per cent. It should be pointed out, however, that the presence of Germanic grave goods in an individual's grave proves nothing about his origin. Obviously, the risk taken by the empire in augmenting its troops by such means could well have unexpected or dangerous consequences. Furthermore, the fact that the Roman army was sustained by an all-providing bureaucracy exerted its own attraction on the Germans, by reason of the perquisites on offer, and stimulated the market economy, along with speculation, while making the burden on the population in general that much heavier. For as well as receiving gifts in gold coin to mark imperial accessions, and being provided with wages, uniforms (manufactured in government weaving establishments) and, in the case of officers, weapons made in government workshops and often ornamented, the troops were furnished with cavalry horses reared on state stud farms (the cavalry made up just over one-fifth of the army) and with rations of bread, wine, meat and oil, not forgetting fodder for the horses. Distribution of the soldier's daily rations – roughly a kilo of bread, over 600g of pork, a litre of wine and seven centilitres of oil – was made from a network of government foodstores. Lastly, under the law of *hospitalitas*, every soldier serving with the field army had the right to be billeted on a local inhabitant, who was obliged to let him occupy a third of his house. This cushioned existence, reflecting the habits of a civilised, sedentary, high-consuming population, must have appeared sheer paradise to Europe's semi-nomadic Germans and Slavs, to whom it would have seemed that serving the empire was an easier and more attractive proposition than life on the other side of the frontier.

But the Germanic peoples can have had no inkling of the gigantic effort required to pay for these services and to cater in advance for the army's every need. A good part of the corn grown in Africa and 'Italia annonaria' was despatched in convoys of ships or wagons to Rome and to the garrisons on the Danube or in the peninsula. 'Italia annonaria', the district embracing the fertile Po plains, owed its name to the *annona*, the vital corn ration which it provided. The troops stationed on the Rhine or in the interior were similarly supplied with corn from the plains of Aquitaine, the Paris basin and the Thames valley. It was therefore essential for the administration to make sure of a steady return from taxation. We have already seen that this could only be achieved with the help of large-scale requisitions. It was necessary to offset the unpredictable incidence of bad harvests and to check the speculation rife at such times by requisitioning foodstuffs at low prices, which did not please the producers. To keep itself well-informed, the government employed spies and allowed them to travel free of charge with the official postal service (*cursus publicus*), which entailed yet more requisitions, of horses and so forth. In short, as an instrument of government the Roman army was as unwieldy as the often overworked civilian services. Low in productivity, high in consumption, the army was a living paradox. It defended the empire with the

The frontier army. Helmet, of which only the silver casing survives, discovered in a peat-bog at Deurne. Its owner, a Roman officer, must have fallen from his horse; the recently minted coins in his purse indicate the date of the accident as around 319–20 (Leiden, Rijksmuseum van Oudheden).

help of large barbarian contingents of whose loyalty no one was certain. Janus-like, its demands worked in opposite directions, stimulating agricultural production in the hinterlands on the one hand, but accentuating fiscal oppression on the other. The greater its technicality and efficiency, the more vulnerable the army became, and the more it attracted the enemy.

A society in flight from the state

The problem is therefore not to decide whether the Roman government was unduly voracious or incompetent, since its objectives were achieved despite the obstacles classically encountered by bureaucracy, but to discover whether it managed to mobilise all its strength in the face of the perpetual threat of war. What in fact appears to have happened is that Roman society, following the example of emperors such as Honorius (395–423) and Valentinian III (425–55), who immured themselves in Ravenna, retreated into its shell in an endeavour to escape from the State, while still enjoying its advantages. If determined generals, authoritarian bishops and censorious monks wrestled with intractable problems and denounced the general apathy, they formed a distinct minority; the reaction of the majority was to evade public responsibilities and seek out alternative political structures which offered greater protection and security, be it the patronage afforded by great senators (the 'patronate') or the charitable institutions of the Church.

Alienation or subjugation of the labour force

We have seen that those who benefited from the State, apart from the heads of Roman households, were the officials and soldiers, whose remuneration in gold coin gave them superior purchasing power. The slaves, too, belonged to the privileged category, since in the eyes of those in flight from conscription and taxation they enjoyed the exceptional advantage of being totally exempt from such burdens. True, slaves were not citizens and in theory they were still merely tools with the power of speech. The majority of household servants were slaves, particularly among soldiers, who often possessed two, if not more. In the establishments of wealthy senators slaves could be counted by the hundred. But outside the household, where it was a question of performing menial, everyday chores no one else wanted to do, slave labour came into competition with the free labour force. Lacking the spur of working for personal gain, a slave worker tended to be only half as productive as his free counterpart, and this holds good for all places where slaves were employed – mines, quarries, state-run weaving factories and foundries, and above all farms. An agricultural slave thus did not furnish the master of an estate with the requisite profit on his investment. Consequently, from the time of Valentinian I it was forbidden to sell a slave without selling the land to which he was attached as cultivator. The object of this measure was to prevent loss of the crop and hence of the tax, but also to secure for the slave opportunity to work the land for personal gain, against payment of rent to the proprietor. The bait of an improved economic status was thus offered to the slave settled on his own plot (*casatus*, domiciled) in order to increase his productivity. From the scanty statistical data assembled by A. H. M. Jones it seems that these rural slaves were in fact not numerous. Arguing from the similarity of the social structure in the eastern and western parts of the empire, it can be supposed on the evidence of certain estates in Asia Minor that slaves only formed ten to twelve per cent of the agricultural workforce. Late-Antique society was thus no longer slavist, except in the juridical sense.

Was this because the number of slaves had diminished? Born slaves, it is true, remained relatively few in number; but there was no diminution in the supply of prisoners of war who were reduced to slavery. At the end of the fourth century the price at which they were offered actually fell, proof of their abundance. They came from frontier regions, principally Pannonia (present-day western Hungary) and Mauretania (Morocco). The barbarians themselves sold their compatriots and prisoners of war to the Romans. None the less, if

Germanic or other captives were set free, they were not necessarily transformed into agricultural slaves. They might be settled on deserted land as soldier peasants (*laeti*), or occasionally even on holdings as *coloni*. The old solution of large slave-gangs living in barracks on great estates no longer answered.

This amelioration of slavery went hand in hand with the worsening in the status of the *coloni*. This latter appellation was given to all free peasants, whether small freeholders or tenants, who were liable to taxes and conscription. The tenants, in particular, must have envied the exemption from these burdens accorded to slaves. The freeholders, who were frequently overtaxed, were permanently at risk from even partial failure of the harvest. Debt, or partition of the property between children, could quickly reduce freeholders to bankruptcy. Tenants, with rent to pay on top of the tax demanded in gold coin, could see half or even two-thirds of their crops being swallowed up in advance. A freeze on rents, as decreed by the emperor Constantine, was of little avail since landlords got round it by using false measures or demanding gifts in kind (*xenia*), usually the products of animal husbandry (pigs, fowls, eggs, etc.). To make tax collection easier, all peasants were supposed to remain in their place of birth, but even though it meant abandoning their holdings, they were quite ready to flee in order to be rid of their debts. As a result, the State became still more persistent in its efforts to tie tenant *coloni* to the soil, regardless of their free status under the law. But for all the government's repeated injunctions, and the support of great landowners for a policy calculated to provide them with a permanent labour force, the situation steadily deteriorated. As for the free peasants, they could find no better solution than to sell their land to a big landowner in return for liquidation of their debt or payment of their tax in gold coin to the tax-collector; or, best of all, to become the tenant of their former property, responsible thereafter only for the payment of their tax and rent in kind. By thus tying themselves to the soil, they lost their property rights and the status of freemen. Legally speaking, they would still be regarded as free, but in their way of life and economic status there was little to distinguish them in practice from 'domiciled' slaves. Worse was to come in the West, for after 451 an ordinary peasant who had worked for 30 years on the same estate was deemed to have become a *colonus* attached to the soil. The reductive process whereby freemen could be turned first into *coloni* and then into slaves is graphically summed up by the monk Salvian: 'Little men robbed of their dwelling and plot of land by brigandage or driven from them by tax-collectors take refuge on the estates of the wealthy and become their *coloni* . . . All those implanted on lands belonging to the wealthy become changed, as though they had drunk of Circe's cup, and are transformed into slaves.'

A free peasant who managed to avoid becoming a *colonus* could try other tactics, such as bribing the local official, or seeking a protector with sufficient influence to win a case on his behalf or to have his tax arrears suppressed. Here it was political rather than economic power that counted. High-ranking army officers or senators with official positions were in fact only too willing to revive the old Roman custom of the patronate. The patron would grant his protection to the freeman he thus received into his following, on the basis of mutual aid. Mostly it was a question of the client's rendering various services or even surrendering land in return for cancellation or suppression of debts, taxes and so on. This contract between equals could be broken off if one of the parties thought he had been wronged, but the dependants, who might be inhabitants of the same village or separate individuals, were often understandably reluctant to forego this protection and its attendant advantages. In this way individuals of every description and entire rural communities passed under the more or less disguised control of the powerful, the *potentes*. This third avenue of escape from the State was never actually prohibited in the West, where the practice of patronage became widespread among the great and powerful.

It should not be concluded from this that medium and small freeholders disappeared completely, or that all *coloni* were reduced to poverty. Many, though how many it is impossible to determine, escaped from this process, and we even come across tenants with the means to rent lands additional to their tied allotment, or to qualify as decurions. The situation was nevertheless serious, since it led not only to the creation of a submerged economy but also to the formation of social groups no longer in contact with the State. An obvious example is provided by the armed retinues with which certain great landowners and army commanders surrounded themselves as a personal protection against forceful counter-measures from officials driven beyond endurance by their abuses. Every Roman legionary, as we know, took an oath of loyalty to the emperor. Similarly, every subject of the empire swore not to harm the emperor's person. But the private bodyguards, known as *bucellarii*, who make their appearance at the beginning of the fifth century are found swearing loyalty not only to the emperor but also to some outstanding military leader or important senator. In practice, they were far readier to obey the general, who fed them on high quality bread, 'army biscuit' (*bucellatum*, hence the name *bucellarii*), than the emperor who so rarely emerged from Ravenna. At this date these bands of personal retainers were quite small, perhaps a hundred or so to any one patron, but their existence is a sign that the army was in grave danger of privatisation.

The Church, the only real refuge?

The poorest were similarly desperate for protection, but sought it elsewhere, in the Church. Under a ruling in force since the First Council of Nicaea (325), a cleric was forbidden to enter the following of a lay patron, but there was nothing which forbade movement in the contrary direction. There were in fact great advantages in taking holy orders. For if the lands of the Church were subject to taxes, the clergy by contrast were exempt from taxation and military service; it is thus not surprising to find a prodigious rise in the number of clergy during the fourth and fifth centuries. Indeed, this is the period when the Church took definite shape as a structure within the framework of the Roman State. Its hierarchy was deliberately modelled on the divisions and subdivisions of the civil administration, so that each province had its metropolitan bishop and every *civitas* its bishop. The *militia armata* (soldiers) and the *militia officialis* (civilian officials) now had as their counterpart the *militia Christi*, soldiers in the cohort of Christ, the clergy. Although the choice of bishop lay with the local people and clergy, the metropolitan bishop and two other bishops from the same province had a right of scrutiny; before consecrating the new bishop they had to satisfy

The clergy, Christ's militia, trace their descent from the Twelve Apostles, seen here with Christ on a fifth-century ivory panel (Dijon, Musée de Beaux-Arts).

themselves that his election had been in accordance with the canons. Lastly, there were the synodical and ecumenical councils in which bishops from a group of provinces and the whole empire respectively met to resolve major doctrinal or disciplinary issues under the increasingly authoritative guidance of the pope of Rome or of his legate. The clergy were paid, each receiving from the landed endowment of his local church a salary commensurate with his status; this meant that clerics, like soldiers and civil servants, were among the privileged. Their superiors could even fall victim to the same ills as afflicted the two other services: corrupt practices were not unknown. The practice of simony (purchase of ecclesiastical office), after being denounced for half a century, was formally forbidden by the Council of Chalcedon (451), a telling indication of the extent to which the Church's social standing had increased.

The custom in Spain was for the revenues of each church to be divided into three portions, one for the clergy, another for the bishop and the third for building work. In Gaul and Italy a fourth part was reserved for widows and the poor. The names of the latter were entered in a register (*matriculum*) similar to that kept of the clergy, and the church in question made itself fully responsible for supplying their needs. The fifth century also witnessed the beginnings of a whole series of charitable institutions: hospitals to care for the sick, hospices for the reception of pilgrims and travellers, orphanages to take in foundlings, and so on. In Rome, with its large floating population, the Church had a more elaborate system for identifying its poor, and the city was already divided into some half-dozen diaconates whose function was to care for the destitute. Basically, then, the Church was the patron of the poor.

So the Church, a veritable State within the State, did not lag behind great landowners and military leaders in evolving its own version of the patronate. For a peasant, there was often more advantage in being a *colonus* tied to an ecclesiastical holding than in preserving his independence. The bishop's court, swifter and closer to hand, was preferred by litigants to the courts presided over by civil servants. It was common for bishops to become the protectors of freedmen devised to them by will, and likewise of the erstwhile *coloni* or clients of some pious benefactor. In this way the bishop became as it were a substitute patron with his own following. In addition, he was careful to preserve the immediate vicinity of his church as a place of asylum for ill-treated slaves or for persons lacking the means to defend themselves against court charges. Burdened with these and other administrative cares, the clergy were thus increasingly caught up in secular affairs and became almost indistinguishable from other potentates.

Such at any rate was the view of certain other Christians, who reproached the bishops and priests with having become too worldly. The fact is that Christians living in society came under strong attack from laymen who had renounced the world to embrace a life of chastity and poverty – monks. Regarding the Roman world, now officially Christian, as Christian only on the surface and in name, they divided their compatriots into two categories: *saeculares*, superficial Christians immersed in the follies and frivolities of contemporary society, and *conversi* or *sancti*, the truly converted, burning with zeal, disowning the wickedness of a world grown too luxurious. It came as a shock, even to Christians, when Paulinus, an aristocratic senator from Bordeaux, together with his wife Therasia, announced their conversion late in the fourth century: having resigned all his offices and sold his possessions to be divided among the poor, Paulinus retired to the sanctuary of St Felix at Nola in southern Italy. It was the same when Melania, an immensely wealthy matron, gave away all her estates scattered over Spain, Italy, Africa and Britain. To many people, however, the gloomily-apparelled, black-hooded figures who haunted the highways, preying on the compassion of passers-by, were no better than parasites, misanthropes or even deserters, who were fleeing city life in order to evade their responsibilities. And when it was proposed as an exception to appoint one of their number – Martin, a senior army officer turned monk and hermit – to the see of Tours, his tattered garments and filthy locks made him the laughing-stock of other bishops. At Carthage monks were even hissed and booed whenever they appeared in the streets.

Of all the groups comprising Roman society in the West, monks certainly appear to have been the most peripheral, the most critical and the least compliant. The proliferating monastic life of the early fifth century was of many different types. Rules were usually lacking and even where they existed tended to be lax. Consecrated virgins lived in spiritual

33

marriage with ascetics, giving rise to much malicious gossip. Bands of hermits kept constantly on the move, in the belief that vagabondage signified detachment. These monks of Egyptian type, known as *gyrovagi*, are to be distinguished from the recluses and other ascetics of the Syrian type, noted for the extravagance of their penitential exercises. Monasteries living on a centralised pattern according to the rule of St Pachomius stand in contrast to those where the monks' cells were scattered and which observed the rule of St Basil. Lastly, we find in some episcopal households the beginnings of clerical communities dedicated to sacred pursuits and the religious life. In short, in the 'desert' as in the countryside, in towns and in private houses, there was everywhere a burgeoning of new modes of monastic life which were as much criticised by laymen as by monks. The most censorious, such as John Cassian, when he arrived in Rome about 405, noted that monks were few in number (presumably by comparison with the East) and that of these the majority were idle and undisciplined.

Town governments, senators and their followings

While the clergy were attracting freemen to their ranks and the monks were attracting criticism, the towns were beginning to empty. Normally, every town serving as the capital of a *civitas* was self-governing. The citizen assembly approved the list of municipal magistrates presented to it by the *curia*, or town council, and it was this latter body, composed of decurions, which in practice managed the city's affairs. Each year on 1 March the members of the town council elected those responsible for the collection of taxes, levying recruits, supervision of mines, imperial estates and staging posts, and the registration in the official records of private legal transactions (sales, gifts, wills etc.). In addition there were responsibilities regarding the upkeep of aqueducts, procuring supplies of wood to heat the public baths, maintenance of the town's walls and public buildings. The council also controlled prices. Lastly, it was the duty of the city councillors to organise the public games, either gladiatorial combats or hunts, for which exotic wild animals were imported from afar. In the West, however, the civic revenues were meagre and by the beginning of the fifth century the landed endowment of the *civitates* even seems to have disappeared. Everything therefore came to depend on the personal fortune of the city councillors, whether to guarantee the city's tax quota or to defray public expenditure on the scale inherited from the Antique tradition of civic pride. So whether they were rich or poor, large or medium landowners, the city councillors tried either to relinquish their decurion status once they had discharged all their civic duties, in which case they were styled *honorati*, or quite simply to flee from their obligations. Often threatened with ruin, they tried to enlist in the army, take holy orders or enter a monastery. If they failed to gain admission to one of these privileged groups, some city councillors, in spite of the protection afforded the poor by the local magistrates, went to the lengths of marriage with a slave so as not to pass on their hereditary obligation. Wherever we look we find the same phenomenon: abandonment of status to escape the clutches of the State. By 458 the ranks of the city councillors were so depleted in the West that the emperor Majorian tried to draft in reinforcements. But it was not chiefly greed or poverty which led to the disappearance of city councillors from towns, but rather their reluctance to be turned into functionaries and to occupy themselves with tasks which kept them from their usual activities.

Their particular ambition was to gain admission to the senatorial aristocracy. The senatorial order was divided into several classes arranged in a strict hierarchy whose designations corresponded to particular offices or titular dignities conferred by the emperor. At the beginning of the fifth century recruitment to the *ordo* was drastically reformed, with the result that very ancient families dating back to the time of the Republic rubbed shoulders with new lineages mostly descended from decurions, but also from common soldiers or even barbarian officers or notaries. Change and continuity were thus the two contradictory features of senatorial recruitment. Lawyers and teachers could also gain admittance. Some senators had barely enough wealth to qualify; others, by contrast, were inordinately rich, especially those in the highest grade which carried exemption from extraordinary taxation and curial obligations. True, they still had the duty and expense of contributing on a lavish scale to the games presented, as in former days, by quaestors, praetors and consuls. But senators took pride in these ceremonial functions, even though they conferred no political advantages. The fact is that senators enjoyed large landed fortunes, and could allow themselves to perform a minimum of administrative functions while continuing to add to their patrimony. Given their wealth and culture, they led an easy and idle existence. Wild beast hunts in the amphitheatre, horse and chariot races, the sybaritic comforts of the baths added up for them to true pleasure and the ideal existence, in which they wanted townsmen of their native city to share. We can hardly be surprised that all aspirations to upward mobility converged on this social group, or that it attracted a swarm of *parvenus*. For this senatorial clique was gradually recovering the political power that to all intents and purposes had been wrenched from it by the Illyrian emperors. Respected for his noble rank and the precedence accorded him in official ceremonies, a senator of the first class could intervene directly with high officials or fob off a curial who demanded his tax contribution. To prestige were imperceptibly added the privileges of influence with the result that people importuning senators for positions gradually became their clients. Here, in the shade afforded by great senatorial families, the patronate made sturdy growth. Having become the indispensable intermediary between government and citizens, the senator in turn removed tax-payers from the authority of the State. When he eventually retired to his estates, while still preserving his links with the court or family connections with important officials, the senator then turned into a local potentate. After a gap of nearly 200 years when such a thing was unheard of, it was more than possible in the fifth century for the head of a senatorial family to obtain the empire by usurpation. This return in force of the senatorial element to the political stage is a sign of the new times just over the horizon.

To sum up, late Antique society saw the birth of a new, powerful and privileged class: officials, soldiers, clerics and senators, along with – and this is not the paradox it seems – domiciled slaves and *coloni* tied to the soil. Between these two social strata, we see free peasants, townsmen, curials and monks tossed this way and that as they struggled either to rise or to descend in the social scale. In all these internal movements, the object was to break loose from the power mechanisms of the State by becoming either protector or protected, patron or client. This general flight from responsibility, this refusal to share in the fiscal and military effort made necessary by war, had its roots in a desire to preserve the way of life achieved under the Roman peace. So attempts by the State to compel every man to do his duty would be wasted, just as the Church's moral exhortations would fall on deaf ears. This is not to ignore the numerous laws enacted to prohibit changes of social status. Thus it was laid down that no slave can become a priest or monk; *coloni* were not to leave their land; members of craft guilds were not allowed to resign; city councillors were not permitted to enlist in the army, take holy orders or become monks; a man marrying a wife of the curial class acquired her status; having received a see, a bishop could not be appointed to another; the daughter of a senator could not marry a freeman or a slave. In a word, these laws, whose purport was to make social status hereditary, prove by their attention to detail and vain repetition that Roman society remained fluid or was slowly coagulating around powerful protectors in a way that made it impossible for the State to harness its energies to the full. It was the same with Christian standards of conduct, which most of the time were ignored or dismissed as impracticable. Many people delayed baptism to the last minute, to be sure of dying pardoned and redeemed. Divorce was still authorised by the law and was not shunned by Christians, despite the proclaimed indissolubility of marriage. Within marriage, the familial structure was often regulated by the practice of abortion. All in all, this non-observance of orders and precepts issuing from State and Church proves that the political and religious values they upheld made little serious impression. The result of this was a flight towards the bonds between man and man and to the untamed solitudes.

The ascendant countryside

Externally, the economy of the Roman empire in the West appears prosperous, if to a lesser degree than that of the East. Internally, it was in the throes of transformation. Whichever aspect we choose to consider – population size, the development of large estates and of the money economy, or the new type of towns – we find distortions emerging which are as much beyond the power of the authorities to control as society itself. That is not to deny that military, fiscal and monetary policy played a preponderant role in the economic evolution of the Western part of the empire; but far from priming the pump, these policies were the cause of serious dislocations at a time when the economy was ripe for expansion.

Few men, many empty spaces

While the population in the East was expanding, in the West it probably remained below the levels attained in the second century; the losses of the third century had not been restored. Notwithstanding disagreements in the estimates put forward by demographers (the population of Gaul is estimated by some at around two-and-a-half million, by others at around six million), it can safely be asserted that the provision of a quarter of a million men to serve in the Roman army, its theoretical size, was perceived to be too heavy a burden for the overall population of twenty million or so inhabitants. Yet whereas this meant that only one in a hundred served, the comparable figure among the Germanic peoples (whose numbers were relatively small) was one in four! This dearth of men was due no doubt to the distaste for military service, but it probably also tells us that certain gaps had not been filled. Otherwise it is hard to account for the determination of the State and landed proprietors to attach *coloni* to the soil and prevent their enrolment in the army. The shortage of agricultural hands and the army's incessant demands meant a continual tussle over men. The policy of importing barbarian troops and of settling Germanic *laeti* on vacant lands enables us to identify the most depopulated areas, first and foremost the border areas behind the fortified *limes*: Illyricum, Pannonia, Noricum, the northern parts of Italy, Gaul and Britain, and Mauretania. Similarly, the distribution of towns pinpoints other areas of underpopulation: Gaul between the Seine and the Loire, western Numidia, and certain parts of the Iberian peninsula, whole regions of which – the central plateaux, the Pyrenean and Cantabrian regions and northern Portugal, apart from Galicia on the extremity – were very sparsely populated; the population of the entire peninsula is estimated by some historians to have been between six and nine million. The Mediterranean lands are certain to have been more populous than might be expected at this epoch, but generally speaking one must be content to interpret the Antique data in a tentative and impressionistic fashion.

The existence of very sparsely populated or even vacant territories is confirmed by the use of official terms such as *tractus* or *saltus*, which apply to all uncultivated lands, forests, marshes, pastures, steppes and so on. Since according to the law such lands had no master, the State regarded them as crown property. The same applied to what lay beneath the soil and hence to quarries and mines. Now it goes almost without saying that the triumphs of Roman land clearances over nature had been confined to areas bordering the Mediterranean. Advances in irrigation and drainage were limited to the eastern littoral of Spain and the coastal regions of Italy. Roman field patterns, in the form of a regular grid set at a right angle to the roads, had radically transformed the appearance of the coastal plains in Sicily and Africa (especially in what is now Tunisia) and were subsequently imposed on the lands to either side of the Po, the Guadalquivir and the Ebro. From Languedoc and Provence these field patterns progressed up the Rhône to Champagne and Picardy and perhaps as far as the Thames valley. But by far the greater part of the countryside was uncultivated and the State's 'domain' must have been correspondingly immense. The plains and mountains of Europe were covered with huge tracts of forest, accounting for perhaps three-quarters of the surface area in the countries under consideration. Timber and resin (for making pitch) from the forests of Corsica, Sardinia, the Apennines, the Sierra Nevada and the Causses were used in naval dockyards, but the resources of the forest went otherwise unexploited. The esparto grass ('Spanish broom') growing on the Spanish plateaux was employed in the manufacture of rope.

But as in palaeolithic times, the essential activities carried on in uncultivated zones were

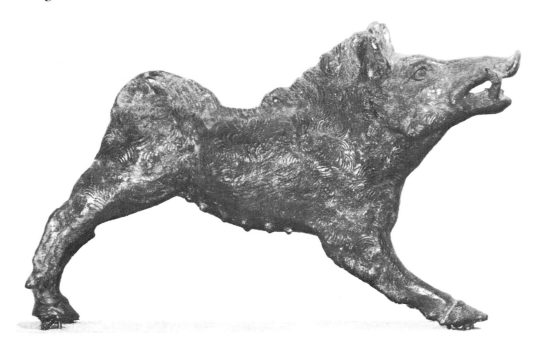

In the hunt, the boar, whose meat was salted for winter consumption, was the most sought-after of the larger animals. Sow in bronze from Cahors (St-Germain-en-Laye, Musée des Antiquités nationales).

those of food-gathering, free range animal husbandry and hunting. Everyone went to gather fruit and berries from the undergrowth, or to graze pigs beneath the oaks and beeches of neighbouring woods. The surplus was often enough to be exported: the pigs of Bruttium kept recipients of the food dole at Rome in meat, while those of northern Gaul found their way to places along the Rhine and the Rhône. Cheese, which along with wool was one of the principal by-products of stock-rearing, was produced in abundance in Illyricum, Dalmatia, Gaul and Britain. Horses were contributed by Africa, Numidia, Spain and Pannonia. While salt pork provided meat in winter, the autumn hunting season, especially on large estates, yielded fresh meat ranging from deer to hare and squirrel, with the boar, greatest of all beasts, taking pride of place. Nor should the food resources of rivers, lakes and sea be overlooked. Fishing, for which nets of various types were employed, was highly rewarding, since the few who were engaged in it lacked the means to exhaust the natural supply.

The fact of this superabundance is confirmed by the particular cases of salt and *garum*, which were found in virtual mass production on almost every coastline of the empire. The existence of saltpans along the shores of the Mediterranean wherever the degree of sunlight permitted led to the establishment of 'salting factories' in which tunny, mullet, mackerel and oysters caught or gathered on the spot were made into a fish sauce, *garum*, a condiment equivalent to the present-day *nuocnam*. It was put into amphoras of a distinctive type and exported up river by the boatload, along with salt, to find its way on to every table. *Garum* was made in vast quantities on the coasts of Mauretania, Baetica, the east coast of Spain from Cartagena to Barcelona, and in Aquitaine.

Two other products of the *saltus* were of direct interest to the State: ores and building stone. When the State did not itself extract them with the help of miners and quarrymen tied by heredity to their craft corporations, it exacted a ten per cent levy on the products extracted and allowed the proprietor of the land to do the same. These advantageous terms were probably the reason why these activities flourished. The most important iron mines under exploitation were on the island of Elba, in Noricum (present-day Bavaria and Austria), in Illyricum, in Berry in central France and in Spain. Gold came chiefly from Galicia and the Cévennes. Tin continued to be furnished by the mines in Galicia and Cornwall, while lead and silver, often found together, were available in abundance from mines in the Sierra Nevada, the Dinaric range in Illyricum and the Pennines. The white marble from Luni (close to Carrara in Italy), and the multi-coloured marbles from the Pyrennees and Africa were highly prized for use in monumental buildings, columns, capitals, and sarcophagi, but these were luxury products. The ordinary stone used for building could be quarried almost anywhere. To sum up, while the *saltus* might appear an almost untracked wilderness, in which the huts of charcoal-burners, wood-cutters, huntsmen and herdsmen were the only landmarks, it was none the less exploited and made a valuable contribution to the daily life and diet of the Romans, as well as to their arts and crafts.

Whither the great estate?

The importance of its role explains why so little of the *saltus* was cleared. We saw furthermore that its arable counterpart, the *ager* as opposed to the *saltus*, was short of labour, in spite of steps taken by the State. The State then issued a whole body of legislation making it possible to enter into ownership of uncultivated or deserted lands. Since the second century Roman law had acknowledged the existence of two titles to the same land: *proprietas*, signifying full ownership, and *possessio*, the right of a cultivator to the perpetual occupation of land he has brought into cultivation for the owner. Recognition of this dual title was common to all parts of the empire. In the fifth century it became possible for anyone who improved a marsh, meander or some other alluvial swamp to become possessor of it in perpetuity without being liable to tax. Similarly, any derelict land taken over by one person from another with a view to rehabilitation became his property at the end of two years. Lastly, a law promulgated in 424 permitted anyone who had cleared a piece of public land, whether *saltus* or a vacant estate fallen into the hands of the State, and had occupied it for 30 years, during which he paid the appropriate rent and taxes, to become its official proprietor. *Possessio* was thus on the way to becoming *proprietas*.

This principle of fundamental importance for the future applied initially, like the law itself, only to the State's cultivated lands. As we saw, these were steadily increasing through confiscations, disinheritances or abandonment. *Agri deserti*, whose desertion was usually the consequence of an unfair tax assessment which failed to distinguish fertile from less fertile land, seem to have occurred in the Campagna and in the Valence region of southern Gaul, but more particularly in southern Tunisia. Many other lands deserted by their lessees lay close to the Rhine or Danube frontiers and had been deserted for reasons of security. Elsewhere, of course, there was keen competition for the public lands. Since the rents could be paid in gold, many great landowners offered themselves as purchasers, seeing this as a convenient means of adding to their patrimony. This is the explanation of a curious phenomenon noticeable in the late Roman world: the tendency of the big estate to increase without causing small and medium landowners to disappear and without additions to the cultivated area. The public lands thus fulfilled the function of a regulator, enabling the demand for land to be met even though no significant change occurred in the size of the labour force.

The lands were bought by all and sundry. But the equality demanded by Roman private law obliged husband and wife to keep their respective properties distinct and to make strictly drawn, unbreakable wills dividing them equally between the children. In consequence, great and small proprietors alike saw the large units (*centuriae*) of the original purchase becoming progressively smaller and more fragmented. To reconsolidate, it was necessary to make frequent exchanges or even to rent or purchase other plots. It also has to be borne in mind that land was the only commodity in which businessmen and merchants could invest their profits. The constant demand for land was thus the final stage of a process which began when those same lands were abandoned. Agriculture, in other words, provided the empire with its principal source of revenue.

Although land was changing hands, the arrangements for its exploitation were still broadly speaking of two types. The peasant proprietors, the tenant *coloni* tied to the soil and the decurions, cultivated parcels that were either compact (*ager*, *agellus*) or scattered over an area (*colonicae*). Little documentary record remains of these small to medium-sized properties and detached plots, which we know must have existed even if the only proof relates to their acquisition by large landowners. The names of the latter were often bequeathed to their principal estate: *fundus Cornelianus*, for example, which gave rise to Corneilhan in Bas-Languedoc. At this date it was very rare for the *fundus* or *praedium* to be all of a piece, and it could be subjected to further division, into two, three or even as many as eight portions, through the vagaries of inheritance or sale. The graduation from small to large estates was thus almost imperceptible. At the very top of the social scale, *fundi* were grouped into *massae*, which emerge like an archipelago from the mass of small and medium sized properties. One senator, Paulinus of Pella, although a native of Bordeaux, possessed *fundi* scattered up and down the Gironde, in Achaea, and in Epirus. In Africa, continuous portions of *saltus* brought under cultivation by a single great landowner could exceed in area the total territory of a *civitas*. But this was possible only on the *saltus*. Elsewhere the great estates were constantly fragmenting into enclaves, whether large or small.

This explains why high-ranking senators were so keen, through the exercise of their patronage, to convert adjoining small freeholds into tenancies, or if this failed, to purchase them at an inflated price, and to enlarge their influence by leasing derelict lands. This twofold attack, consisting in the elimination of neighbours and the creation of new

Gallo-Roman villa at Montmaurin (Haute-Garonne), laid out between the second and fourth century. The buildings occupied about 18 ha, of which the master's dwelling took up four. Two hundred rooms have been counted, excluding outbuildings. The semi-circular entrance court was bounded by a portico and housed a shrine. A colonnade also surrounded the large inner court (600 square metres). Included in the complex were thermal baths and a nympheum.

cultivated areas or rehabilitation of old ones, culminated in the emergence of large landowners who were at the same time *possessores* or leaseholders of public lands, cultivated or not, of which under the 30-year rule they eventually became proprietors. By the end of the fourth century St Ambrose, bishop of Milan, was already castigating the monopolistic appetites and thirst for aggrandisement of landlords who were officials, patrons and judges all rolled into one, and who, thanks to the efforts of their bailiffs (*actores*) and head leaseholders (*conductores*) drew in enormous rents in cash and in kind. In the case of corporate ownership, when the proprietor was the State or the Church, adoption of this system was well-nigh indispensable, and on private estates with absentee landlords the administrative arrangements were bound to be equally complex. At the beginning of the fifth century it was still the custom for wealthy senators to live in town and to manage their estates at a distance through stewards on the spot. It was essential for them to keep abreast with market prices. It has to be remembered that 'Italia annonaria' furnished the state-subsidised grain and wine issued to Roman citizens and the army, that Africa, and to a lesser extent Baetica, sent regular supplies of corn to Italy, and that Aquitaine and Champagne provisioned the armies in Gaul and on the Rhine. This steady demand thus gave large landowners an incentive to expand their undertakings. Better informed than petty producers about current prices, in a position to hire temporary labour for the harvest and vintage, they came increasingly to monopolise the market.

A still flourishing agriculture

Crop yields were thus central to their preoccupations. We have already touched on the deployment of the labour force and on the reasons why the *colonus* attached to the soil came to be preferred to the agricultural slave, and why the latter was likewise settled on a particular plot. But although small in proportion to the whole, slaves could still be found in considerable numbers: for example, in 409, as an emergency measure and in defiance of the law, kinsmen of the emperor Theodosius mustered a sizable army from their servile labour force against barbarian invaders. But since in fact labour was in short supply, it became necessary to innovate. The great landowners turned accordingly to the writings of the agronomists, Columella, Varro and Palladius, whose works were frequently recopied. The treatise on agriculture written by Palladius, an Aquitanian who was praetorian prefect at Rome in 458, well illustrates the growing interest of senators in agrarian practicalities. For cereal crops the system of biennial fallowing was accompanied by frequent hoeing and ploughing; spring cereals needing only three months to mature were sown to offset a poor winter harvest.

The cultivation of leguminous plants, peas, beans, and lentils, and regular manuring in certain cases, must have improved production. Two implements were used to turn the sod, the *aratrum*, a light wheel-less plough, and the hoe. Gardens and vines were tended with particular care. The former produced an abundant supply of cabbages, onions and root vegetables, but vines were usually preferred because of their high yield and the speculative opportunities offered by the wine trade. The practice of 'domiciling' slaves probably began with vineyard plots, where it was obviously in their interest to produce as much as possible: from the profit on the wine they were allowed to keep, they were able to add to their little store of savings. Cultivation of the olive had spread to Africa, Spain and Istria.

It is hard to estimate the yield from cereals. Columella held that an average yield could only be obtained when there were sixteen workers to the square kilometre. Yet it seems that in the late fourth century, because of the labour shortage, the proportion in most places was half this ideal figure. It was therefore important to increase the yield in other ways. Where Columella had advised sowing four measures of seed for every hectare, Palladius was in favour of six. The latter was the equivalent of twenty hectolitres to the hectare, a standard figure for land of average quality. According to Columella, the yield in a poor year was in the proportion of four to one, that is between five and seven hundredweight per hectare. This is probably a safer guide than Varro's figures for Etruria, where, he says, yields were in the region of between ten and eleven to one, giving a yield per hectare of between thirteen and twenty hundredweight or thereabouts.

To maximise the efforts of a labour force deficient in numbers, the Roman agronomists advocated the use of machines. Palladius strongly recommends the construction of water mills 'in order to grind corn without having to call on animal or human labour'. We know that in fact there were several floating water mills on the Tiber at Rome and that at Barbegal, close to Arles on the Rhône, there was a complex whose capacity was of truly industrial proportions. In northern Italy use was made of the *serra*, a kind of cart with saw-toothed wheels, to thresh the grain. In northern Gaul the *vallus*, a kind of harvester with frontal blades which sliced the head of grain from the stalk, was propelled by mules and needed only one man to guide its progress: it thus took the place of several reapers. It even seems possible that the wheeled plough was known in the plains of the Danube and Po as well as in northern Gaul. These are all instances of thinly populated regions which were obliged to supply grain to the army and where innovation was therefore essential.

The late fourth century thus presents a picture of high productivity and prosperity, attributable to these efforts. It is Palladius, after all, who insists that 'the presence of the owner makes the estate prosper' and who advises him to maintain 'a full complement of blacksmiths, carpenters and potters, so that the peasants will have no excuse to leave their normal work for errands in the town'. The trend towards self-sufficiency was the price paid for the estate's contribution to productivity. As in the case of their refusal of public office, the senators' exodus to the countryside by no means signified an abdication of responsibility. Rather, it was a clear proof of their revived interest in agrarian methods and in agricultural speculation. In their size and organisation, the great rural estates of the fourth century revealed to us by archaeology and aerial photography can well stand comparison with those of the empire's classical era.

Towns in decline

By contrast, the urban constructions of the period are unimpressive. The pagan temples had been destroyed, and some of the public buildings allowed to decay. If we leave on one side the cities of Africa and the East, and Rome, which must have numbered around 800,000 inhabitants, and also exclude Ravenna, Milan, Arles and Trier, the towns of this period had very little to show in the way of newly built churches or civic monuments. Beginning in 395, the praetorian prefects of Italy and Gaul had to take measures to prevent city councillors from deserting their posts on the town councils. This movement, like its senatorial counterpart, had the effect of minimising towns as centres of consumption. Since the only permanent residents now consisted of a handful of decurions, the episcopal and monastic clergy, merchants and craftsmen, the town was reduced to the functions of a market for peasant exchanges, temporary barracks for soldiers on campaign, local seat of justice, and fortified refuge in time of trouble.

Townscapes are no longer open, with avenues leading up to impressive public edifices. With the exception of Africa and a few cities in Spain and Italy, towns were now based upon a stronghold. This reshaping served the purpose of enabling the town's centralised administrative functions to be maintained, and provided a place where the surrounding rural population could meet and do business with the priests, officials and craftsmen resident in the town. In times of peace the suburbs must have been relatively populous, 43

Milestone on the Roman road from Agen to Cahors.
These markers were set up at intervals of a
thousand Roman paces, equivalent to 1,481 metres.

especially after Christian cemeteries and basilicas came to be established there in the fifth
century: the discovery in 415 by the priest Lucian of the relics of St Stephen, the first
Christian martyr, led to the building of several cathedrals dedicated to his patronage. At
Milan the commercial quarter was outside the city walls. Yet it is hard to arrive at even an
approximate figure for these urban populations. For one thing, the area covered by the
suburbs is unknown. Some fortifications were large enough to include gardens and unbuilt
spaces: this was so at Toulouse, Vercelli, Bologna, Modena, Piacenza, even at Rome.
Furthermore, in times of unrest or invasion, only part of the population took refuge in the
stronghold, leaving the rest to flee to the surrounding countryside. The town of the late
Roman empire seems to have had elastic capacities. Places like Bordeaux, which in normal
times may have numbered 16,000 inhabitants, or Paris, with about 20,000, could empty

Wine-barge being hauled on the Durance. Although the capacity of ships was small, it was easier and more economical to transport goods by water than by land (Avignon, Musée Calvet).

at a stroke in time of war. Here we touch on one of the most serious of the distortions between town and countryside, the displacement of productive and economic forces from urban centres to the rural areas.

In fact we know of very few *civitas*–capitals which still contained craftsmen and continued to sell their artefacts. The minting of coins, as we saw, was confined to six of the very largest towns. The glass-making carried on at Cologne was perhaps the only urban manufacture of any importance – the clothing factories at Amiens and Bourges were state-run concerns. The *navicularii*, or corporation of ship-owners, who transported the corn levies, were also subjected to state control, whether their port of call was Ostia, Carthage, Aquileia or Barcelona. Especially revealing is the case of the large ceramic workshops, all of which were sited either in open country, in close proximity to the army camps which were the main consumers, or in the hinterland of great ports. The town, in short, came increasingly to represent the State and the Church. Even when it acquired the function of a local market, it was rivalled by the *vici*, large villages to which the peasants more often gravitated to sell their produce.

With the running down of their economic activity the towns in the western part of the empire thus became stagnant, drained by degrees of their craftsmen and resident landowners but still continuing to wield authority in the governmental and religious spheres. A similar imbalance is to be found in the sphere of commercial and monetary exchanges. External trade with the barbarian countries, Iran and the Far East, was heavily taxed at the frontiers where a statutory toll of twelve-and-half per cent was imposed. But the trade with central Europe was in Rome's favour, because of the demand there for artefacts of all types. On the other hand, the deficit due to the import of incense from the Yemen, spices from India and silk from China was not large enough to upset the empire's trading balance. This luxury trade was of quite a different order from the trade carried on inside the empire.

If the government encouraged internal trade, it was as always for fiscal and military reasons. The Roman road network was then in its heyday. Its coverage of the West was so comprehensive that troops and the couriers of the *cursus publicus* could cover distances at a remarkable speed: the journey from Milan to Rome, for example, could be made in six days. It has to be said, however, that for commercial purposes land transport was scarcely worthwhile. The wagons capable of transporting a load of 600 kilos and drawn by a pair of oxen worked out as more expensive than loading the same freight on to two pack camels: hence the presence of camels in all parts of the empire and their exclusive use in the baggage trains of the army. Water transport, if available, was both more practicable and more economical. The average capacity of the grain ships was 150 tons. But with an eye as always to evading the State's demands, the *navicularii* preferred to use ships of twenty tons on which they had less to pay and from which they could make more profit. Barge-owners on the Tiber, the Po and the Rhône were under similar administrative constraints.

Thus only transport by river or sea was economical and significant in scale, especially since the largest consumer was the State. Even though the navigational season was short, lasting from 31 March to 10 October (sometimes until 11 November), and the voyages were slow – five days from Narbonne to Carthage, 30 from Alexandria to Marseilles – the sea routes continued to be much frequented, especially for the transport of grain, wine and oil. Ships called regularly at all the major ports. This trading economy was still concentrated on the Mediterranean, with two exceptions: tin imported from Britain was brought around the Iberian peninsula, and grain fleets carrying corn from the Thames basin plied regularly from London to Mainz. But the latter was again a case of trade promoted by the State. Private dealers appear in fact to have been few in number, judging by the meagre returns from the *collatio lustralis*, the tax to which they were subjected. In addition to itinerant traders from Gaul, Spain or Africa, we notice in particular the activity of Syrian and Jewish merchants. As is only to be expected, however, the producers were eager to negotiate the sale of their cereal or wine crops in person. In northern Italy the chief suppliers of the grain distributed as rations were the great senatorial landowners, who played the market high or low according to whether the time of year was one of scarcity or plenty: over a period of six months prices could triple – or the reverse. Small peasant freeholders still had the power to dispose of their own surpluses. The understandable temptation to speculate was made all the stronger by the offer of loans or advances on the harvest. The net return on an estate in northern Italy appears to have been in the order of ten per cent. Since the rate of interest was officially twelve per cent, and usually a good deal higher, a surge in the demand from the State gave a stimulus to the private money-lending market and produced a crop of borrowings at extortionately high rates – the reason, no doubt, for the diatribes of contemporary bishops, St Ambrose in particular, against usury.

These loans, at rates which for a maritime venture went as high as 33 per cent, implied cash payments in coins of unimpeachable quality. Such coins were abundant in the early fifth century through the issue of the gold *solidus*, a coin with high purchasing power which won general acceptance. Since the bronze coins, the *folles*, continued to depreciate in accordance with Gresham's law that 'bad money drives out good', the State, its officials and soldiers, and the merchants all insisted on payment in gold. The practice of *adaeratio*, the commutation of taxes to gold *solidi*, became general. But the tax-payers, especially *coloni* whose output was small, did not have these coins at their disposal. Starting in 383, the emperors began to strike *tremisses* (gold coins weighing 1.51g, one-third of a *solidus*) in an effort to keep up with the demand. Paying the Rhine legionaries in nothing but the tiny silver coins, the miserable *minimissimi*, had been shown to be out of the question. The brutally deflationary effect of the gold coinage forced free peasants into becoming *coloni* attached to the soil as the dependants of a landowner or patron to whom they rendered their tax in kind, for forwarding in specie to the fisc. The circulation of gold with a purchasing power which was too high in comparison with productivity thus had the effect of promoting the return to a natural economy. It was inevitable that a stable monetary system would lead sooner or later to the breakdown of the empire's unitary economy, depending on the economic forwardness or backwardness of the different provinces. The wealthiest regions – Africa, peninsular Italy, the islands, southern and eastern Spain, southern Gaul – were not adversely affected, but the automatically destructive effect of the imperial government's ignorance of basic monetary laws was beginning to weigh on the poorer regions. Here is yet another instance in which the disparity between the State and the towns on the one side and the rural areas on the other carried the seeds of an eventual breakdown. The East escaped this threat through the revaluation in 498 of the bronze currency. Nothing of this sort happened in the West.

A superficial prestige

One phenomenon in particular blinded contemporaries to reality. This was the cult of Roman civilisation, which conferred such prestige on Rome that its shortcomings in the matter of romanisation passed unnoticed. An urban civilisation formed on the Greek model, Rome had never sought to question the Hellenistic culture it disseminated through-out the West, having accepted the claims of that culture to be universal and universally applicable. The only strangers to it were barbarians and slaves. Only individuals not in those categories would count themselves as being truly free.

An elitist, humanist, outmoded culture

Certainly these were the only ones to benefit from the humanistic Graeco-Roman scheme for transforming man from his savage state into a civilised being. Once the basic elements of literacy and numeracy had been inculcated, the ultimate aim, calling on the resources of both languages, Latin and Greek, was to train men in the arts of eloquence (rhetoric) and to equip them to reflect on human destiny (philosophy). But in a civilisation where oral articulacy still held sway, despite a growing tribe of bureaucrats and notaries, not to mention shorthand writers who noted down the debates, it was inevitable that the teacher of eloquence, the rhetor, had pride of place. Hence in municipal schools there were often only two teachers, one for grammar and one for rhetoric, because nothing more was demanded. Teaching of the other subjects, philosophy, law and medicine, was confined almost exclusively to Rome. It is to be noted that law was always taught in Latin, philosophy and medicine in Greek.

This education, subsidised by emperors who were aware that it formed the basis of Roman patriotism, fostered an elitist, uniformly literary culture in which subtlety and wit were applauded, the sciences were despised, and the ideal way of life was identified not with business (*negotium*) but with studious leisure (*otium*). The school was an institution essential to the State in that it furnished lawyers, officials and even, in due course, bishops. Equally, however, it encouraged disdain for the mechanical arts and for manual labour. In this respect Roman schooling was no reinforcement to society, even if it did produce the eloquent speeches and flowery language with which the rhetors and the authors of imperial constitutions dazzled the barbarians. The regular addition of more and more authors to the syllabus made the fourth and fifth centuries a golden age for the compilers of textbooks, of which the grammars of Donatus and Priscian are characteristic examples. Furthermore, it was also at this time that Martianus Capella produced his vast compendium *The Marriage of Philology and Mercury* (410–29), an allegorical treatment of the disciplines making up the seven 'liberal arts'. Five of these, dialectic, arithmetic, geometry, astronomy and music, filled the gap left by concentration in the schools on grammar and rhetoric. To sustain a Graeco-Roman edifice of learning which with the addition of this further load now reached completion, technical improvements were needed. As in agriculture, innovations made their appearance: the book (*codex*), with pages to be thumbed through or annotated, began to replace the roll; parchment competed with Egyptian papyrus; the goose quill, while not displacing the reed pen (*calamus*), enabled scribes to write a more rapid, cursive hand. But none of this alters the fact that education was in a state of crisis: schoolboys were refusing to be saddled with Greek. Augustine knew practically none, for all that he was professor of rhetoric at Carthage. The learning of both languages, said Paulinus of Pella, was such a strain that he became ill and devoted himself instead to the pleasures of the chase. When learning became a drudgery, the typical reaction of the senatorial aristocrat was to return to nature and country pursuits.

The crisis was further aggravated by a barrage of monastic criticism. Lay Christians were too admiring to wish for any alteration to the classical humanist programme. In monastic circles, however, there was a keen awareness of all the ways in which the Graeco-Roman culture acted as a vehicle for paganism. John Cassian, founder in about 415 of the community of St Victor in Marseilles, called for an intellectual culture based on the Bible. Egyptian monks, usually men of humble origin, could see no use in a humanist education because of its immorality. It was to these criticisms, which profoundly divided the episcopate, increasingly penetrated by members of important senatorial families, that Augustine addressed himself in his *De doctrina christiana*, written between 396 and 427. He took the view that a grounding in classical culture is essential training for understanding of the Bible. The Christian scholar must first be a grammarian and a rhetorician before he can hope to attain perfection as an exegete or shine as a preacher. Augustine thus retrieved the whole of Antique culture and made it the servant of Scripture. At the same time, however,

The most popular author in the Middle Ages: St Augustine. This miniature in a manuscript from Marchiennes abbey, founded on the Scarpe in the sixth century, shows him throned as bishop, framed by medallions depicting the patrons of the abbey (Douai, Bibliothèque municipale).

the need to be understood by the people dictated the use in sermons of clear and simple language, and may therefore mean that a large part of the preacher's rhetorical training had to be ignored. This more relaxed stance, this abandonment of the charges against Latinity, was in fact the only way to overcome the crisis. But for the moment nobody in the West realised the import of this solution or appreciated its genius.

The universalist ideal thus remained inviolate and all the elites were at one as they worshipped, along with the panegyrist Pacatus Drepanius, at the shrine of Rome's eternity. The cultural uniformity, the unanimous acceptance of the benefits of civilisation, the similarity of life-style between East and West, almost irrespective of the difference between Greek and Latin, blinded members of the educated class to the geographical realities of a many-hued *romanitas*. Whole areas could be described as sub-Romanised; it may be chance that they correspond to regions lacking in resources. In Africa, Roman civilisation was slowly losing its hold, from Carthage to Tangier. The mountainous regions were quite untouched by Roman influence. In the north-west of Spain, the *civitas*–capitals were not towns but tribal meeting-places, *conventus*. In the Cantabrian mountains and the Basque country, romanisation had made no headway at all. Gallic survivals show up strongly in Gaul, especially in Armorica. In Britain, the Celtic stock was still vigorous and in Wales remained in the ascendant; in Scotland, north of Hadrian's wall, it was triumphant. In regions only superficially Romanised – the district of Tarragona, the Pyrenees, the Alps and the territory between the Loire and the Seine – bands of peasants, or as some say brigands, erupted at intervals in revolt against the fisc; the most usual name for them, '*bacaudae*', comes from a Gallic word signifying solidarity as a group. Nor should we forget the Germanisation of northern Belgium by the Franks. The Roman consensus hence had its dark patches, which the highlighting of literary and artistic achievements is apt to camouflage.

In this sharply contrasted picture we thus see a self-confident *romanitas* sublimely unaware of its internal fissures. A world under siege but believing itself at peace, Rome developed three instruments calculated to keep the peace: the law, with its distinction between public and private affairs; the army, with its dual character (field and frontier troops); and the civilian administration responsible for justice and finance. But in order to maintain a culture and preserve its urbanity, Rome created a fiscal system whose effects were corrosive. Its remedy for the shortage of manpower was to enrol barbarians in the army. In order to maximise profits it attached *coloni* to the soil and promoted a monetary economy. It used the educational system and the support of the Church to heighten devotion to Rome. But in thus putting a strain on society without being prepared to sacrifice any part of the Antique inheritance, it created privileged groups at the two social extremes and caused serious divisions to appear: between decurions and peasants on the one side and the State on the other, between monks and clergy, between town and country. In the patronage wielded by the newly powerful – generals, senators, bishops – society found a means of evading the State. The rural economy placed itself in the van by short-circuiting the towns and emptying them of producers. The State, the only large-scale consumer in a world unable to keep pace with its demands, thwarted the incipient expansion through a currency with an excessive purchasing power.

We can thus liken the Roman empire of the early fifth century to a lizard in the act of casting its skin: still encumbered by the old, exposed and fragile in the new. Change and resistance to change, archaisms and innovations vie with one another for possession of the body politic. A malign fate decreed that the barbarian appeared on the scene before the process was complete. With his sword he sliced off the caudal appendage, and in so doing saved the life of Byzantium, which started to expand. It is at this point that the destructive side of the barbarian intervention reveals itself. So we next have to see what was preserved and what was destroyed through this dialectic of wars and the structures of civilisation.

2 Break-up and metamorphosis of the West: fifth to seventh centuries

The lasting and long-term consequences of the Germanic invasions were not visible to contemporaries. The vanquished, where they remained in the majority, tended to minimise the importance of these events and to look on the new arrivals as though they were Roman soldiers, except, of course, on the rare occasions when the invaders drove them from their homes. There were thus regions – Spain, southern Gaul and Italy in particular – where Roman influence remained predominant and indeed continued to evolve under its own momentum. We see Roman civilisation handed on, as though in a relay race, to the Church, in whose hands it is at once preserved and transformed. Thanks to the Church's missionary influence, *romanitas* made headway where even Rome had failed. In these regions, therefore, the specific contribution of the barbarians was apt to be played down or even positively rejected. In England, northern Gaul, Germany and northern Italy, by contrast, this contribution was obviously irrefutable. One might therefore expect a geographically-based conflict between Roman continuity and Germanic innovations, fought out region by region until one or the other emerged victorious over a zone. Nothing of the sort occurred: the Church, having decided that unity was the aspect of *romanitas* that must at all costs be perpetuated, brought victors and vanquished together in the quest for a new unity, which purported to be identical with the old. This produced a hybrid which for want of a better name is referred to as 'the civilisation of the barbarian kingdoms', though a better description would be 'Romano-Germanic'. It can certainly be concluded that the work of acculturation performed by the Church taught the Germans how to preserve their own identity, since they made sure of keeping the upper hand over the former Romans and members of the clergy.

From empire to kingdoms

Starting from 375 when the Huns, a nomadic people from the steppes of Central Asia, crossed the river Don, a series of chain reactions resulted in the displacement of entire tribes from east to west and their entry into the Roman empire. Because the empire in the East fended off the initial shock by getting rid of the intruders, deflecting them to the West, the

West was doomed to a lingering death and then to reconquest by Constantinople when the latter recovered its strength; left to fend for itself, the West had the problem of achieving a balance between the various barbarian kingdoms that had carved up its territory. All these kingdoms underwent serious crises from which one of them, the kingdom of the Franks, emerged aspiring to hegemony. The fall of Rome, by a curious route, led to its restoration.

A lingering and painful death

The Hunnic tribes had crossed the Don with the aim of subjugating the Alans, Ostrogoths and Visigoths. The defeated Visigoths sought to instal themselves on Roman territory as *federates*, but their formal alliance with the Romans proved to be of short duration. In 378, at Adrianople, the Visigothic cavalry charged the Roman army in the flank and cut it to pieces. Attempts by this Germanic army, with an entire people in its train, to renew the Roman alliance were consequently doomed to fail. Led by Alaric, the Visigoths roamed the empire of the East in search of a place to settle. After plundering Illyricum, they pushed on to Italy, were rebuffed by the invincibly anti-Germanic court at Ravenna, and in 410 captured Rome. The fall of the eternal City sent enormous shock waves throughout the West.

Meanwhile, finding the Rhine not only denuded of troops but also frozen over, the Vandals, together with groups of Sueves and Alamans, crossed the river on 31 December 406 and proceeded to pillage the whole of northern Gaul. In this emergency the Roman troops in Britain elected as emperor their own commander, Constantine, who crossed to Boulogne and gathered Frankish federates to consolidate the Rhine frontier. The Vandals and Sueves slipped out of the net by making for Spain, which they pillaged without hindrance. At the same time the *bacaudae* once again rose in revolt against the exorbitant fiscal levies to which they were subjected, while the Armoricans, seeing themselves abandoned, rallied to the usurper. It took time, and the efforts of another Roman commander, Constantius, for this tangled web to be unravelled. After deploying them against the Vandals in Spain, Constantius finally settled the Visigoths in Aquitaine, between Toulouse and the Atlantic, granting them the official status of *federates*, allies of the empire. This was in 418, and from that date, which marks the creation of the West's first barbarian 'kingdom', a degree of stability begins to emerge. But the damage done had been enormous, encompassing the extinction of up to two-thirds of Rome's tactical army and the abandonment of a good part of its fiscal revenues.

The marvel is that the empire managed to survive, which it did thanks to the system of *federates*. The Sueves, for example, were installed in this capacity around Braga, at the mouth of the Douro in southern Galicia. But the Vandals, having settled for a time in Baetica, left Spain in 429 (bequeathing their name to Andalusia) and in a host 80,000 strong crossed over into Africa. Making a leisurely progress from west to east, they captured Hippo Regis (where St Augustine had just died) in 430, obtained *federate* status in 435 and ended by sacking Carthage in 439. Although a *federate* kingdom, the Vandal

Anglo-Saxon voyages. The Nydam ship, discovered on the Baltic coast of Denmark, is thought to date from the fifth-century. Oak-built, it measures 22.84m × 3.26m at its widest point. Its rudder is nothing more than an oar, and it has neither mast nor keel. It was propelled by 30 oarsmen, but could not voyage on the open sea. Boats of this type, hugging the North Sea coasts, would have carried the Angles and Saxons to Britain.

kingdom under its leader Gaiseric differed from the rest in the assertion of its independence. With a stranglehold on Rome's grain supplies, it was the foe most to be feared, especially when the Vandals succeeded in occupying all the islands in the western Mediterranean.

Indeed, Gaiseric aimed at a pincer strategy in which Rome was gripped between the Huns, who in 420 had reached the Danube, and his own forces. But he was pitted against Aetius, the ablest Roman commander of the age, who had spent his youth as a hostage at the Hunnic court. The ties of friendship he had formed there enabled him to employ Hunnic *federates* to stabilise the situation in Gaul. In 443 he crushed the Burgundians who had settled around Worms and transplanted them to the southern Jura and the area around Lake Geneva, in the region known as 'Sapaudia' (whence the name Savoy). This brought the number of *federate* kingdoms up to three. With the Visigoths held in check and the Frankish alliance still secure, Aetius was able to withstand concerted attacks from Attila, king of the Huns, and Gaiseric, king of the Vandals. From his encampment deep in the plains of what is now central Hungary, Attila launched an attack with the aim of wresting tribute from all the Germanic peoples who had migrated to the Roman empire. Preceded by a reputation for terror and eager for booty, he destroyed Metz and besieged Orleans, but on the news of the approach of Aetius with Roman troops he withdrew to Champagne. But the soldiers of Aetius did not come alone: with them came Visigoths, Alans, Burgundians, Bretons from Armorica, *bacaudae*, Saxons who had settled in the Boulogne and Bessin regions, and all the Frankish tribes. The character of this coalition suggests a fundamental change of outlook. It was a predominantly Germanic army which intercepted the retreating Huns at Moirey and fought the famous battle of the 'Catalaunian fields' near Troyes on 20 June 451. On his descent into Italy the following year Attila was dissuaded by Pope Leo from attacking Rome; and with the sudden death of the 'khan' in 453 the assortment of tribes assembled under his control immediately disintegrated. To all appearance, the Roman West had once again been saved. But with the murder of Aetius in 454 by the emperor Valentinian III, jealous of his general's successes and fearful for his throne, the slow but fatal process of disintegration resumed. Followers of Aetius retaliated by cutting the emperor's throat; and at Ravenna a barbarian patrician, Ricimer, made and unmade emperors at his whim. And so the fragmentation of the empire continued.

In Great Britain, now unprotected by Roman troops against Pictish raids and 'Scottish' (i.e. Irish) piracy, the Britons, after vain appeals for help, ended up enlisting as *federates* Angles and Saxons from Jutland and the mouths of the Elbe and Weser. These troops, joined to some extent by Frisians mustered from the Rhine delta and Franks they encountered in the Boulonnais, at first did what was required of them, *c.* 450–5. But it was not long before they took advantage of their position to dominate the Britons, installing themselves in particular in Kent, around the Wash and on the Humber estuary. British resistance was fortified, however, by a migration back to the continent and succeeded in blocking Anglo-Saxon progress until the end of the fifth century. At the same time, the Irish established their hold on Celtic Caledonia, to which they gave their name: Scotland, land of the *Scotti*.

Crumbling at the edges, the empire received another blow to the heart. In 455, Gaiseric landed near Rome and plundered the city for over a month. Amid the general apathy there were Romans here and there who organised revolts against the barbarians, in the Auvergne, in Sicily, in Illyricum, but these failed through lack of co-ordination and external support. Between the Loire and the Somme three Roman commanders, Paul, Aegidius and Syagrius, continued to depend on the Bretons to keep the *federate* kingdoms within bounds. We nevertheless find the Visigoths fanning out towards the Loire, the Pyrenees, the Mediterranean and the Rhône; in 476 they captured Provence. Called in by Ricimer to subdue the Sueves, who were now spreading into Spain, the Visigoths drove them back and took their place. The Burgundians captured Lyons, from which they ascended the Saône as far as the Langres plateau and descended the Rhône to its confluence with the Durance.

As to Italy, the last 'Roman' army, whose commander, Odoacer, was a Germanic (either Skirian or Rugian) chieftain, finally rose in revolt and demanded the same status as the *federate* peoples. The young emperor, Romulus Augustulus, was stripped of his insignia and on 4 September 476 he was sent into exile. The Roman empire of the West had expired, but at the time nobody noticed its passing. So far as contemporaries were concerned, there was again only one emperor, residing at Constantinople, who had reassumed responsibility for the West. The emperor Zeno refused, furthermore, to recognise Odoacer as king. The latter, unable to hold the right bank of the Danube, allowed the Lombards to occupy what is now lower Austria. When the Ostrogoths, installed as *federates* in Pannonia since 471, exhausted that country's resources, and threatened to attack Constantinople, Zeno, invoking his claim to be emperor of the West, commissioned their king, Theodoric, to take his troops to Italy and oust Odoacer on his behalf. Acting once more in the official capacity of 'Roman' troops, the Ostrogoths eventually eliminated Odoacer in 493, after much fierce fighting. The Ostrogothic kingdom was the last *federate* kingdom to be created in the West. Setting store by his representation of the imperial power, Theodoric sought to extend his hegemony as far as the Danube, and pursued a policy of matrimonial alliances whose scope included all the barbarian kingdoms, Visigothic, Burgundian, Suevic, Vandal, and even the newly emerging Frankish kingdom.

The surprise sprung by the Franks, 486–535

In fact, this new equilibrium, based on a fictitious lordship of Constantinople over the West, exercised through Gothic intermediaries, was about to be upset by the Franks, a Germanic people whose fidelity to the Roman alliance had endured until 465–8. Up to that date it used to be thought that they were divided into at least two groups: the Ripuarians, more correctly described as Rhenish, who guarded the river's left bank; and the Salians, who came originally from the Salland, a small pocket of land on the lower Rhine, now part of the Netherlands. As we saw, the Salians were originally installed in northern Belgium. It is now, however, doubted that such strongly ethnic differentiation between groups of Franks can be made. From there they gradually advanced to Tournai and Cambrai, where they settled around 430–40. One of their 'kings', Childeric, made an abortive attack on Paris; he died sometime before 481 and was buried in his capital of Tournai, where his tomb was discovered in the seventeenth century. His son Chlodweg, known to posterity as Clovis, suiting his actions to the role of Roman general in command of an abandoned territory, overthrew Syagrius in 486 and took possession of his capital, Soissons. Clovis next set about the unification of the Frankish kingdom, disposing of neighbouring petty kings by murder or trickery; the Bretons of Armorica were mollified by his recognition of their virtual independence. Lastly, Clovis drove the Alamans back towards the upper Rhine, probably in consequence of the battle of Zulpich (better known as Tolbiac), the exact date of which (496? 500?) is debated.

But when it came to attacking the Burgundian and Visigothic kingdoms, Clovis realised he would need the support of their Gallo-Roman inhabitants. The latter had rejected the heterodox teachings of Arius, known as Arianism, the form of Christianity adopted by their masters, and most of all by the Visigoths. Clovis therefore agreed to accept baptism in the Catholic faith from Remigius (Remi), metropolitan of Rheims (some time between 496 and 506 and possibly 25 December 498 or 499). Overjoyed to have found an orthodox king, the Catholic bishops of the Visigothic kingdom issued an appeal to Clovis. He responded with a campaign whose triumphal progress, starting with the battle of Vouillé (507) and ending at Toulouse, was hailed by the Aquitanians as a war of liberation. Clovis had been supported in this undertaking by the approval of the emperor Anastasius, who had recently fallen out with Theodoric, king of the Ostrogoths; the latter, having staved off the threat of a Byzantine landing in Italy, despatched forces to the aid of his Gothic brethren and so prevented the total collapse of the Visigothic kingdom. Theodoric halted the Frankish advance and by the recapture of Provence and Septimania (lower Languedoc) denied Clovis and the Frankish chieftains access to the Mediterranean.

Nevertheless, when Clovis died at Paris, his new 'capital', on 27 November 511, having already convened a 'Gallic' council at Orleans, he left behind a new type of Germanic kingdom in which relations between conquerors and conquered were of a more cohesive nature than in any other. This is proved by the fact that the momentum he imparted to it survived the partitioning of the 'kingdom' between his four sons in accordance with familial tradition. The Burgundian kingdom, at its apogee under King Gundobad (485–516), was dismembered in two campaigns launched in 523 and 534 and partitioned in turn. Even Provence was eventually surrendered by the Ostrogoths, once again in difficulties with the empire.

But the Franks scored their greatest successes east of the Rhine, where territories emptied of their populations by the migrations had been occupied by new arrivals. The Alamans, of diverse origins as their name indicates (*alle Männer*, 'all men'), had gained a foothold in the present-day Palatinate and Alsace as early as 406, without relinquishing their hold on the territories between the Rhine and the Danube. From there they spread into the Franche Comté and into Switzerland (i.e. into that part known today as *la Suisse alémanique*, German Switzerland) as far as a tributary on the right bank of the Danube, the Iller. In the meantime the Bavarians had settled between 488 and 539 in the territory between the Iller and the Enns, all along the right bank of the Danube and as far as the Alps. Lastly, to the north there were the Thuringians, on either side of the Saale. All these peoples were brought more or less completely under Frankish control – the Thuringians in 531, the Alamans in 536 by Theudebert, the Bavarians in 555 by Chlothar. In this way, the whole of southern Germany became subject to Frankish tribute and Frankish influence. For the first time, Gaul and Germany were drawn together within a common political framework. Chlothar I, who became sole king of the Franks after the deaths of his brothers, presided from 558 to 561 over the largest political entity in the West. Thenceforward the Frankish kingdom enjoyed an unrivalled hegemony in the West.

The three Arian Germanic kingdoms which had survived cut a poor figure by comparison. In Africa, the tyrannical rule of Gaiseric's successors was made doubly so by their persecution of the Catholics, which was ferocious under Huneric (477–84) and still severe under Thrasamund (496–523). Slowly the Vandal monarchy came to lose all its internal support. In Spain, to which the Visigoths had retreated after their defeat, the Ostrogothic tutelage did not extend to the task of reconstructing the monarchy. Incapable of agreeing on a single king for the whole people, or of conquering the south with its anti-Arian, Catholic population, the Visigoths were on the point of collapse when a military faction

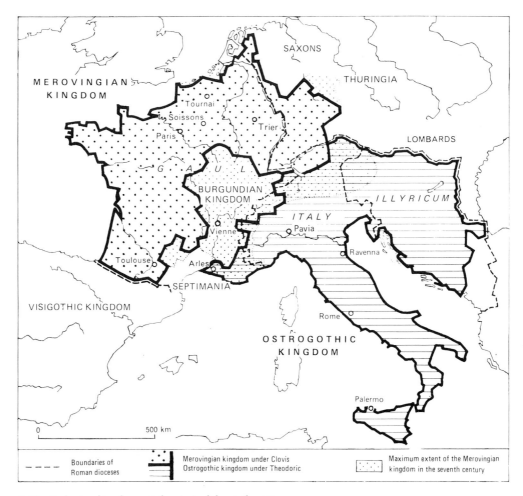

2 The Barbarian kingdoms at the start of the sixth century

brought Athanagild to power in 551. Lastly, in Ostrogothic Italy, Theodoric's brilliant and astute reign ended badly. His strict policy of segregating the two peoples, Arian Goths and Catholic Romans, rebounded on him. Just before his death he failed to prevent the eruption of religious conflict, and the exasperated Goths brought Theodahad to power. He reverted to a policy of exclusively Germanic domination.

Return of the 'Romans', 533–610

Freed from the menace of Germanic invasions, the Roman empire of the East had recovered its strength. Justinian (527–65), aware of the crises in the three Germanic kingdoms bordering the Mediterranean, decided the time had come to reconstitute the Roman empire of the West and so restore the Roman world to its former unity. His general Belisarius, after a surprise landing on the coast of Africa in 533, annihilated the Vandal kingdom so completely that not a trace of its ethnic origins survived. Gaining a foothold in Sicily, the Byzantine imperial forces went on to attack Italy in 535, but the Ostrogoths put up dogged resistance. For twenty years the two adversaries subjected the peninsula to the ravages of their alternating successes and reverses, Rome itself being four times captured and recaptured. By about 554 Italy was once again officially Roman. In that year, furthermore, Justinian won back the south-eastern provinces of Spain as the reward for his support of Athanagild with Byzantine troops. By far the greater part of the Mediterranean had thus been restored to the empire. Without Frankish Gaul, however, the reconquest would remain incomplete. In the event, Justinian's successors lacked the capacity either to sustain his momentum or to profit from the civil wars between the Merovingian kings which were a constant feature of the period from 561 to 613.

In addition, plague-ravaged Italy put up no resistance to the Lombard invasion of 568. It took only four years for the Lombards to capture the plain of the Po and to set up principalities in Tuscany, at Spoleto and at Benevento. Effective Byzantine resistance was confined to a narrow strip of territory running from Venice to Rome and taking in Ravenna and Perugia, while Naples, Calabria, the *Bruttium* and Sicily were left untouched. Italy, and in particular southern Italy, thus remained a channel through which the Eastern Mediterranean could continue to influence the West. This circumstance, of vital importance in Europe's later history, is thus a legacy from Justinian; and it is scarcely an exaggeration to say that it determined the particular destiny of the *Mezzogiorno* down into the nineteenth century. The area in the Danube plain which the Lombards had vacated was very quickly occupied by the Avars, nomadic horsemen from the steppes, who established base camps from which they launched numerous plundering raids on the Germanic world, which was forced to move increasingly into the Frankish orbit in order to protect itself. Thereafter the situation in the barbarian West remained more or less stabilised for the next two centuries.

Despite Justinian's return in strength, the Roman empire of the West thus took over two centuries to disappear – the reward, no doubt, of adherence to the tactic of enlisting the Germanic armies as allies. The fact that death was so long in coming made it possible for Roman civilisation to survive, even if the first Germanic kingdoms were eventually alienated from it by their Arianism and their relocation. The survival of *romanitas* as a political presence in Italy is a result of the disappearance of all the first-generation Germanic settlements except that of the Visigoths in Spain. In contrast, the foundations of the second generation – those of the Anglo-Saxons, the Franks, the Alamans, the Bavarians and the Lombards – retained their vitality thanks to the Germanic hinterland by which they were supported.

A precarious balance, 610–87

The seventh century is characterised by a consolidation of the new political relationships between the Germanic kingdoms, which in turn gives a new look to the strategic map of the former Roman West.

Northumbrian casket made of whalebone. On the right, the defender of a besieged castle, the legendary archer Egil (Örvandill in Scandinavian mythology). The piece was found at St-Julien-de-Brioude and dates from the end of the *seventh* century. (London, British Museum).

While Africa remained Byzantine, Visigothic Spain emerged as the first region to overcome its divisions: Athanagild established his capital at Toledo and kept control of Septimania, Leovigild (569–86) conducted a vigorous offensive against the Suevic kingdom and succeeded in suppressing it in 585, although his campaigns against the Basques merely deflected their pillaging raids on to the northern slopes of the Pyrenees. Reccared (586–601), by publicly converting to Catholicism in 587 and more or less compelling all the Visigoths to follow suit in 589, unified the country internally but failed to expel the Byzantines completely from Baetica and Cartagena: evacuation of the last ports by imperial troops and ships was delayed until 624. From that date the Iberian peninsula was united under Visigothic kingship. The only problems still outstanding were the perennial ones of the Basque country and Septimania, neither of which fully accepted rule from Toledo.

If Visigothic Spain remained isolated, the same cannot be said of Merovingian Gaul. In 613, having emerged from its civil wars, the Frankish kingdom entered a period of great stability under Chlothar II (584–629) and Dagobert (629–38), who by an accident of succession ruled as sole monarchs for 25 years. Like the Visigothic kings, they pacified their frontiers; but having made a definitive break with the Basques and the Bretons they were forced to establish militarised zones at the gateway to their territories. Above all they succeeded in controlling the regionalist tendencies beginning to emerge in Aquitaine and Burgundy. To the east, Dagobert made contact with the Slav kingdom under Samo (a Frank) and obtained an annual tribute from the Saxons, who had extended their territory from the Elbe to the Rhine. After this, however, except for a brief period under Childeric II (between 673 and 675), this unity of command ceased to exist. Two large blocks emerged as distinct entities: Austrasia, stretching from the Rhine to the Meuse and with Metz as its capital; and Neustria, extending from the Meuse to the Loire and centred on Paris. Burgundy, Aquitaine and Provence, resistant to control by a king of any kind, maintained a delicate balancing act between the two. Neustria, where the bulk of the Merovingians' private estates were situated, managed to retain the initiative until 687. But while the quarrels between the rival kingdoms dragged on, the subject Germanic peoples seized the opportunity to upset Frankish rule. From the sixth century onwards, and particularly from 650, the Frisians, a coastal people who had occupied Zealand and taken part in the Anglo-Saxon invasions, began to expand towards the Danish coast and the Rhine delta, where they captured the ports of Utrecht and Dorestad. From 641 we find Thuringia regaining its independence. Not long afterwards, in the Garonne region, incessant warfare with the Basques gave rise to an independent principality in Aquitaine, under the leadership of Duke Lupus from 671 or 672. These are all signs of a developing crisis in a Merovingian kingdom which was still inadequately governed.

The Anglo-Saxons went through a similar process, without in their case making any serious effort at unification. Restricted by the Britons to the island's eastern flank since about 490, around 550–60 they took advantage of conflicts with the Franks on the continent to resume their progress. Different bands, each with its own warleaders, drove the British westward step by step. Soon there only remained the rump of three British kingdoms, Cornwall, Wales and Strathclyde, while the Anglo-Saxons had reached the Irish Sea at two points. Left with nothing but infertile hill country, the Britons stepped up their migration to Armorica, to continental 'Britain', Brittany as it came to be known. As regards the Anglo-Saxon kingdoms – Kent, Essex, Sussex, Wessex, Northumbria, Mercia and East Anglia – these were colonised in force by individual chieftains who then vied with one another for supremacy, without much positive result. By the end of the seventh century these kingdoms were all more or less stabilised, after a period in which Kent, Northumbria and Mercia had each successively achieved a fleeting predominance.

Did Italy suffer a similar fragmentation? Restored after a decade of internal crisis, the Lombard king sought to bring the independent dukes into submission. To achieve this, the best course was to make war on Byzantium. With the imperial forces making their inexorable retreat and the increasing erosion of Byzantium's Italian possessions, the papacy put itself forward as the real master of Rome as early as the time of Gregory the Great (590–604) and tried to check the Lombards' expansionist tendencies by allying with the independent dukes and converting the Lombards from Arianism to Catholicism. The Lombard kingdom entered the fold of the Roman Church with the conversion of king Agilulf in 607, and finally abandoned Arianism in 671. In 680 the Lombards' conquests in Italy were recognised by the emperor, with the result that only the southern extremities of the peninsula, the Romagna and Latium, linked by a strategic corridor, remained officially Roman. The pope became more and more isolated.

Rome: what survived?

Officially the empire no longer existed and the Roman central administration had correspondingly vanished. Roman civilisation, however, like a decapitated goose, continued on its way. The Germanic kings on their side had little choice but to assume the responsibilities of the former praetorian prefects. This continuity is evident above all among the most

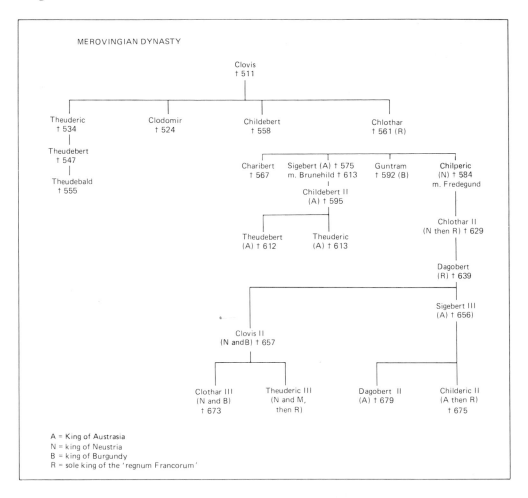

MEROVINGIAN DYNASTY

Clovis
† 511

| Theuderic † 534 | Clodomir † 524 | Childebert † 558 | Chlothar † 561 (R) |

Theudebert
† 547

Theudebald
† 555

| Charibert † 567 | Sigebert (A) † 575 m. Brunehild † 613 | Guntram † 592 (B) | Chilperic (N) † 584 m. Fredegund |

Childebert II
(A) † 595

| Theudebert (A) † 612 | Theuderic (A) † 613 |

Chlothar II
(N then R) † 629

Dagobert
(R) † 639

Sigebert III
(A) † 656)

Clovis II
(N and B) † 657

| Clothar III (N and B) † 673 | Theuderic III (N and M, then R) | Dagobert II (A) † 679 | Childeric II (A then R) † 675 |

A = King of Austrasia
N = king of Neustria
B = king of Burgundy
R = sole king of the 'regnum Francorum'

civilised of the Germans, those who had been in close contact with the empire before they settled on its territory: the Visigoths, Ostrogoths, Burgundians and Franks. The main features of late *romanitas*, let us recall, were the law and civil administration, the tax system, the army, slavery, the senatorial order, the system of landed property, town life, currency and commerce. We shall see that drawing up the balance sheet is a task of considerable complexity.

Continuity in law and administration

Wherever the conquerors were installed under the legal fiction of a treaty of alliance, like a 'Roman' army, and continued to respect this agreement, they became committed in effect to the protection of the occupied population, and to the maintenance of the existing political and social structures. This was particularly true wherever the legal system was founded on Roman law. The settlement of the *federate* peoples had taken place in confor-

62

mity with the law of *hospitalitas* which applied to Roman civil and military officials. We saw how Constantius, short of money and men, was obliged in 418 to enlist the Visigoths as federates. But instead of allotting them pay and temporary quarters, as was usual, he converted the former billeting orders into outright titles of ownership. Indeed, because stability was needed if they were to provide a permanent army, and because the Goths had been familiar with private ownership for more than two centuries, it seemed more profitable to grant them two-thirds of a Roman estate than one-third of a habitation. The Visigoths were thus introduced to this change of proportion when they were settled in the area between Bordeaux, Toulouse and Saint-Gaudens, and they themselves repeated it when they were installed in Spain, in the area bounded by Calatayud, Toledo and Burgos. The Burgundians obtained the same terms for their settlement between Geneva and Lyons. In Italy, on the other hand, the old rule of one-third was adhered to in respect of Odoacer's Scirian troops and again when Theodoric's Ostrogoths were settled in the region round Pavia. The terms of the contract varied according to the people concerned. Among the Burgundians, all Roman landowners were expropriated. Then a levelling out was effected between large and small landowners. Each head of a large family was allocated two-thirds of the *ager*, or arable, one-third of the slaves and half the woodlands, buildings and orchards. Among the Visigoths, on the other hand, the *saltus* was left undivided between the old master and the new. In general, the contract of *hospitalitas* was intended to enable the newcomers and the Romans to live side by side, but this purpose was often frustrated. In Aquitaine, unauthorised encroachments led to stormy relationships; elsewhere, when the two populations became intermixed following the devolution of German allotments by inheritance or sales, the barbarian community still retained its identity. Protecting *romanitas* as best it could, the regime of *hospitalitas*, wherever it was practised, played an instrumental part in preserving Roman agrarian structures.

A still greater role in the protection of *romanitas* was played by the Roman law codes. To make themselves acceptable, the Germans allowed the legal system of the conquered to be perpetuated. It is possible that it was King Gundobad of the Burgundians himself (*c.* 480–516) who had a summary made of extracts from the Theodosian Code and other late Antique legal compilations in order to provide Romans in Burgundian territory with their own law (the *Lex Romana Burgundionum*). In 506, King Alaric II of the Visigoths had an abridgement of the Theodosian Code made for the Aquitanians (the *Brevariarum Alarici*). King Theodoric II of the Visigoths did something similar at an earlier stage in his edict summarising Theodosius II's most important prescriptions *c.* 460, though this text is thought by some to have been issued by Theodoric the Ostrogoth in Italy *c.* 500. In any case, Italy led the field in regard to the maintenance of Roman law, receiving from Justinian at the time of the Byzantine reconquest the famous Code which bears his name (published 529–34), together with the *novellae*, the new laws promulgated between that date and his death in 565. From then on, the peninsula (or at least those parts within the Byzantine sphere of influence) remained a centre for Roman law, both public and private, without interruption. Africa and Byzantine Spain were naturally also drawn in. The exercise and practice of Roman law undoubtedly helped to extend the influence of the conquered. The humanist ideal of a society in which the rights of private persons remain inviolate so long as the State's interests and public safety are not endangered was thereby perpetuated. In countries where Roman influence was dominant, the conception of a State which in return for universal obedience metes out justice on behalf of the individual, the family or a social or religious group, was kept alive and made headway. A fundamental difference with the Germans was apparent wherever men went to law rather than war to settle a dispute. Lastly we have to remember that Roman law remained the law of the clergy, even in Germanic territory, and that it was propagated by the bishop's jurisdiction. Traces of its influence are therefore to be found in Celtic, Frankish, Gothic and even Lombard legal codes. Apart from this, Roman law survived in isolated pockets such as the law of Chur (*Lex Romana Curiensis*) in the mountains of the present-day Swiss Canton of Grisons, drawn up in the late eighth century.

The Germanic kingships likewise made attempts to adapt their practice to the Roman concept of the State and its apparatus of salaried officials. Kings who had been installed by treaty were scrupulous in their regard for Roman institutions, none more so than Theodoric. Officially commissioned by Constantinople to order affairs in Italy, the king was in fact a kind of deputy emperor and assumed the purple. Designated '*augustus*', adorned with the title of patrician, in the annual consular elections he chose one consul out of the two. The last to be appointed in the West was Basil in 541. Theodoric intervened directly in the administrative departments still functioning at Ravenna under the control of the *magister officiorum* and continued to use the *quaestor palatii* for official correspondence, the *comes sacrarum largitionum* for control of finance and the government workshops, and so on. Local administration remained in the hands of two praetorian prefects, one for Italy, based on Ravenna, the other for the Gauls, residing at Arles, each with their own staff. Each province still had its governor, each city its count. Rome kept its venerable magistracies and the lustre of its Senate, even if the latter had ceased to play any real role and was reduced, pending its final disappearance in the late sixth century, to the rank of a municipal council. After the reconquest by Justinian the peninsula was reannexed to the empire in 554, but the ineptitude of the Roman administration in Italy at the time of the Lombard invasion forced the emperor Maurice (582–602) to introduce reforms. He appointed an 'exarch', based on Ravenna, and furnished him with extensive civil and military powers, which included authority over the dukes and counts as his military subordinates, although the civilian hierarchy was left intact. These dispositions continued unaltered into the eighth century.

Africa and Spain were treated to the same form of Byzantine reorganisation. Here too it is fair to say that the Vandals and the Visigoths had tampered very little with the Roman administrative arrangements. The Vandal kings relied on the Roman secretariat of the vicar of Africa and retained the system of provincial governors. The Visigoths, whether in Toulouse or Toledo, adhered likewise to the Roman framework of provincial administration and they also had a kind of *quaestor palatii*: Leo of Narbonne, who acted in this capacity in the reign of Euric, seems to have been the Germanic king's chief political and legal adviser. It is evident, however, that the Vandals and Visigoths, not to mention the

Lhodari, king of the Alamans, presides at an assembly of lay and ecclesiastical magnates to commit to writing in Latin the Law of the Alamans, hitherto transmitted orally. Thanks to his intervention, the heritage of Roman law will be preserved (early ninth-century manuscript of the *Breviarium Alarici*, Paris, Bibliothèque nationale).

Burgundians with their much smaller kingdom, did not have at their disposal all the means of government available to an ordinary praetorian prefect. It was necessary for them to invent some form of 'consistory' and to create a 'royal patrimony' for themselves from an assortment of confiscated estates and public lands formerly administered by the empire. Theodoric was unique in maintaining a strict separation between the two types of lands, which he also extended to Spain. In general, therefore, these 'dualist' realms, where the occupant admired the civilisation of the conquered to the point of adopting the Latin language, Roman titles and Roman methods for the purposes of government, appear to have contributed to the maintenance of imperial political practices in the countries bordering the western Mediterranean. Even the Frankish realm, master of its territory more as a result of conquest than of diplomatic understanding with Rome, was served by Roman officials with the ranks of master of the offices and referendary, the latter having responsibility for the royal seal and official correspondence. What strikes us most, however, is the continuing presence in these territories, without exception or interruption, of the

65

count, the *comes civitatis*. In the Merovingian kingdom, this institution did not penetrate to the Germanised parts until the seventh century.

Continuing struggle against fiscal oppression

The same effort at continuity is to be observed in the fiscal system. Goths, Vandals, Burgundians, and indeed Franks, that is to say the core of Rome's former *federates*, were normally exempt from taxes because they counted as soldiers in the imperial service. Roman civilians, clerics excepted, were therefore required to shoulder tax obligations on their behalf, and the sharing out of estates under the *hospitalitas* arrangement was intended to ensure that the flow of tax payments was maintained.

And it is a fact that the Germanic kingdoms everywhere, in Italy, Africa, Spain and Gaul, took steps to organise and perpetuate the imposition and collection of the land and capitation taxes, with the help of cadasters and polyptychs, registers in which census returns and individual dues were recorded. The fact that the Bretons, associated with a part of Gaul long productive of anti-fiscal revolts, in particular by the Armoricans and *bacaudae*, concluded their alliance with the Franks on the express condition that they would pay them no taxes did not prevent the independent Breton kings from levying tribute on their own account; and as we know from their law codes drawn up some time between the sixth and the late eighth centuries, they retained the services of an official *tributarius* to organise its collection. So we find no changes of practice either at the centre or at the level of the *civitas*. In Italy, Theodoric saw to it that all the taxes cited earlier continued to be levied and collected in gold. In Visigothic Spain, the taxes on merchants and the tolls on internal and external trade were also regularly collected. The king of the Ostrogoths was especially punctilious in maintaining the food doles to the citizens of Rome, in certain cases by means of requisition. The bureaucratic machine had thus not budged, and for that reason the complaints of curials and ordinary citizens continued to be heard. In Ostrogothic Italy, for instance, the official measure used to weigh up taxes in kind before their conversion into gold was half as heavy again as the standard measure; in Merovingian Gaul the tax registers were not brought up to date every fifteen years (the period of the indictional cycle). In short, almost everywhere there were anti-fiscal revolts, especially in times of epidemic, war and famine. At Trier in 548 Parthenius was lynched because he had raised taxes; in Neustria in 584 Audo escaped a similar fate by taking refuge in a church. To be given the task of collecting the income due to the king from fiscal properties was regarded as a death sentence, as in the case of Bertald's mission west of the Seine in 604. Riots were everyday occurrences, and so was their corollary, the flight of tax-payers and abandonment of their lands. This happened, for example, at Limoges in 579, in Corsica, in Sardinia and in Sicily in 595. These islands were the subject of a plea from Gregory the Great to the Byzantine empress to have their taxes reduced. The machinery of the Roman *annona* had however disappeared with the death of Theodoric. Nevertheless, fiscal demands appear to have wrought havoc in the countryside and even in the towns. In 534 a demand for post-horses was enough to empty Como of its population. In Spain, King Chindaswind (642–53) decided to transfer responsibility for the collection of taxes from the town councillors to the counts; in Aquitaine, Eudo *princeps* made use of the Jews. All these efforts were useless in the face of populations whose determination to sabotage the system became all the more obstinate when they succeeded in having the rates of taxation normalised, that is to say nominally fixed, but in practice declining in value year by year; they regarded payment as a mark of servitude. Indeed, with the reduction of the *coloni* to the level of slaves, these two categories became almost the only ones affected. In Spain, King Egica achieved nothing by his law of 702 forbidding under direst penalties the flight of slaves. In the eighth century the Roman land-tax was still in being, but regardless of whether it was derisory, collected only sporadically in deference to exemptions wrested from the princes, or whether it was levied in what had become Muslim Spain, every time it was collected there were catastrophic social consequences, particularly in 722 and in 756, on which occasion a terrible famine ensued. To sum up, under the combined onslaught of the people and the clergy, one of the mainstays of the Roman State, its fiscal system, was gradually undermined, in spite of the intention of Germanic kings to preserve it. It survived only in the countries directly administered by Byzantium or in regions such as Spain and Aquitaine which had been thoroughly romanised. The traces of it in the Asturias and in the Gallo-Roman south were very slow to disappear.

This tendency for Roman principles to be diluted can also be seen in relation to the army. The most sacrosanct of all was the principle that warfare was the business of the Germanic federates and should concern the former Roman population as little as possible. The Byzantine army, where Latin, not Greek, remained the language of command down to the eighth century, perpetuated and reinforced these attitudes in Italy, Africa and Spain, and it continued to number federates among its troops. Theodoric had expressly debarred Romans from the army; the Vandals and Lombards did the same. But in Visigothic Spain and southern Gaul the principle was still upheld that all freemen, including the *coloni*, who were of the same legal status, were liable for conscription to military service. Furthermore, in the heyday of the Germanic realms in the eighth century, with the obvious exception of the Lombards and the Anglo-Saxons, their armies still contained a high proportion of autochthonous elements, *'federate* barbarians' – Basques, Bretons, Avars or Saxons as the case might be – and private bodyguards clustered around their commander-in-chief. Belisarius always had at his side a band of some 7,000 trusted personal retainers, an example later followed by the exarchs. The Roman practice of maintaining private retainers (*bucellarii*) was imitated by the Ostrogothic and Visigothic kings and became so usual that a number of powerful senators, not to mention bishops, followed suit. Soldiers' pay took a new turn. In Italy, the Byzantine government granted its soldiers possessory rights on public lands as their *stipendium*. This system of soldier–peasants (*stratiotes*) was not without influence on developments in the West. Similarly, the Byzantine treatment of the *limes* as a frontier zone bristling with strong points and manned by permanent garrisons was imitated by the Visigoths and the Franks. The best known example is that of the *guerches* erected against the Aquitanians and the Bretons, a suffix still attached to a number of villages in western France. Defensive measures of this kind had the effect of perpetuating zones of indigenous barbarism and still more of accentuating the internal divisions of a formerly unified Roman West, especially in the Italian peninsula. In short, in a sphere where the Germans might be expected to enjoy total superiority, certain Roman features nevertheless survived intact or with very little modification.

Slaves and patrons: a polarised society

Slaves and senators, as we have said, were among the 'privileged' in late Antique society. The former probably saw an increase in their numbers as invasions and warfare became more frequent. Even if there were bishops who produced ransoms in gold to buy back captured members of their flock, the conquerors persistently rounded up labour for transport to their settlement areas. As the result of Vandal, Anglo-Saxon and Frankish raids, Italians, Gallo-Romans and Hispano-Romans might end up in Africa, Britain or Austrasia. Nor was there any cessation in the slave trade as such, which was fed by Moors, Saxons and finally, from the time of Samo (early seventh century), by Slavs. In countries with a Roman tradition their status remained unchanged and their ranks were swelled by *coloni*, tied like themselves to the soil. The gulf between liberty and servitude was still so wide that in Visigothic Spain a free woman who had sexual relations with a slave was regarded as depravity incarnate: flogging, followed by burning alive, was the fate of both partners. By contrast, the free landowner, master of numerous slaves, was allowed by law to breed from servile women as many children as were needed for his agricultural operations. The Roman law issued by Augustus which prohibited the emancipation of more than 100 slaves at a time was still sedulously observed in order to avoid sharp falls in the level of production. For the emancipated there were two possibilities: full freedom as defined by Roman law, or more commonly freedom with *obsequium*, that is the duty of obedience to his former master, now his patron, except where the latter was the patron saint (revealing expression) of a church or monastery. In practice therefore the freedman received his liberty on licence, knowing that the least misdemeanour on his part could mean reduction to his former status. In short, while economic conditions in the slave world may have been tolerable, the same can hardly be said of its legal situation. If slave couples were no longer forcibly separated, and if slaves aspiring to holy orders were duly manumitted, this was only because of the Church's intransigence in all matters connected with marriage and ordination.

In Roman societies subjected to Germanic kings a new, more profound division appeared at this time, between *humiliores* and *potentiores*, the lowly and the powerful, or in another frequent designation the *pauperes* and the *potentes*, the poor and the powerful. The category of the lowly or poor in fact embraced freemen of all types: small and medium landowners, workers of every description, people without protectors in high places. Meanwhile the ascent of the great senatorial families continued, facilitated by the progressive disappearance of the expensive offices of state reserved for them under the empire. Nursing the wounds of their most recent efforts to usurp the empire (Avitus, 455–6) or of their fierce opposition to the Arianism of the East Germans, (Boethius, 524), the senators retired to their country estates. Furthermore, the description 'senatorial' now applied to members of any family that was rich, noble and of Roman origin, whether ancient or modern. Expelled by the Vandals and Lombards, but protected by Theodoric and taken into partnership by the Visigoths and Franks, these former upstarts took root in central Italy, southern Gaul and Spain. In the course of the seventh century, however, they dropped the Roman tripartite nomenclature in favour of the Germanic style. They parcelled out the important positions among themselves, some taking on secular functions while others assumed episcopal office. The example of Gregory the Great is revealing: one of his great-great-grandfathers had been pope and his family was descended from the Gordiani. As late as the tenth century, count Gerald of Aurillac was claiming two sixth-century senators among his ancestry: Caesarius of Arles and Aridius of Limoges, the one a Burgundian, the other from Aquitaine. Intermarriage with the Germanic nobility caused some of these families, originally numbering between 3,000 and 4,000, to disappear. In Italy, one of the Ostrogothic kings, Teias, massacred senators he had been given as hostages. In Spain, the senatorial lineages were already extinct at the beginning of the eighth century. Nevertheless, they unquestionably formed an element of continuity in the transmission of the Roman and Christian cultural heritage.

The power they wielded was political and social as well as economic. Indispensable officials, episcopal protectors of the poor through their extension of the patronate, the senators, whether they willed it or not and despite their devotion to the State, fostered relationships which led increasingly to the privatisation of public power. In Italy, these great landowners were escaping the control of municipal magistrates even in the time of Theodoric, and granting protection to large numbers of free peasants turned *coloni*. The Church of Rome did the same on its Sicilian and Italian estates: a grain merchant, for example, commended himself to St Peter, represented by his steward. Mention has already been made of the importance of the armed retainers serving Byzantine officials in Italy and the leading men in southern Gaul. In Visigothic Spain, *bucellarii* seeking protection from a noble patron surrendered their land and received it back from him in tenure. At the same time they received from him arms to use in his service. As freemen, they were at liberty to break off the contract unilaterally and to join themselves to another magnate, provided they gave back the land and weapons. Otherwise they were entitled to bequeath these possessions to posterity, provided that the heir, male or female, was in a position to render the same obedience and loyalty. Again, the fact that patrons held such a power over their slaves, freedmen and free clients, meant that they were judicially responsible for criminal acts carried out by these dependants on their orders. Once again we find a Roman custom rebounding against the State. For in virtue of the economic and military power they were able to subtract from the king's authority, many nobles would henceforth bypass the law or even, as in Aquitaine, found a new royal dynasty. The written contract of Roman law, the *convenientia* or pact between equals, demonstrates that the forging of ties between man and man in Roman fashion depended on an abstract conception of social relationships. The law was father to the deed . . . and by the same token, divided society into manifold pressure groups. The Church was in no position to intervene, for though clergy were forbidden to become clients, it extended its own patronage to the poor. Indeed, the Church added to the solemnity of oaths of fidelity by allowing and encouraging them to be sworn on the relics of patron saints.

Recovery of the land

As against the changes affecting the army and the State, brought about by the fall in fiscal revenues and the rise of clienteles, the system of landownership remained as it was. The ravages of war and fiscal oppression certainly left many deserted properties in their wake. At the beginning of the Byzantine occupation, the Church of Ravenna was required to hand over to the fisc 57 per cent of its agricultural revenues. On rented holdings, the free peasant with rent to pay on top of his tax was losing two-thirds of his harvest in this way. Land with a poor yield was therefore apt to be deserted in favour of more intense cultivation of the most fertile plots. The phenomenon of the *agri deserti* inevitably became more widespread and contributed to the enlargement of the *saltus*. Especially at the beginning, these abandoned lands, by their sheer extent, added considerably to the royal patrimony of the Germanic kings. Acquisitions of deserted lands for the State were made by the Frankish kings north of the Paris basin, by the Visigothic kings in the centre of the Iberian peninsula, and above all by the exarchs in Italy and in Africa. Once the storm was past, cultivation resumed in altered circumstances. The disappearance of the *annona* for the provisioning of Rome, together with the end of the requisitioning of grain and forage for field and cover troops, held out the prospect of greater profit, even in those places where the Roman land-tax, frozen at the customary rate, still remained. The second favourable circumstance was the persistence of the fundamental distinction in law between ownership and possession, together with the fact that save in Africa the 30-year rule (referred to in the previous chapter) had become general. Agricultural expansion could recur at any time, even if bringing land back into production needed five years of unrewarded expenditure and ten years of assiduous toil. The first essential was to reassemble the *instrumentum massae*, the servile labour force: as we saw this was not a problem since numbers were not diminishing and patronage permitted the tying of more and more *coloni* to the soil alongside the domiciled slaves. Next, in zones where peace was quickly restored – Numidia, Byzacena, Baetica, Sicily, Romagna, Umbria, Campagna, Provence, Aquitaine, Champagne – the underlying structure of large estates divided into scattered or contiguous parcels, small freeholds and a multitude of emphyteutic tenures (99-year leases) survived or was being reconstituted. This can be demonstrated from the Albertini tablets dating to the Vandal period in Africa, found on the borders of Algeria and Tunisia: they prove that tenures dating back to the heyday of the empire were still extant and that large landowners were purchasing them in order to consolidate their estates. Again, the Ravenna papyri of the sixth century reveal that large estates could be so fragmented that the yields fell below those of the Sicilian *latifundia*. In Spain, the so-called Visigothic Tablets depict a similar fragmentation, while the will of St Remigius (St Remi), bishop of Rheims, shows that the cultivation of his family estates was in the hands of a mainly free population of tenant *coloni* and free tenants. It was thus through their willingness to accept the payment of many dues from slaves and *coloni* at least partly in kind, and through the buying in of leases or clearance of uncultivated land, that the great lay and ecclesiastical landlords of the late sixth and seventh centuries gradually built up substantial estates. The cathedral of Ravenna made an assault on coastal marshlands and river swamps; the basilicas of St Martin at Tours and St Martial at Limoges became owners under the 30-year rule of large tracts of *saltus*. But alongside the *colonicae* we see a proliferation of small and medium-sized properties carved out by administrators of large estates (*actores, conductores*) or by freemen who had contrived to retain their independence. In times of renewed disturbance the tendency was to retreat to formerly fortified sites, the Celtic or Iberian *oppida*, but the general trend was towards desertion of the larger rural centres, the *vici*, in favour of dispersed dwellings in the countryside. Although not much is known about agricultural techniques and yields at this date, there is little doubt that prosperity returned to Italy under Theodoric (493–526, with effects lasting perhaps till 534), to reappear in the seventh century in the parts of the peninsula under Byzantine rule. In Spain and Gaul, too, this period was remembered as a time of resumed expansion. Considered as a whole, the surface area under cultivation must have returned to its pre-invasion level. Nearly everywhere, the ruralisation of the economy which had begun here and there in the fourth century became more or less general, while the accumulation of landed property by the Church, an institution which knew nothing of division by inheritance, emerges as one of the dominant motifs in a pattern of landownership still true to its Roman origins.

Towns are not moribund . . .

This ruralisation completed the transformation of the towns. They ceased to function as centres of consumption. Rome was literally emptied of its inhabitants for 40 days by the Ostrogothic king Totila in 546–7. Perhaps at most 25,000 returned from the countryside, very few by comparison with the late fourth-century population of 800,000. The great capitals (Arles, Trier and Milan) ceased to signify as political centres. Milan was recaptured by Uraia, an Ostrogothic chief, in 539, its population massacred, its women sold as slaves to the Burgundians and transplanted to the Valais and Savoy. Milan's city walls, enclosing an area of 133 ha, were completely destroyed, and the Byzantine general Narses, when he came to rebuild them, could not match their ancient magnificence. Urban life at Trier did not revive until the sixth century, following the reign of Clovis. Only Ravenna remained unscathed, to be embellished first under Theodoric and then under Justinian with the dazzling array of monumental churches still to be seen today. New political capitals came to the fore; Pavia, Toulouse, Barcelona, Toledo; and in Gaul, Paris, Soissons, Rheims and Metz. Aping Roman imperial residences, these cities, all of them walled, housed the *palatium regis* and a royal retinue made up of the king's friends and companions, a kind of reconstituted 'consistory'. Similarly, the household offices corresponded to the emperor's *sacrum cubiculum* and the chancery to the secretariat of the former 'master of offices'. As capitals, these cities did not owe their importance to administrative functions, since central

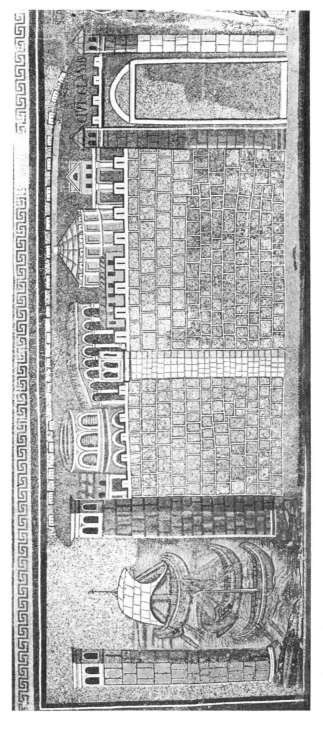

Situated on swampy ground a few kilometres from the sea, Ravenna had a sea-port at Classis, depicted with its defensive towers and fortifications in this mosaic at St Apollinare Nuovo (fifth century).

Irish metalwork. Bronze plaque of the Crucifixion, tenth century. Clonmacnoise, Co. Offaly.

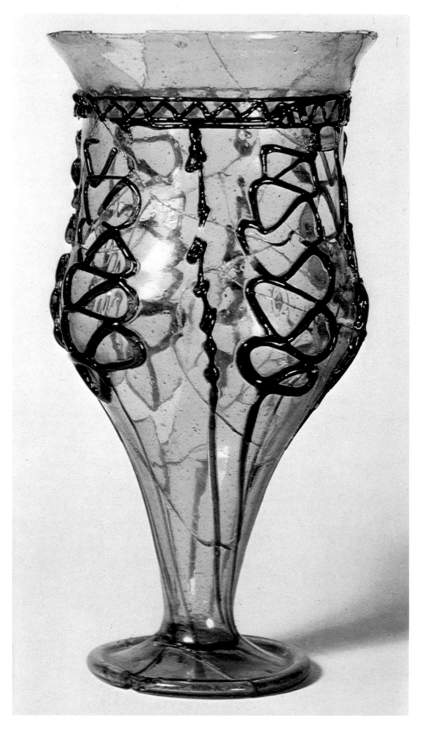

Roman art in Germania. Footed glass, early fifth century, from the necropolis of Vireux-Molhain, Belgium.

Imperial art in Gaul. The 'Port' dish from the Kaiseraugst Treasure. Silver with gilt decoration, mid-fourth century (Augst, Römermuseum).

Lombard art. Frontal plaque of a gilt bronze helmet, *c.* 600, showing King Agilulf enthroned (Florence, Bargello Museum).

government in the usual sense was lacking, but rather to their identification with the royal court. Nevertheless, the commercial sector was still well-represented. The capitals usually boasted a royal burial place incorporated into a basilica outside the city walls, dedicated at Toledo to St Leocadius, at Paris to St Denis, at Metz to St Martin; St Salvator's at Pavia and St Augustine's at Canterbury were the last in this line. In this way the old Roman towns became places where politics and religion intersected. Even when they lacked a royal palace, towns were still the seat of the count and the bishop. From now on an official career started at court and led on to civic office rather than the reverse, but none of this detracted from the town's continuing function as the meeting-place of pilgrims and merchants arriving for the feasts, fairs and markets held in honour of the patron saint, not forgetting the suits heard in the count's courts.

In short, with a few exceptions, there is a noticeable continuity between the Antique and the medieval town. Justinian himself was responsible for the fortification of those towns in Africa, Spain and Italy which had hitherto been left open. More positively, the return of agricultural prosperity enabled bishops to invest their surpluses in new constructions. While the Roman civic monuments fell into decay, the towns of the sixth and seventh centuries witnessed a proliferation of basilicas built with triangular pediments, timber roofs and detached bell towers. A new urban geography took shape. Certain towns to the west of Carthage, on Spain's south-eastern seaboard, between the Pyrenees and the Garonne, in Brittany and Normandy, in Provence, Latium, the Po Valley and southern Italy went into a decline or disappeared. Others started to expand: Merida, Evora, Tarragona, Barcelona, Naples, Gaeta, Marseilles and the towns along the Rhône–Moselle axis. Orleans, Tours and Nantes were rivalled by Limoges and Bourges, where even the suburbs were fortified. Episcopal cities in particular contained a dozen and more sanctuaries within their walls, not counting the monasteries and cemetery chapels outside. The original cathedral complex comprising a church for the catechumens, a baptistry, and a sanctuary reserved for the bishop and the faithful, was now surrounded by other ecclesial buildings: shrines dedicated to a local saint, a hospice for invalids and travellers (*xenodochion*), a hostel for the poor, and so on. These, with their continual comings and goings, made the town more animated. It was here that sale contracts and wills were concluded and committed to writing in the presence of the notary, while the members of the town council, when they ceased to levy taxes, had nothing to do apart from registering and authenticating such acts. Lastly, the town in its new aspect provided a home for the last surviving representatives of craft corporations, the masons and the moneyers.

. . . nor are currency and commerce

The moneyers, indeed, become more numerous during the sixth and seventh centuries. The first generation of *federate* kings hesitated for some time before taking over the supreme imperial privilege of issuing coinage. Obviously there was a risk of upsetting the balance of trade. The Vandals, Sueves and Ostrogoths contented themselves with the issue of silver coins, in deference to Constantinople's monopoly. The Frankish king Theuderic I (511–34)

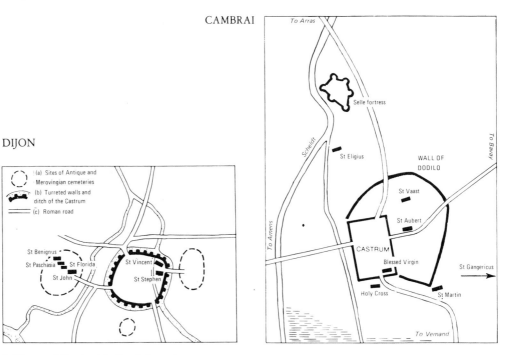

3 Dijon and Cambrai in the sixth century

was the first to strike *solidi* and *tremisses* bearing his name, (a pseudo-imperial coinage) made from gold mined in the Cévennes, but of the same weight and fineness as Byzantine issues. In Spain, following Euric's example (466–84), Leovigild (568–86) was probably the first king to issue *tremisses* bearing his own effigy. Lastly, we should not overlook the re-establishment of mints by Byzantium in its reconquered territories, at Ravenna, Rome and Syracuse. Milan disappeared, but Byzantine coins with the emperor's effigy continued to circulate at Ravenna down to 751 and at Rome until 775. This persistence of a monetary medium common to West and East once again points a high degree of continuity. The Lombards, when they came on the scene, were also very quick to adopt the Byzantine monetary standard.

For reasons so far unexplained, the Germanic kingdoms failed to develop a silver and bronze coinage with low purchasing power. The errors of the past were therefore perpetuated, and only feeble remedies applied, in particular the issue of the *triens* or *tremissis*, one-third of a *solidus*, weighing 1.3g. This lowering of purchasing power, which did not take place in the East, was presumably intended to harmonise supply with demand. Something needed to be done to counteract the deflationary effects of gold coinage while preventing the return to the practice of barter for all but the largest transactions. But the results were disappointing, since in practice the *triens* continued to deteriorate in weight and value in sympathy with actual trading requirements. Lack of gold was not a factor, since the mines

Solidus of Sigebert III, son of Dagobert (seventh century).

in Spain and Aquitaine continued to be exploited. Furthermore, the money economy was spreading, with coins being struck in many more places than under the late empire. In Spain and Gaul nearly every *civitas*–capital had its own mint. Villages, even abbeys and some of the large estates saw the royal monopoly of minting slipping out of the hands of the Merovingians into those of private moneyers who stamped the coinage with their own names. The abundance of coin-hoards can thus safely be used as a guide to the intensity of economic activity.

Indeed, it is thanks to the discovery of *solidi* and *tremisses* all along the main European arteries, especially where the coins are alien to the territory in question, that the trade routes of the era can be reconstructed. The presence of Byzantine coins near the coasts attests that long-distance trade with Constantinople, Antioch and Alexandria by way of Carthage and Ravenna had not dried up. Merchants in Ravenna purchased silks from the imperial workshops at Constantinople. Egyptian papyrus found its way to Marseilles, Indian and Chinese spices to Narbonne. Natron imported from Egypt enabled the glassmakers of Cologne to continue selling their delicate wares to the Anglo-Saxons and the Scandinavians. There is evidence, too, of traffic in the other direction to show that the West was not squandering its gold in unequal exchanges. Examination of a wreck dating to the seventh century found recently in the roadstead off Fos confirms that this vessel was carrying grain in bulk, pitch in *amphorae* and stamped earthenware, all intended for some eastern destination. Marble from the Pyrenees was exported to Constantinople. Convoys of Saxon slaves were despatched from Verdun to Spain or Greece. Bronze liturgical vessels of Coptic origin travelled in the opposite direction, and some Byzantine ships even entered the Atlantic in search of Cornish tin.

Comparison with the long-distance trade of the fourth century shows that the only real changes applied chiefly to Italy. Because Theodoric had called on Spanish and Provençal merchants to alleviate the cessation of grain imports from Africa, and because the State's trading role had disappeared, speculation on the Italian grain market was a thing of the past. The meagre Roman population was now dependent for its corn on a free mercantile trade which fell increasingly into the hands of important Jewish and Syrian merchants. This commerce was confined to the trade-routes connecting Constantinople with Sicily and Rome, while with the installation in 568 of the Lombards in northern Italy the routes through the Alpine passes were closed until the end of the seventh century. In consequence, the axis Fos–Marseilles–Chalons-sur-Saône–Metz–Trier regained its importance. Since the networks of Roman roads were still maintained by the Merovingian and Visigothic kings, the ports of Narbonne, Barcelona and Cartagena remained in contact with Africa and with the towns of their own hinterlands as far as the Atlantic seaboard. Oil and *garum* from Spain were exported to northern Gaul. Salt from the saltpans of the Atlantic and Mediterranean travelled down the Seine and Moselle; wines resinated in the Greek fashion, whether from Samos or the Paris basin, were purchased all the way to the mouth of the Rhine. True, a coinage whose purchasing power was too high was bound to be more of a handicap in these internal exchanges than in long-distance, seaborne commerce, and barter must have played a part. Nevertheless, the increasing frequentation of the river-routes, the widespread use of dromedaries as freight animals in Africa, Spain and Gaul, and the sizeable colonies of Greek and Jewish merchants in large towns and even at La Cluse, at the foot of one of the Pyrenean passes (Perche), all prove that commerce between the barbarian kingdoms with a strong Roman element in their population did not diminish and was even diversified.

To sum up, in the countries where the Germans had found a place as *federates* or to which the Byzantines had returned as masters of the empire, continuity with Rome is plain to see: in the law, in the practice of slavery and its close relation the colonate, in the patronate and in the senatorial oligarchy, in the agrarian system and the gold coinage. The Mediterranean was still a Roman lake. On the other hand, parts of the Roman heritage wore less well. The State, vehemently resisted by victorious or vanquished populations, was shorn of all but its local officials, and its fiscal system faced an inexorable decline. Towns, even where they remained in being and made a fresh start, finally shed all pretensions to be centres of production. Their lead over the countryside had been lost. More positively, changes in the Byzantine East had repercussions in the barbarian West, influencing in particular the public offices, the army, the Church and even patterns of trade. This continuity was the product of healed ruptures, of regressive evolution, as with the return to the patronates of the Roman republic, or of progressive evolution, as with the deepening of Rome's imprint. The late Roman society which we saw striving to escape from the State had at last achieved its goal.

What did the newcomers contribute?

Taking shape in contrast to this old Mediterranean Europe was a younger Europe, continental and insular, in which *romanitas* no longer predominated. Whether they came from the Celts or the Germans, habits and attitudes totally unknown to the Romans were introduced into the erstwhile empire. We shall trace the demographic and linguistic effects of this process on the subject populations the barbarians found *in situ* and then go on to consider the nature and novelty of their contributions to the law, kingship, the organisation of warfare, the relations of man with man and the exploitation of the soil. From their religious outlook we shall discover, in relation to Arianism, that these barbarian peoples were all to a greater or lesser extent at odds with *romanitas*.

A gradual merging of peoples

It should not be imagined that the barbarians descended on the empire like an 'ethnic whirl-wind' upsetting everything in their path. In reality, the Romans came into contact with Germanic armies accompanied by women, children and slaves, followed by their baggage trains and sometimes by a straggle of renegade Romans or detribalised Germans. The military core, whose ethnic cohesion was apt to be weak, thus trailed behind it a floating population which could well be dispersed by the slightest defeat. When the Vandals crossed to Africa they numbered some 84,000. The Visigothic settlers in Aquitaine barely attained 100,000. The Burgundians certainly numbered even fewer than that. As for the Ostrogoths, some authorities put their numbers at 100,000, while the Lombards are thought to have amounted to no more than 20,000. But all these figures are sheer guesswork. Isolated as they were in the midst of conquered populations and uprooted from their countries of origin, it is understandable that these groups should have gone in perpetual fear of becoming submerged. Hence the rule introduced by the Ostrogoths and Lombards forbidding Romans to bear arms, and the adoption by the Ostrogoths and Visigoths for their own benefit of a Roman law prohibiting mixed marriages. This policy of segregation explains why some of the Germanic kingdoms give the impression of garrison-states encamped in hostile territory. When they eventually disappeared they left no trace, as happened with the Sueves, the Vandals and the Ostrogoths. On the other hand, peoples who had maintained contact with their homeland – the Franks, the Alamans, the Bavarians, the Anglo-Saxons and the Celts, the latter through constant communication by sea – were able to replenish their numbers with regular reinforcements. Although this is impossible to quantify, one fact seems obvious: their lack of Romanisation by comparison with the preceding peoples explains the new look they gave to the territories they occupied.

These assertions can be substantiated from the various modes of settlement. We know of only three instances in which Roman landowners were dispossessed of their properties blatantly and by force. The Vandals seized estates in proconsular Africa around Carthage and used them to organise what amounted to a military occupation, backed up by garrisons in the hinterland. The Lombards did the same in the plain of the Po, where a heavy military colonisation was accompanied by confiscations and massacres of the inhabitants. In Britain, the Anglo-Saxons advanced along the river-valleys until the Britons were penned into the western and northern parts of the island or forced to submit. In consequence, Britons emigrated to Brittany where they settled on vacant lands. The encroachment of the Franks, Alamans and Bavarians was of this latter type. The presence of large tracts of deserted or virgin lands accounts for the relatively peaceful manner in which these peoples of the Rhine and Danube made their advance. As they abandoned their original settlement areas, others such as the Thuringians and Saxons moved up behind them to take their place. But certain areas were so empty that in the seventh century the Franks could return to the right bank of the Rhine and colonise a region, Franconia (Franken), which for that reason bears their name. Similarly, Frisians and Franks crossed over to Kent or the Danish coasts, while Irishmen emigrated to Scotland.

These gradual infiltrations therefore produced more lasting results than in the case of peoples like the Anglo-Saxons and Lombards, who had to fight every step of the way. Fusion of the Franks with the Gallo-Romans must have been relatively swift, since the territories north of the Seine were known collectively as Francia by the sixth century, even though the Frankish occupiers were still in the minority. A study of cemeteries reveals the many different forms of fusion. Cemeteries between 400 and 550, from the Rhine to the Loire in fact contain different types of inhumations, of which the arrangement of the graves in long rows is the only dominant feature. Here the Roman custom of burial in a coffin is combined with the Germanic practice of burying the dead fully clad and armed, with food offerings, in varying alignments. Working from north to south, we find the pagan Saxons and Frisians north of the Rhine still practising cremation, horse burials and the making of burial mounds. South of the Somme, burials of exclusively Frankish type diminish, weapons and pottery become less frequent and chieftains' tombs are set apart. On the left bank of the Rhine and in Alsace, the presence of longswords and spherical pottery proves the existence of an Alamannic element. In the Paris basin, Christianisation had made rapid progress and the rows of tombs contain less and less grave furniture. In Burgundy, weapons and ornaments have disappeared, but Gallo-Roman ceramic ware and inscriptions testify to a high level of Romanisation, and the same is true of Aquitaine, where traces of the Visigoths are virtually nil. Furthermore, the few anthropological studies which have been undertaken show a surprising persistence of the old neolithic stock. Indeed, two or three Burgundian cemeteries in the central and southern Jura, the northern Alps and around Lake Geneva reveal the presence of a Germanic population by virtue of mongoloid dental characteristics. But elsewhere, in Normandy for example, the cemetery of Frénouville shows an unbroken continuity with Gallo-Roman skeletons. The height measurements are identical (an average of 1.67m for males and 1.55m for females) and the cranial characteristics are quite dissimilar to those of the very few Anglo-Saxon specimens from Fleury-sur-Orne, who averaged 1.8m in height. Anthropological studies of the Franks are lacking, but it seems that very few of them, perhaps only a few noble families, lived south of the Somme. In reality, the dominance of the Franks was not ethnic but political. In view of their former contact with the empire, it is perhaps best regarded as the achievement of Gallo-Romans who were Frankish by origin and descent.

This may be the reason why their influence on the language was so slight. Spoken Latin, after all, yielded very little of its territory, retreating perhaps only 200 or even 100 kilometres from the Rhine. The Germanic linguistic frontier was stabilised as early as the sixth century. Starting at the coast of Picardy, it made a detour north of Tournai and then ran parallel with the Sambre and Meuse as far as Maastricht and Aachen. From there it curved south, leaving Trier and Metz as a Latin enclave, followed the ridge of the Vosges, cut Switzerland in two east of Avenches and terminated at the watershed formed by the Alps. More or less identical with the linguistic frontier as we know it today, it does no more than reflect the zones most heavily populated or influenced by Germans. For in places unfrequented even by Frankish officials speaking their heavily-accented Latin, language was slower to evolve and a more important factor in conservation. South of the Loire, it is

Convex tombstone, made of granite from the
excavations of the church of St-Similien in Nantes,
seventh to eighth century (Nantes, Musées
départementaux de Loire-Atlantique).

true, another linguistic barrier was in the process of formation with the emergence of
Occitan; but in all essentials this was a continuation of Latin. A zone between the Somme
and the Loire thus emerges as the meeting-point and melting-pot of the two civilisations. A
similar outcome was not possible in northern Italy, where the Lombard language disappeared in the ninth century. Britain, on the other hand, can from now on justifiably be
called England, since the division of the country into two linguistic domains was an
established fact. East of the dividing line, everybody spoke Anglo-Saxon; the spoken
language in Scotland, Wales, Cornwall and Ireland was still Celtic, just as in Brittany. In
short, Latin receded only a little, and its pronunciation and spelling were already undergoing the multiple transformations that would give birth to the romance languages.

A tribal society geared to war

This meagre success of the Germanic languages was also true of the legal domain. When the barbarians invaded the empire, although each of the peoples had a law of their own there were obvious features in common. These laws were not written down; instead they were committed to memory by experts, called by the Franks *rachimburgii*, who were consulted when cases were tried. The need for written texts first became apparent when the *federates* came into contact with the conquered populace, especially when judgment had to be given in 'mixed' suits (those involving parties living under different laws), and later other Germanic rulers reached similar conclusions. First in the field were the Visigoths with the Code of Euric, followed by the Burgundians with the Law of Gundobad, and the Franks, whose Salic Law was written down in a primitive version before 511. All are in Latin, and this also applies to the Edict of Rothari promulgated for the Lombards by the king of that name (636–43). Latin was also the language used by the Bretons when they set down their laws in writing some time between the sixth and the late eighth century. The Anglo-Saxons were unique in using their own language for the laws of Ethelbert, king of Kent at the beginning of the seventh century, and for the Laws of Ine, king of Wessex between 688 and 694. Victors and vanquished were thus able to co-exist because of an individual system of personalised laws. In a 'mixed' suit, each party had to invoke his own law. Only one kingdom, Visigothic Spain, eventually abandoned this principle in favour of territoriality; this happened when King Reccesuinth (648–72) amalgamated the two legal traditions, Germanic and Roman, to produce a unified code, the *Liber Judiciorum*. Generally speaking, these Germanic codes plainly fell short of the more ample Roman traditions. The notion of public law was unknown; article by article, questions of public and private law were jumbled together. A patriarch usually had a right of justice over his kinsmen, household and slaves; he was the possessor of *Mund*, a mysterious sacral power of pagan ancestry, which endowed him with strength and brought him victory. He had at his disposal the *Mund* of others, in particular the *Mund* of a daughter, which he sold to her future husband. The morning after the marriage, the husband gave his wife a dowry, the *Morgengabe*, in thank-offering for her virginity; otherwise, he sent her home. In default of public prosecution, the onus of proving innocence fell on the accused, who could call on his kinsmen to testify on oath, as 'co-jurors', on his behalf. When, as frequently happened, the judges were unable to decide between two opposing testimonies, the only solution was for the accused to undergo an ordeal, which meant immersing his hands in boiling water or, as an alternative, placing them on a red-hot iron. If at the end of a stipulated period his flesh remained intact, it proved that the gods had decided in his favour. Finally there was the matter of punishments. A thief caught in the act was hanged on the spot. But the criminal who killed the member of an opposing kindred, exercising in this way the sacred duty of vengeance (*faida*), risked a series of private wars stretching over several generations. To put a stop to such never-ending disputes, a murderer could break the chain of vengeance by paying blood-money, or *wergild*, the exact amount of which was prescribed by a tariff corresponding to the various types of physical injury. Barbarian justice thus tended to punish the thief more severely than the murderer and to favour property above persons.

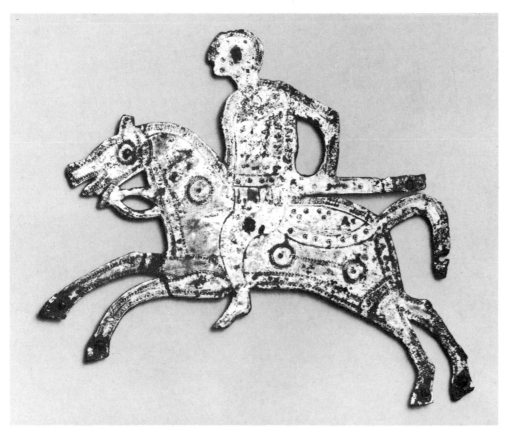

Lombard mounted soldier in cast bronze; he holds a spear and is riding bareback without stirrups. Decorative plaque from a large circular shield. Found near Stabio (Ticino), it dates from the seventh century (Bern, Historisches Museum).

This confusion between public and private affairs was also the source of confusion between civilian and military responsibilities. The tribal chief, even in the guise of Roman general, and later of king, remained a warrior. He was a warleader (*Heerkönig*) elected by all the freemen of his tribe. Victory in battle proved that he was endowed with an authentic pagan charisma, with *Mund*, that magical force symbolised by the genealogies showing descent from the gods, and in the case of the Merovingians by their long hair. But apart from the Merovingians, and the Balts among the Goths, in the majority of cases the royal *Mund* was not proof against the elective principle, for the king had only to suffer one setback to lose his sacral character and along with it his potency. He was no longer the dispenser of booty, the guarantor of the harvest. This being so, he was automatically deprived of his 'ban' (*bannum*), the right to punish and command which was normally ascribed to him, along with its correlative, the power to declare war and make peace. It is no wonder that 'absolutism tempered by assassination' has seemed an apt description of these regimes. The instability of Lombard, Visigothic, Anglo-Saxon and even Frankish kingship is there to prove it. Founded on military prowess, Germanic kingship was inevitably subject to its

This seventh-century terracotta plaque, found at Gresins (Puy-de-Dôme), depicts a foot-soldier and his weapons. The depiction of his phallus and the serpent suggest the warrior's potency in fertility rites (St-Germain-en-Laye, Musée des Antiquités nationales).

vicissitudes. Yet without this foundation, the barbarians could hardly have succeeded. Exaltation of the aggressive instinct as the means of survival underlay their entire system of training. The goal, to win at any price, found expression in the *furor teutonicus*, a frenzy which drove warriors to fight like men possessed. Germanic civilisation was thus founded on violence as the supreme virtue. The word 'Frank' comes from the Old High German *frekkr* meaning bold, courageous, just as 'Gallic' is the equivalent of brave. Every free man was automatically a warrior, usually from the age of fourteen. German personal names, often adopted by the conquered Romans, reflect this mentality: 'Chlod-weg' (modified by scholars to Clovis, and the ancestor of our modern Louis) signifies 'path to glory'. And it cannot be over-emphasised that all the military vocabulary of modern French is descended from Frankish.

Because of this general training in warfare any king could summon at will all free men in their tribal contingents, which were subdivided, especially among the Goths, into units of ten, 100, 500 or even 1,000, these last being under the command of a *millenarius*. The *thiufadus* was in charge of the train which followed the army with provisions and equipment. The Franks and Anglo-Saxons were particularly redoubtable as foot-soldiers. Each man had to carry his own weapons. Of these, the shield, the throwing axe hurled to break the enemy frontline, the bow and spear, the barbed lance and the javelin were all for combat at a distance. For hand-to-hand fighting there was the scramasax, a kind of dagger 50cm long with a single blade, and the longsword. The techniques used in forging these blades made them especially formidable. The centre was fashioned by welding alternating bands of untempered and wrought iron into a damascene pattern. It was extremely supple. In contrast, the cutting edges which were soldered to it were made of very hard steel and were razor-sharp. Employed as a slashing weapon (it was too pliable for thrusting), the Frankish sword was capable, after being whirled several times around the swordsman's head, of slicing through body-armour. The latter, known as a byrnie, was a leather tunic covered with iron plates, but it was relatively rare and usually owned only by mounted soldiers. Weapons of this Germanic type undeniably conferred a clear advantage on their possessors, which accounts no doubt for the exceptional prestige enjoyed by blacksmiths in these warrior societies.

Cavalry was still less important than infantry, but was especially common among the Goths, Alamans, Lombards and Avars. The latter were nomadic horsemen armed with a bow, a quiverful of arrows, a round shield and a sword. Their basic tactic was to feign a general charge and then, after a brief combat, to make off at high speed. When the enemy pursued, inevitably in dispersed order, they were peppered with a lethal hail of arrows which the Avars shot behind them while continuing to gallop in the same direction. The same tactic was used by the Visigoths and Basques. It was also adopted by the Roman army in Italy under the generalship of Narses, and proved especially effective against the Ostrogothic heavy cavalry. The latter, in which horses and men were both heavily armoured, was better suited to close combat in which spears could be brandished at arm's length. Having originated in the plains of southern Russia, heavy cavalry was also known to the Taifals, Alans and Lombards. Costly to equip, these armoured horsemen were few in number, but their intervention could sometimes be decisive.

Men bound by ties of service and fidelity

Since everything was geared to victory, it is not unusual to find the Celts and Germans making use of slaves as soldiers, a practice the Romans shunned on principle. It was customary according to the law of the Bretons for a master to have a slave to carry his weapons. Among the Franks, the Celtic word *gwass*, Latinised as *vassus*, designates a slave charged with a particular duty, which might entail the bearing of arms. *Vassus* produced the diminutive *vassalus*, which gave rise to 'vassal'. The 'lads' who clustered in battle around a 'veteran' (in Latin *senior*, meaning older, which later gave rise to *seigneur*) eventually came to form a kind of private bodyguard in which the comradeship of arms was strong enough to break down juridical barriers. The warmth of fellow-feeling experienced in these moments of crisis could lead naturally from friendship to freedom. Under the Romans, as we saw, it was the law which defined, indeed created, social relationships; among the Germans, on the contrary, changing social relationships produced modifications in the law. The gulf between the free man and the slave was thus easier to cross. Furthermore, even the slaves domiciled by Germanic landowners on their estates were

83

allowed full independence. It was only by slow degrees, in the course of the seventh century, that this earlier blurring of social distinctions gave way to the threefold categorisation: slaves, free men and nobles.

Freedom, innate or acquired, in fact typified the majority of retinues surrounding kings, chieftains and other great personages. The Visigothic and Ostrogothic kings had their *saiones*, all-purpose retainers whose job was to see that orders were executed. Essentially they were members of the king's following, with the capacity to give the weak the protection they themselves received from their royal master. Later, in reference to the palace at Toledo, there is mention of *gardingi*, royal guards who owed the king fidelity and military service. The Lombards had their *faramanni*, possibly originally members of a single clan installed, garrison-like, in a fortified encampment, and obedient to the commands of the king or a duke; distinct from these were the *arimanni* (literally 'men of the army'), liable to be called-up for military service at any moment and obliged in that case to leave the land on which they had settled. In a separate category were the *gasindi* (literally serving-men), usually slaves or freedmen, who performed sundry duties about the palace and owed fidelity to their prince. Bodyguards of similar type and with a similar name, *gesiths*, are found among the Anglo-Saxons. Those of lowly condition received food and clothing from their master, as his name indicates (*hlaford*, giver of bread, whence 'lord'), while others received a grant of land, in temporary or permanent ownership. All owed military service to their protector. Turning lastly to the Franks, we find the same phenomenon. As well as his *scara* or permanent corps of warriors, the king had his *antrustiones*, who were in a way his bodyguards. They went through a special ceremony in which they commended themselves to him, kneeling with their hands placed between his. They swore their fidelity and '*truste*' (the Old High German '*treue*' means the same). Placed from now on under the protection, or 'mainbour', of the master who maintained him, the antrustion defended his master by force of arms. Anyone daring to kill an antrustion was liable to the enormous *wergild* of 600 *solidi*. This gives an idea of the importance of the antrustions and of the bonds between man and man, in this instance between superior and inferior. Another practice found everywhere among the Celts and Germans is that of adoptive paternity, whereby teenage boys were taken into another household to be trained as warriors and servitors, and at a later date even as officials. Known to the Anglo-Saxons as 'fosterage', this system created real physical bonds, with adolescents undergoing rapid initiation into the adult world. Faithful in life and death to their foster-father, these 'nurslings', as they were often described among the Franks and Visigoths, were a force to be reckoned with, especially when their more than ordinary solidarity was underpinned by oaths of commendation. Friends, followers, young men: such were the characteristics of these gangs of fighters, who were soon to be found in the service not only of kings but also of clan chieftains and heads of extended families.

An unshaped habitat in process of definition

The rise of these vassals maintained at their chief's table corresponds to a particular manner of occupying the land, quite different from Mediterranean practices. Whereas in

Mediterranean countries the boundaries between fields or separating the *ager* from the *saltus* were distinct and rectilinear, and indicated by stone markers, the Celts and Germans, by contrast, preferred their territory to be delimited merely by woods or hedges. Among the Bretons, it was forbidden for anyone selling an estate, house or garden to include the hedges surrounding the arable and meadow, which had to remain as fixtures. The Saxons surrounded their villages with a hedge, *Zaun* in Old High German, from which the word town is derived. Along the coast of Boulonnais there are still villages whose names, ending in '-thun', such as Baincthun, Offrethun and so on, evoke this primitive aspect of their origin at the hands of Saxon emigrants. Settlers in romanised territory, on the other hand, were likely to be presented with a ready-made habitat which could be one of two types: the remnant of a large estate in the 'Gallo-Roman' style, consisting of the master's *villa* and the dwellings of *coloni* or slaves; or else a haphazard scattering of huts and halls such as archaeologists have discovered east of the Rhine. They would therefore fit into these pre-existing moulds, merely giving their own name to the inhabited or newly-created place. Place-names composed of a proper name with the suffix '-ingos' enable us to pinpoint the settlements of the newcomers.

In Lorraine one still comes across villages such as Dudelange or Hayange which are proof of Frankish assimilation. The Burgundian occupation of the Franche-Comté and Savoy left its mark in place-names such as Bavans and Sermorens; in Aquitaine, even the Visigoths left traces in the names Brens, Escalatens etc. In Flanders, places of Frankish occupation whose names end in '-ingue' (Bonningues) are evidence of group settlement. Others, when they were surrounded with hedges, were called Le Plouy, from the interwoven branches of saplings which enclosed the dwellings. The element 'ham', whence 'hamlet', points to a settlement in which the dwellings were dispersed. Parallel instances are to be found in Lombardy, on the Spanish Meseta and in south-east England, where Celtic place-names were superseded by names ending in '-ings', for example Hastings. England and northern Gaul were obviously the regions most affected by these changes.

The principal materials used by the newcomers in the construction of dwellings were wood and thatch. In Ireland, protection of the cultivated areas was provided by the countless 'ring-forts' which scatter the countryside. Differing forms are found – in some cases drystone walls, in others a ditch with an earth rampart or timber palisade. The 'crannogs', artificial islands built on lakes or bogs, were linked to *terra firma* by narrow dykes. These lake-dwellings, constructed from criss-crossed beams plastered with clay, housed the wealthiest families, along with a quantity of manual workers. The hamlets of Anglo-Saxon England were enclosed areas containing several homesteads, huge cabins held up by posts and occupied by men and beasts. The Frankish houses excavated by archaeologists present a similar aspect: a floor below ground level with drains to carry off rainwater, and sometimes a hearth (otherwise found outside); low walls; a thatched roof, supported by two or four posts, which must have come down to the ground, forming in all a large habitable area of 70 to 90 square metres. Round about were the grain stores, either in pits or on stilts; rudimentary sunken huts reserved for smithing and weaving activities, whose use is proved by the discovery of balances; well-shafts, and finally the hedge surrounding the whole. In Scandinavia, where climatic conditions meant that animals had to be kept indoors, farmsteads were bigger, about 30m in length. One-third of the habitation would thus be assigned to human occupants and another third to the livestock, while the remainder served as a grain store. But when sudden danger threatened it was easy for these stock-raisers to retreat to ring-forts with stone foundations, where they could hold out against any adversary. Or again, like the Frisians, they could seek refuge on the artificial mounds (*terpen*) which rise up at intervals behind the dunes from the mouth of the Elbe to the Zuider Zee. Excavation of these mounds has disclosed the same type of timber-built homestead, about 20m long and 5m wide, devoted essentially to stock-raising. To sum up, Celtic and Germanic settlements made their greatest impact on the countryside, while the predominantly pastoral or woodland economy they encouraged was still very close to that of the Iron Age.

Nevertheless, the presence of Saxon huts on urban sites such as Boulogne and Canterbury should not make us jump to the conclusion that the intruders were backward compared with the existing population. The emphasis should rather be on the rapidity with which the two intermingled.

A woodland–pastoral economy, new trading ventures

With so much of their northern habitat covered by vegetation, the Celts and Germans are naturally found giving precedence to the woodland and pastures: hunting, fishing and food-gathering were fundamental resources. The Merovingian kings in particular had a passion for the chase. The Lombard king's chief huntsman still figured among his most influential advisers. Hunting was furthermore a direct extension of war, indeed a preparation for it. It was but a short step from the hunting of large animals to the hunting of men. The Anglo-Saxon, Frankish and Lombard kings were therefore keen to monopolise the Roman inheritance of the *saltus*, formerly public lands, for their own use. Any untilled, wooded, marshy or abandoned land passed as a rule into the ownership of the royal fisc. It must also be borne in mind that the disappearance of the Roman legions from the frontiers removed the obligation to produce corn for their support. Along certain Roman roads stretches of forest reappeared, in some cases swallowing up former estates: between Cologne and Jülich, between Bavay and Saint-Quentin (the present-day forest of Mormal), from Pevensey and Hastings towards London. The latter was of course the Weald, a vast hunting-ground which separated Kent from Sussex over a distance of about 200km from north to south, 50 from east to west. Another forest zone stretched from the coasts of Essex north of the Thames to the Chilterns. Although few traces of it remain today, at its fullest extent this belt of forest covered a breadth of 60km. Along the German borders some forests were even used as defensive obstacles, and care was taken to make them impenetrable. The Kentish laws of Wihtred (695) and the laws of the Wessex king Ine (688–94) ruled that any stranger or foreigner who journeyed through a forest off the track without blowing a horn could be regarded as a thief and be killed or redeemed – another excellent opportunity for training in combat! Entire zones, for example the forests of the Ardennes, passed into the hands of the Germanic kings. A special designation came to be applied to such places: *forestis*, meaning that they lay outside (*for*) the cultivated zones; the Lombard term was *gahagio*. It was naturally of importance to the rulers, whose dietary regime depended more on meat than on bread, to make sure of supplies of fish and game for their tables. To this end, they made use, like the Gauls, of the *brolium*, a wood reserved for hunting and usually enclosed. The point was to ensure a regular supply, according to season, of venison, boarsmeat, salmon, partridge and rabbits. The dish most fit to put before a king was evidently the aurochs, a primitive ox of enormous size, a veritable walking larder. Falcons and storks, for catching frogs, and of course hunting-dogs, were protected by appropriate penalties under Germanic law, as were the wild animals.

The uncultivated wastes were thus of much greater importance to the Germans than to the Romans because as stock-raisers they made more intensive use of their resources: as opposed to the civilisation founded on the olive, one might say that theirs was based on butter. Since it was physically impossible for the rulers to grab all the wastelands for themselves, the peasants in fact enjoyed a share. They, too, were ready to leave a large proportion of the soil untilled, since it was to the waste that they went to graze their pigs, look for wild honey, make charcoal and cut wood for use as stakes, beams and roof-shingles. Lastly, and most significantly, they pastured their oxen and cows on the wetlands and their sheep and goats on the heaths. It is even said that the buffalo was introduced by the Lombards into the Po valley during the sixth century. These domestic animals were reared less for their meat than for their butter, cheese, milk, wool and hides. Horses seem to have been less commonly raised than pigs or sheep, but their rarity and scarcity made them of great value. The numerous articles in the Salic and Breton laws which deal with thefts of horses or cattle illustrate the importance attaching to these products of animal husbandry. Among the Irish, cattle-stealing was considered a sport for nobles, because of the violence and danger involved. None of this is to say that the cultivation of cereals was neglected – study of the pollen residues in peat-bogs from all parts of the Rhineland proves the contrary – but rye, barley and oats now played a supplementary, rather than an essential, role. Grain used for the making of bread and beer was stored in granaries raised on piles. To set beside the regime of bread, wine and oil there was thus the contrasting diet of meat, beer and butter.

The only Germans amongst whom no change occurred at this time were the Scandinavians, whose way of life remained that of the Iron Age, in what is known as the Vendel period. Peasant hunters and cultivators roamed the north and made contact with the Lapps, with whom they established a trade in furs and salt, bartering by sign-language. From the evidence of funerary mounds dating to the sixth century, the kings of Uppsala had a vast accumulation of treasure. In fact it is known that between 400 and 700 the port of Helgö in Sweden, near Lake Mälaren, was in communication with continental Europe and the British Isles. The presence of goldsmiths working in bronze and iron as well as in precious metals points to a substantial volume of trade, which was undoubtedly seaborne. The deckless boats of the period, without keel or mast, were powered by oar and covered long distances by hugging the coast. The most intrepid seafarers appear to have been the

Scandinavian ornament on the gold mount of a sword scabbard characteristically combines geometrical and animal motifs in a strictly symmetrical linear pattern. Provenance: Amdal, Lista, Vestagder (sixth century).

Saxons and Frisians, who were prepared to traffic in anything and equally to turn to piracy. Some of the *terps* seem to have specialised in commerce. When they disembarked on invaded territory, these Germans of the north borrowed the Latin term *vicus* for the new ports they established. In the form 'wik' or 'wich', this suffix appears in the mid-sixth century in the name Quentovic ('the port on the river Canche'), Salperwick and Andruicq, to which there are counterparts on the English side of the Channel in Hamvic or Hamwih (ancestor of Southampton), Sandwich (sandy port), Woolwich (wool port) and several others. The new ports which lined the shore with wooden houses, wharves and slipways fashioned from tree trunks probably did not compensate for the hiatus of about a century revealed by the subsoil of Britain's Roman villas. In the particular cases of London and Canterbury, however, the interruption can only have been of short duration.

Kent, indeed, is the first barbarian kingdom not in contact with Rome to strike gold coins, 'shillings', in imitation of the Roman *tremisses*. The Frisians likewise imitated the Byzantine or Roman *tremisses* in order to expand their trade. But this did not mean that they gave up barter or the use of gold rings, Roman coins made into jewellery, cut fragments of bracelets and so on as substitutes for coinage. Scales for the weighing of precious metals turn up in a number of Germanic and Scandinavian burials, evidence that an embryonic monetary economy based on gold or silver existed even in barbarian countries where the striking of coins was still unknown, preparing those peoples for the new means of exchange. Moreover, countries such as Brittany and Ireland employed tin, by the ounce or pound, and heads of cattle as the unit for reckoning fines. Lastly, although foreign coins did not circulate in countries where coinage was struck, they were accepted in all the kingdoms where none was issued. Natural and monetary economies thus closely intermingled, as is well illustrated by maps which plot the distribution of Germanic fibulas, Coptic bronze vessels and Byzantine *solidi*.

Unification in the faith

Whatever the innovations brought by the Celts and the Germans, it is noticeable that in two spheres, property and religion, there is no definitive discontinuity. Even if many tribes still attached most value to chattels, precious stones and heads of cattle, and continued to exploit the uncultivated areas on a communal basis, the primitive agricultural communities constantly shifting from one clearing to another had long since disappeared. Indeed, so well-known was the practice of private property among the peoples who invaded the empire that the idea of public ownership was almost beyond their comprehension. On this point, therefore, there were considerable grounds for agreement between victors and vanquished.

It might also be thought that the prior conversion of these peoples to Arian Christianity would have made it easy for Germans and Romans to unite. It did nothing of the kind. The Visigoths, the Sueves, the Vandals, the Burgundians, the Ostrogoths and the Lombards, already alienated from the vanquished by their language, by their settlement in precisely defined areas, by their military profession, their law and their pastoralism, were even more detested for their adoption of a heresy which had just been extirpated from the empire in the late fourth century. Proclaimed by Arius in Egypt early in the fourth century, this doctrine reduced Christ to the status of a superhuman creature, not eternal but created by the Father. While acknowledging Christ's special position as God's son, it refused to accept his divine nature. It was thus possible to deduce from Arianism a political ideology assimilating the leader to the envoy of Christ. It is understandable that a Gothic priest, Ulfila, should have opted for this form of Christian religion as more comprehensible to warrior-bands to whom power itself was sacred. It enabled them at the same time to equate their Germanic culture with Christianity and in this way became part of their identity.

So, with the exception of the Burgundians, who remained tolerant in their attitude towards the Catholic Gallo-Romans and whose king, Sigismund (516–23), became a convert, the majority of the Arian populations lived in a state of latent or overt hostility towards the conquered populace. The Visigoths, for example, under Euric and Alaric II persecuted the Catholics in Gaul, and their elimination from Aquitaine was in essence due to the appeal from the Aquitanian Catholic bishops to the recently baptised Clovis and the Franks. In Spain the Visigoths came up against the same problem. Having eliminated the Sueves, who in the middle of the sixth century had just been converted to Catholicism, King Leovigild (569–86) was confronted with the rebellion of his newly-converted son

Hermenigild. In order to deter other Goths from following suit, he crushed the revolt and sent Leander, bishop of Seville and instigator of the conversion, into exile. It is hard to imagine that this policy could have succeeded, for his second son, Reccared, converted in 587, was able, notwithstanding uprisings by some of the nobles, to proclaim Catholicism as the religion to be observed throughout Spain at the Council of Toledo in 589. The progressive disappearance of Arianism under his successors made it possible, furthermore, to eliminate the Byzantines from the south-east corner of the peninsula. In fact, the Byzantine Catholics were no longer needed by the Spanish. The result was the genuine unanimity lauded by Leander's brother, Isidore, his successor in the see of Seville, since in the minds of contemporaries religious unity and the unity of the kingdom were one and the same.

In Africa, the Vandals did not shrink from violent persecution of the powerful Catholic Church of Carthage. Huneric (477–84) attempted to convert the Catholics by force and deported them in their thousands to southern Tunisia. Thrasamund (496–523) reverted to this policy and exiled a number of bishops. It is easy to see why the African populations finally called on the Byzantines for aid. The fanatical Arianism of the Vandals was thus the root cause of their disappearance. In Italy, Theodoric, an admirer of Roman civilisation, sought to avoid clashes through strict segregation. By constructing a dualist regime, whereby each city had both a Gothic and a Roman count, Arian and Catholic districts were kept separate, and pro-Arian propaganda in any form was forbidden, Theodoric hoped to make the religious difficulty disappear – at bottom a thoroughly Roman solution. But in ordering the execution of the philosopher Boethius and his father-in-law, Symmachus, president of the Senate, who were charged with defending a senator accused of conspiring with the emperor, Theodoric alienated the Catholics, all the more so when, having imprisoned the pope, who died in captivity, Theodoric instituted his successor by force. So when Theodahad (534–6) began to lay still greater stress on the connection between Gothic national pride and Arianism, he inevitably provoked the Justinianic reaction which led before long to the total destruction of this people. By now the only Germans still clinging to Arianism were the Lombards. Although equally detested for the disruption they caused, the Lombards escaped the fate of the Vandals and the Ostrogoths for two reasons: the inability of the Byzantines to crush them, and a change in papal policy. To save Rome from capture by the Lombards, Pope Gregory the Great chose to disregard his alliance with the exarch in favour of direct negotiation with the barbarians, from whom he obtained two truces, in 598 and again in 603. He had hopes that the baptism of the son of King Agilulf according to the Catholic rite, thanks to the influence of his Bavarian mother, Queen Theodelinda, would bring the Lombards round to orthodoxy just as Clotilde had influenced Clovis. But the opposition was too strong and the Lombards still too disunited for his hopes to be realised. The first Lombard king to be baptised was Aripert I in 652/3, and it was not until the 680s that the last traces of paganism and Arianism disappeared among the Lombards, whether those of the Po plain or those further south. There could from now on be no question of the expulsion of the Germanic peoples from the territories they had conquered, since all the obstacles to fusion had disappeared.

We are now in a better position to gauge the extent of the upheavals produced by the Celts and Germans in the Roman empire. Their innovations are plain to see but limited. Relatively few in number, they left only a faint impression on the linguistic habits of former Roman territories. But the primitive character of their constitutional law, devoid of a conceptual view of the State and the public domain, the greater indulgence shown to murderers than to thieves in their system of justice, and their cult of the war-leader, explain the central role occupied by warfare and constitute the essential reason for their success. Whether they fought on foot or on horseback, with the redoubtable longsword as their weapon, they imposed a predominantly military society where even the slave could become a professional warrior, fighting from loyalty to his master. In the absence of any distinction between soldiers and civilians, armed followings of every description sprang up: *gardingi, gasindi, gesiths, antrustiones* and so on, capable of fragmenting kingdoms into as many autonomous groups as there were chiefs. By favouring the dispersed type of habitat through their hamlets consisting of carefully enclosed houses, they produced a well scattered population in cultivated as well as uncultivated zones. More attuned to the life of woods and pastures than that of the fields, they were none the less capable of an impressive dynamism and, given the close-knit solidarity of their small groups, they were remarkably swift to integrate their territories in the expanse of the former empire, as is proved by their commercial initiatives in the North Sea and their adoption of a monetary economy. In short, once the Arian obstacle had been surmounted, the Germanic and Romanised populations, already to some extent united by their common Celtic stock, could start to make real contact and aspire to a fusion which varied from region to region.

A Christendom is born .

This rapprochement was made possible by the Church, which bridged the gulf between the two populations. The Church was the one structure still intact in the midst of the migrations and transfers of power. By swiftly setting evangelism and acculturation in motion the Church can be seen to represent not only continuity but also change. By endeavouring to modify the political conduct of barbarian kings, by assigning to the bishop an increasingly political role and to the monk that of privileged intermediary with God, the Church attempted to construct a Christendom in which every act was impregnated with the new faith. In northern Europe, from Ireland to northern Gaul, from Britain to Frisia, Christianity gradually gained ground. In every kingdom, bishops and monks participated in the consolidation of political institutions and the creation of a new culture. As H.-I. Marrou has put it, by this 'spadework on the Western soul' the ground was cleared for the emergence into history of European man.

Missionary zeal

Following the lead given by St Augustine, Christians were quick to interpret the barbarians' entry into the empire as an opportunity to baptise those who were still pagan. Celtic

The persistence of paganism: Wotan, Germanic god of war. In cultivated Germanic circles, pagan symbolism would not be slow to combine with Christian concepts (Stele from Hornhausen, seventh century; Halle Museum).

Ireland had been evangelised in the fifth century, first by Bishop Palladius and then by Patrick (died *c.* 461), a Briton who had once been captured by Irish pirates. Influenced by Egyptian and Martinian monasticism, with its strongly eremitical tendencies, the apostle of Erin created a Church outside the usual pattern. In the absence of towns, he could only institute monastic bishop–abbots. Armagh, the most important of Ireland's many monasteries, became the metropolitan see. The monasteries consisted of drystone huts, one for each hermit, loosely grouped round a small chapel. Mostly the monks chose to settle as far as possible from other habitation, usually on an island. While Irish Christianity had a strong attachment to Rome, it remained highly ascetic and individualistic in tone, clinging to distinctive liturgical practices and strongly-held prejudices.

This attitude quickly becomes noticeable in regard to the Anglo-Saxon invaders who were depriving their fellow Celts and Christians in Britain of their native land. Faced with a paganised England and a northern Gaul relapsed into paganism (the conversion of the Franks after 496 was official rather than real), the Irish preferred to let the Anglo-Saxons go to perdition, and set sail for Galicia or Brittany, where monasteries of their own type were beginning to flourish. Then they made contact with the Merovingian kings, with a view to the re-conversion of northern Gaul. There can be no doubt that north of the Seine paganism still exerted great power. Based on the veneration of springs, trees and other natural forces, it may have lacked the priests and temples found among the Saxons and Frisians, but in the forms of animism and magic it was deeply rooted in men's minds. Paganism across the Rhine was equipped with a mythological pantheon whose chief members were Odin, the universal father, Thor, representing elemental strength, and Freya, the fertility god. When St Colombanus began his travels through Europe in 590, he was the precursor of a stream of Irish missionaries. Luxeuil, which he founded as a base from which to evangelise the countryside, quickly became a nursery of ascetic monks. On his expulsion from Burgundy he set about founding other monasteries east of Paris, then journeyed down the Moselle and up the Rhine, preaching as he went. At Bregenz he left behind his companion, Gall. On the site of Gall's hermitage the monastery in present-day Switzerland which goes by the name of St Gall was founded in the early eighth century. Colombanus ended his wanderings in the Ligurian Apennines where in 612 he founded Bobbio; he died there in 629. On the heels of this trail-blazer came other Irishmen who expanded his work. In 615 a monk from Luxeuil restored the see of Basel. Others established Péronne in Picardy, Fosses near Liège and Honau on an island in the Rhine north of Strasbourg. In many cases little is known of these itinerant bishops, roving monks and obscure recluses, but the impression they made was great enough to inspire others to follow their example.

Among their imitators from about 630 onwards were a number of former Merovingian 'office-bearers', laymen who became priests or bishops. Natives for the most part of the Romanised regions, Aquitaine in particular, they left their homes to work in barbarian territories, and this trend continued until about 730. Most of them made for Picardy, Flanders or the Rhineland. The most famous example is St Eligius, bishop of Noyon-Tournai from 641 to 660. Not content with the re-christianisation of his original diocese,

Noyon, he ventured into Germanic territory as far as Antwerp, undeterred by his ignorance of the language. Eligius's mission there was a failure, like that of St Amand, a Poitevin who in 630 had been consecrated bishop without a fixed see. Amand founded the monastery of Elnone on the site of a pagan sanctuary over thermal springs, now called Saint-Amand-les-Eaux. After being equally unsuccessful in the bishopric of Tongres-Maastricht, he wandered through several other regions, and died in 675 or 676. By the time this second wave of missionary activity began to die down around 690 all the country south of a line running from Ghent to Cologne had become part of Roman Christendom.

Meanwhile, since the British, Welsh and Irish were still unwilling to evangelise their Anglo-Saxon foes, Pope Gregory the Great (590–604) seized the initiative by sending to England a mission led by the monk Augustine. He landed in Kent in 597. To consolidate the initial results, a second mission under Abbot Mellitus was sent to reconstitute the ecclesiastical provinces of London and York and to give authority to the Roman monks over the Celtic clergy, who were still hostile to the Anglo-Saxons. Early successes in Essex and Northumbria were checked in 634 by a pagan revolt which forced the missionaries to retire to Kent. By the end of the seventh century only Wessex and East Anglia had been reclaimed for Roman Christianity.

Meanwhile, however, the Celtic monks had at last begun to take a hand in the conversion of the Anglo-Saxons. An appeal by Oswald (c. 605–42), king of Northumbria, to the monks on the island of Iona led to the establishment of the monastery at Lindisfarne by Aidan. As a result of this collaboration, the liturgical differences between the Irish and the Romans were gradually resolved. Monks in the south of Ireland had adopted the Roman method for calculating the date of Easter as early as 630. At the synod of Whitby in 664 another group of Celtic monks was won over, thanks to the mediation of an Anglo-Saxon monk, Wilfrid. And it was Wilfrid, some twenty years later, who baptised the remaining pagans of Sussex and the Isle of Wight. In 704 the northern Irish agreed to abandon their aberrant practices; in 716 the monks on Iona did the same, followed in 755 by the British in Cornwall and Wales. In this way all the Celtic and Anglo-Saxon churches came to recognise the spiritual authority of Rome.

Barely converted, England took up the Roman torch and set out to evangelise brother Germans on the continent. Willibrord, born in Deira in 658, was despatched by Egbert, an Anglo-Saxon visionary, to Frisia where he landed in 690. Aided by Pippin of Herstal and the pope, Willibrord in 695 was consecrated archbishop of a new ecclesiastical province with its seat at Utrecht, formerly a Roman camp. It was perhaps intended to cover the whole of Frisia. Willibrord secured as his base the estate of Echternach (in Luxemburg) where he founded a monastery.

When Willibrord died in 739, Christianity had been brought to all the countries as far as the Rhine. St Lambert, assassinated in c. 700, was succeeded by St Hubert who transferred the see of Maastricht to Liège and completed the conversion of the Rhine's left bank. A network of monastic houses covered the entire region and all the sees existing in late Roman times had been restored. Christianity had also returned, more or less, to Alamannia and Bavaria, thanks to the work of Italian missionaries or monks from the West: Emmeran at Regensburg, Corbinian at Freising, Rupert at Salzburg. Penetration of the wholly pagan regions outside the former Roman empire only began with the arrival of another Anglo-Saxon monk, Wynfrith. In 719 the pope changed his name to Boniface and commissioned him to set up a Frankish church in Germany under the auspices of Rome. Boniface's activity soon revealed itself to be comparable with that of St Martin in Gaul. He reorganised the Bavarian sees, baptised thousands of pagans in Hessen and Thuringia and after his consecration as bishop by Gregory II in 722 attempted to organise the German Church, by improving recruitment to the episcopate and setting up more bishoprics beyond the Rhine. Although invested with the archiepiscopal pallium in 732, Boniface was without a fixed see until 747, when he established himself at Mainz. Too exacting in the eyes of the early Carolingians, despite a series of reforming councils (741–7) aimed at the regeneration of the Frankish Church, he eventually found his advice unheeded and dedicated the last three years of his life to the evangelisation of Frisia, where he was murdered by Frisian brigands in 754. As a result of his efforts, huge territories had been won over to Christianity and the foundations of numerous bishoprics had been laid; his tomb at Fulda, a monastery which he had founded, became one of Germany's major pilgrim centres.

A simple faith, a fixed framework, a powerful bond

The chief result of these missions was to promote the Church of Rome and the see of St Peter to an undisputed primacy. Rome once more had an empire, this time of a spiritual order. 'We Irish,' said Colombanus to the pope, 'are joined to the see of St Peter.' The pope on his side took care to embody these spiritual ties in a concrete symbol, the *pallium*, a band of white woollen material which was draped across his shoulders during the divine office and was sent to every archbishop he appointed. Besides this, many missionary bishops such as Amand, Willibrord and Boniface made several pilgrimages to Rome to test their orthodoxy and have their authority confirmed.

Furthermore, their methods of evangelism initiated converts at the same time into the Romano-Christian philosophy and civilisation. A summary exposition of God's plan in Creation, of the fall of Adam and Eve, the Flood, and the Salvation brought by Christ, made up the instruction given immediately prior to baptism and was thought to be sufficient. The essence lay in the prestige of one God and of a superior civilisation. Gregory the Great advised Augustine of Canterbury to destroy idols but to transform temples into churches. Since many of the latter were built of stone, they were much more imposing than the preceding structures, which were built of logs or planks and open to the elements. In about 670 Benedict Biscop fetched masons and glaziers from Gaul who introduced Mediterranean building techniques. It was around these new edifices, the churches, that the town would make its reappearance. At the same time, chapels were multiplying on the sites of springs formerly regarded as sacred; usually dedicated to local saints, by the continuity of their location they eased the transition from one mode of worship to the other. Another even more effective method of evangelism was the purchase of gangs of slaves. Enfranchised, baptised, instructed and then ordained to the priesthood, they provided living proof

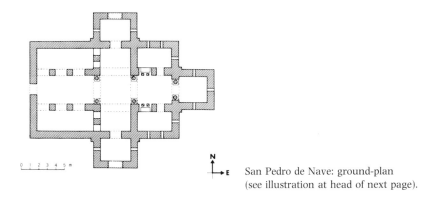

San Pedro de Nave: ground-plan
(see illustration at head of next page).

that the new religion could set men free. This was a practice for which there is some evidence on the part of Irish and Anglo-Saxon missionaries. These neophytes were frequently successful in securing mass conversions, especially when a chief or king was the first to accept baptism and the solidarity set up by the links binding man to man came fully into play. Religion was not at this date a matter of personal choice.

This meant that implantation of the Church, and of the civilisation which went with it, entailed the creation in barbarian countries of a new kind of society, without making a complete break with the old. It was in an effort to improve moral standards that the Irish at this time devised the penitentials, in imitation of the graded fines prescribed in the Germanic and Celtic law codes: anyone who confessed to a fault would automatically receive a penance of so many years of dry bread and water or a certain number of fasts. In a world where gorging rather than mere eating was the order of the day, fasting and abstinence imposed the severest of constraints. The penitential code was thus an instrument of discipline, a code of permitted and forbidden practices which was intended to contain men's tumultuous energies rather than transform them.

To this regimentation of the inner life was added the external support of the parochial system. Except at Christmas, Easter and Ascensiontide, when everyone was supposed to attend the bishop's church, the rural parish was the regular meeting-place of the faithful. From *plebs*, the Latin word usually applied to it, has come the Italian *pieve* and the countless place-names in Brittany beginning with *plé* or *plou* – Plougastel, Plélan and so forth. In peninsular Italy the parochial system stopped short at a line running from Viterbo to Chieti, the explanation being that the dioceses further south were themselves not much bigger than parishes. But in Lombardy, in the Engadin, in Friuli and in the parts of Europe where the Antique framework of the Roman city was less in evidence, the parochial system took hold, starting with the *vici*, the larger villages, and spreading to the great estates. Primitive churches were often grouped in threes: the first was reserved for the catechumens, the second consisted of a baptistery where adults were baptised on Easter Saturday, and the third was open to all professing Christians. By the beginning of the eighth century, however, the practice of baptism by immersion had virtually disappeared from the barbarian kingdoms, a sign that adult members of the population were all officially members of the Church. The institution of the rural parishes thus results in the weaving of a

San Pedro de Nave, Zamora. Built in the late sixth century in a Visigothic area, this chapel marries the Hispanic, Roman and Byzantine traditions with certain Visigothic features. The design represents a compromise between the type of basilica with a nave and clerestory and the basilica in the form of an equal-armed Greek cross, with a tower at the crossing of the transepts.

proper social fabric in which populations were brought together for religious and also for social purposes, since the priest exercised certain judicial and financial functions delegated by the count. The elementary unit of European civilisation has made its appearance.

With the multiplication of private chapels, in northern Europe this basic unit takes on a particular aspect. To obtain support from a great noble or king, missionaries had very often agreed to the request to found an extra-parochial church on a royal fisc or private estate in order to meet the spiritual needs of their peasants. Since the great man in question was building the church at his own expense and on his own land, he regarded it as his property and expected to be able to bequeath, sell or exchange it as he pleased; eventually he might even withdraw the church's ministrant from episcopal supervision. Churches of this type, known in Germany as *Eigenkirchen* and in England as 'private churches', are also found in Spain, Gaul and northern Italy. The system was of value as a means of implanting Christianity in depth, in spite of drawbacks not apparent till later, and at the same time it points to the markedly ruralising tendency of the new civilisation.

Conservation, action, salvation: the Church sets the standard for the world

For the moment, the episcopate was not inconvenienced by these private churches, given the great authority it still wielded. For it must not be forgotten that during the invasions only the bishops kept their place, with the obvious exception of those in England and

97

northern Gaul and those who were expelled by Arians. As the great Roman officials disappeared, the bishops came to symbolise continuity, which they embodied through their skill in negotiating accomodations with the newcomers and their financial capacity to ransom members of their flocks led away by the conquerors to slavery. In the eyes of pagan converts to Christianity, such men must have appeared to lord it over all that was sacred and to hold the keys to eternity. Bishops were powerful in the temporal as well as the spiritual realm; in 507 they opened the doors of Aquitaine to the Franks, and nearly all were of senatorial origin. There was in fact a growing tendency for the episcopate to be regarded as an office reserved for the great families, and the first Germans to be consecrated bishops came as a rule from royal dynasties or their kindred. During the sixth century it was quite common to see men from such families, after holding secular office, separating voluntarily from their wives around the age of 40 to take charge of a diocese. Since ordination to the priesthood was forbidden below the age of 30, many bishops had thus had practical experience of political affairs. Again, because the donations made by bishops to the cathedral churches, sometimes representing their entire inheritance, passed into the church's patrimony, which in the absence of division among heirs was constantly growing, the temporal power of the bishops correspondingly increased. This called for a well-argued defence of the church's property ownership, based on the principle that it was the patrimony of the poor. As we saw, there were indeed many ways in which the bishop of the late Roman empire had become the patron of the poor. In the sixth and seventh centuries this role was continually growing as a result of the spread of assistance to *matricularii*, of *xenodochia*, and of other charitable works such as the adoption of abandoned children and orphans in the wake of each successive wave of disasters or epidemic. The bishop's patronage is made all the weightier by the existence of his tribunal and of the right of asylum within the perimeter, ever more precisely defined, of the *atrium* preceding the cathedral. It was indispensable to peasants who were seeking to dedicate themselves to the patron saint of the diocese, or who were freedmen, whether by touching the altar cord in the Roman fashion or by the throw of a denier like the Franks. Lastly there were bishops who made their mark as builders, Nicetius and Magneric, for example, who carried out extensive restorations at Trier between 527 and 596. In short, the bishop was becoming so powerful a figure in the barbarian kingdoms that certain kings sought to control their appointment and were no longer content simply to approve the candidate chosen by the metropolitan and the other bishops of the province. Especially in Gaul and Spain, where councils were, furthermore, regular occurrences, it becomes evident that the kings would dearly like to bring the episcopate within their power.

There is a corresponding change in the status and position of monks. Having been marginal figures in the fifth century, they became by contrast a model made all the more compelling because less compromised with the world. In the sixth century many more reverted to the old rules of Basil and Pachomius or indeed became hermits in the style of St Antony. The Mediterranean lands saw the flourishing of rural and urban monasteries on the model of Marmoutiers and Lérins, in which asceticism was combined with all manner of cultural activity. Dividing their time between prayer and learning, monks now came to the

Irish monks were active in copying manuscripts. St Matthew, from the Lindisfarne Gospels, which were copied and decorated by Eadfrith in the late seventh century. Matthew is writing in a bulky codex. His Latin name is written above in large, angular, ornamental letters, preceded by *oagios*, Greek for 'the saint' (London, British Library).

fore as counsellors and prophets, as spiritual protectors of the great and as material defenders of the poor. A Burgundian king, Sigismund, founded the monastery of St Maurice d'Agaune to offer up the *laus perennis*, the unbroken song of praise to God's glory, chanted daily by three teams of monks in relays. Monks at this period were not well-endowed with properties, and the monastic complex, not counting the churches, consisted merely of a scattering of cells and workshops for the production of mats, baskets and parchment, made from treated hides, and above all for the copying of manuscripts. The gardens and adjoining fields supplied food for the community and any passing travellers. The solitary hermit cleared a patch for himself on virgin or deserted land and soon found himself with companions; indeed they came in such numbers that he very often abandoned his original settlement to these lay disciples and moved further away, still careful to keep at a distance from inhabited places but never severing all contact with his fellow men. Whether living as coenobites, hermits or total recluses, monks and nuns remained none the less laymen. Ordinations to the priesthood at this period were in fact very rare. The essence of the

99

monastic vocation was prayer and abstinence. Communal prayers were offered daily and throughout the day in accordance with a by now well-established pattern: first there was the night office (Matins), then the dawn office (Lauds), followed by Prime at sunrise, Tierce at the third hour, Sext at the sixth, None at the ninth, the evening office of Vespers (or *Lucernarium*, when the lamps were lit) and Compline before retiring. These men and women who lived apart from the world were regarded no longer as traitors but as trustworthy guides to bliss and salvation in a sea of troubles and catastrophe. Their forthright condemnation of the world and their serene detachment conferred on them an aura that shone out as truly charismatic. The ease with which the monasteries attracted disciples also led to the virtual demise of episcopal control and to the disappearance, along with the Roman bureaucracy, of the rule requiring aspirants to the monastic life to obtain permission from the civil authorities.

Coenobitical and eremitical vocations derived especial stimulus from the advent of the Irish, because of the greater freedom and prestige attached to their missionary way of life. The rule of St Colombanus, possibly propagated from Luxeuil, laid great stress on the vows of chastity and poverty and on extreme forms of penitence, flagellation not least among them. But this rigour was compensated in practice by a constant call to missionary activity or to pilgrimage for God's sake to distant countries, and by a great latitude in dealings with political and spiritual authorities. Peripatetic preachers, divinely-inspired prophets, scholars extraordinary, the Celtic monk and his imitators sometimes ended up as martyrs, more often as popular saints, especially when they had the foundation of a church or a monastery to their credit. Among the more extreme imitators was the type known as the *gyrovagus*, the vagrant monk with no known superior or house of origin but recognisable from the peculiarity of his tonsure, cut in a horse-shoe from ear to ear; footloose, he wandered from place to place, disseminating a religion in which miracles of healing or of punishment for sin took pride of place. Irish monasticism formed the ideal meeting-point at which the Germanic and Roman mentalities could most easily converge and combine. Proof of this is provided by the early appearance of a mixed rule in which the rules of St Columbanus and St Benedict were amalgamated. The first known example is the rule given by Donatus of Besançon, a monk of Luxeuil, to the nuns of Jussamoutiers around 620.

St Benedict, 'father of the monks'

At this point we therefore have to consider the work of St Benedict of Nursía (born about 480, died 553/6), which played a substantial part in the transformation of monasticism. At the time, the rule he composed during the last 25 years of his life passed unnoticed in Italy because of the prevalent disorders. A pure-bred product of Roman civilisation, Benedict desired to create order among the welter of existing rules. After experience of the eremitical and the coenobitic way of life, he eventually founded a monastery at Monte Cassino. Probably of senatorial origin, Benedict judged the Christianity of his day to be unredeemedly pagan. Through his rule he therefore sought to raise up a new militia,

Abbot Desiderius presents books and properties to St Benedict. Dedicatory miniature in an illuminated manuscript from the abbey of Montecassino, *c.* 1070 (Vatican Library, Codex Latinus 1202).

neither civil nor military in the Roman fashion, nor indeed a *militia Christi* as in the pretensions of an over-bureaucratised clergy, but an 'army of the heart'. Benedict's monastic community, powered by an ever-deepening relationship with God, revolved around one simple injunction: '*ora et labora*', 'pray and work', the latter being possible only through the former. This rule, at once rigorous and flexible in its demands, enjoined obedience to the father abbot and laid constant stress on care for the weaker brethren. The diffusion of the rule had to wait for the upheavals brought about by the Lombard invasion of Italy to die down, but once things were calmer the account of Benedict's life and miracles given by Pope Gregory the Great in his *Dialogues*, composed about 593/4, soon reached a

101

wider public. Paradoxically, the regions most influenced by the old Roman civilisation – Italy, Spain, Provence, Aquitaine – were the most resistant. Mixed Colombano-Benedictine communities such as Solignac, founded in 632 by St Eligius, thus represented a necessary intermediate stage. Some Aquitanians, Franks, Anglo-Saxons and Celts, convinced of its superiority, disseminated it so widely that in the eighth century the rule of St Benedict was probably the predominant one in force.

At this time monastic expansion exhibited various new features. In succession to the great noble families which had supported Colombanus in his efforts to found and endow monasteries, some noblemen sought permanent seclusion in monasteries or indeed became their abbots. Others, in times of political insecurity and sudden reversals of fortune, retreated there to await better times. In consequence, the patron saint might be an aristocratic founder, wealthy landowner and pious monk rolled into one. The basilica of the Holy Apostles, founded at Metz some time before 630 by Arnulf, ancestor of the Carolingians, and afterwards reconstructed as a sanctuary around his tomb, is a case in point: in about 715–17 the dedication of the church was changed to St Arnulf. As with the episcopate, we thus witness the transformation of monasticism into a princely ally. In Merovingian Gaul, it would even transfer its support and loyalty to another dynasty, in contrast to the legitimism of the bishops. With the exception of Boniface, all the great Anglo-Saxon monks were the allies and protégés of the Pippinids.

Whatever the reason for this reversal in the respective influence of bishops and monks, the rise of monasticism was remarkable. From locations now exclusively rural, these new establishments, regardless of whether they were Anglo-Saxon (Lindisfarne, Jarrow, Monkwearmouth), Austrasian (Weissenburg, founded c. 660, Nivelles) or German (Fulda, Reichenau), served as the base for missionary activity. In Spain, Fructuosus of Braga founded a chain of Galician monasteries that later preserved the concept of Spanish identity. Italy was eventually won over, with the foundation in the early eighth century of Novalese, Nonantola and Farfa, all deep in Lombard territory. The year 720 saw the resurrection of the abbey of Monte Cassino from its sixth-century ruins. The monastic adventure thus came full circle, returning to base by a strangely circuitous route after an astonishing progress through Europe from the shores of the Mediterranean to the northern seas.

So from the clash of the two civilisations, the Roman and the Germanic, there emerged survivals, losses and fusions. We have seen Roman societies enduring, becoming stronger, even branching out in new directions, succeeding little by little in emancipating themselves from the State. On the map they trace out the limits of an old Europe, comprising Spain, peninsular Italy and Gaul south of a line from Nantes to Besançon. Over against it we find a young Europe, that of the isles and the northern continent, climatically much harsher: it includes the plains watered by the Po, the Seine, the Meuse and the Rhine. Here the contributions of the Celts and Germans are very evident and of lasting effect. They were frequently in conflict with Roman conceptions. But once the religious obstacle disappeared, the momentum of the missionary movement, and in particular of that inspired by the Anglo-Saxons and the Celts, as good as compelled the barbarians into the Church, custodian in many respects of Roman traditions. Interposed as a third party between victors and vanquished, the Church wove the fabric of a new society through its parochial network. It transformed mental attitudes, but by the same token aroused political rivalries. While the bishop fell under the power of the king, the monks succeeded in their turn to the guardianship of all that is holy, no longer on the fringe but integral members of the new Romano-Germanic society. Yet it was not only the rule of St Benedict which contains the essence of these essentially Christian innovations. It took the crisis of the late seventh century to reveal how the choice that had to be made between Germanic chieftains and Christian masters gave rise, after this period of rapprochement, to new and unexpected solutions.

3 Prologue to a history of the East: early fifth century

The year is 395. Theodosius I has just died, on 17 January. Two emperors succeed him, his sons Honorius and Arcadius, the one reigning in the West, the other in the East. This is not the first attempt at dividing the exercise of supreme power over an empire which is too large for Antique means of communication. Never again will a single sovereign wield authority from the Euphrates to the Rhine, from the Danube to the Maghrib. The history of the Roman empire in the East now properly begins: the history, that is, of 'Romania' as it called itself, or Byzantium as we call it after the provincial town, in decline since the civil wars at the end of the second century, which Constantine chose in 324 to be the site of his city of Constantinople, the New Rome. Like any other history, that of the empire in the East bears at its birth the marks of both a recent and an age-old past. In this instance they are more than usually pronounced, for two reasons. First, this is a history founded explicitly on the eternity of Rome, of the empire, of the imperial, and from now on Christian, ordering of the world, which means that the constitutional resistance of any political and cultural system in face of the changes brought by time is made doubly strong by the conviction that nothing could change and that nothing should be changed. Second, we are here dealing with a slow-moving history, in which continuity plays a very large part, and in which trends taking a century or more to develop are punctuated by catastrophes, but very little affected by minor fluctuations. This makes the usual introductory survey more indispensable than ever as the key to everything that follows. The century preceding 395 was prolific in major changes, grafted on to a permanent, Antique stock. So if the reader is seeking a history of Byzantium and thus of medieval Christianity, he will perhaps have a sense of marking time on the threshold.

The conventional date of 395 is to be taken not as the start of a narrative but as setting a scene. The picture it presents is the outcome of recent or more remote happenings and becomes progressively sharper as we move through the first half of the following century. After 460 the rhythm of events and the play of internal forces become more closely interlocked and the story moves at a faster pace, until it is brutally checked in the last decades of the seventh century by the loss of the southern domain, Syria, Palestine, Egypt and Cyrenaica.

There is also a sense in which the whole of any history can be deduced merely from a

The old and new capitals of the Roman empire, Rome and Constantinople, juxtaposed in symbolic fashion on an ivory diptych of the late fifth century. The crown worn by Constantinople (left) portrays the city walls. The figure's veil and the thyrsus carried by Rome (right) would be emblematic of marriage (Vienna, Kunsthistorisches Museum).

map, since nothing is more lasting and determinative than the network of routes around which it is structured. Layer upon layer of history lies embedded in the territory on which Byzantium's history starts to unfold, the sediment of independent cities planted long ago by the Greeks on the coasts of Asia Minor, of ancient oriental despotisms, of the kingdom carved out by Alexander's lieutenants in the wake of his dazzling conquests and relegated by the Romans to the rank of provinces. But the great connections within this territory are more than just the antecedents of Byzantine history, they provide its very continuity.

The Byzantine domain

Byzantium's territory in its early days can be defined as the countries in which the dominant language was Greek. It followed the eastern curve of the Mediterranean from

Tripoli and Ptolemais on the African shore round to that indeterminate point on the Adriatic where, to the west of Durazzo, it encountered the boundary between Greek and Latin, which was also from 395 the administrative boundary of Illyricum, the name given at that date to the great mass of Rome's Danubian possessions. The Byzantine Mediterranean took in Cyprus, Rhodes, Crete and the Aegean archipelago. It was traversed by sea-routes, from Alexandria to Beirut, to Antioch, to the Straits of the Dardanelles, and also along the coasts. Byzantium's other seaward face was the southern shore of the Black Sea, bolted at one end by the Straits and backed up at the other by the foothills of the Caucasus. On the western shore Byzantine authority extended as far as the Danube delta, while the northern shore offered bridgeheads already known and exploited in Antiquity, to which Byzantium would return. Byzantium's limits on land are less easy to define. Broadly speaking they were marked by the *limes*, the series of fortifications uncovered by archaeologists in Tripolitania, Palestine, Syria and along the Danube. The frontiers were also dotted with customs posts, whose location can be pinpointed by the discovery of tariffs engraved on stone, or, from a later period, of the seals of the officers in charge. Even so, the image of a ruled-off line is inapplicable to Byzantine frontiers, which should rather be thought of as a fringe, susceptible to the ebb and flow of history. Each of the empire's principal regions faced outward on its own frontier, and because of the routes followed by traders and armies, was of a piece with the territory beyond. Or it might be better to describe the empire of the East as an articulated living organism, consisting of its internal connections, its borders, and the more distant orientations of long-distance trade.

The body of the empire

In the far south-west, the *limes* of Cyrenaica protected the empire against the nomadic resurgences which were characteristic of the epoch in both the east and west of white Africa. Egypt, granary of the empire in the East, was equally vital as a corridor from the Mediterranean and its great port of Alexandria. It also controlled access to the Red Sea, which was hemmed in on one side by the kingdom of Aksum (Ethiopia) and on the other by the Himyarite kingdom (Yemen), and then led on to the Persian Gulf; alternatively, by ascending the Nile, it was possible to reach Sudanese Africa and its gold. At the empire's other extremity lay another region rich in corn and gold: Thrace, situated between the Danube, the only river-route of any consequence in the empire of the East, and the sea, to which there was access at Thessalonica or Constantinople. Beginning in the fourth century, invaders crossed Thrace in both directions, favouring in particular the route through the valley of the Maritsa from Philippolis (Plovdiv) to Adrianople (Edirne), while the north-westerly route along the right bank of the river continued to serve as the main overland connection with the empire in the West.

The provinces of the East lay between these African and Balkan extremities; for when our story opens, the Greek peninsula was still sunk in the provincial torpor induced by the Roman conquest, enlivened only by the intellectual activity of Athens, a magnet to students from far and wide. The 'East' was made up of regions differing greatly from one another in physical geography, climate and civilisation. The transition from Palestine to Egypt is barely perceptible, thanks to the continuities of coast and desert: from Pelusium up to Gaza and the small market towns of the Palestinian *limes*, scenes of great activity in the fifth and sixth centuries, reckonings of time and measurement are found to be identical. Caravans traversed Egypt's eastern desert and in the south penetrated as far as the Sinai peninsula. The ancient ports of Palestine and Syria were linked by a coastal route which ran from Ascalon to Antioch by way of Tyre, Berytus (Beirut) and Laodicea. A parallel route from Homs and Damascus to Aïla (Eilath) dotted the edge of the Syrian desert with cities which marked the western limit of nomadic trading or raiding expeditions. The routes taken by the nomads varied. Palmyra and Petra were past their peak, but Bosra, Gerasa and Resafa were flourishing and would remain so until the beginning of the seventh century.

Between these two north–south arteries we have to place a third, connected with the traffic generated by Jerusalem as early as the fourth century. In northern Syria, however, the route from Homs to Antioch passed by way of Apamea; then, after Antioch it made another, twofold, change of direction. On its coastal side Antioch stood at the defile of the wooded Taurus range, haunt of Isaurian brigands, which barred the way to Asia Minor. After Laodicea the road along the coast in fact turned inland in order to reach Antioch, situated not far from the mouth of the Orontes, and found its way back to the coast at a point north of Tarsus. Antioch was not merely the centre on which traffic converged from northern Syria, a region made up of hills and valleys and a great producer of olive oil, but also the western terminal of the route to Edessa and Nisibis, and so to Mesopotamia. It is hardly surprising that Antioch figures so often in the pages of history.

Asia Minor, a second piece in the collage of the Romano-Byzantine East, was itself quite complex. Its ragged coastline was dotted with flourishing cities as far as Constantinople; the prosperity of some, Attalia (Antalya) for example, dates only from the Byzantine era, but there were others, such as Ephesus and Smyrna, which had been famous in Antiquity. By contrast, the Black Sea coast would only begin to play an important part, with Sinope and Trebizond, in the last centuries of the empire and in a different context. What is remarkable about Asia Minor at this early stage of Byzantium's history is the importance, for all the difficulties presented by the terrain, of its interior. For the wooded mountains of Pamphylia and Pisidia, opening out here and there into plains, and the tableland of Cappadocia could be said to form a crucial bridging zone for military and commercial purposes. The route running from the capital – or more precisely from Nicomedia and Nicaea – to the foothills of the Armenian Caucasus and the valley of the Araxes can be seen as a backbone of the region's history. At Sebaste the road met two others, one leading to the sea by way of Cappadocian Caesarea and the other into Mesopotamia, passing through Melitene (Malatya) and Edessa (Urfa). At this point we reach the marches of the Roman empire of the East, constantly fought over, and the object of dispute with the Persian empire until the latter's fall in the seventh century. To one side lay the countries of the Caucasus, Armenia and Iberia, gateways to the steppe or to the shores of the Caspian, to Azerbaijan, and to one of the major far-Eastern routes. To the other side stretched the ancient fertile plain between the Euphrates and the Tigris, with its settlements at Callinicum, Edessa, Amida and Nisibis, for centuries a bone of contention between Rome and Persia. But here it will no longer suffice to define the area of our story in terms of axial routes. Another way of piecing together the picture is needed, by considering the peoples, their languages and their civilisations.

The Greek language had penetrated to the East following the conquests of Alexander, having previously been confined to Greece itself and its Thracian and Macedonian marches, the islands, and the great cities on the coast of Asia Minor. The most illustrious products of that expansion were Antioch and Alexandria. From that time onward it seems to be a general rule that the hold of Greek and Hellenism diminish the further one moves from the coast to the interior and from the town to the country. With the Roman conquest Latin was added, as numerous inscriptions bear witness. But with the division of the empire into two, Latin was doomed in due course to disappear, for obvious reasons more quickly in the East than in Illyricum; by the sixth century, Greek was already the language of the empire and of orthodox Christianity. Even so, it was Greek which carried the burden of *romanitas*, although Latin was still in common use as the language of law and administration. What is more, from the beginnings of Byzantine history, the East was remarkable for the vigour of its many other written languages.

Coptic, the form now taken by the language of ancient Egypt, derives its alphabet from Greek. The Hebrew of Judaic Palestine lived on as a cultural language, penetrated to some extent by Greek expressions, and comprehensible to anyone familiar with a closely-related vernacular tongue, Aramaic, thus making for ease of communication between Jewish communities in Palestine and Iran, where they were numerous. Further north we come to a vast Syro-Mesopotamian region in which the written language, at least from the end of the third century, was Syriac, a dialect of Aramaic used in Christian circles on either side of the political frontier in the same way that the Jewish communities on either side used Aramaic. Arabic at this period was confined as a written language to the one or two alphabets evolving in the sedentary kingdoms which had recently emerged in the area of present-day Jordan and the Yemen. Lastly, in the extreme north-east, the ancient kingdom of Armenia, ceaselessly coveted by Rome and by Persia, had been converted to Christianity by Cappadocian missionaries at the end of the third century and in about 400 had found an alphabet appropriate to its language. Within the empire, Syriac and Coptic constituted, in short, thriving entities that were not merely linguistic but cultural, which did not coincide with political frontiers but which spread Hellenic influence in the East; at the same time, however, these entities represented areas of dissidence, or at any rate of insularity, most of all over the now dominant question of religious profession. Syriac Christianity, in this regard as in others the most important of these communities, was to give proof of this attitude in the centuries following the Council of Chalcedon (451). There is, moreover, an irrefutable connection between precocity in the committal of a vernacular language or dialect to writing and the advance of Christianisation. The connection is plain in regard to the Armenian mission and we shall see it repeated in the case of the Slavs. But from a social and cultural viewpoint the languages were so intermixed that their territorial boundaries became blurred. Syriac was spoken right up to the gates of Antioch, and in the fourth century was heard in the city itself: John Chrysostom, a Greek-speaker, refers to the presence in his congregation on a great feast-day of country people unable to comprehend him; the rhetor Libanius, official spokesman for the city, was unashamedly Hellenic in all his discourses. At Jerusalem, prayers were offered in the vernacular languages of the East. In Palestine, the Jewish teachers debated in Hebrew, conversed in Aramaic and understood Greek; moreover, in Jewish inscriptions from Palestine, Greek and Hebrew are intermingled. On the other hand, fourth-century inscriptions from the synagogue at Sardis are all in Greek, and many communities used in their services the Greek translation of the Old Testament known as the Septuagint, a practice which Justinian sought to make universal.

These references to the diversity of languages should be a reminder that we are dealing with a world of the written word. The forms taken by the latter are as various as its functions. In urban communities, the classical custom of inscribing on stone or in mosaic a record of legislative decisions, village boundaries, even tax assessments, was sedulously observed down to the beginning of the seventh century. Of the several languages employed, Greek was the most common, and this not merely in towns but even in remote parts of the country. While it is still not clear who was expected to benefit from these written announcements, their sheer quantity presupposes a certain degree of literacy; it has been supposed that a noticeable decline in the number of inscriptions, beginning in the eighth century, together with a difference in their content, reflects a cultural change of attitude toward them in the territories remaining under Byzantine control. Next there is papyrus, a fibrous substance made from the broad-leaved aquatic plant of that name, used by administrative departments, notaries, private individuals and monasteries for their business, correspondence and accounts. It was produced in Egypt, the plant's natural habitat, where its manufacture was already a royal monopoly in Hellenistic times. Egypt itself has yielded several thousand documents on papyrus dating from the Byzantine epoch, fortunately preserved by the dryness of the climate. Several also survive from Constantinople and from an important find at Nessana, a village in southern Palestine. Here written down for us to read are the everyday details of business transactions, contracts, methods of measurement and methods of accounting, varying from one region to another in accordance with local custom. Unfortunately, papyrus is a fragile material and very little has survived from other parts of the Eastern empire. It was in any case already being superseded, for the production of books, by parchment, sheepskin 'treated in the manner of Pergamon' (*pergamenum*). Moreover, it was in the fourth and fifth centuries that the book in the form we know it, an assemblage of bound sheets called a *codex*, came into existence. But handwriting was not yet adapted to the task of making speedy and legible copies and we have very few manuscripts of the period. Writings in this form can only have had a restricted circulation, within an elite of the powerful or the learned, which is not difficult to understand in the case of some historical work or doctrinal treatise, or in the case of biblical texts intended to be read in churches. But for works as widely appreciated as the lives of certain respected saints, how are we to determine the relative importance of the written and the spoken word in their dissemination? The question awaits an answer.

However that may be, one presumes that public oratory did not reflect the language of

A Sassanid ruler. With its winged crown, tufted beard and neck ornament, this bronze bust of the fifth to sixth century displays the characteristic attributes of royalty. Neighbour to Constantinople, the Persian empire, with its spectacular and influential culture, was at this epoch also a dangerous rival (Paris, Louvre).

ordinary speech, since it remained faithful both to the rules of rhetoric and to the fine language of the classical texts read in schools. In this form, for which we naturally have only written testimony, it retained on the eve of our period the time-honoured importance assigned to it in civic life, when it was traditional for all cities to appoint a rhetor to act as their spokesman and to teach rhetoric. This office still flourished in the fourth century, Libanius of Antioch, who died about 393, being the prime example. In the fifth century it faded away, though without disappearing completely, as the examples of Procopius, rhetor of Gaza in the time of Anastasius, and Chronicus, rhetor of the same city under Justinian, bear witness. By the fourth century, the use of public oration had already passed in part to the local bishops, who were drawn from the same social background and had the same classical education. But even in this guise the practice declined in the fifth century.

Beyond the gates of the Romania

In 395, the empire of the East faced sparring partners at very varying levels of political development and whose history was in a state of flux. The main lines radiating from this initial constellation, which can still be traced as far as the geopolitical changes of the seventh century, extended most directly down to about 460.

We come first to empires. For the Roman empire of the East had to deal not merely with the empire of the West, its *alter ego* with a difference, but also with the vast Persian empire, stretching from Mesopotamia to India and from the Caspian to the Persian Gulf, the one barbarian State that Byzantium was prepared to recognise as an equal in the spheres of diplomacy and war. Persia, after all, possessed the distinctions of a divinely-inspired ruler, a

State Church, served by priests of the centuries-old Zoroastrian religion, an administration and culture based on writing, city-dwellers and great landowners, and a coinage circulating far beyond its boundaries. The cities of Mesopotamia passed back and forth in the constant tug of war between the two powers, as did the kingdom of Armenia, whose limits and liberties fluctuated with the tides of battle and whose hope of preserving a political identity was already based upon a national Church. Between Byzantium and the outlet of the Red Sea into the Indian Ocean lay other kingdoms: Ethiopia on the African shore, converted to Christianity from Alexandria in the fourth century, and on the south-west corner of the Arabian peninsula the Yemen, an urban and trading principality, missionised from Ethiopia, again in the fourth century. Lastly, roaming the frontier with the Syrian steppe, there were Arabs loosely grouped into two tribal confederations, led in one case by the Lakhmids, in the pay of Persia, and in the other by the Ghassanids, in the pay of Byzantium.

The first extension of the movements begun in the fourth and even the third century took place in the Balkans. Byzantium's territorial connections with the empire of the West hinged on the Danube lands and so, strangely enough, did the problem of the Germans. The Goths had crossed the fateful barrier of the Danube in 376, fleeing from the Ukraine where the Huns were hard on their heels. Starving, lured on by the peace and prosperity of the imperial provinces, they swept over Thrace, where renegades and fellow-tribesmen previously brought there as slaves came to their aid, in particular by revealing hidden stores of grain. In 378 the Goths reached Adrianople, winning there a battle in which – an unprecedented event – the emperor Valens, responsible for the East, lost his life. For the next two decades the whole region as far as Constantinople teemed with Goths and other Germans, in the guise of soldiers, bandits or invaders, depending on one's viewpoint. But in 400 the Goths stationed in the capital under their leader Gainas were massacred, and in the following year the authorities succeeded in diverting the Gothic chieftain Alaric to Italy, relieving the pressure on Byzantine Illyricum. The latter nevertheless remained vulnerable throughout the fifth century, until the problem was solved by admitting Germanic warriors to the army and even to the emperor's bodyguard.

The migration of the Huns is significant for another reason. In the debate over their origins, it cannot be denied that they spilled out of that reservoir in Central Asia from which successive waves of mounted tribesmen, Avars, Bulgars, Magyars, Turks, and Mongols, would launch themselves, by varying routes and with varying success, over the centuries. The objects thought by archaeologists to shed light on their material culture show traces of Siberian, Iranian and Hellenistic influence. In 370 the Huns were at the Volga, which they crossed in 375. Their expansion into the Ukraine and the lower Danube region displaced the Goths. Their advance then took several directions: westwards into Pannonia (present-day Hungary) in 405; southwards, where their passage through the Caucasus was of concern to both Persia and Byzantium, not to mention Armenia in the middle; lastly into the Far East, where the Hephtalites carved out a kingdom on the borders of Persia and India known to us from its coins. Like all the barbarians on the move at this period, Hunnic warriors sometimes engaged themselves as mercenaries, taking service with Byzantium,

The practical exercise of sovereign power is further ensured by an administrative system and an army. Augustus, inaugurating the regime of personal power, had superimposed a form of administration still not far removed from that of the private estate, or indeed of the private household, on the republican network of senatorial offices. The administrative and bureaucratic system was clearly in place by the late first century, only to undergo far-reaching modifications in the third century, which continued into the fourth. The traces of this early history would always remain. At the time we first meet it, the system consisted on the one hand of an imperial entourage and central departments, on the other of provincial sub-sections based on the different administrative districts. This draws attention to the importance not only of the road network, whose layout was an Antique heritage, but also of the imperial courier service (*cursus publicus*) whose rest houses (*mansiones*), placed at regular intervals, were reserved in principle for civil servants and bishops travelling in their official capacities and for government couriers, but were much envied and used unofficially by others. The upkeep of roads and the supply of post-horses thus constituted a considerable fiscal burden.

The emperor was aided by a council, which also formed the imperial tribunal. The members of the council included the emperor's spokesman (the *quaestor* of the sacred palace), the two treasury ministers, one for the fisc and the other for the imperial patrimony, and the master of the offices, superintendent of the central departments, each of which had a specialised function but which together made up the imperial chancery, that is to say the two-way channel of communication between the supreme power and the empire. Those who worked there needed a mass of skills and knowledge which young men aspiring to civil service careers could acquire, for example, at the School of Law in Beirut: law, administrative formulae, accounting procedures, special scripts. But for all its apparent striving after uniformity and efficiency, the system never fully achieved those ends. Official positions were salaried, but they were also venal, with far-reaching consequences in the sphere of taxation. Moreover, no distinction was made between what pertained to the State and what pertained to the emperor. These two observations will suffice to show that we are dealing with a living historical system, and what is more, one which endured, since we find it continuing throughout the whole of Byzantium's history.

The army of the Eastern empire at the start of the fifth century comprised two categories: mobile field armies (the *comitatus*) under the direct command of the central power, and provincial garrisons, stationed in particular on the frontiers. Papyrus documents from Egypt and Palestine, and also inscriptions from Cyrenaica and Syria, illustrate the life of these sedentary garrisons, usually stationed long enough for son to succeed father, possessing and indeed tilling plots of land. From this it seems that in the fifth century the East experienced some expansion in the numbers of *limitanei* or frontier troops, whose land was exempted from the ordinary fiscal obligations because military service came under the heading of a specific obligation. The mobile force on the other hand drew its recruits either from peasants levied under the arrangements for rural taxation or from barbarians, engaged as mercenaries and paid from the same fiscal source. The contribution of barbarians to the imperial army had long been considerable, from common soldiers to

Mail-clad horseman (bronze statuette, fourth or fifth century). The heavy cavalry was one of the spearheads of the Byzantine army (New York, The Metropolitan Museum of Art).

commanders-in-chief in the emperor's entourage. They fought in accordance with their own methods, and what is more the imperial armament began to show signs of enemy influence. In particular, the development from about the fourth century of a mailed cavalry was to have important consequences in Byzantine history, both because of its efficacy and because of its cost.

Since Constantine, imperial power at Byzantium had been synonymous with the power of the *solidus*, the gold coin whose stability, maintained down to the eleventh century, testifies to its primarily political function. The *solidus*, and its multiples of account, the pound (72 *solidi*) and the *centenarion* (100 pounds), parcelled out into sealed leather bags, provided coin for the payment of tribute to the barbarians, for the purchase of silk and other imported commodities (for its circulation was international), for large-scale disbursements,

119

as on building works and in imperial gifts, and for an increasing proportion of civilian and military salaries, which in theory also included the provision of food rations and equipment in kind. The importance of gold to the empire explains the bitterness of the struggles for control of the mines. The gold of Armenia was an issue in the wars between Byzantium and Persia in the fifth and sixth centuries, even though Persia's internal monetary system relied to a much greater extent on silver. It was all the more coveted when, for various reasons, Balkan gold became less accessible to the Byzantines after the sixth century. In the sixth century gold from the Sudan also entered the Byzantine orbit, if the evidence of the merchant Cosmas Indicopleustes ('the voyager to India') is to be believed. But as the favoured form of private savings, gold was above all the main object of fiscal demand. *Solidi* and *tremisses* were to the fore in all the payments, dues, offerings and other expenditures above a level which could be met by the low-denomination coinage in everyday use. The latter, struck in bronze or in copper lightly alloyed with silver, appears to have been as volatile and as responsive to economic changes as the gold coinage was stable. The proliferation of smaller and smaller coins, which in the first decades of the fifth century were sometimes cut into two, is indicative of an upsurge in petty transactions. Weak, and possessing no more than a fiduciary value, the bronze coinage presented the one element of elasticity in the system. There was thus a conflict of interest between the government, which periodically sought to institute a relatively strong bronze coinage in order to relieve the circulation of gold, and the mass of unmoneyed consumers. Between the two poles of the gold and bronze coinages, the role of silver in the fifth century was virtually non-existent.

The crushing weight of the Church

Constantine had converted the imperial government into a Christian power. By the end of the fourth century the state that had been reached was as follows: it had been made possible for the Church to own landed property; the existence of a new social category, that of the clergy, had been acknowledged; the Church had been assigned a public duty of a specific and also a novel kind, that of rendering charitable assistance; the Church's authority in the domains of moral discipline and especially the definition of dogma had been endorsed by the imperial power. Submission to the Church's doctrines hence became a civic duty, and their rejection an offence against the State.

Which Christianity?

Having said this, at the beginning of the fifth century Christian influence was visible on several different levels. To begin with, there was the diffusion of the Christian faith. The old polytheism, the vehicle in its day of the historical values bound up with Rome's eternity, had been dispossessed. In 392 it was finally proscribed and the remaining possessions of its temples confiscated. The Christianisation of the empire of the East was making marked progress in the countryside and towns by the fourth century, and even in the third. Pockets of paganism nevertheless persisted. The town of Gaza, for example, formerly possessed a famous temple, the Marneion. So when Porphyry, bishop of Gaza, began his episcopate (he died in 420), he was violently attacked by villagers unwilling to pay his church its due. The *Historia Religiosa* of Theodoret, bishop of Cyr in northern Syria (*c.* 393–*c.* 466), makes reference to the evangelisation of a village in the vicinity even at that late date. The Arabs on Syria's borders received a bishop only in 430. On another front, even if the elite of the court and the public services from now on professed Christianity, this did not prevent the cultivation of Neoplatonic philosophy in many educated circles. Justinian found it necessary to suppress adherence to the old cults at differing levels of society, and as late as 580 a charge of 'Hellenism' was levelled at no less a person than the patriarch of the capital. The fact is that in practice the question is not reducible to the hard and fast categories of official reports, but should rather be thought of in terms of a continuity as profound as it is obscure. The feasts, or rather the carnivals, of the old calendar, celebrated with indiscriminate revelry, were to hold out for centuries against Christianisation, in the capital as much as in the countryside. In time of stress, Byzantines continued to utter magical incantations invoking the names of the ancient deities. Devotion was increasingly paid by all to saints whose nebulous authenticity – St George and St Demetrius come to mind – remained quite divorced from the place they held in the piety of the Byzantines and their Slav converts. The attributes of these saints, their iconography, and sometimes their cult places, echo those of powers venerated in former times, and yet are by no means reducible to those prototypes: the question is less simple than it appeared to scholars at the beginning of the present century, which makes further investigation all the more necessary. Nevertheless, a movement was afoot which gradually excluded all dissidents from the empire's collective life, or to put it in another way, which defined *romanitas* ever more strictly by the orthodoxy of the creed. It inevitably excluded polytheism, for all its resilience, but also affected the Jews, who found themselves suffering civic disqualifications and a deterioration in their everyday relations with Christians; and lastly it affected heterodox Christians, some of whom would in any case be severed from the empire by the advance of Islam.

The Christian picture of the world and of the human condition as it was conceived in Byzantium at the start of the fifth century was the product of an already lengthy evolution, the course of which was by no means run. Its main features emerge from the sermons of the great urban bishops of the late fourth century, to whom we shall return, and with still greater effect from the host of pious narratives and saints' lives, mostly of monastic origin, composed for the edification of the laity and of the monks themselves, or intended to adorn the walls of monasteries and places of pilgrimage. These features were derived from a profound cultural transformation which came about in the second and third centuries, and which was thus contemporaneous with the first rapid expansion of Christianity, but without necessarily resulting from it. The first trait to be noticed is an intense preoccupation with personal salvation. An account of what Christians could expect in the next world had been available since the second century in an apocryphal work, the *Apocalypse of St Peter*. A more elaborate *Apocalypse of St Paul*, given currency by Syrian monks at the end of the fourth century, although initially suspect in the eyes of the ecclesiastical hierarchy,

Figurine of a woman stuck with pins. The official adoption of Christianity concealed the survival of pockets of paganism, whose magical practices are eloquently recreated for us in this Coptic statuette of the fourth century (Paris, Louvre).

became the basis of Byzantine tradition. At this date, however, the after-life was not yet the dominant theme of Byzantine religious sensibility. That part was taken by demons, whose multiform ubiquity was another inheritance from the earlier period. Sometimes demons merely made themselves felt or heard while remaining invisible; at other times they appeared under a borrowed shape, as a black dog, for instance, a mouse, or an enormous 'Ethiopian', or again they might be seen but defy description; they caused accidents and sickness, led people into sin, and brought on the morbid state known as demon possession, through which men of the time found an outlet for their aggressions and inner tensions. Even in the absence of demonic intervention human existence was felt to be precarious: the threat of bad weather or invasion by locusts hung over the harvest, populations were a prey to epidemics, the future was dark, usually with the menace of punishment for collective sins which needed to be brought to light.

This is where the mediator came in, the holy man with power to heal the sick, succour the infirm, multiply food for the hungry, protect the fields, foretell the future, in short to perform miracles precisely in the manner recorded in the Gospels. This power, exclusively male apart from some trivial exceptions, was the fruit of a solitary sojourn in the wilderness, in the course of which the holy man had submitted himself to an ascetic regime setting him totally apart from the common rut: abstinence from food, deprivation of sleep, exposure to the cold, wrestlings with demons, and above all complete sexual chastity. The last of these was another, and perhaps the most important, element in the cultural transformation mentioned above: salvation and sanctity, in more everyday terms moral merit, depended from henceforth on voluntary and sustained chastity. Here we are not concerned with the causes of this evolution, which are less simple than may appear, but with its important cultural and social consequences. Whatever the reason, the fifth to seventh centuries stand out as the heyday of these 'holy men', who in this time of transition, and hence of instability and unease, were invested with a social function which, without ever being institutionalised, none the less acquired a central importance. From his village or from the retreat where men sought him out, the ascetic freely extended his mediation to society as a whole. Men of every social rank flocked to the feet of the Stylite ascetics, to Symeon the Elder on his pillar not far from Antioch, to Daniel on his in a suburb of the capital. After death, the benign influence of the holy man continued to be exercised from his tomb, and was one of the justifications for monasticism, just as it was the vindication of his ascetic retreat to the desert. It can well be imagined that in reality these movements were a great deal more complex, and that they relate to an aspect of social history already touched on, the forms of spatial organisation.

The religious imperatives of the period extended equally to the honouring of martyrs, from whose real or supposed tombs the same benefits were expected, and whose feast days provided occasion for social celebrations on a greater or lesser scale. Later on this collective devotion would attach itself to other saints, and in particular, towards the end of the sixth century, to the Virgin Mary. All of this draws attention, on the eve of Byzantine history, to vital and enduring elements which pervade the collective consciousness of society from top to bottom. When the emperor Anastasius consults Daniel the Stylite, when Procopius, the great historian of the sixth century, draws up a secret indictment of his master Justinian, crediting him with a demonic nature and powers, then it becomes clear that the belief-system just described knows nothing of the social, or as we might say the cultural, barriers our modern rationality would lead us to expect.

As well as influencing beliefs, the change in attitudes going back over several centuries and commonly associated with christianisation had an effect on sexual, conjugal and family life. In this sphere they are noticeable as early as the second century. In rating virginity above abstinence and both above marriage, St Paul reflected a trend already developing in the imperial culture of his time but absent from rabbinic Judaism. By the second century it had become dominant. Voluntary virginity, refusal to contract second marriages, cessation of conjugal relations by mutual agreement, spiritual marriage, from which such relations were presumed absent from the start, all appear to have found some favour as ascetic options in the fourth and again in the fifth century, and did not entail the

123

The *martyrion* of St Symeon Stylites, now Qalat Seman, one of the most important Byzantine sanctuaries in Syria. The edifice was constructed to a cruciform plan around an octagonal chamber containing the saint's pillar. Late fifth century.

abandonment of social or even family ties. The Church nevertheless viewed them with disquiet, preferring the stark choice between marriage and total withdrawal from the world that it was gradually to impose on Christians over the centuries. The Church was thus violently opposed to spiritual marriage and tended to put virgins, like widows, into a group qualifying for assistance once they reached the canonically specified age of 60, when their state could be presumed definitive. Another expression of sexual abstinence is to be seen in the proliferation of solitaries and of monks living in communities. But this raises problems on its own account, to which we shall return. The Church was of its epoch, an epoch well-disposed towards voluntary celibacy, but which at the same time saw the tightening of family bonds. The difference in this latter respect between Rome, with its relative laxity, and the customs of the imperial East was doubtless of long standing. In any case, the Church asserted itself in formulating two points: the constitution of the marriage bond, and the impediments to marriage. Nuptial blessing did not become obligatory in law at Byzantium until the end of the eighth century, and the freedom to divorce afforded under Roman law only gradually faded into the background, without ever disappearing completely. But the increasing habit of attaching validity to betrothals, which reveals an oriental and perhaps a specifically Jewish influence at work, and the immature age at which girls in particular became affianced, testify to the social importance of marriage. The multiplication of impediments on the grounds of blood relationship, kinship by marriage or through baptism points in the same direction. The society of the Eastern empire appears to have had a tendency at the beginning of this period to reinforce kinship ties by those of marriage, particularly by the union of first cousins. The Church's strictness in this matter went further and further beyond the impediments enunciated in the Old Testament, and the imperial legislator followed suit. The extension of prohibitions continued until the end of the tenth century; but whether the code was honoured in the breach or the observance, the underlying tendency was the same – reinforcement of the kindred as the basic social unit. What seems much less evident is that attitudes towards conjugal morality itself were undergoing any marked alteration at the turn of the fourth century. Here the turning-point had come as early as the second century, affecting the empire as a whole; it also has to be pointed out that the condition of women in Greek and Hellenised societies was not, and never had been, on a par with that of Roman women, whatever the sermons of preachers such as John Chrysostom may imply to the contrary.

And which Church?

Christianisation means that the Church defines a distinct if complex group in society, and on the other hand that a connection exists in public law between the Church as an institution and the imperial power. At the beginning of the fifth century, the organisation of the Byzantine Church already displayed in broad outline the features which were to become definitive. Its administrative divisions followed those of the empire, with bishops presiding in the cities and a metropolitan in the provincial capital. In 381 the Council of Constantinople initiated a system of patriarchates, with the result that a pre-eminent position was accorded to the sees of Rome, Constantinople, Alexandria, Antioch and Jerusalem, by reason of their honoured place in Christian history, and in the case of Constantinople its imperial associations. Each of these patriarchates exercised jurisdiction over a particular region of the empire. The system was then endorsed by the Council of Chalcedon in 451, which placed the patriarchates of Rome and Constantinople on an equal footing. It became fully-fledged in the sixth century. The patriarchate of Constantinople styled itself 'ecumenical' (universal) and later played a role of the first importance in political and diplomatic affairs. The urban-based bishops had under them *chorepiscopi* or rural bishops, placed in charge of country districts and in particular of the larger villages. After them came the priests serving the urban and village churches. In inscriptions and other documents they figure among the village notables. Even nomads were not neglected, as is shown by the appointment in 430 of a bishop to minister to the 'Saracens' on the edge of the desert. In law, the status of cleric also extended to deacons, sub-deacons and readers. The virgins and widows referred to above can be regarded as belonging to the same milieu. Deaconesses might be widows with adult children, as we know from inscriptions on provincial tombs.

All these persons composed the Church of the clergy, a ministry at once urban and rural. As to its means of support, the problem of Church properties, of the personal possessions of the clergy, and of the relationship between the two, had constantly been aired ever since Constantine's recognition of the legal status of ecclesiastical establishments. There was no lack of idealists to urge that priests should not engage in paid employment, but should live by and for their calling, in the manner of the old Jewish priesthood serving the temple; the *Apostolic Constitutions*, a utopian work of the fifth century, is still imbued with this idea. In practice, however, we know from fourth-century legislation and provincial tomb inscriptions that it was quite common for priests, and still more for deacons, to follow a trade. Moreover, since the fourth century, the churches themselves had owned properties and revenues: these no doubt included lands confiscated from the temples of Asia Minor, but more important was the continual flow of gifts in property, cash and revenues contributed by the faithful, from the emperor down to the lowliest peasant, and which the churches, if only tacitly, expected in acknowledgment of their spiritual intercession – a thank-offering, as it were, for the hope of salvation and grace already received. The *Life* of Olympias, a lady in John Chrysostom's circle of correspondents who had voluntarily chosen celibacy and become a deaconess, is loud in its praise of the fabulous fortune in money and property she bequeathed to the church in the capital. The possessions of the latter, for example, included several hundred craftsmen's shops; at Jerusalem, the Church of the Resurrection drew an income from tenements in the city. In the sixth century, the patriarchate of Alexandria fitted out its own fleet of merchant ships. On a smaller scale, the village churches found themselves in similarly easy circumstances, except where the village in question formed part of an estate, as was frequently the case in Egypt.

The cardinal principle underlying the Church's ownership of property had been clearly enunciated since the time of Constantine: to make possible the provision of charitable assistance to a newly-identified social group comprising the poor, the homeless, the aged and the sick, to which we shall return. This was reflected in the regime governing the administration of the Church's patrimony, starting with the rule that ecclesiastical property was inalienable, from which official dispensation was granted only in special circumstances. The Church of Moesia, for example, was authorised to sell some of its properties to obtain the money needed for prisoners' ransoms, a recognised form of charity. The usual practice, however, was for churches to let out their properties on very long leases. Second, churches and clergy came within the scope of the fiscal system, whose nature has already been explained; within it, they formed a special category of tax-payers with specific duties to perform and therefore qualified for compensatory immunities. The position regarding the Church's charitable duty is clear; but over the question of ecclesiastical immunities the legislators long remained hesitant, influenced no doubt by the importance of the Church's possessions and of the private wealth remaining in the hands of the clergy. The same question was soon to arise in relation to the monastic foundations, with their differing origins and evolution, the existence of whose endowments was first acknowledged by the Council of Chalcedon in 451. From then on the fiscal and patrimonial regulations or the arrangements regarding gifts referred to above applied equally to monasteries and to the charitable establishments served by monks which started to proliferate at this period. In the early fifth century the monks were already a social and cultural force of great importance, resulting from a unique conjunction of a mass exodus by peasants and the spiritual aspirations of the more cultivated, but it is still too soon to speak of monasticism as an institution; the time for that comes later when, as we shall see, monks had a crucial part to play in the shaping of Byzantine society.

Possible hazards, definite deviations

The official jurisdiction of the Church extended over its own internal discipline, the conduct of Christians in general, and over questions of dogma. The Church reached its decisions in councils, some regional, some ecumenical, where the emperor had the right to preside. Bishops travelling to councils were authorised to use the imperial courier service, which underlined their official character. On the other hand, some of the Church's most respected teachers, chief among them Basil of Caesarea, who died in 379, had already laid down the foundations of Byzantine canon law through their answers to questions which had been raised or their opinions on concrete cases. The Church had its own code of exclusively spiritual punishments, of which the most severe was the exclusion of the offender for a period proportionate to the gravity of his fault. But the Church was supported by the secular arm, or rather there was a single power, in part spiritual, in part political, which defined and punished errors, as much in matters of conduct (persistence in magical practices, marital misconduct, deviant sexuality) as in Christian belief. Such, at any rate, is the principle of government in Byzantium. As can be imagined, the reality was sometimes different.

In the first place, there were occasions for conflict between the public authorities and the requirements of the Church. The legislator's hesitations on the subject of clerical immunity show this to have been the case. A still better example is the right to asylum on ecclesiastical precincts; its existence was recognised in principle and its exact physical limits publicly displayed; at the same time, the imperial power endeavoured to restrict it in the name of preserving social order, as for example in the case of slaves, and the Church generally speaking fell into line. Again, entry into holy orders or into a monastery could be interpreted as a device for evading curial or guild obligations. The legislators had already attempted to close this loophole in the fourth century, by stipulating that in such cases the patrimony of individuals should remain with the association, because of the collective responsibility mentioned earlier.

Finally, the Church was far from united in subscribing to the doctrine which commanded recognition of the secular power. The heresies dividing the Church were in fact of two very different kinds. There were heresies which defined entire regions of the empire whose inhabitants had ceased to share the beliefs of the capital, and there were those which, while going under different names, boiled down to a single and powerful challenge to the Christian social order in the name of radical Christianity.

The great theological debate spanning the fifth century turned on the relationship between the persons of the Trinity, or in other words on the nature of the Incarnation. According to the Arian doctrine already being preached in the fourth century, the Son is a creation of the precedent Father; as Word, he in turn creates the Holy Spirit. Arianism, which takes its name from the Alexandrian priest Arius, had been condemned in 325 by the Council of Nicaea, the first ecumenical council, and again in 381 by its immediate successor, the Council of Constantinople. The difficulty for us today lies not so much in following this debate but in understanding the widespread commotions it caused. Two observations may be helpful. First, that Christ was now adored so fervently that ordinary Christians looked for teachings which exalted both his divine power and his proximity to men. Second, that the debates of the fifth century assume a regional dimension already noticeable in the Arian controversy: the see of Antioch and the see of Alexandria, the capital, the Syrian and the Coptic monks, and behind them their respective populations, formed in this debate a network of deeply-rooted particularism so enduring that it survived the Arab conquests. Nor should it be forgotten that the Germanic West had been converted to Christianity in its Arian form, which had incidentally been a factor in the hostility between the *federate* Goths and the inhabitants of Constantinople around the year 400.

The progress of the theological debate is known to us from the polemical literature, from conciliar decrees and from church histories, in particular the one composed by Theodoret, bishop of Cyr, which goes down to 428. The fifth century witnessed the continuation of the controversy, which now revolved around the terms 'nature' (*physis*) and 'person' (*hypostatis*). The school of Antioch maintained that the two natures, divine and human, were co-existent in the person of Christ but remained totally distinct, so that it was only in his human nature that Christ was born of Mary and suffered on the cross. Nestorius, chief proponent of this doctrine, acceded in 428 to the patriarchal see of Constantinople and therefore was supported by imperial authority. In contrast, the school of Alexandria insisted on the union of the two natures in the person of Christ. The attack on Nestorius was led by the patriarch Cyril, supported by Rome and by the Coptic monks, among whom Shenoute, abbot of the White Monastery of Atripe in the Thebaid, was pre-eminent. The third ecumenical council, which met at Ephesus in 431, decided in favour of the Alexandrian doctrines and condemned Nestorius. The next two decades witnessed the political as well as the theological triumph of Alexandria, as not only Cyril, who died in 444, but also the Egyptian patriarchate, rose in prestige. Alexandria's position became still more extreme, to the point of maintaining a single nature in Christ, at once human and divine, but more divine than human. And so Monophysitism was born. It was condemned in 451 by the Council of Chalcedon, the fourth of the ecumenical councils, at which a compromise supported by Pope Leo I was adopted. The beliefs upheld at Chalcedon remained the yardstick of orthodoxy both at Constantinople and in Roman Christendom, which at this time were united in opposing the all too successful rise of Alexandria. From now on, the provinces of Syria, Mesopotamia and Egypt formed by contrast a dissident monophysite block, irrespective of social distinctions, to which independent Armenia formed a kind of appendage. Monophysite beliefs defined for centuries to come the space occupied by Eastern Christianity, and more immediately the space in which Islam was to triumph over Byzantium. As for Nestorianism, it penetrated to Iran and Central Asia, by means of missions despatched from its Syrian homeland.

Our knowledge of the 'socially subversive' heresies comes from condemnations of them by orthodox believers, from polemical literature, conciliar canons, formulae of reconciliation and a few direct testimonies. In 1945 a whole library of heterodox writings was discovered at a site in Upper Egypt, amongst them the apocryphal *Gospel of Thomas* in Coptic, dating perhaps to the third century. The Syriac *Acts* of Thomas (known in the fourth century) and *Book of Degrees* (pre-350) form part of the same tradition. Lastly there are narratives which although absorbed by the Greek Church into its hagiography are imbued with the same ideas. They continue a radical strain descended from the gnosticism of the second century, whose wide-ranging speculations, drawing on polytheistic philosophy, Judaism and Christianity, had led to belief in the duality of the divine power and a creator of the world, which meant in effect the divorce of the soul from creation. Conduct based on these principles ran counter to the fundamental norms of the existing social order. Thus we hear of men and women wandering footloose, and sleeping together in various combinations, of women cutting their hair and dressing as men, of family ties being severed. Slaves run away from their masters, monks from their superiors and their places of retreat. Marriage is condemned, married priests are rejected, private celebrations replace the Church's regular services and festivals. The *Book of Degrees* describes a hierarchy of the 'Just', on whom everyday tasks devolve, and the 'Perfect', who alone are permitted to see God. It is easy to imagine how a movement of this kind could span the centuries and we shall come across it later. But in the fourth century Epiphanius of Salamis was already

129

making the comment, in his treatise on heresies, that the movement merely carried to extremes the Gospel injunction to abandon all worldly possessions: there was little difference, in other words, between their attitude and orthodox asceticism.

A solid rural base

Having seen the nature of the central power and the main characteristics of the culture, we can now look more closely at the society to which these applied. The numerous and relatively small provinces each had a governor at the head. The provinces in turn were grouped into dioceses headed by vicars, the deputies of the praetorian prefects. The praetorian prefects, of whom there was always one for the East and usually another for Illyricum, formed the apex of the provincial hierarchies. These arrangements were subject to revisions, which are not our present concern. The aim here is to examine the oldest forms of social organisation existing in the Roman and Byzantine East: the cities, whose Antique vitality persisted down to the brutal changes of the seventh century; the villages, whose settled occupation of the countryside dated back to time immemorial and suffered little disturbance under the Roman and later the Byzantine empires; and the uninhabited space, which reveals so much about historical changes.

The production and consumption of food

Continuity should not be taken to imply uniformity, which could hardly be expected over such a vast expanse. On some points, however, it is safe to generalise, starting with the agricultural products for which there was universal demand. Bread made from wheat formed part of everyone's diet, from the poorest peasant or slave right up to the emperor: consumption of fresh bread increased the higher one rose in the social scale, while the poor, soldiers and hermits in the desert fed on biscuit or gruel. Barley, which was consistently sold at two-thirds of the price, was resorted to when times were bad. Wine, of varying quality, mixed to a lesser or greater extent with water, was the universal drink. Sweetness was supplied by honey, dried fruits, and dates, whose consumption was widespread in Egypt and Palestine. Fresh fruit on the other hand appears to have been a luxury. Everyone ate vegetables, of the green or root varieties. But when we come to proteins and fats, social divergences begin to appear. Oil was used for cooking and seasoning, principally olive oil, varying in quality, but the poorest had to make do with oil extracted from seeds of various kinds. Cheese was scarce, as were the other milk products consumed in such quantity by the people of the steppes. There was fresh or salt fish, and the fish sauce, *garum*, mentioned in an earlier chapter, a few eggs and poultry, and meat, if only in the form of sausage: it is to be noted that inhabitants of the Byzantine world, or at any rate of its southern portion, Egypt, Syria and Palestine, were not pork-eaters, differing in this respect from the populations of Italy and Gaul. This is probably less true of their contemporaries in Asia Minor and the Balkans. Consumption of fish can be assumed to have been greatest near to the coasts, even if river fish are taken into account; fish and meat were more accessible to townsmen

This mosaic in the Great Palace at Constantinople (sixth century) gives a realistic illustration of agricultural work. Here, two peasants turn over a plot with a two-pronged hoe.

than to country-dwellers; and soldiers were issued with meat as part of their ration. In town and country alike, those who could not afford meat subsisted largely on pulses, 'the meat of the poor' as it has been termed by two experts working for the United Nations.

The picture so far appears to be of a flourishing rural economy, but three observations are needed by way of qualification. First, there were great natural hazards to contend with. Cereal yields could reasonably be expected in the proportion of 4 or 5:1, but were at the mercy of the seasonal catastrophes which punctuate the pages of contemporary chronicles. An autumn or spring drought placed the crops in jeopardy, plagues of locusts ate them up. The excessively severe winter of 401 devastated regions already a prey to barbarian attack, famine, epidemic and a proliferation of wild animals, doubtless a product of the circumstances. The harsh winter of 443, which was followed by an epidemic among humans and animals, ravaged the area around Constantinople. Famine, defined as always by the dearth of grain, whether wheat or barley, hit the countryside harder than the towns, where people were less dependent on local supplies for their food and communications were better. The second point to note is that an immense effort was required to provision the capital, the great provincial cities and the army. Lastly, the delays and difficulties experienced in transporting produce over long distances, a direct consequence of the priority accorded the fiscal levies, gave peasants everywhere the incentive to grow all the necessary kinds of produce, both for themselves and for the market of the town in whose locality they lived. For their own consumption, for the urban market, and when required for delivery to the fisc, peasants also produced articles other than food. In Egypt and southern Palestine, palm fibres were woven into sandals, matting, baskets and containers for use as measures. In the mountain forests of Asia Minor there was timber to be cut, in contrast with the Anatolian plateau where its scarcity was such that, as today, dried cow-dung was burned to give warmth. Other products of the countryside included leather, where there was stock-rearing, wool, and textiles made from plant fibres, of which the fine Egyptian linen is an example. Egypt, of course, was also the source of the papyrus used throughout the Mediterranean world, including the West.

This gives an idea both of the productive capacity of rural areas and of the problems posed by their economic and social organisation, or by their links with towns. Here again there is a picture of geographical diversity, from which certain common characteristics emerge. The basic unit of production was the peasant household known to us from the fiscal returns and the laws: the menfolk are to be seen at work in mosaics of the period, the women figure in the tax censuses, and a law for Pontus in 386 counts women as halves when calculating the capitation tax, but of their precise activities we know nothing. One or two slaves, with perhaps a few hired hands, completed the household. Oxen were used for ploughing, carting, and for threshing, by dragging a heavy spiked plank across the threshing-floor. Donkeys also served on occasion as draught animals, but were more often used as beasts of burden. Horses, requisitioned by the army and the public courier service, and mules provided transport for humans. Tools were apparently rarely made of metal. The form of plough used was the *aratrum*. Otherwise there were hatchets, pruning-knives and hoes of various types. It is when we come to the larger pieces of equipment that we begin to glimpse the social appearance of the countryside. Where such devices could be installed, threshing-floors, wine or oil presses, mule-powered millstones and water-mills belonged in some cases to a peasant 'master of the house', in others to a village or again to an estate proprietor.

The rural settlement was usually compact, although some texts mention outliers. It was surrounded by multiculture 'gardens', vineyards, arable and coppices: the plots of individual holdings were thus dispersed over the territory as a whole, without there being any discernible effort at collective farming – though this may be hinted at in a Palestinian tale where a boy takes all the village cattle out to pasture. But there are infinite variations: the Isaurian hideouts of mountain brigands, the large villages of Syria, equipped with baths and churches, the remote villages, cut off in winter, which witnessed John Chrysostom's last days in exile. If the archaeologists have so far found little trace of village industries, except in Thrace, the texts point to a degree of commercial activity: a certain village in Syria was reputed for its walnuts, others set up a market or an inn at a staging-post on an important highway or in the neighbourhood of a celebrated holy man and his monastery. Furthermore, peasants went to the nearest town to sell their products. There they procured the gold and bronze coins required for purchases, tax payments and rents. There, too, they earned money by hiring themselves out on the town's building sites, where a man with a donkey could expect better pay than a man on his own.

Flourishing village communities

The existence and scope of the rural commune in Byzantine society has been the subject of more than usually impassioned debates, the reason being that these originated in Russia in the late nineteenth century, where the rise of Byzantine studies coincided with a debate over contemporary agrarian problems. To obtain a clear understanding of the matter we have to distinguish between the village in its physical, social and institutional aspects.

The starting-point of the discussion has to be the nucleated character of the settlement, which we shall understand more fully, irrespective of regional differences, as more sites are investigated. The results so far obtained, and likewise the written texts, indicate a sense of community firstly by means of the buildings themselves: the watch-towers of villages on the Syrian steppe, the farming equipment already mentioned, the bath-house and church where such existed. Next, we have good reason to believe in the existence of commons, clearings, woodlands, and boundaries between territories. When we turn to village society, however, we find it composed not only of peasants but also of landlords, priests, soldiers, and here and there a few craftsmen. In other words, it is an unequal society, in which the scale of wealth no doubt bears some relation to the land and the means of exploiting it: for example, one finds in the countryside labourers with no land at all, while soldiers or the priest can cut a figure as petty notables, and great landowners have a residence there. This inequality finds clear expression in the government of the village by 'heads of household', 'from the smallest to the greatest', with a foreman and spokesman who was often the priest. Village solidarity could also manifest itself through a decision to construct a building, which will be recorded in an inscription, the concealment of an abducted maiden, adherence to a heretical creed, the practice of brigandage. Between individual households and the commune there was also the intermediate solidarity between 'neighbours', whose importance is underlined by fifth-century laws which granted them a pre-emptive right over plots put up for sale. To judge from examples of partitions by inheritance which have survived, the neighbours as a rule were also kinsmen, so that when the law speaks of the 'nearest' it does so in all senses of the term, which shows that we are dealing with a group of some complexity. But above the collective spirit loom those who hold the village in their power.

Here we touch on institutions as ancient as they were fundamental to a society and economy where land was the essential ingredient, namely the fiscal role of the village community and the dependent condition of the peasantry. It should first be explained that there was no necessary correspondence between the status of the village and that of its inhabitants, that not all villagers were necessarily of the same status, that an individual peasant could be both independent and dependent, owning some of his plots but not others, and lastly that the village could be entirely independent, that is to say composed exclusively of peasant freeholders, or entirely dependent, on one master or on several. In a word, peasant independence signified that the land and the individual were subject to no obligations and levies apart from the public, that is to say, fiscal ones: the independent peasant paid his land-tax directly to the fisc. Dependence on the other hand implied that peasant cultivation was subject to a levy to the master of the land and figured in the tax

133

register under his name, as the intermediary who paid the land-tax. Legally speaking, however, the dependent peasant, or *colonus*, remained no less liable for the contribution and no less amenable to justice. He might even take the master of the land to court if he considered the levy, generally fixed by custom, to be excessive. For the *colonus* was bound not to his master but to the land, in accordance with the formula enunciated in a law of 393. The sole diminution of his personal liberty arose from the rule forbidding him to migrate and thereby to deplete a labour force which, because of the backwardness of technical resources, was never over-abundant. At the same time, forced services, other than public duties, were not demanded at this period, the Byzantine East remaining faithful in this respect to its Classical tradition. The master of the land thus benefited from peasant labour only through the share of its product which he was entitled to take, levied in kind or in cash; the latter implies that the peasant had direct access to the market. This is another sphere in which the solidarity of the village could manifest itself, especially where it was independent. The fisc in fact held it to be collectively responsible for the land-tax, another reason for the rights of pre-emption mentioned above. And it was as a collective that the independent village went in search of a patron, to act as its protector against fiscal oppression.

The fact is that the rural history of Byzantium in this initial period is to be read not in the static condition of the peasantry but in the changes affecting the social group comprising the masters of the land. Traditionally this was made up of city-dwellers, to whom we shall return, of great landowners, the greatest of whom was the emperor, and lastly of churches and other religious establishments. The upsetting of this balance to the detriment of the urban bourgeoisie came about through the practice of patronage, which encouraged peasants to seek effective protection against the fisc; as we saw, this was just as vital to dependent peasants, who were no less answerable to the fisc, as it was to freeholders. The protection afforded by patronage extended equally to the courts. Indeed, the importance of patronage as a key to the social practices of the time can scarcely be over-stressed. Patrons wielded their influence by various means: through religious supremacy, as in the instance of the holy man who according to Theodoret secured the collective conversion of a pagan village in northern Syria in return for his patronage; or through force, as in the case of those magnates who in the late fourth century were already the target of laws which fruitlessly forbade the maintenance of private armies and private prisons, or the harbouring of deserters, but who were the first to benefit from the regime of autonomous tax-collection, *autopragia*, introduced for Egypt in 409, which promoted an estate into the category of a separate fiscal unit, marked off by physical boundaries. Patrons could also bring their credit and official contacts to bear on those law suits from which *coloni* formerly emerged the losers. Needless to say, these same methods could be invoked to impose protection where it was not wanted. However that may be, one is left with the impression that a redistribution of effective rights over the products of the soil was definitely in progress, generally at the expense of the land's rightful owners. In a word, the true hallmark of the peasant condition in this society, as in many others of the same type, was the tendency for rent and tax to be combined in a single levy.

While some monks prayed, others did manual work. This duality was portrayed by many illustrations depicting the form of monasticism which developed from the fourth century onwards, from Egypt to Asia Minor (Vatican Library, Ms Vaticanus graecus, eleventh century).

The wilderness

We do not as yet possess, and probably never will, an archaeological coverage sufficiently comprehensive to allow reasoned conclusions to be drawn about the occupation of Byzantine territory at this epoch or about its variations. It is possible to put forward some general hypotheses, which find their place in the next chapter. It is also possible here and now to make a positive statement of a structural nature: the occupation was discontinuous, more so in some regions than others, of course. But the texts point to the existence of wastelands everywhere: the term 'desert' applies to the wooded mountainside, infested with wild beasts, to which an anchorite brought the first human presence, where brigands robbed travellers with impunity, and from which they descended in spring to pillage the surrounding countrysides; it applies equally to the barren steppe where nomadic camel drivers supported themselves by turns as caravan escorts, hunters and bandits, whether on the borders of northern Syria, along the great highway plunging into the Sinai peninsula, or in the Egyptian desert; and lastly it applies to the uncultivated areas, no matter where, which had been abandoned to the demons lurking near villages, or evacuated, as in Thrace, under the more substantial threat of barbarian attack. The historian has the inclination to scrutinise these fringe areas for signs of fluctuations in the population. The way in which the men of the time completely reversed their attitudes towards the wilderness is one of the great cultural and social facts of the age. The change is first

135

noticeable in Egypt in the late third century, manifested in Antony's haunted solitude and the barrack-like regime of the Pachomian monks, going out to till the fields in gangs, kept under perpetual moral surveillance and with their every moment accounted for. In the fourth century Egypt's western desert was populated by ascetics, whose way of life, miracles and sayings became known through the dissemination of pious narratives. But as these make clear, their solitude was only relative; ascetics were found sharing their primitive stone cabins with a 'disciple', or indeed living in the close vicinity of another ascetic, and they sold their handiwork, for instance, ropes and baskets, in the villages. Others followed a system which prefigured the *lavra*, typical of the semi-communal form of orthodox monasticism, acording to which the members lived apart but came together on Saturdays and Sundays to draw their rations and celebrate the liturgy communally. Lastly, monastic communities were already in existence which merited the description *koinobia*, 'places of the common life', such as Wadi Natrun, and the monastery of St Catherine, established in the fourth century at the foot of Mount Sinai. It was also in the fourth century that the movement first spread to Syria and Palestine, and then into Asia Minor, with the earliest Cappadocian initiatives. Visitors from the West, such as Etheria of Aquitaine and the Marseilles monk John Cassian, carried back with them their zeal for these modes of life and spread it among their compatriots, while Jerome succeeded in attracting some of his female Roman penitents to his settlement at Bethlehem. Whether it took the form of a solitary or communal life, monastic withdrawal represented a fundamental challenge to the village as much as to the town: even if in one sense the desert was not far distant from either, even if the town was willing in this initial period to accommodate a specifically urban monasticism, the fact of withdrawal implied above all the negation of family life, of the basic cell of contemporary society, and this remains true even where men united by ties of kinship joined together in pursuit of an ascetic life.

In reality, because of its flexibility and lack of a uniform rule, the monastic movement in this initial phase raised questions to which no clear answers were forthcoming for several generations: at issue are the conflicting claims of the desert, with its path to salvation, as against those of the town, with its temptations and innate wickedness, but also with its many sinners to be saved; of solitude as against the fraternity of the communal life; of work as against contemplation; of inner conviction and spiritual spontaneity on the one hand, and hierarchical authority and the constraints of dogma and the priesthood on the other. As it evolved, Byzantine monasticism had to grapple with these questions, which it never fully resolved because the terms in which they are posed altered from one century to the next. The answers reached between 450 and the beginning of the seventh century left an especially strong imprint on the century that followed.

Tenacity of civic values and urban realities

The cultural and political values of the Greek Mediterranean world had for centuries past been those of the city: gregariousness, as practised by men, ease of social intercourse, discussion of political and literary topics, material comforts, such as piped running water

Woman with pitcher. Detail from a floor mosaic in the Great Palace, Constantinople, fifth century.

Man's head. Church of St George, Salonika, detail of dome mosaic, fifth century.

The Empress Theodora. Detail from choir mosaic, San Vitalis, Ravenna, sixth century.

Virgin and Child. Mosaic on a gold ground in the apse of St Sophia, Constantinople, ninth century.

for drinking and bathing, and the market, with its provisions catering to the demand for wheaten bread and biscuits, for olive oil, wine, fresh vegetables, meat or fish. We can therefore begin by defining as towns those places where such amenities continued to exist down to the beginning of the seventh century. Our evidence is contained in the historical sources, in the eulogies of towns composed by professional rhetors, in numerous inscriptions, in the decrees and sermons through which the Church of the bishops, itself quintessentially urban, endeavoured to Christianise the towns, and in the tales told of holy men; to these can be added the images furnished by certain mosaics, and the results obtained from the excavation of urban sites such as Sardis, Ephesus, Apamea and Antioch, better known to us than the capital, where the fact of continuous habitation has made any real archaeological investigation impossible. It is nevertheless difficult to propose a league table of fifth-century towns, because of the dearth of statistical criteria and also because the documentary sources are as varying in character as are the reasons for urban prosperity and growth. From a cultural and commercial standpoint, Antioch and Alexandria are towns of equal importance; the attraction of Jerusalem is solely religious, though that is saying a great deal; and a town as small as Corcyrus of Cilicia is revealed by its cemetery inscriptions, which are careful to indicate the trade of the deceased, as a hive of activity. There is nevertheless some truth in the claim that the age stands out as an age of 'great cities', in the sense that above a certain threshold urban life takes on an entirely different character. This is true above all of Constantinople, no ordinary town or even the largest town among many, but the capital, and in every way unique.

The Antique town lives on

With these reservations, it is still true to say that the traditional picture of the provincial city is the one to emerge from our sources: here are the warm baths constantly fed with hot water, where unescorted boys ran the risk of amorous advances; the fountains; the squares, where the statues and inscriptions celebrating the emperors and other personages were arrayed; the arcaded streets, where makeshift booths of wood and canvas, perpetual fire hazards, were set up between the columns; the taverns where a meal and a woman could be found; the cheap cookshops and takeaways where rumours circulated and riots sometimes broke out; the theatre, whose lascivious and comic spectacles aroused the enthusiasm of the populace, the disgust of the cultivated and the hostility of the Church, but where the provincial governor came to be cheered or booed by a public with little other chance to make its voice heard; here sometimes, as at Caesarea in Palestine, there is a hippodrome, in imitation of the capital; and lastly there is the basilica, that vast rectangular hall, whose architectural form predated its adoption for Christian worship, where business was transacted and law suits heard, and where the governor, representative of the central power, might have his seat. The churches, some inside the town, some in the suburbs, encouraged a new sociability, which is however merely a continuation of something older; people flocked to them to attend services and hear sermons, and sallied forth from them in procession, or sometimes as a riotous mob. Beggars camped at their entrances. In the fifth

Scene from everyday life in a provincial city: two diners in a cheap eating-house having a discussion. Fifth-century mosaic depicting a street in Antioch (Antioch, Museum of Antiquities).

century the first urban monasteries appeared and the charitable establishments which began to be founded at the end of the preceding century became more widespread.

The Roman government had found it easy to transform the civic assemblies of notables, which were made up of resident landowners and were responsible for taxation, into provincial town councils. The cities had their own sources of income: rent from properties located in their territory or from urban plots, let out for example to stall-holders, and from tolls. Nevertheless it was customary for the most important needs to be met by the municipal magistrates themselves, whose offices, far from being paid or even venal, depended on the wealth, liberality and appetite for fame of their holders. Actions such as the building of a bath or the relief of a famine would be duly commemorated by the erection of a statue in the main square, with an inscription hailing the magistrate in question as 'father of the city' or 'benefactor' (*euergetes*). The Roman State had taken over and adapted this system, delegating to the municipal councils (*curiae*) tasks such as the upkeep of roads, the provision of the army and the collection of all fiscal levies, for which the members were made individually and collectively responsible. Under the Severan emperors the system became noticeably more rigid, while membership of the *curia* became hereditary, both trends being in line with the military pressures and centralising tendencies which marked the first third of the third century. This policy could not fail to have social consequences, which were already clearly visible in the fourth century.

True enough, the *curia* was able to resist the central power through the forces of inertia and solidarity. The officials appointed by the central government to supervise council affairs inevitably ended up being recruited from among the curials themselves. In similar fashion, the councils placed themselves under 'patronage'. And the patron in his turn derived profit, or at any rate prestige, from this equivocal role, which although perfectly legal bypassed the normal judicial and fiscal processes. It was possible for the emperor himself to be patron of a town council. Very often, however, the role devolved on one of the council's own 'principals', whose existence bears witness to an increasing social differentiation within the *curia* at this period. The burden of municipal responsibilities brought impoverishment to the least affluent, who either did their best or fled to the estate and service of a great landowner. At the other end of the scale a select group of 'principals' emerged – 'the top ten'. Lastly, the wealthiest of all sought to break out of the local frame, judging it too humdrum with its boring round of municipal duties, by gaining entry to the senate of Constantinople or the upper reaches of public office. The urban bourgeoisie, meanwhile, resented the admission to town councils of persons whose fortunes were derived from commerce rather than the land. It is thus possible to discern elements of decline in municipal institutions. It should be stressed, however, that the process was a very gradual one, even though the first signs were already visible towards the end of the fourth century.

The central power was represented in the largest cities by the provincial governor, in secondary cities at the very least by the tax office. The governor's powers were essentially of a judicial and administrative nature. Governors as a rule were not natives of the province, where they were forbidden to acquire property, and they seem to have been anxious to conform to the old stereotype, since numerous inscriptions from provinces throughout the East testify to their munificence as builders. This activity is placed in a less glorious light by a series of laws forbidding them to plunder marble columns from other buildings for their own works or to attach their name to projects begun by their predecessors. But there is more to this than a thirst for the traditional prestige. If governors kept a careful watch on food supplies, the reason was their perpetual fear of riots. But they very quickly joined the ranks of the true rulers of provincial society. Here they rubbed shoulders with more recent arrivals, who were nevertheless of primary importance, namely the bishops.

Emergence of the urban episcopate

In the beginning, the episcopacy was not necessarily based in the towns, but there can be no denying that from the fourth to the sixth centuries the urban episcopate enjoyed its golden age. Even towns of secondary importance might be served at this period by bishops who came from the families of provincial notables or were the sons of highly-placed officials, and who shared the Classical culture common to everyone in that milieu. It is significant that the fourth century and the first half of the fifth should have witnessed the brilliant if ephemeral flowering of bishops with great literary accomplishments, authors of letters on administrative or spiritual matters, of polemical and theological treatises which **139** demonstrate their training in Classical rhetoric and philosophy, notwithstanding an already discernible monastic tinge: Basil of Caesarea (*c.* 330–79), perhaps the most important for the Byzantine Church because of the richness of his contributions to canon law, Gregory of Nazianzus (*c.* 330–95), briefly bishop of Constantinople (380–1), and Basil's brother, Gregory of Nyssa (*c.* 335–94), expositor of Christian Platonism, were thoroughly rooted in the fourth century but remained permanent landmarks for the future. They cast a glow not only over Cappadocia, the most quintessentially Byzantine province, but also over that fleeting and privileged moment when Hellenism was already Christian and had not ceased to be Antique. Their contemporary, John Chrysostom or 'Golden-Mouth' (344/54–407) was from Antioch, where his father held the most senior military rank of *magister militum*; and he spoke for the church of Antioch, alongside Bishop Flavian in the years between 386 and 397. At that date he became archbishop of the capital, where he entered into conflict with the palace and above all with the empress Eudocia. He died in exile in 407, in the depths of Cappadocia. John Chrysostom typified another aspect of this unique cultural juncture, the employment of all-powerful rhetoric to vindicate the all-powerful nature of the priesthood. In this way he earned his reputation as defender of the Antiochenes, preacher of Christian standards, and public judge, in this sense, of his imperial opponents. Synesius, bishop of Cyrene (*c.* 370–*c.* 413) cut the same social and cultural figure in his remote corner of the Libyan Pentapolis as his Cappadocian brethren in their sphere. The series concludes with another Antiochene, Theodoret of Cyr (*c.* 393–*c.* 466). But in his *Church History*, his treatises against heretics and pagans, and his edifying tales of holy men in northern Syria, where his impoverished diocese was situated, Theodoret already gives the impression of a man more at home in the study than on the public platform, and it becomes harder to penetrate to the Classical culture beneath the episcopal persona.

Chosen by popular acclaim and experienced in worldly affairs, bishops of this period thus took their place quite naturally within the civic system while combining in a novel way certain of its functions. In one sense they were successors to the rhetor, the town's traditional spokesman, and they took a growing share in the direction of affairs, especially in towns of secondary importance. Maintenance of food supplies, upkeep of the town walls, interventions with the fisc on behalf of their clergy or of their diocese, and arbitration in law suits, which Justinian was to make statutory, all required their attention. Like the other notables, bishops also went in for building, naturally in order to meet their specific needs. All of this activity continued into the sixth century, as we know from inscriptions, and in the larger cities developed on an even grander scale. Even the *Life* of John the Almoner, patriarch of Alexandria from 610 to 619, composed by one of his circle, Leontios, bishop of Neapolis, still paints an astonishingly vigorous picture of the Church's activities, which included the conduct of overseas trade. In the Syriac and Coptic world the pre-eminence of monastic leaders asserted itself at an earlier date and with greater profundity than in the Greek cities. In the latter, lastly, the effectiveness of episcopal power also depended on its success in facing up to new social needs as they began to declare themselves within an apparently unchanging social framework.

An urban 'people', reflection of Antiquity

Everything that has just been said about the prevailing powers in this first Byzantine society seems to show the town dominating over the countryside, source of its nourishment. In other words, the seat of power was urban, and the tribute it levied came from the land. And it is true that the axis of political power in this first phase of Byzantium defined itself in these terms. A more complex situation is revealed, however, when we try to visualise how the economic life of this society functioned in practice.

Once again we have to begin with the organisation of the Antique city. While the urban landowners jointly made up the *curia*, the urban producers of goods and services, and those engaged in overseas commerce, were organised in *collegia* according to their crafts or trades. These associations had a long history, since the associative principle can be seen as the basic building block of Classical Mediterranean society. Here it will suffice to pick up that history in the time of the Severi, when the system of delegating public services as a fiscal obligation, in the way already described, was made explicit. In the early part of the present century, this system evoked from historians who were disposed to trust in the limitless opportunities open to private enterprise, page upon page deploring the merciless constraints which supposedly chained each member of society in the late empire to his original station. In fact the system was far less rigid than it appears. First, it is by no means certain that enrolment in a *collegium* was obligatory, since, as we have seen, for every constraint there was a corresponding privilege. Next, it was not really practicable for a son to secede from his father's guild, or from his own. In any case, as in the *curiae*, the rule of collective responsibility applied more to properties than to persons. The workshops run by the State, such as the mints, the arms factories, and the textile mills which produced army uniforms and the purple silks destined for the court, have to be placed in a different category. Conditions for the workers in these establishments, which are to be found not only at Constantinople but also at Antioch, Cyzicus and in other places besides, were truly harsh, not far removed from slavery.

Yet on the other hand the various sources all point to the existence of an apparently independent urban artisanate, of a family rather than an individual character, to judge from tomb inscriptions which couple father with son or brother with brother. How much this artisanal activity contributed to the empire's global output is open to question. It is noticeable that consumer goods easily predominate over items such as tools, which would have aided further production. From this it can be concluded that most of the implements used in farming were made in the countryside, and that output here was generally low. Although craftsmen produced between them a great range of everyday goods, the output of each was highly specialised: confectioners would make only one kind of cake, shoemakers only one kind of shoe. The production of luxury articles, for example the superbly crafted ivory caskets intended as wedding gifts, was also highly specialised. In fact, for evidence of economic activity in towns, and to a lesser extent even in villages and the countryside, we need to look at the building sector, the particular indicator which is of specific value in regard to societies of this type, as will be apparent in the period following 450.

It is true that in the largest cities, Alexandria, Antioch, and above all Constantinople, great mercantile fortunes could be made, in particular by shippers and merchants engaged in long-distance trade, importers of spices and raw silk: the sea-routes through the Red Sea and the Persian Gulf were known from as long ago as the land-route through Central Asia and Iran which brought silk from China to the Mediterranean. The profits from long-distance trade, above all by sea, were commensurate with the risks run by those who undertook or underwrote it. There are also the 'silver-merchants', dealers in precious metal, who combined the functions of assayer, money-changer and manufacturer of objects which received an imperial hallmark and ended up in private treasuries and monasteries alike. But the balance of political power was not affected by these fortunes, nor did they enter into the mainstream circulation of goods.

Integral to the constitution of the Antique city had been a common people, the Greek *demos*. Its role was to make its voice heard – in the most literal sense – in approval or disapproval, in demand, in an electoral or at least in an acclamatory capacity: its roar, in short, had the force of legitimation. To this one political category belonged all townsmen who were not part of the *curia*, from the great merchants and most skilled craftsmen down to those whom a law of 312 exempted from all fiscal obligations because of their penury. The history of the common people in cities of the East from the fifth to the seventh century thus proceeds at two levels, political and social, which the historian has difficulty in keeping apart. The people traditionally enacted its political role in urban settings privileged for the purpose: the theatre at Antioch, the hippodrome at Constantinople and elsewhere, but also the public squares; to these must be added the newly-privileged setting of the church, where the body of the faithful responded to the preacher, and from which it might erupt to demonstrate outside. These popular demonstrations, while violent, in fact adhered to a repertory of gestures which were tantamount to a code of violence: vandalism of public statues, stone-throwing, rhythmic chanting. After 450–60 the outbreaks became more serious and the code crystallised around the rivalries of the Blue and Green factions, which were fought out in the racing-stables, streets and neighbourhoods.

In an effort to shed light on these rivalries we must digress for a moment and revert to the hippodrome at Constantinople, whose cosmic symbolism, and that of the races run there, has already been touched on. Of the four racing colours initially inherited from Rome and sported by the competitors, only the Blues and the Greens were still current. Truth to tell, we do not know what these colours signified to contemporaries, which makes it impossible to say why men gave their allegiance to one faction rather than the other. As a group, the adherents of the colours were a mixed bunch. Primarily of course they were recruited from those who worked in the racing-stables and from all the people who gravitated around the spectacle, such as coachmen, but also dancers and actors. All this gave rise to uncontrollable excitement which was a danger to public order. This is borne out by the fruitlessly applied policing measures, the constant brawling in the hippodrome, not to mention the small lead plaques bearing magic spells, which were intended to bewitch a particular opponent. On the other hand, it is possible that the Blues and the Greens corresponded to divisions of opinion, or perhaps social divisions; but if so, which? For all the ink that has

The Hippodrome, symbolising with its games and its factions the socio-political life of the capital, is shown here on a fragment of a fifth-century ivory diptych. The obelisk is visible in the centre; the horse race is the gift of the Lampadi family, seen above in a box (Brescia, Museo Cristiano).

flowed on the subject, the question still lacks a precise answer. The Blues are taken to represent the palace, the higher echelons of the civil service and Chalcedonian orthodoxy, the Greens to represent the city, heresy where applicable, and a markedly anti-semitic tendency.

Between 460 and 610 the factions, or more probably their henchmen, carried their brawls into the streets, and from 530 onwards they descended into crime. But the causes of this rise in tension are to be sought in the social history of the sixth century, and more precisely in that of the towns.

The objectives of the urban riots enumerated in the historical sources for the first half of the fifth century should warn us not to take too simplistic a view. Undeniably there were sometimes food riots in the capital. They happened in 409, 412 and again in 431, directed against those held responsible: in 412 the rioters burned down the house of the urban prefect, Monaxius; in 431 the emperor himself, to quote a contemporary source, was 'pelted with stones thrown at him by the starving populace'. But it seems that individuals who were popular with the mob could equally provide occasion for riots. For example, when John Chrysostom eventually paid the price for his outspoken moral criticism of the empress and was condemned in 403 by the Synod of the Oak, the city rose in defence of its archbishop; and when in 404 he took the road to exile his supporters burned down St Sophia. It seems therefore that religious agitation could be precipitated by motives other than the passion for theology so often attributed by historians, for no very obvious reason, to the Byzantine man in the street. The brawling between Arians and Orthodox or between Christians and Jews, sometimes ending in deaths, is probably an indication of the growing importance of the confessional factor in building up the consensus which early Byzantine society, like any other society, was striving to achieve. And this factor was later to become dominant.

It is easy to see that these demonstrations, sometimes successful and always feared had a genuinely political function in a society which had not lost the Antique habit of identifying public life with town life. This makes the social composition of the urban populace an object of still greater curiosity. We are aware of it as a definite entity, or rather as two entities, one Antique and the other Christian, since in the first half of the fifth century the distinction was still visible. The common people of Antiquity were those who benefited from the public bread rations (*politikoi*) dispensed at Constantinople and Alexandria, and from the remnants of traditional liberality. They were also the members of the urban militias, the 'youths' who mounted guard on the city walls, and who at Constantinople appear to have helped to build the Theodosian fortifications, and lastly they were the activists in the factions – possibly while also manning the militias. An urban underclass, maybe, from the petty traders down to the street urchins, but clearly not powerless. Its vitality extended, furthermore, beyond its assigned constitutional role. Writing towards the end of the fourth century, Libanius depicts the instigators of the riots at Antioch, and the 'three hundred wolves of the theatre' in particular, as the urban dregs, the hearthless and homeless, no part of the *polis*. However Classical the formulation, the ready availability of rabble-rousers who represented, in a literal sense, 'the townspeople', lends it a certain substance; we shall be reminded of it when we see that the swelling of the towns after 460 coincided with the increased frequency of riots.

The scourge of poverty and the monks' intervention

In Christian homilies of the late fourth century there are already increasing allusions to the need in towns for charitable assistance and the relief of suffering, while in contemporary legislation the connection was made, with reservations that are not our present concern, between the delegation to the Church of responsibility for dispensing charity and the fiscal immunities granted to the clergy and to ecclesiastical property. The poor, the homeless, the sick and infirm, the beggars and aged were brought together within an original and perceptive definition of poverty as an incapacity to provide for oneself. The response to their needs, also original, was an establishment which provided the poor with shelter and where necessary with medical attention. Unknown to Classical Antiquity, despite the prevalence of medical skills, the hospice and its counterpart the hospital were creations of the fourth century and hence represent a major innovation of the later period. Establishments of this kind in private households, the product of individual initiative, are already found in the fourth century. The first example of an ecclesiastical initiative is the hospital provided by Eustathius, bishop of Sebaste in Armenia, from 356 to his death in 380. In this as in other ways Eustathius gave a lead to Basil of Caesarea, who in 370 became bishop of his native city and created what might be described as a hospital complex, the Basiliad, by the city gates. Each made arrangements for their establishment to be served by monks, and this feature became integral to the model, which was thus urban from its very beginnings. Houses of charity staffed by monks then started to multiply, especially in the capital, during the first half of the fifth century. It would be hard to ignore the cultural significance of this development, whereby this Christian institution opened its doors to people for whom there was no place in the normal categories of contemporary society. It will be recalled that the Church was already providing something of the kind for the disadvantaged in the Christian community – virgins and widows for example – in the second and third centuries. But the role played by circumstance is not to be underestimated. From about 360 the poor in need of help seem to have been on the increase, in step with the growing size of the towns, whose attraction, particularly in the case of the largest, became greater than ever. People fled there to escape official exactions, oppressive landlords, and the unjust sentences of provincial governors, or out of hunger in time of famine, in the hope of eking out a living from the traditional handouts of the notables or from the new Christian charity. The main centres of attraction were once again Constantinople, Jerusalem, Antioch and Alexandria, though obviously for differing reasons. There may even have been some deterioration in the health of the population, since the slow but steady increase in numbers was not matched by a corresponding expansion of resources. Specific illnesses followed a rhythm of their own: leprosy, hitherto dormant, made a reappearance in the last third of the fourth century; the disturbances attributed to demonic possession become everyday occurrences, and those afflicted were indeed 'invalids', unfit for regular work. Curiously, the sources relating to the years 400 to 450 show no evidence of a growth in criminal activity; that came later, in the time of Justinian. All we know is that 'able-bodied beggars' were forbidden to reside in the capital, with what success it is impossible to say. Above all, the distress of the poor assisted or deserving to be assisted by charity conferred an entirely new dimension on the urban population.

The fundamental incompatibility between the monastic model and urban values has already been mentioned. But here again the reality exceeds the model. Monks irrupted into towns as shock troops in the doctrinal conflicts, at Antioch as much as at Alexandria. In 438, the 'band of forty', in its descent from Samosata towards the Holy Places in the retinue of Barsauma, destroyed the synagogues of towns on the way, before decimating the throng of Jews assembled at Jerusalem for the Feast of Tabernacles. Alexander the Acoemete ('the sleepless') was expelled from Antioch, before arriving in the capital around 425 to head a monastic movement of which charity was only one aspect. Another monastic concern was asylum: monasteries admitted the socially distressed, runaway slaves and insolvent debtors, for example, to the refuge which the Council of Ephesus in 431 prescribed as the enclosure between the monastic building and the outer wall. The State accepted this in principle, but was at pains to preserve its rights. Heretical subversion, by contrast, admitted of no compromises. For in the fifth century the antithesis between monasticism and the city still overlapped in part the antithesis between regulation and liberty. The monk came to town in order to sacrifice himself, according to the pious narratives. At the opposite pole, heretical subversion found embodiment in the roving bands, often of both sexes, which mingled with the world, that is to say the town. The first examples of monasticism at Constantinople were not always of orthodox complexion. In any case, they give the appearance of having been independent and informal. A rule in the Western sense was lacking, apart from an ascetic code whose elements went back to Basil of Caesarea, and discipline was even more lax than in some of the desert establishments. Sacerdotal involvement was small or non-existent. In the town as in the desert, the monk stayed outside the normal governmental and social categories. This accounts for the vigour with which the monastic 'force' intervened in theological conflicts, for the accompanying violence, for its association with the poor, and for its aggressive stance in regard to the episcopate, for example towards John Chrysostom in the capital. As a rule, moreover, monks came from a rustic background, in the cultural as well as the social sense. It was through them that the Coptic or Syrian world broke into the civilised milieu of Alexandria or Antioch.

In this sense the monks of the early fifth century, like the poor, can be said to have introduced an entirely new element which irremediably altered the old conception of the 'people' as a component of civic order. Far from being encased in rules, the urban monasteries of this period were open and accessible. The monks sometimes lived in small groups of two or three, in a manner comparable with the fourth-century ascetics who went on living with their families, or more precisely, since only men were involved and the family framework was absent, with similar groups in the desert. All this explains the increasing severity of the laws which attempted to check the free movement of these men from one town to another. The Council of Chalcedon, in 451, forbade them to wander and subjected the accessibility and activities of their establishments to the surveillance of the local bishop – evidently without success, since an attempt was made by Justinianic law to banish them from towns completely. Meanwhile, the first half of the fifth century clearly reveals the existence of an urban face to the monastic Church which we saw developing in the desert, and no less clearly reveals the antagonism between this Church and that of the bishops, which will only be resolved, through the triumph of the former, when we reach the ninth century.

4 The empire in its glory: mid-fifth to mid-seventh centuries

The great epoch which begins with the accession of Leo I in 457 and ends with the death of Justinian in 565 does not owe its coherence to the reigning emperors. It forms one of those exceptionally rich periods when events and innovations multiply, when the mass of more or less latent social and cultural potentialities come to fruition, when the society concerned seems, in short, to have a unique superabundance of men and resources which could account for the features just described. The first stage of this epoch lasted until the accession in 518 of Justin I, whose reign did no more than usher in the great reign of the century, that of Justinian I, who succeeded him in 527. An examination of the period highlights first the mechanisms of imperial succession, which in their own fashion illustrate a sharper definition of the supreme power, and also the new posture adopted by the empire of Byzantium from the time of Leo I. We see the West becoming a frontier region, a possible objective of foreign policy. But Persia was likewise asserting itself, and Byzantium continued to encounter its adversary on the land-routes and seaways of the East. But successive emperors relied, as had been the case for centuries, either on the Balkans in the north, or on the provinces of Syria, Palestine and Egypt in the south, a south which began, it should be remembered, on the southern borders of Asia Minor, in the mountains of Isauria. At the heart of this choice between north and south lay the 'sovereign city' of Constantinople and its populace, whose political role was mentioned in the preceding chapter.

The attraction of the east

The reigns of Leo I and of his son-in-law and successor Zeno witnessed the elimination of the problem posed by the Germanic armies to the empire of the East, and more specifically to the palace on the one hand and in Thrace on the other, with the result that yet another difference was opened up between the empire and the West.

Isaurian disorder

In 457, when a successor had to be found for Marcian, the most powerful figure in the empire was perhaps the 'master of the soldiers', Aspar, an Alan of Arian persuasion. His

Sixth-century marble bust, probably of the empress Ariadne. The double row of pearls mounted on a cap is certainly typical of imperial headgear. Daughter of Leo I, Ariadne had her two successive husbands, Zeno and Anastasius, placed on the throne (Paris, Louvre).

father Ardaburius, consul in 427, and Aspar himself, consul in 434, had been Theodosius II's leading generals, and although the Alans were people of the steppe, the two men had intervened with the emperor on behalf of the German *federate* troops, professional soldiers and Arians like themselves. And it was Aspar who determined the choice of Leo, a Thracian from his entourage, as emperor. To counter-balance the German troops, Leo began to recruit as soldiers those 'barbarians' of the interior, the Isaurians. He it was who created the new regiment of palace guards known as the *excubitores* ('those who sleep at the door'), composed of Thracians, Illyrians and Isaurians, which plays an important role in later centuries. In 466 or 467 an Isaurian chieftain, who took the Greek name Zeno, married Leo's daughter, Ariadne. In 471, when Aspar and his son (another Ardaburius) were assassinated at the palace, Thrace was ravaged once more by one of their kinsmen, Theodoric Strabo ('squinter'), who had the backing of the federate Ostrogothic army installed there since 454, and who became in turn *magister militum* in 473. Zeno, however, by playing the Ostrogothic leaders off against each other, later succeeded in deflecting their armies toward Italy.

In the absence of a marriage linking him to the reigning family, Leo took the novel step of adding to the acclamations by army and people the gesture of coronation by the patriarch of Constantinople, recently placed by the Council of Chalcedon (451) on a parity with the

149

see of Rome. A familial pattern was already beginning to take shape around the throne, which included succession through the female line. The marriage of one of Leo's daughters to a son of Aspar was followed by the marriage of the eldest, Ariadne, to Zeno, who in 474 succeeded Leo. Leo's widow, Verina, interrupted Zeno's reign in 475, persuading first her lover and then her brother, Basiliscus, to seize power; but Basiliscus in turn had to contend first with his wife and then with his nephew, her lover. Zeno then regained power in 476, and remained on the throne until his death in 491.

The elimination of the Ostrogothic problem from the Balkans and the disappearance in 476 of the empire in the West can be seen to favour a new balance of power, based openly on the East, in which the Isaurian highlanders held a place whose importance is best, but not solely, illustrated by the rise of Zeno and his entourage. The turbulence of the Isaurians had been demonstrated as far back as the second century, and similarly their chronic insubordination. In these respects, the second half of the fifth century appears to have been a peak period. Even before Zeno's accession, that is to say between 467 and 470, there is mention of their acts of violence at Rhodes in the form of kidnappings and murders, while the common people of the capital bombarded them with stones and slew many out of hand.

Doctrinal rifts

Above all, Zeno scored by playing on the specifically eastern and provincial character of monophysitism. The confessional rift opened up at Chalcedon now begins to take clear shape as a rift between the capital and the eastern provinces. At Constantinople the populace was Chalcedonian. The advent to power of Basiliscus and his monophysite position sparked off a conflict in which the monks and people of the capital, mobilised round their patriarch, Acacius, confronted the troops – and we need not doubt that they were monks – of the patriarch of Alexandria, Timothy Aelurus. Meanwhile, however, monophysitism was making headway in the eastern provinces, in Syria, and above all in Egypt, its birthplace. In 482, Zeno and the patriarch Acacius put forward a 'formula of unity' (*henotikon*), which was accepted neither by Rome (which led to a rupture in 484), nor by the Chalcedonians in the empire, nor for that matter by the monophysites. But at least it demonstrated that the emperor could count on the support in doctrinal matters of the patriarch of Constantinople. This in turn exposed, in more brutal fashion than before, the problem of the power relationships between the emperor and the patriarchates and between the patriarchates themselves, a problem which was far from being solved. The patriarch of Alexandria, Peter Mongus, tried at first to steer a course between the imperial *henotikon* and the monophysite pressure exerted by Egypt's many thousand monks. His own sympathies, however, were with the latter, and in the eyes of the masses he confirmed himself, in the years following 482, as the real power in Egypt, against whom the governor, the representative of imperial authority, was powerless to act. Around 490, relations between the patriarchates of Constantinople and Alexandria were severed, while monophysitism also claimed the see of Antioch, where Peter the Fuller, who died in 488, had become patriarch for the third time in 485. On the other hand, Zeno succeeded in closing the school of Edessa, centre of Nestorian teaching, whose teachers then emigrated to Persia. The religious divide thus became a little more clear-cut.

Disturbances in central Palestine stemmed from a revolt by the Samaritans, who as a people had remained faithful down the centuries to a Pentateuch more or less identical with that of the Jews but transcribed in a different alphabet, and to a holy place which they located on Mount Gerizim. Their main centre, Neapolis (Nablus), had in 456/7 been the scene of a massacre of monophysite monks by Samaritans and Chalcedonians which was instigated by the patriarch of Jerusalem. A Samaritan revolt which broke out at Caesarea and at Nablus around 484 was accompanied by an attempt at usurpation, which was repeated in 529. In that year a decree suppressing the Samaritan cult provoked a rising in the countryside, which came out in massive support of the Samaritans and swept a certain Julianus to power. The revolt spread to two urban centres, Nablus and Scythopolis (Beth-Shean), where there was a mixed population and the rebels set fire to properties and churches. According to Procopius 100,000 people perished in the revolt; in any event the landowners of the region, Christians to a man, were deprived of their peasants and left to face the fisc alone. The members of Palestine's numerous Jewish population supported the Samaritan movement. Later on, in 555, both groups fell on the Christians at Caesarea, killing among others the governor and demolishing the churches.

When Zeno died of an illness in 491, his widow chose as emperor a palace official already in his sixties, the silentiary Anastasius, and took him as her husband. His first action was to embark on a war to subdue Isauria, which dragged on until 498. The hour of the Isaurian ascendancy seemed to be over but it was to return. The fact that Anastasius was born at Dyrrhachium (Durazzo), on the fringe of the Latin-speaking world, seems however to have been of lesser account than his previous career as an administrator and the time he had spent in Egypt. While he reigned the imperial power remained emphatically in the monophysite camp. In religious matters he relied on Philoxenus, bishop of Hierapolis in the patriarchate of Antioch, a Syriac-speaker and one of the great exponents of monophysite doctrine, and still more on Severus, originally from Sozopolis in Pisidia, a Greek by culture and language, whose contribution and influence are important in the history of Christian doctrine, and who in 512 became patriarch of Antioch. In short, Anastasius looked toward Syria, to the extent of welcoming Severan monks to the capital in 508 and appointing Marinus, a Syrian from Apamea, praetorian prefect in 512. His relations with the patriarch of the capital were consistent with this. Euphemius, having exacted the emperor's promise to respect the beliefs affirmed at Chalcedon as the price of coronation, was deposed in 496. His successor Macedonius, who adhered, as did the emperor in theory, to the official line of the *henotikon*, eventually suffered the same fate: in 511 he was sent into exile. In this way Anastasius drew down on himself the open and violent hostility of the populace in the capital, pro-Chalcedonian and fiercely loyal to their patriarch. At the empire's other pole the emperor's partialities were not calculated to win him support. In 512, while in the capital the people rose in revolt against the intrusion of a monophysite formula into the liturgy and sacked the house of the prefect Marinus, Chalcedonian bishops in Illyricum made an appeal to the pope. In 513, another sensitive area of the empire, Thrace, saw the

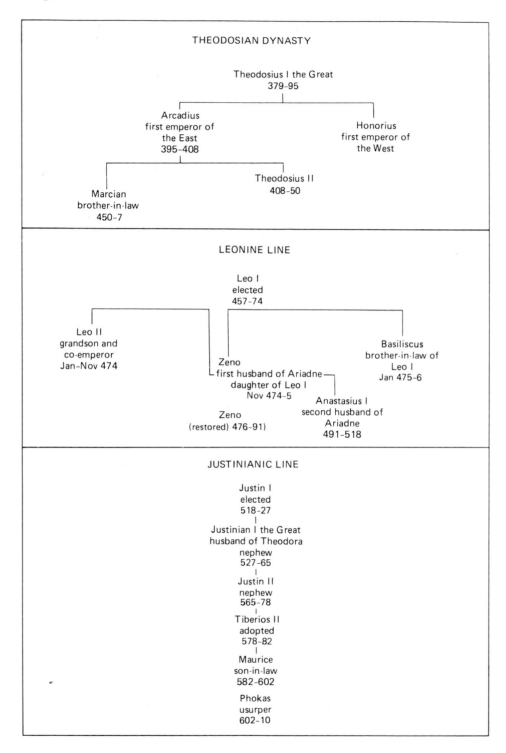

THEODOSIAN DYNASTY

Theodosius I the Great
379-95

Arcadius
first emperor of
the East
395-408

Honorius
first emperor of
the West

Marcian
brother-in-law
450-7

Theodosius II
408-50

LEONINE LINE

Leo I
elected
457-74

Leo II
grandson and
co-emperor
Jan-Nov 474

Zeno
first husband of Ariadne
daughter of Leo I
Nov 474-5

Basiliscus
brother-in-law of
Leo I
Jan 475-6

Zeno
(restored) 476-91)

Anastasius I
second husband of
Ariadne
491-518

JUSTINIANIC LINE

Justin I
elected
518-27

Justinian I the Great
husband of Theodora
nephew
527-65

Justin II
nephew
565-78

Tiberios II
adopted
578-82

Maurice
son-in-law
582-602

Phokas
usurper
602-10

outbreak of Vitalian's rebellion. Count of the federates and kinsman to patriarch Macedonius, Vitalian rallied behind him the discontented barbarian soldiers of his command, their numbers augmented by peasants of the region, and made overtures to Rome. On three occasions his army advanced as far as the capital. Initially victorious, and able in 514 to dictate terms to the imperial authorities, he suffered defeat in 515. But in spite of this setback and the repression which followed, a section of the Balkan episcopate persisted in its opposition to monophysitism, supported at a discreet distance by Rome.

It is interesting to speculate whether Anastasius opted for monophysitism as the result of personal conviction and the intellectual arguments of theologians such as Philoxenus and Severus, or whether he merely went along with a creed emerging as the dominant culture of the eastern provinces, which would imply that he judged those provinces to be more important than the approval of the capital. But since the inner life of emperors in that remote society is perhaps even more of a closed book to us than that of the poor, the question must remain unanswered. In any event, at the end of his reign, the eastern patriarchates were united in their separation from Rome. But the attitude of the ecumenical patriarchate was guarded, that of Alexandria defiantly monophysite, and in Syria the victory of monophysitism was not complete: in Palestine it had made no headway, since the mass of the population was not even Christian but remained predominantly Jewish or Samaritan, with the consequence that Palestinian monasticism, perhaps originally more heterodox, had little difficulty in upholding the Chalcedonian position. But wherever we look there is discord, in which monks are everywhere protagonists, in Syria even fighting on both sides. Everywhere, too, save in the special case of Palestine, or of individuals such as Severus, it becomes apparent that the doctrinal cleavage coincides with linguistic, and therefore to some extent social divisions, though precisely how far remains to be seen. Coptic or Syrian culture is synonymous with monophysitism, Hellenic with the beliefs of Chalcedon: the map of the future is already drawn.

Predeceased by his wife, Anastasius died in 518. We find the choice of successor once again being decided inside the palace, before receiving formal confirmation first by the Senate, then by the people and army, lastly by the patriarch. The man who seized power in this way was the count of the *excubitores*, Justin, a native of Skoplje in Latin-speaking Illyricum, already well into his sixties. He had no children by his consort Lupicina, crowned under the name Euphemia, and so almost immediately associated his nephew, Justinian, born about 482, with him as co-ruler. As it happens, the same pattern recurred in 565, again in the absence of imperial progeny: that is to say, Justinian was succeeded by his nephew, Justin II. So the succession, although lateral, remained within the family. And here again an empress was to the fore, not in the sense of determining the succession, since she died before her husband in 548, but because of her part in the government of the empire and the maintenance of its equilibrium. This empress, Theodora, daughter of the capital, daughter of a bear-keeper in the hippodrome, seems once to have been a *scenica*, a show-girl, in other words a prostitute, and hence traditionally ineligible for a man such as Justinian, whose office placed him in the category of the *illustres*. The law enacted in 520–4 which relaxed this prohibition was manifestly designed to permit their union. Theodora's early

153

adventures had taken her all over the East, and in a manner she represented the East, its monophysite sympathies included, in the conjugal, shortly to be imperial, partnership, while Justin I and Justinian, uncle and nephew, adhered to a Chalcedonian position, for what reasons it is again impossible to guess.

Justinian: the splendour

With the accession of Justinian the curtain rises on the second act, more dramatic and more spectacular than the first half of this great epoch, and undeniably more famous. Everyone is familiar with the imperial silhouettes, flanked by court dignitaries, in the procession depicted on the walls of St Vitalis at Ravenna, and equally with the whiff of scandal attaching to the name of Theodora, though it should be pointed out that her participation in supreme power seems less extraordinary when restored to the context of the imperial reigns as a whole. In actuality, and precisely because of the extent of Justinian's power, the period yields an abundance of narrative and iconographic sources, of which received opinions about the imperial couple are merely a false epitome. The process starts with an official historian, Procopius of Caesarea, a pointed and impassioned critic who after spending many years recording his sovereign's wars and building exploits was goaded for some reason, around 550, into writing the *Secret History*, which contains the celebrated account of Theodora's childhood and teenage years. The work also casts a shadow over other personages, including Belisarius, the great general, and John of Cappadocia, praetorian prefect from 531 to 541. In the same way, the praetorian prefecture is also the subject of the third book of the treatise *On the Magistracies of the Roman People*, composed by John the Lydian. He was born in about 490 and attached for many years to the staff of the praetorian prefect in Constantinople, in which, in order to attack John of Cappadocia, this virtuous but unimportant official depicts scenes of violence and obscenity.

The century of Justinian

From these and other sources the circle around Justinian and Theodora comes to life as individual personalities. Furthermore – and this again is characteristic of the epoch – the mass of surviving literature, hagiography apart, emanates from the capital's ruling and administrative classes, whereas that of the late fourth century came from the milieu of the rhetors and the urban bishops. As a result, the sources not only contain a record of events and governmental measures, but also reveal the constitution of an imperial model whose characteristics, evolving since the time of Constantine, now became fixed for the future. In this double perspective the monument of Justinianic legislation stands out as a prime source, and brings into view another of the epoch's great figures, the jurist Tribonian. He was editor-in-chief of the *Code of Justinian*, published in 529, and of the *Digest*, published in 533, a revised compilation of Classical Roman law, declared from henceforth untouchable. Thereafter the legislator's will was expressed in 'Novels', laws issued independently; the reasons adduced for them and the resulting judgments determined developments in the capital, the provinces and the conquered territories. If the *Code*, with the exception of a few laws enacted after 450, still stands before us as a Latin text, the Novels are dominated by Greek: the handful of Latin texts presumes a western destination, Italy, Africa, Illyricum. In addition, the reign lasted long enough to set a political standard, or at least to leave a decisive imprint on the model that had been evolving since the time of Constantine. This model was developed within the frame of juridical discourse, in which the emperor described himself as inspired 'by love for the human race' entrusted to his care from on high, and by his foreknowledge of what was for the good of mankind, in accordance with the divine will. Hence the assertion in the preamble to the *Digest* that he never slept, an image which Procopius in the *Secret History* presents as literal fact and in equally bizarre fashion turns back to front, ascribing Justinian's sleepless nights to his demonic nature.

Justinian's authority further manifests its splendour in buildings and their ornamentation, throughout the provinces but above all in the capital, where Justinian had two symbolic edifices constructed, a palace and St Sophia. Like the palace of Constantine and the palaces of the ninth and tenth centuries the Great Palace of the sixth century is known to us only from fragments. Excavations have uncovered some exquisite rural mosaics in the Hellenistic style, one of which shows a water-mill across a river, a novel image in this period. On his own initiative, Justinian's master of offices, Peter the Patrician, collected together the orders of ceremony observed at the court in the fifth and sixth centuries and thereby produced a guide so much in keeping with the trend towards ritualised expression of the imperial majesty that fragments of it have come down to us in the *Book of Ceremonies* compiled four centuries later by Constantine VII.

Begun in 532, consecrated in 537, rebuilt in 558 following the collapse of the dome, and reconsecrated in 562, St Sophia, the Church of the Holy Wisdom, on whose fabulous construction and treasures no expense was spared, became and remained the religious heart of Byzantium's imperial power, and this in the eyes not only of the emperor and the people of his capital but equally of foreign nations – as the capitals of the Slav nations will later bear witness. So lofty is the dome, rising to a height of 55m above ground, and so spacious its span, 77m, that the choir of Beauvais cathedral could be accommodated with ease. Thus was fixed for centuries the archetype, gigantic and unrivalled, of the Byzantine church on the centralised plan, weighty in construction, crouching in almost ungainly fashion on the ground, but whose interior, clad in the splendour of its mosaics, offers to God a setting in which His power must call to mind that of the prince. If at Ravenna, in Italy, St Vitalis happens to be smaller, or if St Apollinare retains the basilical layout, this is merely a regional variation: there, too, the connection is made between the emperor, present in person, surrounded by his ministers, and the power from on high.

Justinian's aims might be summed up as unity and *romanitas* – and resistance to change. The imperial power thus set itself to eliminate all dissidence and discord in relation to a standard set by the Christian empire. It saw itself as born from a tradition, but not of a tradition that it was at liberty to change. Looking backwards rather than forwards, preoccupied with perpetuity but blind to the future, it adopted a stance scarcely comprehensible to the modern mind but which explains many of the directions that Byzantine policy took from this time onward. This position was asserted, for example, in the legislative sphere: once the *Digest* and the *Code* had been compiled, all the contributory material was destroyed and further commentary forbidden. In actual fact, paraphrases and Latin translations circumvented this ban, while Justinian's Novels give proof in themselves of a response to current pressures and show new practices being initiated. Even though the language of the Novels was henceforth Greek, and Latin appears to have been demoted from its official position, cultural contacts were not interrupted, since they also had a political aspect – as is illustrated by the influence wielded from Rome to Constantinople by the Anicii, one of the great Roman families of the day, which possibly numbered Pope Gregory I the Great among its descendants. But the reconquest of the West remained Justinian's over-riding historical, or rather cultural, aim.

Extent and limits of a 'Roman reconquest'

Right at the beginning of the period, notice was served of a return to global policies by the intervention of Leo I, backed by powerful resources, in Africa – in reply, be it noted, not to any immediate threat but to a request from the empire of the West, then on the point of collapse. Anastasius concentrated on wars that were primarily defensive, in the Caucasus against the warrior tribe of the Tzani, ensconced in its mountain redoubt, on the frontiers with Mesopotamia, where he undertook an important programme of fortification, and lastly in the Balkans, where since the time of Zeno the Slavic Antae and 'Sklavenes', along with Turkic elements already designated 'Bulgars', had been exerting a pressure which in the reign of Anastasius became more intense. Otherwise, Anastasius exerted his influence over the Arab tribes of the Syro-Palestinian steppe to protect neighbouring provinces from their incursions, at this time frequent, and to deflect their raids against Persia. In much the same way the emperor supported the conquest of Himyar by the Ethiopians, which was reinforced by the conversion of the region by Christians who were from Alexandria, and therefore monophysites. This had the effect, for Byzantine sea captains, of freeing the vital sea passage from Eilath to the Persian Gulf and so to India. The conflict was reopened in the reign of Justin I, because of the Himyarite king's conversion to Judaism, which signified his rejection of tutelage by Ethiopia and the patriarchate of Alexandria; furthermore, he sought support from the Arab principality of Hira, for its part still faithful to traditional pagan cults. But a new Ethiopian offensive subdued the rebel kingdom, not without benefit for Byzantium. Justin I was equally active in strengthening the empire's position in the Caucasus. Henceforth, however, we know that offensive and defensive operations were mounted by the empire using its own manpower resources. It seems that the Isaurians, when they were not harassing the population of Constantinople or Rhodes, in the years immediately preceding their war with the central power, had found seasonal employment on the large monastic building-sites in northern Syria. After the fall of their mountain stronghold, the Isaurians were deported to Thrace to strengthen its defences. And from the reign of Leo I they figure as men-at-arms in the private troops raised by great landowners to guard their estates, and which the landowners often drafted, as the need arose, into the

St Sophia in all its splendour: interior view. Built under Justinian in the sixth century on the site of an
earlier basilica also dedicated to the wisdom of God, '*Haghia Sophia*', the church was built by no less than
10,000 workmen, and was intended by the emperor to surpass all existing buildings.

157

regular armies. These *bucellarii* (literally 'men entitled to army biscuit') played a significant part in Justinian's wars – and we are speaking not just of Isaurians but of provincials such as Thracians. At his accession, Justinian thus disposed of an army which was primarily provincial rather than composed of barbarians, although the latter would never be absent. They even represented a majority in the Italian expeditions, as they did elsewhere after 540, which is hardly surprising.

Justinian bequeathed to the imperial tradition at Byzantium a model, a goal: restoration of the old unity through reconquest of the West. Summoned in the course of dynastic conflicts, in 533 he intervened in Africa, where his general, Belisarius, carried all before him; and in 535 he intervened in Italy, where the same general landed in Sicily, crossed the Straits of Messina, and entered Rome in 536 and Ravenna in 540.

We should avoid falling into the common error of belittling these achievements because of their unequal duration. The 'triumph' of Belisarius in the old Rome, the reappearance of 'Romans' as far north as the Po, does this not represent a return to Constantine? Gaul and Spain were still wanting, it is true. But must this always be so? These are the expeditions which reveal most clearly the importance of the *bucellarii*, recruited in their thousands and placed at the disposal of generals such as Belisarius or Justinian's cousin Germanus: they indicate at one and the same time a certain abundance of manpower and the growth of the private power of which we shall discover other indications in the countrysides.

But although the historic memory of Byzantium remained fixed on the West, its present and future history was to be played out in the Balkans and along the eastern frontier. At the start of the reign the war with Persia was being waged, not without some success, in Mesopotamia, Lazica, and above all Armenia. It was punctuated by major enemy offensives, which in 529 carried the Persian forces as far as Antioch, and in 540 delivered the city briefly into their power, in violation of the treaty which had been concluded between Byzantium and Persia in 533. From 531 to 579 the throne of Persia was occupied by Chosroes I, whose reign, like Justinian's, marks a great political and cultural epoch, that of Sassanid Persia, which the Islamic conquest was to engulf but not efface. Did Persia, too, profit from an abundance of men and money, silver coinage in this instance? It seems possible. All around the two imperial powers were restive barbarian peoples. To the north, Justinian finally subdued the Tzani of the Caucasus. Asia Minor suffered the disturbance of a 'Hunnic' irruption like the one under Anastasius, but it was their stranglehold on the overland silk-routes from China that chiefly enabled the Huns to exert pressure on both Byzantium and Persia, when they were not serving as mercenaries on one side or the other. The 'Bulgars' were pressing on the Balkans and in 540 they ravaged Thrace and Macedonia. On the other hand, Byzantium consolidated for its own advantage and against Persia the confederation of Arab tribes led by the Ghassanids, who made a base for themselves in the Syrian steppe at Sergiopolis, the town of St Sergius (Resafa), while a rival confederation headed by the Lakhmids fought for the Persians. Lastly, in the south Justinian continued to apply the diplomatic, evangelistic and military pressures which constituted Byzantium's foreign policy, focusing attention on the one hand on Nubia and on the other, as before, on

the Ethiopian and Himyarite territories which commanded access to the Red Sea.

Resafa, Syria, choir of St Sergius (fifth century). The use of small arches to carry and reinforce a larger arch was widespread in Byzantine architecture of this period.

The military turning-point occurred a little earlier, it seems, than in the financial and social spheres, which would suggest that the former was a cause of the latter. The pace of reconquest in the West began to flag as early as 540. In Africa its cultural gains came under threat from a Berber insurrection lasting from 544 to 548. In Italy, the new king of the Ostrogoths, Totila, mounted resistance which dragged on from 541 to 555. And yet in 552 Byzantium embarked on a war in Spain, once again sparked off by a dynastic and religious conflict, which delivered part of the peninsula into Byzantine hands. In 561 the conquest of Italy was completed at the Venetian Alps. In the same year, a ten-year peace treaty was concluded with Persia. It is true that in the Balkans the pressures became greater after 544, **159** as new waves surged forward, altering the political landmarks: Kutrigur Huns, 'Bulgars' with Sklavenes under their power, made ever more serious incursions into Thrace and threatened the capital, where the Huns penetrated to the suburbs. In 558 Constantinople received its first embassy from another Turkic people, the Avars, who in 561 were installed on the Danube. Occupying the last decade of Justinian's reign, this succession of incursions, battles and negotiations in fact marks the beginning of a new era in Balkan history.

Justinian: the dark side

The times between 457 and 565 are not all of one character. They begin with a period, lasting perhaps until 518, which generated within a few decades, and simultaneously, wars far afield and closer to home, urban upheavals, an astonishing growth of monasticism and progress in building activity of every description, all to the accompaniment of alterations in the basic structures of society and of production. A gradual rise in population during the fifth century, reaching a critical threshold around 450–60, might well account for such a concurrence of developments, provided that we can assume it was based on an abundant coinage, particularly in gold, the instrument of internal and external policy. With this movement on the historical plane went an increasing social rigidity. Undeniable signs of movement and of rigidity became apparent with Justin I, and with Justinian: to be more specific, after 550 things were at breaking-point.

The weight of men and of gold

It goes without saying that we have no reliable population figures, or more accurately no plausible overall estimates, to help us evaluate the stray information to be gleaned from the documents: how many monks there were in a monastery or tax-payers in a village, the number of men in an army as reported by a reliable witness, and so on. The archaeologists can give us some idea of demographic variations in a particular region, but investigations along this line are incomplete. What follows is therefore purely conjectural, its sole justification being the desire to find the best explanation for the largest number of known facts. It is certain that the fourth and the first half of the fifth century had known no disruptions or catastrophes on a very large scale. This was sufficient for the population to grow, even in the face of infant and seasonal mortalities, frequent famines, a meagre diet and indifferent sanitation. Inscriptions from family graves show that provincial families were often successful in rearing as many as four or even six children beyond the stage of infancy. Now a society whose productive capacity was both inelastic and heavily dependent on human energy was bound to be unduly sensitive to fluctuations which the figures, if we had them, would perhaps show to be in reality quite trivial. Sudden disasters would thus be one of the negative factors, as would a second phenomenon, of which the first need not be the only cause, an excessive decrease in the number of child-bearing couples.

This decrease could have demographic causes. One very important cause might be plague. The bubonic variety is described in medical texts, but cannot be identified as having occurred in the history of the early Roman empire, where the exact nature of two serious epidemics of the late second and mid-third centuries remains uncertain: they may have been smallpox. By contrast, when the first outbreak occurred in 541, brought from Ethiopia by way of Egypt, Procopius and other writers described the illness with a minuteness which indicates its novelty. In the spring of 542 the plague reached Constantinople, to rage through the empire and for that matter the West. A law promulgated in March 544, decreeing the return of wages to their former level, marks its official termination. But in fact the threat of plague continued, further outbreaks being recorded in 557–8, 572–4, 590, 599 and sporadically into the seventh century. There can be no doubt that the outbreak of 541–4 did enormous damage, which was made greater by the social disruption the plague brought about and which, because of the children who died, affected future generations. Moreover, the decade which opened with the plague was struck by other calamities, in particular a catastrophic animal epidemic in 547–8. And the whole of Justinian's reign was punctuated by more frequently recurring famines. It is possible that these betoken a period of prolonged drought, which might also account for the more aggressive behaviour of the nomads on the empire's eastern borders. Yet it is also conceivable that the extent of the ravages from plague and famine, great by any standard, was linked with the slow growth in population which we postulated above, which had proliferated by comparison with its resources and fell back after 550. Yet the decline, too, was only a gradual one. For among the contributory causes were socially-determined factors of demographic imbalance and failure to procreate which became evident from 450–60 and reached their peak in the reign of Justinian, but whose cumulative effects continued in the medium and long terms. If one sets aside the military undertakings of the period, and the problem of regions constantly exposed to barbarian attack, these causes write themselves into the history of our three types of territory – the desert, the countryside and the town – and of their inter-relationship. They will therefore be considered when we come to deal with the period in its social aspect.

Military activity, the internal development of towns, the growth of monasteries, and building works would not have been feasible without an abundance of gold coinage to sustain them. Leo I's war with the Vandals, and the construction of the monastic complex of the Miraculous Mountain to the west of Antioch, in Zeno's time, show the way the wind was blowing. But here it is the financial and fiscal reforms of Anastasius which mark a turning-point, following on from these already heavy expenditures. In 498 he abolished the tax in gold and silver levied on goods and services, in which prostitution was included, while insisting on collection of the land-tax in gold. In addition, he created a heavy bronze coin, the *follis*, designed for use in the largest of petty transactions, so as to enhance their value and to ease the circulation of gold. Lastly, he systemised the collection of customs duties, and that part of it which allowed customs officials to receive gratuities *pro rata* – or at any rate he tried, like many after him, to restrain officials from abusing the system. In actuality, the *follis* did not cease to depreciate in relation to gold, notwithstanding a revaluation undertaken by Justinian in 539. The dowries of provincial brides, the treasure accumulated by monasteries, the rents made over to them and the gifts they received were

161

Gold solidus and reverse of a copper follis (from the beginning and middle of the sixth century respectively); the follis was minted to relieve the monetary system based on gold (Paris, Bibliothèque nationale, Cabinet des Médailles).

reckoned more than ever in gold, as were the savings accumulated by workmen who received their daily wage in bronze.

Claims have often been made that in the fifth and sixth centuries the empire's gold was being drained off in tributes paid to the barbarians, purchases of foreign goods, spices from India, silk from China brought in through Persia, and the hiring of Scandinavian mercenaries, even though export of the metal was officially forbidden. Finds of *solidi* in places ranging from Sweden to the Ukraine seem to confirm this hypothesis and it is true that according to Cosmas Indicopleustes, the merchant whose testimony has already been cited, the Byzantine gold *solidus* ranked above the Persian silver coin in a market as far away as Ceylon. But it is possible that part of the gold paid out to barbarians and mercenaries re-entered the empire in the form of purchases. The silk problem was solved by the introduction of the silkworm into the empire in 553 or 554. Further, stocks of gold could be replenished from the metal mined in the Sudan, but above all by the ever-present possibility of melting down articles hoarded by the palace, the magnates and religious establishments. Lastly, Justinian's government used and abused all the traditional methods: sale of offices, creation of a monopoly for the guilds of the capital, in return for payment; an imperial monopoly over raw silk when it still had to be imported; confiscation of properties belonging to pagans and heretics, especially in Asia Minor; aggravation of the fiscal burden by the methods already described; delays in paying soldiers their wages – though some officers, it is true, cheated the authorities by not removing dead men from their lists. All these pressures seem to have come to a head after 540, just at the time when the population was hit by the plague and a number of other calamities.

Towns in ferment

From 450 onward, and especially under Justinian, towns experienced a marked recrudescence of internal conflicts which pose problems for demographic, social and political historians. That the relative population of towns was increasing seems beyond question. Archaeological investigation bears witness to the fact, from Aleppo to Jerusalem. And the documentary sources make it clear that the growth was not benign. People took refuge in

Beggars. Plague, animal epidemics and serious
social upheavals led to a rural exodus. The Church
tried to provide for the welfare of these people,
whom the capital could not absorb (Syriac Gospel-
Book, late sixth century, Florence, Laurentian
Library).

towns to escape the social difficulties of the countryside, and in the metropolis to escape
those of the provincial capital. The Novels of Justinian, much concerned to check a
movement which after 530 had become a flood, give a good indication of the problem.
Many of the new arrivals were the victims at one and the same time of landowners, the fisc,
and the corrupt justice of provincial governors. Allowance should also doubtless be made
for vagrancy pure and simple, the rootlessness of the poor, and the restlessness which
peopled the streets and highways with those 'vagabond monks' whom the canons
repeatedly but ineffectually condemned, and also for the attraction held for all such groups
by famous sanctuaries such as the Miraculous Mountain, and by the Holy Land. The
capacity of towns to absorb this influx was very limited. Apart from employment on the
construction-sites of buildings, reservoirs and walls, that is to say in the public services,
there were practically no openings for the unskilled labour offered by newcomers. Skilled
craftsmanship, on the other hand, appears to have become scarcer, perhaps because it
failed to expand in face of an increased demand. The craft associations in fact show a

tendency to develop into pressure groups bent on defending a monopoly, or at any rate an assured position. At Sardis, as early as 459, a stone inscription published the rules for the settling of disputes and breaches of contract which had been agreed between the building workers, members of the craft association, and their employers. A Novel of 538 makes special concessions to market gardeners who brought into cultivation plots situated outside the capital. At this same period, Justinian was granting, or rather selling, to the associations in the capital the right to a monopoly, well before the plague which according to a Novel of 544 sent wages rocketing. In 539 a special magistrate, the *quaesitor*, was appointed in the city to control the new arrivals, sending them away if their presence was not justified or putting them to work on public building or in the bakeries. The law creating this office refers to the danger of a rise in crime, while another denounces the misdeeds of procurers who brought in peasant girls of tender age. When no work was to be had, newcomers fell back on charity. If occupation of properties in Constantinople and Alexandria still carried an automatic entitlement to 'bread from the State', charity in the proper sense was from now on an attribute of the Church. Fugitive slaves and fugitive *coloni*, debtors to the fisc and unsuccessful litigants took refuge within the enclosure offering asylum, there to kick their heels while awaiting better days. Rustics, vagrants, invalids of every description turned to the charitable establishments that were springing up in the large towns, served by monks, and in more and more cases built and endowed by the emperors. Some of these were run on the lines of a hospital, and they all distributed food to the needy, at any rate on feast days. Associations of pious laymen made their contribution by gathering up the destitute, living or dead.

Population movement of this order inevitably posed a political problem which the traditional civic establishment was unable to accommodate, but which manifested itself in the recrudescence of riots. There is certainly some significance in the fact that the explicit causes rarely relate to material demands. To be sure, food shortages, governmental failings, unpopular measures could all give rise to violent agitation, arson, stoning of officials, sudden deaths; and people might kill each other round watering-points during a drought. But the 'revolt of the poor' at Constantinople, in 553, against an 'interference with the petty coinage' remains a rarity. And when we are told that the *demos* of Antioch rose in 540 on the approach of the Persians, 'in expectation of the revolution', it is safe to assume that in the minds of the participants any social motivation was overlaid, in this particular instance, by expectations of an eschatological kind. Much more typical, by contrast, appear to be the bloody skirmishes between adherents of differing religious persuasions, and the attacks on Isaurians. It is also to be noted that street-fighting with the Jews was on the increase, in Antioch and elsewhere. The only response of the establishment was to increase and systematise the role of the factions of the hippodrome.

It will be recalled that the symbolism of the four colours – which before long were regrouped into two, the Blues and the Greens – and of the hippodrome, as the image of the world and of its enthroned sovereign, goes back, so far as our present history is concerned, to the fourth century, though its antecedents were very much older. The role of these factions is most conspicuous in the fifth century, and more precisely from the time of

Anastasius, before it fades out early in the seventh century, or dwindles, rather, into an innocuous component of the emperor's symbolic attributes. In their heyday members of the factions manned the urban militia, which maintained and guarded the city walls, and took the leading roles in the ritualised dialogue between the emperor and his people in the hippodrome. The factions appear to have been properly constituted bodies, with a commander, administrator, council, spokesman and funds. The Greens had some distinguished patrons. But the activity of the factions was not limited to the capital; neither was it restricted to the spectacle nor confined to the hippodrome, where the factions evidently enacted the part of the Antique populace face to face with the imperial power. The Blues and Greens fought battles which could spill over into the streets, and stirred up trouble in a variety of circumstances, on occasion against the emperor himself. The most significant episode of this kind was the famous Nika riot (*Nika* = 'Victory to . . .!') which in 532 put Justinian in mortal danger, and which was whipped up by both factions following a clamp-down due to excesses perpetrated by the Greens. Procopius, if we can believe him, claims that around this time, and perhaps with secret encouragement from Justinian before his accession, the factions and their gangs of 'young men' had turned openly to organised crime, blackmail, robbery and contract murders. Their deployment was thus in no way linked with the increase in the poor and the uprooted; on the contrary, the factions attracted recruits from the best of families. And here perhaps, in this devolution of all antagonisms, in this formal polarisation of the latent violence which the conditions of urban life perpetuated, we have the town of late Antiquity in a nutshell.

Rural depression

While the towns, particularly the largest ones, began to bulge, the countrysides did not empty. Yet if the village community retained its identity, in a form which endured over the centuries, the development of dependent estates and the growing incidence of monastic farming in certain regions – northern Syria, Mesopotamia and the area around Bethlehem – are responsible for some noticeable changes. The estates which developed in fact depended much less on direct exploitation than on rent collection, and still more on the privatisation of public power, that is to say the assumption by landowners to their own advantage of policing and fiscal demands, usually, it is true, by way of delegation. Testimony to the existence of private troops, police and prisons increases after 450. In some cases they formed a legitimate constituent of the proprietary regime, in others an abusive extension of it through the exercise of patronage, which might either be imposed by force or on the contrary entered into willingly. The Egyptian properties of the Apion family, whose archives have been preserved, represented in the sixth century a miniature State within the State. The attitude of the central power was in the last analysis ambiguous, for it found itself torn between frustration of its fiscal demands and a feeling of natural solidarity with the great landowners – of whom the emperor of course was the chief – and ecclesiastical proprietors such as the Church of Alexandria, more especially since their wealth took the form instinctively recognised by contemporaries as the basis of political and social power.

Thus the Novels of Justinian could complain, after 530, that the prosperity of mountain villages made a mockery of the public power from which they were shielded by some local protector; by force of arms is the implication. In this instance, therefore, the central power endeavoured to strengthen public order by uniting the military and civilian powers, traditionally separated, in the hands of one person, in anticipation of the system that was later to become general. On the other hand, under Justinian and Justin II there were many more concessions of fiscal autonomy, indicated by boundary-stones marking an estate which agents of the fisc were forbidden to enter and from which the landowner levied and delivered the land-tax himself, a system tantamount to according him a chunk of public power and the right to deduct sums with no external restriction. To the peasant's burden was also added his contribution to the Church, exacted in virtue of another power-relationship, which consisted of regular and occasional voluntary offerings, not forgetting the extortion practised by one or other village priest under threat of withholding the sacraments from the recalcitrant. This form of taxation was thus supported by the system of belief. Furthermore, where the church was private, as was often the case in Egypt, the offerings went to swell the revenues of the estate.

We can imagine that from now on the harshness of the peasantry's condition varied according to the place and time. The peasants of Asia Minor were crushed, after 545, by a combination of a drop in population due to plague, the growing weight of fiscal oppression and a series of bad harvests. In Thrace, the peasants found it harder and harder to withstand barbarian pressures of increasing severity. The central power set about the suppression of regional religious dissidents, such as the Samaritans in Palestine and the heretics and pagans in Asia Minor, in the interests of ideological unity and to replenish the treasury through confiscations. These sects had an important rural dimension. Nevertheless, although we hear of violent resistance by the Samaritans, of massacres and self-immolation among heretics, of peasants in Thrace flocking to swell the ranks of Vitalian's rebel army, there seems to be no trace of genuine peasant revolts. Peasant society reacted by disintegrating; and this took place not by recourse to brigandage, which in regions such as Isauria was a normal way of life, but by flight. Whichever power was responsible, aggravation of the peasant's burden beyond endurance resulted in its total abandonment, the dispersal of his family and the desertion of his land. The countryside was driving its sons into the town, into the armies raised by the magnates, and doubtless above all into the monastery and the desert.

The world of monks

Something has already been said of the nature of the wilderness, and of the reasons which impelled men to leave the world to live there in solitude or with a single companion, eking out an eremitical existence by means of their handicrafts, or to join others in communal life. Reference has also been made to the rise of urban monasticism linked with the dispensation of charity. But the most distinctive feature of the period under review is the remarkable growth of monasteries outside the towns, in the form either of a *lavra* or of a *koinobion*. The *lavra* was semi-communal: the monks each had a separate habitation, but shared a common patrimony, came together on Saturday and Sunday and were subject in material and spiritual matters to the direction of one individual, the *hegoumenos* ('leader'). The workings of this model are described in the *Life* of the most famous of the Palestinian monks, Sabas, who died in 532, and whose foundation survives into our own time. Established in barren territory, for example the Judaean desert, a *lavra* had to limit its productivity to artefacts, but even so would have a 'garden', in this case on the shores of the Dead Sea. Its resources were supplemented by cash donations, which for example made it possible to purchase or erect permanent buildings: this was how Sabas was able to build his *lavra* and acquire living-quarters in Jerusalem for his monks. Establishments in the arid zone of Egypt and Palestine followed the same pattern. In regions more suitable for cultivation, such as the fertile part of Egypt, the country around Bethlehem, northern Syria and Mesopotamia, there was a proliferation of monastic communities engaged in the production of corn, wine and olive oil. In this case, the archaeological evidence points clearly to communal habitation. In addition, these establishments fulfilled a charitable and medical function, which could become highly important if they were sited near an important and busy route. Their monks were the backbone of the Chalcedonians in Palestine and the region around Antioch, and equally of the monophysites of Egypt and Mesopotamia. They attracted cash offerings in lump sums or regular donations, in sufficient quantity to maintain and develop their activities. Their lands, like all ecclesiastical property, were inalienable, and were sometimes acquired through clearance. Stones planted in the Syrian or Pamphylian countryside to mark the limits of asylum indicate a possible reason for the attraction they exerted. The *Life* of Simeon Stylites the Younger, who died in 592, tells of workmen often travelling there from afar, of men cured of their afflictions offering so many days' labour because money was not accepted, and of uninterrupted building work, the scale of which is confirmed by the excavations carried out at the Miraculous Mountain near Antioch. But at this period there were also monasteries already following the example of other landowners, that is to say collecting rent.

The impetus towards the founding of monasteries clearly has its place in the annals of the 'great century' which began in 457 and closed in 565. The crusade entrusted to the monophysite bishop John of Ephesus, in 542–3, thus resulted in the colonisation by monks of lands confiscated from the pagans of Asia Minor. There is a marked decline in foundations after 550, presumably to be connected with the easing of human pressure and the contraction in financial resources. Nevertheless, many centuries would pass before some of the monasteries already in existence became extinct, and from these must be excepted those which survive into our own day – Mar Saba, St Catherine of Sinai, completed in about 556, and several more – to maintain the historical presence of Byzantine Hellenism in countries adhering to Eastern Christianity and Islam.

Failure to solve the religious problem

The goal of reconquest did not include according the pope the place of eminence on the world stage held by ancient Rome: the New Rome was master now. Following the reconciliation effected at the start of Justin I's reign, the pope retained his value as a

A desert monastery: St Sabas in Palestine. Founded in the fifth century by Sabas, a monk, this monastery followed a strictly regulated communal regime, very different form of monasticism from the life of the solitaries in their caves.

potential arbiter, and as a reference which Justinian was at pains to obtain in his search for a compromise that would resolve the monophysite problem, which was a task he undertook in virtue of the emperor's doctrinal competence. In his efforts to build religious unity round an imperial creed Justinian met with mixed success. The monophysites represented a cultural force too coherent, and already too closely identified with the twin poles of national feeling, Syrian and Coptic, to be restored in any true sense to the bosom of orthodoxy. Egypt, however, was divided by a doctrinal dispute between Severus of Antioch, who had taken refuge there, and Julian of Halicarnassus, whose radical opinions on the suffering and body of Christ attracted a large monastic following. Justinian first intervened by introducing a hierarchy in doctrinal conformity with himself, known even to this day as Melkite ('emperor's men'). Ephraem, who occupied the see of Antioch from 527, was a senior official, Count of the East; Apollinarius, Melkite patriarch of Alexandria from 551 to 570, held the rank of *dux* (military commander). Because of their qualifications, the central power was inclined to confer on them full authority over their province. In the meantime, the monophysite Church took on a new and lasting form under the stimulus of Jacob Baradaeus ('the ragged one'), who in about 528 had arrived in Constantinople in the monophysite circle protected by Theodora, and who was consecrated bishop of Edessa in 541 through her influence. He in turn used this office, which he retained until his death in 578, to revive a clergy on the way to extinction and which from then on went by the name 'Jacobite', still in use today. The tribal confederation (phylarchy) of Syrian Arabs, and the missions which penetrated up the Nile as far as Sudan added to the political stature of monophysitism, whose intellectual flowering was especially evident in the Syriac domain, for example in the historical and hagiographical writings of John of Ephesus, in the mystical philosophy of Stephen bar Sudaile, and in other ways. In these circumstances there was no chance of success for the compromise proposed by Justinian in 543–4, which turned on the condemnation of 'Three Chapters' extracted from the decrees of the Council of Chalcedon. Neither side would assent, even though Pope Vigilius was summoned for the purpose to Constantinople, where he arrived in 547 when the Byzantine campaign of reconquest was in full swing. Thus in regard to the monophysite problem the reign achieved nothing. It is true that the see of Alexandria remained in Chalcedonian hands following the death of Apollinarius, whose tactic had been to mingle force with persuasion, but neither the peasants nor the monks were won over. The situation in Antioch and in Syria was similar, while in the capital monophysitism appears to have made some headway towards the end of the reign. The victory of Islam, or to put it more accurately the defeat of Byzantium in Syria and Egypt, can perhaps already be perceived beneath the surface of this episode.

The same point can be made in regard to the Jews, who were affected by civil disqualifications but whose religion was not proscribed, although marriage with Jews and conversion to Judaism were forbidden. Invoking the principle of his imperial competence, Justinian intervened in a debate that was splitting the Jewish communities, and indeed had a bearing on their relations with the empire. For the Jews of this period were divided between the Greek tradition, descended from Alexandrian Judaism, and the rabbinical stream, dependent on the Hebrew and Aramaic tradition of exegesis, and dependent therefore in the sixth century on the illustrious Jewish communities of Persia. The Babylonian Talmud appears to have been completed by around 500, but the work of exegesis continued. In other words, there was on the one side the cultivation of Classical culture, and Greek philosophy in particular, and on the other adherence to a monumental mass of traditions, not uninfluenced by the imperial culture, though in a less intellectual form, but dominated by an intensified concern with the jurisprudence and the religious concepts which had the general, and perhaps increasing, effect of setting the Jews apart from the rest of society. The Novel of 553, which permitted the reading of the Law in synagogues in Greek, preferably in the translation known as the Septuagint, and forbade the use of rabbinic commentaries, evidently had as its aim the reduction of Judaism to the norm apparently closest to Jewish Antiquity, but closest also to the Christian imperial culture, and thus most suitable for a possible realignment. The welcome extended by the Jews of the East to the Persians, then to the Arabs, was to show that their history, like that of the rest, was not tending in that direction.

The savage repression of the Manichaeans from the very start of the reign, in parallel with that of the Phrygian Montanist heresy, with its undercurrents of symbolic or actual subversion, and also the measures directed against polytheism, are manifestations of the imperial desire to purge the cultural heritage once and for all. But here again the realities of the situation spelled defeat. Manichaeans and Montanists took their place in the depths of an age-old current too fundamental to be eliminated in this way; we shall meet it again. The problem with paganism was its subsistence at different social levels. The ban imposed on pagan teaching in 529, and the consequent closure of the school of philosophy at Athens, the great centre of Neoplatonism, struck at an intellectual milieu which had hitherto lain outside the doctrinal authority of the Church. Some of those affected eventually migrated to Persia, where Chosroes received them with open arms. By contrast, the mission conducted by John of Ephesus among the pagan highlanders of Asia Minor, around 542, has the crude appearance of a monastic colonisation. In any event, the old cults remained part and parcel of the collective heritage, to resurface in sensational affairs such as the one in which the patriarch of Antioch was rightly or wrongly thought to be implicated around the year 580.

Turning point of an age: 565–610

One major reign came to an end in mid-November 565 with the death of Justinian, and another began in 610 with the advent to power of Herakleios. Between these two dates there is nothing to break the momentum. The movement of history proceeds in the same direction, indeed it accelerates under pressure from the Persian empire and the barbarians in the Balkans, bearing the emperor and his Church, the capital and its provinces towards another Byzantium. The phase of political, cultural and military transition which opened in 565 lasted in reality until around 615–20, and its importance, which is great, is unconnected with the personality of the rulers. The only reason for putting them first is to clarify the sequence of events.

A dynastic policy doomed to failure

Just as Justinian succeeded his uncle Justin I, Justin II succeeded his mother's brother. His wife, Sophia, had a part in the imperial power, as is signified by her depiction on the coinage. Incapacitated from 574 by mental illness, Justin II nominated as Caesar the Thracian Tiberios, count of the *excubitores*, appointed from within the palace as Justin I had been by Anastasius, and adopted him. Tiberios succeeded Justin II, who died in 578. Tiberios himself died in 582, having designated as his successor the Cappadocian Maurice, count of the *excubitores* like himself, but subsequently supreme commander in the East (*magister militum per Orientem*) in the war against Persia. Maurice married Tiberios's daughter, Constantina. The couple produced an ample progeny: in this way it typified the imperial family of succeeding centuries and was in contrast with the childless emperors of the century then drawing to a close. Yet Maurice did not become the founder of a dynasty: his reign was marked by factional conflicts so violent that they amounted to civil war; furthermore he may have been a heretic. In any case, notwithstanding his military prowess, in 602 he was overthrown by Phocas, a non-commissioned officer described by contemporary chroniclers as a 'tyrant' (meaning pretender), and massacred with all his family. The confusion of the period and his own brutality prevented Phocas from holding power for long. His son-in-law, the patrician Crispus, appealed to Herakleios, exarch of Carthage. But it was the latter's son, another Herakleios, to whom the factions accorded a triumphal welcome from the walls of the capital in 610. For the next century Herakleios the Younger and his direct descendants occupied the forefront of Byzantine history.

There is no lack of sources to set this series of emperors in context. In addition to the narrative histories of Evagrios, Theophylaktos Simocatta and others we have a number of memorable hagiographical writings. The *Life of the Patriarch John the Almoner* (died 620) composed by Bishop Leontius of Neapolis reconstructs for us the considerable financial and commercial activity of the church of Alexandria. In the collected *Miracles of St Demetrios*, patron saint of Thessalonica, an account is given in the first book, composed not long after 610 by a bishop of that city, of a major attack on Thessalonica by a combined force of Avars and Slavs, the 'Sklavenes' of the Byzantine sources, which probably took place in 597. The purported autobiography of Jacob, a Christianised Jew, shows him embroiled in the factional disputes of the early seventh century, while George of Pisidia's poem on the capture of Jerusalem by the Persians in 614 again refers to the trouble stirred up by the factions and alludes to the support given by the Jews to Byzantium's eastern enemies. The results of archaeological investigation, although localised and incomplete, also contribute to the dossier.

After the decline which had set in with Justinian's old age, Justin II undoubtedly began to redress the situation. His building works, his largesse and the revival of the consulship at any rate suggest that such was his intention. But the times were more than usually troubled, especially under Maurice. Irregular pay and other grievances made the armies restive. When in 588 the troops of the Eastern army received no pay, they disbanded and took to marauding and pillaging the countryside. It was the mutiny of the Balkan army in

602 that brought Phocas to power. In straitened circumstances, the large towns seem to have remained full, or even over-full, of people. The factions of the capital played a part in the fall first of Maurice and then of Phocas. Referring to the reign of Phocas, the hagiographer of St Demetrios blames them for an outbreak of seditious and criminal activity afflicting all parts of the empire, prompted, he says, by the Devil. Religious tension forms part of the picture. Maurice pursued an aggressively Chalcedonian policy, perhaps in an effort to recapture the unity that was slipping away. He tried to impose the imperial creed on Armenia after his victory in 591 and allowed his cousin Domitian, bishop of Melitene, to carry out a savage, and as it turned out fruitless, persecution in Mesopotamia. In 580 an upsurge of paganism, in which the patriarchs of Antioch and Constantinople were implicated, manifested itself in a rising at Heliopolis and the offering of sacrifices at Edessa. In 594 there was yet another Samaritan revolt. To crown it all, the end of the century was punctuated by a series of natural disasters: serious outbreaks of plague in 573–4 and a still worse one in 599, severe famines in 582 and from 600 to 603. Yet the sombre mood of the epoch was due above all to the pressure from the barbarians. It made itself felt in the countryside and along the roads, it set towns and armies on edge, it sharpened the disputes between communities and between the central power and disaffected regions. A contemporary *Treatise on Tactics*, for centuries mistakenly attributed to Maurice himself, describes the weapons and tactics of Byzantium's various assailants with a closeness of observation and attention to detail that tells its own story. And there was certainly a great variety of ethnic groups both among the attackers and among the mercenaries hired to defend the empire. Around the frontiers, it seems, there was no shortage of men, relatively speaking – for once again we lack satisfactory figures from which to measure the scale of these movements of peoples.

End of the reconquest

The regions reconquered by Justinian – Italy, Africa, and, remotest of all, Spain – occupy the fringes of our story. Spain, the last and most fragile of the reconquests, was the first to crumble away under Visigothic counter-attacks. Africa was under constant threat from the 'Moors'. Italy had proved easy prey to the Lombard invaders in 568, but the scattered segments of Byzantine rule which survived around Ravenna, Perugia, Rome and Naples, in Calabria and on the Adriatic, together with Sicily, remained an essential element in Byzantium's military, and still more its political, dispositions. The reign of Maurice brought an important innovation. Africa and Italy (the former before 591, the latter at latest by 584) were raised to the status of exarchates (governments) whose governor was responsible for both civil and military affairs, with a separate administration for Sicily. Justinian had initiated this regime for especially troublesome mountain provinces. It was revived by Maurice for outlying territories, and in Italy it created a situation that was fraught with consequences: for the late sixth century, and more specifically the pontificate of Gregory I the Great (590–604), saw the pope laying claim to sole power in the old Rome, while the exarch ruled from Ravenna. This duality was fated to end with the fall of the exarchate, and

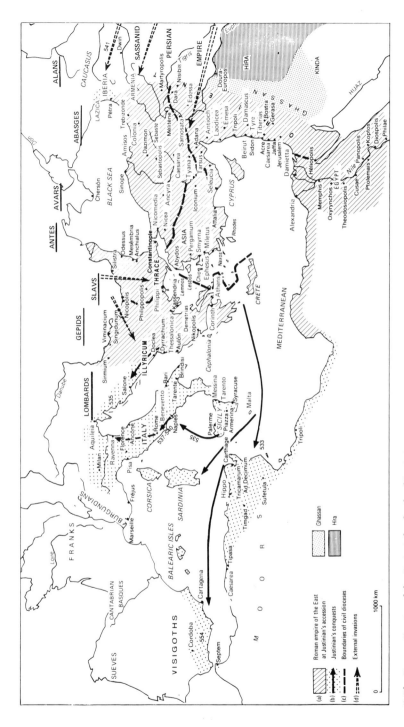

5 The Roman Empire of the East at the death of Justinian

St Demetrios, protector of Thessalonica against Slav attacks, remained the town's patron saint and one of Byzantium's most popular warrior saints (Gold cloisonné, eleventh century, Paris, Musée de Cluny).

the birth of the papal state in the eighth century. To the south of the empire, the Berbers laid waste the Scetis (present-day Wadi Natrun) in 583–4, irreparably destroying a monastic centre of prime importance to Egypt and to the East in general.

On the Balkan front, the situation had been marked since the beginning of the sixth century by the influx of Slavs under Turkic domination: in the second half of the century they appeared in ever greater numbers. The Turkic element was formed by the Avars, ruled by a chieftain and a warrior elite. They headed from east to west, and settled in 570 on the Hungarian plain, where they remained until their political power, menacing but insubstantial, was destroyed by Charlemagne. Justinian and his successors received their embassies. Unable to defeat the Avars, the Byzantines paid them a heavy tribute, and in 582 they were obliged to surrender to them the key position of Sirmium. All through this period the Slavs were spreading in increasing numbers over the Balkan peninsula, starting from the mouths of the Danube, and in 578 they reached Corinth. Thessalonica first came under siege in about 586, and again in 597; for a time the fighting was pushed back beyond the Danube, but in 602 the river frontier collapsed. Tiberios and Maurice transplanted

174

populations from Asia Minor for the defence of Thrace, the region having become depopulated because of the chronic insecurity. If the Avars, with their military and political organisation, merely represent a chapter in the advance of the Turkic peoples, the Slavic impregnation of the Balkans was to be a continuous process, and for the East constitutes the great event of the European seventh century.

On the eastern frontier, the system which had served in the sixth century was also falling apart. The Arab kingdom of the Ghassanids, in the event a faithless ally, was dismantled in 580. In 572 Persia started on a period of ostentatious military activity, aimed in the first instance at Armenia, which had rebelled against the Persians with Byzantine support; a treaty concluded in 591 nevertheless ceded the greater part of it to Byzantium. The Persian offensive resumed after the fall of Maurice and was triggered by the revolt of the commander of the garrison at Edessa against Phocas. In this campaign the Persians broke through into Byzantium's eastern provinces; in 609 they reached Chalcedon, directly facing the capital, and their triumphal progress, far more serious than before, occupied the first part of the reign of Herakleios. It has been seen how the gulf separating Byzantine authority from both the Christian monophysites and the Jews had widened. The Persians, perhaps even more obviously than the Arabs a few decades later, were the beneficiaries, since as a great power they had long been seen as a possible source of deliverance. Feverish anticipation of their coming may thus account for the bloody uprising of the Jews against the Christians at Antioch in 609.

After 560–70, we thus see the beginnings of the unprecedented redistribution of peoples and sovereignties which reached its peak in the seventh century with the Muslim expansion, followed by the birth of the first Bulgar kingdom. Next to the texts with their reiterated descriptions of the devastation of Thrace, archaeological investigation is probably our only means of discovering the true extent of the disruption to Byzantium's social organisation. Excavations have shown that a town as large as Antioch never fully recovered from the Persian invasion of 540, nor for that matter did Aleppo. At Ephesus, at Sardis, at Gerasa, examination of the buildings shows the impoverishment which came with the second half of the sixth century. The samples of stray coins on a site, which give a rough picture of the local monetary circulation, frequently attest to a decline starting under Herakleios. The seventh century unquestionably ushered in a period of eclipse for the town in its economic and social aspects, abruptly inaugurated for some, Sardis for example, by the Persian invasion of 614, but witnessing more fundamental changes elsewhere, such as the obliteration of the Antique town plan through the encroachment of private buildings on public squares, or the construction of defensive ramparts using stones from ancient monuments. Lastly, the bishops now quite definitely surpassed the curials in importance, and had long had more affinity with imperial officials than town councillors. Our analysis, furthermore, can only be regional, and chronologically spaced out. For example, the olive-producing hinterland of Antioch appears to have declined in the seventh century – at the same time as the urban market which provided its outlet or the seaborne trade in which Antioch was the leader. Contrariwise, some small town in southern Palestine or monastery in the Holy Land could plod peacefully along even during the initial years of the Arab conquest. The solution to this conundrum is not obvious, nor can we expect it to be unique, and the question in any case is twofold: are we dealing with changes in territorial and social organisation, or with variations due to circumstance?

The cultural importance of the epoch is nevertheless considerable. The literature expressive of regional religious dissidence has already been touched on. In Greek, Chalcedonian Christianity produced at this time some of the most important works of popular edification, above all *The Meadow* (*Pratum Spirituale*). Its author, John Moschos ('the Lamb'), who died at Rome in 619, gathered together in the course of his pious wanderings a collection of tales in which fact mingles with fiction; this compendium was drawn upon down the centuries by a whole range of medieval literature. Also committed to writing at this period were stories relating to icons and their miraculous properties, since representations (icons) of Christ, his Mother and the saints were increasingly becoming the focus of belief and veneration. These images, whose typology was fixed, were executed in mosaic or more commonly in encaustic applied to a slightly hollow wooden surface, usually of limewood. Among their antecedents have been cited the custom of funerary portraits, such as those which adorned the already Christian mummies of Fayum; the images placed on the tombs of martyrs; and the image of the emperor which, as a token of the sovereign's real presence, appeared in the law courts and the hippodrome and on the silk robes the emperor offered as gifts. From the late sixth century it was believed that images of Christ existed which were 'not made by human hands'. First the town of Edessa in 544, then an army marching against the Persians in 586, attributed their deliverance to an image of this nature. At the same time the cult of the Virgin made a decisive advance, with the completion by Justin II of her churches of Blachernae and Chalkoprateia in the capital, and his provision within the latter of a chapel for her girdle.

These sanctuaries acquired an importance in the religious life of the capital that would never be effaced. The iconography of the Virgin, for which the model was said to be a portrait executed by St Luke, developed in parallel. The cult of holy men, living or dead, equally contributed to the new proliferation of images. Edifying tales of the late sixth and seventh centuries credit them with the powers, not merely of protection, but of direct intervention in public and private affairs. There is a sense in which the exaltation of the emperor's person links up with this development: he begins to be spoken of at this time as the true 'image of Christ', to employ the language of a text describing the enthronement of Justin II. The latter was crowned in his own palace, and the encompassing ceremonial laid stress on his links with the patriarch, while the patriarch, under Maurice, claimed the title 'universal' (*oikoumenikos*). In all of this there is more than a hint of the fully-developed theory of the ninth century. It was again Justin II who constructed the 'Gold Chamber', as a shrine for the imperial presence while ceremonies were in progress. Significantly, the image of Christ was placed there above the imperial throne, to demonstrate the structural bond uniting the two powers. The factions, after the last and worst spasm of their urban violence, were invested with the ceremonial role which they were to occupy from now on in the palace ritual and in the emperor's public appearances. Their members, having been the protagonists in urban conflicts, now began to play leading parts in the representation of

176

One of the rare surviving examples of sixth- or seventh-century icons, and also one of the oldest, this painting on wood, representing St Chariton and St Theodosius, is preserved in the monastery of St Catherine on Mt. Sinai.

the imperial majesty, while retaining, at any rate down to the beginning of the eighth century, their responsibilities in the defence of the capital.

In a word, everything that typifies the century of Herakleios and Justinian II is already explicit in the pattern emerging from the years which bring the century of Justinian I to a close. Yet one element was missing from this evolution which was capable of accelerating it, or even of brutally developing its characteristic features. While the Roman and Persian empires tried to recover their equilibrium, a catastrophe was on the way, a bolt from the blue: the soldiers of Islam came bursting out of the desert.

'Fill His vast spaces and feed on His providence' (the Koran).

PART 2

The building of new worlds in the East: seventh to tenth centuries

From the Hegiran model to the Arab kingdom: seventh to mid-eighth centuries

5

The Islamic world of the early medieval centuries is defined, even more than by a common thread running through its economic, social or technological organisation, by the absolute predominance of a system of values, of a political and cultural model which disrupted the 'units' formerly in occupation of the geographical area in the East and around the Mediterranean, obliterated their memory, reduced and isolated their remnants. And yet, as it evolved and became more elaborate, this new world displays the same general characteristics as the Byzantine and Sassanid worlds it replaced, whose economies, indeed whose societies – in so far as it is possible to trace and understand their evolution – did not in fact form autonomous units of which their political or cultural system can be regarded as the more or less faithful reflection. The Muslim conquest went beyond the superimposition of a common language on the worlds it served to unify, or of a fiscal code as a badge of effectual subjection; as in Antiquity, the State was at once a mirror of inequalities and a repressive instrument which codified and preserved them; it was also the driving force behind the circulation of goods and of values. It was through the State that a privileged class of public pensioners came into being, composed initially of all Muslims who had participated in the conquest, later of faction members or the clients of particular dynasties; it was the State which controlled the monetary economy, whose metals had no other function than to reinforce the hierarchy, by draining off the surplus of small peasant units.

Like the Antique world, whose main features the Dar al-Islam would perpetuate, sometimes to the minutest detail, the new world presented itself as a whole: everything in it cohered, and the sense of belonging was fundamental, essential: doubt was the chief enemy, raising the spectre of social anarchy and the curse of personal disintegration. The driving forces of social evolution were power, factionalism, the family and religious belief; ownership of the means of production or one's place in the economic cycle were negligible factors since they were subordinate to the exercise of governmental power, and this necessitated total ideological commitment to a ruling dynasty, guarantor of justice, social harmony and salvation. The theocratic system embodied in the Prophet would weigh impartially on all subsequent experiments, revolutionary or conservative; but it was through drawing on the thought of Antiquity, *gnosis* in particular, that this thirst for unity and salvation, and the hope of their apocalyptical fulfilment, came to take shape in political programmes. An analysis of the mutations of the Islamic world between the eighth and the eleventh centuries in terms of bourgeois – 'feudal' conflict may bring out certain well-worked aspects of reality, but otherwise can only obscure an achievement of astonishing originality and permanence.

A divided Near-East face to face with a religious revolution

In 610, when Islamic prophecy begins, the Near-East was parcelled out between two great empires, two monarchical societies equipped with an aristocracy in the service of the State and a centralised clergy, but lacking in ideological or religious unity; and the monarchy in either case was identified with a dominant people and a hegemonic culture. The Byzantine Near-East had subjected to the authority of the Greeks and to the definition of orthodoxy fixed at the Council of Chalcedon in 451 a string of ancient, semi-Hellenised nations. The religious preferences of the latter, their 'heresies', prompted them to draw on the arsenal of religious polemic for whatever could reinforce their identity as national groups; the 'melkite' persecution had probably not been uniform, nor were heretical tendencies merely a reflection of linguistic particularities and ethnical traditions, as we have seen. In Egypt, where the melkites were few in number and support for the monophysite Church was solid, the Coptic language was an effective cement of the union and a sign of opposition to the Greeks; around 610, moreover, an atmosphere of terror prevailed, following the exiling of Patriarch Benjamin and the enforced apostasy of the bishops, priests and monks, constrained to subscribe to the solution imposed by Herakleios (638) to the christological problem, 'monothelitism'. The Syrians and the Mesopotamians, speakers of Syriac and Aramaic, were divided by contrast into three parties: the melkites, of whom there were many in the aristocracy of service at Jerusalem, where a lone patriarch upheld the position of Greek orthodoxy; the monophysites, subscribers to the 'Jacobite' tendency defined by Severus of Antioch and disseminated by the itinerant preacher Jacob Baradaeus, who looked to the patriarch of Antioch and owed their strength to a firm monastic base; and lastly the Christians of Iraq or Iran, whose bishops had chosen since 484 to follow the theology of Theodore of Mopsuestia, setting up in 485 a Nestorian *catholicus* at Ctesiphon. The expulsion of Nestorians from the empire by the emperor Zeno, around 491, only strengthened the position of this semi-official Church which commanded the allegiance of all Christians living in the Persian empire. If the Jacobites of Syria were in communion with the Copts in Egypt, they were separated from the Syriacs of Mesopotamia as they were from the Armenians, who adhered, for the most part, to the official Church – as did the monothelites of Antioch, centred on the monastery of St Maro.

The unity of the Sassanid empire appears to have been equally lacking in substance: and the matter goes further than the 'horizontal' barriers between the Persian aristocracy and the conquered subject peoples of Iraq and Armenia, in that the Iranian world was itself only superficially converted to Zoroastrian orthodoxy. If the sacred fires of other descendants of the ancient teaching of the Avesta had been extinguished, they nevertheless smouldered on in the unconscious or in popular fervour, finding expression for example in Zorvanism

This astonishing brick-built vault, among the remains of the royal palace of Ctesiphon (in present-day Iraq), explains the attraction exerted by the Sassanid superpower, already in decline when the Arabs captured its capital.

and other heretical movements that had taken root in court circles and appealed to the masses. In the third century, prince Mani had advocated a syncretic religion and morality based on the absolute nature of truth, and on the total separation between the principles of good and evil, extending to the rejection of meat, of the flesh and all things corruptible. Executed in 276, Mani left a vast ideological posterity, which nevertheless found itself defenceless in the face of repression. Around 500, in the time of Shah Kubadh, the philosopher Mazdak plunged the empire into a disastrous war: the fact that the senior heir to the throne was his chief supporter precipitated that prince's downfall and encouraged his younger brother, Chosroes I, in his bid for power. As a result, the whole of the north-eastern part of the empire slipped out of the Zoroastrian net: all around Balkh (Bactra), Bactriana and the old Iranian lands beyond the Amu-Darya (Oxus), the Ferghana and mountainous Ushruana, the Sogdian principalities underwent a profound conversion to Buddhism. Balkh is famous for its more than a hundred pagodas (*viharas*) and 3,000 Buddhist monks, and in particular for the Nawbibar, 'the new *vihara*', whose chief priest founded the powerful family of Barmakid viziers, prominent under the Abbasid caliphs.

So there are weaknesses here of a structural order: latent opposition among great masses of the peasantry, their solidarity sustained by a network of monasteries and itinerant

183

preachers; the combined moral and fiscal resistance of entire provinces; and above all the theological divisions prevalent among the political and religious elites in court circles, always in pursuit of a universalist solution, always ready to persecute a new 'heresy'. To all this is added, in the decade 600–10, the exhaustion resulting from the all-out war between the two empires: this was kept going chiefly with the aid of warriors from the client Arab principalities, the Ghassanids on the Syrian borders and the Lakhmids on the banks of the Euphrates, both of them Christian. In this way the Arabs, hitherto secluded in the desert – that preserver of values and emblem of freedom – became gradually involved in the great theological and political conflict of the East.

These Arabs whom we now encounter, were by nature and by etymology nomads: in the south, 'pure' Arabs, in the north 'Arabised' tribes, brought together in a loose federation by the caravan and religious centre of Mecca, guarded by the Quraysh tribe. We see in the north a pastoral society, conservative, loyal to values born of the independence forced on them by their tribal way of life and constant feuding; in the south, an urban society, cut off from the cultural and religious currents of other Semitic lands by the barrier of the Arabian desert, proud of its traditional independence (and in fact the only Semitic people to remain autonomous), and characterised by archaising social and cultural institutions (city-States, local pantheons). The wars, by throwing new forces against the Yemen, arrested the trend developing in the Himyarite kingdom towards a military empire and a Judaising monotheism; on the other hand, the whole episode served to strengthen the solidarity between southern and northern Arabs. In 525, at the instigation of the Byzantines, the Ethiopians of Aksum invaded the Yemen and put an end to the Himyarite monarchy; but the survivors allied with the northern tribes and built up around Mecca a confederation which in 571 was strong enough to overthrow the Ethiopian occupation. Pride in the uniqueness of their language and culture, in 'Arabism', was undoubtedly a factor in precipitating this resistance: but if it deployed the resources of a 'tribal humanism' which made a moral virtue out of honour, independence and virility, it also underlined the contradictions between this set of values and the demands of monotheism.

Muhammad

If their weakness or state of crisis, definable *a posteriori*, are not considered sufficient reasons for the collapse of the Near-Eastern empires, it is still the case that Islam burst in like a revolution. Nevertheless, this was not a social revolution, since Islam saw no particular virtue in poverty, even if acts of revenge and the settling of old scores here and there entered into its expansion, nor was it a 'national' revolution by minority peoples in thrall to great empires. This was a religious revolution, which is to say it was at once political, intellectual and philosophical, turning on the 'recall' to the essential oneness of God, and stamped by the indelible experience of Prophethood, of direct contact with the divine. The Meccan call for a transmutation of values, the break with a paganism in the process of becoming institutionalised, let loose the extraordinary power of monotheism, while in the Medina period the prophetic current was contained, channelled into the creation of a State, but of a

State which remained for ever unrealised, an ideal model uncertain of its legitimacy, convulsed by the explosive forces which had been unleashed and activated in response to the Prophet's call. In the space of two decades a set of principles was forged on which a culture, a faith and a law continued to repose, in the face of a constantly disputed State.

There may be some astonishment at the widespread adhesion of the Christian world of Asia and Africa or the whole block of territories governed by Sassanid Zoroastrianism to a religion mediated by a group as small in numbers as the Arabs of the Hijaz, marked out neither by any unusual philosophical capacity or by a history of close contacts with the cultural centres – Antioch, Alexandria, Haran, Ctesiphon, Djundishapur – where the Classical heritage and the main impulses of monotheism had combined. The intellectual 'scandal' of Islam's birth outside the areas already converted to monotheism is in fact reminiscent of the equally subversive and marginal character presented by the majority of those same religious impulses on their first appearance: Islam recaptured the radicality of primitive Judaism or primitive Christianity facing the pantheistic cults or elaborate philosophical constructs of their times. In Islam the Graeco-Semitic culture discovered for the first time its true voice: it rid itself of stifling, alien modes of expression and, for a time at least, of philosophising theologies.

When Muhammad's preaching began at Mecca, central Arabia was still in a state of tension generated by the invasion of the Yemen by the Christian Ethiopians, possibly in reprisal for persecution suffered by the Christian Arabs of the oases from the Judaising Yemenite princes. The symbolic value of the victory before Mecca won by the combined Arab forces in the Year of the Elephant (571) can scarcely be overestimated. For the sanctuary contained the idols of the clans and tribes, which were assembled under the guardianship of the Quraysh tribe in the 'enclosure of Abraham' surrounding the Ka'ba, the 'cube', the first, rudimentary home of Abraham's son Isma'il. This concrete link with the very beginnings of monotheism was a justification for the attempts by the *hanifs*, devout men who related their belief in a single God explicitly to Abraham, to strike out independently along a new and specifically Arab path. Serving also, unofficially, as a federal sanctuary, Mecca awaited and desired a prophet qualified to establish a hierarchy of deities, in order to consolidate the hegemony of the tribes and of the Qurayshites. The influence of the latter was on the increase, following the shift in trade-routes: for the decline in the use of the Red Sea route and of the caravan-routes converging on the Euphrates bend, brought about by the Perso-Byzantine wars, had favoured the development of a new caravan-route, taking in the oases of the Hijaz, to connect the Yemen, producer of aromatics and importer of spices from India, with Syria. The sudden riches and the encroachment of the money economy were threatening the traditional equilibrium of the clans and the inter-clan relationships; the substitution of monetary values for the values of 'tribal humanism', virility, generosity and agnatic solidarity, was an inevitable consequence. It is for this reason that the movement unleashed by Muhammad's preaching presents itself both as a revolution, with its radical commitment to a new ethic of the family, and as a reversion to the fundamental values of monotheism, which throughout the whole history of the Near-East had appeared to be undergoing progressive mutilation. Construction of a 'total' faith

185

thus went hand in hand with an Arab revolution to bring the One God back in triumph to the temples from which He had been driven by man's neglect of the original covenant, whether through idolatry or through the complex speculations of theologians intent on defining his nature. Muhammad thus placed himself first and foremost in the tradition of the great prophets of Judaism and of the other branches of the Revelation: Shu'ayb, Salih, Hud, prophets of Moab and the Arab peoples of the north, who play an essential role in the Koran and who had proclaimed the omnipotence of God and the imminence of Judgment.

From words to weapons

The breaking away of this merchant, rich, monogamous and respected within his community (he organised the rebuilding of the Ka'ba), has been compared with the destinies of other mystics: embarkation on a lone voyage bears fruit which after long meditation takes shape in preaching. We need not doubt that in the first place the Prophet was following a personal quest for salvation. For him, the revelation of 610 came as a message to a needy soul, a spiritual message, a call to righteousness, a call to respect the imperatives of the old clan morality, purged however of its pride and exclusivity: by his condemnation of consanguineous marriage, by pronouncing a curse on the exposure of female babies, Muhammad would encourage the disintegration of tribal society, through the consequent population explosion or through the breakdown of clan solidarity. In this first dawn, the Prophet's Revelation thus joined itself to the evolutionary trend within Meccan society, without seeking to remodel it, but also without becoming part of it: there was no question of assuming the garb and functions of a soothsayer (kahin). Gradually, however, as Muhammad enters into contact with the other hanifs, and indeed into rivalry with another prophet, Maslama, and as he becomes the focus of the 'young and the weak', for whom there was no place in tribal society, we notice a change in the prophetic function: from proclaiming as his message the pre-eminence of the God of salvation, Muhammad moves by slow degrees towards political and social reform.

The Qurayshites who invited Muhammad to head a reforming movement and establish a new pantheon, to be their Lycurgus and Hesiod rolled into one, were not really mistaken. The Prophet in fact agreed to draw out this pedigree for the gods, but assailed by the consciousness that God spoke through his mouth, and under pressure from his first group of converts, he subsequently drew back. It was only the tribal ethic of solidarity which saved him, and this despite his condemnations of Qurayshite pride and violence. Gradually disclosed as belonging to the monotheistic tradition, the message took more definite shape with the adhesion of the first followers, 'the people of the Household': among his close relatives his wife Khadija, Ali, at once his nephew and his son-in-law, his freedman Zaid, who was like an adopted son, then neighbours such as the Umayyad Othman and Omar ibn al-Khattab, followed by more humble people like Bilal, the black slave purchased by Muhammad from a cruel master. Distilled in the rite of communal prayer, the message, for so long diffuse, gave rise around 619 to a primitive community of a distinctively egalitarian and revolutionary character. The death of Muhammad's uncle, Abu Talib, who had shielded the small band without actually subscribing to the new religion, was the signal for a more fundamental rupture: emigration, which Muhammad deemed necessary to escape persecution. The women and children departed for Christian Ethiopia, which confirms the existence at this period of links with Christianity and is to be set beside verses in the Koran exalting the Virgin and recalling the conception of Jesus by the Spirit, thus conferring on him a special place in the line of prophets. Muhammad meanwhile looked to the *hanifs* and to the Arab clans centred on Yathrib, 'the town' *par excellence* (Madina, Medina) as it became on his arrival; a number of Jewish tribes were settled there and he was offered a role as arbiter. It is his departure for a place of refuge (*hijra*) on 24 September 622 which founded Islam as a universal community: this is the 'Hegira', a rupture, a temporary emigration, a voluntary exile. Islam, a religion in which the only certainty is that nothing escapes the omnipotence of God, declared itself through this founding act as a religion of exile, of total abandonment and of utter dependence on the divine will.

The welcome accorded by the Medinese, the 'helpers', to the *muhajirun*, the emigrants who had made the Hegira, and then the fairly rapid conversion of the former to the Muslim faith, resulted in the *umma*, a congregation sworn to total fidelity, an intimate band of brothers overshadowed by a divine omnipresence. For at Medina God spoke through the mouth of his Prophet with less formality than in the early days of the Revelation. Once this is grasped, it is easy to see why, throughout Islamic history, this 'Hegiran' community, the *dar al-hijra*, the 'house of Refuge', should have aroused such intense feelings of nostalgia: in every century one finds initiatives or even breakaway movements seeking a return to the purity of 'Hegiran' relationships between men and between men and God, and to that simple form of State in which the common purse was fed by voluntary contributions or the booty captured in wars against the infidels, while the wars themselves were fought by a quickly assembled people's army of equals, reflecting the fundamental equality of Islamic prayer. This was the 'model' which would unfailingly sustain the onward drive of Islam to its frontiers, in close harness with the 'recall' of souls to God, less by conversion than through conquest, less through preaching than by hastening to defend God's due. It would inspire all movements claiming to return to the primitive state of Islam, from the Kharijite secessions to the Qarmatian insurrections and the Fatimid 'manifesto', and so on down the centuries, cropping up again in the Sudanese Mahdism of the nineteenth century or the *Sanousiya* movement in present-day Libya.

Also tested and defined at Medina was the relationship of Islam to the monotheistic religions: the Prophet evidently found contact with Judaism fruitful since he showed no hesitation in adopting Jewish customs, dietary prohibitions and observance of an annual fast (on the tenth day of the month of *muharram*) and emphasised the similarities between his teaching and the religion founded on the Law. In this way Islam escaped from the orbit of Christianity, which had only moral precepts to offer, useless to the founding of a State, whereas the Judaising elements could immediately be called on to join the *umma* in its war on the pagans of Mecca; their presence was a demonstration, like the orientation of community prayer towards Jerusalem, of the unity of the Muslim 'combatants' in upholding the Faith and the Law. But this unity was achieved on the basis of an astonishing

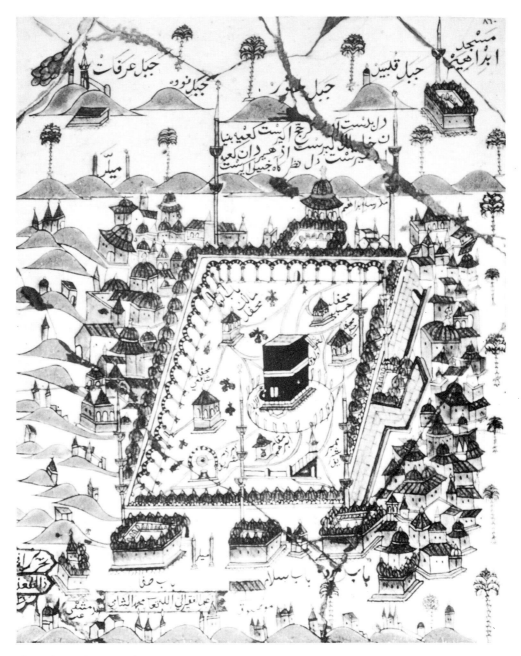

The Ka'ba, at the heart of Mecca's sacred mosque, pole-star of the Islamic religion, is seen draped with its traditional covering of black brocade. The rebuilding of this cubic edifice was directed by Muhammad in the seventh century (eighteenth-century faience tile, Cairo, Islamic Museum).

misconception: seeing himself as a prophet in the line of descent from Noah, Abraham, Moses and Jesus, Muhammad joined his own message to the proclamations and the vision of God vouchsafed to these forerunners and from the beginning asserted the universality of his role; he was thus going against the idea of the 'chosen people'. In the eyes of the Jews and Judaisers of Medina, Muhammad was no more than an Arab prophet, appointed to present to the Arabs, in Arabic, a mirror image of Judaism. Following a period of successful military collaboration, the rupture came about in two stages: in 625 the Jewish tribes were expelled from Medina, and in 627 the Qarayze, suspected of treason, were massacred. Muhammad's prophethood thereafter became more narrowly attached to the person of Abraham (Ibrahim) and of his son Isma'il, and this in turn reaffirmed the central role of the Ka'aba at Mecca: the direction of prayer was changed towards Mecca, while the fast was replaced by the more strenuous ordeal of an entire lunar month of abstinence and continence by day, timed to fall in the month, *ramadan*, which coincided with the anniversary of the first prophecy. Lastly, the dietary laws were abandoned, although not to the point of relaxing the more traditional prohibitions regarding pork and the flesh of dead animals; the Jewish horror of consuming blood, implanted at Medina, was to be equally a trait of the Muslim.

The most important consequences of the Hegira, however, were the militarisation of the community and the dependence on booty, developments attributable to the hegemonial rule of an aggressive *umma*: in January 624, in disregard of the sacred truces protecting the Ka'aba for three months in the year, Muhammad started a partisan war against the Meccans in which he ambushed their caravans, thereby altering the whole character of warfare: for in place of the 'gentlemanly' engagement intended to take prisoners and force tribes into submission which could be disguised as familial dependence, Muhammad introduced total warfare, with no quarter given, calculated to destroy the political and religious framework of the Meccan world. In the event, the failure of the Qurayshite army commanded by the Umayyads Khalid and Amr in 627 was sufficient to demoralise the tribe. Without going back on its militarisation, the Medinese community urged a return henceforth to the fundamental values of the Arab people: after the conversion to Islam of the Umayyad generals, an agreement was made, in 628, between Mecca and Medina, which reopened for the following year the pilgrimage route to the Ka'ba. This made it possible for Muhammad to revive and sacralise the pilgrim rites, which he restored to their context in the story of Abraham: seven circumambulations of the Ka'aba, seven courses between Safa and Marwat, a sojourn for prayer on Mount Arafat, the stoning of Satan in the valley of Mina, and lastly the sacrifice, the 'great festival', which commemorated still more exclusively than the Jewish passover or Christian Easter the fundamental sacrifice offered by Abraham. The peaceable pilgrimage of 629 thus offered the Quraysh a way out, a guarantee that in exchange for a definitive Islamisation of the sanctuary Mecca would remain the political and commercial centre of Arabia. Furthermore, the forays of the Medinese had widened the Muslim sphere of influence from the tribes of the Hijaz to large tracts of the south and the Syro-Palestinian borders. In 630, a Muslim army numbering 10,000 undertook the pilgrimage, conferring on the *hajj* the aspect of a triumphal entry;

the idols were suppressed and harmony was re-established between the Quraysh and their most famous son. In the following year non-Muslims were formally excluded from the pilgrimage, making complete the identification of Islam with the place sacred to the preceding regime. Mecca, however, was never to become the capital of the Islamic state: between 630 and the Prophet's death in 632, and again under the first caliphs, the capital remained firmly fixed at Medina, which was to remain the touchstone of legitimacy, the natural focus of insurrection for several anti-caliphs, inasmuch as it was the chosen residence of the Prophet's closest kin, the descendants of Ali.

The Hegiran model

The Medinese State found embodiment in the monument *par excellence* of primitive Islam, the first 'mosque', the *masjid* of Medina: the form of this special 'sanctuary' (though the whole earth, of course, was sacred to God) would be perpetuated in a type of building specific to Muslim culture, the mosque and its enclosure, at once a religious and secular centre, where the community assembled for the performance of collective functions and ceremonies. On a patch of land with a slightly irregular shape, the Prophet laid out a large, square courtyard whose surrounding brick wall was pierced by three entrances; a portico supported on rustic columns made from palm trunks was originally placed against the north wall to mark the direction of Jerusalem, but was transferred after 624 to the southern wall (the *qibla*) facing Mecca. Defensive stronghold, place of assembly for political and military purposes, and – like Muslim private dwellings – inward-looking, the sanctuary of Medina was dominated by the Prophet's seat, his *minbar*, and included his house and a series of rooms along the eastern wall. For prayer, the faithful ranged themselves in rows running parallel with the wall indicating the *qibla*, in a manner consistent with an egalitarian community of believers; an exception was made only for the *imam*, 'leader' of this worship which consisted of praise and adoration. But who, after the death of Muhammad, would sustain the contact between the transcendent God and the community of his worshippers? How could the unity of the believers still find expression and answers be found to new questions? How was the divine message to be amplified and safeguarded, when the Prophet alone had enjoyed direct access to God and had alone borne witness, in his judgments (*hadiths*) and by his exemplary life, to the divine will?

The State encapsulated in the Mosque

The example of the mosque illustrates both the unity of function which lay at the heart of an institution unique to the Muslim society-*cum*-State, and also the conservatism of a system which tamely reproduced the Medina model throughout the Dar al-Islam. Everywhere, the Muslims set up sanctuaries which preserved the squareness, the fortified enclosed space and the asymmetrical layout of the prototype, as well as its chief internal features. From the *minbar*, central to the Friday midday worship which expressed the militant solidarity of a people under arms, the preacher, himself armed and attired in ritual garments, proclaimed the legitimacy of the ruling dynasty: it was this ceremony, the *khutba*, that welded the community together. A vacant niche, the *mihrab*, marked the 'spiritual direction' of the prayer, just beside the *minbar*; the arrangement has been interpreted as the residue of a specifically caliphal chapel, but this hypothesis is to be rejected although without losing sight of the idea of a close connection between the mosque and the caliph's or governor's palace. An exception must be made for Jerusalem, where the Dome of the Rock recalled the place of sacrifice, already consecrated by David's [Solomon's?] Temple, and the Aqsa, the last mosque, was a reminder of the Judgment and the end of time; everywhere else, however, the Friday mosque (*jami*) stood cheek by jowl with the palace, linked to it by a passage which opened into the *maqsura*, the enclosure, screened off from the communal area, where the caliph or governor came to pray. As at Medina, the Friday mosque for a long while fulfilled the functions of rallying-place for the army, hospital, law-court and public Treasury, as at Damascus, where the small structure housing the Treasury was perched on a column set into an angle of the Umayyad mosque.

In 632, when the founder died, the fundamental prescriptions for a Muslim State and society had already been laid down. Most basic of all were the 'Five Pillars': profession of the monotheistic faith, prayer, the fast of Ramadan, pilgrimage, and lastly almsgiving (*zakat*), amounting to one-tenth of the believer's income and essential to the smooth working of the State. Next came the 'good practices' deduced from the example of the Prophet and from his sayings, the *hadiths*, which at Medina represented the prophetic function in its everyday aspect, when it was necessary to make rulings on mundane matters. These many sayings were graded in Muslim practice, then reviewed, shaped into a corpus by the first teachers of the Law and rearranged into a recitation, the *quran*, or Koran, where verses (*suras*) recording the Revelation transmitted to the Prophet alternate with others applicable to tribal morality. One of these good practices, the *jihad*, the armed 'struggle' against pagans and others who deny God his due, soon achieved a standing almost on a par with the Five Pillars. Other traditions, in a more or less Islamised form, became incorporated into religious practices and the conduct of family life: circumcision, for example, and the wearing of the veil by women, which was prescribed by the Prophet only for members of his own household and the wives of believers, but also endogamy (although condemned by Muhammad), which in a clan-structured society was the guarantee of noble birth and a protection against the dispersion of patrimonies, such as might have ensued from the application of the Medinese rule for inheritance (one share to each son, a half to each daughter); or again the custom of polygamy, sanctioned by Muhammad's multiple marriages, contracted as much from political as from amorous motives, but strictly limited by precept to four wives whose rights were to be respected and equally apportioned, including the right to sensual enjoyment, the value of which Islam took for granted.

The reinstatement of the customs of the Meccan aristocracy and their diffusion as a model throughout the Dar al-Islam reflects a compromise between the egalitarian society of believers, which was still horizontal in structure, theocratic, and wholly dependent on the voice of God for guidance in administrative and legal matters, and the Meccan society whose values, such as purity of family descent, tribal hierarchalism, and agnatic solidarity,

191

Ground-plan and aerial view of the Great Mosque of Kairouan. Rebuilt in 836 on the site of a seventh-century mosque, it nevertheless remained true to the model, inspired by the Medinese mosque, which was followed at this time throughout the Islamic world.

all had their roots in a distant past, and carried a tremendous charge, but equally a risk of instability. The fact of the matter is that the tribal system superimposed itself on the Muslim army and proceeded to colonise the Umayyad State: it relied for its success on a well-tried network of dependences and loyalties – a 'republic of Cousins' – but was fundamentally aristocratic in principle. With the death of the Prophet, Islam, carried on the shoulders of the Umayyad generals, also became a vehicle for bringing great families to power. A genealogical model everywhere became the norm, in perpetuation of the old agnatic, patrilinear customs of the Mediterranean; polygamy, for its part, was to act as a powerful solvent on conquered societies, which were forced to hand over their women. Paradoxically, and in a spirit largely alien to the Prophecy, military conquest and the rights of the family created a new society whose governance required a prodigious effort of adjustment and reflection. But from the moment of this society's inception, and even before it had triumphed over its enemies, the seamless mantle of Medinese Islam was being rent into 'schools', which were divided over the principles concerning the devolution of power, the relations between free will and the sovereignty of God, and the relationship between faith and human reason.

The 'Family' in conflict with the 'Powerful'

The 'family row' occasioned by the succession to the Prophet, with its episodes of tragedy, pettiness and factional in-fighting, reveals the fundamental weakness from which Islam

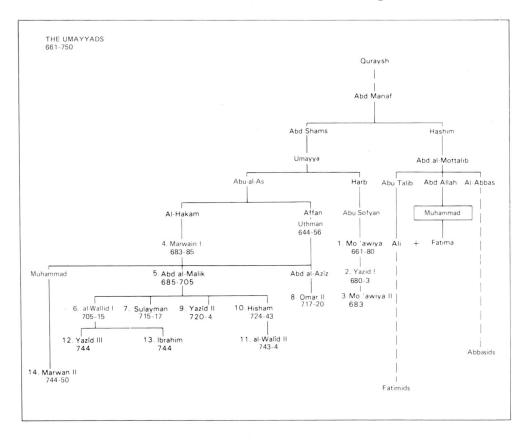

THE UMAYYADS
661-750

suffered for many centuries: how to define the legitimacy of power. It gave rise to the formulation of countless political and therefore religious doctrines, probing ever more deeply into the problem, enriched by contributions from outside and frequently verging on heresy, if only in the form, common enough in Islam, of 'exaggeration'. On the death of the Prophet, a conservative and serviceable solution permitted the transmission of power to senior, highly respected Muslims related to the Prophet by marriage, Abu Bakr and then Omar, who launched the great conquests. This meant that other, closer, relatives of the Prophet were passed over: Abbas, Muhammad's uncle, whose descendants were later to eulogise his merits and revive his claims, and above all Ali, the Prophet's nephew, the first convert after Khadija, a scrupulous and zealous believer, around whom a party began to form when, on the death of Omar, power passed into the hands of a third 'deputy' (caliph), Othman, an Umayyad who had the backing of his clan and whose supporters were already permeating the State. Othman encountered opposition among the old guard of believers, faithful to the original *umma*, or the witnesses to the Revelation, the 'sayers' of the Koran; by authorising only a single version of the Book of the Revelation, from which the curses formerly called down on his clan had been erased, Othman precipitated his death by assassination in 656.

So Ali was coming rather belatedly to power, in an atmosphere of intrigues and vengeance. Accused by the governor of Syria, Muʾawiya, of having instigated the murder of his kinsman, Othman, Ali temporised and lost some of his support; dragged into a civil war between his own forces, based on Kufa, and the army in Syria, he avoided a bloody engagement by agreeing, at Suffin, to submit his putative responsibility for the assassination to arbitration; but the weakness of this response aroused the fury of those who challenged the validity of human judgment in such an affair. Islam became split in consequence into three parties. Former partisans of Muhammad's son-in-law, among them 'graduates' of the initial *umma*, formed a party of intransigents known as the 'Kharijites', puritanical in outlook, condemnatory of sinning imams or lapsed believers, preaching purity of conscience as the only way. Around Ali there survived only a faithful remnant of his following, soon to become a sect, who failed to shield him from the knife of a Kharijite assassin; the elder son of the murdered caliph abandoned the struggle, but the younger, Husain, took up arms against Muʾawiya and the Umayyads; his martyrdom at Karbala in 680 led to the formation of an Alid 'party' (*shiʾa*). The Shiʾites, a legitimist minority, succumbed to a mood of tragic, theatrical remorse, while to the victorious Muʾawiya flocked the moderates, the opportunists, the indifferent and the ambitious, eager to lend support to this military power, a reflection of the Quraysh and the old tribalism: the Umayyads had arrived.

In general, however, the trend of the philosophical and political doctrines evolving in Muslim circles was not favourable to the Umayyads. The Siffin scandal, and the ejection and martyrdom of the Alids, led to reflection on the validity of the imamate, on the extent of human responsibility, and even on the nature of the Koran and the attributes of God. By a process for the moment specifically Muslim, reason, *kalam*, was used to assert human freedom against the 'compulsion' implicitly preached by the Umayyads, and against predestination. Those who stressed the inaccessibility and oneness of God came to constitute an important school of thought, 'muʾtalizism': a clandestine organisation opposed to the anthropomorphism and immorality of the Umayyad caliphs, by emphasising the duty of 'good government' and of rebellion against unjust or immoral leaders, it prepared the way for the propaganda of the descendants of Abbas who infiltrated its ranks. While differing widely from the Kharijites on the condition of the sinning Muslim, the muʾtazilites were at one with them on the idea of a just imam and of an imam removable by the faithful; on the other hand, their philosophical contacts seem to have been closer with Shiʾite circles.

The development of Islam thus consists chiefly of an increase in depth, a reasoned reflection on the elements of the faith. Its contacts, its borrowings and its polemics are of limited extent. It is, of course, true that Islam came under attack from Christian theologians of the Syrian schools such as John of Damascus and Abu Qurra, but the chief concern of Muslim thinkers was rather the radical scepticism of the 'libertines', the *zadiqs*, inheritors of Iranian dualism: for the problem of evil aroused them more than that of the Greek *logos* propounded by the Christians in Syria. Muʾtazilite theories exempted God from any responsibility for evil, which originated solely in human free will; as for the doctrine of a 'created Koran', this was intended to refute the arguments of enemies of Islam who seized on the imperfections in the sacred text, which was nevertheless held to be the word of God. In this climate of intellectual investigation, philosophical choices still could not escape having a direct political application. In this respect Islam, both religion and State, placed a responsibility on each individual Muslim. With the formation of parties, and the party of the Alids in particular, ideas began to penetrate which by origin were quite alien to Islam.

Although the pro-Alid movement long persisted in presenting itself as a family movement headed by the senior members of the clan, and thus as a 'lawful party', sectarian elements sowed or nurtured in it the seeds of 'exaggeration': to wit, millenarist expectations, which led to the ascription of a prophetic function to the imams and in particular to anticipations of the appearance of the 'rightly guided one', a *mahdi*. When the imams recognised as *mahdis* failed to live up to expectations, the idea gained ground that the 'return' of a saviour–*mahdi* descended from Ali must be preceded by a period of concealment; in this way the group came to recognise incarnations of the divine in the chain of hidden imams, which led in turn to acceptance of Hellenistic notions of metempsychosis, and opened their minds to the gnosticism of the Christian world. Around 760, in Shi'ite circles at Kufa, the cult of prophecy and millenarism, clothed with the memory of the Mecca and Medina era, exploded into a constellation of volatile sects: partisans of Ali and fervent believers in his probably messianic return; partisans of Ali's son, Muhammad ibn al-Hanafiya; partisans of Abu Hashim; devotees of the branch descended from Husain; activists who rallied to the Hasan branch of the Alids and pressed for military opposition (the Zaidites). No very obvious boundaries separated the legitimate 'party', the Shi'a, which was prone to frequent revolts of a violent but ephemeral kind, from the minor groups with their pronouncedly mystical character, doomed in the end to impotent obscurity. Even before Islam was able to reap its full harvest, tares were already growing among the wheat.

Islam's harvest

The government of the Umayyads thus took shape in an atmosphere of continual conflict – political, ideological, familial – between warring factions in the bosom of the Arab people; solutions to the triple problem of power within the community, relations between conquerors and conquered, and the definition of juridical principles would give them effective control over the Islamic world, swollen by conquest to dimensions as vast as those of any empire in Antiquity. The eventual failure of the dynasty should not blind us to its creative capacity, which found expression in achieving a synthesis between contradictory elements, between the egalitarian, universalist Message and the realities of the hierarchical structure and client relationships traditional to the Arabs. The Umayyads, it is clear, were no ordinary generals sprung from the Qurayshite aristocracy: they would always bear responsibility for the rupture with the more prestigious Alids, and they laid themselves open to charges of luxurious living and immorality; but one has to take into account the necessities which drove them to set up a personal power base, court and administrative apparatus which distanced them from an intractable people's army in the grip of nostalgia.

The figures of the three sovereigns overwhelmed by the Arab advance, the Byzantine emperor, the Sassanid basileus and the Visigothic king of Spain can still be made out in this badly damaged but remarkable painting from Qasyr Amra in Jordan.

Yet they were conscious both of their duty to the community – to set a standard of morality, liberality and justice – and of their uncertain legitimacy, or at least of the fact that it was shared by other branches of the Family. Under the Umayyads, once the fateful day was passed when Husain, son and heir of Ali, met his death at Karbala, insurrections were never repressed with the ferocity that would later be displayed by the Abbasids.

From Turkestan to Libya

The building up of the Medinese State and the difficulties posed by Muhammad's succession are to be viewed against a background of expansion, conquest and the founding of a universal empire. Here events came thick and fast. If the first campaigns, within the Prophet's own lifetime and in the time of Abu Bakr, sealed the adhesion of the Arab tribes to Islam and aligned them with the first converts in a common military enterprise, the phenomenal successes of the Qurayshite generals had the effect, within six years of the Prophet's death, of creating a new empire in the Near East and disrupting its traditional frontiers.

In 636, the battle of Qadisiya marks the brutal ending of the Sassanid dynasty: after that, it would take only a few years for Muslim domination to be extended to the Zagros (642), Fars and Khurasan (651). On the other horn of the fertile crescent, the capture of Damascus

(635) and Jerusalem (following the victory at Yarmuk in 636) opened up Egypt, Upper Mesopotamia and Armenia (641) to the ambition of the conquerors, almost without opposition. Here it is necessary to stress that it was the Meccans, belated adherents to Islam, and in particular the Qurayshite Umayyads, strongly imbued with the traditions of tribalism and tribal warfare, who directed these operations and then took charge of the conquered territories: Muʾawiya was governor of Syria from 637, Khalid and Amr controlled the provinces in Iran and Egypt. They thus established precedents for the exercise of a wide measure of autonomy by local governors, made wider still by the diversity of the agreements concluded with local populations. The existence of these tribal armies and decentralised commands underlines the importance to the Muslim State of its fundamental political and religious consensus: an ideological unity which persisted, although marred by the bitterly contested struggle over the legitimacy of power.

Thus when the great quarrel (*fitna*) between Ali and the heirs of Othman broke out in 656, the essential nucleus of the Islamic empire – Egypt, Syria, Iraq and Iran – was already in being. Expansion into Khurasan and Sijistan continued, thrusting forward to the Iranian marches in the north-east, which bordered Turkish territory and the outposts of the Chinese empire. Violent tribal confrontations went hand in hand with the progressive subjugation of these ancestral Iranian lands of Transoxiana, a mosaic of Zoroastrian and Buddhist principalities, made first into tributary states and then suppressed. The all-Arab army of conquest, mobilised from Kufa and Basra, was soon split into factions quarrelling over the division of booty between warriors and the central Umayyad administration, to the extent that the Banu Qays, in command of an assortment of tribes from the Hijaz, sided with opponents of the Umayyads and after 691 turned them against Arabs of Yemenite origin. The ranks of all these tribes were soon swelled by 'clients' (*mawali*): mercenaries, former Iranian slaves, or prisoners of war, whose enfranchisement was conditional on a duty of loyalty and devotion towards the tribe of which they henceforth formed part, albeit in an inferior position (the word *mawla* implies the dependent relationship of a subordinate to his master). After 705–15, contingents of *mawali* that is, of Arabised Iranians, took part in the conquest of Bukhara, Samarkand, Khwarazm and the high valleys of the Ferghana facing China. In 731, 1,600 *mawali* foot-soldiers and 1,000 Samarkand converts assisted the regular Arab army, perhaps 40,000 strong, in removing the threat from the Turkish khan of Turgesh. The frontier was by now solid; and the Chinese, when they attempted a counter-offensive to regain control of their former Transoxanian fiefdoms in 751, were thrown back to the river Talas; it seems, however, that Islam was for its part not in a position to press further into Chinese territory. Wherever the line is drawn, the territory on the far side, whether we are speaking of Turkish country, the Caucasus, the sub-Caspian mountains, Afghanistan or Nubia, ranks as the 'home of war' and of raiding, where the volunteers of the faith operated alongside the regular army; as a result, with the settlement of the Arabs and the diminished role of the official soldiers, these volunteers, or *ghazis*, etymologically speaking 'pillagers', gradually grew in importance and acquired an ever-increasing prestige: in the time of the Abbasids, *ghazis* from the Iranian frontiers were to

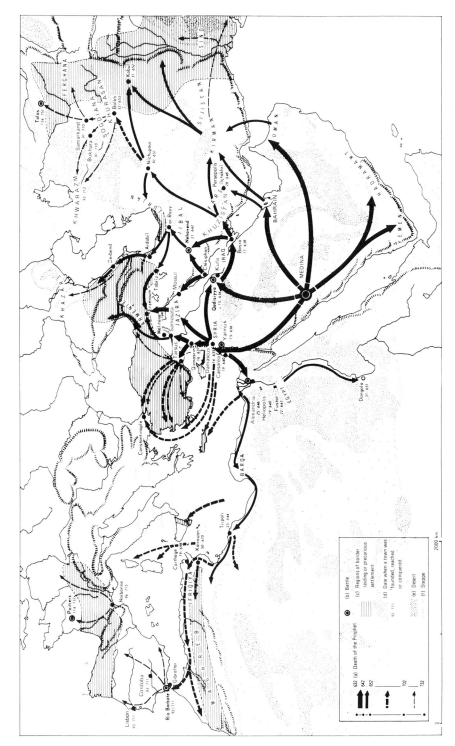

6 The great campaigns after the death of the prophet

come to the rescue of the tribal Arab army struggling to hold its own against Byzantium in the Taurus.

It was above all on this side, and against the islands of the eastern Mediterranean, that the thrust of the conquest had been most continuous: for the burgeoning aspiration to a universal empire was very soon joined by a fascination with the sacred role of the New Rome and the belief that the capture of Constantinople would resolve certain eschatological obscurities and crown Islam's triumph – hence the immensity of the Umayyad effort to achieve it. But once the first, semi-miraculous victories had run out of steam, and the fighting had moved to the Greek terrain of Asia Minor, the Muslim armament and tactics were found to be on a par with the Byzantine forces, which had proved easy enough to expel from regions such as Syria and Egypt, no less Christian, but profoundly hostile to Constantinople. As things now stood, the war could not be waged without heavy cavalry, a costly investment in swords, lances and mailcoats, and a skilful co-ordination of troops: it was expensive, and brought little return. To cut their losses, the Umayyads eventually felt obliged to disband contingents of the regular army and remove them from the pay-roll, provoking ferocious opposition. At sea, however, the Arabs had been relatively quick to master the techniques of ship-building and naval warfare: by 648 they were already mounting expeditions against Cyprus; in 655 they won a decisive victory, the 'battle of the masts'; and less than twenty years later they appeared before Constantinople, from 673 to 680. This first 'siege', which in fact was not a siege in the strict sense, was resumed with more serious intent in 717–18; it failed on both occasions, however, since the Arabs had not reckoned with the formidable defences or with the efficacy of 'Greek fire'. This was a naphthalene compound which enabled the Byzantines to set fire to enemy ships, to clear the area and to regain, at least until about 825–6, genuine naval supremacy.

And from Libya to Aquitaine

Extension of the conquest beyond the Libyan deserts probably formed no part of the Umayyads' original intentions; it is true that the extreme fragility of the Byzantine garrisons in Ifrikiya had been brought to light when Abd Allah, son of Az Zubair, made a foray as far as Carthage in 647, but so had the difficulty of controlling the Berbers of the Atlas, proverbially endowed by God with more than their share of unruliness, waywardness, love of disorder and violence. Even if it is not literally true that Oqba ibn Nafi made a lightning march through Barbary to the south of the Wadi Sebu (the river Sus) and rode his horse into the Atlantic (681–3?), he is certainly to be credited with the establishment of a camp to the rear of Carthage at al-Qayrawan (Kairouan), despite opposition from neighbouring Berber tribes. Systematic conquest, backed up by a force said to have numbered 40,000, began after 692. Carthage, like the other Byzantine positions, fell to the attack of Hassan ibn al-Nu'man. Perhaps, although nowadays doubts are cast upon the story, there was an organised resistance in the Aures led by 'al-Kahina', a woman of the Djerama; what is certain is that it took more than a decade to make the road between Kairouan and Volubilis tolerably secure. Even so, it was possible for governors of the

Maghrib such as Musa ibn Nusair to play their cards independently, confident of being out of reach.

Possible reasons for the Iberian venture continue to excite speculation. Did Greek and Jewish merchants send for help against Visigothic oppression? Was it a commercial transaction? Was it a personal venture on the part of Tariq ibn Ziyad, a Berber *mawali* in Musa's following? Roderick's recent usurpation of royal power in Baetica and the disarray in the court at Toledo could well have tempted an opportunist on the lookout for gain. In the summer of 711, Tariq crossed the strait, bequeathing his name to the mountainous rock which guards the northern side (Jebel al-Tariq, Gibraltar), and in a battle at the Rio Barbate dispersed Roderick's army and killed its commander. A year later Musa followed him, this time with Arabs, who captured Seville, Merida, Toledo and Saragossa; resistance was sparse, flight panic-stricken, and this 'lightning conquest', requiring two or three years at the most, was altogether typical of the way in which the Muslims combined prudence with audacity. In about 714 the flood washed over the foothills of the Cantabrians, where a handful of warriors had taken refuge, and around 720 seeped into Roussillon and reached Narbonne. The rapidity of this 'revolution in the West' and its subsequent lengthy duration seem, however, to call for explanations going beyond the skilful deployment of force or surprise attack.

In fact, the Muslim armies encountered in these regions a state of upheaval which should be linked with a more profound crisis in the basically Roman socio-political order which still prevailed in Byzantine Africa and the greater part of Spain. There were already areas – the Basque Pyrenees, the Cantabro-Asturian zone and most notably Berber Africa – from which the institutions imposed by Rome had all but vanished, giving place to reconstituted tribal or 'segmentary' groupings which appear to tie in with the forms of social organis-ation in existence prior to romanisation. As elsewhere in the West, the symptom pointing most clearly to this degeneration of the Roman inheritance is the decay or disappearance of towns. This is noticeable not only in fringe areas where the Roman way of life was particularly vulnerable for ecological reasons, for example the pre-desert zones of north Africa where tribalism was regaining its sway, but even along the shores of what had once been *mare nostrum*, the 'Roman Sea' of Arab texts. On Spain's Mediterranean coastline, so great had been the decline between the period of the third-century crisis and that of the Islamic invasion that long-established towns like Sagonta and Cartagena, once bustling with activity, had been reduced by the beginning of the eighth century to the status of unimportant villages. The wars lasting into the beginning of the seventh century between the Visigoths and the Byzantines may have contributed to this decline – Cartagena was destroyed by the rulers of Toledo – but are not sufficient to account for a trend so all-embracing as to include the disappearance of Tarragona, Rome's third great east-coast metropolis, which vanished completely from the map between the time of its destruction during the Muslim conquest and the repopulation of the site by the Catalans in the twelfth century. The former towns of the African coast also disappeared, with the exception of a few places close to the Strait where a Byzantine presence was maintained for rather longer, Tangier and Ceuta for example.

The Dome of the Rock, Jerusalem, the oldest standing Muslim building, built 688–91.

The minaret of the Great Mosque of Cairouan. mid-ninth century.

The famous spiral minaret of the Great Mosque of Abu Dulaf at Samarra, Iraq, 859–61.

Columns in the prayer hall of the Great Mosque of Cordoba, Spain, late eighth to tenth century.

The death throes of the Latin Sea?

In fact it is the sea which appears to have been the scene of the most bitter and prolonged conflicts. The de-urbanisation of the Mediterranean West in the period before the rise of Islam had been accompanied by a decline in normal maritime relations which affected the entire western basin. This part of the Mediterranean, formerly criss-crossed with traffic, became an economic and political vacuum, given over to the operations of pirates; and this remained the case until regular traffic slowly began to revive in the ninth century and more particularly in the tenth. The situation in these coastal regions was only to change very gradually as a result of their attachment to the Muslim world, since the major seats of Islamic power in the West – not one of which was located in a maritime city before the eleventh century – did not much concern themselves with affairs in places of such minor political and economic importance. Except at the two obvious crossing-points between southern Europe and northern Africa, that is to say the Strait of Gibraltar and the Sicilian Strait, neither Andalusia nor the Maghrib could boast of any coastal town worthy of the name from the time of the Muslim conquest down to the tenth century. Between Nakur and Tunis there was nothing to be seen but the ruins of old Roman towns, and beyond Malaga on the Iberian shore the prospect was little better. Tortosa, because of its strategic position in relation to the Franks, constitutes the sole exception, but even here no trace of commercial activity has been discovered before the tenth century. Like the great metropoleis, the urban centres which became integrated into the cultural domain of Islam, to take the lead in the political, economic, social and cultural life of the central and western Maghrib and of Andalusia (al-Andalus, country of the Vandals), were all located in the interior: Tubna, Msila, Achir, Tahert, Tlemcen, al-Basra, Sijilmasa, Seville, Toledo, Saragossa.

The case of the Balearic Isles could be cited as a fairly typical illustration of this political vacuum and its depressive effect on urban life and regular exchanges. Subjugated in theory, in 707, by the newly-created Tunisian fleet, the islands remained free of control by any external political power for close on two centuries. Attacked in 798 by pirates probably operating from the coasts of Andalusia, they were deemed by the Cordoban government to be protected by a *sulh* or truce, the rupture of which in 848 prompted the despatch of a semi-official punitive expedition. They were still considered a battle area of the holy war, and therefore not part of the Muslim world, as late as 902, when a wealthy individual obtained permission from the emir of Cordoba to organise a private *jihad* with a view to their conquest. Islamisation followed, but for the next three decades or so they constituted a quasi-autonomous emirate, whose incorporation into the Cordoban administrative structure was delayed until after the proclamation of the caliphate in 929. It was only after the conquest of 902 that urban life revived on Majorca with the foundation of Palma (Madina Mayurqa), whose growth was rapid in the Western Mediterranean, where long-distance trade was beginning to recover.

The picture is the same in the Eastern Mediterranean. In 723, when Willibald set out for the Levant, he found ships plying from Gaeta, Naples and even Sicily to the Aegean and

Cyprus, which had been accorded a tributary status by the Umayyads and remained in contact with Byzantium. On his arrival in Syria, however, Willibald was immediately arrested together with the crew of his Cypriot ship, accused of spying and only exonerated when an old man was able to identify him as a pilgrim. Rearrested and again released, this time on the testimony of a Spanish convert, Willibald had to wait a long time for a ship to take him directly from Tyre to Constantinople. It seems, therefore, that communications were not completely severed; but the multiplicity of dangers and obstacles that served from now on to fragment the unity of the Mediterranean and of the luxury trade it formerly carried are plain to see. The naval blockade seems to have been flouted only by the Cypriots; it had not been imposed with an economic objective, but the recovery of Greek supremacy over the sea until 826 led to the decay of urban centres all along the Syrian coastline and to the attenuation of sea voyages, though not, as Pirenne once claimed, a complete cessation of navigation. A 'continentalisation' of the Arab empire appears then to have been the first, and disastrous, consequence of Umayyad warfare.

On land, and until expansion finally came to a halt, warfare has no doubt still to be regarded as an essential ingredient in Muslim society; but from now on there were great differences from the Hegiran epoch. Whereas at that time the entire Arab people had launched and participated in a campaign of armed expansion, the progressive reduction in the role of the tribal element had by now restricted military service to a small group of professionals, representative for a time of all the tribes but under the Abbasids drawn solely from the Arabs of Khurasan, the 'children of the Revolution'. Yet awareness of the military obligation laid on them by the *jihad*, the armed assertion of God's rights, remained very strong among Muslims, whether as a spontaneous emotion or because it was fostered by the jurists. Furthermore, the Umayyads themselves gave a lead by establishing the model of a combatant caliph. An apparently convenient solution was found in the creation of a volunteer troop of *mujahedīn*, maintained by the caliph, which satisfied both the doctrinal and the practical requirements; for one thing it spared the government, save when invasion threatened, the evidently troublesome or all too inadequate procedure of a general mobilisation. But the practice meant that the army had two parallel intakes, of professional soldiers, soon to be supplied by mercenaries or slaves housed in barracks, and of self-righteous volunteers. It thus distanced the great mass of Muslims, except in emergencies, from the Hegiran model of a military democracy; and it increased the likelihood of a conservative revolt aimed at recovering for the 'rank and file' Muslim his imprescriptible right and lost prestige: hence the strength of support for the Kharijite or Alid secessionist movements and their derivatives.

Could there be an 'Arab kingdom'?

The Umayyads' challenge to the claims of the Byzantine empire is made patent by their confiscation of two symbols expressing its claim to universal sovereignty. Even as late as 687, the Syrian caliph was still undertaking to supply the emperor with papyrus carrying the distinctive imperial markings and with robes of honour and office woven in the

Egyptian workshops; a few years later, in 692, Abd al-Malik made a radical departure by suppressing the invocations to the Trinity and the sign of the cross on the papyrus, and by putting a *tiraz*, trademark of the State workshop, on the imperial vestments. And it is Abd al-Malik who introduced a monetary reform which disrupted the prevailing scale of values and substituted a new and purely Muslim type for the Byzantine monetary types retained by the coinage of earlier caliphs: his first gold *dinar*, issued from 691 to 696 and showing the standing figure of the caliph, was followed from 696 by the purely epigraphical type of *dinar* which became standard. This could only be regarded by Byzantium as usurpation of a privilege inseparable from its imperial sovereignty, the issue of gold coinage. The new Muslim coins, the gold *dinar* of 4.25g and a silver *dirham* of 2.97g unified two systems which had long been circulating independently of each other: the Byzantine *solidus* of 4.55g and the Sassanid silver *drachma* of 4.10g.

How could this multiplicty of peoples be unified?

These equivalences had a convenience value, but the chief message they conveyed was of a religious order, a declaration of faith: 'There is no God but God; He is one, without associate, and Muhammad is the messenger of God'; 'God is one, God is eternal, He begets not, He was not begotten, none is equal to Him'; which is the 'Umayyad hallmark'; or in an alternative, 'prophetic' formulation, 'Muhammad is the messenger of God whom He has sent with direction and a religion of truth so that it may triumph among the religions.' These inscriptions, which occupied the central field and at first made no concessions to anything but the name of the caliph, of his agent, usually a client or *mawali*, and an indication of the mint and date, manifest a marked preoccupation with religious propaganda, with unshakeable affirmation of the faith, and with Arabisation. The existence of a genuine gold-silver bimetallism was supplemented by an ample copper coinage (the *fels*, successor to the Byzantine *follis*) and testifies to a market that was complex and many-tiered, rural, local, inter-regional, and to an early attempt at economic unification of the Muslim continent, henceforth cut off from the old Mediterranean domain.

This symbolic unification was accompanied, in reality, by rigorous domination of the conquered peoples – whether ethnic or religious groups – whose surprising collapse bears witness to the weakening of traditions in the face of pressure from a universalist ideology. Even Iran, which was by tradition a nation of fighters, accustomed to dominate and called equally, by Mazdaism, to a universal role and a perpetual struggle against evil, totally disintegrated. True, in the province of Fars a few 'noble' lineages held out, preserving the proud spirit of their race and nursing memories of national dynasties. But it was the mountain region bordering the Caspian, with a long history of independence and belatedly Islamised into the bargain, that retained its autonomous power for longest: their 'marquesses' (*ispahbadhs*), in Tabaristan for example, who were heirs to the Sassanid governors, and one or two others, who were encased in 'war territory' ravaged by repeated Muslim raids, or badgered by missionary efforts, for a while managed to hold their own. Further east, Islam was willing to make concessions to win the submission of the Sogdian

Early Islamic coins. Left, a transitional coin of the late seventh century; in imitation of Byzantine coins, it bears the effigy of Abd al-Malik, author of the monetary reform. Right, an eighth-century epigraphic *dirham* of the classical type, devoid of imagery. (Paris, Bibliothèque nationale, Cabinet des médailles).

and Bactrian princedoms: at Balkh, a local dynasty kept exclusive hold of power until 736, the Arabs even being made to occupy barracks in a neighbouring town, and then in competition with the emir, prior to being eliminated around 870. The same degree of autonomy was to be accorded to the princes of Ferghana and Ushrusana, or to the Afghans of Ghazna, and later still, down to 995, to the shahs of Khwarazm. Generally speaking, these partial and precarious agreements between the Iranian aristocracy and the Islamic government did not amount to the constitution of a national 'refuge': Islam was all-pervasive, the Persian languages heavily Arabised. All that remained to the Iranians was the memory of their glorious poetic, architectural and politically dominant past, which found a reflection, once the Umayyads started recruiting scribes of Persian origin to their bureaucracy, in the polemical literature known as the *shuʿubiyya*: against the Arab humanism of Basra, the Persians reaffirmed – but in Arabic! – the literary and heroic values of the Iranian past.

In the Christian countries of Iraq, Syria and Egypt, the assertion of religious freedom and the ending of Byzantine persecution resulted in a renaissance of the minority churches, the rebuilding of monasteries, and the recruitment of many monophysites as officials, while a great cultural upsurge, centred on Severus Sebokht, breathed new life into the Syrian Jacobite Church. Fiscal pressure, it is true, quickly put an end to this 'Islamic honeymoon', leading to numerous Coptic revolts and encouraging the caliph to play on the sectarianism of the minorities, for example by sending Zoroastrian tax-collectors into the Jazira. Thus divided, the sects were in no position to resist the strict enforcement, on orders from Omar II ben Abd al-Aziz, of rules reflecting the Islamic ascendency: the obligation to behave with deference and discretion (no bells to be rung, no public worship, a humble bearing to be adopted) and to wear a distinguishing mark. Muslim law had to be applied in any suit between a member of the minority and a Muslim or between adherents of different minority sects, and a member of the minority was forbidden to possess a Muslim slave or to bear witness against a believer. In these circumstances the fiscal and judicial systems might have been effective instruments of conversion, but the caliph held back, from fear of exhausting the fiscal reserves on which the community depended. In general, therefore he protected the *dhimmis*, the subjects, against intolerance, and intervened as arbiter in a long-running debate between doctrinaire Muslims and teachers of the minorities on the liberties at issue: the right to rebuild churches and synagogues, but not to construct new ones; the right to *waqf*, that is to say to undisturbed possession, granted to religious institutions; the right to inherit from distant kinsmen or even to inherit under the will of a Muslim. Attempts would be made by Christian scribes, Nestorians in particular, who took service with the Umayyads, and for a long while afterwards with the Abbasids, to enlarge these liberties; but an early defection by Syrian scribes of the Greek rite made the opposition to Byzantium implacable and helped to place an entire sector of Eastern Christendom under suspicion of spying for the Greeks.

In the West, even outside the Islamised tribal milieus which were already close in structure to traditional Arab society and therefore receptive of its ideals along with its language, one is struck by the rapid diffusion of Arabic among the indigenous Islamised communities, including those which had remained faithful to Christianity. In Toledo, notorious for its recalcitrance towards the Cordoban emirate and apparently numbering few Eastern immigrants among its inhabitants, the *muwallad* (native convert) poet Ghirbib was already composing verses in Arabic to stiffen resistance among his fellow-citizens towards the end of the eighth century. Well-known, too, are the mid-ninth-century lamentations of Eulogius, a mozarab ('a person living among Arabs') cleric, over the neglect of Latin letters by the Christians of Cordoba and their fondness for Arab culture. Doubtless it was a long while yet before the indigenous Romance dialects ceased to be used in the peninsula, relegated though they might be to the status of a spoken rather than a written language, and required to compete, even at that level, with spoken Arabic, which perhaps only superseded them completely in the eleventh century. This semitisation of linguistic habits was undoubtedly accompanied by the penetration of customs, ways of life and mental attitudes which served to distance the Andalusian population from its native roots. For example, it is interesting to find that endogamous marriage, presumably practised in imitation of Arab customs, was a controversial issue among the mozarabs in the ninth century. Over the whole of the Mediterranean coast, the many examples of tribalised toponymy, no doubt introduced from the ninth and tenth centuries, display an eastern or maghrebi style of relationship between human communities and the land, which supposes a deep-seated change in kinship structures in comparison with the local tradition of Romano-Visigothic origin.

The problem of resources

The Umayyad 'Arab kingdom' thus combined the political structure of the army–State with the compartmentalised structures traditional to the empire: the Muslim people, basically Arab in language and culture, still organised in tribal groupings, and with its needs supplied by an assured income from taxation and booty, devoted its energies to conquest or to defining the intellectual, philosophical, juridical and political positions which justified its ascendancy. This Islamic society thus had an 'Athenian' quality and visibly depended on the exploitation of conquered societies, trapped by their essential diverseness and inferiority.

205

The system of stipends reveals above all the superiority of the Muslims as a whole – and not just the military class: the tribes were enrolled in their entirety in the Books, the *diwans*, kept by the treasurers from the time of Omar, and this without any precise reference being made to a service they owed to the army. The stipend, or *ata*, of the soldiers, veterans or free Muslims who could all be mustered in the army, tended to replace the portable booty (*ghanima*) of the era of the initial conquests: it formalised the superior rights of the Arab people and reduced the temptation to raiding and irregular warfare. Enrolment by tribal contingents in addition served as a forcible reminder of Islam's origins since for a long while it ignored non-converts, who were furthermore constrained, as the price of integration into the 'pure' Muslim society, to become clients, *mawalis*: indeed, even their participation in military campaigns, which as we saw was active, did not entitle them to pay but only to a minor share of the booty.

Another disposition, that of conquered land, was to add to the inequalities within Muslim society and perpetuate, through the quasi-ownership of vast estates, the existence of tribal chieftaincies and military commands. In theory, booty in the form of landed property, the *fay*, was shared out between all the combatants, apart from one-fifth due to the Prophet, later to the Community, which was given to religious foundations. In practice the Muslims can be seen hesitating between two forms of apportionment. The first respected the principle of division and resulted in large-scale distributions of land, which continued to be cultivated by their possessors, now become subjects, or *dhimmis*, and placed on an inferior legal footing; they paid the customary taxes while Muslims owed the State a tenth part of their revenues. The second, adopted in the Sawad, the 'black earth region', the especially fertile zone around Baghdad, provided for the preservation of the land, by granting it in *waqf*, or mortmain, to the community as a whole; the inhabitants paid tax under the double heading of poll- and land-tax, which contributed to an 'endowment fund' earmarked for Muslim needs. In both cases, however, the prince, in virtue of the special position accorded thechieftain under tribal laws, amassed for himself a large reserve of landed property, the *sawafi*: these consisted of lands confiscated from the Sassanid State, churches, temples of fire-worshippers, and indeed the possessions of disinherited noble families or lands left abandoned. At first not very extensive, this reserve brought in only 4 million *dirhams* in the Sawad out of annual revenues amounting to between 124 and 128 million; but it was continually augmented by further confiscations or through the application of the caliph's right of possession over grazing lands.

The caliph was at liberty to make grants from these *sawafi* lands to deserving Muslims: the concession carried with it the obligation to cultivate the soil; it remained revocable and therefore did not constitute full ownership, but it nevertheless led to the formation before long of large estates (*dayʾa*) on which it became difficult to distinguish between the original usufructuary grant and subsequent purchases. Without going so far as to establish a landed aristocracy, since in accordance with Muslim law the inheritance was divided among the children, this system undoubtedly encouraged the settlement of a median class of Muslim landowners. In general, however, the financial resources of the State rested on the system of impositions which had developed piecemeal in step with the conquest.

With the evolution of the tax system and the attempts of the jurists (*fuqahas*) at rationalisation, this anarchical situation was gradually bought under control, leaving two universal taxes: the *jizya*, the poll-tax levied on subjects, or *dhimmis*, as the price of their protection and falling only on adult males of fighting age, to the large amount of between 1 and 4 dinars; and the land-tax, *kharaj*, assessed most frequently, especially in Iraq or Iran, on the extent of the land (*misaha*) and payable either in money or half in money and half in kind. The progressive conversion of the *dhimmis* obviously posed a considerable problem, since the poll-tax could then no longer be imposed. It was for this reason that jurists now tended to connect the land-tax with the land rather than with the status of its possessor: the tax was due to the community and could be neither diminished nor alienated. As a casuistical refinement it was proposed that lands should be classified according to their original status. But opinions among the legal experts were so divergent that the caliph remained definitively in charge of taxation.

For a long while the Muslims themselves remained exempt from taxation; beneficiaries from its income, their obligation was limited to voluntary alms-giving, the *zakat* or *sadaqa*, whose amount was fixed by custom as equivalent to a tenth. The cost of this to the individual should not be underestimated. The *Chronicle* of Dionysius of Tell-Marhe enables us to put a figure on the various items of which it was composed: we learn that in Islam's second century a tenth of the harvest, commuted in the Jazira at the high rate of two *dinars* per unit of land, was a burden equal to the *kharaj* in neighbouring Iraq; and that a tenth on Bedouin flocks, levied not on the revenue but on the capital and payable in coin, was so oppressive that the rate had to be lowered to $\frac{1}{30}$ or for smaller herds $\frac{1}{40}$. So in the matter of taxation the Muslims were not as privileged as might be supposed: all they were spared was the poll-tax, which was deemed to be ignominious. Nevertheless, the mass of conversions, accompanied by the growth of non-productive towns and an exodus from the countryside, were to reduce the revenues of the State from what it had been in Umayyad times: the fiscal revenue from Egypt, which under Omar and his successors averaged 12 million *dinars*, rising to peaks of 14 or 17.5 million, was to fall under Harun's caliphate in the ninth century to around 4 million, and under the Fatimids to hover between 3 and 4 million. In the Jazira, with its Jacobite population, the decline came later, from 58 million under Harun to 17.3 million around 870. Similarly, the fiscal revenue from Iraq, stabilised around the 120 million *dirhams* it yielded at the time of the conquest and still keeping to that level under Harun, shows a steep decline in the ninth century, to 78 million around 870. This impoverishment of the State no doubt had several causes, among them the granting out of *sawafi* lands and the changing fiscal status of tax-payers. Without seeking to play down the immensity of the fiscal demand and the drain it represented on economic activity or personal incomes, one understands the State's concern to let nobody escape and to arrest the downward trend.

This concern encouraged the development of a pettifogging bureaucracy: from time to time a veritable inquisition, the *taʾdil*, was conducted in order to check the information in the tax register; in the Jazira after 690 this took place every ten years and was ruthless, most of all towards illicit occupants of public land. Nobody could travel without the tax-

Frequent tours of inspections by officials of the central government, as in this illustration of notables visiting a village, helped to maintain the grip of the new Arab administration on conquered populations (*Sessions of Harîrî*, ms arab 5847, early thirteenth century, Paris, Bibliothèque nationale).

collector's receipt, which served as protection against arrest and interrogation. This was in order to check the tendency to evade tax by flight, which threatened to become widespread; and to make assurance doubly sure, travellers were later required to give proof of their tax clearance by wearing a lead seal on a cord round their necks. The oppressiveness of taxation was further increased by the arbitrary nature of the assessment carried out by officials of the central government, who were chosen as a rule from a minority different from that of the tax-payers. Another aggravation was the obligation to pay in gold or silver, since to procure the necessary coin it was necessary to sell the crop direct from the threshing-floor, naturally at a lower price than it might have realised several months later. The temptation was therefore strong for the headmen in the villages, responsible for handing over the tax, and themselves substantial landowners, to set themselves up as money-lenders; the usury which accompanied this practice made a dent in the egalitarian structure of the rural community and led to the forging of vertical bonds between headmen and the impoverished labourers indebted to them for protection. Tax evasion and usury were alike responsible for peasant revolts, directed against the speculators, but equally at the 'tax exiles', who were pursued so as to be hauled back to the community made poorer by their defection. Shades of Byzantium!

Taxation in the West follows the same pattern

It should go without saying that at the highest level of government and administration, the structures erected in the West were copied faithfully from the models being elaborated in the East. A very early example was the *diwan al-jund*, or register giving details of the various tribal contingents in the army and the pay they received. In the sphere of taxation, the desire to conform with the system evolving in the East is evident from the start: hence we meet the *jizya*, specific to Christian tax-payers, the *kharaj* or land-tax, and the tithe (*zakat* or *ushr*) demanded from Muslims. As early as 701, for example, the governor of Ifriqiya, Hassan ibn al-Nuʾman, is found entering on the land-tax register the names of *Rum* (Romans) who had declared their intention of remaining Christian. In al-Andalus, a treaty which has become famous as the treaty 'of Tudmir' (Theodemir) was made with a Gothic leader of that name, based on Orihuela, guaranteeing to Christians in the south-east of the peninsula the continued possession of their lands and the status of *dhimmi*, against payment of a *jizya* in coin or in kind, which is virtually identical to Eastern texts of the same type.

Remoteness might easily have given rise to abuses and the taking of liberties; in reality, the control of the Damascus caliphate over the first governors appears to have been as tight as distance and the technical resources of the period would permit. There can be no mistaking the will both of the empire's central government and of the local authorities to bring the organisation of the newly-conquered provinces into line with Islamic norms. The Latin chronicle of 754 known as the *Mozarab Chronicle* stresses more than once the efforts by governors of Cordoba to bring the anarchical reality of the conquerors' appropriation of the land into conformity with legal requirements. For example, it is said that al-Samh, governor from 719 to 721, ordered a new distribution of lands which the Arabs had been holding '*indivisum*', that is without having gone through the formalities of a legal apportionment. And it is said of Yahya ibn Salam, governor from 725 to 727, that he actually compelled Arabs and Berbers to restore 'peace lands' to the Christian inhabitants – presumably a reference to lands which had been seized from them in spite of the guarantee of continuing possession given in a peace treaty (*sulh*) at the time of their submission. The same source also mentions the creation of fiscal registers by these early governors, of whom it is said that several made a *descriptio populi*, presumably in order to regularise collection of the *kharaj*.

In Africa as much as in Spain, the monetary system, which was a corollary of the tax system, was introduced with remarkable rapidity. The coin-types imposed in the East by Abd al-Malik's reform of the currency in the late seventh century were in fact preceded in the West by a number of hybrid Latino-Arab coinages, but if the presence of the latter

The problem of irrigation, crucial to the revival of an essentially agrarian economy, encouraged the Arabs to develop machines such as the *noria* seen in this illustration (*Hadith of Bayad and Riyad*, Arab ms 368, thirteenth century, Vatican Library).

indicates awareness by the authorities of the need for a transitional stage, the briefness of the emissions (in Africa from 703 to 716) demonstrates an intention to move as quickly as possible to the Eastern system. In al-Andalus, the break with the Visigothic coinage was immediate and total, and the Latin or bi-lingual transitional coins, imitated from African models, lasted only from 711 to 717, after which one finds only *dinars* which in their epigraphy and metrology conform to the type fixed by Abd al-Malik's reform. What is still obscure, however, is the reason for the interruption to the gold coinage in al-Andalus in the mid-eighth century. Starting in 745, after a gap of about fifteen years which is no doubt attributable to the mid-century political crisis, the Andalusian mints began to emit nothing but *dirhams*, similar to the types previously issued by the Damascus caliphate, and this remained the situation down to the proclamation of the caliphate at Cordoba in 929. In this and other institutional respects, Spain appears as a sort of repository of Umayyad tradition. It is conceivable that, just as they did not venture to assume the caliphal title straight away, so the sovereigns of Cordoba thought themselves equally unauthorised to challenge the Abbasid monetary monopoly over gold. It may also be relevant that gold was scarce at this period throughout the West, and worth noting that emissions in gold ceased in al-Andalus at the same time as in Gaul. In the Maghrib, the Idrisids likewise confined their issues to *dirhams*, no doubt for the same reasons. As for the *dinars* minted by the Aghlabid rulers of Ifriqiya, these were presumably chiefly destined for the tribute due to the caliph; internal circulation would have been based mainly on silver.

A painful economic recovery

It is unlikely that the rural base in those parts of the Near-East which were affected by the Islamic conquest underwent any immediate transformation. The conqueror's principal concern, as should now be clear, was fiscal in character: he inherited local conditions, including the taxes imposed by the Byzantines and Sassanids, and relied on peasant communities to raise them. Even if the Arab invasion produced a modicum of tribal settlement in Syria, the Jazira and Egypt, this implantation of a rather small number of Bedouin, perhaps no more than the 150,000 who fought in the battle of Siffin, was unlikely to have had consequences for the empire's rural base; much more unsettling to rural communities, and the cause of a wave of desertions, was the appeal of the non-productive towns. Living off the fruits of the soil and of taxation, crowned with military and religious prestige, the Islamised city attracted the mass of new converts who resented the weight of rural taxation: in the towns they were able to escape the *kharaj*, which assimilated them to the subject *dhimmis*, and to enjoy the blessings of freedom and anonymity, or even the privilege of admission to a tribal sub-group as *mawalis*.

A narrower, devitalised rural base

Desertions from the land had thus become considerable: they are explicitly referred to and dated in the *Book* on the land-tax compiled about 790 by Abu Yusuf for the caliph Harun: in central Iraq, in the Sawad, fiscal heart of the empire, he claims that 'they go back a hundred years or so'. His testimony is corroborated by the findings of modern archaeologists: these include a wholesale abandonment of canals in central Iraq between Baghdad and the Zagros or between the Tigris and the Euphrates; a decrease in the number of villages in the plain of the Diyala 'behind Baghdad', and in northern Mesopotamia. Similar indications of ancient desertion are found in other regions of the Near East, principally on the Nabatean fringes of southern and eastern Palestine and in eastern Syria between Homs and Palmyra. The settlement in the Jazira of the Mudar, Bakr and Rabi'a tribes, all from northern Arabia, in Syria of the Qaysites and the Kalbites, originally from the Yemen, and in Egypt of Qaysites and several Yemenite groups who penetrated as far as the Sudan, clearly made a difference to the lives of the native inhabitants. It has been stressed that this should not be interpreted as a conflict between nomads and sedentaries: the ecological balance of the regions was not upset by the herdsmen, who on the contrary made a contribution by exploiting complementary resources and promoting exchanges between the desert fringe and the agricultural zone. By comparison with these implantations, the waves of rural desertion were more wholesale and later in date: it was deforestation and then the demographic crisis that

211

together bled white the urban markets and produced the reversion to tribal values in the face of an oppressive State; for Syria, it was the displacement after 750 of the empire's political centre to Iraq; in Egypt, the reduction in the irrigated area and the abandonment of the Delta's western, and more particularly its eastern, fringes would be the long-term consequences in the tenth century of the silting-up of the Nile's connection to the sea – though it is by no means certain that greater care and forethought by the Muslim State could have avoided this, since of the seven main branches of the Nile which had been navigable in Ptolemaic times only three, with their outlets at Pelusium, Damietta and Rosetta, remained open when the Arabs first appeared on the scene.

But we should not paint too black a picture: on the fringes of the desert, especially in Syria, the Umayyad period saw a proliferation of palaces, serving both as hunting-lodges and as centres for large-scale agricultural operations: these depended on meticulous regulation of the water supply, which was trapped in reservoirs and fed into the extensive cultivations, enclosed within high walls of stone and unbaked brick. Qasr al Hayr al-Sharkî, meaning 'eastern', built by Hisham in 728, was a large fortified site, with walls 71m long and a central courtyard measuring 45m × 37m, the whole being defended by twelve round towers; designed for luxurious living, magnificently decorated with frescoes and a stucco of vine-leaves, it was supplied with produce from an orchard and garden (*hayr*) 7km long and 1.5km wide. Other early efforts at agricultural management, such as dyke-building, digging canals, or the building of new palaces or even whole villages, are ascribed to the Umayyad princes Saʾid and Maslama. They bear witness to a shift in the interest of the powerful towards the irrigated lands of lower Iraq that would be the centre of agricultural experiment and revolution in the Abbasid period. Ibn Washiya, in his *Nabataean Agriculture*, gives us an early description of these exploitations, or *daʾayas*, which were managed by a master and an overseer and worked by an unskilled, largely non-Islamised labour force; one must assume, however, that the help of engineers was needed to dig the canals and construct the huge bucket-wheels to draw up the water. Villages and large farms rolled into one, they necessarily included an artisanal sector of blacksmiths, potters, carpenters and so on. Firmly rooted in an Antique tradition of agricultural management, although as a rule no longer reliant on slave labour, these large exploitations kept to the pre-Islamic solar calendar and preserved a body of technical lore impregnated with magic.

The status of the peasants, viewed as a whole, presents a picture filled with contrasts: the large estates employed a paid labour force, at any rate fed and kept in semi-servile dependence, but this was an exception. Rural communities were still vital forces in Syria and the Jazira, where they exercised a right of joint ownership over the soil, implying periodic redistributions, while in Egypt it was the State which annually imposed on a community, as its intermediary, the duty of reallocating the irrigated land and the compulsory cultivations. Since large-scale landownership was inhibited, as we saw, by the rules of inheritance, the burden of taxation and fiscal abuse tended instead to reinforce the patron–client relationship between the notables and inhabitants of the countryside: the peasant cultivator might seek the protection, *taldjia* or *himaya*, of a 'man of power', who

The impressive ruins of the fortified palace of Qasr al-Hayr al-Sharki in the arid wastes of the Syrian desert. It is hard to imagine that this was once the centre of a vast agricultural domain chiefly comprising gardens and orchards.

paid the tax and enjoyed a superior right over the land of his protégé, perhaps transforming it into a share-cropping tenancy or making it more profitable by exacting a full or half tithe as the price of protection. It should not be supposed that this practice resulted in the permanent constitution of large estates split up into tenures: the peasant community put up stubborn resistance, made all the more effective by family solidarity; the possibility of escape into the town remained open, and the reason for this was bound up with the precarious standing of the 'men of power'. Coercive power and wealth went with political fortune, an all too volatile commodity; ownership of the land was constantly being disrupted by falls from grace and confiscations. Was this perhaps the way in which the Islamic social regime preserved its natural checks and balances? A reminder of the centrality of the State in the age of conquest? A means of averting the creation of a class of rich and powerful men capable of exerting pressure on the caliph and appropriating his superior and imprescriptible right over the land? Quickly assembled and quickly divided, large estates could survive only in the form of *waqf*, religious endowment: the pious foundations destined for the poor, for mosques, and for the public good (caravenserais, baths, conduits) were not large in themselves, but the way in which they were managed by family trusts could lead to the formation of a formidable landed base: it is true that these were chiefly urban properties and that the effect on the countryside was negligible. The

213

status of the peasant, already lowly and insecure under the Byzantines and Sassanids, in general seems to have worsened: the word *raqiq* commonly applied to it has a servile connotation, as of a person undeserving of respect. Where lands were held in tenure, that is on old estates or those enlarged through the operation of patronage, the share of the cultivator was modest in the extreme: a share-cropping tenancy (*musaqah*) allowed him to keep back, on lands that were fertile, only between a half and a quarter of the crop; under the *mukhabarah* contract, a species of partnership in which, in addition to the land, the proprietor supplied tools, seed-corn and the use of his oxen, the peasant partner was allowed only one-fifth of the grain harvest; and the situation was the same in the Maghrib, where the *khamessat* followed the same pattern. This depressed social and economic condition was doubtless neither universal nor evenly spread: the countryside had both its rich and its poor, its landless labourers and its vagrants of whom we catch only a glimpse. Doubtless, too, there was a sense in which the large estate and the rural community were complementary: the former was able to absorb and set to work on the irrigated lands any surplus members of the rural population, or to offer younger sons, when the community had reached its ecological and demographic limits and had no more land to share out, a small plot to work with the loan of seed-corn and oxen.

Towns old and new

The Muslim society of the conquerors was above all a society of town-dwellers, living in organised military encampments, easily aroused by the tumultuous assemblies for communal prayer, an armed community whose life was focused on two essential centres, the mosque and the palace. At the terminus of the caravan routes followed by the Arab armies, and beside the great rivers of Egypt and Iraq, the settlement of the Bedouin gave rise to new and important agglomerations: Kufa, in 636, at a point where a pontoon bridge over the Euphrates opened the way from Hira to central Iraq; Basra, in 638, at the confluence of the Tigris and the Euphrates; Fustat, in 640, close to the Byzantine fortress of Egyptian Babylon, where the first bridge upstream from the Delta was situated. These new towns, the *amsar* (singular *misr*), bore witness to the strength and unity of the conquerors; they had no need of fortification or protection of any kind, and when Basra was eventually provided with a rampart and ditch in 771, this was not from fear of the conquered populace but because of Kharijite disturbances among the Bedouin themselves.

A new, if varied, urban layout was adopted in these *amsar*: its basis was the tribalism which determined the division of the site into districts corresponding to the various clan groupings in the army. At Basra there were five such districts or quarters, each allotted to a tribal confederation: Azd, Tamin, Bakr, Abd al-Qays, Abd al-Aliya. At Kufa the layout resembled that of a Roman camp, with four principal avenues intersecting at right angles at the centre, marked by the mosque and the palace; the streets were up to 25m wide, and at the centre of each tribal concession or *khitta* was the cemetery of that group. At Kufa, the topography was to remain consistent with the divisions fixed for this initially semi-rustic settlement of reed huts and tents, which were not replaced by permanent structures until

The town-palace established by caliph Sulaiman in 717 at Anjar in the Lebanon. Despite the persistence of Byzantine traits in the decoration, it exemplifies the inventive qualities of Umayyad urban architecture.

some 30 years after its foundation. At Fustat, the archaeological evidence points to a similar chronology, beginning with a tented town criss-crossed by streets separating the tribal *khittas*; but here the layout is more confused, consisting of a maze of little streets leading into blind alleys or squares, sometimes enclosed, in the shape of a crowsfoot or a star; this pattern, which no doubt reflected tribal particularities, influenced the whole topographical development of Fustat down the centuries. At Fez, whose foundation as the Idrisid capital dates to the turn of the eighth century, the layout again seems to have resulted from a tribally-determined partition.

Certain common features characterised the way of life in the new towns: reliance on the tribal group, which was controlled by its own chiefs and led a more or less independent existence, fortified in its identity by 'elders' revered for their all-important knowledge of a tribe's genealogical lore; an uncomplicated structure, geared to rapid mobilisation of a populace paid for military service; a very attenuated judicial and political apparatus, since questions of inheritance lay within the jurisdiction of the tribe; a religious and intellectual centre, the mosque, in a constant state of ferment. This simplicity was gradually obliterated by the advance of economic activity, whose main objective remained the provisioning of the urban groups; thus the organism became more complex without losing its fundamental significance as a stipendiary metropolis, 'gobbling up booty'; and to booty must be added the income from the land, principally in the form of the tax due to the community of the conquerors. Buildings sprang up everywhere: a mint, a treasury, at Kufa even a storehouse for booty; Basra was equipped with a harbour looking to the Persian Gulf, and before long to India; at Fustat, commercial activity founded on the tradition of local merchants and on Meccan expertise began to flourish around a local agricultural market, whose wares were gradually augmented by products imported from India or China. This urban transformation was admittedly very slow to affect the tribal look of these towns, but it accentuated the differences in wealth between the great 'houses' at the head of the clans and the lesser lineages.

The new agglomerations, while they were the ideal of urban life for the Arab immigrants to the ancient lands of the Fertile Crescent or to Egypt and Spain, controlled an extensive network of towns inherited from the past. Apart from a few probable additions under the first caliphs and the Umayyads, especially in Iraq and on the frontiers, the picture is essentially the same as under the Byzantines or Sassanids, continuity of toponymy and habitation being especially apparent in northern Syria, on the borders with Anatolia and in Iran. In the east, where the installation of large Arab contingents gave a sudden spur to urbanisation, the tendency was for old agglomerations to be duplicated: alongside Persian towns, usually citadels of minor importance, the newcomers built themselves a suburb (*birun*), adjacent to the highway, in which the essential organs of an Islamic city – the great mosque, palace and market – were located. At Nishapur, on the route through Khurasan to Transoxiana and China, the citadel and the 'inner town' (*madîna* or *sharastan*) were incorporated into one vast whole. The long-continuing autonomy of the former Sassanid 'marcher' lords delayed the Islamisation of numerous towns such as Merv, Balkh, Samarkand and Bukhara. One notes everywhere the divided structure of cities which succeeded

Entrance to the *suq* at Damascus, still flanked by the colonnades of an avenue dating from Roman times. Chosen by the Umayyad caliphs as their administrative capital, Damascus underwent some alteration in their time, but its foundation goes back to Antiquity and its layout to the Byzantine epoch.

in resisting the unitary pattern and were only gradually reordered: at Merv, which the Arabs encamped in the oasis were long forbidden to enter, it was Abu Muslim who eventually constructed a new political centre (*Dar al-Imara*), around 750. The region of greatest continuity was Syria, where the Arab occupation adapted itself to the pattern of military districts, *junds*, found in the former cities; admittedly the coastal towns, as attested by the archaeological evidence, suffered a rapid decline at the time of the great forays into the Mediterranean; on the other hand, the number of copper coins bearing the marks of

217

Tahir, marched on Baghdad and laid siege to it from August 812 to September 813, meeting heroic resistance from the population. These dynastic conflicts were further inflamed by the jealousies of the secretary–tutors and the ambitions of the queen–mothers, each wanting to get the better of her rivals in the women's quarters of the palace. The atmosphere of unbridled intrigue finally undermined the very nature of the caliph's power: Mahdi was perhaps assassinated, the same dark suspicion attaches to the death of Hadi, and Amin met his death at the hands of Tahir's soldiers.

Which path was an 'Islamic' monarchy to follow?

The conflicts within the Family obviously had their repercussions on the court and contributed to the stormy history of the viziership, punctuated to the end of the Abbasids' personal rule by cruelly vindictive disgraces and excessive confiscations. The fragility of their position drove the secretaries to frantic attempts to consolidate their standing, and to an insensate accumulation of riches, with the result that the viziership increasingly became a private power, in which authority was delegated to one individual: the favourites were distinguished by significantly grandiose titles ('brother in God' under Mahdi for Ya'qub ben Dawub) which gave proof of integration into the Family and masked their insecurity. One example stands out: the Barmakids, descendants of a Buddhist prior at Balkh, who governed from 786 to 803, having risen to eminence with Yahya, tutor to Harun, who was afterwards responsible for bringing his pupil to power. The exceptional duration and extent of this family's success enabled long-term policies to be worked out: reconciliation with the Alids, recruitment of a new army in Khurasan, imposition of peace with Byzantium. A convention was established whereby the vizier reigned supreme in Baghdad and the caliph devoted himself exclusively to the *jihad*: a true division of political labour. It was the fiscal burden this policy entailed which brought about the downfall of the Barmecides, and their execution in 803.

Ominously for the future of the dynasty, the members of the Family were quite soon assailed by doubts regarding the legitimacy of their power: the Alids had not been slow to intensify their propaganda and refine their arguments. They continued to boast of the purity of their pedigree, untainted by misalliances; they laid stress on their irreproachable female ancestry (whereas the caliphs were the sons of slave concubines), and before long on Fatima – even though the genealogical model common to the Arabs was strictly patrilinear. Above all, in certain circles at least, they invoked the support of messianic ideas that were once again in circulation: these centred on the imminent apocalyptical appearance of the *mahdi*, the 'rightly-guided one', the 'Lord of Time' who should establish a Reign of Justice, the Imam endowed with almost supernatural knowledge and virtue, a bridge between the human and the divine. To counteract these beliefs, which echoed themes previously harped on by Shi'ite extremists and which harmonised with the Neoplatonist cosmology just being discovered by Arab thinkers, the Abbasids resorted to the ineffectual tactic of imitation: the regnal name Mahdi adopted by Mansur's son, who already bore the forename Muhammad ben Abdallah, which was associated in pious tradition with the

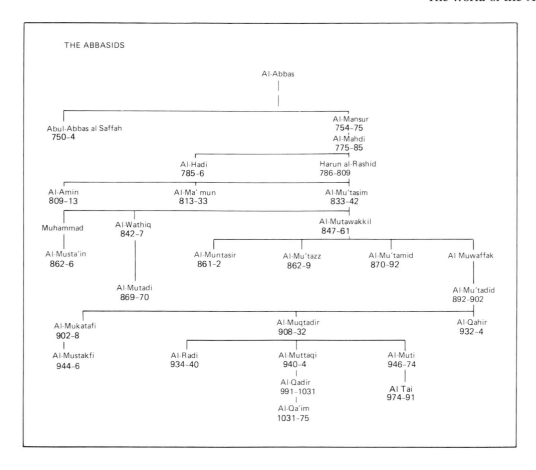

THE ABBASIDS

Al-Abbas

Abul-Abbas al Saffah
750-4

Al-Mansur
754-75

Al-Mahdi
775-85

Al-Hadi
785-6

Harun al-Rashid
786-809

Al-Amin
809-13

Al-Ma'mun
813-33

Al-Mu'tasim
833-42

Muhammad

Al-Wathiq
842-7

Al-Mutawakkil
847-61

Al-Musta'in
862-6

Al-Muntasir
861-2

Al-Mu'tazz
862-9

Al-Mu'tamid
870-92

Al Muwaffak

Al-Mutadi
869-70

Al-Mu'tadid
892-902

Al-Mukatafi
902-8

Al-Muqtadir
908-32

Al-Qahir
932-4

Al-Mustakfi
944-6

Al-Radi
934-40

Al-Muttaqi
940-4

Al-Muti
946-74

Al-Qadir
991-1031

Al Tai
974-91

Al-Qa'im
1031-75

saviour Mahdi, and Ma'mun's adoption of the title imam, and even *kahlifat Allah*, 'vicar of God', are portents of an extraordinary inflation of the Abbasid regnal titles, each with a greater religious significance than the last; in a language not yet grown stale, they express the approval, good fortune and victory bestowed by God on his protégé. But while not yet stereotypes, these titles were none the less impostures, and the sense of the Alids' superiority began to make headway even among the caliphs. Between 816 and 818 Ma'mun reached the point of deciding to transmit the caliphate to the Alid Ali al-Rida, who became his son-in-law and appointed heir; but this dream of reconciliation was frustrated by the armed opposition of Baghdad, and the imam-elect was removed by death, probably poisoned.

Following this setback, one last effort to give meaning to the Islamic monarchy was made by Mu'tasim and his son Wathiq, through their attempt between 827 and 847 to impose a common ideology on the Muslim empire in the form of Mu'tazilism. The adoption by Ma'mun in 827 of the doctrine of the 'created Koran' was followed in 833 by the establishment of the *mihna*, the inquisition: carried out by the prefect of police of Bagdad, with the authority of the chief qadi and by provincial governors, it purged the dynasty's service of all ideological opponents of Mu'tazilite thought: the Iranian dualists and those

227

heretics known collectively as *zindiqs* who denied the oneness of God, anthropomorphists who accepted the corporeality of the divine attributes and the vision of God in Paradise, and those who denied the existence of human free will. The repression extended to teachers, who were interrogated by the authorities, on occasion even by the caliph, and made to subscribe to the Muʿtazilite dogmas. The majority submitted, with varying degrees of sincerity, but a traditionist resistance grew up around Ahmad ibn Hanbal, who was twice interrogated and imprisoned. A number of executions provided Hanbalite propaganda with martyrs, and on the accession of Mutawakkil the inquisition was brought abruptly to an end. The chief qadi, Ibn Abi Duʾad, was deposed in 852 and the caliph was reduced to condemning, by decree, all study of dogmatic theology, *kalam*. This defeat, while not ruling out future theological and philosophical enquiry, nevertheless helped to make it suspect in the eyes of many traditionists and led to the formulation of a doctrine whose horizons were bounded by literal agreement with the sacred Book. The failure of the experiment also makes evident the failure of another form of government, which had brought the chief qadi to the forefront at a time when the power of the viziers was restricted to their fiscal and financial prerogatives.

With Mutawikkil, this parenthesis was closed and the Islamic monarchy returned to the instability and dangers of the Barmakid era. In addition, new perils made themselves apparent through the systematic recruitment of an army composed of Turkish slaves: it should be explained that the dynasty had given up the direct administration of Khurasan, which was handed over to Tahir and his descendants, and had thus cut itself off from the traditional source of recruitment. From now on, as well as nurturing the intrigues of the caliph's 'adoptive brothers' and the secretary–tutors, the palace was to excite the ambitions of Turkish army officers, who could rely on the unquestioning obedience of their troops: the story of violent successions is resumed with the assassination of Mutawakkil in 861 by the palace guards, opening the way for further conflicts between the Abbasid princes. The failure of the Islamic monarchy was total: it laid bare the foundations of the State, exposing the dependence on pure force which underlay the hypocritical persiflage of the caliph's titles; and it opened the door to contradictory currents of public opinion, lending reinforcement to Shiʾite millenarist beliefs in the coming Reign of Justice, but at the same time adding weight to the *ulama*, the circle of religious teachers who were determined to speak in the name of the community and to oppose the abuses of the military. In their quest for a profound and lasting political and moral transformation, it might appear that the West offered more fertile ground. It is indeed the case that the political evolution of the western part of the vast Muslim empire shows a number of distinctive traits. For all practical purposes, the independent States which formed in al-Andalus and the western and central Maghrib as a result of the crisis of the mid-eighth century and in Ifriqiya after 800, no longer acknowledged the authority of the eastern caliph. Though the ethnic factor represented by the Berbers undoubtedly played an important role in the emergence of the Tahert and Fez emirates, the constitution of the Cordoba and Kairouan emirates appears to have been unconnected with any local indigenous element of particularism. Everything was run by a ruling aristocracy of eastern origin, with or without the support of Arab or

228

The army, at once the strength and weakness of the caliphs, and essentially alien in its composition, played a primordial role in politics throughout Islamic history. This stone slab carved in Daghestan in the twelfth century depicts an officer of alien origin, perhaps a Turk (Paris, Louvre).

Berber tribalism. Furthermore, even in the 'Berber' States of Tahert and Fez, the respective dynasties were Iranian and Arab. And there may also be some truth in the claim of the petty emirs who ruled the Salahid 'princedom' of Nahir to be of Arab origin. It is only on the still indistinct margins of western Islam that we come across quasi-independent political chieftains of indigenous descent, for example the Berber Midriades of Sijilmasa or the Muwallad 'lords' of the Ebro valley. On the political plane, therefore, all the forces which ruled over tribal segmentation and local fragmentation were of eastern provenance, which means that we should first try to measure the actual extent of Arab and Eastern influence over the Muslim States of the western Mediterranean at the time of their establishment.

Berberisation or Arabisation: which was it to be in the West?

Almost nothing is known of the exact processes by which the ethnic elements imported from the Middle East – Arabs or Arabised clients incorporated into the army and its tribal organisation – were settled on the land. In theory, these warriors should have received not land but pay, in accordance with their rank order in the *diwan-al-jund* or military register. In actuality, whether in Ifriqiya or al-Andalus, they very soon received substantial landed endowments, whose distribution the governors sent by the Damascus caliph found it difficult to regularise. The means whereby the native inhabitants were dispossessed, the proportion of the land appropriated in this way by the conquerors, the system of allocation (whether on a clan or individual basis), are matters on which our ignorance is well-nigh total. A great number of questions can be asked about the application in practice of the legal norms – themselves still ill-defined at this period – which should have governed the appropriation of lands by the conquerors and their allocation, but we are unlikely ever to be in a position to give an answer. As regards the actual cultivation of these estates or *diya*, we can presume that their new possessors were chiefly concerned to continue the regime in force on the eve of the conquest; this seems to have meant, at any rate in Spain, that on the **229** large estates of the ruling aristocracy the rural workforce was maintained in a juridical condition still close to Roman slavery. It would be reasonable to suppose that as the result of conversions to Islam, and in keeping with the spirit of the new regime, the condition of these dependent peasants evolved towards forms of the colonate less disadvantageous to the cultivator, allowing him a share of the produce. All the same, Ibn Hawqal, who though writing shortly after the middle of the tenth century appears to be referring to the period of social, political and religious disturbances experienced by the Muslim part of the peninsula at the end of the ninth, can still point to the existence of large estates worked by Christian peasants of servile status, from whom revolts were always to be feared.

We are equally in the dark about the number of Arabs or Arabised easterners who finally settled in the West. Talbi puts at 180,000 the total strength of the armies from the East which penetrated Ifriqiya. In Spain, the figure is certain to have been less (perhaps 50,000?), and the eastern contingents entering al-Andalus should not be added to those of the Maghrib, since it is likely that many had come from the latter country and not directly from the East. We can only speak in terms of tens of thousands of warriors, of whom the majority can be presumed to have settled permanently in the West, in most cases with their families. They were concentrated mainly in Ifriqiya, in the south of the Iberian peninsula and the northern march (Ebro valley), with a smaller concentration in northern Morocco around Tangier. Later, Arabs from al-Andalus and Ifriqiya went to populate Fez, newly-founded by the Idrisid dynasty. But what is more important than attaching a numerical weight to the Arab element in the population is to gain an insight into its social role, which was considerable. In Ifriqiya, it has been pointed out, the Arabs succeeded not only in protecting their identity as an ethnic group against dilution by the surrounding mass but also in asserting themselves 'as the leading group in society, which they pervaded with their language, religion and ideals. Of their physical fecundity there can be no doubt, so that if the appearance of generations of *muwallidin* and *hjana* (descendants of Arabs and native women) points to fusion of a biological kind, it also signifies an expansion of the Arab element in society at large'.

These observations are equally valid for Spain, where, for two centuries and more, the Arabs continued to form an active aristocratic element, distinct from the rest of the population, and sufficiently numerous, especially in the southern regions, to be more than a match for the Islamised natives (*muwallads*) and Christian mozarabs who revolted against their domination in the late eighth century. Particularly in Spain, it can well be imagined that the patrilinear and endogamous structure of the Arab clans, 'in the market for women', and in any case politically and socially dominant, put them in a very strong position vis-à-vis an indigenous aristocracy enfeebled by defeat, without strong cultural roots, and whose family structures were much looser. The indigenous aristocracy appears in fact to have been progressively marginalised, eliminated or absorbed, so that after the ninth century it ceased to play any visible role.

In North Africa, the socio-political system proposed by the conquerors differed from that of Roman imperialism in that it was not fundamentally destructive of native institutions. The Arab tradition embraced a tribal system fairly close to that of the Berbers, which the military organisation of the *jund* helped to preserve. The Arabs' greatest affinity was

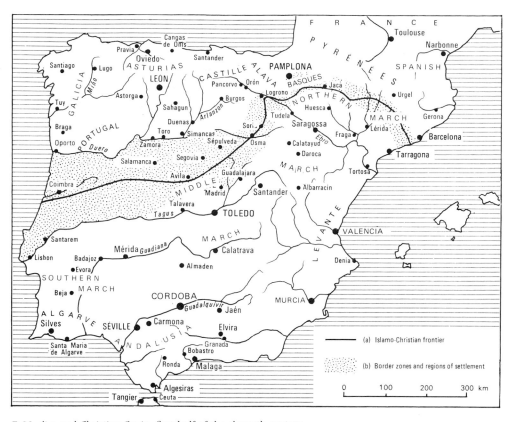

7 Muslim and Christian Spain, first half of the eleventh century

probably with the large tribal groupings of 'eastern' Berbers, with whom assimilation was rapid. This affinity was noted by al-Ya'qubi, writing towards the end of the ninth century, who says of the Hawwara that 'they claim to be descended from Yemenite tribes whose name they have forgotten', and adds that 'the separate groups join together in the same way as the groups in Arab tribes'. The sedentary *Baranis* of eastern Algeria, while no doubt leading a more village-based existence than the nomads or semi-nomads of the pre-desert steppes, appear to have had a social structure not unlike that of the ancient Arabs, to judge from answers given by members of the Kutama tribe of Little Kabylia to enquiries as to their customs when they visited Mecca as pilgrims around 900: 'We branch out into various tribes, clans and families . . . There is not much co-operation between us . . . We fight and then make up; we make peace with one branch and declare war on others.' They further explained that they were ruled by assemblies (*djemaas*), and that their law-suits were settled by arbitrators, 'persons who have acquired some learning and school teachers'. They lastly asserted that they were not subject to any State and that they paid the 'charitable tithe' required by Islamic rules directly to the poor.

A synthesis of this kind between Muslim requirements and the traditional modes of tribal society must have been achieved over a large part of the Maghrib, including the whole of the Kharijite zone where the tribes were subject merely to the distant and ill-defined authority of the imam of Tahert, like the Nafusa in the south of Ifriqiya, who according to al-Ya'qubi resisted payment of the land-tax to any government. He also makes it clear that in his day (late ninth century) the Nafusa did not speak Arabic; and it is of course to be expected that preservation of the indigenous social structures would encourage the retention of Berber as the language of everyday speech. But what is also obvious is that these Berbers were thoroughly Islamised, meaning that they had accepted Arabic as their cultural language, with all that that implied in terms of the gradual modification of social standards, attitudes and habits which were not in line with those purveyed by the new 'official' language. An already advanced level of Arabisation among the Kutama of Lesser Kabilyia is revealed by what happened when Fatimid missionaries arrived around the year 900 to spread Shi'ism in this rural region, situated on the borders of the Aghlabid emirate but still set in its tribal ways and jealously preserving its independence from the Kairouan government. For even if the Kutama recoiled from the political authority and fiscal constraints which officials of the Aghlabid state, living in the towns at the foot of their mountains, sought to impose, the success achieved by the Fatimids shows their fascination with the East as the source of all knowledge, and this could only have encouraged the spread of Arabic and of the social ideals which went with it.

What has just been said of the Berber tribes of the Maghrib is even more true of the tribes transported to Spain at the time the peninsula was conquered in the early eighth century. In al-Andalus the Berber tribal milieu was neither so important nor so cohesive as in the Maghrib, but the texts leave us in no doubt as to its existence. There were many parts of al-Andalus which received a large Berber influx – the Andalusian mountains, the valleys of the Guadiniana and the Tagus (*Djawf*, or the Merida region and the southern March), the Sierra Morena (*Fahs al-Ballut*), the northern *Gharb* (the centre of present-day Portugal), the mountainous country between Toledo and the Valencian region (Santaver), not forgetting a large area of the Levante – traces of which still survive in place-names. Mestanza, in the mountains north of Cordoba, Moquinenza, in the Tortosa region, Cehegin, in the province of Murcia, and the several places called Adzameta in the Valencian region bear witness to the settlement of organised groups of the Mistasa, Miknasa, Sinhaja (*al-Sinhajiyin*) and Zanata tribes; and it would not be hard to find many similar examples. Certain towns or rural districts in the southern March, the Levante and the Andalusian mountains went by the name of other tribes, the Nafusa, the Maghila, the Lamya, whose settlement must usually have resulted from a *de facto* occupation of territories they had conquered, which the authorities then legalised as best they could. It is thus easy to see how the Ifriqiyan jurist of the late tenth century, al-Dawudi, in the part of his book on landed property, *Kitab al-amwal*, dealing with the Muslim West, came to echo traditions that during the occupation of Spain each group of conquerors – who came in tribal contingents, it will be remembered – took possession of whatever lands fell into their hands, without first submitting to any legal form of division. This was why changes, especially of an economic order, were slower to follow the occupation of the land in the West than in the East, where legal reforms precipitated an agrarian transformation that was both durable and rapid.

Production

Fiscal reform, belatedly undertaken and unconnected with the political upheaval of the Abbasid revolution, affected only central Iraq, the Sawad or black earth region around Baghdad which formed the kernel of the caliph's empire. It was introduced in the hope of putting an end to the impoverishment of the treasury and to the abandonment of cultivated lands. Defended by Abu Yusuf in his *Book* on the land-tax written for Harun al-Rashid, it had been initiated by his predecessors, under Mahdi: it was a response to the realisation that Iraq's rural areas were being deserted, which increased the burden on peasants remaining in the village community, and to the social conflicts generated by the necessity to pay in coin, at a time when the crops were still awaiting measurement on the threshing-floor. The caliphal jurists further pointed out that the tax levied on abandoned plots rebounded on the community, thus depriving peasants of the financial resources they needed to bring the lands back into cultivation. So in response to petitions from peasant communities in the Sawad, the caliphal government agreed to return to the system of a tax levy proportionate to the harvests.

A fiscal reform, a cultural revolution

This apportionment, the *muqasama*, was made on the threshing-floor. This does not mean, however, that the tax was being exacted in kind; the only difference was that the assessment was made on the crops actually harvested, on the basis of which the prince's share was then translated into money. But was this calculated by the tax-collectors in relation to an ideal price, after allowing for variations, or the actual market price? We should probably work on the former hypothesis, since the theoretical exponents of Islamic law were afraid to dabble in the irregularity of the market price, which was God's business, and viewed it with suspicion because of the illicit gains it could encourage. But the prince's share was much greater than in the case of the tax levied on the cadastral unit: three times as much, a difference which represented a considerable increase in the burden of taxation; the necessity for a quick sale of the crops did nothing to alleviate the fiscal burden, and the picture was further darkened by speculation, the purchase of grain at monopolistic prices by bankers who came round with the tax-collectors, and usury. The fact that peasant communities had actually pressed for the reform indicates that the burden of the deserted lands and their tax must indeed have been crushing.

The reversion to the *muqasama* system was accompanied by a fiscal policy deliberately intended to encourage agricultural expansion and by a virtual revolution in farming practices. The suppression of the taxes on uncultivated lands gave inducement to communities and individuals to enlarge the boundaries of their cultivations; at the same time, 'dead lands' were granted out to whomever brought them back into cultivation. More important still was the systematic reduction of the tax on irrigated lands to take account of the costs involved: on land subject to the *kharaj*, the State demanded 40 per cent of the corn and barley grown on non-irrigated land but only 30 per cent where irrigation was

233

Age-old methods of irrigation: top right, using the current, as with this *noria* at Hama in Syria; bottom left, using animal traction, as with this camel-operated pump at Zem Zem in Tunisia, or top left, as with this primitive Algerian balance-beam.

practised; again, a levy of 33 per cent was imposed on vines, forage crops (clover and lucerne) and other produce grown in naturally-watered surroundings, and of only 25 per cent on 'summer' crops (vegetables, water-melons, sesame, colza, aubergines, cotton and sugar cane). When we turn to tithed land the intention of the policy becomes even more obvious: ten per cent on cereals watered 'naturally' (that is by rain, flooding or gravity, without mechanical intervention), five per cent on cereals dependent on costly machinery for their water, ten per cent again on dried fruits, dried vegetables, textile fibres and cereals of secondary importance (millet, rice, sesame), and nothing on fresh vegetables and forage crops: included in the latter were summer crops (melons, marrows, aubergines), catch-crops such as cucumbers, carrots, spinach and spring melons, and the forage crops whose value to the soil had been recognised by agronomists (in addition to trapping nitrogen, they provided green-mulch or cattle fodder, thus liberating grazing lands and producing manure).

The breadth of its economic objectives makes this complex reform seem well in advance of its time: the regressive rate of taxation, linked as it was with the productivity of the soil, was a stimulus to increased output, and a means of encouraging development without loss of revenues to the State, which benefited from the larger harvests to be expected and which in addition controlled the construction or digging of irrigation channels. The reform encouraged the adoption of new species, the rehabilitation of the productive capacities of the soil, and the multiplication of harvests during the year (catch-crops, 'summer' crops). Those products on which the tax was reduced were, furthermore, the ones most saleable on the urban market: durum wheat, an irrigated 'summer' crop in demand for making pasta; rice, whose future in the Muslim world was assured; fruit and vegetables, whose consumption was supported by culinary fashion and for which there were standard recipes in Abbasid cookery books (meat dishes seasoned with dried fruit, spices and herbs, meat cooked with almonds, pistachios, pomegranates and so forth, confections of rice and meat with sugar and buttermilk, meat cooked with a variety of vegetables – leeks, onions, chickpeas, aubergines).

But in spite of new signs of life in a food-producing economy which had been suffering, especially in the East, from over two centuries of neglect, it would be wrong to suppose that the condition of the rural populations was any better than it had been in the Umayyad era: whether he was a petty proprietor, a share-cropper or, more rarely, a slave, the tiller of the soil was subservient both to the wealthy landowner who was his patron and to the demands of the nearest town. The town, therefore, still played a fundamental role, as it had in Antiquity. But before exploring its nature, we must take another look at the West.

Greater confusion in the West

The fact that public authority was more disjointed in the West certainly gave rise to many local contracts and much confusion of classes. In the biographical collections we come across references to men of learning, some of them quite eminent, living in country districts, like the *faqih* of the early ninth century from somewhere near Moron who was held in such respect by the *muftis* (jurisconsults) of the qadi of Cordoba that when he visited the capital they kept silence in his presence, not daring to voice an opinion. This important personage, who ended up as *qadi* of Ecija, was of Berber descent, attached to a tribal group which had undoubtedly settled near Moron at the time of the conquest. Ibn al-Faradi, our informant on these matters, says that the *faqih* was living in a *qarya*, that is a village, and hence not on a large estate. The existence of large estates belonging to the urban elites of al-Andalus and Maghrib is not in doubt, but we are ignorant of what proportion of the land they represented, and almost equally in the dark about their methods of cultivation. Reference was made earlier to Ibn Hawqal's claim that a number of $di^{\circ}yas$ in al-Andalus were worked by Christians of a genuinely servile condition, but this does not appear to have been the general rule, and these estates probably tended to evolve in the direction of a less rigorous, share-cropping form of colonate. Above all it seems reasonable to ask whether the most usual regime may not have been that of the small or medium-sized property, in individual or collective ownership, in the context of a village.

One of the most illuminating texts on landed status is the already-mentioned treatise by al-Dawudi, which gives useful information relating to Sicily and to a lesser extent Spain. Most cases in it concern groups of cultivators complaining of unjust decisions to the central power, which, for a variety of reasons (of a politico-administrative nature) has confiscated lands granted as *iqta*, or granted them out anew following their temporary desertion in time of war, making it necessary for the original recipients or their heirs to reclaim them. We thus become witnesses to law-suits between the State – which, in its capacity as representative of the Muslim community, exercises some kind of superior right over the land – and holders of concessions that have been transformed into agricultural plots, which they may not cultivate themselves (even if there are sometimes indications to the contrary), and who as land-holders look much more like military *coloni* than great landed proprietors. For example, the government may want to saddle Sicilian *coloni* with the duty of cutting timber for ship-building, which they resist by saying that they are bound only to military service, the *jihad*. The government tries to impose its will by force, but this merely leads to the lands being abandoned. Again, Berbers in al-Andalus find their right to possess an *iqta* contested, resort to arms, and are eventually expelled. The interest of these disputes lies less in their outcome than in the trials of strength they reveal between the government and groups in possession of the soil who are ready at a certain level to resist the State's demands, if necessary by force.

The level of the State's demands, which was defined in principle by Islamic law itself, and which given the ubiquity of legal experts could probably not be raised to infinity, no doubt varied with the capacity of different groups to resist. If the *dhimmis* who had been left in possession of their lands were hardly in a position to resist an increase in the *kharaj*, the same does not apply to the soldiers of the invading armies who had been installed on *iqtas*, or to the Islamised Berber tribes of the Maghrib, fortified by their cohesive tribal or village structures. Even excluding the independent Kharijite tribes of the Tahert emirate, or the tribes of the western Maghrib, it is clear that there were many inland places where tribal organisation had survived even within the confines of the Aghlabid State. For example, al-Ya°qubi mentions the existence near Beja of a territory occupied by the Wazdaja Berbers, a people 'of an independent disposition who refuse obedience of any kind to the Aghlabid prince'. The autonomous Arab rulers of Setif and Balazna boasted of having 'tamed' the Kutama and of having 'well-nigh reduced them to subservience and servitude', because of a temporary success in exacting from them the Koranic dues which the Kutama insisted they fulfilled by paying the sum directly to the poor as alms. It appears that the Kutama had a very high threshold of resistance to the State's demands, since they in fact rejected taxation in any form.

Situations of this kind were certainly not unique to the Maghrib. In Sicily and Spain, large tracts of conquered territory had been made over to groups of conquerors, amongst whom there were some ready to take advantage of the remoteness or weakness of the public power by refusing, in the fashion of the Kutama of Little Kabylia, to admit any fiscal obligation: it is again from al-Ya'qubi that we hear of the Berber tribes in the Valencian region who refused to recognise the authority of the Umayyad emirs of Cordoba. During the great crisis of the late ninth century, most of al-Andalus was outside emiral control. Yet generally speaking it does not seem that the inhabitants then fell under the yoke of oppressive 'feudal' lords: indeed, we see them everywhere offering violent resistance to attempts to restore the emiral authority, in the castles beginning to pepper the countryside, which were more in the nature of high places of refuge or fortified villages than of 'feudal' castles. It appears that the majority of these populations were Islamised, and the few glimpses we have of them scarcely bear out the common idea, especially in regard to al-Andalus, of masses of impoverished tenant-farmers subject to fiscal oppression or the arbitrary will of great landowners. If such may have been the condition of the most disadvantaged sections of the peasantry, for example the Mozarabs left stranded on the estates of the urban *khassa* after the conquest, it certainly did not apply to the majority of landowners, who were either descendants of the Arab and Berber conquerors or native converts, and who lived within the framework of villages or *qura* and were subject merely to a State levy about which we admittedly have little information, but which equally does not appear to have been particularly oppressive or in excess of the norms prescribed by Muslim public law.

Agricultural expertise applied to a difficult terrain

Overall, the agricultural economy which benefited most from the fiscal reform was that of Iraq, where there was an abundance of water and a knowledge of irrigation techniques. In the form of solutions to simple arithmetical problems, an eleventh-century manual compiled for surveyors in the government's fiscal and irrigation departments gives details of the labour required to dig canals, together with its cost, and calculates the effort needed to operate the machines, powered by humans or oxen, which made it possible to irrigate fields above the level of canals or rivers. This in fact was a State service, run by a staff of experts and employing gangs of free workmen, several hundred at a time, who were paid on a piecework basis, according to the amount of earth extracted or piled up to form an embankment; depending on the terrain, they would dig or gather huge bundles of reeds and scrub, which were stuck together with clay. The use of two machines in particular permitted continuous watering and repeated harvests: the noria, a bucket-wheel capable of watering 35 ha a day and adequate for summer cultivations extending over 100 ha and winter cultivations of 150 ha; and the cross-beam, requiring four or five men to manipulate it, which ended in a scoop with a capacity of up to 600 litres, enough for summer cultivations of from 44 to 78 ha and for winter cultivations of from 100 to 138 ha. In parallel, the diffusion in foothill country of an Iranian device, the *qanat*, (an underground conduit which tapped the water table higher up and followed a course marked on the

Harvesting dates. Fruit-tree cultivation played a considerable part in the agricultural expansion of the eighth and ninth centuries (detail of an ivory casket presented to a Cordoban prince in 967, Paris, Louvre).

surface by a chain of ventilation and maintenance shafts), made it possible on the one hand to irrigate light, 'hot' soils reclaimed from the mountain, and on the other to drain the *marjs*, marshlands where water was stagnant. There can be no doubt that this hydraulic engineering was in the hands of experts, who understand the dangers of uneven delivery of water and the risk to poorly-drained soils of salinisation.

Over the Muslim empire as a whole, however, a pluvial agriculture prevailed. Depending for water solely on rainfall, or at best on such lesser hydraulic devices as wells, cisterns, and the small water-wheels used to draw up water for gardens, this was nevertheless a regime not lacking in expertise: it understood how to 'close' the soil by harrowing, so as to prevent evaporation, it knew how to make use of a slight slope to regulate the distribution of rainfall over level ground, and it was aware that successive ploughings were needed to 'break up' the ground – after the first rains – to allow the spring breezes to circulate and expose the turned-over sods to the sun. The knowledge accumulated by the ancient agronomists (Varro and Columella, translated into Arabic in the ninth century, the Byzantine Cassianus Bassus, author of a *Roman Agriculture*, and the Pseudo-Constantine VII), and the Persians (Kustus ibn Askouras-Kina), based on Aristotelian cosmology but combined with careful observation and in some cases experiment, was diffused through an agronomical literature which has recently attracted scholarly attention in relation to al-Andalus: farmers are advised to use straw and ashes as fertilisers and mulches, to grow turnips as a catch-crop on arable resting between cereals, to employ more than one type of plough implement, to keep animals grazing on the fallow in mobile pens, so as to avoid over-manuring, and more

238

generally to practise a rotation between natural pasturage and arable, to prevent the trampled-over soil becoming hardened. A body of knowledge tried and tested by experiment, for which the garden of the princely courts no doubt provided the ideal setting, was diffused in the form of books which adopted an eclectic approach, collecting and listing the various techniques in accordance with the method of the traditionalists (which was to maximise the number of examples in the absence of total certainty) and testing them by practical experimentation.

The urge to innovate and experiment which is so patent in the work of the agronomists helps to explain the success of the cultural revolution; the 'new crops' introduced or selected in the horticultural centres of Iran, Syria and Egypt were rapidly to spread throughout the whole Dar al-Islam. This enrichment to the native flora forms part of a centuries-long process by which sub-tropical plants unknown in Antiquity were introduced to the Mediterranean. In the first instance the new products were plants with a short season: spinach, known as *isfanakh*, the speciality of Isphahan, colza, and aubergines, again of Iranian origin and whose Persian name, *badinjan*, is still recognisable elsewhere in forms such as *melenza*, *melinjano* etc. They could be cultivated as catch-crops, provided the soil was well manured and turned. Still more important was the introduction of summer cultivations, rice, cotton, melons, sorghum, durum wheat, and cane sugar, which, with the same provisos, could be made to yield a second harvest in a single summer, something previously unknown. Other plants again would be adopted by growers around the Mediterranean: fruits such as lemons, oranges, bananas, coconuts and mangoes, dye-plants such as henna and indigo, and lastly plants with tap-roots like the turnip, again as catch-crops. Dissemination was rapid and extensive: by the eleventh century Arab Sicily had mastered the specialised techniques of cultivating cotton, henna, indigo, Persian sugar cane and the manufacture of refined sugar; it was perhaps familiar with the banana, and certainly with the date palm, not to mention the mulberry, which also proliferated in the Byzantine empire for the rearing of silkworms.

The farming calendar drawn up for Egypt by Makrizi illustrates the importance of the new cultivations: the annual inundation by the Nile, which begins in June, the Coptic month of *abib*, and reaches its height in *tut*, September, was immediately followed by the sowing of cereals, corn and barley, for harvesting in April, of vegetables for picking in November, and by the sowing of chickpeas, lentils, flax and clover for harvesting between April and June, prior to the collection of the first instalment of land-tax, which was assessed in accordance with the inventory of flooded areas made in September. Fields to which machines brought water from the Nile and its adjoining canals – chiefly in the Delta, where the flood waters accumulated in the natural reservoir formed by Lake Karun at Fayyum and were controlled by sluices inherited from Antiquity – would be sown in March and April with rice, for harvesting in October, colza, aubergines, cucumbers, melons, sesame, spinach, *lubīya* (the haricot bean of Antiquity), and in May with indigo, with a growing season of 100 days. The harvests on the summer cultivations, or *sayfi*, would coincide with fruit-picking (cherries, figs, peaches, pears, bananas, lemons, grapes), and with the levying of the second instalment of the land-tax.

These new crops tied in with the policy of developing by more intensive farming the productivity and profitability of the soil: sugar cane, colza and coconut improve briny soils and reduce their salinity, cotton enriches poor soils. Together, fruit trees, vegetables and industrial plants suppose a prosperous urban market, already well supplied with grain and other basic produce, and a refined cuisine; they are consistent with the increasingly sophisticated character of the town and help to diversify and improve the quality of urban diets. These sub-tropical plants were greedy for water and required multiple ploughings, together with large quantities of manure; they therefore had the effect of concentrating the effort at improvement, irrigation and agricultural innovation in the well-watered suburbs of great cities, leaving to 'dry-farming', in its way equally expert, the task of producing the basic necessities.

In the irrigated zone, the farming revolution was dependent on the supply of water and manure: inundation and irrigation by gravity no longer sufficed, and all inventive efforts were dedicated to extending the season of irrigation by machines and canalisation, and to renewing the productive capacities of the soil. Although the science of fertilisation made no great strides, empirical knowledge was gained of the nitrogenous properties of leguminous plants (beans, lentils, lupins, chickpeas and vetch) and of the value of green forage crops (lucerne, grey peas, Alexandrian clover) as fertilisers, in the form of mulches or compost mixed with ash, while the employment of a variety of hoeing and ploughing implements made it easier for water to penetrate and for the cultivator to break down the clods and eliminate weeds. The haunting fear of creating impenetrable surfaces encouraged the cultivation of plants with tap-roots, whose capacity to loosen the soil was well understood, and the mixing of manure with straw and ashes, in particular with cinders from the furnaces of bath-houses. Close observation prompted the choice of leguminous plants with short roots, in order to fertilise the top layers of the soil, so essential in the cultivation of cereals. Another necessity, that of keeping soils supplied with calefactory elements, was served by the application of bird droppings, those of doves being particularly sought after; pig dung was ruled out for obvious reasons, likewise human excrement.

In general, fiscal reform – limited to Iraq, where it was essential to the caliph's finances – and agricultural revolution (worthy of comparison with England's in the eighteenth century) appear closely connected, and their pursuit of a common economic objective seems almost like a premonition of physiocratic ideas: exploiting the notion of intensive farming, they made it possible for peasant societies not to be crushed by the burden of taxation, heavy as it remained, and for numerous, heavily populated metropoleis, with high consumer demand, to be fed. They were very closely bound up with the existence of the free urban market, and in one sense they circumvented the necessity for an *annona* system and governmental distribution of surpluses. But this Abbasid agriculture, which produced yields in proportion to the seed sown that seem incredibly high to any historian of the Western Middle Ages (in Egypt an average of 10:1 with maxima of between 20 and 30, in medieval Sicily, which inherited Arab methods of farming, an average of 8 with maxima of between 20 and 22), and high returns in proportion to the area sown (from 2 to 20 *irdabbs* of wheat per *faddan*, that is between 3.6 hl and 36 hl per ha, an average of 18 hl), was also precarious: in its irrigated sectors it depended on constant regulation of the water supply, and it depended everywhere on ample supplies of manure. It could thus be damaged by the destruction of canals or losses of livestock when these were more than isolated occurrences. The 'Asiatic' vision of a hydraulic society hardly applies: Egypt, Iraq and Khurasan were served by regional irrigation systems, based on the *nome*, *comarq* or district, and only repeated catastrophes could put them out of action. On the other hand, this was an agriculture on which shifts of population and the desertion of village sites made little impact: in a world which was still largely uncultivated, with huge reserves of land to draw on, technology and control of the water supply were the greatest capital assets.

Triumph of the Muslim town

The Abbasid revolution symbolised its triumph through the creation of a monumental capital, the circular city of Madinat al-Salam, the City of Peace, whose name evokes the Islamic character of the new monarchy. The site was remarkably well-chosen. Like Nineveh to the north and Basra to the south, the new capital was situated at the outlet of one of the three routes allowing access through the Zagros to Khurasan (Nineveh at the outfall of the Great Zab, Basra by way of Ahwaz, Baghdad by way of Hulwan, Nehavend and Hamadhan). There were easy river communications, by the Tigris and Euphrates, with the Jazira and Syria; and the region commanded the last convenient crossings of the two great rivers before the opening out of the valley and the swamps of lower Iraq. Lastly, sea-going vessels with a shallow draught could navigate the rivers as far as the site of the new town. In 758 Mansur envisaged it as 'the crossroads of the world': 'Ships from Wasit, Basra, Uballa, Ahwaz, Fars, Oman, Yumana, Bahrein and adjoining regions will come there by the Tigris and drop anchor; merchandise will come from Mosul, Azerbaijan and Armenia, brought thither by the Tigris; ships on the Euphrates will bring products from Diyar, Mudar, Raqqa, Syria, the marches of Asia Minor, Egypt and the Maghrib. And this town will also be on the highway of populations living in Jibal, Isphahan and the provinces of Khurasan.' Since this prospectus seems so much concerned with the provisioning of the future capital, we may also call to mind the fertility of the Sawad and the Zagros foothills.

Enormous capitals

The site chosen in 758 offered a series of ready-made entrenchments ideal for a military encampment and the residence of a revolutionary dynasty: ancient canal systems, the Sarat and the Nahr Isa, which made a kind of island between the two great rivers. But the site had one great drawback: the area on which the round city was founded escaped the high water of the Tigris by only a few dozen centimetres, and flash-floods were to undermine the palaces built of sun-dried brick. The only quarter not affected was Karkh (the 'town' in Aramaic), founded at an earlier date on a mound the water did not reach; it was to remain the heart of the town's western sector, while the combined effects of flooding from the Euphrates (a rare but devastating occurrence) and from the Tigris (annual, and

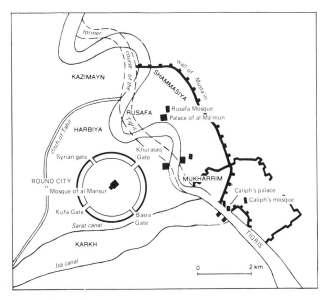

8 Plan of Baghdad

always dangerous: the rate of flow increases from 1,200 to 8,000m³ per second and can be as high as 25,000m³) made it desirable to transfer the hub of the town to the higher ground on the eastern bank, protected by ancient earthworks but with no natural defences.

The round city, founded in 762 and completed – by dint of mustering a force of craftsmen and labourers some 100,000 strong – in 766, was built in concentric circles: perfectly round, it inherited from the Iranian cities a mystical conception of cosmic kingship (hence its four gates, 360 towers and uncompromisingly astrological orientation, which necessitated the 'disorientation' of the mosque adjoining the caliphal palace), which gave special prominence to its defensive and symbolic aspects. Fringed by a ditch twenty metres wide, a wall nine metres thick was followed by an open space, 57 metres wide, leading to the main rampart, which had a height of just over 30 metres and a thickness of 50 metres at the base, fourteen metres at the top. Each of the fortified gateways gave access through angled passages to the exterior and on the inner side opened on to segments of the inhabited ring, which were strictly isolated from each other and from the outside world. Within the main rampart, a width of 170.7 metres was occupied by the built-up ring, which was reserved for Abbasid supporters and the military and closed off on its inner side by a wall seventeen and a half metres high and twenty metres thick. At the centre of the entire complex, which had a total diameter of 2,352 metres, was a vast esplanade: here, on the intersection of the two axes passing through the main gateways, stood the Golden Palace, 200 metres square, with its copper dome, flanked by four colossal iwans, and the Great Mosque, 100 metres square. No one entered this central space except on foot and with orders to do so. The obsession with security led to a multiplicity of grills, guard-rooms and covered ways watched over from the vaults; commercial activity, in particular, was confined to the four

242

roofed-in 'avenues', each housing 108 shops, and was eventually banished to the Karkh quarter, where Mansur built a second Great Mosque. In consequence, the town became quite literally the caliph's personal domain.

A capital of partisans, peopled exclusively by the promoters and pensioners of the Abbasid revolution, Khurasanian warriors, the *Abna al Dawla* or 'Sons of the Regime', and members of the Family inclusive of its Alid cousinage, the town made rapid growth in two directions. The caliph's court shifted first to the east: even in Mansur's lifetime, it deserted the round city in favour of Khuld, 'the Garden of Eternity', planted at the bridgehead leading to the east bank, before moving under Mahdi to Rusafa, and then under Ma'mun to the Hasani. Each caliph made it a point of honour to build a new and more ostentatious residence, an ambition facilitated by the building materials, unbaked brick faced with the more expensive kiln-fired brick and panels of stucco. After the 50-year sojourn at Samarra, and with the return of the Abbasids in 892, the Hasani became the unrivalled centre of caliphal power, for whereas the palaces of earlier Abbasid caliphs had been unitary structures, the Hasani precinct embraced several smaller complexes, the *Taj* ('Crown') and the *Firdaws* ('Paradise'), as well as eleven other pavilions. A dazzling profusion of wealth reinforced the symbols of power: 38,000 silk curtains, 12,500 robes of honour, 25,000 hangings, 8,000 tapestries, 22,000 carpets, 1,000 horses, four elephants and two giraffes, 5,000 cuirasses and 10,000 pieces of armour made up the offerings presented in 917 to the Byzantine ambassadors. For his personal protection the caliph of this period had a guard of 20,000 page-soldiers, and the domestic staff, of which little else is known, was augmented by 10,000 slaves. Under Muqtadir (908–32) the household would still consist of 15,000 slaves and the Mujarite guard, as well as a garrison of 14,000.

The development of the capital in other directions included the west bank, where members of the Family had been assigned lots to build villas and outbuildings. Whole districts, complete with apartment blocks and markets, were constructed on the land which went with these palatial villas, but so were private hippodromes, polo grounds and houses for the clients of the Abbasid princes. It becomes noticeable that the caliphal palaces were no grander in many cases than the villas of the *khassa*, while the great boulevards on which these were situated became the focus of urban planning. On the east bank, parallel with the Tigris, the Grand Avenue was laid out in the tenth century in a style very similar to Samarra: villas with a view over the river and direct access to it lined the embankment; opposite were the soldiers' quarters, the stables and the private mosques. This open townscape, intersected by gardens, menageries and hunting reserves, with its broad vistas and the horizontality of its one-storey buildings, forms a marked contrast with the narrow streets of the shut-in, closely supervised quarters, and in particular with the markets. It was unprotected by any fortification, apart from the earthwork hastily thrown up in 865 by Musta'in, which held out for a year against the troops of his rival, Mu'tazz, and protected the right bank.

Samarra ('happy he who sees it'), founded in 836 as a second Baghdad by Mu'tasim, partly in self-protection (following the civil war and the Baghdad insurrection) and partly to revive the dynasty's prestige, evolved with the same characteristics: a somewhat ill-considered

Samarra, the abandoned megalopolis. Founded in 836 to supplant Baghdad, its lifetime as the Abbasid capital lasted only a few decades, but its impressive dimensions well illustrate the originality and grandiosity of Abbasid town-planning. Vestiges of two Great Mosques, whose spiral minarets were frequently imitated, still stand out among the ruins. The town was enlarged to the north, towards the Tigris.

site (it lacked drinking-water, and had previously supported only a few hamlets and Christian monasteries) and one which did not have the same geographical advantages as Baghdad – a foundation, therefore, 'from scratch'. First there was an isolated palace, the Qatul (in this instance built on an octagonal plan), which was followed by another, of vast dimensions, around which the Great Mosque and plots of building land were laid out, where Muʿtasim installed himself in 838; and finally a second city, Jaʿfariya, was built by Mutawakkil between 859 and 861, with its palace and mosque (the so-called Abu Dulaf mosque), left unfinished at the time of his assassination in 861, and with several palace complexes (Balkuwara, the Castle of the Betrothed) built for the princes. Systematic defences are conspicuously lacking from the plan, which, while it reveals no fortifications and not many canals, shows enormous palace complexes and broad avenues, one of them extending over seven kilometres, villas separated from the road, in the Khurasanian fashion, by a bridged conduit, huge hippodromes, vast hunting parks, and lastly, on the irrigated west bank, villa–estates. Markets are indistinguishable on the plan, which is dominated by the right-angles of private roads; if a merchant quarter existed, to supply the needs of the caliph and the *khassa*, it is evident that Samarra, with its line of villas and barracks strung out over 35 kilometres and in simultaneous occupation, served primarily as an administrative and military centre, even though Baghdad was never abandoned in favour of the new capital – a capital which bears the marks of a dynasty in full vigour, addicted to sport, bellicose, but also on its guard against the military and wary of conspiracies, and where seven successive caliphs would rule in only half a century. Over this enormous area, the segregation of the ethnic groups enrolled in the army served to prevent any fusion or even contact with the civilian population and to keep alive the mutual antagonisms on which the caliph's personal safety depended, while in case of a coup the sheer size of the town guaranteed time to escape: a whole day was needed to cross the capital on foot.

Samarra, and then east Baghdad, after 892, carried to extremes the tendency towards the colossal and grandiose already adumbrated by Mansur's original foundations: the lavishness of the layout, the vast amount of ground taken up, borders on the grotesque. At Samarra (6,800 ha), the caliph and the notables were scrupulous in acquiring land of little value: the site was vacant, unencumbered and enormous, and in both capitals the employment of unbaked brick at least kept down the costs, high as they were. Apart from stucco panels and frescoes, all the decorative features, executed in marble, mosaic, cedar and teak, were easy to dismantle; and even the facings and arches were broken up to extract the kiln-fired bricks (expensive because combustible materials were scarce), leaving a rubble of unbaked brick which was quickly eroded by wind and flood. The expenditure was nevertheless commensurate with the vast scale of the enterprises: the cost of the round city is put at between eighteen million and a 100 million *dirhams*, depending on the source, while the Palace of the Pleiades was to cost Muʿtadid 400,000 *dinars*, and the building of the Buyid palace would cost Muʿizz al-Dawla one million. Mutawakkil's extravagance evokes comment from the Muslim historians: al-Yaʿqubi estimates the cost of his unfinished canal at Jaʿfariya as at least one-and-a-half million *dinars*. In both towns, the extension to the built-up area through the addition of new districts serves to emphasise the personal and autocratic character of the original foundations – without there having been any conscious decision to abandon the old palaces and districts. The caliph manifested an implicit faith in his own destiny, reinforced by the favourable predictions of astrologers, with which his architects, merely obedient to the caliph's will, were made to comply, even at the expense of adding to the technical problems – as at Samarra, a site without water, with no convenient bridge, exposed to flooding and remote from the empire's main arteries. For this reason, after the departure of the court and the army, Samarra could not sustain the prosperity enjoyed by Baghdad during the prince's absence and its surface contracted in consequence to a minute area in the neighbourhood of Mutawakkil's great mosque.

Centres of acculturation

Headquarters of the *khassa*, the Abbasid capitals lived principally on imperial taxation: when Baghdad was founded, each of the caliph's uncles received a subsidy of a million *dirhams*; between them, the Family had at their disposal a sum of ten million *dirhams*; and the 700 Companions each drew a monthly pension of 500 *dirhams*. In accordance with the policy of geographical segregation, the Bedouin contingents in the army were assigned to separate tribal quarters while the Khurasanian regiments (composed equally of Arabs) were grouped according to their town or region of origin (Khwarazm, Rayy, Merv, Kabul, Bukhara) and stationed alongside the palaces and apartment blocks inhabited by kinsmen of the Abbasids and their leading supporters. The swelling town, whose markets did not cease to multiply, before long attracted an underclass, chiefly of Iranians who were quickly Arabised, and these too established their own quarters: one such was exclusive to craftsmen from the Ahwaz (Tustars skilled in the weaving of silk and cotton). Along with an administrative, military and religious elite, Baghdad and Samarra thus saw the burgeoning of the *amma*, a turbulent and only partially productive urban mass (weavers, masons, wood-carvers, brick-makers and potters), the remainder being idle or sporadically active (as porters, boatmen, bodyguards, mace-bearers and in many cases thieves), obsessed with politico-religious conflicts and imbued with municipal patriotism. Profoundly Islamised, Arabised, the *amma* could put up a brave show: they were the 'defenceless' ones who in 812–13 held out for fourteen months, armed with sticks, against the forces of Tahir, at the time of the civil war between caliphs Amin and Ma'mun.

The large town in fact played an essential role in the phenomenon of acculturation: though Baghdad remained an important Christian city, through the presence there of the Nestorian patriarch and of monasteries and churches of the Nestorian, Jabobite and Melkite obediences, though it remained the capital of Judaism, with its Talmudic schools and the presence at court of the exilarch, the religious feeling in the quarters polarised around the mosques which doubled as *martyria*, the tombs of the Shi'ite imams at Kazimayn, the shrine of the teachers persecuted by the Mu'tazilite inquisition, and the mausoleum of Ibn Hanbal. In parallel with the flourishing astrological, astronomical and medical culture to be found in the palaces, the observatories, the public hospitals and the

246

The mosque of Ibn Tulun at Cairo: courtyard, colonnade, fountain and minaret. Built of brick between 876 and 879, when Egypt was distancing itself from the central power, this mosque is remarkable both for its spaciousness and sobriety of line and for its wealth of stucco decoration.

'House of Wisdom' founded by Ma'mun to garner the accumulated learning of Greek Antiquity, there developed (but not without the interplay and circulation of ideas and people) a popular Islamic culture, vigorous, attentive to philosophical debates, apt to be intolerant, and continually inflamed by conflicts between the various schools of thought. Shi'ism made its appearance at Baghdad as early as 780, to embark in due course, with Hanbalite encouragement, on what amounted to a puritanical campaign against immorality in high places.

Epitomes of the luxurious and hedonistic court life which aroused revolt in puritanical quarters, Baghdad and Samarra set the tone for the provinces: the architectural and decorative style evolved by the caliph's architects left its stamp on the capital of Tulunid Egypt. The great mosque of Samarra, built between 849 and 852, and the mosque of Abu Dula (859–61) were truly immense (measuring respectively 100m × 160m and 104m × 155m), standing out, with their massive walls and facades punctuated by corner towers and rounded buttresses, and with their towering minarets, like giant fortresses in a vast and empty space. In the mosque of Ibn Tulun (879), although of a different shape (square), the enormous scale, the huge rectangular pillars of brickwork, the positioning of the minaret at the centre of the mihrab, and above all the decoration of the plaster facing with rosettes and inscriptions, all hint strongly at a migration of artists from Baghdad. In

247

the same way, Baghdad's culinary tastes, manners, deportment and music infiltrated into Spain through Ziryab, the former slave of Mahdi who was variously talented as cook, dancer and teacher of etiquette, 'the Andalusian Petronius'. It was these large towns, in fact, which fostered the ideal of the Muslim 'gentleman', the *adib*. His extensive knowledge, which enabled him to shine in conversation and which was governed by the rules of good taste, coincided to a large extent with the accomplishment expected of the secretary, the *katib*.

Arab encyclopedic literature in fact arranges a great mass of eclectic and somewhat disparate knowledge, invaluable for those sessions of talk and poetry where a pedantic and extensive vocabulary was called for. An inexhaustible memory, eked out as needed by mnemonic devices, a store of historical, biographical, genealogical and geographical knowledge which could easily be tapped for moral anecdotes and wondrous tales, and lastly an urbane manner of presentation, were almost exactly what was required of a secretary. If the latter needed in addition to be versed in the law (that is to say the tax and land law and 'governmental statutes'), in calligraphy, and in the rhetoric of administration, it was nevertheless through his general cultivation, his *savoir-vivre*, that he would make his career, through poetry, the culinary arts, music or astronomy, all in the cause of *adab* (good taste). And just as the capital had garnered the cultural gains of Iran and Hellenism and subdued them to the norms of Islam and Arabism, so would the code of civilised conduct align the etiquette prescribed in Persian Princes' Mirrors with Aristotelian learning – transmitted for the most part through the Syriac translations of the Pseudo-Aristotle. This was the reply to the ironic criticisms voiced by secretaries of Iranian origin: the forging of a new humanism in accordance with Arab traditions.

It is obviously as a result of the syncretism beginning to take hold in the East that the towns were able to play their role as the chief catalysts of learning. In this respect, Ma'mun's foundation of the 'House of Wisdom' at Baghdad in 832 is an important landmark in the history of human thought, signalling as it does the moment when the philosophy and science of the Greeks made contact with Arab–Iranian and Hindu culture. The Muslims received the great Greek authors with avidity and treated them with respect: the translation, in particular of Plato and Aristotle, but also of Hippocrates, Galen and Dioscorides, Ptolemy, Euclid and Archimedes, Hero of Alexandria or Philo of Byzantium, gave a spur to the teachers reflecting on the 'revealed content' of the Koran, or who were engaged in less abstruse speculations on the potentialities of language, empiricism in medicine or astronomical observation. Al-Kindi (died 873) and al-Farabi (died 950) were the first to make use of Aristotelian logic, from which the Mu'talizite movement already mentioned derived part of its force. The sheer size of the 'libraries' being assembled at this period seems astonishing: Fustat at the start of the Fatimid era possessed, we are told, 18,000 ancient manuscripts, 40 repositories and 400,000 volumes, while the same claim is made for Cordoba in the West.

In the scientific domain, syncretism was of the essence. Furthermore, the thinkers of this time did not function as specialists, but were philosophers, biologists and mathematicians all in one. Ishaq ibn Hunayn (died 910), the 'Arab Ptolemy', assembled and developed the

Antique theories on vision, optics and light, while his contemporaries Abu Mashar (died 886) and Thabit ibn Qurra (died 900) did the same respectively for the movement of the planets and for trigonometry. It should however be noted that at this stage, prior to the great Iranian syntheses of the eleventh century, scientific activity was essentially a matter of assimilating, verifying and propagating existing knowledge: for example, no challenge had yet been offered to the Greeks' geocentric theory of the universe. On the other hand, in one essential department, that of arithmetical calculation, Muslim mathematical thinking departed from Greek tradition, being less influenced by Ptolemy or Diophantos than by Hindu discoveries. Nothing shows this more clearly than the work of al-Khwarizmi (died 830), a prolific scholar well ahead of his times: as well as introducing the decimal system and the Hindu zero, he disseminated knowledge, derived from India, of quadratic and cubic equations, and in his book *al-djabr*, meaning 'the number which restores', he later covered all aspects of 'algebra'.

An urban civilisation without parallel in the Middle Ages

The imperial foundations (Baghdad and Samarra, but also Raqqa, Harun al-Rashid's capital close to the Syrian frontier, Tyana, and Tarsus in Cilicia where Maʾmun resided) and the provincial capitals (Fustat, and later Ibn Tulun's Egyptian capital) were grafted, with varying degrees of success, on to an obvious urban trend. Many new agglomerations were forming in Iraq (Haditha, Qasr Ibn Hubayra, Rahba, Jazirat Ibn Umar), in northern Syria (Hisn Mansur, Haruniya, Masisa and Iskandaruna, all rebuilt in defiance of the Byzantines) and in Palestine (Ramla), while the Iranian towns were beginning to blossom around their Arab 'suburb'. It is important, however, not to be deceived by the false appearance of urban expansion: a few brilliantly successful examples may conceal shifts of population away from other centres and the decline of former metropoleis. This is illustrated in Egypt by the almost total desertion of Alexandria, reduced to less than half the space enclosed by its ancient walls and clinging from now on to the spit of land overlooking the Heptastadium, a port of only minor importance, lacking even a mint, and in Syria by the decline of Antioch. Very little is known of the actual demographic trend; whatever calculations are made remain in the realm of hypothesis. The one reliable fact is the cessation of the great epidemics under the Abbasids, after renewed outbreaks of plague in the last decades of the seventh century and again down to about 745. It may therefore be assumed that urbanisation did not make such catastrophic inroads on the rural population as it had under the Umayyads, or at any rate that the losses were more easily made good.

If in general it was a question of one urban network being replaced by another (as in Syria, where many coastal sites were abandoned, in Egypt, on the Anatolian borders, and perhaps in Iran), in Iraq urbanisation took place on a truly colossal scale: Baghdad, in 892, extended over an area of between 6,000 and 7,000 hectares, at least four times the size of Constantinople and thirteen times as large as Ctesiphon. And its population may well have numbered half a million: at the beginning of the tenth century, it is said that in two out of the four mosques where the *khutba* was proclaimed (to which, in theory, all adult males were summoned), a total of 64,000 worshippers was in attendance. This massive population was quite new, for the growth of Baghdad had not been accompanied, or at least not before the burning down of Basra by the Zandjs in 871, by the decline of middle-sized towns; growth of this order is only to be explained by a mobilisation of the financial resources of an empire, which permitted the great capitals to 'take off', and by increased agricultural output from the lands subject to intensive cultivation, which made it possible for these huge agglomerations to survive at a time when the activity of urban craftsmen made only a very modest contribution to fiscal revenues and the creation of wealth. The cities did not sell their products to the countryside and the circulation of goods between town and country was purely fiscal. The dead weight of the towns in fact set an impassable limit to the urban expansion.

The widespread progress of urbanisation in the Abbasid empire does not mean that all towns followed the same plan. The idea of a 'typically Muslim' town, with a mosque at the centre and a pre-ordained hierarchy of markets, is one we have to discard; the Umayyad and Abbasid capitals present us with the contrary example of a town centred on the palace. The topography of Baghdad and Samarra, where the spacious avenues were quite distinct from the narrow confines of the market quarters, is very different from the jumble of streets and dead ends at Fustat, where the tribal pattern had survived, and different again from that of towns whose Antique layout had been disrupted by privatisation and encroachment on the streets. Everywhere, however, dwellings seem to have been built in accordance with a single model, with only minor variations: that of the Samarran *bayt* discovered by excavation of the caliph's capital, which took the form of a large habitation enclosed by windowless walls and arranged internally as a series of rectangular apartments opening on to a central court. Analysis of the remains at Fustat has confirmed the ninth-century dating: the basic module consists of three chambers running parallel with a three-bayed portico or ante-chamber, in which the middle room contains two lateral recesses (hence its description as the 'inverted T chamber'). The courtyard was adorned with a fountain, and because the arrangement was often asymmetrical, the paving of the rooms and courtyard made no attempt at regularity.

This pattern, to be found all the way from the Maghrib to Siraf, was subject to modifications dictated either by necessity or by chance. The ante-chamber is lacking from the merchant houses at Siraf, where stout walls taken up to a considerable height carried upper storeys used for storage. At Fustat, as in the princely palaces, two courts, composed in some cases of two opposing *bayts*, were combined to produce sets of apartments with differing functions, perhaps to separate public and private apartments (*harim*), or winter and summer quarters. The excavated dwellings all bear the marks of wealth: high-quality workmanship and building materials (good stone, kiln-fired brick, well-executed masonry using only the best mortar), stucco decoration, and above all an abundant supply of water, however hard this was to contrive. At Siraf, the town sweltering in the desert heat was fed by water brought down from the mountain by two aqueducts. At Fustat, reservoirs ordained for different purposes (street-cleaning, washing, drinking) and hewn from the bedrock were complemented by an efficient system for the removal of dirty water through canals and brick-lined drains which were regularly cleansed from outside the houses (proof of this is provided by the homogeneity of their archaeological content, which is contemporary with the abandonment of the site). The inventiveness, the concern for cleanliness, and the efficiency of which there is further evidence at Fustat in the construction on the terraces of a means to trap and channel cool breezes, was to lead in the tenth and eleventh centuries to a proliferation of hydraulic contraptions: in a house built symmetrically around a network of open channels, a grotto, complete with waterfall to humidify and freshen the atmosphere, leads to a pool with fountains and goldfish ponds, surrounded by flower-beds and trenches for trees. This arrangement, with its dual symmetry, already Fatimid in style, supposes houses of very large dimensions.

The diversity in type, origin and topography of Islamic cities should not blind us to characteristics which this generation of Abbasid towns have in common, in particular the formation of what has been described as a 'patriciate', a rising class composed of rentiers of the soil, men of religion and merchants, which took its place alongside the representatives of the central power, the civilian secretaries and the military. Drawn originally from a wide variety of religions (Nestorian, Zoroastrian, Muslim) and social backgrounds (jurists and *hadith* teachers, *dihkans*, former Sassanid officials, silk-merchants using the route from Khurasan to China via Transoxiana), but welded together in time by inter-marriage and joint participation in family enterprises, the patrician dynasties of Nishapur combined the prestige of descent from the Arab Muslim conquerors (the judicial family of the Harashi, for example, was descended from caliph Othman and took his name) with control of the local economy: by marrying the daughters of officials, the Harashi-Othmani acquired numerous estates, and in the tenth century they allied themselves with the Balawi, a merchant family of Persian descent.

An exceptionally precise archaeological image of the dominance of the ruling class is conveyed by the excavations carried out at Fustat and at Siraf, which testify to vast, fortress-like houses, with a janitor's lodge and in some instances a zigzag passage to guard the entrance. They are surprisingly extensive; at Siraf, the floor area of the houses excavated ranges from 210 to 540m², an average of 361m², not counting the upper storey. At Fustat, although the layout is less clear (many of the walls have been razed to their foundations) and the divisions are of irregular shape, several huge sites have been identified. The evidence points to the existence of two modules: one a simple type, with only one court, of between 180 and 200m², and one with a double court, varying in size from 400 or 500 to 1,200m². On both sites, the Iranian emporium as much as the Egyptian metropolis, these enormous houses take up all the space, at Fustat B running the full length of the excavated site (350m × 50–100m) and embracing large industrial complexes (potteries and glassworks). There is no sign of any lesser habitations, apart from a few traces of later 'squatters' in the much-ruined islets around the main intersection. The patrician houses, which at Fustat have been dubbed 'castles', appear to follow on without interruption, leaving no space for an infilling of smaller dwellings. Nor is there any sign of tenement buildings of the *insula* type known from Antiquity, which were marvelled at by visitors on account of their many storeys. So where did the 'common' people, the underclass, live? And where were the shops? If it is permissible to conclude that newcomers inhabited rented rooms on the terraces of the patricians, and that craftsmen lived in their workshops, these archaeological findings limit still further the supposed exuberance of the markets, and the development of the artisanal middle class. The picture which emerges is of wage-earners in a state of domestic dependence; it also points to the incorporation of the weak into these great households, and draws attention to the existence of family clienteles, and more generally to the familial base of urban societies.

Dynamic crafts, a burgeoning art

Urban development could not fail to stimulate a growing trend towards diversification of occupation, under the patronage of the 'elite' houses; the Muslim town inherited from Antiquity an extensive range of craft trades, which a scrupulous concern for the quality and price of products had no doubt served to particularise and multiply. It is important to dismiss any idea of a guild system of the type in which master craftsmen regulated their trade through private associations, or of democratic occupational groupings, entered by initiation, which originated in a craftsman's 'pact of honour' supposedly sworn under the auspices of the Prophet's barber, Salman the Persian, called 'the Pure'. This has been shown to be a later conjecture, which confuses the origins of the *futuwwa*, a political association devoid of occupational connotations but infected by the initiatory rites of the Isma'ilians, which came into existence only in the latter part of the ninth century, with the State's system for overseeing urban crafts.

This system had a long history, dating back in the case of certain crafts to the time of the Umayyads. Under the Abbasids they came under the control of the *mutasahibs*, the masters of the market: specialised craftsmen were appointed to check on the quality of the products, keep watch on prices and ensure that the masters were enrolled on the fiscal registers. Under this leadership, the crafts remained open: apprenticeship, admission to the craft and the right to practise it were not subject to any restrictive or coercive regulation; nor did individual crafts have particular locations assigned to them, even if it was considered desirable for trades of the same kind to be grouped together to facilitate supervision. If a certain degree of *esprit de corps* appears to have come into being, the reason is surely to be found in the social ambience which encouraged sons to follow the trade of their fathers or uncles, and no more than a few examples of factional disputes involving different trades can be cited (as when the lessors of bath-houses clashed with the salt-suppliers at Mecca, or the victuallers on the one side took issue with the shoemakers and cloth-merchants on the other at Mosul in 919 and 929). The artisanal world did not display any particular desire for democracy, either within this institutional framework or in opposition to it, and there is nothing to show any massive penetration of its circles by 'Isma'ilian' ideas, while literary references to manual work can be taken as little more than a scholarly reflection of Antique culture.

In cities throughout the Islamic world, satisfaction of consumer demands required the services of tradesmen specialising in the supply and processing of food; to furnish the tables of the aristocratic households there were fruit and vegetable suppliers, usually specialising in a single product, grain-merchants, dairymen, vinegar-makers, vintners, purveyors of palm wine, fishmongers, specialists in shellfish, butchers and poulterers, as well as all the trades linked with particular stages of production: cattle-dealers, slaughterers, knackers and so on, down to the butchers, tripe-dressers and sausage-makers; grain-merchants, millers, flour-merchants, ending with the bakers and an infinite variety of confectioners. At the same time, cookshop keepers in the market, the *suk*, did an increasingly brisk trade in a great variety of ready-made dishes intended for the poorer classes, who from fear of fire, or because they lacked the means to buy in bulk, did not cook for themselves. Dishes of fish, rice, vegetables, meat with gravy (beef or camel, since mutton was the meat of the wealthy), offal, fritters and honey pastries could all be procured in this way. This cuisine of the streets created a common social and cultural bond extending all the way from al-Andalus and Sicily (some of the dishes, still known by their Arab names – *calia*, *sfincio* for example – remain firm favourites in the Palerman cuisine of the twentieth century) to Iran. Equally ubiquitous were the *hamman* ('Turkish' bath), its Greek origin forgotten, but reactivated by Islamic ritual requirements, and all the specialised craftsmen: those connected with building, of which there were many, cabinet-makers (turning out chests, chairs and cupboards), leather-dressers (essential to the manufacture of furnishings and receptacles), workers in fabrics – the degree of skill required of tailors was reflected in a high wage and an elevated social standing – blacksmiths and potters.

The inter-regional traffic in artisanal products consisted not only of a wide range of non-perishable and easily transported food specialities (jams, crystallised fruits, dried fruits, pickled vegetables), but also of high-quality manufactured goods, in particular textiles, weapons, paper and ornamental pottery. In spite of the political unity, the diffusion of techniques was only gradual: it was achieved more often by the migration of craftsmen than through imitation (at Fustat, for example, the linen handkerchief-makers were natives of Amida in Mesopotamia) and tied in with the remarkable visual capacity of customers to recognise the qualities, distinctive features and turn of hand acquired by generations of working in an uninterrupted tradition. Special appellations had to be found for the products executed by immigrant craftsmen in accordance with the standards and techniques traditional to their countries of origin (*Tabari Ramli*, for example, for the tapestries woven at Ramla in Palestine by immigrants from Tabaristan). The location of these 'specialities' depended to a large extent on the raw materials, which if they were bulky posed problems of transport. Metal-working was thus chiefly concentrated in mining areas, which accounts for the location of armourers' workshops in Armenia, Afghanistan and Transoxiana, of steel-working at Damascus, within reach of the iron ore in the Taurus and Cilicia, of ironworks in Daghestan, Azerbaijan, Nishapur and Isphahan, of copper-smithies at Mosul, and of brass foundries at Herat and Baykand. But Damascus, where a copper industry developed, and the Egyptian Delta, where Tinnis made a speciality of cutlery and scissors, demonstrate the role of a long-established tradition of artisanal activity and highly-skilled workmanship in fixing the location of such industries and establishing their reputation.

253

The textile sector – at once the largest industry and the one which tied up the lion's share of family investments, which constituted the working capital and a potential reserve – shows the same picture of specialised centres of production, their location again being dictated by that of the raw materials: wool from Egypt, Syria and the semi-circle of mountains from the Taurus through Armenia and Tabaristan to Iran, flax from the Egyptian delta, cotton from Khurasan and the Jazira, raw silk from Khurasan and the Ahwaz. The fact that some of the most prized materials could be transported with relative ease led to multiple centres of production and extreme diversification: Tiberias, Armenia, Azerbaijan, Tabaristan, Khurasan and Transoxiana specialised in carpets, Fars in embroidered carpets, striped coats came from the Yemen, cotton goods from Kima, handkerchiefs from Tabaristan, satins from Khurasan, brocade and *dibaj* (where the warp and weft are of silk) from Tustat, the *attabi* taffetas made of silk and cotton from Syria, robes from Fars, *siqlatun*, a cloth patterned with large ornate circles, from Baghdad, *sharb* and *qasab*, gauzes of Egyptian flax, from the Delta. This short list gives only a glimpse of the enormous variety of products on offer, in which were included some avowed imitations of famous originals, for example the 'Armenian' belts that were manufactured at Tib in the Ahwaz.

We are witnesses, furthermore, of the first stirrings of an original decorative art which can be described as 'Muslim', in the same way that the art of the Achaemenids had ultimately become 'Persian'. It should first be explained that in the presence of ancient and often still powerful artistic traditions, such as the floral exuberance of the Hindus, the animal art of Mesopotamia or the 'historiated' representations, in sumptuous materials, of Byzantine Egypt and Syria, neither the caliphs nor their entourage thought of imposing an external tradition, and in any case they had no such tradition inherited from pre-Prophetic Arab art on which to build. They summoned artists from the most diverse regions, without discrimination, and for a time were content for them to work from indisputably Byzantine or Sassanid models, as at Damascus or the Dome of the Rock at Jerusalem. In 722, the Umayyad Yazid II tried, it is true, to bring pressure to bear on artists by proscribing, even before the Byzantines, and perhaps under the influence of a rigorist attitude peculiar to the Middle East, any representation of creatures, as manifesting a spirit of 'emulation' quite inadmissible in regard to the Creator. But even if buildings used for worship appear to have been adapted to these requirements – which were reiterated in more moderate form by the Abbasids – enough private decorative schemes, ceramics and miniatures survive in which the human figure appears and which predate the tenth century, such as those found at the palace of Qasyr Amr in Jordan, to make us doubt the complete efficacy of this Muslim version of 'iconoclasm'.

Hence, and at a later stage, the confluence of the various aesthetic currents served to release a fount of original inspiration, which was after all remarkably homogeneous from one end of the Dar al-Islam to the other. From the moment when it ceased to be necessary for every wall, doorway, column or platter to serve as commentary or illustration, say of a holy text or a legal maxim, there was no longer any reason to aim at the representation of concrete reality. The Muslim mode of artistic expression will therefore be abstract, detached from the world of experience, wholly dream-like and mysterious, with no signifi-

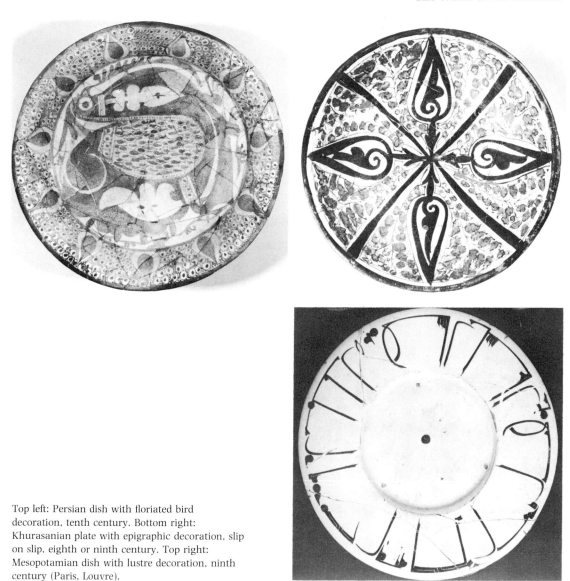

Top left: Persian dish with floriated bird decoration, tenth century. Bottom right: Khurasanian plate with epigraphic decoration, slip on slip, eighth or ninth century. Top right: Mesopotamian dish with lustre decoration, ninth century (Paris, Louvre).

cance beyond the harmony of its forms. Stylisation, geometry, overlapping and infinitely repeated shapes, are all fundamental to its theme; and because of an abhorrence of empty space, which as it happens is wholly 'medieval', the curves, counter-curves, lozenges, interlaces and foliated scrolls applied to the decoration of stucco, wood, ivories, glazed tiles, textiles and dress will appear in a profusion almost too overwhelming for our Western aesthetic taste. The two features which might break up this luxuriant monotony in fact make little difference. The 'arabesque', that is to say the pious inscription rendered in stylised characters, merges into a decoration already influenced by the Arabic script, with

255

its loops and abbreviated hooks, and is often hard to disentangle from nearby floriated scrolls. And the introduction of typically 'oriental' animal motifs shown in combat, affronté, or in line, whether they were real creatures, such as elephants, camels, lions and peacocks, or imaginary ones, such as the phoenix, dragons, unicorns or firebirds, is so stylised that a good part of their 'visual' interest is sacrificed for the benefit of the recognisable symbol they embodied.

It is perhaps somewhat artificial to base our view of the origins of this art on the town; many of the rural palaces are no longer extant. But the richness and probable expense of court or religious art make it justifiable to link the phenomenon with the basic centres of acculturation, that is, the great conurbations.

In the West, revival rather than a new departure

In the West, the fairly numerous indications concerning the development at Cordoba and Kairouan of the function of the *sahib al-suq*, the master of the market, need to be seen in conjunction with more general aspects of urban development, which again conform to the pattern of urbanisation common to the whole of Muslim civilisation. Here, too, it is justifiable to emphasise the precocious flowering of the town structured on the oriental model.

Kairouan's origin, like that of Kufa, Basra or Fustat, was as a 'camp town', at which time the tribal quarters and the monumental nucleus were laid out. The building of the cathedral mosque and the governor's palace was actively pursued by governor Hassan ibn al-Nu'man (692–705), and it is known that by the time of caliph Hisham ibn Abd al-Malik (724–43) the mosque was complete: with its mastery of brickwork techniques and systematic redeployment of Antique columns, it is one of the most beautiful in all Islam (the whole complex, courtyard and prayer hall combined measures 85m × 135m), with seventeen flat-roofed aisles, and a cupola above the vault with an opening for the *mihrab*. The decoration of faience tiles with a metallic glitter is directly copied from Samarra. Alterations were made after 774, and again in 836 and 862, when the mosque was further enlarged and its square minaret raised to a height of 30m. It was also around this time that the central *suk* formed along the *simat*, a broad avenue which divides the city in two, and it was Yazid ibn Hatim (governor from 772 to 787) who shortly afterwards organised it and separated the various crafts. Independently of this official town-planning, however, the town was expanding in a more spontaneous fashion around suburban *suks* and mosques, a fair number of which were evidently in existence before the middle of the eighth century. The capital of Ifriqiya went on developing at a rapid pace under the Aghlabids, who, however, duplicated it with sumptuous princely foundations in the manner of the Abbasids, al-Abbasiya at the inception of the dynasty's rule, Raqqada towards the end of the ninth century. The elaborate network of storage tanks and conduits which kept the metropolis supplied with water was begun in the governors' time and added to by the Aghlabids; traces of it can still be found in the vicinity.

The general line of development is the same throughout the Muslim West, with the

Testimony to the mastery achieved in popular art: terracotta jar of the Abbasid epoch (Mosul Museum, Iraq).

qualification that it was more often a case of revitalising and restructuring Antique towns which had fallen into decay than of new foundations. The most important and most obvious exception is Fez, founded under Idris I in about 789, then developed early in the ninth century by Idris II, who in addition assigned tribal quarters to Arab colonists from Ifriqiya and al-Andalus. At Tunis, the cathedral mosque (the Zaytuna), built by Ibn al-Habbab (governor from 732 to 741), was soon surrounded by *suks*. On the edge of the Maghrib, urbanisation was pursued under the auspices of Idrisid principalities which were centred on towns such as al-Basra, founded in the ninth century, or on small pre-Islamic settlements. Many of them were mints, whose abundant issues of *dirhams* testify to the progressive 'monetarisation' of the economy.

At Cordoba, almost as soon as the town was captured, the governor, al-Samh (719–21), ordered the Roman stone bridge over the Guadalquivir to be rebuilt and the partially-demolished ramparts to be restored. The history of successive enlargements to the great mosque, material as well as spiritual heart of the conurbation, testifies to the growing importance of the great Andalusian metropolis; this edifice occupied in Spain a position comparable to that of the Kairouan sanctuary in the Maghrib. Begun in 766 or 768 on the site, purchased from the Christians, where the cathedral had stood, and continually extended until the middle of the tenth century, the Cordoban mosque was of grandiose proportions: the prayer hall (180m × 120m), larger than its counterparts at Samarra or Fustat, consisted of nineteen aisles whose roofs were supported by more than 850 marble columns, linked by a two-tier system of arches in white stone and red brick; domes with a covering of mosaics, floral decoration with a stucco base, and alabaster panels engraved with pious texts point to a more purely autochthonous source of inspiration – 'Visigothic',

257

or not to put too fine a point on it, Roman. This mosque, the largest edifice left by Islam from the Middle Ages, is proof enough in itself of the ample resources and political and economic strength of the Umayyad emirs who found asylum there after the massacre of 750. In the accounts of Arab travellers, Cordoba rates as the only possible rival to Baghdad. The celebrated 'suburban revolt' of 818 is evidence that the popular districts facing the old Roman town across the Guadalquivir had already begun to expand. It was not until the first half of the tenth century, however, in the time of the caliphate, that Cordoba, like Kairouan, was duplicated by a princely foundation, Madinat al-Zahra.

These towns, or at all events the most notable of them, quickly developed into centres of intellectual life, and this is true not only of the political capitals but also of other important places. Tunis, for example, like Kairouan, had its complement of scholars and traditionists, and its mosque had won repute as a religious and educational centre even before the Aghlabid epoch. Even a town as geographically remote as Saragossa, on the frontier with the Frankish world, appears to have been more than a mere fortified outpost and trading station: the impression left by the Andalusian biographical compilations is of a flourishing religious and intellectual life from the early days of the Islamic conquest and throughout the period of the Cordoban emirate, to judge from the 30 or so religious, legal or literary worthies, natives of Saragossa or long resident there, whose names the biographers saw fit to include from the period prior to the proclamation of the caliphate (929). A similar claim can be made for Toledo, a city which had only a small Arab population and which was in a constant state of rebellion against the Cordoban government, to the point of allying on certain occasions with the Christians in the north. Early on in the emirate, a group of Toledans had become so addicted to the study of literature and the religious sciences that they departed for the East, there to sit at the feet of Malik ibn Anas (died 795); on their return, these students set themselves up as teachers and disseminated the fruits of their learning among their compatriots. A little later, in the first half of the ninth century, another group made the voyage to Kairouan to study under Malik's great disciple, Sahnun. It should go without saying that all wisdom, at Toledo as much as Saragossa, came from the East, acquired either at first hand by the many who journeyed to the sources, or through the intermediary of Cordoba and Kairouan, where the teaching ultimately derived from the Eastern masters. In important centres, the group of scholars dedicated to the religious and legal sciences was evidently one of the most active elements in society, as is exemplified by the important role they played in the Cordoban rising of 818.

Headquarters of government and administration, place of residence for the military aristocracy, centres of industry and commerce, hubs of intellectual activity, disseminators of Islamic culture, the towns of the Muslim West came quickly to life, and as they did so they raised the level of civilisation and integration into the Muslim world of these distant margins of the Dar al-Islam. It has been said with regard to Ifriqiya, where the urban factor was dominant, that there has been too much of a tendency to regard these towns as amorphous organisms, tamely submissive to authority. Yet the Ifriqiyan town of the ninth century was, in contrast, the nerve centre which united all the vital forces of the region, the place where any number of aristocratic or bourgeois clans lived in permanent tension and in an environment calculated by its very nature to give rise to perpetual ferment: for illustration we need look no further than the troubled histories of Kairouan, Tunis, Tripoli or Palermo during the Aghlabid epoch. This state of tension can also be seen in al-Andalus, but it should perhaps be stressed that in both cases it seems to have been spent in agitation, whose logic we scarcely understand, and which was signalled by seemingly sterile revolts and clan rivalries which we should perhaps relate to the absence of any inherent autonomy in the structure of the medieval Muslim town.

. . . but a similar urban society

The standard Western account of Muslim society depicts it as made up on the one hand of the mass, or *amma*, composed of artisans, small traders, day labourers and wage-earners of every description, and on the other of the elite, or *khassa* – the paradigm we saw exemplified in the East. At the head of the elite we find the group holding the reins of power, which in the Western emirates of the ninth century was more or less equivalent to a clan of the ruling dynasty's paternal kinsmen and their clients; they monopolised the key positions in the government, the administration and the army, and represented, as in the East, several hundred persons in receipt of the highest pensions and endowed with large landed estates. Also included in the elite was the former military aristocracy, principally of Arab descent but with some *mawali* of eastern origin, and in Ifriqiya a fair number of Khurasanians, in its ranks. Some elements from this nucleus of the original army were kept on the payroll, in recognition of their relatively frequent participation in military campaigns (the Syrian *junds* in Spain, for example), while others, who had been lavishly rewarded with grants of land, were thereby 'demobilised', in the sense of being less immediately dependent on the State for subsistence. For policing operations and campaigns with limited objectives the government in any case preferred to call on the prince's bodyguard, or on contingents of mercenaries or soldiers of servile condition, recruited from the Berbers, Slavs (i.e. slaves of European origin) or blacks, who were housed in barracks; these, after all, were constantly at its disposal, and in the light of repeated mutinies in the traditional army were also considered more dependable. For a major campaign, however, or in an emergency, it was still possible to muster the traditional army.

One should also place in the elite the highly important category of the *fuqaha*, that is to say the intellectuals, experts in the juridico-religious sciences or *fiqh*, whose names fill the pages of the biographical dictionaries and who, often from quite humble origins, could rise through their learning to the highest positions in the State. The *qadi* of Kairouan Asad ibn al-Furat, appointed in 827 to lead the army embarking for Sicily, in addressing his companions made allusion, surrounded as he now was by honours, to his early career as a modest *faqih*, exhorting them to cultivate the legal sciences as the key to all doors, army commands included. Many acceded to official functions, chiefly in the judiciary (as *qadi*, judge or *mufti*, judge's assistant), or to positions linked with the conduct of the mosques

259

(leading the prayer and preaching). The most respected joined the sovereign's councils, but there were some who made a point of refusing any compromise with governmental power, which did not fail to enhance their reputation with the people. Thus fortified, they could on occasion voice forthright criticism of or even opposition to governmental measures. And finally there were some who devoted themselves exclusively to teaching, deriving at least part of their income from this source.

This group, united by a common educational background and common function (essentially to pronounce on the law), if not by a common social origin and attitude to the power of governments, played a major role in Muslim society between the end of the eighth century and the beginning of the tenth. It was through their agency that the Malikite doctrine, one of the strictest of Muslim orthodox schools, was disseminated in Ifriqiya and al-Andalus. These *fuqaha* could spring from a great diversity of social backgrounds, but it seems that the majority were drawn from a kind of middle class which the hard and fast division between *khassa* and *amma* serves to obscure, that of the merchants, a *de facto* bourgeoisie, but one which went unrecognised in the official hierarchy, even if at Cordoba some of its most affluent members, who had made their mark in the quarters and the bazaars, sometimes occupy a place at the bottom of the ceremonial order. From the biographers' laconic statements on the subject, it seems clear than an appreciable number of *fuqaha* came from merchant families and earned their living in similar fashion, this being a civilisation which attached no social or religious stigma to the practice of commerce – in fact quite the contrary.

Many studies draw attention to the overlapping interests of the merchants and the *fuqaha*, stressing the deference paid by merchants to legal learning, the similarity between the routes travelled by merchants and intellectuals which is revealed by their itineraries, and the fact that the Islamic law had been codified at a time when Muslim society was dominated by a commercial mentality. Among the Andalusian *fuqaha* of the ninth century one can detect a difference between an earlier group, composed of narrowly specialised jurists, fascinated by the exercise of power, and a later generation whose minds were open to the new developments in religious studies, some of whom had travelled to the East and in so doing acquired a prestige unmatched by their rivals. This second generation was perhaps the product of a growing integration of al-Andalus into the Muslim world's network of exchanges, and of the rise of urban classes geared to the expansion of industry and commerce. Identification of the merchant and intellectual classes should not, how-ever, be pressed too far, principally because merchants fell into varying social categories (the *tudjdjar* who carried on long-distance trade were allied to the ruling classes, while the petty traders of the urban bazaars were part of the *amma* and subject to the jurisdiction of the *sahib al-suq*: the concerns of the two categories were emphatically not the same). The prosperity of long-distance trade, a large part of which, especially in the West, was in any case carried on by non-Muslim merchants, Jewish or Christian, was largely uninfluenced by the regional or local economic context. Furthermore, it would be misleading to imply that the *fuqaha* were an exclusively urban class, even if they were closely bound up with the urban milieu through their education and often through their subsequent careers.

The bonds of commerce

The movement of craft techniques and craftsmen from east to west is to be seen as playing a major part in the cultural unification of the Islamic world, denoting the presence of common tastes and underlining the role of the ruling classes in the diffusion of products.

The textile industry, which recruited workmen, spinners, weavers and dyers in large numbers, inherited the ancient Coptic, and still more the Sassanid and Byzantine technical and artistic traditions (satin-weave, in which warp and woof are clearly distinguished), and then branched out, for example by inventing the multi-textured damask-weave. By this means new fibres, cotton and silk, gained in popularity and spread quickly from east to west: cotton, introduced in the eighth century from Khurasan, had before the eleventh century reached Spain, Tunisia and Sicily, whence it was to be exported – in its raw state – to the Egyptian manufacturing centres. The silkworm, already known to the Byzantines and the Sassanids, and the complex technique of rearing, unwinding and spinning the cocoon, which the Chinese captured in 751 on the Talas are supposed to have introduced or perfected, reached Spain at a very early date; perhaps because of its settlement by Arabs from Syria, Spain became the chief centre of sericulture, while Sicily, from the tenth century the other main producer of raw silk in the Muslim world, along with the Reggio region of Calabria, became one of the chief suppliers of the raw material to the Byzantine silk industry. Paper manufacture presents a close parallel: its introduction is similarly attributed to the Chinese taken prisoner in 751; and it is a fact that paper-making in the Islamic world first began in Samarkand, which at the beginning of the tenth century was still producing papers of high quality, imported by the Ikhshidids into Egypt. At the close of the eighth century (799 is the first firm date) paper was introduced into government offices, to the eventual exclusion of other writing surfaces on which alterations were less easy to detect. The main varieties of paper took their names from princes or their officials: 'pharaonic', *sulaymanî* (after the treasurer of Harun al-Rashid), *ja'farî* (from Ja'far, Harun's vizier), *talhî* (from Talha, son of Tahîr), *tahirî*, and *nouhî*, (from Nouh the Samanid). Production of paper began at Baghdad in 794, in Egypt during the tenth century and shortly afterwards in Spain, where it was based in particular on Jativa, from which high-quality papers were exported to Egypt. To produce this paper, rags were shredded, pounded to a pulp, with starch added as a sizing agent, then smoothed out over a shallow bed of flour and starch, and often coloured as part of the same operation. A whole gamut of colours (yellow, blue, violet, pink, green, red) attests to the degree of technical mastery attained, while the popularity of the product at the lower end of the market is demonstrated by its use from the twelfth century (in triangles or squares) for wrapping purposes.

The same east–west progression can be traced by archaeologists even for a product as widely diffused as pottery: the Byzantine and Sassanid traditions (lead-glazing and superimposed decoration) were first combined in order to imitate the Chinese porcelains imported through the Gulf (T'ang celadon and stoneware); this led to the birth of several schools, in an atmosphere of technical discovery and excitement which reveals extraordinary inventiveness. The Iranian school produced imitations of T'ang splash ware (polychromatic with streaks of colour under the glaze) and added a specifically Islamic variant, the incised or *sgraffito* pattern under the coloured decoration. Susa, Rayy and Samarra, in an effort to imitate Sung white porcelain (vitrified at a high temperature by a process which remained undiscovered) produced a white faience delicately incised beneath the lead-glaze: against the opaque white of the faience, a pseudo-epigraphical decoration and floral patterns in cobalt blue constitute one of the Islamic potters' greatest triumphs, which was to be adopted in return by China and ultimately to inspire the factories at Delft. The pottery of Nishapur and the surrounding region is characterised by the use of coloured slips on white and a decoration of Kufic inscriptions around the Tao motif. Samarra, lastly, is noteworthy for its precocious mastery of the art of giving pottery a metallic sheen: the firing of glazed earthenware in reductive conditions brought to the surface an excess of metallic salts in the glaze, resulting in products which looked like metal vessels, the use of which was disallowed by rigidly orthodox teachers. Allied to the luxury of the caliphal capitals, these products (Khurasanian slipware excepted) rapidly blazed a trail from east to west. Some of them were exports, for example the lustrous polychrome tiles used in 862 for the mosque at Kairouan and another batch which arrived in 936 in the Spanish capital of Madinat al-Zahra. But there were also imitations, for example the tiles in two colours produced at Kairouan, and the metallic sheen and *sgraffito* of Fatimid Egypt (where Coptic potters were producing religious objects). As early as 771, a lustre-painted glass produced by a similar process was being manufactured at Fustat, and around 900 glass decorated with splashes of colour is found alongside products made by the traditional methods of wheel-cutting and engraving. These last examples illustrate the close connections set up between arts in which firing played an essential part, underline the provincial capitals' function as intermediaries, and confirm the vigour of the trade relations between all parts of the Islamic world.

Production, but for which clientele?

The luxury market obviously played an essential role in the elaboration and diffusion of these artisanal products: luxuries for the poor in the case of lustre-ware or imitation celadon, but very costly luxuries when it was a question of working in rare and expensive materials: ivory, the gold and silver needed by jewellers and weavers of brocades, pearls, the coral used in carpet embroidery, the 'sea-wool' obtained from conches for weaving into opalescent fabrics (for which less expensive colouring matter was soon substituted), dyeing materials imported from distant parts (brazil-wood from India, lacquer, gum Arabic). The demand for products of the greatest rarity accounts for the staggering prices quoted by contemporary authors – 50,000 *dinars* for a length of brocade produced for the mother of Harun al-Rashid, 1,000 *dinars* for a jacket of the same material for Ma'mun's doctor, 400 *dinars* to cloak the jurisconsult Abu Hanifa – which critics were quick to compare with the more than modest price, five *dirhams*, of the suit worn by Ibn Hanbal. The accumulation of artisanal products in the cupboards of the elite – the jurist Abu Yusuf accumulated 200 pairs of silk trousers – and still more of the prince, was presumably a precaution: in the amounts quoted, the huge stocks in the Abbasid palaces can have been of no practical value, and because they were only partially negotiable did not even represent a genuine capital reserve. Their value was purely symbolic.

The caliphal treasure, which issued a continuous stream of gifts, particularly in the form of the ceremonial robes (*khila*) distributed to officers and officials or presented to foreign princes by ambassadors, was replenished by the official workshops of the *tiraz*. Better known in connection with Fatimid Egypt than with the Abbasid empire, this organisation which supplied the textile needs of the State was bipartite: at the caliphal and emiral palaces there were tailors to make up the ceremonial garments; away from the centre, in factories renowned for the production of a particular fabric, officials controlled by the Master of the *tiraz* were empowered to conscript craftsmen, in return for a decent wage, to do work for the State. The caliphal workshop was thus not a factory but an administrative department; in each centre, there was a warehouse-*cum*-residence which connected a chain of *tiraz*, a link symbolised in Egypt by the Nile barge which conveyed the Master on his rounds of collection and inspection. The high standing of this dignitary is underlined by his presence at the caliphal ceremonies, where he presented the vestments worn only by the commander of the faithful.

The *tiraz* (the name comes from the Persian word for 'embroidery') in fact formed one of the rights exclusive to the sovereign majesty, on the same level as the prayer and the coinage. All three cases involved exaltation of the prince's name: the *tiraz* was a band of woven material on which his *alama* or device was embroidered in gold or coloured thread. It could be worn only by the caliph or, at his command, by those enjoying his special favour; its political character was emphasised by the inclusion of prayers and blessings specific to the dynasty, and under the Fatimids in some cases of phrases from the Ismaʾilian creed, and by the incorporation of the names of the viziers or trusted agents of the caliph – his *mawalis*, or clients – who commissioned the making of the *tiraz*. As a prerogative of the sovereign, the *tiraz* was linked in caliphal law with the right to drape the Kaʿba with a silken veil woven in the official workshops and the practice of presenting a black robe and turban to the preacher appointed to lead the prayer; it is thus not surprising to find Harun bracketing the *tiraz* in his will with those other cog-wheels of the State, the land-tax, the courier service and the treasury, for the precise reason that it manifested the caliph's glory. Maʾmun's action in removing his brother's name from the embroideries of Khurasan was thus to be the first sign of his revolt. From Umayyad times onward, Egypt seems to have had more than its fair share of *tiraz* establishments: Akhmin, followed by Fustat, and lastly Bansha and Dabiq, as well as the *tiraz* of the Saʾid in Upper Egypt. The evidence of the textile fragments discovered at Samarra and in Egypt points to the difference between an agency concerned with products reserved for the caliph, *tiraz al kassa*, and another, less exclusive, the *tiraz al amma*, of which there is evidence at Fustat under Amin, whose products were in wider circulation, presumably because they were distributed to officials, servants of the caliph (in particular to official preachers) and the military, and perhaps even put on sale.

Bird in flight. Chinese silk of the T'ang era. The graphic expression and array of techniques commanded by the Chinese had a considerable influence on Islamic luxury art, even if the latter, in keeping with the characteristics of Islamic decoration, did not aim to reproduce the model (Paris, Musée Guimet).

Eleventh-century tiraz with the name of the Fatimid caliph al-Mustansir (Paris, Musée de Cluny).

The existence of this commercial element remains conjectural: it appears to be ruled out by the evidence of Nasir-i-Khosraw, relating to Tinnis in 1047, but it might account for the widespread distribution of the finds.

Illusory aspects of the commercial 'take-off'

A convenient and traditional way of looking at the Abbasid empire is to regard it as the golden age of Muslim trade. The political unification of regions which before the conquest had been separated by rigid frontiers, the upsurge of towns and the inflow of money made possible by the capture of booty, the conversion of treasure into coin and the availability of gold from the Sudan have inspired visions of a 'melting-pot of time and space, a point of intersection, a vast conjuncture, a miracle of convergence'. The reality is more modest and the chronology above all more spaced out: the pace of expansion was tightly controlled by the resources and demands of the ruling social classes. Attuned to the caliphal society of the great capitals, it paid no attention to mass circulation. This first point becomes self-evident when it is realised that the caliphal empire coincides with the disappearance – for the next 1,200 years, barring a few regional exceptions – of wheeled transport (even the word now used in Arabic for a cart, *araba*, is of Turkish origin). This lack, in a mountainous and geographically divided world, reflects and serves to emphasise the absence of any traffic in bulky commodities. In particular it meant that movements of grain could take place only within well-defined geographical units, accessible by river or by sea: Egypt was able to feed the Hijaz, following Amr's reopening of the canal between the Nile and the Red Sea, but the export of Egyptian grain to Syria was perforce reduced to the few tonnes which could be transported by a caravan of camels. The Jazira supplied Baghdad, Sicily supplied Tunis, but in general the volume of grain exports was small: the Muslim world consisted of a great continental mass, and the inland seas, apart from the Red Sea and the Gulf, which in any case adjoined desert regions, were not available for inter-regional exchanges – only the Euphrates filled this function, while the Mediterranean front remained deserted. A camel,

Transporting salt by caravan in the desert. In such conditions, the volume of trade was inevitably restricted.

depending on the type of harness, could carry a load of between 70 and 240kg, and a caravan – of perhaps as many as 500 camels – shifted between a quarter and half of the cargo carried by an average ship (250 tons).

Furthermore, political unification, for all its rapidity, long remained incomplete, especially in Central Asia, where there was a history of close trading relations with China, and did not extend to commercial unification: internal customs barriers subsisted between the provinces, for example the *ma'sin* levied at Jeddah on merchandise coming from Egypt. Coinage issues, furthermore, continued for a long while to respect the monometallic silver and gold currencies traditional to particular regions. Unification of the two systems was only gradual, as is proved by coin-hoards, while considerable differences in price levels, between Iraq and the Jazira on the one hand and Syria and Egypt on the other, make it clear that these continued to form distinct trading areas. On its own, an abundance of coinage could not have given a decisive spur to the circulation and production of goods: in the absence of a technological revolution – of which there is no trace except in ceramics and belatedly, in the tenth century, in luxury textiles – the empire's economy was doomed to rigidity, and the creation of new outlets only came about through the democratisation, presumably at an even later date, of the silk factories, which is attested by the Jewish documents from the Geniza in Egypt. In consequence, the dethesaurisation of precious metals merely stimulated a rise in prices: from patiently amassed evidence it can be deduced that the scale of this was unprecedented, in as much as the price of grain and bread appears to have at least quadrupled in the course of the eighth century. The rise may also have been due in part to the reduction in areas under cultivation and possibly to a growth in population, but there is no reason to doubt the truth of Harun al-Rashid's assertion that a *dirham* in Mansur's time was worth more than one of his own *dinars*, issued 30 years later.

In general, the result of the Muslim conquest was thus merely to consolidate the merchant class and to give sharper definition to the various types of merchant and trading institutions, in particular to the forms of commercial co-operation described in works of jurisprudence from as early as the eighth century. Alongside the craftsman who sold his products directly to the consumer, the Muslim world gave greater scope to the middle man, liberated from the institutional restraints which had hampered him in the past: the State's hold on distribution was greatly diminished (disappearance of the *annona*), and under the stimulus of fiscal changes the self-sufficiency of the great estate and the peasantry was giving place to the free market. Relaxation of the traditional constraints also benefited the merchant, who was no longer obliged to enrol in a corporation or to sell to the State or corporation at monopolistic prices. He was nevertheless not free of all restrictions: when abroad, he had to reside in a trading-post and undertake spying missions, and he was morally obliged by his ties with the government to make his services available as banker and tax-farmer. Finally, just as in the ancient world, his rapid rise to riches was kept in check by sweeping confiscations, with the result that the merchant could suffer brutal inroads on his wealth: in 912, the Egyptian merchant Sulayman was saddled with a fine of 100,000 *dinars*.

A merchant hierarchy formed in the eighth century. At the very bottom was the itinerant trader who collected finished goods from the workplace and took them to the regular markets. Above him was the 'traveller' who went to inspect merchandise in distant countries, taking commissions and capital in coin or in goods with which to do business on behalf of a great merchant, representative of a third type. This was the 'sedentary' merchant, for whom the respected appellation of *tadjir* was reserved, who operated from the great commercial centres, engaged in trading by commission but also collecting and disseminating commercial intelligence by letter, and entering into partnerships of the informal, friendly type which were to flourish above all in the world of the Geniza. It was within this select group of *tadjir*, few in number, and like Sulayman the Egyptian fabulously rich, that the stock of costly products circulated, as did the fiduciary money: orders to pay, always drawn on the bearer, and orders for deferred execution of payment (*suftadja*), payable on sight by the merchant's agent. These letters of credit and cheques (*sakkas*) circulated freely in the most distant places, at a time when the lending of money at interest remained a rarity and was reserved for grave emergencies of a non-commercial kind. Probably condemned as immoral, lending at interest would make a belated appearance on the scene only in the twelfth century, while the bill of exchange continued to be unknown in the Muslim world, which clung to its monetary unity and numismatic standard, reckoning transactions in its own money of account, the 'pure' *dinar* or *dirham*, to which all actual coins were related.

The various forms of commercial partnership are recognisable from a very early date: the works of Malik ben Anas (died 795), founder of the Malikite school of jurisprudence, and of the 'Hanifite' Shaybami (died 803), author of a *Book of Partnership* and of a *Book of Commission*, anticipate the forms that were introduced – or rediscovered – in Italy during the tenth century. First and foremost there was the 'partnership', *sharika*, formed from a pooled capital, limited to one operation, one commodity, and a fixed amount of money, or conversely unlimited and universally applicable, in which case it had the solidity of a family undertaking. The contract imposed on the partners a duty of collective guarantee and reciprocal representation, which also had its counterpart and roots in a mode of partnership that was friendly, informal and patriarchal. In the commission (*muqarada*, *qirad*), known in the Hijaz by the sixth century, the great merchant entrusted goods or capital to a 'traveller' who would share the profit (receiving a third, unless he accepted liability for possible losses) as compensation for his effort and the personal risks run on the journey. Obtaining commodities by commission was in theory forbidden precisely because of the uncertainty over the setting of prices, but was nevertheless condoned by the Hanifite school as a matter of practice. In general this school promoted respect for the traditional commercial practices and the development of juridical forms which amounted to 'legal tricks' designed to circumvent the ban on usurious practices which the rival Shafite and Malekite schools were only too eager, by contrast, to detect.

In this small, close-knit mercantile world, where everyone knew everyone else's business, it was customary for a merchant to undertake on behalf of a correspondent the heavy responsibility of handling his merchandise, without compensation, *pro-rata* commission or profit, but simply on the basis of reciprocal good will. To perform this service, he had to help the 'travellers', see to the despatch, supervision and transportation of goods, and above all keep his distant friend informed about price movements, the quality and quantity of goods available on the market and the likely departure dates of ships and caravans.

The commercial handbooks, like the one Dimashqi produced in the eleventh century among the Fatimids, and the letters of the Cairo merchants recommend untiring diligence in seeking out reliable information and speed in acting on it as the only way to achieve the high profits desired: in the order of between 25 and 50 per cent of the merchant's outlay, with purchase price, carriage and other expenses included. These sources exclude from their sphere of action and interest the commercial transactions of the masses, and trace for us the picture of a great merchant dealing solely in valuable merchandise (gems, rare imported spices, expensive fabrics) and especially in the raw materials which supplied the most up-market forms of craftsmanship (goldsmithing, perfumery, pharmacy, gold-thread embroidery). He is equally a business man, well-versed in the 'capitalist' techniques of borrowing, lending, and commission, and keen to reinvest his profits in tax-farming, property transactions and agriculture: in short, he forms part of a merchant aristocracy by no means restricted to its commercial function, geared to the conspicuous consumption of princes and the aristocracy.

The sovereign market

Everywhere, the State tax system kept alive the local market, whose golden age, the seventh and eighth centuries, is reflected in the abundance, particularly at Basra, of the low-denomination coinage, the Umayyad and Abbasid copper fals. It amazed Western pilgrims such as Arculf, who visited Alexandria in 670, and Bernard the Monk, who in 870 saw a market-place laid out in front of St Mary of the Latins at Jerusalem where anyone

Taking ship on the Euphrates, one of the few routes by which goods could be sent by water (*Sessions of Harîrî*, ms arab 5847, early thirteenth century, Paris, Bibliothèque nationale).

could set up a stall for an annual payment of two *dinars*. In reality this phenomenon signified the incursion into the town of the rural market, under the spur of the land-tax, which with its demand for monetary payments placed the rural producer at a disadvantage, obliging him to sell at any price; this market gave the necessary stimulus to the countryside without creating new outlets for urban enterprises, since peasants had to conserve their profit and could rarely afford to make purchases, which left little scope for the merchant. These markets – the *Mirbad* at Basra, the *Kunasa* at Kufa, the Tuesday market at Baghdad, the Wednesday market at Mosul, the Monday market at Damascus – were at first generally accessible, with no places reserved: the best went to the first to arrive, 'as in the mosque'. However, there was a gradual tendency, under the Umayyads, for the *suk* to become enclosed: places were reserved and stall-holders paid a rent to the 'Master of the *suk*'. Next the *suks* became specialised, as *khans* or *funduqs* took on the role of miniature commodity exchanges, each for a single product; the *qaysariya*, an enclosed, guarded market for luxury articles (the Caesar's house of Antiquity), appears as early as the eighth century, while the food market, displaced from the town centre, became localised as the *suwayqas*, the 'little markets' of the suburbs.

While the topography of the Muslim town precluded any hierarchical distribution of the *suks*, commercial activity became highly specialised: like the craft bodies, from which they were barely distinguishable, mercantile occupations were minutely differentiated by names derived from the product being traded. In his book *The Key of Dreams*, Dinwari enumerates nearly 150 mercantile trades in Baghdad in 1006, and 90 are mentioned by name in the Geniza documents. Under the supervision, in Umayyad times, of a *wali*, found in the principal towns (Mecca, Medina, Kufa, Basra, Wasit), and then of the *mutasahib*, who fixed the prices, collected the tithe and rent for the space occupied, controlled weights and

269

measures and judged the honesty of transactions, the market was completely monetarised. But the interplay of supply and demand did not determine the price of basic foods; these were calculated by the 'Master of the market' with reference to the needs of the turbulent masses, and the effort to peg them, when it took the form of a public granary to bring down high prices, can sometimes look like an early example of government intervention: this was the *rahba* system ultimately inherited in the twelfth century by Norman Sicily. The rural market obeyed different laws: sellers were obliged to dispose of bulky and perishable produce at no matter what price, so as to have the coin needed for payment of the land-tax. The market in artisanal goods, taking account as it did of the quality, originality and amount of labour put into the article, was obviously speculative: it was not productivity or supply and demand which determined the price, but the style and technical accomplishment of the maker, more artist than artisan, and the history of prices is inevitably limited, on the one side, to that of the upper price ranges in an economic climate uniformly favourable to the urban consumer, and on the other by the extravagant impulses of the rich, or demands for ostentatious display.

Long-distance trade routes to the East, exotic products

The development of the great Iraqi power centres and of certain provincial capitals stimulated the well-established long-distance trade in articles intended for consumption by a cultivated elite with vast financial resources. As well as in the caliphal capitals, such a clientele existed at various times in the big towns of southern Iraq, Kufa, Basra and Wasit, whose merchant circles had become assimilated through their wealth with the privileged elite, in Fustat in Tulunid Egypt, in Rayy, Nishapur and the large towns of Transoxiana; the direction of the trade-routes came to be dictated by the demand emanating from these centres, and more particularly from the emiral capitals. Syria remained for a long while excluded from this circulation; the archaeological evidence confirms the absence, after the precocious opulence of the Umayyads, of Iraqi and Iranian wealth west of the Euphrates, and the slow response to the fashions for tin-glazed faience and pottery with a metallic sheen, imported from China by way of Iran.

A much-quoted passage in which Jahiz lists the goods imported into Iraq describes a trade in expensive articles – horses, spices, slaves, fruit and preserves, clothing, fabrics and weapons – which fall into three categories: articles for military consumption, as is only to be expected in view of the fundamental character of the Abbasid State (horses from China and Arabia, Afghan, Khazar and Yemenite weapons, horse harness from China, swords of Indian and also Frankish provenance); articles for conspicuous consumption, including tropical products (spices, drugs, ivory, precious woods, Indian teak in particular), northern goods (furs brought from Siberia via Khwarizm) and others that were still more exotic (Chinese paper, silks and celadon wares, menagerie animals, felts from the Dzungarian Turks); and articles of everyday consumption, though still luxuries, traded between different regions. These consisted of manufactured and agricultural products special to particular regions: Egyptian papyrus; the sugars and sweetmeats of Khwarizm and Ahwaz; Ahwaz

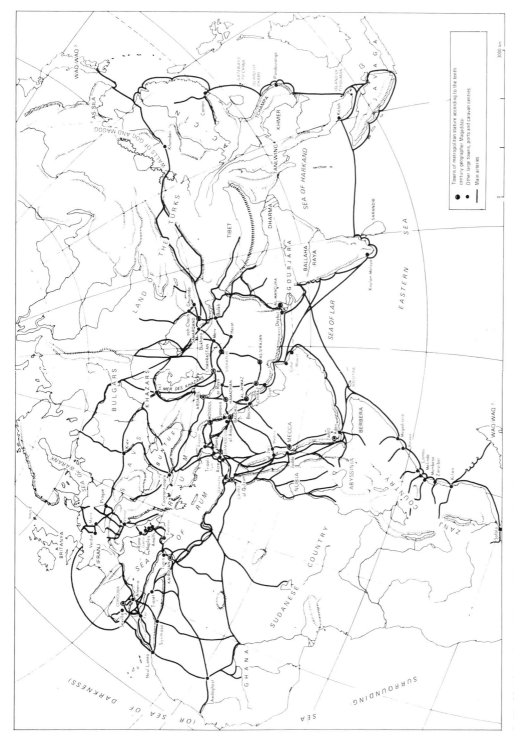

9 Worldwide trading relations of Islam during the Abbasid epoch

silks, Egyptian linen, carpets and woollen goods from Armenia and the Jazira; and the many varieties of choice foods: pickled capers from Bushanj, Gurgan pheasants, truffles from Balkh, plums from Rayy, apples and quinces from Isphahan. There was lastly an enormous traffic in the most valuable of all commodities, slaves: Indians (with engineering skills), Zandjs from the East African Sahel, and Slavs and Turks sent through Khurasan by the Bulgars and Khazars. Around 870, Bernard the Monk departed from Bari, capital of a slaving emirate, at the same time as six ships loaded with Lombard captives from southern Italy: there were 9,000 prisoners in all, 3,000 destined for Tunisia, 3,000 for Tripoli and 3,000 for Alexandria. It is thus hard to avoid the general impression that the commerce of the Muslim world consisted of imports flowing in from all directions, heedless of trading balances and based on the pleasure principle.

It therefore comes as no surprise that in developing this traffic the earliest routes to be exploited were those which brought the rarest and the most valuable products from the most far-off places: excavations at Satingpra in the Malay peninsula, the obligatory crossing-point from the Indian Ocean to the Gulf of Siam, have demonstrated the presence between the sixth and ninth centuries of Chinese stoneware and T'ang celadons together with glassware from Alexandria. In the Chinese sources, 'Persian' merchants are mentioned as early as 671, and again in 717 and 748. Relations between the Gulf and China were severed for a time when Muslim mercenaries burnt down Canton in 758, after which the China route remained closed until 792. Trade was then resumed, only to be abandoned again following the massacre of 120,000 Muslim merchants by Cantonese rebels in 875–8: although this is clearly an inflated figure, the Arab sources testify not only to the importance of the port (where the minaret served as a lighthouse), but also to the early date at which it became a goal of trading expeditions (aloes were being purchased there around 750) and to their regularity. A maritime 'guide-book' entitled *An Account of India and China*, first published in 851 by Sulayman the merchant, was revised in 916 by another merchant, Abu Zayd of Siraf, and complemented, in 950, by the *Marvels of India*, which was compiled by Buzurg, a merchant in the port of Ram-Ormuz. It traces the route from Basra to the gulf ports (calling first at Suhar and Muscat, then at Siraf and Ormuz) and thence to the Malabar coast, being careful to avoid the pirate-infested coasts of Baluchistan and Sind, and so to Ceylon, where a Muslim colony had been in existence since 700, and Kalah in Malaysia, the place where after the events of 875–8 the Arabs made contact with the Chinese. From Kalah, sailing round Champa, the ancient country of the Khmers, the Muslim ships arrived after a three-month voyage at the ports of Canton or Zaytun at the mouth of the Yangtze. Along the entire length of this route the Muslim presence was being consolidated, with the foundation of colonies in Sind (Daybul and Mansura), on the coast of India (at some time before 956, Mas'udi visited a town, Saymor, with 10,000 Muslim inhabitants), in Sumatra and Java. Sulayman and Abu Zayd make it clear that only a small number of ships was involved and that the purpose of the voyage was to fetch back rare and costly commodities – aloes, teak, porcelain, camphor, brazil-wood, Malaysian tin. Confirmation again comes from the archaeological evidence, which shows the presence at

Samarra, Rayy, Susa and Nishapur of the Chinese translucent white porcelain and celadon wares.

Activity on the other main trading front of the caliphal empire had already begun in the Sassanid era: intensified by the Tahirids, it reached its apogee under the Samanids, only to go into abrupt decline after the year 1000. This route was the source of furs from the Russian, Polish and Siberian taiga, and of slaves. The slave trade was organised from the urban centres of the Turkic peoples around the Volga: Bulghar, capital of the Bulgars, not far from Kazan, and the town of the Burtas near Nijni-Novgorod. The chronology and geography of the traffic can be deduced from the finds of Islamic coins: one hoard, at Novgorod, exactly dated by dendrochronology, provides good grounds for thinking that there was only a short interval (not more than fifteen years) between the striking of the most recent coin and the burial of the hoard; and, out of 66 dates determinable in this way, two fall in the eighth century, twenty in the ninth, 41 in the tenth and only three in the eleventh century, a chronological distribution confirmed by analysis of those hoards which have been fully published, which reveals a still more overwhelming predominance of tenth-century Samanid coins. Our picture of the geographical distribution of these coins is in part distorted by a heavy concentration of hoards along the shores of the Baltic (eleven were listed in 1910 in the governorate of St Petersburg and 42 in Livonia), which are generally regarded as Viking war booty or trading profits, drawn from the riches accumulated by the peoples acting as middlemen. But a find-map shows that hoard deposition coincides in particular with the southern limits of the great forest: the former governorates of Kazan (fourteen hoards), Viatka (fifteen) and Jaroslav (eleven). The vastness of the riches buried not only in Russia (deposits with more than 1,500 *dirhams* are not uncommon and the Vladimir hoard contained no less than 11,077, composed of 140 Abbasid *dirhams*, four Tahirid, sixteen Jaffarid, two Sjid, sixteen Buyid and 10,079 Samanid), but also in Poland, in Scandinavia, and in places as remote as the British Isles and Germany, to the total of half a tonne of pure silver – 120,000 *dirhams* in Russia and more than 40,000 in Scandinavia – and which can represent only a modest sample of the flood of Islamic coins, reveals the scale of this commercial activity, and also its one-sided, importative character.

More doubtful prospects in the West

In the tenth century, the activity on these trading fronts was to be matched by the commercial expansion of the African Sahel, which until then had merely been served by a few trading-posts on the shores of the Indian Ocean (where colonies were established at Berbera, Zayla, Sofala and Zanzibar), or at the southern termini of the routes across the Sahara, perhaps reconnoitred by Sidi Uqba as far back as 666, but explored and Islamised by the Sanhaja Berbers in the tenth and eleventh centuries. At the same time, the Mediterranean coastline appears to have been made sterile by wars and razzias. The sea had in fact been abandoned to Saracen 'pirates', who first appear on the scene with their attempted invasion of the Balearic Isles in 798. After this we hear of raids on the small

273

The many hoards found even as far away as Scandinavia (in this instance at Väsby in Sweden) contain coins of very varied provenance. Tributes levied from conquered peoples make up only a minor part; these hoards rather give an idea of the geographical extent of commercial exchange, which, in the case of Islam, peaked around the ninth century.

islands off Sicily and southern Italy, on Sardinia and Corsica, and in 812 on Civitavecchia and Nice. It seems that these attacks were mounted by large and well-organised fleets coming from the east coast of Spain and less frequently from the western Maghrib, and that they were manned chiefly by Berbers, to judge from the description *mauri* applied to them in Carolingian sources. The Arab chronicles dealing with this period, which usually rely on semi-official annals, tell us nothing of these engagements, presumably because of the private nature of the enterprises, launched as a rule from regions no longer subject in practice to the control of the political powers established in the great capitals of Western

Islam, or in a state of open revolt. This Andalusian piracy developed in the second half of the ninth century into attacks on the coastline of Provence, and then into a continuous occupation, lasting from 890 until 970, with the establishment of the Saracen base at Fraxinetum.

Italy also experienced serious harassment from the Saracens. The damage was done not so much by seaborne raids, such as the celebrated attack on Rome in 846, which was probably the work of Andalusian pirates, but rather by the bands of Muslim mercenaries which had been recruited in the first half of the century by the petty dynasts of the south and had quickly got out of control. Here too the Muslims would establish permanent bases, in the case of the emirate of Bari (841–71) even taking the form of a miniature State. The object of all these Saracen raids was primarily to capture slaves for sale at a good price in the markets of the Muslim world where there was a strong demand. The merchants of southern Italy had been in the habit of exporting slaves to Ifriqiya since the late eighth century, but it may be that a short supply and hope of greater profits tempted interlopers to help themselves by force. The prince of Benevento had no chance of success when in 836 he forbade Neapolitans to engage in the traffic. Attempts have been made to justify the expeditions to the islands by the need to procure timber for ship-building. While it may be true that the Saracen fleets neglected no opportunity to capture any merchant vessels they chanced to encounter, this was certainly not their main objective. This piracy cannot therefore be used, as it sometimes is, as an argument in support of the existence at this date of a still significant degree of commerce in the western Mediterranean.

The situation was different in the central Mediterranean, where Sicily and the towns of southern Italy preserved close links with the Byzantine world, at a time when Ifriqiya differed from the rest of the Maghrib and al-Andalus in remaining directly within the political and economic orbit of the Abbasid empire. In this sector, the sea had never ceased to be traversed by important commercial currents, and to be patrolled by Byzantine fleets, to an extent which the governments established at Kairouan could hardly ignore. The connections between the trading-ports of the former duchy of Naples – Naples itself, Gaeta and Amalfi – and the African shore were maintained even after the Muslim conquest, which, as we saw, may well have given a stimulus to certain kinds of traffic – for example in slaves. The Aghlabids of Tunisia were therefore at pains not to be outdone by independent ventures which threatened to escape their control, and in 827 they seized the initiative by launching the conquest of Sicily, under the auspices of the *jihad*. Even in the Aghlabid emirate, however, urban centres and regions of the interior such as Mila, Laribus, Sbiba, the Zab and the Nafzawa made a greater contribution by and large to the stability of the country than did the coastal centres of Tunis or Sus, while coastal towns such as Gabes or Tripoli played a more significant part as staging-posts or termini of the overland caravan routes from Egypt than they did as ports.

It was also as caravan towns that Tahert (founded in 761) and still more Sijilmasa (757), the great trading-post on the edge of the western Sahara, achieved their importance. Both were situated on routes traversing the Maghrib from east to west, but their chief importance was as the departure-point of a flourishing trade with black Africa, in which salt and man-made products were transported across the desert in exchange for slaves and above all gold. This trade was responsible for the development of towns in southern Morocco such as Aghmat or Tamdult, which was founded by an Idrisid emir in the ninth century. It also helps to explain the growth in importance of towns on the Saharan fringe of the Aghlabid emirate, Tozeur in the Qastiliya and Tubna in the Zab. But very little is known about the chronological development of this commerce, which was monopolised by the Kharijite Berbers of the Tahert emirate. In particular, it seems that Sijilmasa only assumed a leading role in the tenth century, when the Fatimids extended their control over the whole of the Maghrib, reducing Tahert, which had previously been one of the nodal points in this trade, to a mere stopover on the East–West route. Another active trading-area for which we lack detailed information is the frontier with the Carolingian empire and its successor states. The towns of Spain's northern march (Saragossa, Huesca, Lerida) were familiar with the sight of Jewish and probably also Mozarabic merchants passing through on their way to the Frankish territories, which they entered in the east from Barcelona and in the west from Pamplona and the Pyrenees, to bring back white slaves (*saqaliba*), furs and possibly weapons.

But foreign merchants penetrate deep into Islam

Although this activity on the empire's 'fronts' demonstrates the initiative and audacity of Muslim merchants and seamen, it by no means indicates the commercial superiority of the Islamic world. It was merely a case of one set of merchants in quest of products to satisfy an aristocratic demand making contact with other groups of merchants, no less capable of taking initiatives. Even if the Muslims were bold enough to penetrate parts of India, Malaysia, Indo-China and China, and explored for commercial purposes the fringes of Africa and Siberia, they steered almost completely clear of the Byzantine empire, which confined its rare visitors to closely supervised trading-posts, and they knew nothing of western Europe. In contrast, concern for the provisioning of the caliphal capitals prompted the Muslim empire to open its doors to foreign merchants, groups of marginal importance in their own less evolved and less urbanised societies, transients whose activity carried no threat of serving the political interests of great enemy States, Byzantium or the Khazar kingdom, and whose movements within the Muslim world came under the scrutiny of the 'counter-espionage' service organised by the officials of the courier network, the *barid*.

It is to one of these officials, Ibn Khurdadhbih (appointed in 870 to take charge of the central bureau), that we are indebted for a detailed description of the routes taken by two of these groups. If his itineraries remain at some points implausible and obscure, the general value of his testimony can hardly be doubted. It entitles us to assume that around 840 (Ibn Khurdadhbih started writing in 844) one such party penetrated deep into the Islamic world, and that another had received permission to cross its central isthmus to gain access to the Indian Ocean. In the first we recognise Russian merchants – of the Slavic race – as those who travelled 'from the most distant parts' (presumably the taiga and tundra regions inhabited by hunters) by way of the Don, the Volga and the Khazar capital to reach the Caspian. Crossing to the Gurgan shore, they journeyed with a caravan to Baghdad, where eunuch slaves acted as interpreters. Other merchants, using the Dnieper and the Black Sea route, fetched up in Byzantium. Their merchandise consisted of furs, slaves (etymologically Slavs), Frankish weapons (swords of superior workmanship) – and their services. These Russians were evidently carrying a stage further the great eastward movement of the Varangians; they were doubtless Slavs under Scandinavian leadership, and Ibn Khurdadhbih makes it clear that they were Christians. In other circumstances, the trade-route was to serve equally well as the path of invasions: the Russians who crossed the Caucasus or the Caspian in the years between 864 and 884, or in 909, in 913, in 943, in 969, and in 1030–2, did so in order to plunder Tabaristan and Azerbaijan, where they occupied the capital. Trade, as we see, went hand in hand with pillage. It is to be noted that the Turkic peoples around the Volga, the Khazars and Bulgars, did not play the intermediary role their geographical situation might indicate (the Bulgars, however, struck a fairly abundant coinage in imitation of Islamic money). Furthermore, this vast displacement of men with their merchandise testifies to the intermittency of the transactions and to their rudimentary nature, which also fits in with the high prices that were commanded.

Of still greater interest, and regarded as much more debatable by historians, to the point that some have even doubted the authenticity of Khurdadhbih's text, is the circulation of the 'Radhanite' Jews: long the subject of controversy, this was at one time held to prove the special affinity of the Jewish community with commerce and more recently their dominance of routes open to all. These two interpretations can be disregarded, and even if it must be accepted that certain details of the itinerary outlined by Ibn Khurdadhbih have been included from other routes by a process of 'contamination', there is no reason to doubt that his text, taken as a whole, sheds light on a brief but significant episode, involving polyglot Jewish merchants (speaking Persian, Greek and Arabic, along with the Frankish, Spanish and Slav languages), who brought from the West eunuchs, female slaves, boys, silk, pelts and swords. Taking ship 'in the land of the Franks, beside the Western sea' (which rules out Narbonne in favour of the Carolingian empire's Atlantic ports), they crossed the isthmus of Suez between the points of Farama (the lock) and Qulzum (Suez) and arrived at the Arabian peninsular ports of al-Jar and Jeddah, to take ship again for India and China; on the return journey, which in this first itinerary retraced the same route, they took back spices and aromatics. A variant route passed through Antioch and went by way of the Euphrates, Baghdad and the port of Ubullah to arrive at the same Far Eastern destinations. Yet a third itinerary started from Spain and the land of the Franks, passing through Tangier, the Sus, Ifriqiya, Egypt and Syria; and lastly there was a fourth, 'behind Byzantium', by way of the Slavs' territory to the capital of the Khazars and thence into the Muslim world through the Gurgan. Continuing through Balkh and the Ferghana, the itinerary finished up in China.

Ibn Khurdadhbih probably included in his description of the Radhanite routes sections of itineraries that were originally unconnected; the journey *via* Morocco and Tunisia seems especially intrusive and out of keeping with the rest. But many other elements fit perfectly with information culled from other sources: in about 825 we find Louis the Pious granting commercial privileges to a number of Jewish merchants, Donat, Samuel and Abraham of Saragossa, and David and Joseph of Lyons, which matches Ibn Khurdadhbih's assertion that the Radhanites returned 'to the court of the Frankish king'. The fact that Alexandria is absent from the itinerary is consistent with its decline as a port and its current status as the seat of a corsair republic. Lastly, the passage of a route 'behind Byzantium' is confirmed by a series of hoards – mostly somewhat later, from the tenth century, and consisting of Samanid and Bulgar coins – in Galicia and Bohemia. The Indian spices and Samanid *dirhams* (dating from 913–15) seen at Mainz in 973 by the Andalusian traveller Tartushi are further evidence of the same route. Some doubt remains over the opening of the Red Sea at this early date, in particular to minorities such as the Jews; one can simply note that Buzurg, in his travels around the Indian Ocean in 950, encountered a Jewish merchant, a *dhimmi*, who was profiting from the 'caliphal peace' well before it was extended to the merchants of the Geniza. The itineraries thus seem plausible and there is no difficulty in accepting the list of products put forward. All that remains is to identify the Radhanites.

They have commonly been regarded as Jews of the Muslim world: Radhan is the name of a district in the Sawad, to the east of the Tigris, and this etymology must be taken as decisive, to the exclusion of the explanation based on the Persian term '*Rah-dar*', meaning 'one who knows the roads', or a still more fanciful derivation from *Rhodanus*, the Rhône. But the text testifies explicitly to the European character of these Jewish merchants, who indeed look very much like 'the King's Jews', and if one bears in mind the particular nature of this venturesome and marginal trade, a liaison which it was bold and hazardous to attempt (even if it was sufficiently regular to be reported by the master of the *barid* to the caliphal secretariat), it becomes conceivable that a name – that of a family or small community – of Iraqi origin should have been retained by a group which entered the Frankish empire either as immigrants or engulfed in the tide of conquest, a group which preserved its links with the Muslim homeland and its familiarity with the Arabic and Persian languages (a detail which lends weight to this hypothesis), and which took advantage of its pivotal position and indeterminate legal status to launch commercial operations that from a Western standpoint seemed unprecedented, but which among the merchants of the Dar al-Islam would probably be considered quite normal. Candidates who come to mind are the Jews of Narbonne after its recapture by Charlemagne, whose prestige in following centuries was to be enormous; there is no real proof one way or the other, and the Radhanites' connections with Spain may be explained by the Atlantic itinerary cited by Ibn Khurdadhbih, going round Gibraltar. But in general it seems safe to say that the *Radhaniya*, to which there was no sequel, coincided with the expansion of the Carolingian empire; it did not survive the crisis provoked by the invasions of the Northmen and the resumption of the Muslim offensive against Provence, but it had broadly anticipated the characteristics of long-distance trade in the eleventh century: the part played by minorities, the role of the Red Sea, and the opening up of the Samanid routes to India.

The development of a social model

As we contemplate the Abbasid world, it appears to be the direct heir of the Umayyad Dar al-Islam: the structure of the ancient world was still intact; the capital city soaked up the monetary revenues drawn in by an effective fiscal apparatus; uncontested power remained in the hands of the State and its administrative class, which was the chief beneficiary of the social redistribution of the land-tax but also well-placed to absorb, in capillary fashion, the wealth and distinctions enjoyed by the aristocracies of ancient name and military repute. A social hierarchy of privileged families excluded interlopers, by the memory of the elders, but could nevertheless accommodate, through the system of adoptive kinship, the upward mobility of slaves. The factional disputes within the most open and most volatile strata of this privileged class reflected the struggle for power, which is to say wealth. The break-up of the Arab army and its tribal aristocracies therefore left the educated and the military in naked competition, in a contest between on the one hand the master of eloquence, calligraphy and fiscal procedures, and on the other the ambitious professional soldier, sprung from the lowliest, most alien and most impoverished of backgrounds, that of a Turkish or Khazar slave. It is not a question, however, of competition and conflicts between social groups but rather between factions which formed shifting and short-lived alliances.

The mass of the Muslim people, now solidified by the conversion and acculturation of the minorities and made uniform by the dissemination and standardisation of Muslim teaching, appears to have been excluded both from political life, where it was oppressed by the autocratic power of the caliph and by the actual power of the coteries, and from all economic influence: one has the picture of a social existence heavily dependent on the clienteles higher up the pyramid, who were clustered around the fortunes of the administration and the merchant class which supplied the *khassa*, the elite. Convincing proof of this dominance certainly exists in the archaeological evidence and the layout of towns; yet there are signs that a social entity, a collective consciousness, a 'horizontal Islam' rooted in the Hegiran model, managed to subsist and blossom anew. The *khassa* proved too changeable, too often disrupted by confiscations to lay down firm foundations; for its true vitality the establishment continued to depend on knowledge, and the common standard of education meant that there were both more candidates and more opportunities, which had 'destabilising' effects on the conflicting elements already *in situ*. In contrast with this fluidity, the common people, whose philosophy was well-accommodated to such swings of the pendulum, exemplified the virtues of stability and humility; they invested their hopes in the religious debate, in millenarism, and in their attachment to the noble Alids who languished in a semi-obscurity, devoting themselves to the study of the 'religious sciences'.

In this way, the figure of the 'teacher' gained in stature and support among the masses. He was no longer merely looked up to as a party-leader, a scholar learned in philosophy, a zealot ready to raise the standard of revolt in the name of purity; he was increasingly valued as an instructor, whose roots in the community were demonstrated by his daily contact, in the mosque or his own home, with the sons of the people, whose poverty and state of dependency was often no worse than his own. Even if the *amma*, the underclass, was forced to stick together and to gather around those currently in power, and was at once protected and exploited, it nevertheless discovered in the cash economy and the market opportunities for a freer existence and a moral independence, which stand in contrast with the hierarchical tribal structures of Muslim towns in the first generation. Earning only a pittance, and deriving no ideological support or emotional charge from their bond with the powerful, they were thus able to slip away to other masters, and above all to recover their freedom through the adoption, at first vociferous, later more secret, of revolutionary ideals. This did not mean, however, that millenarism was invested with a social purpose, apart from the reversal in the role of master and slave which was expected as the remote consequence of a return to the Hegiran model. It is hard to deny the existence of two models: one realistic, in which power alone created wealth, and only knowledge gave access to power; the other idealistic, in which power was subservient to knowledge, and knowledge the only justification for power. The privilege of establishing and imposing the criteria, of weighing up the results, remained that of the teachers.

A new Byzantium in the making? 7
Mid-seventh to mid-ninth centuries

The Heraklids were to hold the throne in the direct line from 610 to 711, with a few digressions. Their succession calls for two comments. First, succession in the direct line was established as the norm; this was achieved by the institution of co-emperors, associated by the reigning sovereign in his power, but it firmly disposed of the claims of brothers to succeed. Second, the disqualification of defeated candidates was governed from now on by a 'code' of bodily mutilations, which made its appearance in seventh-century judicial practice and even under Justinian, before receiving legislative endorsement from Leo III and his son in 726. 'Code' seems to be the right word, since the type of mutilation was seen as symbolically corresponding to the offence: nasal mutilation was charged with a sexual significance, which explains its application in the law of 726 to adulterers of either sex, and it therefore signified a loss of potency, of which sovereign power was another expression; hence its use, not as absurd as it sounds, to disqualify rival contenders for the throne during the seventh century.

Mutilation

A married man at the time of his accession, made a widower in 612, Herakleios took the step of associating his son Herakleios, 'the new Constantine', with his reign as early as 613. In 614, he entered into a new union with his niece Martina, by whom he had nine children. In making this consanguineous marriage he was probably following a provincial custom, condemned by the Church and by imperial legislation of the fifth and sixth centuries. The transmission of the name from father to son, and not from grandfather to uncle, is equally suggestive of a family foreign to the ruling culture, if not Armenian, as is asserted by a contemporary Armenian chronicler. For whatever reason, the marriage evoked public disapproval; in consequence, following the deaths of Herakleios and of his son and co-emperor in 641, Martina and her son Heraklonas were forcibly ejected from power. The throne then passed to the son of Herakleios the Younger, Constans II, 'the Bearded' (641–68), and thence to his son Constantine IV (668–85), who had been co-emperor from 654, but in association from 659 with his younger brothers, Herakleios and Tiberios. The latter remained associated with him until 681, when he deposed them, subjecting them to nasal

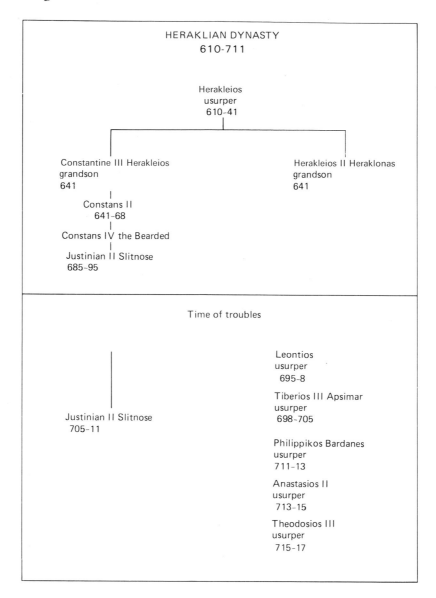

HERAKLIAN DYNASTY
610-711

Herakleios
usurper
610-41

Constantine III Herakleios
grandson
641

Herakleios II Heraklonas
grandson
641

Constans II
641-68

Constans IV the Bearded

Justinian II Slitnose
685-95

Time of troubles

Justinian II Slitnose
705-11

Leontios
usurper
695-8

Tiberios III Apsimar
usurper
698-705

Philippikos Bardanes
usurper
711-13

Anastasios II
usurper
713-15

Theodosios III
usurper
715-17

mutilation. His son Justinian II reigned from 685 to 695. Deposed, and subjected to the same mutilation, whence his nickname of 'Slit-Nose', he nevertheless returned to the throne in 705, with the help of the Bulgar khan, and retained it until 711. In the interval an Isaurian general, Leontios (695–8), marked the re-entry on the scene of that warlike province, with the backing of the Blue faction. The war at sea against the Arabs provoked a revolt in which, with the backing of the Green faction, Leontios was replaced by a naval commander, Apsimar, who ruled under the name Tiberios III (698–705). Mention of the Arabs and the Bulgars is enough to indicate how the pieces on the chessboard have changed since the beginning of the seventh century, to which period we must now return.

This lengthy chain of successions from father to son, the first obvious difference from the sixth century and the first similarity with the eighth, in fact counts for less than the territorial changes which permanently altered Byzantium's historic situation, and the structural changes which, at the same juncture, separated the future from the past. Yet the seventh century, needless to say, is the offspring of the sixth. The latter had already worn the aspect of a series of military aggressions. But, under pressure in the north from waves of Slavs in search of a homeland and of Turkic horsemen in search of booty, and as a result of the Justinianic reconquest in the West and of the rivalry between the Byzantine and Persian empires in the East, we shall find that from now on warfare is everywhere accorded an identical social and cultural value. This value in a sense provides the key to the seventh century, which is characterised by the annual spring campaign, and also unites in a single civilisation Byzantium, its Balkan assailant, which is in the process of taking shape, and its Persian antagonist, shortly to be replaced by Islam.

Persians, Arabs, Slavs: the assault

The history of Byzantium at this time is made on three territorial, ethnic, or – it is not too soon to say – national fronts, often on more than one at the same time: the Orient, stretching from the Caucasus to Egypt; the countries lying on the right bank of the Danube, Macedonia, Thrace, the Greek peninsula and islands; lastly, what remained of the reconquest, very soon reduced to the Italian territories and Sicily.

Persia's energies had revived, as we saw, in the time of Justin II. In 612 the Persians took Cappadocia and Armenia, in 613 Damascus, and in 614 Jerusalem. The repercussions of this event were magnified by the fact that the victors carried off the relic of the true Cross, and by the status of Jerusalem, in the eyes as much of Jews as of Christians at this time, as a city of greater eschatological and symbolic significance than historical importance. Contemporary descriptions of the final conflicts which tore the city apart while it was still in Byzantine hands, and of the opposing reactions of the different confessions to its fall, are to be interpreted from this perspective. In 615, the Persians reached Chalcedon; in 619 they were the masters of Egypt, where, as in Palestine, the ground was already prepared. In the north, in 617, the oncoming Slavs made headway in the west of Illyricum, in Thrace, in the islands and in Asia; and they laid siege to Thessalonica. In 619, they joined forces with the Avars, appearing once more before Thessalonica, and before Constantinople. The symbolic significance of the capital of the empire, the New Rome, was comparable with that of Jerusalem, if not even greater because more immediate. This becomes more obvious on the occasion of a second siege some years later.

Several measures betray the strain the war imposed on Byzantium during these first years of Herakleios. We can point to the striking in 615 of a silver coin, the *miliarision* or hexagram – an innovation indeed for a monetary system which, in opposition to the Persian silver currency, had in the sixth century demonstrated its determination to stick to gold. The coin vanished with the Heraklids. In 615, an increase was decreed in the price of the bread sold at favourable rates to the palace guard, the *scholae*; in 618, the traditional privilege of bread donatives linked with residence in the capital was abolished, 283

Constantinople's corn supply being already threatened by the Persian advance. As a positive contribution, the treasure of the Church of Constantinople was handed over to the emperor by the patriarch, Sergios, and melted down. And in 622, fortified no doubt by this access of precious metals, Byzantium went on the offensive. Herakleios launched his attack on Persia with a series of spring campaigns through Armenia and backed up by the Christian peoples of the Caucasus. In 628, the forces of *romanitas* captured the Persian royal residence of Dastagerd, and looted its fabulous treasure: Theophanes, who compiled his chronicle early in the ninth century, knew of its riches, spices, silks and carpets, as well as silver and gold. In the same year, the Persian king was deposed in a plot involving his son, Shiraw, who succeeded him and sued for peace. The empire recovered Roman Mesopotamia, Syria, Palestine and Egypt, and Herakleios returned to Constantinople in 629 laden with booty. The relic of the Cross was restored to Jerusalem in 630. To all appearances, therefore, the Persian empire had been crushed by its age-old adversary. The empire of the Romans was triumphant, and its sovereign was free to adopt the title *basileus*, long current in Byzantine practice but the property in theory of the Persian king. This marks the end of an evolution extending over several centuries, which to enhance the personal power of the emperor had vested him with cosmic symbols borrowed from the iconography and ceremonial of the Iranian model, and ended by bestowing on him a title taken from the same source.

But only four years after the ending of this conflict, Islam mounted its attack. The Byzantine defeat at the river Yarmuk, in 636, and the capture of Caesarea in Cappadocia in 640 encompassed between them the conquest of Syria. The capture of Dwin, in 642, made a bridgehead for the Arabs into Armenia. Jerusalem fell in 638, though Palestine held out longer. Lastly, the conquest of Egypt, begun in 638, was achieved with the capture of Alexandria, symbol of Hellenism and the empire, in 642. From now on, until the tenth century, the caliphate filled the ancient role of Persia as Byzantium's military foe, political and cultural counterpart, and geographical neighbour, the latter over an unprecedentedly wide area, since from the time of Constans II the caliphate's land conquests were to be augmented by victories at sea. It would be a mistake, however, to think of relations between the two powers over this period in terms of a hard and fast boundary: on the contrary, the history of their relationship can scarcely be understood without taking into account the fringe area, running from the Taurus through Mesopotamia to Armenia, which, defined by its linguistic and confessional particularities, was to be both the arbiter and the object of future conflicts.

On the Balkan front, Slavs and Avars at first continued their advance. The *Miracles of St Demetrios*, patron saint of Thessalonica, identify a siege of that town, to be dated between 610 and 626, as the first occasion on which the 'Sklavenes', as the Byzantines still called them, took to the sea, in a distinctive type of craft made from hollowed-out tree-trunks (*monoxyla*). In 626 Avars and Sklavenes jointly besieged the capital but failed to take it. The important religious repercussions of this event at Byzantium will be seen later. The point to be noted here is that it marks the decline of Avar power in that part of Illyricum, but does not stop the peaceful penetration of the Slavs, who it is generally agreed probably travelled in tribal groups at this time. They seem to have settled chiefly in the country around Thessalonica.

In the West, lastly, the extreme fragility of Justinian's reconquest was becoming clear: between 616 and 631, almost all the territory recovered in Spain had to be abandoned. Still more clearly apparent, however, is the problem that was to beset Italy in the seventh and eighth centuries, that of a religious and historic centre relegated to the periphery by the foundation of Constantinople. Latent until the end of Justinian's reign, the problem had been overt since the Lombard invasion and the pontificate of Gregory the Great. The exarchate of Ravenna could not provide Byzantium with a solution, which increasingly lay in Rome, in the hands of the pope. In 616, a certain John of Conza seized power after raising a rebellion in the Campagna, while at Ravenna the exarch (another John) and other officials were massacred, perhaps because of a delay in the payment of wages to the troops, who from this time were recruited on the spot. Eleutherios, charged by Herakleios to restore order, proclaimed himself emperor in his turn and was sent by the archbishop of Ravenna to be crowned by the pope. He was murdered on the way, but the episode boded ill for the future.

A list of military events gives us only a partial account of Herakleios's reign. There can be no war without ideology. The war which Herakleios conducted in person was perceived as a holy war. This was the consequence of the contemporary identification, current since Constantine, of *romanitas* with Christianity. Constantine was the reference-point: the return of the Cross to Jerusalem linked him with Herakleios, whose son and successor, furthermore, was dubbed 'the new Constantine'. The holy war ideal is expressed in the work of the court poet, George of Pisidia, and the speech put into the mouth of Herakleios by Theophanes, writing early in the ninth century, shows that this was the role permanently assigned to him in Byzantine's historic consciousness. The role of the patriarch is seen to be evolving in the same direction, when the Church can sacrifice its treasure, and when the patriarch Sergios can share in the delegation of imperial authority over the capital during the sovereign's absence on campaign, above all during the fateful episode of 626. In that year Constantinople was besieged by the Persians and the Avars acting in concert. The emperor was far away. Sergios gave orders for the pictures of Christ and his mother, which for decades past had been the object of mounting devotion, to be paraded on the ramparts. At this precise moment, say contemporaries, a female silhouette was seen moving on the selfsame walls, firing darts at the assailants. On that day Constantinople entered into a permanent bond with its protectress, whose robe, removed from the Blachernae church on account of the Avar threat and kept until 619/20 at St Sophia, had already become a cult object. During the siege of 626 the hymn in the Virgin's honour, the *akathistos*, '(to be heard) without sitting down', was chanted in the definitive version which still forms part of the Orthodox liturgy. There could be no better illustration of the future course of Byzantine Christianity than this entire episode, remembered for ever more as one of its reference-points. And then there is the fact that Justinian II placed on his coins the image of Christ, instead of the Cross by itself, which had been substituted, but only under Tiberios III, for the ancient effigy of Victory. The sequence is significant.

The unity of *romanitas* thus manifests itself as the unity of a religious belief. Herakleios, who banned Jews from Jerusalem after its recapture, issued a decree making their conversion obligatory in the empire, a step which none of his predecessors had dared to take: the argument of Antiquity, which had protected Judaism after a fashion, was thus shown to be obsolete, superseded by a new system of values. On another front, the victories of the Persians and then of the Arabs in the East are part of the same trend as the provincial divisions already opening up in the fifth and sixth centuries. Herakleios clearly recognised the danger. Quite early on, in 616, the patriarch Sergios produced a conciliatory formula, aimed at the monophysites, based on the idea that Christ's two natures were united by a 'single energy'. After making some headway with the Armenian and Antiochene clergy, and having secured the goodwill of Pope Honorius, the central power was baulked by the Chalcedonian intransigence of Jerusalem's new patriarch, Sophronios (634), and the intransigence of the more extreme monophysites of Alexandria, persecuted on that account by their own patriarch, Kyros. A new document, the *Ekthesis*, on the subject of Christ's 'single will' (monotheletism), published in 638 and approved by a council held in the capital, was accepted at Alexandria and conversely rejected by Pope Severinus, to be synodically condemned under his successor, John IV. The doctrinal alignment of the emperor and his patriarchal colleague in opposition to the pope was once again a portent of the future, while the monophysite East entered into the condition of recognised religious minority under an Islamic power, in which it would remain for centuries. Even so, the flickerings of orthodox Hellenism were not so easily extinguished. In Palestine, and without counting Jerusalem, many Greek monasteries went on gently declining until the ninth century, while others, such as St Sabas in the Judaean desert, survive to this day, as does St Catherine on Mount Sinai. It is appropriate to mention that in the seventh century the Sinai peninsula, depicted in a half-real, half-imaginary light, figures in the tales of the Greek monk, Anastasios, which he fills with demons and wandering 'Saracens', and that the same author composed a 'Guide' (*Hodegos*) to the Chalcedonian arguments against the monophysites.

Resignation and adjustment in the East

Under Herakleios's successors the new world continued to take shape. Islam followed up its victories, again helped by the existing breaches between Byzantium's central government and the outlying territories. From Egypt, the Arabs advanced through Cyrenaica and Tripolitania, and in 647 reached Byzantine Africa, while in 642 the disaffection of an Armenian leader opened the way for a complete conquest of the country in 654. But although a Muslim administration was set up at Dwin, Arab domination was confined in practice to fiscal and military demands, which in keeping with a treaty concluded in 653 left the warlike, aristocratic and Christian character of Armenian society intact. Above all, the sea became from now on a theatre of Muslim warfare, thanks to the ports, ship-building timber and men of the coastal regions, Syria in particular, captured from the Byzantines: the first Arab squadron was fitted out at Tripoli in Syria, in 645. The loss of Rhodes followed in 654, while Cyprus hung in the balance. In 659 the internal problems of the caliphate led to the conclusion of a peace treaty, and even to the imposition on the Arabs of a tribute in gold *solidi*. When hostilities resumed, they broke out in Africa but most of all at sea. In the reign of Constantine IV, the Arab fleet, which was now familiar with navigating the Aegean, launched an attack against Constantinople. In 673 it penetrated the Hellespont, and from its anchorage off Cyzicus it mounted an annual blockade of the capital during the navigation season (April to September), desisting only in 677, when reverses elsewhere obliged the caliphate to come to terms. The Byzantine resistance had owed part of its success to the deployment against the Arab ships of the weapon the Crusaders would later call 'Greek fire': an inflammable mixture of naphtha, sulphur and pitch, blown through tubes and combustible even on water.

The maritime conflict which followed the emergence of the Arabs as a sea power had been one of the incentives for the radical reorganisation of the fiscal and administrative system which sustained the Byzantine war machine, of which more will be said shortly. When the peace treaty came up for renewal in 688, Justinian II agreed to the removal from the frontier of the Mardaites, a bellicose mountain people of the Amanus massif who formed a buffer between Byzantium and Arab-conquered territory, protecting the former by making raids on the latter. In so doing he left Asia Minor more exposed, while the Mardaites, transplanted to Pamphylia, and later migrating in swarms to Greece, provided recruits for the empire's maritime forces.

In the Balkans, the Slav settlements in Moesia (on the right bank of the Danube) and most of all in Macedonia were sufficiently substantial to be recognisable from now on as genuine enclaves, the *sklaviniai* of the Byzantine texts. There has been much impassioned debate in Greece, going back to the nineteenth century and the reawakening of national consciousness, over the extent of the Slavicisation. The pro-Greek hypothesis admits dense Slavicisation around Thessalonica, which is however regarded as forming an effective barrier to further progress, and an advance into the western Peloponnese, but denies that there was any lasting penetration of central Greece and the eastern Peloponnese, or into any part of Thrace. The latter was in any case at the receiving end of the acts of population resettlement which were a familiar practice of the Byzantine government, as we saw in connection with the late sixth century. It is important to distinguish between the population of an area and its culture, and the real issue is the progress of Slav acculturation. The archaeological and place-name evidence, which is obviously crucial, does not at present permit the establishment of a very exact chronology. The texts are naturally concerned with the undisguised acts of aggression: raids as far as Epirus and into the Taygetus range, piracy, descents on islands of the archipelago, and above all the series of attacks on Thessalonica, close at hand and a tempting prize. In 658, to free the latter, Constans II conducted a regular war of subjugation against the Slavic enclaves – it is at this point in his narrative that Theophanes first uses the expression *sklaviniai*. Another campaign, against the Slavs of Macedonia, was undertaken in 689 by Justinian II, who recruited from them a unit to defend the passage across the Strymon, while part of the population was deported to Asia Minor as a reinforcement against the Arabs. And on top of this, the closing decades of

287

A fortified monastery in the Sinai desert: St Catherine's, founded by Justinian in 527, is more than 1,500m above sea-level and could only be reached by pulley. The numerous buildings on the site now include a mosque.

The griffins featured on these plaques from a tenth-century diadem form part of the traditional imagery of Bulgar art (Preslav, Archaeological Museum).

the seventh century witness the opening of a new phase in the history of the Slavs on Balkan territory.

For to these decades belongs the birth of the first Bulgar state, or more exactly of the first chieftaincy to be recognised by Byzantium as a partner in dialogue on the Balkano-Danubian front, an event of decisive importance. From the same Turkic stock as the Huns and Avars, related possibly to the Utrigur and Kutrigur Huns of the early sixth century, the Bulgars, or rather one of their branches, had been pressing against the left bank of the Danube, the threshold of the empire, since the time of Herakleios. Like other ethnic groups of the same origin, they made their appearance as an elite of mounted warriors, whose culture bore the marks of Siberian and Iranian influence, led by a khan whose power was hereditary. In 626 they took part in the siege of Constantinople. Around 635, the Bulgar Kovrat rebelled against the overlordship of the Avars, and was rewarded by Herakleios with gifts and the title of *patrikios*: the day of the Avars in the Balkans was passing, that of the Bulgars just beginning. In 679, the khan Asparuch crossed the Danube, under pressure from another Turkic people, the Khazars, of whom we shall speak later. When he installed his tribe between the river and the Balkan range, he found himself in a predominantly Slavic region, where the Bulgars were to become a ruling minority. Next, in 681, he concluded with Constantine IV a treaty which recognised his authority over this officially imperial territory, the former province of Moesia, backed up by payment of a tribute. Bulgaria, as the Byzantine authors now start to term it, was poised to play its historic part in this region of the medieval world wedged between Byzantium and the barbarian lands on the far side of the great river, whose lower reaches it commanded. At Pliska, which became the capital, excavations have revealed a civilisation still characteristic of the Uralo-Altaic world and showing traces, like others, of Iranian influences: a mysterious script, yet to be deciphered; solar symbols, amulets with animal motifs; horsemen armed with bows, and the depiction of a shaman, the traditional witch-doctor of the Siberian steppe, complete with his little bells. The khan held his power from a sky-god, and resided surrounded by his

289

dignitaries in a palace. Bulgarian intervention in imperial affairs began as early as 705 when khan Tervel, Asparuch's son, assisted Justinian II, a refugee on Bulgarian territory, to regain his throne. He received in reward the title of Caesar. As much the result of cohabitation with the Slavs as of contacts with Byzantium, the acculturation process was already under way in the eighth century, with results that became visible in the ninth. Lastly, following hard on the heels of the Bulgars, came another Turkic people, the Khazars, who reached the Black Sea around 679, and gained a foothold in the Crimea. From now on they occupied the middle course of the Volga. Justinian II, when first driven from the throne, took refuge with the Khazars and married the sister of their khan. Their hour was to come in the eighth century.

Alienation and incomprehension in the West

The problem of the West defines itself ever more sharply as an Italian and papal problem. We saw how the Arab conquest, like its Persian precursor, served to detach from Constantinople regions of the empire whose culture was already tending to make them disaffected. The same pattern was repeated in the West, in that part of Italy which to the end represented Byzantium's stake in the West. And it continued to repeat itself until the rupture of 1054. Secessions on the part of exarchs – that of Gregory in Africa in 646, those of Maurice and Olympios in Italy in 642 and 650 – show us the military and political side of this centrifugal movement, made all the more unstoppable because of the guarantee offered by the presence of papal power, which since Gregory the Great and the end of the sixth century had become considerable. The papacy, which had rejected the *Ekthesis* of Herakleios, was just as unwilling in 648 to accept the *Typos* of Constans II, which forbade further discussion of the Herakleian proposition. Pope Martin I condemned the *Typos* at the Lateran synod of 649, and in so doing relied on the exarch Olympios, who proclaimed himself emperor. But when Olympios was killed fighting the Arabs in Sicily in 652, the pope was arrested in the Lateran church, taken to Constantinople, put on trial and banished to Cherson. Martin received the support of the Church in Africa, and although this Church followed the Latin tradition, the spokesman for its orthodoxy was a Greek, Maximos, 'the Confessor', born about 580 to an aristocratic family in Constantinople, who after holding high office in the civil administration had become a monk. Driven by the perils of the times from his monastery at Cyzicus, he went to Egypt and then to Africa, to throw himself into the battle against monophysitism, and then against the monothelite compromise. As the moving spirit of the Roman council of 649, Maximos shared the fate of the pope: arrested, condemned, and sentenced to the amputation of his tongue and right hand, he died in exile in Lazica in 662. Subsequently revered as one of the great authorities of the Greek Church, in his own times Maximos prefigured the stand the Byzantine monastic Church would make all through the ninth century against the political integration of the patriarchal Church, and in favour, as a necessary consequence, of obedience to Rome. Italy again became the focal point of imperial policy when Constans II left Constantinople and based himself at Syracuse, from 663 until his assassination in 668, after crossing the south of the peninsula, now under Lombard domination, and being received at Rome by the pope. This migration, which was inspired by difficulties in the capital as well as by the threat from the Arabs of Africa to Byzantium's Italian possessions, gave the emperor opportunity to bring Ravenna into play: the archbishop of Ravenna obtained from Constans recognition of his see's independence (autocephaly). The rupture between Rome and Ravenna was brought to an end, officially at least, in 680, the year in which Constantine IV convened in the capital the sixth ecumenical council, which abrogated the monothelite propositions, and in which the legates of pope Agatho participated.

But the course of history was set towards separation. In 692, Justinian II convened the council 'in the domed hall of the palace' (*en troullō*), of fundamental importance in the history of Byzantium and its progeny. Following the doctrinal councils of 553 and 680–1, its purpose was to perfect the disciplinary code of the Church; the decrees it produced then became the basis of Christian order at Byzantium, just as they represented the summation of earlier canonical development. The council found its inspiration in the seemingly beleaguered situation of the New Rome, beset by Islam and by the still pagan Slavs and Bulgars, defied within its own borders or on the margins by the Jews, the Armenians and the collective adherence to the old rituals and festivals, but equally by the unchecked exuberance of the Christian imagination. Marriage was subjected to regulations never since altered: a system of prohibitions was laid down on the grounds of affinity through blood relationship, marriage or the spiritual kinship arising through godparentage, which went far beyond the scheme sketched out by Justinian; authorisation to maintain an existing conjugal relationship was granted to men who become priests, but not to those acceding to the episcopate – a reason, no doubt, if not the only one, for the essentially monastic character of subsequent recruitment to the Byzantine episcopate. Some of the prohibitions affecting the clerical order, the priesthood in particular, were not new, such as lending money at interest, keeping a tavern, or frequenting theatrical performances and the hippodrome, which was tainted in this instance with paganism; the criminality of simony and the sale of the Eucharist was made plain. Other canons testify to the attraction still exerted by the Jewish model of priesthood, especially among the Armenians, who made the priesthood a hereditary office and honoured it by the appropriate offerings of cooked meat. The council was at great pains to separate priests from laymen, and at the same time to ensure that laymen observed the liturgical seasons and attended Sunday worship. Although it upheld the Old Testament prohibition on the drinking of blood, it proscribed, in conformity with a long-standing tradition, all contact with Jews: Christians were not to take part in their passover, frequent their baths, live with them or consult them in illness. But most of all its decrees shed light on a twofold anxiety, acutely felt and only at first sight contradictory. On the one hand the council condemned adherence to the old rites and festivals: celebrations of the new year, carnival masquerades, the cult of Dionysos, oaths sworn in the 'Greek' – that is, pagan – fashion. On the other, it turned its face against free – and therefore to say the least suspect – forms of Christian observance. When the council forbade laymen to preach and teach, and the administration of baptism in a private chapel, and forbade monks to roam, it was following a well-worn path. But the need to stipulate

291

that a layman could not administer communion to himself, or that a hermit should submit himself to a monastic novitiate, reveals a process of Christianisation which was becoming more and more difficult to subject to the normative power of the Church, precisely because of its much deeper penetration. It is moreover a fact, as has just been indicated, that as Christianisation went deeper it absorbed elements of the Antique calendar, to be so thoroughly digested by the collective consciousness that the essential core would be retained down the centuries, even to the Greek and Balkan observances of our own day. Customs such as giving communion to corpses and serving dishes made of semolina on the day after Christmas, as nourishment fit for the new mother, tell the same story. As for the miracle-workers, sybils, bear-leaders and holy fools, real or fake, who figure in the condemnations of 692, they too were to crop up at Byzantium in later centuries, as is shown by the commentaries of the great twelfth-century canonists, Theodore Balsamon's in particular.

In all these dispositions, the council paid no regard to the dispute with the pope, or rather it made its decisions independent of him. Claiming to be the continuation of the sixth ecumenical council of 680–1, it in fact addressed specifically eastern questions, and furthermore placed Constantinople on the same level as Rome. For its part, Rome rejected the practice of clerical marriage, and gave endorsement only in 721 to the inclusion of spiritual affinity (through baptism) among the impediments to marriage. All the same, there was no repetition of the scenes enacted in 649: the attempt to arrest pope Sergius failed, the Roman militias and the troops of the exarchate having closed their ranks in his defence. Indeed, during Justinian II's second reign the pope, Constantine I, paid an official visit to Constantinople and an accommodation was reached. Nevertheless, and despite the strength of Roman propensities towards Hellenism in the seventh and eighth centuries, this pacification was only temporary, and the individual physiognomy of the two Churches became increasingly distinct.

'The Empire of the East' takes shape

Justinian II was the last of the Heraklids; his son Tiberios, when still a child, had his throat slit when Justinian was deposed for the second time in 711. Competition for the succession occupied the next few years, in which victory passed in turn to Philippikos Bardanes, an Armenian (December 711 to June 713), Artemios, crowned as Anastasios II (June 713 to August 715), Theodosios III (715–17) and finally to Leo III, proclaimed on 18 April 716 and crowned on 25 March 717. Each of these men relied for support on differing forces, recruited from the large military and administrative circumscriptions, known as 'themes', which made their appearance in the closing decades of the seventh century, as will shortly be explained. Leo commanded the Anatolikon theme, and received help from Artavasdos, commander of the Armeniakon theme and – to judge by his name – of Armenian descent; he was rewarded after victory with the hand of the new emperor's daughter. The accession of Leo to power thus brought to the forefront the key sector of the eastern front, his own place of origin since he was born in Germanikeia. His descendants in the male line kept the throne until 797. His son Constantine V succeeded him in 741, having been associated in the empire since 720, when he was only two years old. In 741–2 he frustrated an attempted usurpation by Artavasdos, who was supported by the themes of Opsikion and Armeniakon, while he himself could reckon on the loyalty of the themes of Anatolikon and Thrakesion. Constantine then reigned until 775. Married in 733 to the daughter of the Khazar khan, who took the baptismal name Irene, he had three sons by her, among them his successor, Leo IV; he had several more from a third marriage. Leo IV, associated with his father from 750, reigned from 775 to 780. He married an Athenian, another Irene, and their son Constantine VI succeeded him. The friction between the latter and his mother and the course she adopted are matters too closely bound up with the whole internal history of the period to be dealt with in summary fashion. Here it will suffice to say that with the blinding of Constantine VI by his mother in 797 the Isaurian dynasty properly speaking came to an end, although Irene herself continued in power until 802.

Unending war

The warfare waged by Byzantium in the eighth century was conducted by the emperors in person, particularly Constantine V. It was carried on against the Bulgars on the lower Danube and the Thracian front, against the Arabs at sea, and on land in a sector which was to be the focal point of all such confrontations down to the eleventh century. Blocked off at one end by Melitene and its environs, this sector is buttressed in the south-west by the massif of the Taurus and in the north-west by the first foothills of Armenia. In short, this is the old monophysite territory, and further to the south, beyond Edessa, the old Nestorian country, which as we saw earlier once formed a march between Byzantium and Sassanid Persia. Armenia itself, dominated by dynasties who controlled the land, the military and the priesthood, had been a prize disputed by Byzantium and the Arabs since the middle of the seventh century, and was very conscious of its strategic value. The Khazars, lastly, whom we saw following on the heels of the Bulgars in the preceding century, had now set up a state based on the Volga and the Caspian, bounded on either side by the Don and the Kuban, which helped to limit Islamic expansion beyond the Caucasus. In addition they straddled important trade-routes, which were presumably the channels through which Jewish influence percolated to the khan and his entourage in about 740, leading to their eventual conversion. Their material support of Philippikos Bardanes, and then the marriage of Constantine V, shows them to have been a force to be reckoned with in that part of the world.

The Arabs had their sights trained on the capital of the empire. The attack by land and sea, which blockaded Constantinople in 717–18, was repelled with the help of the Bulgars; it was to be the last. For although the Arab offensive was resumed in 726 with a series of annual assaults, the impetus was broken by the Byzantines' victory on land at Akroinon (near Afyon Karahissar) in 739, and at sea the Egyptian fleet was put out of action for a long while in a battle off the newly-recaptured Cyprus in 747. In 746, Constantine V invaded Syria and recovered Germanikeia. The events of the following decade are significant.

Armenia revolted in 751 against the Arabs: the emperor recaptured and destroyed Theodosioupolis and Melitene, and in 755 resettled the population in Thrace, with the evident design of reducing pressure in the sensitive area of Asia Minor and reinforcing the Balkan frontier; as a result, the emperor refused the tribute due to the Bulgars in virtue of an earlier agreement, thereby rekindling the war. In 755, the Bulgars reached the outskirts of the capital, but Byzantium regained the initiative and the displaced population contributed to the defences. In 758, a Slav uprising in Thrace and Macedonia was put down, and it was the turn of the Slavs to be deported, in their case to Asia Minor. The struggle was also waged on the Black Sea. In 733, the Byzantine fleet sailed up the Danube, and the khan Telerig capitulated. The reader should not be misled by this highlighting of a few selected dates: we are dealing here not with a Byzantine offensive or defensive struggle aimed at the restoration of peace, but rather with the underlying trend of contemporary societies, for whom warfare, whatever its explicit motives, was an activity taken for granted. To be sure, it was not the only form of international relations, even leaving aside the Italian and papal problem, a supposedly internal affair. Treaties, the Khazar marriage of Constantine V, the Byzantine marriage of khan Telerig (baptised at Constantinople in 777), the summoning of craftsmen from Constantinople to work on the Umayyad mosque at Damascus – all these go to show the alternating and ambiguous character of such relationships; but above all they define the place of war among other customs in effecting the gradual and permanent relocation of the peoples and States which form the subject of this history. And that warfare acted as an agent of internal social change seems clear: the transformations already in train are there to prove it.

New institutions for a new empire

The impending divorce between two epochs of Byzantine history which was already foreshadowed in the closing decades of the sixth century was made absolute in the course of the seventh and eighth centuries by a whole set of social and cultural transformations. Taking place against the backcloth of Slavo-Bulgar and Arab movements, and of the changes in the economy, these transformations prove to be as fundamental as they are badly documented, until their effects can be seen in a different order of society, in the early years of the ninth century. In consequence, the origin, purpose and sometimes the timing of these transformations have been keenly debated.

Let us start with the administrative organisation. The concentration of all civil and military powers in the hands of a single administrator was a practice not unknown in the sixth century, when Justinian had adopted it for the unruly mountain provinces of Asia Minor, and it formed the essential basis of the Italian and African exarchates. From obscure beginnings in the time of Herakleios, there gradually developed the system of 'themes' (from the Greek *themata*), each with an all-powerful *strategos* at the head. The military system in force from the time of Diocletian had provided for a mobile army commanded by the central power (the *comitatus*), complemented by sedentary provincial and frontier troops. The central army can still be seen to exist in the form of regular regiments (*tagmata*).

294

And the word *thema* is the term used from now on to designate both the provincial army and the area of its responsibility. Starting out with a military meaning, the word thus came to be applied, in a fashion understandable at a time when the whole of Byzantine society was geared up for war, to an administrative unit. The partition was flexible, dictated by circumstances and subject to modification, particularly to subdivision. The oldest and largest of the themes date back to the late seventh century: Asia Minor, heartland of the empire, was divided into the theme of the Armeniakon in the north-east, apparently created between 669 and 692, and the theme of the Anatolikon (the eastern theme), of much the same date, and matching it in the south-west; the Opsikion theme, extending over the north, faced Constantinople; the theme of Thrace was carved out of it between 680 and 685, following the Bulgar invasion. In 732 there is mention for the first time of a *strategos* of the maritime theme of the Cibyrrhaeots, of which Attalia (Antalya) became the principal town.

The organisation of the naval forces followed the same pattern. At first, in the last quarter of the seventh century, the fleet of *Karabisianoi* (modern Greek *karabi* = ship) pitted by Byzantium against the Arab fleet simply formed part of a general naval command. But its ineffectiveness during the siege of Constantinople in 717, combined with the fact that it had sided with Artemios-Anastasios in the struggle for the throne, was cause enough for the victor, Leo III, to suppress it. From then on Byzantium's maritime forces were comprised partly of an imperial fleet, which from its bases at Abydos and Hieron guarded Constantinople and the Straits, but was also available for offensive expeditions, and partly of provincial fleets, in the role of coastal patrols, which were reinforced by the creation of coastal themes: the Cibyrrhaeot (from the 730's), the themes of the Aegean (from the 840's) and the Dodecanese ('the twelve islands'; from the mid-tenth century), and those of Chios and Samos in the late ninth century. The theme system is seen at its most effective in the ninth century and in the first half of the tenth. The huge circumscriptions of the early days became progressively smaller through division and subdivision. And in the middle of the tenth century, the strategic importance of the eastern frontier favoured the adoption of a new scheme: in contrast to the major or 'Romaic' themes of the interior, frontier or 'Armeniac' themes made their appearance, no bigger than a fortress and its surrounding territory. The various jurisdictions continued to be combined in the hands of the *strategos*, until the moment when the institution started to decline. By the late tenth century there was already a tendency for him to be subordinated in military matters to the duke, who commanded the *tagmata* over an entire sector of the frontier, and for the judicial authority of a praetorian magistrate to become distinct from that of the *strategos*. In the eleventh century the system became obsolete. It posed, as is clear from the start, a problem of financial resources and recruitment; and this was none other than the problem posed all through this period by the relationship between society and war.

Under the fiscal system introduced by Diocletian and still in force, the furnishing of men and their equipment to the army represented fiscal burdens, which fell essentially on the rural areas, while taxes commuted to money made it possible to hire mercenaries: to them should be added the barbarian *federate* troops, who were parties to agreements which

St Sophia, Constantinople. General view of the central dome, piers and buttresses, sixth century.

Syria: west facade and single apse of the church of Qalb Lozé, sixth century.

Cave church in Cappadocia (probably ninth or tenth century).

plots allocated to the *limitanei*, troops stationed on the frontiers. But the 'military' properties attested from the ninth century onwards were dispersed throughout the empire, more precisely through all of its themes.

The more specialised nature of maritime recruitment entailed the conscription of coastal populations, at this time chiefly the Mardaites from Mt Amanus, transplated to Pamphylia by Justinian II. The fighting unit was the *dromon*, an oar-powered vessel tapered fore and aft, which was capable of carrying between 100 and 200 men and which from now on would be equipped with 'Greek fire'. There is no explicit reference to the funding of the fleets of the coastal themes, but the same principle of especially exempted properties presumably applied. Later on the usual tendency to recruit mercenaries asserted itself, which is how Russian sailors came to be employed.

Birth of a new social order: fighting-men, countrymen

The recruitment of combatants for the land armies is obviously the most important problem for the social historian. *Lives* of ninth-century saints, tactical treatises of the ninth and tenth centuries, and the whole trend of legislation from the ninth to the eleventh centuries, all reveal the soldiers as a social category diversified by the unequal size of their properties, but in every case as cavalrymen, with a military – and hence social – standing not far removed from that of their contemporaries in the Carolingian capitularies. The evolution of the warrior class in this period of Byzantine history poses an essential and difficult question. The system of miitary properties proved inadequate for the recruitment and financing of the armed forces, and in the tenth and eleventh centuries the traditional option of commuting military service to a cash payment became increasingly popular, which led to an ever greater dependence on foreign mercenaries. Furthermore, the 'military households' appear from the outset to have been distributed throughout the social scale and not, as was once thought, concentrated on the peasantry with its reinforcement of Slavs; it will be seen later what further diversification ensued. The ethnic dimension, finally, is not to be discounted, in so far as there was a gravitation from the borders to the centre on the part of those seeking their fortune in the empire, which usually meant fortune in war. Hence the stress that has been laid on the role of Armenian immigration. The mass of the population was affected only when emperors followed a campaign with deportations of the kind effected by Constantine V in the middle of the eighth century. But there was a long tradition of individuals coming to volunteer their services, and this became more marked in the eighth century, reflecting inter-dynastic struggles inside the empire. A typical case is that of Smbat Bagratuni: first he received sovereignty from the Arabs to whom he surrendered the country, to the detriment of rival dynasties, the pro-Byzantine Mamikonians and Kamsarakans; then, grown too powerful for the Arabs to tolerate, he changed over to Byzantium around 700, but only for a few years, because of his dissenting religious position. In the wake of Philippikos Bardanes and of Artavasdos, Leo III's son-in-law, the historical record reveals a growing number of personages with Armenian names: the trend will become still more obvious after the middle of the ninth century, but it is already noticeable. It presumably reinforced, through the advent of newcomers of the same type, the by now pronouncedly military character of Byzantine society, or rather of its politically dominant class. For example, there is Bardas, *strategos* of the Armeniakon theme, who after the death of Leo IV took part in a plot to bring the late emperor's brother Nikephoros to power; or Alexis Moselè, *dronggarios* or commander of the watch (the corps responsible for the security of the emperor and the palace), sent by Irene to suppress a revolt in the Armeniakon theme, of which he became the *strategos*. These two examples, and there are others, suggest a correspondence between the role of the Armenians in the imperial entourage and that of the eastern march in Byzantine strategy. Lastly, as will appear later, historiography gives us grounds for thinking that the preoccupation with lineage which characterises the ruling class in the ninth century first made itself felt in the time of Constantine V. The aristocratic orientation of the Armenians may have been a factor in this evolution.

This embattled society was becoming less and less urban. The empire's losses in the south had already deprived it of regions traditionally rich in urban life, Syria and Palestine, and the great cities of Alexandria and Antioch. The towns which remained, in Asia Minor and Thrace, suffered considerably under the blows inflicted in the seventh century, invasions by the Persians, and to a lesser degree the Arabs, in the case of Asia Minor, or by the Slavs and Bulgars, in the case of Thrace. These effects are clear from archaeological investigations, which testify to alterations in the urban environment and its organisation, and to the decrease in monetary circulation on the site: the decline in activity went together with a decline in the urban population, which thus accounts for the discovery in the eighth-century layer at Corinth of graves on the acropolis, that is to say in the heart of the inhabited area. The reorganisation of the empire into themes modified the administrative functions of towns, while bringing benefits to some, for example Attalia. The great days of the urban episcopate were past, while monastic establishments, hitherto an attraction, were dispersed by Constantine V's persecution to the mountains of Bithynia, among other places. There was no respite from aggression, whether in the running battle with the Arabs which impeded the commercial activity of coastal towns such as Athens, or in the Bulgar attacks which repeatedly threatened Corinth. Nor, finally, should the effects of the plague which ravaged the empire in 746–7 be overlooked. And yet, as is plain from the *Lives* of certain saints, the older cities were not dead but had entered into an eclipse, which lasted until the ninth-century revival. The capital went the same way, so far as we can judge. In this instance no systematic archaeological investigation has been possible, but the texts state that the population in the eighth century was too small to maintain the city walls, and that certain cisterns fell into disuse, indicating that the demand for water had shrunk. It did not escape the plague, following which Constantine V brought in population replacements from the islands, the Peloponnese, and the theme of Hellas (eastern and central Greece). And it suffered its share of Arab attacks, the prolonged naval blockade of 673–7 and the combined land and sea siege of 717–18. In addition, Arab activity in the Mediterranean cut it off from its traditional overseas markets. But the severance was probably not as complete as was once believed. If Constantinople ceased to be supplied with corn from Egypt, it continued to import Egyptian papyrus. Most important of all, it was still the capital, and as such had unrivalled chances of survival. Thessalonica, for its part, retained the importance conferred on it by the ethnic movements on the right bank of the Danube and continued to act as the commercial and cultural threshold of the empire, the role in which it starred in the ninth century.

Nevertheless, the substance and continuity of the empire lay for the time being in the rural areas, a point stressed by the system of military properties. The net result of the population movements in the seventh and eighth centuries was probably in their favour, especially in those regions where the influx of Slavs and Bulgars coalesced with the emperors' strategic concerns. The latter made use of the new arrivals to protect the frontier against succeeding waves, and, as a further precaution, from the end of the sixth century adopted the policy of transferring populations between Thrace and Asia Minor. In the eighth century, the Slavs of the Aegean region, granted the status of 'allies', constituted autonomous and culturally distinct communities, whose religious and linguistic contours would become blurred only in the ninth century. Other groups of Slavs installed themselves, around the middle of the eighth century, in the Peloponnese. As a result of his campaigns, Constantine V transferred Slavs to Asia Minor, and moved to Thrace a number of Armenians and Syrians from the region of Germanikeia, Melitene and Erzerum, which at the same time weakened a pocket of religious dissidence. All this is suggestive of a sizeable demographic insertion, but not of wholesale transformation by the Slavs, affecting even the social structures, as many historians have postulated. There is in fact an almost total dearth of documentary evidence to shed light on this domain in the unsettled period between the late seventh and the ninth centuries, with the result that scholars have combed with more than usual thoroughness a solitary text, known as the *Rural Code*, which has survived in numerous manuscripts with a legal content but whose precise date and region of origin cannot now be ascertained. In essence a compilation of customary law, it deals with agrarian contracts of various types, law-suits, crimes such as the theft of farm implements, emphasising their particular gravity during the period of seasonal works, and with matters of common concern such as tree-lopping, harvesting and wood-cutting. The setting appears to be a village community in which private property, joint possession and communal ownership exist side by side. It is clear furthermore that the community is charged with a collective fiscal responsibility, especially in the case of deserted holdings. And it is on this last point that much of the scholarly debate has turned. The fact that several articles in the code make reference to 'sharing out the village land' has been taken by the Russian school as proof that the Slav type of commune, based on the periodic redistribution of holdings, had penetrated to the Byzantine countryside. Leaving aside the question of whether such a commune even existed at that period or in those regions, others have pointed out that sufficient explanation for these articles is to be found in the workings of the Byzantine tax system, which required deserted holdings to be reallocated by the fisc, or by the community in virtue of its collective responsibility. And when the written sources of the

Foot-soldier and cavalryman. Although Hellenising in tendency, these ivories reproduce in relatively realistic fashion the items of military equipment in standard use over several centuries. (Foot-soldier: detail from the triptych of the Forty Martyrs, eleventh century, Leningrad, Hermitage Museum; cavalryman: eleventh century, Troyes, Cathedral Treasury).

ninth to eleventh centuries come to our aid, enabling us to form a fairly precise picture of Byzantine rural organisation, the uninterrupted history of the fiscal institution is confirmed.

Images

The eighth century is famous above all for the the prohibition of the cult of images, which marks a crucial stage of development in Byzantium's history, although the record was irremediably damaged when the cult triumphed again in the ninth century. The conciliar decrees and polemical texts survive only in the fragments which scholars have painstakingly reconstructed from passages quoted at the Council of Nicaea, which temporarily restored the cult in 787, and in the polemical outpourings of supporters of the images during the second 'Iconoclasm' (813–43). For the same reason, almost no trace of church decoration survives in the monuments. This silence even extends to historiography, perhaps because the century is over-full of events, and our principal source is the chronicle of the monk Theophanes, son of a confidant of Constantine V, and himself a fervent supporter of images, which was written in the time of Leo V (813–20). Furthermore, between the initial iconoclastic action (iconoclast = 'destroyer of images') of the basileus in 726 and the permanent restoration in 843, the movement and the debate passed through several phases. Therefore the first essential is to be clear about the order of events, since this is also the key to the issues at stake.

Destruction of images in the eighth century

The accession of Leo III took place in an atmosphere of messianic expectation induced by the struggle between the empire and Islam and in particular by the siege of Constantinople, which subsequently acquired the aura not just of the New Rome but also of the New Jerusalem. The expectation was shared, on the first count, by the Jews themselves, as is shown by the rising in Iraq against caliph Hisham, of which the ring-leader, Severus, was a Syrian Christian converted to Judaism. In 721–2, Leo III decreed the forced conversion of the Jews.

Then came the year 726; the Arabs resumed their annual raids on Asia Minor; Leo III, in association with his son and co-emperor Constantine, promulgated a legal code entitled the *Ekloga* ('Selections'), the first systematic compilation since the Code of Justinian of 529. But one cannot fail to be struck by the difference between that venerable monument and this successor, which in a modern printed edition runs to little more than 60 octavo pages! In the content, however, there is less of a discrepancy. The *Ekloga* gives proof of certain fundamental changes in the practical application of the law which had become operative since 565, or indeed since 529: insistence on the equal culpability of both parties in the crime of adultery and in the infringement of the age of consent, the importance assigned to betrothals, the elaboration of corporal punishments and in particular of mutilations symbolic of the crime. As a preamble, a definition of imperial authority is proposed in which the legislator figures as one inspired directly and uniquely from on high, like a new Moses.

Yet, in this same year, Leo III ordered the removal of the image of Christ displayed above the Bronze Gate of the Great Palace and its replacement by a cross. The official sent to carry out the order was killed by the mob. In 727, the theme of Hellas rose in revolt, but the movement was crushed; the prohibition of images provoked the first written defence, the three *Discourses* of John Damascene. Mansur, as he was originally called, had been born at Damascus to an influential Christian family and held important positions at the caliphal court, before becoming a monk, under the name of John, at St Sabas in Palestine. The supporters of images took from him the line of argument which became standard, and in which a radical distinction was made between the idols condemned in the Scriptures and the Christian image, which was a bridge between the divine and the human made possible by the Incarnation. And it is around this distinction that the fundamental controversy continued to revolve, even when it became overlaid with propositions inherited from the philosophical schools of late Antiquity.

The discourses of the monk of St Sabas draw attention to another aspect of the matter, in as much as they challenge the emperor's competence to decide on an issue of theological significance. An exchange of letters between Leo III and Pope Gregory II between 727 and 729 shows that the emperor in fact made an effort, vain though it was, to obtain the pope's agreement. This correspondence, preserved in a Greek translation, demonstrates the appellate function which the pope long continued to serve in Byzantium's religious affairs; but it deepened the gulf which had opened up in the seventh century. For it was indisputably the case that the emperor could not decide such matters on his sole authority,

Iconoclasts whitewashing the image of Christ. This miniature perhaps seeks to draw a parallel between the iconoclasts and the soldiers who offered Christ vinegar at the crucifixion (Chludov Psalter, ninth century, Moscow, Historical Museum cod. 129).

even though in practice he had just done so. Furthermore, it is clear that he lacked the agreement of the patriarch, Germanos, enthroned in 715: the texts have survived of reprimands addressed by the latter to two bishops of Asia Minor, Constantine of Nakoleia and Thomas of Claudiopolis, who had taken the initiative by destroying the images in their respective dioceses. The *silention* (council) of 17 January 730 deposed Germanos and replaced him by his own *synkellos* (the head of the patriarchal administration). The decree was then promulgated. It was condemned in Rome at a synod promptly convened by Gregory III, elected pope in 731. Next, probably in 732–3, the emperor restored to the jurisdiction of his patriarch the papal patrimonies of Sicily, Calabria and Illyricum, which signified the return of their revenues, but also the opening of a serious quarrel with Rome. On his death, in 741, armed competition for the throne was resumed, this time within the imperial family. Artavasdos, son-in-law of the late emperor and *strategos* of the Opsikion theme, attacked Constantine as he passed through on his way to the front. Victorious, Artavasdos had himself crowned at Constantinople, in association with his elder son Nikephoros, and appointed his younger son, Niketas, supreme commander over the armed forces. Artavasdos also had on his side the Armeniac theme, which he had commanded, and the theme of Thrace. In contrast to Constantine V, he restored the cult of images. But the latter withdrew to Amorion, power-centre of the eastern theme, formerly commanded by his father, and from there regained the capital, which he entered in November 743.

The reign of Constantine V, to which the remarkable victories mentioned earlier form a backcloth, was distinguished by doctrinal formulation, in which the emperor himself played a leading role, and by a crystallisation of the conflict between the power of the

Iconoclasts (below) persecuting a supporter of images who is publicly declaiming his convictions (ms Vaticanus graecus 372, Vatican Library).

emperor and that of the Church which was a practical result of their respective evolution. In 754, a council was convened at Hieria, the suburb where the emperors had their summer palace. The patriarchal see being vacant, the chair was taken by Bishop Theodosios of Ephesus, son of the emperor Tiberios III, and the doctrine of iconoclasm was defined. The ground had been prepared in a written disquisition by Constantine V, which can be reconstituted from extracts quoted by the ninth-century patriarch Nikephoros at the time of the second iconoclasm. The sovereign stressed his perception of the logical impossibility of portraying Christ: the image cannot depict his divine nature, nor should it be limited to showing his human nature; therefore the only true image of Christ is the Eucharist. The council of 754 affirmed its veneration of Mary and the saints. But according

303

to ninth-century sources Constantine developed his argument as follows: Mary, a woman, could bear only what was human, and after the birth reverted to being an ordinary woman, just as an ordinary purse has no intrinsic value once the gold pieces it holds are removed. The cult of the saints was indeed a major target of Constantine's offensive. It has been seen how, in the late sixth century, the growth in the veneration of images was coupled with the prestige of the saints, and hence of the monks who served and mediated their cult. The iconoclasm of Constantine V was essentially a battle against the power of the monks, starting from 760. On this point we have the testimony of the *Life of Stephen the Younger*, composed in 806, according to which his martyrdom in 764, by a mob in the capital, was inflicted on orders from the emperor; and of the *Chronicle* of Theophanes, written under Leo V (813–20), which vouches for the cruelties and indignities inflicted on monks from 766 onwards by Michael Lachanodrakon, *strategos* of the Thrakesian theme, who, for example, forced monks and nuns to join in matrimony. Monastic buildings were handed over to secular use, monastic properties were confiscated. In place of the monks, Constantine sought to rely on the episcopal hierarchy. A primary consequence of his policies was the conclusive choice by Rome of the Frankish alliance, with the treaty concluded at Quierzy in 756 between Pippin and Pope Stephen II. Henceforward, therefore, the pope found himself politically independent, and thereby confirmed in the appellate function that was guaranteed to him in any case by the historic dignity of his see. We shall see later how the Byzantines made use of this in the ninth century.

The council of 754 gave Constantine justification for widespread destruction of images and of decorative schemes which carried the offending representations, which were in any case probably not numerous at this date. As regards the coinage, we saw that Justinian II adopted an image of Christ in place of the cross which Tiberios had substituted for the Antique figure of Victory. On the coinage of the eighth century, Christ was replaced in turn by imperial effigies, which were retained even during the short-lived restoration of images under Artavasdos. In buildings, too, the accent seems to have been placed on imperial iconography, for example through the depiction of scenes from the hippodrome. But on the death of Leo IV in 780, power was left in the hands of his widow, Irene, their son Constantine being too young to govern. Then, in 784, the iconoclast patriarch was made to step down; in 786, a council convened at Constantinople in the Church of the Holy Apostles was broken up by the palace guard; another council was convened at Nicaea, in 787. This council restored images, and in addition arrived at a series of decisions on ecclesiastical discipline, in themselves an essential testimony to the cultural and social condition of the Byzantine Church in the closing years of the eighth century.

Why this particular crisis?

The first iconoclasm, as it is usually described, was thus at an end. What it really signified has given rise to much argument. Explanations invoking Jewish influence, or the example of contemporary Islam, are almost certainly to be discarded, since the facts are not comparable. Islam, as we know, forbade the representation of any living creature in places of worship; mosaics that were effaced have indeed be found in certain Palestinian churches from between the sixth and eighth centuries; nevertheless, in synagogues of the same period, the figures of benefactors, although small, are not excluded from the decoration. Still more to the point, the significance attributed to such representations, which unlike the Byzantine icons were not portable, is in no way comparable with the belief focused on the images of the saints, Christ, and Mary, and with the reference in the two latter cases to the doctrine of the Incarnation. From the cultural angle, Leo III's Syrian origins may be of greater relevance, since his reservations about the representation of Christ as human could have a monophysite connotation. Constantine V, because of the particular line of argument he pursued, will even be accused of Nestorianism. It has therefore been suggested that the iconoclast policy was adopted as a gesture to the monophysite provinces, which in the eighth century were in the front line against Islam. The monophysite hypothesis is to be preferred to that of a 'Semitic' aversion to images, which is pure fabrication. But this still does not exhaust the question, since we also have to account for the preferences of the capital and the provincial armies. Now the revolts by which the latter made and unmade emperors all through this period, seem in the last analysis to have been dictated not by any sort of doctrinal preference but solely by the personal loyalties which for centuries had been one of the keys to the imperial succession. As for the population of Constantinople, it reacted violently to the initial moves of Leo III, yet demonstrated its attachment to the official position under Constantine V, if we are for example to believe the account given of St Stephen the Younger's martyrdom. The truth of the matter is probably that no single definition of its allegiance can be assumed, and more particularly that iconoclasm managed to implant itself more firmly with the passage of time.

Still to be considered is the imperial motive for iconoclasm. When Leo III ordered the image of Christ over the Bronze Gate to be replaced by a cross, he reversed a trend which had only recently become established, since it was Justinian II, it will be recalled, who placed that same image on his coins in substitution for the cross, which the iconoclast emperors removed in their turn to make way for their own effigy. A sequence of this kind is indicative of a debate over the fundamental relationship between Christ and the emperor, revolving round the emperor's twin roles as incarnation of the law and bringer of victory: these aspects had of course always been present, but since the end of the sixth century the Christly interpretation of them had become more specific. In replacing Christ by the cross, Leo III removed Christ, as it were, to a transcendental realm and thereby emphasised the terrestrial power delegated to the basileus. In the same way, the prologue to the *Ekloga* presents the basileus in the guise of a new Moses, an interpretation which clearly owes its inspiration more to the Pentateuch than to any contemporary Jewish influence. An association of this kind also casts its radiance over the earthly sovereign, the hero to whom all eyes turn in a time of acute anxiety inspired by the Arab advance, and intensified a few months previously by a violent earthquake in the sea off Crete. The return of the cross marked the reappearance of the sign which had beckoned Constantine I to victory.

With Constantine V we come closer to the heart of the matter. For signs are visible of the conflict which was to outlive the first restoration of images and the second iconoclasm and agitate the whole of the ninth century and the first half of the tenth. It is less a question of direct conflict between the emperor and the Church than one of a conflict within the Church itself, which pitted the increasingly powerful and ultimately victorious monastic party against an episcopate whose head, the ecumenical patriarch, shared with the emperor in the governance of the world. In this controversy, Constantine V seems to have played the dominant role, claiming for the imperial power a cultural, and no longer merely legislative, competence which anticipated Leo VI and Constantine VII, for whom it would be of the essence. In the present case its essential concomitant was the theoretical impotence of the patriarchate of the capital. In the provinces, the voice of the episcopate was scarcely heard, or at any rate not as a corporate body. This relative silence, perhaps due to the decline of urban life, left the field free for the monks. The *Chronicle* composed by the monk Theophanes relates episodes which certainly indicate that at every opportunity Constantine V directly attacked monastic power as incompatible with his own, and the cult of the saints which most obviously sustained it, while finding support among the secular clergy. The nuptials staged by Michael Lachanodrekon made a mockery of the *schema*, the black robe worn by monks since the fourth century which earned them the respect and veneration of Christians. The destruction of the books containing the 'sayings of the fathers', a compendium of edifying or miraculous tales from the early days of monasticism, indicates that by opposing icons the basileus was indirectly attacking the local and familiar prestige of the 'holy man', the phenomenon we saw developing in the fifth and sixth centuries and which was still in evidence. Theophanes claims furthermore that Constantine had recourse to sorcerers, in other words to the opposite of holy men. The murderous assault in 764 on Stephen, abbot of the monastery on Mt Auxentius near Chalcedon, is interpreted by the monastic chronicler, writing in 806, as the crime of an emperor and capital city still obeying the old calendar and its rituals.

But to discover the vital forces of monasticism in the time of Constantine V we must look outside the capital. Perhaps it was persecution which caused an exodus of Greek monks to Italy and Rome, which had noteworthy cultural consequences: for example, the *higoumenos* of St Sabas on the Aventine is to be found among the signatories to the council of 787. Above all, it is at this time that the monastic personalities who were to enter the scene in 787, in conjunction with the first restoration of images, began to emerge. Plato, born at Constantinople to a wealthy family, lost his parents in the great plague of 746 (or 747). He was brought up by an uncle, and through the patronage of the latter he entered the office of weights and measures in the imperial finance department, before becoming a monk in a monastery on Mt Olympus, of which he became *hegoumenos* in 780; we shall come across him later. His nephew and spiritual son, Theodore the Stoudite, born about 759, was to be the prime architect of the definitive triumph at Byzantium of the monastic Church.

Irene, a woman emperor

The great era of iconoclasm came to an end with the death of Constantine V, in 775. His son Leo IV, called 'the Khazar' because of his maternal ancestry, seems to have been the sole survivor of three sons from the first marriage, since the names of the others, Christophoros and Nikephoros, were also given to sons of the emperor's third wife. A moderate iconoclast, Leo IV sought and obtained adherents among the monks through promotions to the episcopate. He died in 780, and his death opened up the possibility of a dispute over succession within the imperial family. His son, Constantine, was ten years old, and Leo IV had associated him with the throne in 776, by crowning him with the agreement of all the political classes, in the words of Theophanes, 'the armies of the themes, the senate, the central army, the whole body of citizens and the heads of the guilds'. An alternative solution, that of a lateral succession from the emperor to his brothers, thus seems to have been ruled out: Leo IV had not even taken the step of making them co-emperors. Because Constantine VI was a minor, the succession from father to son had to be achieved through the expedient of his mother's regency, and hence through the attribution of imperial power to a woman. Considering the importance of war and victory to the imperial persona, it can well be imagined that all would not go smoothly. The palace intrigues, the religious preferences, and the positions adopted by the provincial armies, all crystallised around this problem, while the actors seem suddenly to come to life for us because the sources are more immediate, more numerous, and more articulate. There is of course a pitfall here which historians have not always managed to avoid. The reproduction of what seems to be a faithful portrait may not be an accurate reflection of long-extinct preferences and grievances, and it is equally wrong to project on to the past the specious rationality of a present-day culture and morality. But to anyone prepared to make the necessary effort of imagination, the ninth century offers an abundance of material: for the early years the basic framework provided by Theophanes in his *Chronicle* is supplemented by the biography of the patriarch Tarasios, composed by the deacon Ignatios, a member of the patriarchal staff, by the family history of Maria of Amnia, wife of Constantine VI, written about 821 by one of her cousins, the monk Niketas, and lastly by the considerable corpus of writings from the pen of Theodore the Stoudite.

What, then, is the truth about Irene? Are we to regard her in the first instance as an anxious mother, concerned to safeguard the future of a son too young to assert himself against the paternal uncles who commanded the loyalties of the eastern armies and of the men who had served Constantine V? Did she glimpse right from the start the prospect of an empire in her own right, to be bitterly disputed with her own son? We shall never know. Born in Athens, did she import into the palace the tradition of a piety which had never been disturbed by regional disaffection, and does this explain her indulgence, displayed even in the lifetime of Leo IV, towards the monks? It may be so. This said, it has to be pointed out that her status as a woman in the imperial household condemned her to a courtly and urban existence, and dictated her choice of tactics and supporters. The period which runs from the death of Leo IV to her deposition in 802 falls into three distinct parts.

In the first, from 780 to 790, Irene was in the position of a regent associated with the imperial power. Her first object was to frustrate the hopes placed in the Caesar Nikephoros, brother of Leo IV. He stood for the continuation of Constantine's iconoclastic and military policies; she brought into play the monks, who had already gained her sympathy, the capital and its civilian populace, and the place staff. And she had to contend with the hostility of the armies in the eastern themes. Of the two men she relied on at this period, one was a eunuch in her household, Staurakios, who became logothete of the *dromos* (minister for the police, the public courier service and external relations), and in 781 conducted the campaign against the rebellious Slavs in Macedonia and Greece, but who by reason of his castration could never aspire to the throne. The other was the head of a department (*a secretis*) in the imperial chancery, Tarasios, a layman whom she made her patriarch in 784, having forced the iconoclast patriarch Paul to step down: she staged the election of Tarasios by the assembled 'people' in the Magnaura palace, thus placing an imperial stamp on a traditional ceremony. Together, they then prepared for the restoration of images by entering into negotiations with Rome and with the eastern patriarchates. A first attempt at holding a council, in the Church of the Holy Apostles on 31 July 786, was thwarted by the iconoclast soldiers of the palace guard. Irene then drafted the capital's iconoclast troops to the Asia Minor front, replacing them with troops in favour of images which she summoned from Europe. This cleared the way for a new council, which met at Nicaea from 24 September to 13 October 787 – the seventh and last council to be recognised as ecumenical by the Church descended from Byzantium. The final declaration was signed at the Magnaura, where the 'new Constantine and the new Helena' were acclaimed, a reference to the archetypal Christian emperor which the choice of Nicaea, scene of the first ecumenical council, had already implied. The Council of 787 emphasised the distinction between 'veneration' and 'adoration' of images, and made or reiterated some general rules regarding ecclesiastical property, clerical discipline and the criteria for validation of the liturgy. It agreed to the readmission of penitent iconoclasts. In reality, the council was neither homogeneous, nor all of one mind.

The problem of reconciliation within the ranks of the clergy initiated a debate which was to drag on in various forms until the tenth century. On the one hand, Tarasios inaugurated the type of patriarch recruited directly from the public administration, and disposed to view his collaboration with Christ's delegated sovereign from an essentially political standpoint. On the other hand Plato and his nephew Theodore personified the claim to the absolute priority of the Church, which was commissioned to lay down the law for all, the emperor included; and the Church in this instance was the monastic Church. Plato had founded the monastery of Sakkoudion, of which he became *higoumenos* on a family estate in the region of Mt Olympus: this he was able to do as early as 781, the start of Irene's regency having given the signal for monastic liberation. The strict regime devised for Sakkoudion was inspired by a wish to return to the origins of monasticism, that is to say to the coenobitic model of Basil of Caesarea. Theodore, born in 759, was Plato's nephew, his sister's son, and his whole family lived withdrawn from the world. He himself became a monk at Sakkoudion, and collaborated in the reform initiated by Plato, whom he succeeded. Their party was opposed to the reinstatement of iconoclast bishops.

In the year after the council, Irene arranged her son's marriage. The bride was Maria, grand-daughter of Philaretos, a landowner from Amnia in Paphlagonia. In 821, another grandchild, the monk Niketas, wrote the history of his grandfather (and godfather), who, he tells us, dedicated him to the monastic life in childhood in order to carry out the task. The

308

resulting narrative, an important source for the social history of the period, is on two levels. The first, an edifying strand, compensates for the absence of an illustrious lineage, at a time when this was beginning to be important, by presenting a hagiographical picture of Philaretos, depicting him as a kind of Christian Job whose over-abundant charity gradually swallowed up all his possessions; his imperial marriage constituted the source of new prosperity, after which the author is able to contemplate him enjoying eternal bliss. The second level is familial: Niketas gives exact particulars of the children and grandchildren of Philaretos, and describes the tour of the provinces by imperial envoys in the quest for a bride whose social origins were less important than her perfect physical proportions. Other instances are to be found at this era of this competitive method of finding a bride for the emperor. It may hark back to the old Iranian custom exemplified by the story of Esther, and is doubtless to be regarded as the female equivalent of the male criterion of victory in war.

The triumph of the monks

The second period of the reign of Irene and Constantine began in 790. Impatient at being held in check, Constantine fomented a conspiracy against Staurakios, the consequence of which was that Irene insisted on being the sole recipient, as long as she lived, of the soldiers' oath of loyalty. While the troops of the capital acquiesced, those of Asia Minor deposed Irene, in a climate influenced by military threats from the Arabs, the Bulgars and the Lombards in Italy. Constantine nevertheless restored her to his side in 792. But his management of affairs was disastrously inept. He suffered a defeat from the Bulgars in 793, and finally eliminated the threat from his paternal uncles by having Nikephoros blinded and the tongues of the others cut out, slighting in this way the very strong attachment still felt for the great Constantine V. In addition he blinded the Armenian Alexios Moselè, *strategos* of the Armeniacs, who had supported him against Irene in 790. The theme thereupon rebelled, and Constantine only regained the upper hand by exploiting a factional Armenian element, which he nevertheless included in the ensuing repression. After losing the support of this vitally important theme, he next forfeited that of the monks. In 795 he despatched Maria to a convent, and discovered a priest, Joseph, who was willing to bless his union with his mistress Theodote, kinswoman to Theodore, the future Stoudite. In so doing Constantine not only sowed the seeds of his own downfall but also sparked off a controversy which clarified the position of the powers involved, and was of capital importance. The point is that Constantine's action went against the law on the separation of married couples as it had been evolved by the Church from the fourth century, and to which Justinian had given formal endorsement in his legislation: in the absence of a mutual agreement, the repudiation of a wife was impermissible save in a small number of strictly-defined situations. The absence of opposition from the patriarch Tarasios was to be expected: as we have seen, he stood in the line of political patriarchs, to which other patriarchs drawn like himself from the public service belonged. In contrast, Plato, *hegoumenos* of Sakkoudion, and his nephew Theodore, saw in the affair their opportunity to affirm the paramount authority of the Church's rulings in every case, and at the same time to assert the superior competence of the monastic Church. Constantine sent them first to prison and then, in March 797, into exile. He therefore found himself isolated in the face of the plots being engineered in the palace by his mother. On a summer day in 797, Irene had him blinded 'in the purple chamber where she had brought him into the world'. At the same moment, the *Chronicle* of Theophanes continues, 'the sun was darkened, ships strayed from their course; and from what men say, all were convinced that if the sun hid his rays, it was because someone had blinded the emperor'. With these words the chronicler offers us the key to a tale whose unvarnished atrocity has too often been a stumbling-block to historians. The 'purple chamber' is of course the imperial birth-chamber, which was to acquire an increasing importance in the ninth century, and most of all for the posterity of Basil I, as criterion of the inalienable legitimacy of power. Constantine VI was thus disqualified through blinding in the very place where he entered on his birthright; and on the other hand, the equivalence – still more explicit in Greek – between the sun's rays and those of sight points clearly to the solar character of imperial sovereignty, an attribute familiar since the third century and the time of Constantine, making it easy for us to understand why blinding was chosen at Byzantium as the mutilation irreconcilable with the possession or expectation of supreme power. Constantine was therefore relegated, like Theodore, to a purely private existence. He left behind two unresolved problems: the conflict stirred up within the Church by his marriage, and the exercise of the imperial power by a woman, who now assumed it single-handed, and without the pretext of a temporary delegation. With this we enter on the third phase of the period, which ended with the fall of Irene in 802.

An event of decisive importance occurred right at the start with the transference, still in 797, of Theodore and his uncle, with their monks, to the capital. An ever-increasing number of monks, too many to be accommodated at Sakkoudion, a threat of Arab attack, but perhaps above all the sense that the time was ripe, made it logical to install the community permanently in the capital, where it reoccupied an old, deserted monastery, the Stoudios or Stoudiou (in the genitive), so-called from the patrician said to have founded it in the fifth century. It will be recalled that Plato and his nephew saw themselves as the promoters of a return to the pristine monastic principles of Basil of Caesarea. In actuality, the Stoudios was provided by Theodore with a system of rules for which there was no precedent. The minutely regulated timetable, the elaborate nature of the monks' penitential code, the diversity of occupations, requiring the monks to be allocated to different workshops and agricultural tasks, the existence of an infirmary for the monks, of a hospice, and even a school, seem it is true to echo the principles of Basil of Caesarea, if not indeed the Pachomian communities, just as they certainly have much in common with the practice of Syrian and Palestinian monasteries in the fifth and sixth centuries. Even so, the exhaustive and coherent nature of the Stoudite *Rule* makes it the first document worthy of the name to appear in the Byzantine setting. The modernity of the Stoudios resided above all in its urban situation, and still more in its location in the capital, which gave it a leading cultural role and accounted for its political influence: inside the imperial structure, the Stoudios, under varying forms, would in future hold its place as monastic spokesman in a dialogue in which

Solidus of Irene, the first female emperor. She restored the cult of images in 787 but in so doing alienated the largely iconoclast army and therefore weakened the empire (Paris, Bibliothèque nationale, Cabinet des médailles).

the emperor was as much involved as the patriarch. From now on the problem of the supreme power was to have three dimensions.

The problem surrounding the elimination of Constantine VI by his mother was not, it must be repeated, of a moral order but of a political kind: when the *Chronicle* of Theophanes equates the sun's eclipse with the blinding of Constantine, the reproach is levelled at an outrage committed against the sovereign with the greatest claim to legitimacy, and not at the crime of a mother against her son. Equally, no comment on Irene's action came from Theodore the Stoudite, in whose eyes Constantine remained guilty of having disrupted the order whose guardian was the Church, and which Irene restored. This said, Irene was still left to grapple in various ways, and in the end without success, with the real problem – the fact that the emperor was a woman: to aggravate it, the empire suffered military and diplomatic reverses connected in part with the rise of the Carolingians, which was consecrated by the coronation on Christmas Day 800. In an effort to solve the problem, Irene resorted to symbols, whose impact on the restricted milieu of the palace, scene of the power game, should not be underestimated. In her laws and on her coins she took the title of basileus ('emperor'). On Easter Day 799, she assumed the purple and gold raiment, appropriated the chariot drawn by white horses, and scattered the coins which betokened the imperial pomp: mimetic gestures which probably had more substance than the project of a marriage between herself and Charlemagne, of which we hear only from Theophanes. On the other hand, Irene continued to bestow favours on her ever-faithful allies, the 'citizens' of the capital, whose fiscal burden she alleviated, and the monks, beneficiaries both of her generosity and her zeal. Her desire to bring the civil law into line with the formalisation of canon law being undertaken by the Stoudites is shown by the law which declared the blessing – which thereby acquired a new importance – to be sufficient for the solemnisation of a marriage between poor people, and by the prohibition of third marriages. She did not visualise her succession, it seems, or at least did not consider continuing the line, since she ordered the brothers of Leo IV who, apart from Nikephoros, still had their sight, to be blinded. Surrounded by the rivalries of her eunuchs, Staurakios and Aetios, and of their followings, after the death of Staurakios in 800 she became more isolated. She finally succumbed to a palace revolution, led by the logothete of the treasury (finance minister) Nikephoros. Banished first to the Princes' Island and then to Lesbos, she died there in August 803.

With the accession of Nikephoros I the ninth century, and the gradual ascent of Byzantium towards the classic splendour of the dynasty founded by Basil I in 867, properly began.

The Byzantine 'Pre-renaissance'

The history of the years 802 to 867 is marked by a second iconoclastic period (from 815 to 843), ending with the definitive proclamation on the role of images; by the founding of the dynasty miscalled the 'Macedonian', descended from Basil I, which began in 867 and became extinct in 1056; by the conversion of the Bulgar ruler in 864; and by the first Russian attack on the capital in 860. At this period, the peoples who burst on the scene in the seventh to eighth centuries, the Bulgars in process of Slavicisation and the Khazars, achieved political stability; the Russians appeared on the Byzantine horizon; long-distance trade began to expand and urban sites showed clear signs of a revival; lastly, the social patterns beginning to emerge in the second half of the eighth century became firmly established. But the most striking feature of these years is a cultural revival, without precedent if not without inheritance, to which the historian is indebted for an abundance of texts. And the historian, whose concern is always to identify determinate causes, is confronted at the outset of his investigation with the culture – in the sense in which the term is to be understood at this period. Integral to his study are the authorities' accounts of themselves, the reference-points of those accounts, the techniques of their diffusion, and the forms of representation established, or at any rate recognised, at the different levels of the social system. Ninth-century historiography poses a difficult problem because we only know of it through tenth-century works, which are wholly orientated, as we shall see, towards justifying the manner in which the dynasty came to power. In addition there is a range of biographical material to draw on, from the *Life* of the patriarch Ignatios, who was at the heart of the political debate, to that of Ioannikios (died 846), a model of Bithynian asceticism, and the tales of Saracen pirates involving saints of southern Italy and the islands.

Byzantium's internal tensions and external relations at this period are thus to be defined in cultural terms: Classical culture in tension with Christian faith; the patriarchal Church with the monastic Church; the capital with the provinces, but equally Hellenism with the minorities; Byzantium with the tribal peoples; and at the apex, summing up, representing and explaining the entire edifice, the figure of the emperor. And this culture finds expression not only in the texts but also, from the middle of the ninth century, in a triumphant iconography. To all this must be added the written sources external to the empire, in particular the substantial contribution made by the Arab chroniclers and geographers, as well as archaeological evidence, which still has many secrets to yield up.

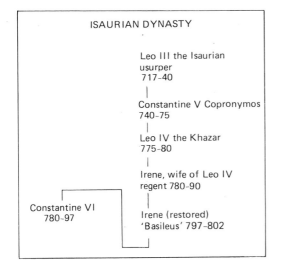

ISAURIAN DYNASTY

Leo III the Isaurian
usurper
717-40

Constantine V Copronymos
740-75

Leo IV the Khazar
775-80

Irene, wife of Leo IV
regent 780-90

Constantine VI
780-97

Irene (restored)
'Basileus' 797-802

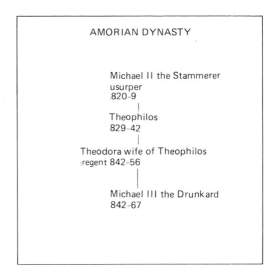

AMORIAN DYNASTY

Michael II the Stammerer
usurper
820-9

Theophilos
829-42

Theodora wife of Theophilos
regent 842-56

Michael III the Drunkard
842-67

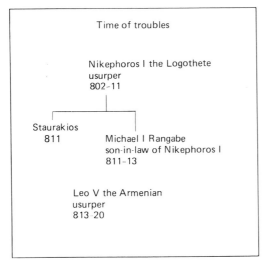

Time of troubles

Nikephoros I the Logothete
usurper
802-11

Staurakios
811

Michael I Rangabe
son-in-law of Nikephoros I
811-13

Leo V the Armenian
usurper
813-20

The succession: new difficulties, continuing confusion

We start as usual by identifying the protagonists: the emperors, of course, whose succession conforms in theory, barring historical accident, to the patrilinear principle; but from now on there are others to be mentioned. The figure of the patriarch assumed an equal importance in the politics of the ninth century. Furthermore, the social trend already apparent under Constantine V came to maturity. The leading men, defined by the holding of high civil, and still more of high military, office began to form a cohesive, though not a closed, class: hence there was a greater emphasis on descent, matrimonial alliances and family connections, as is shown by the new attention paid to these details in historical

313

writings. Confirmation is provided by the emergence of the family name, which from the late eighth century increasingly denoted, among the governing circle, those whose distinction already went back to a previous generation. Sometimes the family name was a personal name, Phokas for example, sometimes a Hellenised foreign name, at this date usually Armenian, more rarely the derivative of a place-name – but often it seems to have started with a nickname which then became permanent. Names which originated in the spoken language, for example Onomagoulos, 'donkey-jowls', give an inkling both of the socially open character of the aristocracy at the time of its formation, and of a linguistic level scarcely recorded in the surviving texts of the period.

We saw that Nikephoros I, who overthrew Irene in 802, was a minister of finance (*logothetes tou genikou*); his success can be regarded as the logical outcome of Irene's female rule, centred on the palace. He emerged triumphant from two attempts to unseat him, by Bardanes Tourkos in 803 and by Arsaber in 808: these Armenian names, and the former's soubriquet, draw attention to Byzantium's eastern pole, politically crucial since the eighth century and for a long time to come. Nikephoros nevertheless married his son Staurakios, associated to the empire in 803, to an Athenian, Theophano, because of her kinship with Irene, and because of her success in the beauty contest which was the female version of imperial victory in war. His daughter Procopia married Michael Rangabe, whose father, Theophylaktos Rangabe, had supported the cause of Nikephoros, brother of Leo IV, and filled the position of *drongarios* (admiral) of the Dodecanese. But in 811 the emperor was cut down in the Bulgar war. After one successful campaign, in which he had captured Pliska, Nikephoros was killed in battle, and the khan Krum had a silver-lined drinking goblet fashioned from his skull. The profound impression made by this battle is apparent from stories like that of the soldier Nicholas, who sees a supernatural figure keeping watch over the battle, and whose life is spared because of his chastity the night before, and who then becomes a monk. Staurakios was wounded, and died a few months later leaving no heir. The throne then passed to Michael, father of two sons and three daughters: attention was drawn in the previous chapter to the tendency, from Herakleios onwards, of imperial families to be prolific. Michael I in his turn was defeated by the Bulgars in 813. Afterwards he is said to have declared, 'the empire of my father-in-law and his line was unpleasing to God', a saying which, if not strictly authentic, is at least fully consistent with the spirit of the age. Deserted by victory, Michael I was despatched to a monastery, along with his wife and children.

The imperial succession then became an object of contention between three men who had all taken part in the rebellion of Bardanes Tourkos: Leo, an Armenian who was *strategos* of the Anatolic theme, Michael the Stammerer, originally from Amorion in Phrygia, and Thomas, called 'the Slav' but born somewhere near Comana in the Armeniac theme. Raised to the throne in 813, Leo V gave out military commands to Thomas, and particularly to Michael the Stammerer, to whose daughter he stood godfather. In 820, a plot to put Michael on the throne cost Leo his life. Michael II was then faced with a rebellion by Thomas, his long-standing rival. Thomas, who passed himself off as Constantine VI, relied on a conjunction of forces: Asia Minor, and in particular the north-west frontier zone, touching on the Iberians, Armenians, and Abasgs; fiscal discontent; the sailors of the thematic fleets. But these were offset by the hostility of the *strategoi* of the Anatolikon and Opsikion themes. He obtained the backing of caliph Ma'mun, and in December 821 laid siege to Constantinople. Michael II regained the upper hand, with the assistance in his case of the Bulgar khan, Omurtag, and of the imperial fleet, which remained loyal, and Thomas died under torture in October 823. More than an echo of the dispute concerning images, the episode is probably best regarded as one of those convulsions which remind us every now and again that Constantinople, posed between Anatolia and the Mediterranean, was not the capital of a homogeneous empire.

Michael II had married Euphrosyne, the daughter of Constantine VI, who was accordingly released from the cloister, forging in this way a link with the great dynasty of the eighth century. He associated his son Theophilos to the empire, and the latter succeeded him when he died in 829. Theophilos had the murderers of Leo V executed, through whose deed his father had come to the throne. This action, like Michael II's marriage, exalted the imperial power above the *de facto* breaks in its continuity. Theophilos married the young woman who won the contest already referred to, and on his death, in 842, left an infant son, Michael, born in 829. His widow Theodora, whose sisters had married into the aristocracy, governed with the help of her brothers, Petronas and more particularly Bardas, and of the Logothete of the *dromos* (minister for external affairs, the courier service and the police), the eunuch Theoktistos, who was implicated many years before in Michael's accession, and baptismal kinsman to Theodora, and according to an Arab chronicler related to her in a more carnal way, despite his mutilation. The reign of Irene, when she was flanked by Aetius and Staurakios, might seem to be repeating itself. The outcome, however, was to be different. These men saw matters in a wider perspective. Our picture of Theoktistos, Bardas, even of Michael III, is gradually being freed of the discredit cast on them by the rumours spread by contemporary opponents and the verdicts of later historians. Also different is the way in which the situation is resolved. It was at first dominated by Theoktistos, until 855, the year in which Theodora showed her intention of separating her son from his mistress, Eudokia Ingerina, and forcing him to take a wife. Theoktistos was assassinated with the connivance of Bardas, and Theodora excluded from power. Next Bardas carried all before him, and received the title of Caesar. And lastly came the meteoric rise to power of the future emperor Basil I, founder of a dynasty which surrounded its origins with a haze of self-justificatory propaganda.

Virtually unknown, a native of Adrianople, and on his father's side perhaps of Armenian descent, Basil had come to the capital to seek his fortune. He became Michael's boon companion, and manager of his stables. Michael then provided him with women, first his sister Thekla, who appeared on coins with Michael and their mother, then his mistress, Eudokia Ingerina, whom Basil married, after his own wife had been sent back to her people. Next, in 865, Basil got rid of Bardas. In 866, he was associated to the empire. And in 867 he assassinated Michael III, whose murder in his bed-chamber following the imperial banquet, connived at by kinsmen or friends who were privy to the plot, is depicted by contemporaries as a scene of positively Shakespearean violence. The sequence of political events which brought Basil to supreme power was confined wholly to the palace.

A religious truce

In their relations with the emperors, the line of patriarchs conformed to the pattern already developing under Irene. Some were recruited from the top ranks of the capital's civil administration, for example Nikephoros I, who had only recently become a monk when he succeeded Tarasios in 806, and Photios, who at the time of his appointment in 858 was not even ordained. The others were monks such as Methodios (843–7), who furthermore had been on intimate terms with Theophilos before collaborating with his widow in the restoration of images, or his successor Ignatios. This alternation expresses the dominant theme of the conflicts of the ninth and even tenth centuries, during which the Byzantine Church acquired its distinctive traits. It does not diminish the personal importance of the ecumenical patriarchs. Those of both types were habitués of the palace even before their appointment, and their family connections are often worth noting: Photios, on his father's side a nephew of Tarasios, was related through his mother to Theodora, wife of Theophilos; Ignatios was none other than Theophylaktos, a son of Michael I, castrated and placed in a monastery at a tender age when his father fell from power. The great patriarch of the second iconoclasm, John Morocharzianos (837–43), came from an already illustrious family; his brother Arsaber (the name is indicative of Armenian descent) married Kalomaria, 'Mary the Beautiful', a sister of the empress Theodora, to whom John himself was related as a fellow godparent. The first iconoclastic patriarch, Theodotos (815–21) belonged to the clan of the Melissenoi, already prominent in the eighth century. In secular life Theodotos had held the rank of *spatharocandidatos*; he enjoyed the friendship of the future Michael II, and his patrician father, Michael Melissenos, was related by marriage to Constantine V.

These details help us to visualise the men and the social circle in which the debates of the capital were personified. Nor should it be forgotten that the patriarch was also the head of an administrative apparatus: after all, it is to the deacon Ignatios, custodian of the patriarchal treasure, that we owe the *Lives* of Tarasios and his successor Nikephoros. Lastly, the Stoudios monastery, installed as we have seen in the capital, also has its part to play in the history of the ninth century. Theodore's *Rule*, composed in verse, envisages the Stoudios as a complete social organism, ranging from the school, for children destined to make their profession there as monks, to the infirmary, passing through a series of workshops, amongst which the scriptorium will soon attract attention. Although Theodore himself belonged by birth to the capital's aristocracy of service, social recruitment to the Stoudios appears to have been relatively open, as is only to be expected from a Church not prepared to compromise with the world. But even if the Stoudios retained the leadership, it did not remain the sole champion of the monastic viewpoint: the period was also remarkable for the rise of provincial monasticism.

316

The conflict between the patriarchal party of compromise and Stoudite intransigence continued in various guises throughout the ninth century; the heart of the matter was still the definition of relations between politics and religion at the fountainhead of power. The attitude of Nikephoros was the exact opposite of Irene's. Stretched by the war effort, and hence in financial difficulties, he put an end to the fiscal privileges enjoyed by monastic and other pious establishments. He had inherited furthermore the disagreements left by the episcopal appointments dating back to the first iconoclasm, and by the divorce and remarriage of Constantine VI: more particularly, the dispute raging over the status of the priest who agreed to solemnise the remarriage. The patriarch Tarasios died in 806, and the emperor replaced him with another of the same type, Nikephoros, who had begun by following his father into the imperial secretariat, in which official capacity he attended the council of 787, before retiring to a monastery of his own foundation. Although the emperor consulted Theodore over this appointment, the new patriarch's willingness to compromise excited Stoudite opposition. In 808, the monastery was occupied by troops; in 809, a synod condemned the Stoudites, while nevertheless declaring Constantine VI's only valid marriage to be his first – proof, if it were needed, that the real issue was less respect for the canons than the assertion of religious authority, or more precisely of its autonomous and determinant position within the power structure in general. The Stoudite leaders departed into exile, and Theodore made a vain attempt to appeal to Rome: a logical stratagem since the pope, the senior of the five patriarchs, was the only conceivable counter-weight to Constantinople, from which Rome remained separated by the quarrel over the papal patrimonies confiscated under Leo III, and by the Frankish alliance. This was from now on a stratagem typical of the monastic party, and was renewed on several occasions, even if there were times when the emperor followed the same course. A reconciliation brought this first episode to an end, under Michael I, who was susceptible to Stoudite influence.

Leo V led the empire back to iconoclasm, in an atmosphere of anxiety caused by the gravity of the Bulgar threat, already evident in the reverses of 811 and 813. In that same year, the populace of the capital flocked to the tomb of Constantine V, of victorious memory. In addition, by their incursions into Thrace the Bulgars were jeopardising the capital's food supply, causing a steep rise in grain prices. Leo V saw himself as a new Leo III, to the point of crowning his son Smbat under the name Constantine. The conscious intention to restore the victorious model of the preceding century no doubt accounts in part for his adoption of iconoclasm. This at once led to the deposition, in 815, of the patriarch Nikephoros, whose co-operation with the government did not extend to the rejection of images. He was replaced by Theodotos Melissenos, kinsman, as we saw, of Constantine V. A month later, a council held in the church of St Sophia at Constantinople issued a definition of the doctrine. It was preceded by research into manuscripts with a view to compiling a dossier of justificatory texts, carried out by a committee headed by John Morocharzianos, the future patriarch. The decrees of the council did not survive the restoration of 843, and our only knowledge of their content comes from the quotations and refutations supplied by the exiled patriarch. Theodore was also banished, after once again appealing to the pope; some of his disciples were put to death. Michael II, an iconoclast in his turn, tried in vain for a

The triumph of orthodoxy. On the right, the iconoclast council of 815, with the emperor Leo V and the patriarch Theodotos, deposing the orthodox patriarch Nikephoros. On the left, Nikephoros triumphs over his enemies, now prostrate at his feet (ms *Pantocrator* 61, ninth century, Mt Athos).

reconciliation, chiefly by recalling the exiles and tolerating the cult of images in private. But Theodore, content with nothing less than the reinstatement of the patriarch Nikephoros and the summoning of a council, appealed over the emperor's head to the authority of the Roman see. In a letter of 824 to the Carolingian emperor Louis I, Michael II justified himself by explaining the abuses to which the cult of icons had descended, and requested support from him at Rome. This produced no results. The Latin Church did not turn a blind eye to the power struggle at Byzantium, in which it remained a court of appeal. But the debate over images, which was one aspect of that conflict, was almost as foreign to the Latin Church, in this period at any rate, as the cult of the images themselves.

After the death of Theodore in 826, and of Nikephoros in 828, the subject was exhausted without being closed. Theophilos took a sterner line. He forbade the painting of images, and he was severe on the monks, who were more than ever identified with the cult. In 836, scurrilous verses were branded on the foreheads of the 'graptoi' brothers Theodore and Theophanes, two Palestinian monks; Lazarus, a monk who painted icons, had his hands pierced. John Morocharzianos, whose role in the events of 815 has been described, became patriarch in 837. But Theodora and her daughters persisted in the veneration of icons in the secrecy of the palace, and imperial iconoclasm did not outlast the death of Theophilos in 842. In 843, John was deposed, and replaced by the Sicilian monk Methodios, who was formerly caught up in Michael II's repression as the bearer of a papal message in support of icons.

The solemn and final restitution of devotion to images took place on the first Sunday in Lent, a day honoured since then and even into our own times as 'Orthodox Sunday' in the Churches descended from Byzantium. At the same time, the continuity of imperial power and the dynasty was assured by reports of Theophilos's deathbed repentance, of the vision in which the pious empress saw Christ pardoning her husband from the judgment seat, while the patriarch, it was said, had found Theophilos's name miraculously erased from a list of heretical emperors placed the evening before on the altar. The Golden Chamber of the palace was restored to its former state: the image of Christ was again displayed above the imperial throne, while the Virgin, together with the emperor, the patriarch and saints, took her place at the west door.

So the second iconoclasm came to an end. It was distinguished from the first by the erudition brought to the debates, which so far as we can judge applied to both camps. To this period belong the philosophical deepening of the case in favour of images, and the drawing of more profound political conclusions from the Incarnation. The works, abounding in Aristotelian references, on which the patriarch Nikephoros was engaged up to the time of his death, in part still unpublished, can be cited as clear evidence. The explanation is no doubt to be found in the maturing of movements which had already built up traditions on both sides, but still more to be found in the intellectual ferment of the first half of the ninth century, a period possibly more brilliant, more creative and more enquiring than the great Classical age which opened with the accession of Basil I.

Towards a new image of the Church

In the first place, there was a decisive change in the means of disseminating book-learning. Paper, although already in use in Islamic lands, was still unknown at Byzantium. But it was at this time that Byzantine copyists abandoned the uncial hand in favour of minuscule, so much more rapid that comparisons have been made with the invention of printing; it will be seen later that the same transition is made, in this same ninth century, in the Latin writings of the Carolingian West. The earliest known Greek manuscript written in minuscule, a Gospel book, was copied in 835 in the scriptorium of the Stoudios. A symptom of an increased demand for books, the employment of the new hand was presumably not unconnected with the scholarly character of the second inconoclasm: this conclusion can

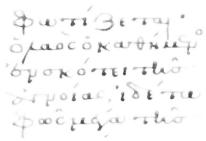

Left: uncial script; right: minuscule script. With the increased demand for books in the ninth century, copyists abandoned majuscule in favour of a more rapidly written hand. (Uncial: *St Matthew's Gospel*, sixth century; minuscule: *Homilies of Gregory of Nazianzus*, eleventh century; Paris, Bibliothèque nationale.)

hardly be doubted, even if the books written from the iconoclastic standpoint are now lost. Going by the sequence of datable manuscripts, minuscule was first employed for works with a scriptural and theological content, then for treatises on practical subjects such as surveying and medicine, and lastly for works of literature in the wider sense.

The reign of Theophilos marks the true beginnings of the ninth-century 'renaissance', which, like all renaissances, in fact represents the blossoming of a contemporary movement. Two men played a particularly important role. One was John Morocharzianos, called John the Grammarian, a man of high birth and Classical culture, whatever his opponents, who refer to him by the popular diminutive of 'Jannis', implied to the contrary. His leaning seems to have been toward Greek science, and hence also towards magic, the two being almost inseparable in contemporary thought. He had a lasting influence on Theophilos, whose tutor he had been and who sent him on an embassy to Baghdad. Leo the Philosopher (or the Mathematician) was born at Constantinople about 790 and was initially trained in rhetoric, though his studies also included philosophy and arithmetic. At first a private teacher, in particular of mathematics, he was given a public teaching position by Theophilos. He became metropolitan of Thessalonica in 840, but returned to Constantinople after the restoration of 843. A moderate iconoclast, we know that he divided his scholarly attention between Plato, amending his own copy of the text, Euclid, and the influence of the stars on human destiny. The future patriarch Photios, born about 810, was already at work under Theophilos. Pursuing a career at this stage in the upper reaches of the civil service, in course of which he too visited Baghdad, Photios found the time, in about 838, to compile for his brother's benefit his celebrated *Bibliotheca*, an annotated list of 279 books he had read; some of these notes, which go into considerable detail, remain the sole testimony to Antique works no longer extant. His cast of mind made him less interested in science and philosophy than in rhetoric, which at this period of course included history. In addition he seems to have set up some kind of study circle for reading and instruction.

The contribution of Theophilos himself went beyond the patronage of the scholars just mentioned, and the initiation of a policy intended to produce a publicly-educated elite and a cultured administration. He included the imperial image itself in the cultural transformation, by adding the intellectual dimension which it was to present in the ninth and tenth centuries; and unlike Constantine V, he did not confine himself to the theological sphere. His fascination with the government and civilisation of the caliphate shows itself, amongst other things, in his borrowings from Umayyad palatial art as an alternative to the Christocentric decorative scheme traditional since the late sixth century, but which an iconoclastic emperor could hardly retain. The theme of imperial victory was enacted in the triumphal entries staged on his return to Constantinople after his successes in 831 and 837; the protocol observed on these occasions is preserved in the *Book of Ceremonies* compiled by Constantine VII. And although Theophilos bequeathed no laws to his successors, his virtues as supreme judge are none the less illustrated in the pious tales about his absolution, and in the collection of imperial *Lives* composed in the entourage of Constantine VII: the posterity of Basil I thus underlined the uninterrupted dignity of the imperial office, circumventing Michael III, who was ruled out by his assassination.

To sum up, the imperial culture of the second iconoclasm was typified by its rereading of the Antique, and by a specifically lay spirit of enquiry, found even in John the Patriarch; Photios, whose scholarly preoccupations remained predominantly Christian, was an exception, and in any case he came to the fore only in the generation following 843. This second generation therefore inherited a cultural model based on Antique authorities promoted to Classical status, and from now on in the hands of a government whose renewed commitment to images was permanent. This is of course not to deny the role of the individual, or of the private pleasure taken in this 'renaissance' by its protagonists. The historian's task, however, is to establish and explain its political relevance.

The second iconoclasm was also – and this will be no surprise – a time of monastic expansion. The Stoudios pursued its way, as is testified by the manuscript mentioned earlier, copied under Theophilos, by the Stoudite hagiography, with its accounts of the ordeals suffered by Theodore and his successor Nicholas, compiled in the monastery under Basil I, and by the fruits of its training, of which the patriarch Ignatios was an illustration. While not unfamiliar with Antique culture, the Stoudios approached it with a different end in view: exaltation of the monastic Church to the prime position in the empire. But the second iconoclasm also coincided with, and no doubt in part caused, a proliferation of monastic settlements in the provinces, which had important consequences. Mt Olympos in Bithynia, not far from Brussa, became a favoured place of retreat, where the ascetic life was cultivated in exemplary fashion. If the influence of Peter, *hegoumenos* of the Atroa monastery (773–837), remained provincial in scope, that of Ioannikios, who was born under Constantine V to an iconoclast family and died in 846, set a standard for the empire as a whole. The contemporary *Lives* of these holy men shed light at the same time on the attitudes of popular piety. The holy men of this generation figured less prominently as healers than their fifth- and sixth-century predecessors, and more frequently as seers. The knowledge of the future and of destiny that men such as Leo the Mathematician sought from astrological calculations was taken by their devotees as a function of their saintliness. What is more, their penetrating vision did not merely travel over space and time: it could also probe the secrets of guilty hearts, wresting from them the confession which was the

Anchorites in their caves. In the sixteenth-century painting on the left (detail from the *Death of St Ephraim*, Vatican Museums), the monks' caves bear a strong resemblance to the peculiar rock formations in the Cappadocian region of Turkey, seen in the view of Goreme on the right, which the anchorites seem to have found particularly attractive.

prelude to penitence. The authority of the 'spiritual father', respected in all ranks of society, became in consequence an essential ingredient of monastic power. Moreover, we find the hagiographers placing a new emphasis at this time on the priestly status of their subjects. This was also the moment when features of the general veneration of images became set in their future, but already traditional, mould. Michael II's letter to Louis I vouches for the living reality ascribed to icons, for example by naming them as godparents. A later anecdote tells how Theodora and her daughters kept their icons in a closet in their private apartments, and how the emperor's jester whispered to Theophilos, 'Watch out, emperor, for the empress's dolls!'

Cultural revival, imperial revival

In defining this period it would therefore be wrong to distinguish between a learned and a popular culture. Let us rather say that the evidence points to a common culture, in which Christian belief and practices stand out, above which was an intellectual stratum of Antique learning, rediscovered by the ruling classes, including the imperial entourage and the Stoudios, although they naturally differed in the aspects of Antiquity they chose to emphasise. However, if the spirit of scientific enquiry seems to have been a characteristic of iconoclastic thinkers, when it was a case of composing, for example, a biographical narrative, the same rules of rhetoric were everywhere applied, and the language was everywhere equally remote from that of the author's everyday speech. Again, it would be wrong to make a distinction between a metropolitan and a provincial culture, at any rate in the sphere of learning: comparison of manuscript hands and illuminations indicates wide diffusion. On the other hand, at what can be called the communal level, a regional culture can be seen emerging: we shall come back to this when dealing with the Eastern frontier in the second half of the ninth century.

The prevailing culture of the years following 843 was thus already being formed during the second iconoclasm, perhaps even since the beginning of the century. The second restoration of images did even less than the first to change the direction in which the imperial image was evolving. Only the theoretical and historiographical work accomplished between the time of Basil I and his grandson Constantine VII went further. But the reign of Michael gathered the fruits of the cultural growth which preceded it. The imperial power continued its support for advanced studies, under the influence first of Theoktistos, who funded a chair in philosophy for Constantine-Cyril, future apostle of the Slavs, and then of Bardas. The latter set up around 855–6 the School in the Magnaura palace, where Leo the Philosopher supervised the teaching of geometry, astronomy and grammar. The same continuity was preserved in the symbolic position of the sovereign and of his power. The palace, with its protocol for the audience of ambassadors, or for the imperial banquet, was still the place where that power was manifested, the hippodrome, the procession, and the hunt still the forms in which it was displayed to the world outside. As early as 843, the patriarch Methodios was inspired by the adoration of images to compose the office for Orthodox Sunday (the first in Lent), celebrated in all the churches of the empire, in which the names of the sovereigns were acclaimed and those of heretics anathematised. In short, the imperial ideology shifted its position in 843, without abandoning its cosmic pretensions. The return to images signified the conclusive choice of the Incarnational interpretation of the supreme power, the return to earth of the 'Christ-emperor'. The tale of the miraculous pardon granted to Theophilos is a clear indication that 843 occasioned no break in the line of descent.

The radical wing of monasticism, equally intent on proving its continuity, took the opposite line in as much as it stressed the clear break between the iconoclastic regime and the restored orthodoxy, with a jubilation well conveyed by the miniatures from a group of psalters dating from the second half of the ninth century. The conflict of authorities, between the conception of a Church auxiliary to the sovereign and the claims of the Stoudites, was therefore restated in precisely the same terms as at the beginning of the century. Methodios, in spite of his monastic background, did not align himself with the Stoudios, where there was anger over the attitude of appeasement following the return to images. On his death in 847, the choice of Theodora fell on the monk Ignatios, the eunuch son of Michael I. This was a concession to the Stoudites, in the person moreover of a man of

323

The angel of St Sophia, or the glory of imagery rediscovered. After the destructions wrought by the iconoclasts, religious art, liberated at last, took off with a fervour and a delight in beauty which have perhaps never been equalled (detail of a mosaic in St Sophia, ninth century).

324

imperial parentage, who thus formed a link between the present regime and a preceding dynasty; but it also signalled the outbreak of yet another conflict, because in making her choice Theodora had bypassed the synod, provoking episcopal opposition to Ignatios in which Gregory Asbestas, bishop of Syracuse, played a vociferous role. In 858, Ignatios was sent into exile by Michael III and Bardas, because he had refused communion to Bardas, accused of incest with his daughter-in-law, and because he also refused to assist in the relegation of Theodora and her daughters to a convent. He was replaced by Photios, head at this time of the imperial chancery, nephew, it will be recalled, of Tarasios, and related to Theodora. Having received all the clerical orders in quick succession, Photios had himself consecrated by Gregory Asbestas, who had been deposed from his see by Ignatios, but who had appealed to Rome. Photios was therefore drawn into a war of mutual accusations of invalidity with Ignatios and his supporters, in which Pope Nicholas was appealed to as arbiter; the latter, who found an opportunity to revive the question of the papal patrimonies confiscated by the emperor Leo III, was simultaneously engaged in rivalry with the Byzantines over the Bulgars, as we shall shortly discover. A synod was held at Constantinople in September 867, under the presidency of Michael III, who added his signature to the decrees. There Photios obtained the assent of the three other Eastern patriarchs to the excommunication of the pope, condemned as a heretic because of the Roman doctrine of the procession of the Holy Spirit, which the Greeks held to be 'from the Father through the Son', and the Latins 'from both the Father and the Son'. This divergence, already made explicit in the sixth century, after 867 came to be regarded at Byzantium as a touchstone of orthodoxy, and figured in the schism of 1054. For good measure, Photios denounced the pope's intervention as unlawful. He ordered the conclusions of the synod to be circulated throughout the East. After this there was not only internal conflict, turning on two differing conceptions of the relations between the sovereign and the authority of the Church; there was also collusion between the emperor and the patriarch over external affairs, adumbrated, it will be recalled, in the time of Herakleios, and from now on widening in scope as new fields opened up to imperial penetration, in particular among the Slavs.

Byzantium resumes the offensive

In this powerfully unfolding sovereignty and its culture, what was to be the fate of the minorities and the marcher lands of the empire? The question is inseparable from that of Byzantium's external relations. A preliminary glance enables us to form an overall picture of the territories in question, their peoples, their changing and unchanging features, and also the warfare of which they formed the object. But it would be wrong to write this chapter solely in terms of the empire's territorial integrity, as has too often been attempted in the past. Warfare remained more than ever a normal and permanent factor in public life, in the sovereign's ideology, in the conduct of international relations. It constituted, along with embassies and trade, the essence of international relations, and the source of their prestige and profit.

Three major theatres command our attention at the start of the ninth century, to some

325

extent overlapping. The first was in the west: it embraced the Aegean and the central Mediterranean, together with their islands, Calabria, the Adriatic and the Dalmatian coast, and the Venetian lagoon, all of which were still officially Byzantine. We come next to the Balkan provinces, with their still partially distinct Slav enclaves, and populations transferred there by government fiat; the Straits, and the western shore of the Black Sea, commanding the way to Constantinople; facing Byzantium, the Bulgar State; and on the northern shore, where Byzantium had the outpost of Cherson, raised to a theme in 833, the zone dominated by the Khazar State, between the Don and the Volga. Lastly, in the east, we find the region which had been vulnerable to attack since the seventh century, the great semi-circle flanked at one end by the Taurus and at the other by the Caucasus, where the empire's borders adjoined the old Christian countries of Armenia and Iberia. Furthermore, at Melitene, Manzikert and Arzen, as at Tiflis, border emirs had been in occupation since the eighth century. They were apt to ignore, or even rebel against, Baghdad, but were on friendly terms with the local Armenian princes and sometimes married their daughters.

Reanimation of trade-routes and coinage

Strategic routes and strong points had a new part to play in long-distance trade, whose expansion, beginning in the ninth century, reflected the expansion of court and urban consumption, and of a mercantile sector with the necessary knowledge of languages, routes and products. The Jews, for whom it was easy to maintain communication in writing with an extensive network of co-religionists, tended to excel in such knowledge, and the same considerations probably still applied to the Karaites (from Hebrew *qara*, to read), dissident Jews who kept to the letter of the Scriptures, turning their back on rabbinical exegesis and its conclusions. At this date they were already to be found in the Crimea. From the middle of the eighth century the Jews occupied a privileged position in Khazaria, in the same region. Muslim merchants were equally in evidence. Two main trading currents can be detected: the first, with a long tradition behind it, brought spices and silk from India and China; the second brought imports of leather, furs, timber, honey and slaves from the Ukraine. The Bulgar State occupied a commanding position on the lower Danube route, which led from the Slav countries. The Khazar State profited from the more easterly route, with outlets at Cherson and Trebizond. But the Khazar ascendancy was vulnerable and declined in favour of the Russians, when they began to navigate the Volga and reached the Caspian at the end of the ninth century.

In the extensive movement of products and coins spreading across the three areas of consumption – the Muslim East, the West, and Byzantium – the trading position of the latter was probably not as disadvantageous as has sometimes been claimed. As redistribution centres, Constantinople and Thessalonica were still unrivalled, and commercial activity there remained in Byzantine hands. Athens and Corinth showed signs of revival early in the ninth century. Lastly, there is the evidence of coinage.

As we already know, from the time of Constantine the monetary system of Byzantium

Coin with effigy of Leo III (Paris, Bibliothèque nationale, Cabinet des médailles).

was based on the gold *solidus*, 72 coins being struck to the pound of about 327g, to the very high standard of 24 carats (*keratia*). The *solidus*, the medium of public payments – taxes, salaries, revenues assigned to individuals or religious establishments, tributes financed by the empire – also reigned supreme on the international markets. At the same time, a bronze coinage, in which copper predominated, was available for everyday transactions: the tendency of the authorities was to make it heavier, and therefore more effective, while its everyday use for smaller and smaller payments drew it downward, continually making it lighter. Between the two, silver coinage made only a fleeting appearance as an occasional expedient. Now, from the eighth century, the Byzantine system based on gold found itself between a Western coinage consisting at this date solely of silver, sign of an inferior financial and monetary capacity, and an Islamic East closer to bimetallism, since the caliphate issued a gold *dinar* inspired by Byzantium and a silver *dirham* inherited from the Persian coinage, which in its turn inspired Byzantine issues. These coins would be found meeting and competing along the new highways of the Scandinavian and Slav world, carried there by mercenaries and brought back by merchants.

Ceremonial silver coins were struck from the reign of Leo III, and began to be adopted for commercial use. Theophilos resumed regular minting of the silver coin (*miliaresion*), temporarily increasing its weight. Michael II's lead in striking a heavier bronze coin (*follis*) was followed by Theophilos, and this coinage remained stable over the next two centuries. These two developments, occurring at a time when the gold coinage remained immobile, point clearly to an increase in local exchanges and long-distance trade. The map of stray coin finds, pieces lost by their users, gives a rough idea of the direction of exchanges, and of their relative importance. Coins were still scarce in Bulgaria in the ninth century, while in Moldavia, as in Transylvania, coins turned up along the drovers' routes, which presumably took livestock to the markets. The incidence of bronze coins along the Black Sea coast is perhaps to be connected with the market for basic provisions in the capital. Only the gold coinage of Theophilos is found in the western Balkans, above all in the interior. Most striking of all is the proliferation of coins along the Aegean coastline and in central Greece, where Arab coinage started to penetrate – copper coins issued by the Arab emirs of Crete, silver *dirhams* reissued as *miliaresia* at Corinth, and more particularly at Athens. It is essential to take note of such things if we are to form a convincing picture of a world in which war and piracy on the one hand, and commercial exchanges on the other, so often consigned to separate chapters in the history books, in fact constituted the warp and woof of a single reality.

Breaking the encirclement in the west and north . . .

In the Mediterranean, the first half of the ninth century was dominated on one side by the victorious Muslim fleet, on the other by the seaward and landward extension of Byzantium's defence system. In 805, Arab ships lent support to a general revolt of the Slavs in the Patras region. Nikephoros I suppressed it and used the opportunity to transfer to the area inhabitants of Asia Minor. A *strategos* of Kephallenia is mentioned for the first time in 809. Meanwhile the Arabs stepped up their attacks on the Aegean islands, descending in 806 on Cyprus, in 807 on Rhodes. The naval theme of the Aegean is mentioned for the first time in 843. In the Adriatic, the Byzantine positions came under threat from Slav pirates operating on the Dalmatian coast, the aggressiveness of the Carolingians, and the expansion of the Venetians. In the event, a treaty concluded in 813 or 814 preserved Byzantine sovereignty while leaving Venice with *de facto* independence; this independence was soon to be substantiated by appropriation of the relics of St Mark, stolen from Alexandria by Venetian merchants in 828, which permitted Venice to claim the apostolic status essential to a town in the game of political precedences as it was played at this period. In 836, we have the first mention of a *strategos* of Thessalonica, possibly in the post since 824, and in 842–3 of a *strategos* of Dyrrachium (Durazzo).

In 825 some Cordoban Arabs, expelled from Alexandria where they had taken refuge, captured Crete: in so doing they deprived Byzantium of a prime strategic and commercial position, which guaranteed them mastery of the sea-routes in the central Mediterranean. A Byzantine expedition in 828–9 met with no success, and the fate of others was the same. The Arabs founded Candia, and remained in control of Crete until the tenth century. In 827, Aghlabid forces from Africa landed in Sicily, taking advantage of a local revolt against Byzantine authority: Sicily, made into a theme around 700, preserved because of its peripheral position a certain degree of autonomy. Its Church, however, was Greek, at any rate since its reannexation to the ecumenical patriarchate by Leo III. The Arab forces laid siege to Palermo in 830 and captured it the following year. The conquest of the island as a whole was evidently protracted, since Syracuse succumbed only in 878 and Taormina in 902. From Sicily, the Arabs crossed to southern Italy, where Byzantium retained the duchy of Calabria, Otranto and – in still more theoretical fashion than with Venice – the duchy of Naples, of which Amalfi formed a dependency until about 839. The Arabs captured Taranto in 839–40, and in consequence posed a threat to Venetian maritime traffic. In 840 a Byzantine embassy made its way to Venice, and in the same year the Venetian fleet attacked Taranto, but to no avail. In 842 the Arabs took Bari. From their island bases they made periodic raids on the coasts of Greece, for example the Athos peninsula. Saints' *Lives* of the period are full of such descents. The disaster of a Saracen invasion thus forms the opening chapter in the *Life* of Theodora, the sainted recluse of Thessalonica, born in 812, who for this reason was forced as a child to leave her birthplace on the island of Aegina. The history of the Arab rule in Crete is singularly devoid of such incidents. It is in any case important not to make too much of the bond existing at this period between Byzantium and its Italian periphery. In Sicily, where the central government seemed remote, the latter's

Pliska, ruins of the Khan's palace. Founded in the seventh century in conjunction with the first Bulgar state, it remained the capital for two centuries. The decision to move the capital to Preslav in 893 was · dictated by the conversion of the Bulgars to Christianity and renunciation of the pagan ways associated with Pliska.

fiscal and military demands were no doubt conducive to a rupture. On the other hand, the history of Venice, Naples or Amalfi is typical of the sphere where *de facto* independence, although undeniable, was not achieved without formal allegiance to the empire, signalled by the titles Byzantium conferred on local rulers, and sometimes honoured by the latter in the form of concrete support – a duality hard for us to comprehend, and yet one which is inherent in the empire's very nature.

In the Balkans, the early years of the century were still dominated – and in no uncertain fashion, as we have seen – by the war between Byzantium and the Bulgar State. The khan Krum struck out in several directions, with varying success, since Nikephoros I had been able to capture the Bulgar capital, Pliska, shortly before the defeat in which he was to meet his death in 811. After threatening Constantinople in 813, Krum himself died in 814, and in 814 or 815 his son Omurtag concluded a thirty-year peace with Byzantium, during

329

which, as was also mentioned, he supported Michael II against the revolt of Thomas the Slav. The problem of the Slav enclaves on imperial territory had not yet been eliminated. Reference was made above to the revolt in the vicinity of Patras in 805. There was a recurrence in 841. On the Bulgar front, however, the peace lasted for several decades: the Slavicisation of the nation, the penetration of Christianity, and the greater maturity of the Bulgar political system called for a less warlike attitude, which began to take shape with the advent to power of khan Boris in 852. And although a new Turkic people of the steppes, the Hungarians (Magyars), reached the mouth of the Danube around 837, they had still to appear on the Byzantine horizon.

Further east, the Khazar domain prompts the same observation. The power of the Khazars was founded on their levies on neighbouring tribes and the users of the long distance trade-routes. Jewish penetration of the Khazar world dates from around 740, and the official choice of Judaism by the ruling group, evidently reflecting the desire to replace their ancestral Turkic polytheism with a form of religion more appropriate to the political maturation of the Khazar State, was an accomplished fact by the second half of the ninth century. This choice, analogous to the one we shall see facing the Slav or Slavicised States after 860, is noteworthy in that it enabled the Khazars to preserve their independence in relation to Christendom and Islam, their two neighbours in the political sphere, while offering for the same reason no guarantee of security. On the northern shore of the Black Sea, relations between the Khazars and Byzantium were peaceful. Around 833, the Khazars sent a request to Constantinople for Byzantine engineers, who built them their fortress at Sarkel on the Don. At much the same time Byzantium raised to the status of a theme its ancient bridgehead of Cherson, the maritime terminus of the long-distance trade-route coming from Kiev. And it was the 'Russians' (Greek *Rhos*) of the Kievan State who posed the new threat in this part of the world, both to the Khazars, whom they eventually replaced in the tenth century, and to Byzantium, beneath whose walls their ships appeared for the first time in 860. But in all these events war played only a secondary part, and we shall come across it again when dealing with the desire of the young nations for integration into the prevailing power system, and the way in which it was met by Byzantium under the form of Christian mission.

. . . and in the east and the south

To the east of Byzantium, the strategic frontier conformed in theory with the line traced out at the beginning of the century by the campaigns of Harun al-Rashid (died 809), following the repudiation by Nikephoros I of the tribute agreed by Irene. The Arab campaigns in Asia Minor during his reign, reaching Ankara (Ancyra) in 806, formed a counterpart to the naval expeditions of the same period. The lull lasting from 814 to 829 suffered little disturbance from Ma'mun's support for the rebellion of Thomas the Slav. The war started up again with Theophilos. But the issues at stake cannot be understood without reference back to the distinctive position of the region in the seventh and eighth centuries, and more specifically to the crisis of the early ninth century, in which the part played in the imperial succession by troops of the Anatolic theme, reacting against Irene's palace government, and in the bid of Thomas the Slav for the throne, must be accounted relevant factors. We mentioned at the time that the notion of a natural predisposition of the east towards iconoclasm was largely without foundation. What cannot be ignored, however, is the religious distance separating the Greek Church of the capital, even under the iconoclasts, from the Christianity of the regions, which owed its vitality to the Syriac-speaking Jacobite clergy. Since the sixth century the Jacobite patriarch of Antioch had in fact been resident in one or other of the fortified monasteries in the neighbourhood of Harran (the Carrhae of Antiquity), Barsauma in particular, on Islamic territory. The first half of the ninth century was a golden age in Syriac literature, in which translations from the Greek, homilies, hagiography and canon law are found alongside an independent historiography, which demonstrates the collective awareness of an individuality of which the Christological difference with Constantinople is merely the sign.

The Caucasian spur formed another element in this straggling frontier. In the reigns of Nikephoros I and Michael I, as indeed already in the eighth century, Byzantium paid as much attention as did the caliphate to the feudal conflicts between the great Armenian families, the Bagratuni of the north-west, one branch of which was dominant in Iberia, and the Ardzruni, whose domination of Vaspurakan extended before long to the whole of the south-east. The two powers kept up their rivalry by bestowing titles, tantamount to political endorsement, but leaving no opening for the establishment in that strategically vital area of a unified State, which could have been a danger or at any rate an embarrassment. In 806 Ashot Bagratuni, installed at Bagaran, received from the Arabs the title prince of Armenia. He married one of his daughters to an Ardzruni, the other to the emir of Arzen. The territory was carved up again between his sons, and they had to fight the emirs of Tiflis. In 813, his Iberian cousin and namesake received the same title. The clan occupied from then on a commanding position in the Caucasus.

Melitene, Tarsus and Arzen were the preserves of frontier emirs, leading members of that border society, stretching from the Taurus to Armenia, which germinated in the ninth century, ripened in the tenth, and until the arrival in force of the Turks in the eleventh century was as typical of one aspect of Byzantium as Constantinople itself, or the region around Thessalonica. It was a world whose inherent nature was as unchanging as its political and military loyalties were fluctuating. Warriors of the empire from time to time crossed to the opposite camp there, as did the *strategos* Manuel, of Armenian descent, who in the reign of Michael II took refuge on the Muslim side after being falsely accused. He returned later to take service with Theophilos, rising to the positions of *domestikos* of the *scholai* (commander of the place guard) and minister of the public courier service, and became linked with the sovereign by ties of baptism and marriage. The emirs made their presence felt all over the region: for example, between 812 and 825 we find them launching attacks on neighbouring Armenia, and bringing away inhabitants as captives, as did Theophilos following his campaign of conquest in 837. Their local fame earned the emirs a place among the heroes of the epic poems, preserved over the centuries and down into our own day in Greek popular poetry, but which are known to have originated in this

331

region during the ninth century, perhaps in the time of Theophilos. They are songs of love and war, with the 'Saracens' admittedly cast as the enemies, but in which the 'emir', enamoured of a Christian lady, is sometimes also shown to be on the Byzantine side – a figure of infinite ambiguity, who a few generations later will crop up in the epic of *Digenis Akritas*, the warrior of 'double race'.

Lastly, this same region, at this same time, witnessed the rise of the Paulicians, a sect of Christians who made a radical distinction between their God and the created world reminiscent of the gnostic teaching of Marcion (second century). Their rejection of images, and in consequence of the status of Mary and the saints, made them resemble the iconoclasts, although they regarded even the symbolic use of the cross as unacceptable. On the other hand, they differed from the iconoclasts in their total rejection of the sacraments and the episcopal hierarchy, which they justified as a return to apostolic Christianity. They bowed to the authority of inspired 'masters', who were sometimes in conflict, and of which the dual line brought to light by an investigation under Basil I can be traced back to the late seventh century: two were executed in 682 and 688. Their denial of hierarchy in any form made them equally liable to persecution under iconoclast rulers: one of their masters was summoned and interrogated by Leo III. Only under Irene does it seem that the sect may have served as a refuge for iconoclasts: her reign certainly marked its high-point. Later, the patriarch Nikephoros persuaded Michael I to put the Paulicians to death, while Theodore the Stoudite opposed such rigorous treatment: in adopting these attitudes, the two men were remaining true to their respective order of values, for the patriarch demonstrated by his severity in this case – as much as by his flexibility over Constantine VI's remarriage – the priority he conceded to the political order of the empire, even in religious matters.

But the Paulicians also had a provincial connection. It is quite possible that the founder was an Armenian. At any rate, the Armenian church is known to have suppressed, and perhaps expelled, some heretics in the eighth century, and these were probably Paulicians. In the course of the eighth century, the wanderings of the masters of the sect took them back and forth along the frontier with Islam, to the region of the upper Euphrates and Melitene, and in one case to Antioch in Pisidia. Under Leo V, the master Sergios and his disciples took refuge with the emir of Melitene. Next, in the propitiously fluid situation prevailing on the borders, the sect found itself a home: around 830 it took possession of the town of Argaoun, under the aegis of the emir of Tarsus. In consequence, the Paulicians took on the character of frontier warriors, enemies of Byzantium. In 843 or 844 a small Paulician State came into being, under the chieftaincy of Karbeas, probably a fugitive from Byzantium, with its capital at Tefrik, founded some time before 856. This had the effect of making the Paulicians auxiliary troops of the emir of Melitene. On his death in 863, Karbeas was replaced by his nephew and son-in-law Chrysocheir ('Golden-Hand'). The names of Karbeas and Chrysocheir recur in *Digenis Akritas*, the heroic epic of the eastern frontier, although recollections of them are vague. On the Byzantine side, the defence of the frontier in the first half of the ninth century hinged on the *kleisourai* (mountain passes), military commands which later became the themes of Charsianon, Seleucea and Cappadocia.

The war resumed in 830 with an offensive by caliph Maʾmun, and was waged in Anatolia. Annual campaigns resulted in alternating successes, of which the highlight was the capture of Amorion by the Arabs in 838: this emotive event, involving the cradle of the reigning dynasty, became quickly surrounded with legendary tales concerning the traitors who surrendered the town, and the 42 martyrs who stood firm in their Christian profession. The deaths of Theophilos and Maʾmun, in 842, were not marked by a break in hostilities, but Michael III's coming of age gave the signal for a more aggressive policy. The Arab offensive of 860, supported by the Paulicians under Karbeas, and the drive by the emir of Melitene as far as Amissos in 863 were followed that same year by two great victories, for one of which the emperor's uncle, Petronas, was responsible.

The Greeks among the Slavs

The Byzantine embassies to Aachen and Baghdad, Venice and Cordoba in 839–41, and the arrival of foreign envoys at Constantinople, are not to be regarded solely as alternatives to military campaigns. They represent steps towards contact between the civilisations, in particular between Constantinople and Baghdad, for which war frequently provided the opportunity, as did Byzantium's unfeigned admiration of the caliphs' material achievements. The borrowings by Theophilos from the art of the Umayyad palaces, themselves the heirs, it is true, to the art of the Hellenistic East, provide a classic example. Even the bargaining over prisoners became a more protracted affair, offering occasion for compensatory gestures and the exchange of gifts. One Arab ambassador recalled that he had arrived, in 861, with 'close on one thousand pouches of musk, silken garments, a quantity of saffron and objects of an unusual and novel kind', items, that is to say, which took the form both of costly articles suitable to offer as gifts and of instructive curiosities. In return, the magnificence and formality of the imperial audiences, and the impressions of the capital formed by those who attended them, were the means of spreading far and wide the news of Byzantium's power and prestige. In the second half of the century, however, these international contacts, which it should be noted followed an age-old pattern, took a new turn with the Christian mission sought and welcomed by the States of the eastern Slav world.

Whatever their ethnic origin, because of their growing political maturity these States found themselves faced with the choice of a religious dimension suited to the development of sovereign power. It is doubtless the case that as a result of their manifold contacts, in particular the presence of prisoners of war, they had among them a growing number of Christians. But this was not the answer to the problem in the ninth century, any more than it had been in the now distant days when Justinian set about the evangelisation of the Caucasus: ever since Constantine, Christianisation had been a sign of *romanitas*, that is to say a necessary qualification for the admission of a barbarian State to the imperial world order in which – and this was perhaps the over-riding consideration – it found the sanction for its own political aspirations. If it is possible to sum up so decisive a development in one sentence, one might say that the ancestral Slav or Bulgar polytheistic religions could not

333

fail to reveal their inadequacy once the figure of the ruler took more definite form, to the detriment of the aristocracy which he then tended to dominate, and also once the sovereign began to aspire to international recognition as of right, and not merely as the by-product of a treaty assenting to some enlargement of territory. The conversion of the Slav States was thus an event stemming at this period from political decision-making at the top; their effective Christianisation is another, and an appreciably longer, story. From the Byzantine standpoint, mission represented a satisfactory means of reducing the periphery to order: a traditional solution, as has just been pointed out, but one to which the cultural movement outlined above would lend an exceptionally high profile and degree of success. Lastly we should note that in the context of the vast and enticing new world opening up between the Elbe and the Danube, the idea of missionary incursion into Slav territory appealed not only to Byzantium but to the Carolingian empire and the pope. This was the starting-point of a conflict leading, in the last resort, to a demarcation into spheres of influence which traced out almost exactly the boundaries between the Greek and Latin Churches. Only the Khazars held aloof by opting, as we saw, for Judaism, despite the survival of 'Gothic' Christianity in the part of their territory extending from the Crimea to the Kuban and the Kerch, and the conversion of their neighbours, the Abasgs, to Christianity in the seventh century. The Khazars were equally unique in their form of political organisation. The missionary impetus first became explicit in 860. In that year, ambassadors arriving from Kiev after the Russian attack on the capital were alleged to have received baptism: such, at any rate, is the conclusion to be drawn from a sermon preached by Photios, patriarch at the time. But this was a formality with no immediate sequel. The real turning-point was reached with the missions of Constantine – known in religion as Cyril – and his brother Methodios.

Constantine and Methodios had been born at Thessalonica, Byzantium's gateway to the Slav world, to an army officer father and perhaps to a Slav mother. Constantine had studied at Constantinople, where he was subsequently invited by Theoktistos to teach philosophy. His knowledge of Slavonic, a language differing little at this period from one country to another, equipped him to solve the mission's essential problem, transference of the language to writing, which was a necessary preliminary to the diffusion of Christianity in its Byzantine form. We find him going first, still in 860, to the Khazars, where it is said he disputed in Hebrew with the Jewish teachers in the presence of the ruler. Whatever the truth about this initiative with no sequel, Constantine and Methodios were sent in 863 to the prince of Greater Moravia, Rastislav, in response to his request for a mission. They succeeded in producing the first version of a Slavonic alphabet, called Glagolitic (*cf.* Russian *glagol*, 'verb'), key to the cultural and therefore the political penetration of the empire. There is therefore room for argument over the place, Moravia or Bulgaria, which formed the setting for the translation of the oldest law code committed to writing, the *Law Concerning the Accused*, which was modelled on the *Ekloga* of Leo III and Constantine V, in other words on the code currently in force at Byzantium. And it was in 865 that the Bulgar ruler, Boris, was baptised. The question had been under consideration since the accession of the latter, in 852, but at that point he was veering in the direction of the Franks and a

Frankish alliance. A Byzantine show of military and naval strength reversed the position, and Boris received baptism, most probably in 865, with the emperor, who gave Boris his own name, Michael, standing as godfather. Boris thus became the emperor's 'spiritual son'. The kinship created by baptism gave new vigour to an older system, dating back in fact to the sixth century, of a hierarchical kinship between rulers, which developed most fully around Byzantium in the ninth and tenth centuries. Another factor relevant to the ruler's conversion was the juridical status of the Church it brought into being. Boris was clearly of the opinion that it should be autonomous, Byzantium that it should depend on the ecumenical patriarchate. In this impasse, in 866 Boris addressed to Pope Nicholas I the famous letter in which he asked questions of the latter about the position of the hierarchy and the rules to be followed in future, and the possibility of retaining certain traditional usages, marriage customs in particular. His requests did not meet with a satisfactory response. It should be added that his baptism had sparked off a revolt of the Bulgar aristocracy, in the ethnic sense of the word – the boyars, who were long to remain hostile both to Byzantium and to the Slav part of the population; this pattern, to be repeated at Kiev, underlines what has already been said about the political significance of royal conversions. But the sequel to the story belongs to the reign of Basil I, when, as the empire recovered its strength, the vital forces of the Christian east blossomed anew.

8

The renaissance in the East:
mid-ninth to mid-tenth centuries

With the seizure of power in 867 by Basil I, after the murder of Michael III, it makes sense to start a new chapter. Today of course we know that the change was to usher in a golden age of the empire, or rather that it would bring to completion the model that in history at large has become the stereotype of Byzantium and its legacy. In actuality, Basil (867–86), his son Leo VI (886–912), and his grandson Constantine VII (913–37) had to vindicate both the breach in continuity brought about by the inaugural murder, and the claim of their own dynasty to remain in possession of the throne. So well did they succeed that the dynasty survived the upheavals of the tenth century, to wit the minority of Constantine VII, which witnessed the reign of his father-in-law Romanos I Lakapenos (920–44), and later the minority of his grandsons, following the death of his son Romanos II in 963. They solved the problem, moreover, not merely as heirs to the previous imperial tradition, going back to Constantine, but as the direct beneficiaries of its ideological and cultural enrichment in the first half of the ninth century. This in fact is the key to the political significance of what has been called the Macedonian renaissance, the Classicising movement which set the seal on the cultural endeavours of preceding generations. In consequence, the texts and images which form our historical sources for these three reigns and that of Romanos Lakapenos are to a large extent the product of a conscious artistry, in which the emperors personally took a hand. This element, plain to see if not yet fully elucidated, is what must first strike the historian as he contemplates the period.

Restoration of the economic and social structures

But let us look first at the context of the political programme, the economic and social development over the century as a whole, in which the year 867 possesses no significance as a dividing-line. A salient and important factor is the revival of towns, which was evident from the time of Basil I and during the tenth century, even if it resulted in part from the expansion of long-distance trade, already noticeable at an earlier date, and which can otherwise be supposed to indicate that any demographic deficit consequential on the upheavals of the eighth century had been made good, or at any rate that the population had returned to a state of equilibrium.

Reawakening of the towns

The evidence on this question is still far from complete, since we lack excavations in sufficient quantity to do justice to the diversity of urban sites in the empire of the ninth and tenth centuries, although this is obviously a matter in which archaeology must have the last word. Furthermore, the overwhelming preoccupation since the nineteenth century with the Antique strata has resulted in irremediable damage to various urban sites, predominantly in Greece, and in particular at Athens. The following inferences are therefore of a partial and no doubt provisional character, although none the less suggestive. Corinth had declined so far in the eighth century that burials encroached on the former agora: the ninth century is marked by the reappearance of local pottery, coins, and official seals, which indicate that the town was again playing a role in the empire's administrative structure; in the tenth century, a church requiring considerable outlay was built, as well as a chapel. At Athens, in spite of the depredations, the discoveries include coins struck by the Arab emirs of Crete, a Muslim place of worship erected on the agora in the tenth century or early in the eleventh, and churches whose decoration – on local marble, and dating from somewhere between the tenth and twelfth centuries – makes use of kufic characters, which suggests the employment of Arab craftsmen. Sardis, too, came to life again in the ninth century, but was quite unlike its former self: medieval, or in any case no longer Antique in its appearance, it now consisted of a fortified refuge, with dwellings on the plain below. In the tenth century, the acropolis was reoccupied and the inhabited area advanced into the city's Antique territory, but only as isolated enclaves with agricultural plots in between. The rebirth of Ephesus dates from the same period, but the once bustling great city reappeared in the shape of a fortified provincial town, though its displacement to the vicinity of the acropolis may in part be explained by the silting up of the port. Attempts have also been made to deduce the level of urban activity from the finds of stray coins on a given site, on the assumption that the proportion of coins lost by individuals remains more or less constant, and that variation in their number from one stratum to another therefore corresponds to the variation in the number of coins in circulation. The method is admittedly not without its drawbacks: it is open to the objection, for example, that an emperor's coins remain in circulation for a long while, half a century at least, after his death. But it is none the less striking that Athens, Corinth, Antioch and Sardis all register the same blank on the chart, extending over the seventh, the eighth, and part of the ninth century, while the same four sites, admittedly to a varying degree, show signs of a recovery which begins by and large with Basil I.

Lastly, there is the function of the provincial towns as producers to be considered, which so far has been less easy to make out. Apart from what it can tell us about public buildings, churches, ramparts and other constructions, the picture presented by archaeological investigation reveals, as might be expected, an urban fabric dotted with plots under cultivation, implying a still incomplete division of labour, and modest urban production to meet the local demand for articles such as weights and pots, while the leather and textile products of the period have left no trace. Nevertheless, the results of the American

The ramparts of Corinth. In the face of the threat from the Slavs, Justininian restored the town's ancient walls, which were further reinforced in the tenth century. These Byzantine fortifications would correspond to the first and second of the three series of ramparts still visible.

excavation of the Byzantine levels at Corinth show that productivity was not insignificant when judged by the standards of the day.

There is also the written evidence, which supplements the findings of the archaeologists and helps in their interpretation. It testifies in the first place to the official functions which were being restored to the towns. The Antique jurisdiction of the latter had been lost with the organisation of the empire into themes, and a law of Leo VI abolished the last remnants of curial responsibility. But here or there, where a town functioned as the headquarters of the theme or the seat of a bishopric, where there was a naval dockyard or a customs-post for the collection of inland or coastal tolls, or where several of these combined, typical urban activities were maintained, although the extent to which these stemmed from local initiatives is admittedly hard to determine. The term *kastron*, which survives in numerous place-names ending in -kastro (Palaiokastro, for example), thus combines the meaning of 'strongpoint' and 'small provincial town', which is doubtless in itself highly significant. The most typical economic activity seems to have been commerce, which we have already seen expanding in the ninth century, but this is true only in favourable circumstances, such as those enjoyed by Cherson and Thessalonica, situated at the outlet of routes from the Slav world, or Trebizond, at the terminus of the Far Eastern route. The *panegyreis*, gatherings at once religious, commercial and sporting in character, had a very ancient ancestry, and were much appreciated by ordinary Christians, if not entirely by the Church. The feasts of St Demetrios at Thessalonica and of St John at Ephesus were traditional; by contrast, that of St Eugenios at Trebizond came into existence only under Basil I. The habit of celebrating these festivals persisted down the centuries, in some cases into our own times. Even if an attraction of this kind was perhaps insufficient in itself to confer real commercial importance on a town, it is often a reflection of it, while the ubiquity of these feast-days in all parts of the empire was one means of ensuring that the towns had a specific role. The same is true of the bureaux of overseas trade set up at this time to control the movement of travellers and goods, which were dependent in their turn on the marine department in the capital headed by the *drongarios*, supreme commander of the fleet, whose new importance underlines the naval strategy of Basil I and his successors. The seals of the 'chiefs and counts' (*archontes cometes*) of these local offices bear witness to their activity in places as far apart as Sinope and Cherson, Smyrna and Ephesus, Thessalonica, Thebes and Athens, Corinth and Patras, Palermo and Cagliari, and naturally in the Straits, where the port of Abydos had already been subject to strict customs regulation under Anastasius, in keeping with the volume of commercial traffic generated by the capital. The hagiographical literature, as well as yielding information about the main arteries of trade, describes the Arab attacks, which on the basis of archaeological investigation of the sites in question prove not to have interfered with the urban revival. The historical texts even leave the impression, becoming still stronger in the second half of the century, that the policy of reconquest acted as a stimulus on certain towns, while constituting a serious drain on grain production.

Byzantium's second spring

Constantinople is in a class apart; in particular, the information we have is of a different order. Archaeological investigation has not been possible, except on the site of the imperial palaces, officially cleared of habitations early in the present century but still only partially explored. To make up for this lack, there is an unparalleled mass of written evidence: the narratives of the hagiographers and historiographers; the orders of ceremony preserved in the *Book of Ceremonies* compiled by Constantine VII; the *Book of the Prefect*, the code for the regulation of industrial and commercial activity addressed by Leo VI to the official responsible for the capital, who is restored to his former importance by the *Epanogoge*, the law code of 879, which ranks him immediately below the emperor and the patriarch; the growing number of descriptions left by Arab travellers and ambassadors; the treaties concluded in 907 and 911 with Kievan Russia, no longer extant in Greek, but preserved in the oldest of the Russian chronicles, the eleventh-century *Chronicle of Times Past*; and lastly the corpus of traditional literature devoted to the miracles specific to Constantinople and their more or less legendary origins. All this does not alter the impression of an evolution which, if we make due allowance for the difference in scale, is comparable with that of the provincial town. Constantinople was protected, it will be remembered, by two sets of

Working in ivory and textile manufacture figured among the crafts regulated by the Palace. (Weaver: ms graecus 747, Vatican Library; ivory: ms 'Oppiano', Venice, Biblioteca Marciana.)

ramparts, those of Constantine and of Theodosios II. The area outside the Theodosian ramparts tended to become depopulated, while the space between the two walls was not inhabited in the ordinary sense until the twelfth century: for the moment it contained only monasteries and the great cisterns. Habitation of the inner area, by contrast, had intensified since the sixth century, through the addition of timber-built dwellings, rarely of more than two storeys, occupied by tenants. To reduce the overall density, however, there were still the streets, squares, parks and private houses, not to mention the central complex of the Great Palace. It has been estimated that even at the most flourishing periods, say on the eve of the plague of 541–4 or under the Comneni, the total population of the city never exceeded 400,000. The demographic decline of the eighth century can be presumed to have had an effect, since we hear that the population was not sufficiently numerous to maintain the walls, and that a number of cisterns fell out of use. On the other hand, there are indications from this same century of recovery and the resumption of activity, starting perhaps as early as 760: in the dry summer of 766, a team of workmen rebuilt an aqueduct which had been in ruins since the siege of 626. But reinstatement of the cisterns which had been filled in since the time of Herakleios began only with Basil I.

It is perhaps significant that it was Leo VI who promulgated the *Book of the Prefect*, the first attempt since Justinian's Novels at systematic regulation of the economic activity of the capital through the trade guilds, from the corporations of pork-butchers and candle-makers to the notaries and silk-merchants. The picture which emerges is of diversified urban consumption, and hence of lively demand. Even the palace had a productive function in the luxury sphere, bound up with its political function. The imperial workshops manufactured the fabrics of damasked silk and the carved ivory plaques and caskets which traditionally served as diplomatic gifts, and which in the tenth century transmitted the images of Byzantine power to the Ottonian court. The palace also employed its own teams of copyists and painters, who executed sumptuously-illustrated codices and made plain copies of the texts needed to stock up the imperial library. The work of the central administration formed another branch of activity specific to the capital: here, too, the palace occupied a position of paramount importance in the ninth and tenth centuries, by reason of the responsibilities for general oversight entrusted to its personnel, the dispensation of justice by the emperor's tribunal, which combined the functions of High Court and Court of Appeal, and the correspondence maintained *via* the chancery with the provinces. The patriarchate was similarly provided with a central bureaucracy. Lastly, the capital itself came under the jurisdiction of the city prefect, charged in particular with the maintenance of order – and he, too, had the backing of an administrative apparatus.

Constantinople was from now on a market for international trade, and perhaps outdistanced all others as a centre of redistribution. The two celebrated documents which summarise the treaties concluded with the Russians, in 907 and 911, bear witness to the significant blurring of the distinction between diplomacy and trade, and to the principle of assigning specified places of residence to foreigners, in this instance the quarter around the church of St Mamas. The Amalfitans were the first merchants from the West to settle in the capital: the presence of their colony is mentioned in 944. They succeeded in exporting to Italy articles that were normally forbidden, for example purple silk. We hear in the late tenth century of a mosque, but Muslims had been finding their way to Constantinople from a much earlier date. The Jews, who had always constituted a well-defined group, undoubtedly found their numbers augmented at this period by Jewish merchants coming from overseas.

The urban tradition of Constantinople, unbroken since the fourth century, retained in the first half of the tenth century many of its Antique features, such as the districts and the hippodrome, representational setting for encounters between the emperor and his people. And yet wherever we look the capital gives the impression of being another city, from the Stoudios monastery to the Blachernae church, favourite sanctuary for prayers addressed to the Virgin; from the palace to the mansions of the nobility, swarming with kinsmen, friends, boon companions, and exposed, like the palace itself, to the gaze of the holy man who sees things from afar and can predict the future; from the craftsmen's workshops to the markets of foreign merchants. No longer troubled by the disturbances of the sixth century, Constantinople had yet to experience those of the eleventh, expressive of a later stage in its development. The Constantinople of this time had lost nothing of its uniqueness in the consciousness of the empire's inhabitants, or on the horizon of the medieval world as a whole. Between the capital and the provinces there was a distinction as significant as that between town and country, and it is to the latter that we now turn.

The enduring village

Rural history has two aspects, both of which need to be kept in view without allowing them to become confused: on the one hand there is the life and labour of the peasants, their habitat, agrarian techniques and subsidiary forms of production; on the other, the levy on that production, and the relationship between the peasants and the masters of the land, wherever the latter are distinct; this is turn raises the question of peasant status, and in particular the exact nature of their dependence. Peasants of the early Byzantine epoch were depicted as living in villages, usually nuclear and with a communal form of organisation that was doubtless of considerable antiquity, certainly older than the appearance of the Slavs, who would in any case have found the eastern arrangements incomprehensible: villages forming a part of estates or made up of peasant proprietors, or even partly the one and partly the other, unless it was the case that the head of a peasant household was registered as dependent in respect of one holding and as owner in respect of another. Documents with a bearing on rural history which become available after 867 make it worthwhile to reopen the file. First there are the earliest charters in the archives of Mt Athos, the oldest of which go back to the reign of Basil I; together with the properties concerned, they passed in 963 into the custody of the Lavra monastery, where they have remained ever since. Next, we have a series of laws (Novels) from the tenth century which deal with disputes between peasants, the fisc and the masters of the land; the dating and reconstruction of these laws in the original text is often difficult, because of the multiplicity of copies surviving in compilations made for the use of lawyers; but to compensate, some of the copies contain marginal glosses which show how the law was applied. Also from the tenth century is an isolated *Treatise* on fiscal procedure, intended to simplify the work of peripatetic officials, which is known from a single manuscript in the Marcian Library at Venice.

The author of this guide makes it clear that the village was normally compact, but that isolated appendages might exist as the result of disagreements between neighbours, or of other circumstances such as over-population and the splitting up of a household with too many members. The village community, cemented by ties of neighbourhood and often reinforced by those of kinship, governed itself through the council composed of the heads of the peasant households. Even a great landowner could form part of the village community if he possessed one or more parcels of land on its territory. Furthermore, the Byzantine estate seems at this period to have consisted in the main of a collection of rents and prescriptive rights, for example to the acorn crop or to pasturage on common land, but to the exclusion of forced agricultural labour. Compulsory public service, to which there is reference in charters of immunity, remained obligatory and was essential for the upkeep of roads and bridges. Direct cultivation by the landowner, where it was practised, relied on the services of domiciled slaves and wage-labourers. To give a completely accurate picture, however, it would be necessary to distinguish between regions, and hence between products.

On the other hand, from the beginning of the Byzantine era the rural areas had also borne the brunt of taxation. The independent village commune, or as the case might be the private or monastic estate, constituted a fiscal unit. The independent peasant paid his tax under the aegis of the former, the dependent peasant of the latter. Peasant dependence was thus defined at this period by the mode of payment, not by personal status, although the

Scenes of rural life in the ninth and tenth centuries: sheep-shearing and ploughing. The latter was used as the yardstick of a peasant's income and so of his tax liability (ms grec 533, Paris, Bibliothèque nationale).

obligation to pay rent and taxes of course still implied, as always, an attachment to the soil. The continuation of the State at Byzantium was in fact incompatible with a contraction of civil responsibility within the ranks of free men, that is to say non-slaves. Russian historians and their Soviet successors could thus rightly maintain that the domanial levy and the fiscal levy of this period were identical in nature. This formulation is a fair summary of social relationships in the Byzantine countryside at the time and of the position of the State within these relationships. The latter in fact behaved like a superior landowner, chasing after tax-payers who took refuge on private estates (which was nothing new), holding the village responsible for plots abandoned by one of its inhabitants, and disposing in full ownership of lands left vacant for 30 years (*klasmata*), in order to transfer them by sale, lease or gift. This structural confusion also harboured the germ of the confusion between public and imperial property which was to become so flagrant in the time of the Komneni, when the evolution of Byzantine society entered its terminal phase. In a word, any variations there might be in the peasant's condition at this period were the result of local circumstances. As in the past, when an assessment was needed for public purposes,

343

the material extent of peasant resources was measured in terms of the means of production, in which ploughing capacity was the major consideration. From the eleventh century, fiscal terminology would itself distinguish between owners of 'a pair of oxen', 'a single ox', and 'none', all of whom were nevertheless entered on the rolls. At a still lower level there was the 'free' peasant who had no claim to independent status, who indeed had no status and did not figure in the scheme of rural taxation, but drifted from place to place. Some documents of the tenth century authorise his inscription on the roll of a monastic estate, for the joint benefit of the fisc and of the landowner, willing as always to enlarge his labour force. Only slaves came lower; they formed the labour-force both in peasant households and on the estates, along with the seasonally-employed wage-labourers.

The principle by which peasants were classed for fiscal purposes will not seem surprising if it is recalled that the countryside functioned above all as a supplier of grain, a commodity vital to the existence of towns and armies. The masters of the land like the peasants themselves had access to the market – a necessary condition for the latter, since most of their taxes and dues were payable in coin. Markets were already held on estates, and seem indeed to have been a privilege greatly coveted by large landowners. For the provisioning of Constantinople, the first call was doubtless on the estates in the hinterland of the capital, in Bithynia, and in Thrace: a land-route ran by way of Thessalonica, while the port of Rodosto received grain transported by sea. Further to the east, a route passing through Trebizond exported to Cherson the grain grown on the shores of the Black Sea. Conversely, the importation of Bulgar corn, through the ports of Mesembria and Anchialos, is not to be ruled out. But it is appropriate to recall here the frequency with which populations from other areas were transplanted to Thrace, a practice which continued: as well as adding to the defence of the frontier, it must have made a useful contribution to the labour-force, that most important of variables in any economy where techniques of production remained unchanged.

The accumulation of wealth

We pointed out that in the exercise of its right to the fiscal levy, the State behaved as though it were a superior landowner. In consequence, two major variables impinged on the rural social order: the actual extent of properties, and the distribution of the levy on the product of the soil between the State and the landowners. The latter can thus be categorised in accordance with the old principle of immunity, which exempted the beneficiary from extraordinary taxes, in practice the heaviest, in compensation for undertaking a particular task deemed to be in the public interest. All monastic properties belonged to this category, whether the foundations in question were independent, owned by other monasteries, or owned by individuals, emperors included, who might well be their founders. The period saw monachism taking off in new centres. The second half of the ninth century was marked by an event of capital significance for Byzantium's cultural development: the beginnings of monastic settlement on Mt Athos, vouched for by the discursive *Life* of Euthymios the Younger (823/4–98) and the earliest official documents. The site was well-protected by its isolation at the extremity of a peninsula, and at the same time possessed easy access to land- and sea-routes. The Slav population of Chalcidice had perhaps already discovered the advantages of the peninsula as a local 'wilderness' in the late eighth century. An obscure hermit, Peter, is the subject of a canon (liturgical poem) from the reign of Theophilos. But the real impetus appears to have come from Euthymios the Younger, who, in quest of greater solitude, moved from Olympos in Bithynia to Athos in about 859. He was the founder, in 871, of the Peristerai monastery, not on the mountain but in Chalcidice, while his companion, John Kolobos, founded the Kolobou monastery at Siderokausia, later advancing its site to Hierissos on the very edge of the peninsula. A judgement handed down by Basil I, dated 883, banned the peninsula to officials seeking to collect dues, and to local inhabitants seeking to exercise their customary grazing rights; but the first intimation of a boundary between Hierissos and Athos comes only in 942, just at the time (940–1) when Athos received its first regular income, deducted by Romanos I from the revenues of a monastery in his ownership. A charter of 908 had made Athos independent of Kolobou, mentioning for the first time, in connection with the appeal by the Athonite monks, a *protos* (Greek word for 'first') at the head of the collective, who was sent to plead their cause in Constantinople. A charter of 958 again refers to the *protos*, and to the holding of three annual assemblies – the form of organisation which was to become traditional. All the contemporary forms of Greek monachism, solitary, semi-solitary and coenobitic, were represented on the mountain. The foundation of the Xeropotamou monastery dates back to a time before 956, but that of the large communities belongs to the period after 963.

When it comes to justifying the immunities granted by the emperor to monastic foundations, and the gifts of land or revenues they received, the accent now falls on the role of monks as intercessors, one aspect of which was the function of 'spiritual father' accorded them by all ranks of society. Their duty of giving charitable assistance was much less in demand than in the Eastern world of the fourth to sixth centuries, or again in the capital during the twelfth century. The shift of emphasis was no doubt connected with the thinning-out of the population, more especially in the towns remaining part of the empire after the seventh century. Conversely, the growth in the estates of the Athonite monasteries from the tenth century onwards can only be explained by an increase in the regional population due to the Slavs. A well-known collection of documents relating to the monastery of Iberes (Iviron) may be cited as an example of this process in the region around Thessalonica in the tenth century, and there are documents in plenty from the same and the succeeding centuries to provide confirmation, by reason of the Slav names borne by certain peasants, and sometimes by place-names.

The military holdings, the source of support for the armed forces in the themes, formed another officially exempted category. Ample testimony to the system, which had clearly already been in existence for at least two generations, is provided by the *Life* of Euthymios the Younger. He, and still more obviously another hero of Byzantine hagiography, Luke the Stylite in the tenth century, appear to be placed at a comfortable level on the landowning scale, scions of a 'house' hereditarily endowed with land in return for the military service furnished by one of its members. Furthermore, such an inheritance was partible among several owners. And the personal service was commutable to money, in accordance with time-honoured practice. A law of Constantine VII brought the social standing of this fiscal class around the middle of the tenth century more clearly into focus. The legislator forbade alienations which would reduce the total value of such a patrimony to less than four pounds in the case of the thematic armies and navies, and to less than two pounds in the case of sailors of the imperial fleet. Comparison with the all too meagre figures furnished by archival documents of the ninth and tenth centuries suggests that the minimal value of four pounds was already far from the bottom line on the patrimonial, and hence the social, scale. At this time the system must certainly have been in its heyday. Yet at no time had it been the sole means of financing wars, still less the sole source of recruitment. It will be remembered that the independent villages and the estates were required to furnish recruits as part of their fiscal obligation. Above all there was a long-established tradition of recruiting frontier tribesmen and foreigners as mercenaries, and from the beginning of the tenth century this practice increased, being adopted even for theme armies, as well as for the navy and the imperial regiments (*tagmata*), where Russians make an early appearance. Lastly, there was the much more complex question of the social standing of the great war leaders, corresponding to their prime political importance, to which we shall return.

The 'powerful' and the 'poor'

The landowners of whom we perhaps know least, when it comes down to it, are the lay proprietors who lacked statutory claims to immunity, since we are still grievously short of archival evidence for this period, and largely dependent in consequence on the legal and narrative texts. The properties in question ranged from those belonging to the emperor, scarcely distinguishable from those of the State, to very modest properties inscribed on the fiscal roll of a town or village, with an intermediate group of sizeable estates, such as those owned by the Maleinoi family in the neighbourhood of Charsianon; nor should we overlook the feudal lordships of the Armenian frontier, which were raised in the tenth century to military commands. In general it seems safe to say that the home of the military and political aristocracy whose rise to power characterised the tenth century, from Leo VI to Basil II, is to be found in the central and eastern parts of Asia Minor, which is where they had their estates, in so far as they possessed them.

The social histories of the peasants and the masters of the land were thus jointly governed by their relations with the State. The grants of immunity conserved in the monastic archives we have at our disposal contain exemptions from precisely specified taxes, in respect of named dependants. In this way the State relinquished a part of its fiscal income. More significant, however, and also the source of more conflict, was the share which it lost merely as the result of current practices. The officials, who obtained their office by purchase and were paid on the spot by tax-payers or litigants, had always inflated the legal levy as much as possible for their own profit, although it is true that they also bore the responsibility for any deficit. At the same time, the aim of the great landowners was to increase the extent of dependence, and to reduce their own fiscal contribution. The Novels

A great landowner, the widow Danielis, carried by her slaves on a tour of inspection. She belonged to a class of magnates which formed in the ninth century, partly at the expense of independent peasants. (*Chronicle of Skylitzes*, thirteenth century, Madrid, Biblioteca Nacional.)

of the tenth century describe certain traditional practices which they then condemn: tampering with the boundaries of an estate as recorded in the fiscal register; entry into the village community through fictitious sales or gifts, in a manner comparable with the precarial arrangements in the West, or through 'adoption' by a peasant member of the community.

Usurping landowners are characterised in contemporary sources as 'men of power', meaning that they possessed a share in the public power, and with it the capacity to coerce or protect other men. The designation could equally apply to members of the episcopal and monastic hierarchy, and for that matter to a peasant who bettered his position. The levy on the product of the soil had thus become an object of rivalry between the State and the 'powerful', the motives of the latter, one strongly suspects, being dictated as much by considerations of political and social prestige as of profit in the strict sense. The tussle was chiefly over landowners lacking in 'power', one effect of which was to place the smaller military properties in jeopardy: hence the law's insistence on their inalienability. But the annexations of the great landowners were made at the expense above all of peasant freeholders, who were singled out by the law-makers, significantly enough, as the 'poor', using the term in its social rather than its economic sense. We thus find at Byzantium the same *potens/pauper* coupling as in the Carolingian West. Using the methods already described, the 'powerful' penetrated the independent villages, which they ended up taking over. Hence the efforts of the legislators in the first half of the tenth century to reassert the right of pre-emption traditionally accorded to neighbours, kinsmen and associates, in short to those who shared a collective fiscal responsibility, which Leo VI had undermined.

In 927–8, a famine following an exceptionally severe winter spelled ruin to many of the

347

'poor': a Novel of 934 sought to revoke the wholesale alienations which had then ensued, and its dispositions had to be reiterated in a Novel of 947. This tug of war between the central departments and local forces, conducted on either side through the medium of the public power, was nothing new: we saw it taking place in the sixth century, and even earlier. What had changed, however, was the complexion of both parties, and the very conception of public power. Is this a stage along the road to a feudal Byzantium? Put thus, the question does not really arise until after 960.

The 'Macedonians' take root

From Basil I onwards, the imperial image benefited from a wealth of theoretical adornment, laid on especially thick because of the dynasty's murderous origins, and also because of the general brilliance of the era ushered in by Theophilos: at the apex of the imperial social order, at the heart of the world as it was viewed from Byzantium, the sovereign called for glorification on an unprecedented scale, for which men of learning and culture would furnish the text, and iconography the illustration. Note should also be taken of the particular objects of imperial devotion: Christ, whose image regained its place above the sovereign in the Golden Chamber of the palace with the accession of Michael III; the Mother of the Lord, protectress of the capital since the siege of 626, it will be recalled, whose cult was promoted with an especial fervour in the ninth and tenth centuries, amongst others by certain sovereigns; St Michael, the warrior saint; St Elijah, whose veneration by Basil may be connected with the celestial and solar traits which appear in Byzantine representations of the prophet, inspired by Elijah's fiery chariot, and perhaps by his name (Greek *helios* = the sun).

Basil and Photios: a fresh start

Basil filled the imperial palace with his presence, ordering representations of himself, with his wife and children, to be depicted on the wall of the Golden Chamber, which was also adorned with scenes from his campaigns. Still within the palace complex, he built the Nea ('new church'), dedicating it in 881 to Christ, the Virgin, the archangels Michael and Gabriel, the prophet Elijah and St Nicholas. And he built another church dedicated to Elijah at the summer palace of Hieria, not far from Chalcedon. But before going further we need to examine his relations with the Church, more precisely with the patriarch Photios.

When Basil seized power, the patriarchal see was occupied by Photios, and in a state of schism with Rome. Basil recalled Ignatios, with a view to winning support from Rome and the intransigents: as part of this plan, he informed Rome of the decrees issued by the council of 867. Rome reacted with vigour. The years 869–70 saw Photios condemned, Ignatios rehabilitated, and all ordinations since 858 suspended, except with the signed authorisation of papal supremacy. Photios, living in exile, nevertheless remained influential. By 873 he was back in the capital, where he almost certainly resumed his teaching in the circle centred on the Magnaura and supervised the education of Basil's sons, the future

Leo VI included. He made his peace with Ignatios. The latter, furthermore, was becoming estranged from Rome over the issue of Bulgar Christianity, on which he sided with Constantinople: the ecclesiastical problem and the political problem had thus become intertwined, but with the positions reversed. On the death of Ignatios, in 877, Photios regained the patriarchal see, which he occupied until 886. In 879, he held a council which was attended by papal legates and which pronounced his rehabilitation in return for concessions to Rome over Bulgaria. After the death of Basil Photios was deposed and replaced by Stephen, brother of the new emperor. He died in exile about 893.

Photios was a key figure in the ninth century, and one who was to dominate the future. We earlier saw him compiling the *Bibliotheca*, at a time when he was committed to a public career in the reign of Theophilos. He acquitted himself equally well as a theologian during his first exile (868–72), when he replied, in the *Amphilochia*, to difficult questions posed by Amphilochius, metropolitan of Cyzicus. Above all, he made heard the voice of the patriarch of the Byzantine empire, and of Christian *romanitas*. Some of his sermons in St Sophia accompanied events of far-reaching significance: the first attack by the Russians in 860, the introduction or reintroduction of an image of the Virgin, which provides factual confirmation of the place held by the latter in the imperial devotions of Basil I. He is supposed to have inspired the prologue to the *Epanagoge* ('Restoration of the Laws'), which is dated to the period after 879, henceforth the most comprehensive guide of the relations between the offices of emperor and patriarch: the former was responsible for the well-being of the empire, the defender of orthodox dogma, the interpreter and sustainer of the laws, leaving the latter to be sole judge in the interpretation of the canons and conciliar decrees. This definition, which well sums up the specifically Byzantine conception of the relations between political and military power on the one hand, and religious power on the other, became the model for the Christian States of the Slav world, notably, later, for the third and Muscovite Rome; equally, it stood in the line of descent from Constantine's premisses, in as much as both powers were still found united in the same capital, which as we have seen had a much more symbolic than geographical significance in the Roman Christian empire. The capital was, however, no more than the New Rome, the second of that name, while all the historic dignity and imperial eminence of the first devolved on the papacy. This fundamental distinction helps to explain the difference between the West and Byzantium in the evolution of the problem posed by the 'two powers'.

The Byzantine solution has no connection with the muddled and unfounded notion of 'Caesaropapism', which is the latter-day invention of certain Byzantine historians. But it lies at the root of the discord between the Latin and Graeco-Slav Churches. From this perspective, one understands how Photios came to be credited with the authorship of the *Nomokanon in Fourteen Titles* (883). The idea of making a concordance of the civil and ecclesiastical laws, presented in systematic fashion, had already been projected in the sixth century, and the first version of the *Nomokanon* dates back to the seventh century. The ninth-century edition gave rise in turn to a posterity which extended as far as the sixteenth century, under Turkish rule, and was also taken up by the Russian Church. Lastly, the biographer of the patriarch Ignatios, writing between 901 and 912, asserts that Photios composed for Basil an illustrious but false genealogy, which he transcribed in 'archaic characters' and hid in the imperial library, where an accomplice pulled it out in the sovereign's presence. We shall return later to the historiography of the dynasty, which was an essential element in its policy. Here we need only point out that in this malicious anecdote Photios plays the role at Basil's side which was his in reality and in which he was evidently a past master: that of theoretical exponent of imperial power.

Unification, legislation, encyclopaedism

The internal history of Basil's reign shows him conforming, in large measure, to the definition of the imperial office we saw put forward at its midway point. His imperial vigilance for orthodoxy found political expression in the mainly successful attempt to suppress religious and cultural differences of every description. The Slavs of Greece and Macedonia were subjected to a systematic campaign of integration, Hellenisation and Christianisation, but with less than total success, as is shown by the revolt, occurring as late as the time of Romanos I, which at the end of 921 or early in 922 opened the Peloponnese to the Bulgar invasion. We learn from a Novel of Leo VI of a decree, dated 873 or 874, ordering the compulsory baptism of Jews, which is corroborated by an unusual Jewish source, the *Book of Genealogy*, composed in honour of his ancestors, in the mid-eleventh century, by a certain Ahima᾽az of Oria, near Otranto. Writing in versified Hebrew, the author recounts tales of miracles and witchcraft which clearly owe much to the southern Italian milieu of his times, and gives some rare indications of the position held by Jews in this region during the ninth century, where they tended to serve as intermediaries between Byzantium, the Arabs and the Lombards, together with an account of this imposition, from which the Oria community was spared, it is claimed, by the intervention of rabbi Shefatya, the author's ancestor. Having journeyed to Constantinople, he is said to have prevailed on the emperor by the display of his polemical skill, and by curing the emperor's daughter, who was possessed by a devil. If the exemption of Oria is authentic, this may have to do with the current situation in southern Italy, where a start had just been made, as we shall see later, on a Byzantine reconquest.

The crusade against the Paulicians on the eastern frontier can be accounted an unmitigated triumph of Basil's reign, at least so far as one judges by the most obvious yardstick of military operations. The war begun in the time of Michael III was resumed with raids which tempted Chrysocheir, son-in-law and successor of Karbeas, to advance as far as Ephesus and Nicaea in 869. The embassy whose findings are reported by Peter of Sicily in his account of the Paulicians seems to have been despatched about this time. In 872, Chrysocheir campaigned in Galatia, and in the course of a battle against the Byzantines was killed by one of his own men. Basil directed further offensives against Melitene in 873 and 876. The fall of Tephrike, in 872, marked the end of Paulicianism as a military and political force, its rise having been encouraged, as we saw, by the emirs of Melitene and Tarsus. This victory is to be seen in the context of Basil's general scheme of reconquest in the East. Between 871 and 882, Byzantium regained control of the passes through the

Taurus and the Anti-Taurus, which were vital to its defence. But the religious problem was not so easily dismissed: the Bogomils, when they surfaced at Byzantium and in the Balkans in the tenth century, like the Tondrakites in Armenia in the eleventh century, may well have represented further offshoots from the old heretical stock, with its contempt for the flesh, hierarchy, procreation and the world in general, which had plagued Eastern Christianity since the fourth century. Here is a problem of continuity still waiting to be unravelled.

Basil I again conformed to the imperial model in being a law-giver, the first in the ninth century. Reference was made above to the *Epanagoge*, which dates at the earliest from 879, and whose implementation remains in some doubt. The *Procheiron* ('Guide to the Laws'), undertaken in 876, summed up the civil and penal laws introduced since the *Ekloga* of the emperors Leo III and Constantine V, and drew in addition on the *Institutes* of Justinian. The *Epanagoge* gives unmistakable proof of the prime importance from now on of the Classical dimension, evident not merely in the theoretical content of the aforementioned prologue but also in the sequence of chapters, which begins with definitions in the realm of public law concerning the emperor, the patriarch and the city prefect; all of these were absent from the eighth-century code, which by contrast opened with betrothals and marriage. Basil also set in motion a revision of the entire corpus of laws (*Anakatharsis*), which came to fruition under his successor. For reading aloud, he chose 'history books' or the lives of famous men, and he showed an interest in the ascetic practices and deeds of contemporary saints. Still extant is a collection of the homilies of St Gregory of Nazianzus arranged for liturgical use which was executed for Basil between 880 and 886. It is adorned with a series of sumptuous illustrations, headed by portraits of Basil and his wife, between their sons Leo and Alexander, and including images of Christian rulership: the archangel Gabriel crowning Basil beneath a large cross with the words 'Jesus Christ conquers!'; Christ enthroned and blessing, book in hand. Bearing all the hallmarks of the imperial workshop, this manuscript exemplifies the iconographic representation of imperial ideology which was to characterise the tenth century, foreshadowing in its form and content the model which would so notably inspire the new Ottonian empire. Nevertheless, in regard to Basil himself it is too soon to speak of a cultivated emperor, even if a set of instructions to his son, a sort of 'Prince's Mirror', goes under his name. For learning and authorship as traits inseparable from the imperial image we have to look to his son, Leo VI, and still more to his grandson, Constantine VII.

The legislative work of Leo VI is not perhaps his greatest claim to fame in this respect, even if it marks an important stage in the engagement with Classicism which underlies the ideology of Basil I's successors. Most of the Novels are addressed to his favourite minister, Stylianos Zaoutzes (died 896), who in a large number of cases, if not all, was probably their instigator, and to whom we shall return; their object, as was usual with this class of legislation, was to clarify or complement the existing law. The monumental *Basilika* ('Imperial laws'), on which work was begun, as we saw, under Basil I, represents by contrast a systematic codification of the Classical law, meaning the law in its Justinianic state, which in turn provided subject-matter for commentaries (*scholia*) and gave rise, probably before the tenth century was out, to a summary (*synopsis*), which was subsequently expanded by the addition of post-tenth-century Novels and of miscellaneous extracts of practical interest to the officials who often owned the manuscripts. Many copies have survived from the eleventh century and after.

It was of course traditional for an emperor to lend his name and his will, if not his hand, to any legal work. But Leo VI is also credited in person with creativity in fields where such precedents are lacking. One thinks first of his military treatise, the *Taktika*, abounding in references to ancient tacticians, but inspired none the less by thoroughly contemporary conceptions, for example of the emperor, whose responsibility for peace obliged him to make war, and most of all the war-leader, whose qualities in that capacity depended on the nobility of his origins. Next, there are the homilies he delivered from the pulpit of St Sophia, among them the funeral oration for his father: a remarkable encroachment by the political sovereign on ecclesiastical terrain, and offering one more proof, if such were needed, of the union of the two powers in Byzantine eyes, even if conflicts could arise between the two titularies or the definition of their respective roles might be disputed. And lastly, there is the insistence of the court historiographers on Leo VI's talents as a copyist.

The cultural accomplishment of the emperor reached its acme with Constantine VII, and is probably not to be explained merely as a personal *penchant*, or even by the inactivity to which he was supposedly condemned, until 944, by the government of his father-in-law, Romanos I Lekapenos, who had become emperor because the purple-born Constantine ('Porphyrogennetos') was under age. On the contrary, it is scarcely to be imagined that ideological responsibility for the sovereign power can have been lodged anywhere but in the hands of its legitimate heir, even when it was exercised in practice by Romanos. Leaving aside for the moment his Novels, speeches, and the already mentioned *Book of Ceremonies*, Constantine was the author of a treatise *On the Themes*, and of another *On the Administration of the Empire* (the title given to it in the first printed edition of 1611). The latter, written between 948 and 952, discusses the principles and practice of relations with the barbarian peoples, which it is suggested may vary from one case to the next. We are treated as a result not only to a complex analysis of Byzantium's international relations, but equally to a wealth of information about the past and present of the peoples in question – Russians, Petchenegs and Turks. On top of this Constantine appears to have been the instigator and organiser of an ambitious work of collaboration, which exploited the resources of the palace library and its copying services. Its chief aim was to assemble extracts from Antique texts with a bearing on particular subjects: agriculture (*geoponika*), ambushes, embassies, and so on; these compilations, like their counterparts in Baghdad, are illustrative of a generalised tenth century taste for encyclopaedias, typical of a Classicising age taking stock of its heritage. This activity also has a historiographical side, which for our present purposes is the more important. Under his direction, an official history was established not just of the dynasty but of the rulers who preceded it in the eighth and ninth centuries: the purpose was to demonstrate the flawless continuity of the imperial power as such, and its unerring transmission to the men most fitted to succeed. From an anonymous team of writers, known to us as 'the Continuators of Theophanes', he

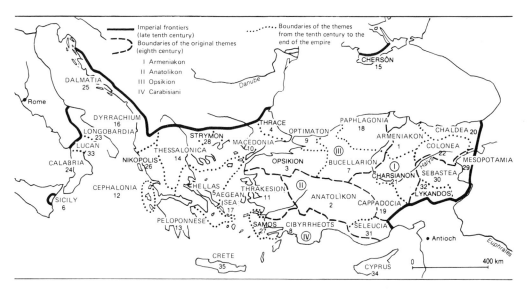

10 The Byzantine themes from the eighth to the tenth centuries

commissioned a series of imperial biographies, starting with Leo V, which again reflect the taste of the age, with its avidity for Plutarch. Constantine himself almost certainly undertook the all-important *Life of Basil*, which is careful to mention the portents revealing his future greatness, ranging from the Classical eagle which hovered over his infant slumbers to the pious visions he experienced, his exemplary virtues as a sovereign, extending to the relief of fiscal distress, and the genealogy which traced Basil's descent from the Arsacid kings of Persia, doubtless the very one projected in an earlier version by Photios. There is a final volume which continues the story down to 961, and also a *Book of Emperors*, commissioned by Constantine from Joseph Genesios, which deals with the emperors from Leo V to Michael III.

The palace and its message

Not for the first time, and however we may regret it, the side of Byzantine history which is uppermost between 886 and 959 is thus centred on the palace. The significance of the palace complex and of the ceremonies there enacted is illustrated in striking fashion by the treatise on precedences (*taktikon*), dealing in particular with imperial banquets, and composed by the master of ceremonies Philotheos in 899. He notes the proper place for each person according to his rank, that of patrician for example, and his office: in this way he arranges in due order the episcopal hierarchy, the military and the civilian hierarchy, the officers of the household and the palace guard, the 'Bulgar friends' and other embassies. The order which governs the feast-days of the palace, as has been recognised, is identical in the eyes of our author with the imperial order itself, which is what makes this document so valuable. Constantine VII in his *Book of Ceremonies* dwells less on the orders of precedence

353

A *bulloterion*. This device was used to set a gold seal, or chrysobull, on imperial documents – privileges, deeds of gift, decrees, contracts – issuing from the Palace (illustrated in G. Zacos and A. Veglery, *Byzantine Lead Seals*, Basel, 1972).

than on the ceremonies themselves, staged to mark the feasts in the Christian or imperial calendar and events in the life of the imperial family, or to honour distinguished visitors. And for the whole of this period we also have the eye-witness accounts of Arab ambassadors.

But as well as providing the stage for the pomp of sovereignty, in the course of these same generations the palace became a living organ of government and administration whose operations can be followed in documents preserved in archives or quoted at second hand: it served for example as court of appeal, or of direct jurisdiction in the case of certain monasteries, and housed the fiscal department where charters of immunity or gift were drawn up. From the end of the ninth century, the imperial chancery is found issuing *chrysoboulloi*, documents sealed in gold with the imperial seal, which were marked by a distinctive hand, the highlighting of words in red ink, and the presence of an autograph signature counter-signed by the 'keeper of the ink-horn'. With all this in mind, it becomes easy to imagine the palace as a nerve-centre of political decision and ideological impulse. The verbal celebration of imperial greatness on the occasion of military triumphs, festal banquets and marriages was entrusted to the palace orator. Arethas of Patras, holder of this office in 901–2, who was born around the middle of the ninth century, shortly afterwards, in 902 or 903, became archbishop of Caesarea in Cappadocia. An investor in manuscripts, particularly of the Antique philosophers – amongst which there figured a two-volume Plato revised in his own hand – Arethas enlarges on the theme of the structural correspondence between Christ and the emperor in a language of such dazzling erudition that it verges at times on the incomprehensible, but which is not to be regarded, or at any rate not exclusively, as pedantic indulgence or affectation: the choice of words and the Antique rhetoric are intended to signify that the present is as great as the past, because the very nature of imperial greatness makes it immobile and immutable. It is to be imagined in consequence that the cultural activity characteristic of Leo VI and Constantine VII was not, for its part, simply the fad of men raised in the purple, but an integral part of their task as sovereign.

Other sources, while not emanating directly from the palace, can only be understood by reference to it: whatever the historiographical narrative, it can be taken for granted that the palace forms its focal point. To the works already cited can be added a chronicle which continues that of George the Monk, written under Michael III, which had stopped in 842. Its manuscript tradition, still not fully unravelled, shows a proliferation of additions, variants and continuations going under names which tell us virtually nothing of their authors, such as 'the continuator of George the Monk', 'Symeon the Magistros' or 'the Logothete' (finance minister), to name but a few. But this matters little, since from internal evidence it is easy enough, especially when Basil and Photios are in question, to identify narratives with a polemical slant, in which the tone and content betray their authors as belonging to the higher reaches of the public administration or to an aristocratic clique in the capital. The palace, as the hub of political life, also forms the focal point of patriarchal biographies. Two are of especial interest: the *Life of Ignatios* and the *Life of Euthymios*, which appeared in the crisis surrounding Leo VI's fourth marriage. This crisis also provides the context for the *Life of Ignatios*, written by Niketas, who had become a monk under the name David; in this work Ignatios is exalted as a model of the Church's resistance to imperial omnipotence, in contrast with the Photian history of compromise. And the same virtuous contrast is implied by the monastic contemporary who composed the *Life* of Euthymios in the Psamathia monastery, which Euthymios had founded.

Implanting a dynasty

The narratives relating to the palace and the imperial power are far from being the only sources at our disposal for the years between 867 and 957. But they dominate as it were the forefront of the stage, and give an account of events within a narrow but not enclosed milieu where the all-important political decisions were made. The emperor had around him a double circle: an outer ring composed of the magnates, the military chiefs in particular, and their kindred; and an inner ring, consisting, apart from his own family, of counsellors, favourites, eunuchs on his personal staff, and monks, all with their own strings of relatives – for in this political jungle no one could survive on his own. Byzantine

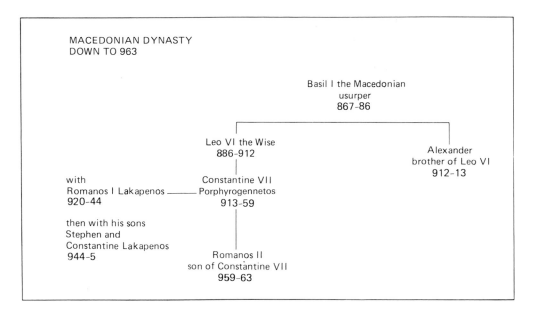

MACEDONIAN DYNASTY
DOWN TO 963

Basil I the Macedonian
usurper
867-86

Leo VI the Wise
886-912

Alexander
brother of Leo VI
912-13

with
Romanos I Lakapenos ———— Constantine VII
920-44   Porphyrogennetos
                                                  913-59

then with his sons
Stephen and
Constantine Lakapenos
944-5

Romanos II
son of Constantine VII
959-63

historians have tended in the past to overlook these connections, although their importance is to be deduced from the attention paid to them in contemporary historiography. The
family networks rise, falter, and fall, or hold their own together at the top, and the history of
the ruling class is therefore directly related to its proximity to the throne and the palace.

Basil had four sons. Constantine, the favourite, born from his first marriage, was
associated with the empire in 869. Leo may not have been the son of Basil but of Michael III.
After him Eudokia bore two more sons, Alexander and Stephen. Basil went on to associate
Leo with the empire, in 870, and shortly after 871 did the same with Alexander.
Constantine died in 879, leaving Leo in consequence as the heir presumptive. The emperor
had married the latter to Theophano, a member of the Martinakios clan, to which Eudokia
Ingerina may also have belonged. Basil was antipathetic towards Leo, even banishing him
for a time. The contemporary author of the *Life of Theophano*, a lay client of the Martinakioi,
ascribed this action to suspicions implanted in Basil by the monk–magician Theodore
Santabarenos. But a formal reconciliation had ensued, on the feast-day of St Elijah.
Moreover, before he died in 886 of injuries received in a hunting accident, Basil designated
Leo his successor. With Alexander still as co-emperor, Leo replaced Photios with Stephen.
This concentration of the highest functions in the imperial fraternity is significant. It set up
a model which the Ottonian empire followed, after its own fashion, when Bruno, brother of
Otto I, was made archbishop of Cologne. Or, to put it another way, for the first time it puts
into practice the familial pattern, to be taken sometimes in the literal, sometimes in the
metaphorical sense, which embodied the political thinking of the age.

Leo deserted his wife: her biographer, or rather hagiographer, subsequently portrayed
her as following an ascetic vocation, rewarded by posthumous miracles at her tomb, and it
is true that she figures from the tenth century in the Byzantine Church's calendar of saints.

Leo 'united himself in friendship', to use the contemporary euphemism, with Zoe Zaoutzina, whose husband is supposed in consequence to have been poisoned, and installed her in the palace. She was the daughter of an Armenian, Stylianos Zaoutzes, whom Leo placed at the head of affairs and for whom he created the title *basileopater*, 'father-in-law of the emperor', although at the time no marriage existed to justify the description. Having been made Logothete of the *Dromos*, and hence responsible for the courier service, internal affairs, and in part for external relations, Zaoutzes played until his death, in 896, a role whose importance is attested by the large proportion of Leo VI's Novels of which he is the addressee. Theophano died in November 897, and Leo married Zoe, who also died, late in 899, leaving a daughter. Zoe's clan, which in any case had been a centre of intrigue, was therefore obliged to vacate the palace. Still without an heir, Leo took as his third wife a young girl originally from the Opsikion theme, Eudokia Baiana, who died, together with a newly-born son, in 901. He had by now stretched the canonical indulgence of remarriage to the limit, without having solved the problem of his succession: he had himself only a few years before renewed the ban on third marriages, which rendered the offspring of them illegitimate, and reiterated the disapproval of second marriages. He lived therefore with a fourth woman, Zoe Karbonopsina ('with eyes like coal'), without first taking her in marriage. She seems to have been a kinswoman of Himerios, who was high admiral of the fleet (*drongarios tou ploimou*) in the early years of the tenth century. In 905, she gave the emperor his long-awaited heir, the future Constantine VII. In consequence, a new chapter was about to be written in the tale of the long-running battle between the integrist party in the Church and the political patriarchs recruited from the public service.

On the face of it, this succession of four imperial marriages certainly seems to exemplify an ill-fated family history, but the emperor's motives for contracting them must also be considered: passion no doubt entered into it, at any rate as regards his antipathy towards Theophano and his attraction to the first Zoe, but anxiety for the continuity of the empire unquestionably played its part, made ever more acute in his case by the setbacks he encountered, and not by any element of novelty; similarly, emulating Theophilos, who had condemned his father's accomplices, Leo gave orders for Michael III, victim of his own father's usurpation, to be reburied in the Church of the Holy Apostles, the imperial mausoleum. Turning lastly to the four women involved, the first, and to a lesser degree probably the last, already had a distinguished ancestry. Zaoutzes, judging merely from his name, was a recent arrival; his family connections lived in easy circumstances until the premature death of Zoe proved the undoing of their still precarious prosperity. There were yet more characters on the scene, or who had just left it, at the time when the birth of Constantine revived a barely-extinguished disagreement. The patriarch Stephen, brother of Leo VI, had died in 893. The ecumenical see had been occupied since 901 by the patriarch Nicholas I, a man in the tradition of Photios, his kinsman and seemingly his godson, certainly close enough to have taken refuge in a monastery at the time of his deposition. Related to the commander of the household troops, 'adopted brother' of the emperor, and in recent years his private secretary (*mystikos*), Nicholas had the kind of experience and connections which should have disposed him towards a compromise

357

favourable to the palace. Leo first prevailed on him, in January 906, to baptise the infant in St Sophia, with the monk Euthymios standing as a godfather. In the following spring, a priest performed the marriage ceremony, and Leo crowned Zoe. This was the signal for open conflict between the patriarch, who forbade the emperor to set foot in St Sophia beyond the sacristy but agreed to devise a form of penitence; the emperor, who at first refused the offer and called for arbitration by Rome; and a rigorist party, headed on this occasion not, as a century earlier, by the *hegoumenos* of the Stoudios, but by Arethas, now installed as archbishop of Caesarea.

But the balance of forces and the subject at issue had changed. Nicholas, preoccupied with the unity of the Church, failed to satisfy Leo, who in 907 forced him to resign, on the pretext of complicity in the recent conspiracy hatched by Andronikos Doukas. In his place Leo appointed Euthymios, who although a monk did not display the intransigence one might expect. The author of his *Life* nevertheless portrays Euthymios as an outstanding example of the 'spiritual father', the director of conscience whose all-seeing vision had since the previous century formed one of the principal strands of spiritual practice: on this score, he is able to credit Euthmymios with an ascendancy over the emperor. In reality, Euthymios gave way in the face of the appeal made by Leo to Rome and the Eastern patriarchates, and, if we are to believe his biographer, in the face of Leo's threat to promulgate a law authorising fourth marriages. The marriage was accordingly legitimised. Leo ordered a mosaic panel to be placed in St Sophia above the Imperial Entrance: it shows him prostrate at the feet of Christ, who is enthroned between the Virgin and an angel, penitent and yet redeemed, since he is placed on Christ's right hand. He died in 912, and Alexander came to power. Alexander restored Nicholas to the patriarchal throne, which entailed the deposition of bishops instituted by Euthymios, a circumstance which earned Nicholas the undying resentment of the Euthymians. Beset by problems arising from Bulgar affairs, Alexander died in June 913. Nicholas had a seat on the council of regency, and indeed the whole burden of the empire fell on his shoulders once he set Zoe aside. In 920, a Tome of Reunion formally concluded the affair, but without allaying the grievances.

The conflict and its outcome raise questions about the conduct of relations between the emperor and the Church at Byzantium in this early part of the tenth century. There is little trace here of the claim to monastic power which was still a factor in the dispute between Ignatios and Photios. Even the politicised patriarchate can be seen in the end to have been subdued by the imperial will. The triumph of the latter is manifested not only in the legitimisation of a union that was contrary to the existing law, but in the threat Leo VI may have used to bring this about. The threat may or may not be authentic, but it is significant that we learn of it from a monk, writing the biography of another monk, who is in fact being upheld as a model.

In May 919, Constantine VII married the daughter of Romanos Lakapenos, who revived the title *basileopater* recently borne by Zaoutzes. Then (September 920) he received that of Caesar, in imitation of Bardas, uncle of Michael III, and in December 920 he became co-emperor with his son-in-law. To understand this turn of events, we need to pick up two leading threads from the preceding decades, which cannot be entirely separated: the

Mosaic in St Sophia inspired by Leo VI's 'contrition' after the somewhat contrived legitimisation of his fourth marriage: even though he had personally prohibited third marriages, the emperor did not hesitate to bring pressure to bear on the Church when his concubine Zoe Karbonopsina at last produced his long-awaited heir. He is seen here prostrating himself before Christ.

international relations fostered by Byzantium, and the interplay of personalities and dynasties in the imperial entourage.

Family power, ruling culture

The dazzling semblance of continuity achieved by Byzantine culture, the undoubted continuity of its political ideals, and the unrivalled sophistication at this time of its administrative process and written procedures have served to conceal from many histori-ans the real mainsprings of Byzantine power at this period. We need be in no doubt that power belonged in part to the educated, and there exists no better proof than the presence of Leo VI and Constantine VII among their number: for the justification of the sovereign power in historical, juridical and Christian terms was their responsibility. But the impor-tance of warfare should not be discounted: we see emerging from its unending series of military episodes the leading actors in the political and dynastic history of the times.

Power-hungry dynasties

As was earlier pointed out, an awareness of lineage – reflected in the adoption of surnames, the tracing out of pedigrees and the praise lavished on an illustrious ancestry – first showed itself in the eighth century, becoming more firmly established in the ninth. It continued to grow during the time between Basil I and Constantine VII, in parallel with the official doctrine making birth in the purple the test of imperial legitimacy. Properly speaking, the question of a 'feudal' Byzantium, or a 'feudal' empire, did not arise until the time of Basil II. But the historical writings from the reigns of Basil I, Leo VI, Romanos I and Constantine VII point on the one hand to the existence and contribution of particular families, some of which would still be on the scene in later centuries, and on the other to the dynamism of a social group in which the military, political and cultural values traditionally associated with aristocracy were still conjoined with complete social openness. We shall take three examples. The first is that of the Doukai, and of their meteoric rise and sudden fall at the beginning of the tenth century. The first Doukas we know of, Andronikos, bore a personal name which signifies 'virility' and 'victory', along with the designation 'Doux', at once a title and a nickname, which seems to have become a surname as early as the next generation. Under Leo VI, he is found alongside Himerios in the war against the Arabs, and invested with an important command in Asia Minor, with a son who in 906 was already adult – Constantine, married to a daughter of Gregoras 'the Iberian', who was at that time *domestikos* of the *scholai*. That same year, Andronikos was denounced, rightly or wrongly, to the emperor by Leo's Christian Arab favourite, the eunuch Samonas, and entered on a rebellion 'along with his kinsmen, children and followers', to quote a contemporary writer. He first took refuge in the fortress of Kavalla, not far from Konya, and later fled to Baghdad. His son Constantine returned however to Constantinople, and in 913, after the death of Leo VI, he allowed himself to be tempted into a bid for the throne, when he held the command of *domestikos* of the *scholai*. The attempt failed, Constantine lost one son in the conspiracy, and another, still only a child, was castrated, an exceptional measure which shows the importance attached to the affair. Yet another Doukas, Nicholas, died in the war against the Bulgars in 917. Even after this extermination, a Doukas family nevertheless reappeared in the eleventh century, this time to stay: there is no difficulty in imagining that it was descended from another branch.

Our second example is none other than the emperor Romanos I Lakapenos. On the basis of a well-known passage from Constantine VII, stress is generally laid on his lowly birth. But although no one disputes his Armenian origin, the facts of the matter are not altogether clear. It is true that we can go back no further than his father Theophylact the 'Unbearable' (*Abastaktos*), whose nickname was hardly transmissible, and of whom all we know is that he saved the life of Basil I during an unsuccessful attempt on Tephrike. Whatever the truth about this episode, it at least tells us that Romanos's father was engaged in war service, even if he did not make it his career. It is in any case certain that a female forebear of Romanos was married to Adralestos, *strategos* of the Orient theme, somewhere around the middle of the ninth century, since she was to be the grandmother of the monk Michael Maleinos, born in 894. But Romanos I was the first of the line to win official distinction. What this meant is immediately obvious from the rank of his 'co-fathers-in-law': while his daughter Helena married the young emperor, his daughter Agatha became the wife of an Argyros, Leo, whose family, which went back to Michael III, was very much in the ascendant; his son Constantine married into the family of the patrician Pantherios, his son Christopher into that of the patrician Niketas. Christopher and Constantine were associated to the empire, as was their brother Stephen, while the youngest, Theophylact, was invested with the patriarchate, following the pattern adopted by the sons of Basil I; a bastard son, Basil the Bird, followed the career of a palace eunuch, and under Constantine VII was to occupy the coveted position of chamberlain (*parakoimomenos*).

After the Doukai and the Lakapenoi, our third example takes us to the very heart of the tenth century. This is the Phokai clan, progenitor of the future emperor Nikopheros II, around which, by means of marriage alliances, was built up cluster by cluster the major aristocratic constellation of the age. Their pedigree, given currency it seems by the Phokai themselves, ascended to a great-great-grandfather of Nikephoros II by the name of Phokas, which is the name of a martyr honoured in the district around Sinope. He is said to have attracted the notice of the emperor (Theophilos ?) on account of his 'bodily strength and nobility of soul', and to have been set at the head of a *turma*, the basic military unit of a theme: a quite plausible origin, comparable with that of Theophylact Abastaktos, albeit without the latter's exemplary deeds, and typical, furthermore, of a society where sucess in war was a common source of new reputations. Phokas gave his name to the line of his descendants: in the reigns of Basil and Leo VI, his son, Nikephoros Phokas, was already one of the outstanding generals – we saw him winning renown in southern Italy. His grandsons, Bardas, whose name hints at an Armenian uncle or grandfather, and Leo distinguished themselves under the regency of Zoe, mother of Constantine VII. By reason of their marriage alliances, they presented themselves as rivals to Romanos Lakapenos. Bardas was married to a member of the Maleinoi clan, which was already attracting historiographical attention under Michael III and Basil I; her grandfather was a patrician and a *strategos*, while one of her grandmothers was related to Romanos Lakapenos. The Maleionoi came originally from the Charsianon theme, where their kinsman Eudokimos, perhaps *strategos* of the theme, had died in an odour of sanctity around 840. Leo, brother of Bardas, was brother-in-law to the *parakoimomenos* Constantine, favourite eunuch of Leo VI in the latter part of his reign. As for the children of Bardas, Nikephoros, born about 912, became emperor, after a career to be described in due course, and which was mirrored by that of his brother Leo; one of their sisters married a nephew of John Kourkouas, the very man whom Romanos I envisaged as the father-in-law of Romanos, son of Constantine VII. From this union was born another emperor, the nephew and murderer of Nikephoros II, John I Tzimiskes; he took as his first wife a daughter of the Skleroi, another powerful family, and one which had been in evidence since the early ninth century. This genealogical sketch is merely intended to demonstrate how in two generations, that of Bardas and the next, the Phokai attached themselves to the handful of families who were serious contenders for supreme power, not one of which, so far as can be judged, went back beyond the ninth century.

The success scored by Romanos Lakapenos through the choice of his daughter for Constantine VII was in fact the result of the replacement of Leo Phokas, who in 917 was leading a campaign in Bulgaria, by the admiral of the fleet, with backing from the palace, in

The path to power at Byzantium was strewn with conspiracies and mutilations. Blinding, as well as being cruel, had a symbolic significance, as did amputation of the hand or nose (*Chronicle of Skylitzes*, thirteenth century, Madrid, Biblioteca Nacional).

the circle around Zoe and the patriarch Nicholas. The imperial betrothal provoked Leo, relieved of his command as *domestikos* of the *scholai*, or in other words ejected from the palace by Romanos, into raising the themes of the Orient in rebellion. His attempt failed, and he was permanently eliminated from the contest by blinding. His brother Bardas on the other hand was not deprived of his command and took part in the counter-offensive after the Russian attack of 941. But the best-laid plans of Romanos, founded on a numerous progeny, were of no avail in securing the future of the Lakapenoi. In 928, a conspiracy in favour of Christopher instigated by his father-in-law was foiled. After the death of Christopher in 938, his brothers Stephen and Constantine got rid of John Kourkouas, the general whom Romanos I wished to have as father-in-law for his grandson, the future Romanos II. Finally, they deposed their father, but were deposed in their turn by Constantine VII, who in January 945 at last achieved real power, and sent to rejoin their father in a monastery. Even though a daughter of Christopher was married to Peter, tsar of Bulgaria, the clan disappeared for good from the political scene, and Constantine aligned himself for obvious reasons with the Phokai. Bardas Phokas was appointed *domestikos* of the *scholai*; his sons

Nikephoros and Leo were appointed *strategoi*. The son of Constantine VII, Romanos, associated with the throne from 945 when he was still a child, had been married during his grandfather's ascendancy to an illegitimate daughter of Hugh of Provence, who soon died. Around 956 he took as his wife the beautiful but obscure Anastaso, a barmaid according to later report, who changed her name on marriage to Theophano. This choice avoided the embarrassment of aristocratic and ambitious brothers-in-law. The historiography of the time represents Theophano as holding Romanos under a spell. Later she would furnish the first example in the literature of the period of sexual passion leading to crime, something hitherto unknown in the imperial circle.

Constantine VII died in 959, perhaps poisoned by his son at the instigation of Theophano. Scholars have allowed themselves the indulgence, in view of his literary output, of depicting Constantine as an intellectual, and so fallen into the common trap of encouraging the modern-day reader to fill out the portrait with his own preconceptions. Constantine was certainly by nature a man of letters and not of war. But it should not be forgotten that, willingly or perforce, he was not alone as emperor. Romanos I and generals such as John Kourkouas discharged the military function of the imperial power with considerable competence, as did the Phokai when Constantine turned to them after the fall of the Lakapenoi. And Constantine, who did not cease to be emperor to the day of his death, for his part discharged a literary function, which was wholly devoted, in his historiographical works, to the vindication of the dynasty founded by Basil, in the *Book of Ceremonies* to the symbolism of power, and in the treatises on the themes and the imperial administration to the definition, once and for all, of the traditions and factual knowledge essential to its universal exercise.

A ruling culture and its limits

In these middle years of the tenth century Byzantium presents a picture of health, if one accepts that for a society around the year 1000 the conduct of warfare and of long-distance trade are the best indicators of that condition. And like any healthy society, it generated cultural activity by which to express and justify its condition.

We have constantly drawn attention to the cultural impulses behind Byzantine political history, and most recently to the way in which Basil I, through his intermediary Photios, Leo VI and Constantine VII elaborated and perfected the time-honoured conception of the imperial power, and more particularly to the historiographical achievement of Constantine VII in providing the dynasty inaugurated in bloodshed by his grandfather with respectable foundations. But we have also seen, beginning with Theophilos, attempts by that same imperial power to justify itself by claiming unbroken continuity with the Classical culture bequeathed by Antiquity, and that claim being put into practice, after the second iconoclasm, with the help of an all-embracing and definitive iconography. The imposition of Classical standards, which was facilitated, as we also saw, by the use of minuscule, is reflected in the philological revision of ancient texts, which was so thorough that our text of Plato, for example, derives to a large extent from the one established in the ninth and tenth centuries. But it would be false to conclude that this correction represents – or rather solely represents – the impartial scholarly activity of a learned culture: what it also and above all reflects is the totalitarian outlook of a ruling culture. This equally explains why the *Menologion*, the collection of saints' lives arranged according to the calendar, was subjected at this time to a draconian revision, which affected both the personages commemorated, weeding out almost all those of recent origin, and to the narratives, which were ruthlessly rewritten in an easily recognisable rhetorical style; fortunately, the mass diffusion of this revision did not lead to the total disappearance of earlier versions. It is possible that the author, Symeon Metaphrastes ('the rewriter'), carried out the work at the behest of Constantine VII. We have no means of knowing whether he is to be identified with the chronicler, Symeon the Magister and Logothete, who is himself so little known, apart from his work, that it is equally impossible to say whether he is to be distinguished from Symeon the Magister whose letters have survived.

The ruling culture was still synonymous, it will be recalled, with the perpetual glorification of the emperor by the palace rhetor, with the sophistication of the imperial and patriarchal administrative apparatus, and with the triumph of orthodoxy. But for all this the palace, the Stoudios monastery and the patriarchate, or in a word the capital, were not its exclusive domain. The ruling culture was centralised, but not localised. Proof is furnished by administrative documents emanating from the provinces, which become available from the time of Basil I, and above all by the letters that have survived from the tenth century. Letter-writing, a means of personal communication, was also by tradition a branch of rhetoric, which was a reason for making exemplary collections, some of which have come down to us: they include letters sent by officials and bishops stationed in the provinces to their friends in the capital or their protectors, sometimes to the emperor himself or the patriarch, and occasionally *vice versa*. Preserved in this way are letters of the patriarchs Photios and Nicholas, and of Theodore Daphnopates, imperial secretary at the time of Romanos I, as well as a very rich collection from the second half of the tenth century. In these letters, as in the musings of Arethas, bishop of Caesarea in Cappadocia from about 904 until his death in 932, can be detected the nostalgia, in part conventional, in part sincere, of educated men separated from their own kind and buried in a rustic milieu.

Lastly, the ruling culture delivered its message through figurative images. Many of these have since disappeared, for example the mosaics in Basil I's New Church. But there is no lack of witnesses to the deliberate reversion to the relevant canons of Antiquity, whether in the revival of carved ivory decoration on caskets and book covers, the production of chased silverware, or the illustration of manuscripts, even where the content is religious, as in the case of the so-called Paris Psalter, a remarkable product of the early tenth century. It is this ruling culture that Byzantium exported, through its artefacts and its craftsmen, to Preslav, and later to Kiev. Nevertheless, it is permissible to ask where the social, provincial and one might even say national boundaries were drawn within the vast corpus of the empire itself.

The first thing we can be sure of is that the language of the ruling culture now finally

Reliquary in gold and enamel, inlaid with gems, supposed to contain a relic of the 'True Cross'. Brought to the West in 1204, this masterpiece of tenth-century goldsmiths' work is now in the cathedral of Limburg am Lahn.

parted company with the language as spoken by all, including the political elite. Phonetically, the changes which led up to the present-day pronunciation of Greek were already occurring long before the tenth century, in particular the tendency to sound the *i* separately when it appears with other vowels and diphthongs. But even the structure of the language, as the result in particular of simplification of the declensions, already prefigured at this time the one we know today. The mistakes made in the copying of manuscripts are revealing in this regard. As to the vocabulary of modern Greek, we find a sprinkling of it – depending on the text, but most frequently in certain saints' *Lives* – well before the tenth century. The classical renaissance of the ninth and tenth centuries, which restored the Antique treatises on rhetoric to a place of honour, accentuated the difference, political as much as cultural, between two levels of language, a difference which had the same function at Byzantium as the separate usage of Latin and the vernacular languages in medieval Western Christendom. The vernacular language was to find its way into the domains of the written word in the twelfth and thirteenth centuries. Nevertheless, the basic idea of a double language has persisted in Greece down to the twentieth century, with an ideological significance which remains more or less unaltered. The spoken language of this first half of the tenth century is therefore only accessible to us by indirect means, such as the mutilated *Life of the patriarch Euthymios*, composed as we saw by a monk in the Psamathia monastery, which goes back to at least the time before the unique manuscript, copied about 1080–1100 and now lost, was amended by its editor. Examples also occur in a number of Anatolian battle and love songs, in sundry verse-couplets from the court preserved in the *Book of Ceremonies*, and, a source too often overlooked, in certain family names which crop up in the historiography of the ninth and tenth centuries, such as Garidas, from 'shrimp', or 'Gongylios' from 'turnip', whose social significance has already been touched on.

Even the ruling culture, one suspects, was not impervious, and absorbed some peripheral influences. For example, a Gospel book copied in the tenth century, but perhaps not decorated until the eleventh, suggests an Islamic influence in the scribe's ornamentation of the headings and in the architectural surrounds framing the figures of the evangelists. This manuscript comes from the eastern frontier, and stands in marked contrast with a manuscript of the ascetic treatise by John Klimakas ('The Ladder') copied in Italy in the ninth century, in which the decoration shows an affinity with contemporary Western motifs. Again, manuscripts produced in southern Italy can be recognised by characteristic traits in their handwriting, ornament and illustration. The architecture of Armenia, which blossomed under the Ani kingdom, began at this time to exert an influence over Byzantium which became more pronounced in the second half of the tenth century, with the advent to power of John Tzimiskes, which is also the moment when the Georgians started to play a role. The marches of Byzantium thus provided fertile soil for the work of acculturation.

The Jews already encountered in southern Italy furnish yet another example, suitably placed as they were, with a flourishing culture of their own, at the intersection of the Byzantine, Islamic and Latin worlds. The case is different for the Jewish minority inside the empire, squeezed by the increasing rigour of the identification between *romanitas* and orthodox Christianity and suspected furthermore, rightly or wrongly, of being implicated in iconoclastic movements. For this reason, the conversion of the Jews appeared more than ever necessary. It was decreed, as already mentioned, by Basil I in 873 or 874, and this measure was reiterated by Leo VI in a Novel making it obligatory on Jews from henceforth to obey the Christian law, their own being rendered obsolete. A hagiographical work composed after the death of Basil assigns to his reign the career of Constantine of Synnada, a Jew who as a boy, having signed his mouth with a cross after yawning, as was the custom, found himself a Christian, and who afterwards became a monk. Whatever lies behind this story, Romanos I was the author in his turn of a decree enforcing conversion, issued in 932, which appears to have started an exodus, perhaps to Khazaria, and subsequently to Kievan Russia where Jewish culture made an immediate and important impact. The Jewish minority was thus not annihilated at Byzantium, either then or later, but neither did it find there soil on which to flourish in the way that it did in Italy, the Rhineland or the Islamic countries at the same period. Yet there must have been some permeation by Byzantine culture of learned or semi-learned Jewish circles, which produced the bizarre description of King Solomon seated on his throne in the Hippodrome flanked by the four colours, which is written in Hebrew using certain Greek words, and whose author has a knowledge of the capital, and even of the palace, which seems to date from the first half of the tenth century. After 960, the Jewish situation at Byzantium underwent a change.

And what, it may be asked, has become of the common culture? The chief essential is to be aware of the ambiguity attached to this term. Suppose we take the material culture. Many articles survive, some of which – ivories, silk fabrics, jewels, high-quality ceramics – point if not to the palace at any rate to the elite. But equally there are others – crosses, amulets and portable icons made of polished stone, pots made of ordinary earthenware – which come from more modest levels of consumption. For all the differences, we cannot help noticing the uniformity of the religious iconographical repertory, and hence of the representational code and the system of beliefs. By contrast, the social range of late ninth- and tenth-century hagiography is usually narrower than that of the fifth to seventh centuries, in which the social scene was very varied, even though the events were similar. The point has already been made that the holy men contemporary with Basil and his successors were monks, spiritual fathers whose conversation was with emperors and great personages. In many such narratives, the common people occupy at most an indistinct place in the background. The case is different, however, when the village folk of the Latros region climb up to Paul the Younger (died 955) to pray for rain, or when the townsfolk of Thessalonica bar the passage of Euthymios the Younger (died 898) in attempts to touch him on the days when he descends from Athos to the town. The triumph of the monks, which was implicit in the restoration of 843, and central to all the disputes from Constantine VI to Leo VI, became final in these middle years of the tenth century. The monk would remain for centuries the communal voice of Byzantine culture at all levels of society. We have to picture him living in a monastery, subject to the *hegoumenos*, because the recluse, the isolated individual, was suspect. He nevertheless existed. The religious practices and representation of the other world which were to be those of modern Hellenism thus become clearly visible in the tenth century.

Byzantium's quest for a protective glacis

Warfare has never long been absent from these pages. The means of waging it remained unchanged: the warships, or *dromons*, spearheaded the maritime offensive; on land, the charge in pitched battles was delivered by squadrons of cavalry, such as may be seen galloping across the page of some eleventh-century Gospel manuscript, the upper part of their bodies encased in a coat of scale armour, their heads protected by an iron helmet, a triangular or round shield on their left arm; more lightly-armed troops, bowmen for example, were thrown in as support, while the Eastern frontier was the theatre for the guerilla warfare of the *akritai*, charged with its defence. Already unfolding were the values that became dominant after 960, from the time of Nikephoros Phokas, otherwise the emperor Nikephoros II, to that of Alexios Komnenos. Tactical treatises, of which the most famous is ascribed to the emperor Leo VI in person, bear witness to this development, as does the historiography of the period. Not that the latter lays as much stress as in the post-960 period on the leading military role of the emperor, and with good reason. But it offers the reader proof after proof that the promotions of individuals and lineages in the political sphere were the result of military prowess. The characters who came by this means to the front of the stage did so, moreover, within the framework of the military institutions with which we are familiar. The units of the central army (*tagmata*) were placed under the orders of the *domestikos* of the *scholai*, the crack regiment. As before, these troops included a number of foreign mercenaries, and at the start of the tenth century these consisted in particular of 'Russians', 'Rhos' (the word refers at this date to the Scandinavian element of the newly founded Kievan State); but recruits from inside the empire were not ruled out. The theme armies depended in part on the service due from the holders of military properties, but also on recruitment by virtue of fiscal obligations. Lastly, the old custom of settling barbarians on plots of land in exchange for military service was still in evidence.

The emperor clearly retained responsibility for the overall conduct of the war, whose many theatres were enumerated in the preceding chapter: the East and the Caucasus; Bulgaria, the nothern shore of the Black Sea, and now Kiev; the eastern and central Mediterranean, the Adriatic from Taranto to Venice. Everywhere, the war proceeded in tandem with the conduct of other relations, such as long-distance trade, evangelisation and diplomacy, and often followed the same paths. As we have already seen, the cumulative effect was to inscribe on the world of that time the divisions – Graeco-Slav Christianity, Latin Christianity, Islam – still recognisable in our own. It should also be remembered that from the ninth century onwards, as Byzantium strove to carve out a peripheral sphere of influence among the Slavs, it came up against the dual Christian might of the papacy and the Carolingian empire, and the latter's Ottonian successor, while Islam was still competing with Byzantium in the East for the ancient Christian communities of the Caucasus and the Mesopotamian marches.

Bulgaria, mirror of Byzantium

From the time of Basil I, the convergence and conflict of the three powers in the central Mediterranean added a new dimension; of all the prizes fought over from the ninth to the eleventh centuries, Sicily and southern Italy were perhaps the most significant. But at the other extremity of Christendom, in the East, the situation as we see it at the beginning of this period carried the seeds of its own transformation: born from the Byzantine model, Christian Bulgaria evolved towards becoming a miniature Byzantium, its partner and adversary, as opposed to the still non-Christian Turkic peoples pressing against the mouth of the Danube, and also as opposed to the new protagonist, the State of Kiev, shortly to become Christian.

The Bulgar State swung finally towards Byzantium in the reign of Basil I. The problem for Boris-Michael, as we saw, had been that of utilising the ideological reinforcement to the monarchy offered by Christianisation in order to counteract the boyars, who were linked with the old polytheism, while at the same time, and for the same reason, equipping himself with a Church which would buttress his authority, and not lead to dependence on an external power – hence his tergiversations between Rome and Constantinople. Dissatisfied with Rome's reaction to his letter of 866, Boris fell back on Byzantium. In 870, a council held in the imperial capital decreed the attachment of Bulgaria to the jurisdiction of the ecumenical patriarchate, while granting a measure of autonomy. And very soon afterwards the spread of Slav literacy by emissaries of Byzantine Christianity offered the ideal solution. In 885, on the death of Methodios, his chief disciples were expelled from Moravia by the mounting success of the Frankish mission. Clement and Naum journeyed to Pliska, bringing with them liturgical books in the Slav tongue. The result was a decisive expansion of the local Christian community. Clement spread the Gospel in Macedonia, around Prespa and Ohrid, which was annexed to Bulgaria in the first half of the ninth century, and became bishop of Ohrid in 893, while Naum, before rejoining him, was active around Pliska and the royal monastery which Boris-Michael founded for himself on the Byzantine model, St Panteleimon near Preslav. In 889, Boris abdicated and became a monk. His successor was his eldest son, Vladimir, who reverted to the boyar party, while persecuting the clergy, and to the Frankish alliance. In 893 Boris-Michael reappeared in Pliska; he had Vladimir blinded and incarcerated, called an assembly which proclaimed his second son Symeon, educated in Constantinople, as tsar, and announced the transfer of the capital to Preslav.

Any remaining connection with the Bulgar past, in the Turkic sense, was thus severed, for the greater benefit as much of the monarchy as of an already strongly Slavicised national identity. The decision taken in 893 extended to the substitution of Slavonic for Greek as the official language of State and Church. The Glagolitic script was replaced by 'Cyrillic', still in use today, which was much less cumbersome and also close to the Greek alphabet. Byzantium pursued a policy which gave the best hope of acculturation, making translations of Byzantine religious and even secular works available, and disseminating its iconography. Symenon, as 'son' of the emperor, stood closest to him in the metaphorical family circle of which the emperor, in Byzantine eyes, formed the global centre. The reign of

369

Constantinople besieged by the Bulgars, at the peak of their power in the ninth and tenth centuries. Taking advantage of a succession crisis at Byzantium, Symeon twice reached the walls of Constantinople, in 914 and 924 (*Chronicle of Manasses*, fourteenth century, Vatican Library).

Symeon (893–927) signified for Bulgaria a political, cultural and military golden age, when the foundations were laid for the critical Byzantino-Bulgar relationship of the tenth century. It was a time when Bulgaria saw itself as a second Byzantium, to the extent that Symeon claimed for himself the title of basileus, and when Bulgaria experienced at its own rear the pressures of Slav and Turkic peoples whose successes and reverses followed the rhythm of Byzantine policy on that same terrain, the Ukrainian and Danubian plains.

The crisis broke out in 894, when the monopoly of Bulgar trade was granted to two Greek merchants, Staurakios and Kosmas, 'friends' of Stylianos Zaoutzes. They transferred its centre from Constantinople to Thessalonica, a move prejudicial to the Bulgarians, in that it bypassed the trade-route from Pliska to Constantinople. On top of this the duties on Bulgarian merchandise were increased. Symeon invaded Thrace, and in 895 Leo VI mobilised against him the Magyars in the region between the Dniester and the Prut, while the Byzantine fleet blockaded the mouth of the Danube. Symeon retaliated by driving the Magyars back across the river and hurling against them the Petchenegs settled on the Dnieper. Demoralised, the Magyars migrated westwards, and their permanent settlement on the Danubian plain marks the foundation of Hungary, with Germanic support and at the expense of the Moravian state, which the Magyars finally destroyed. Two more Turkic peoples had thus appeared on the scene. The Magyars were not new arrivals, since they had first reached the Danube in 837. The Petchenegs followed in their turn the classic trajectory of peoples from the steppe, and they were found throughout the tenth and in the first half of the eleventh century, holding the military balance of power north of the Danube, even if their nomadic structure never crystallised into an organised State.

Peace was re-established in 896, on the condition of an annual tribute from Byzantium. But after the death of Leo VI in 912, his brother Alexander suspended payment of the tribute, before he himself died in 913. Armed with this pretext, Symeon went over to the attack, and in September of the same year he appeared beneath the walls of the capital. But the root of the problem lay elsewhere. The political example of Byzantium and the triumphs of his own reign, in conjunction no doubt with the minority of Constantine VII Porphyrogennetos, had fired the Constantinople-educated Bulgar with another ambition: to become basileus himself. This ambition was to be fulfilled not by a mere downgrading of the imperial power to the level of a basileus of the Bulgars, but by centring the power of the basileus of the Romans on Bulgaria. This extraordinary adaptation of the model goes to show how far the latter was still regarded as unique in tenth-century eastern Christendom. The patriarch Nicholas, placed by Constantine's minority at the head of affairs, touches on this matter in letters to Symeon which have survived. The attack of 913 gained him entry to the capital, where he received the promise of a future marriage between Constantine and one of his daughters, and where the patriarch placed on his head a crown, albeit using, so it is said, the formula 'basileus of the Bulgars'. But this is not how Boris understood it: at all events, we know of one seal, admittedly of lead rather than gold, on which the Greek legend gives him the title 'basileus of the Romans'. Hostilities were thus resumed, and were inevitably further embittered by the marriage of Constantine VII to the daughter of Romanos Lakapenos, of which they had been a cause. From September 914, and the opening of hostilities by Symeon, until his last assault on Constantinople in 924, there was a decade of unbroken warfare, in course of which both powers, Byzantium and Bulgaria, brought secondary peoples into play, the Christian Slavic Serbs, and the pagan Turkic Petchenegs. Symeon died in 927, and his son Peter made peace, accepted the compromise title spurned by his father, together with an annual tribute from Byzantium, and received as his spouse a grand-daughter of Romanos I Lakapenos, Maria: an ingenious solution, which allowed a privileged ally to marry an imperial descendant, but not one born in the purple, and in so doing reinforced the family aspect characteristic of the international system centred on Byzantium. Attention was drawn earlier to the marriage of Constantine V in the eighth century to the daughter of the Khazar khan, and to her baptism in the name of Irene, and to the fact that Boris of Bulgaria became at his baptism the spiritual son of Michael III. The empire, unique by definition, seems to have envisaged the growing body of sovereign rulers as a single family. Within that family, the Bulgar marriage cautiously paved the way for matrimonial alliances in the proper sense, to which Constantine VII gave lengthy consideration in his treatise De administrando imperio. Unless they were with the 'Franks', he judged such alliances to be forbidden in the line of the purple-born: a principle that would be breached when Basil II secured an alliance with Svjatoslav of Kiev through the marriage of his sister Anna.

The peace of 927 enabled Byzantium to reassert its authority over the Serbs. Bulgar society continued to evolve, chiefly along the lines of Slavicisation, which from now on permeated the old boyar aristocracy, and Christianisation, which made headway outside the towns and offered a means of cultural and national unification. Increasingly complex, Bulgar society was also increasingly subject to the influence of other cultures, as is shown by the development of the Bogomil heresy during the reign of Peter (927–69). Its birth is assigned to this period in general terms by the Bulgar priest Kosmas in his well-known *Sermon* against the sect, composed in the reign of the emperor John Tzimiskes, and more precisely in a reply by the patriarch Theophylact (933–56) to an enquiry put to him on the subject by Peter. The teachings of the heresy, imputed by Kosmas to a certain priest Bogomil ('on whom God takes pity', or 'God-implorer'), a name too telling to be invented, come remarkably close to the dualist ideas of the Paulicians, for example their condemnation of the world and of earthly powers, those of the Church included, and of the flesh and procreation. Ideas of this kind, as we know, had been circulating in the East for centuries, but it is legitimate to link them with the introduction of a form of Christianity new to the Balkans: one naturally thinks of the deportations of Paulicians to Thrace in the ninth century, following the conquest of their territory, and of their later employment there to swell the ranks of the imperial armies. But the *Sermon* by Kosmas gives an insight at the same time into the local situation, where the movement was evidently coloured by a strong and socially-motivated hostility toward the Church, with its well-endowed bishops and monks, and toward the rich in general. This was far from being the full extent of its influence, however, since the Bogomils would reappear later on at Byzantium, in the unsettled religious climate of the eleventh century.

Christianisation beyond the frontier

Byzantium and Bulgaria were no longer the only parties engaged in confrontation – the Russians already came on the scene in the previous chapter. After their surprise attack in 860, a letter was sent by Photios to the eastern patriarchs announcing their conversion. But this was presumably a formality, since in 874 a pact looked forward to the Christianisation of the principality, for which purpose the patriarch Ignatios appointed an archbishop. The project was nullified through the advent to power of Oleg, son of Rurik: the history of the Scandinavian influence on Kiev is comparable in this respect with that of the proto-Bulgarian influence on Bulgaria. The conversion of the ruler had to await the maturation of the State, in the late tenth century. At the beginning of the century, Russian ships posed a threat both to the Khazars and to Constantinople. Reference was made earlier to the treaties concluded with the Russians in 907 and 911, which formulated the rules for the conduct of future embassies and trading relations in the capital. These are known to us solely from the *Chronicle of Times Past*, the Kievan chronicle whose textual transmission and evaluation raise a multiplicity of problems. The Russian attack of 941, by contrast, is also referred to in Byzantine sources. It is once again the Russian *Chronicle* which preserves the text of a treaty concluded in 944. This sets out the tariff for the ransom of prisoners captured by the Russians, the quota of silk that the Russians were entitled to purchase, and provisions for the protection of Chersonnese fishermen. The importance of the Russians on the Byzantine horizon is shown by the space devoted to them in Constantine VII's treatise on the administration of the empire, written in the middle years of the century. Their evolution confronted them with the question of Christianisation: in 957, Olga, Igor's widow, received baptism at Constantinople, in the name of Helena, which was also, it may be recalled, the name borne by the wife of Constantine VII. Here again the Bulgar story seems to be repeating itself, to the point that in 959 Olga in her turn tried out the Latin solution, and sent a request for a bishop and priests to Otto I.

The Christianisation of the Slavs continued to be a bone of contention in the power struggle with Rome and with the Carolingian empire. In these more westerly parts, the Serbs, converted long ago under Herakleios but having since relapsed into paganism, asked for missionaries and received baptism somewhere between 867 and 874, which strengthened Byzantine influence in the north-eastern corner of the Adriatic. Here Byzantium came up against Venice, and against the problem of Slav piracy: the *Narentani* pirates were converted in the reign of Basil I. More important still, Byzantium clashed in Croatia with Rome and the Franks. But the islands and the Dalmatian towns remained part of the Byzantine 'commonwealth' until the twelfth century. Lastly, the Adriatic was also to be a stake in the war with the Arabs. Byzantium's progress in the region was signalled by the setting up between 868 and 878 of the Dalmatian theme, while a *strategos* of Strymon figured in the list of precedences drawn up by Philotheos in 900.

In the Caucasus, the recognition of an Armenian kingdom has to be seen as an incident in the centuries-long struggle between Byzantium and the Arabs in the frontier region stretching from the Taurus to Armenia. Back in 867, it will be remembered, the Paulician war was the chief item on the agenda. After some failed attempts, Basil I conducted a successful campaign of reconquest, lasting from 871 to 882, which won back for Byzantium the key positions on the frontier, the Taurus and the Anti-Taurus, as well as the crossings of the Euphrates. It was in the course of these operations that the territorial base of the Paulicians was wiped out. In 885, Baghdad sent a crown to the Armenian Achot Bagratuni, against payment of a tribute, and Basil naturally did the same. Bagaran, the seat of the dynasty, became the kingdom's capital. Achot, who died in 891, and his son Smbat (892–914) battled against the emirs of Mesopotamia and Azerbaijan, from whom the rival clan, the Ardzuni of Vaspurakan, received in consequence occasional support. The Bagratid kingdom, now with Ani as the capital, nevertheless experienced from the first third of the tenth century an intellectual and architectural golden age, which coincided moreover with the ascendancy of the Armenian generals – John Kourkouas chief among them – at Byzantium.

Start of the counter-offensive against Islam

The war in Mesopotamia continued. Romanos I followed in the footsteps of Basil I by launching a serious campaign of reconquest in the east. In 934, after several vain attempts, John Kourkouas captured Melitene. In 942 he campaigned successfully in Armenia, and in 943 in Mesopotamia, in which year the Byzantines recovered places of great antiquity, Daras, Amida, and Nisibis. They laid siege to Edessa, and the town yielded up the *mandylion*, the image of himself which Christ reputedly sent during his lifetime to King Abgar. The relic was brought back in triumph to Constantinople on 15 August 944. Ranged against Byzantium were the emirs of the region, in particular Saif ad-Dawla, emir of Aleppo and Mosul, member of the local Hamdanid dynasty and legendary hero of the Arabs in northern

The church of the Holy Cross at Aghtamar (in modern Turkey) is one of the finest examples of the artistic flowering of Armenia in the ninth and tenth centuries. The four symmetrically-placed apses, duplicated by four apsiodoles in the angles, form the shape of a cross, surmounted by a cupola.

Syria. The Christians figured in the struggle both as objects and agents. Armenian lords and chieftains became integral to Byzantium's frontier dispositions, which continued to evolve, the *kleisoura* ('defile') often serving as the preliminary to the constitution of a theme. Such appears to have been the origin of the themes of Lykandos, mentioned in 908 and again around 916, and of Sebasteia, mentioned before 908 and again in 911. In addition there is mention as early as 873 of a theme of Charsianon and, between 899 and 901 (at the latest 911), of a Mesopotamian theme; the latter was in fact identical with an Armenian principality ceded to Leo VI and the Armenian prince of Taro was appointed to it as *strategos* between 900 and 930. As always, therefore, these frontiersmen passed from one allegiance to the other, without making any lasting commitments. Byzantium for its part made deliberate use of the region's Christian faith. The Armenians repopulated the fringes of the Melitene emirate, left vacant by the defeat of the Paulicians, early in the tenth century, and provided garrisons for the Mesopotamian theme. After 950, and even earlier under Romanos I, Armenian migration westward took on a more regional and more concerted character than in the days when individual Armenian warriors departed to seek their fortunes at the court of an eighth- or ninth-century emperor. The frontier themes after 950 consisted as a rule of little more than a fortified position, where the *strategos* had his base. By comparison with the 'great' themes of the interior they were indeed 'small', and went either by that description, or by that of 'Armeniac', in significant contrast with the 'Romaic' themes. Their forces were composed of Armenians, Syrian Jacobites and even Paulicians, who were familiar with the terrain but incapable of posing a threat to the capital. Lastly, during the same period, the wars of the great Armenian clans, their Georgian cousins, and the emirs of Melitene, at the start of the ninth century, have a history all their own; enacted on the fringes of Byzantium and the caliphate, this history is known, or rather accessible, from Armenian, Syriac and Arab (Christian and Muslim) sources; they have more to tell us on the subject than the Byzantine sources, whose role in this instance is complementary. But it should at least be mentioned that here, on the margin of eastern Christendom, we have the history of rich and important national societies, which – despite some promising and already fruitful philological and archaeological researches – remain too little explored.

In the later years of Constantine VII, however, Saif al-Dawla regained the advantage. In 954 Nikephoros Phokas replaced his father Bardas at the head of the army and brought victory back to the Byzantine camp. In 958, the nephew of Nikephoros, John Tzimiskes, entered Samosata. Both had their feet firmly on the path that would lead to the throne.

More uncertain progress in the West

In the Mediterranean, the situation was different, in terms both of the opponents and of issues. At sea, from Rhodes and Crete to Sicily and the Gargano, Arab piracy threatened the security of coastal dwellers and maritime traffic. In Sicily and southern Italy, any Byzantine initiative was bound to follow the contours of the reconquest, Justinian's grand design, which over the lifetime of the empire was periodically revived, in the ninth and tenth centuries to the glorification of Basil and his dynasty, in the twelfth to that of the Comneni. Here too, however, the picture in 867 is dominated by the story of Arab progress, and is altered, where the Justinianic model is concerned, by the fact of the Carolingian empire and the presence of the Lombard principalities in the south. That the two situations are intimately connected should therefore be obvious, and can be verified by studying for example the *Lives* of two monks of the period, one a Sicilian, Elias the Younger, who was born about 823 at Enna and died in 903 at Thessalonica, and the other a Calabrian, Elias the Cave-Dweller (Speleiotes), who was born between 860 and 870 at Reggio and died around 960 in his monastery. Both set up monasteries at the foot of Aspromonte, on the tip of Calabria. Both had connections with Rome, emphasised by the place given to a stay in Rome in their biographies. And both made many voyages, and were driven in particular towards the Peloponnese by force of circumstances. Elias the Younger was nevertheless on good terms with the governor of Calabria and with Leo VI.

This said, the history of the Arab raids on the Greek and Italian coasts is of a different order from that of the naval campaigns against southern Italy. The Arabs' mastery of the sea is reflected in attacks of varying intensity. In 896, the inhabitants of Aegina fled to the mainland following a raid, known to us from the *Life of Luke the Younger*, which carried on into Greece. In 904, an expedition led by a Byzantine renegade, Leo of Tripoli, got as far as the Dardanelles with the aim of attacking Constantinople, then sheered off to capture Thessalonica. The eye-witness account of this event, by the cleric John Cameniates, shows that one motive for such forays was to take captives for sale. He refers to the assailants in a way that conforms to the Byzantine stereotype of the savage, but this does not disguise the very violent nature of the occurrence, whose impact was all the greater because of the particular town that was affected. In 925, Oria suffered an attack described in a letter written (in Hebrew) by Shabbetai Donnolo, a Jewish physician and philosopher who belonged to the local community, which we have already come across in connection with Basil I's decree of conversion. Nevertheless, alongside the deaths and disappearances resulting from such raids, life in proximity to the Arabs had its more domestic aspects. A manuscript dating from 916 gives the story of Athanasia of Aegina, who eleven days after their marriage had lost her husband through an Arab invasion, and who then obeyed the imperial decree enjoining the island's widows and spinsters to take a 'barbarian' husband. Admittedly, this story has an exemplary ending, since the second husband eventually agreed to become a monk. But the circulation of Arab coins, for example of the Cretan emirs, whose presence at Athens has already been noted, and the discovery in Athens of a Muslim place of worship, not to mention the ornamental use of kufic characters in the church decoration of that region – all bear witness, around the tenth century, to a peaceable Arab presence. In short, there is a coastal Byzantium, stretching from Sicily to Apulia, from Calabria to Thessalonica, and including the Aegean, where the spectrum of relations with Islam is comparable in many ways with the picture we painted of Byzantium's land frontier in the East. In actuality, by reason of the competition for Cyprus and the maritime activity of the emirs of Tarsus, this Byzantium of the islands and sea coasts can also be said to impinge on Asia Minor.

Imperial policy in fact had two goals: the reconquest of the sea-routes and the reconquest of Italy. The first was scarcely be accomplished before the second half of the tenth century. Basil started off, it is true, with a run of successes in the Adriatic. He liberated Ragusa in 868 and in 876 recaptured Bari from the emperor Louis II, who had taken it from the Arabs in 871. This victory sowed the seed for the later theme of Langobardia, first mentioned as having a *strategos* in 911, which was created, as the name implies, at the expense of the Lombard princes in the region – or to put it more precisely, it subjected them to a superior authority. A victorious campaign by Nikephoros Phokas in 885–6 delivered Amantea, Tropea and Santa Severina to the Byzantines, while in 901 the Arabs captured Reggio. Until the middle of the century, the administrative nomenclature remained that of the Sicilian theme, but the terminology then changed to take account of the facts: the treatise *On the Administration of the Empire* (948–52) mentions a *strategos* of Calabria. Byzantium can thus be seen asserting itself once again as a political presence and military foe in southern Italy from the reign of Basil I. And beneath this official history lies the history of a provincial Hellenism whose political allegiance was pledged to Constantinople, but whose religious allegiance was to Rome. We learn of it from the monastic literature already referred to, a part of which has been destroyed through later misfortunes, but whose vestiges are sufficient to show the rich complexity of a border culture that only gradually declined following the Norman conquest of the eleventh century. Traces also survive in the archaeological remains, still not fully inventoried, and in a handful of archival documents whose number may yet increase. Lastly there are the Calabrian Greek dialects, living languages to this day, which in spite of the problems they present are certainly to be included in the evidence.

This Byzantine expansion into southern Italy did not solve the general problem of seaborne contacts. On the contrary, in the course of the tenth century, the Arabs succeeded in occupying Sicily, from which they menaced Calabria, and where Hellenism nevertheless survived. Everything hinged in fact on Crete and Cyprus, and here Byzantium failed, as it had failed in 904 at Thessalonica. The Byzantine fleet under its admiral Himerios landed on Cyprus in 910 following a great victory in the Aegean in 905 or 906. But in 911, returning from a fruitless campaign to Crete, his fleet was destroyed off Chios. Nevertheless, the second half of the ninth century saw important changes in the organisation of Byzantine naval forces. The *drongarios* of the imperial fleet became commander-in-chief, with the department of naval affairs beneath him. The first reference to a new naval theme, that of Samos, occurs in 899. To match it, a large ship-building programme was put in hand, and attention was paid to the reinforcement of key coastal positions such as Thessalonica, following the disaster of 904, and Attalia.

Byzantium is thus to be seen around 950 as embodying Eastern Christianity, a model of empire, a coinage, a ruling culture, and their peripheral attributes, but equally as a society of warriors and clergy, townsmen and peasants, which invites comparison with the contemporary West. A society without problems? Assuredly not. But we must be content to decipher them from the fiscal discontent of a province, the dissent reflected in a heresy, the divergence of a regional culture, or the ambitions of a war-leader. These make up the driving force of a history which pursued its course after the death of Constantine VII towards what has to be called, despite a contradiction in terms more apparent than real, a 'feudal' State.

377

Restoration of the empire in the West. This bronze-gilt statuette, said to be of Charlemagne, probably represents one of his victorious successors, orb in hand, in imperial raiment, or else the ideal image of a Carolingian ruler (*c.* 860–70, Paris, Louvre).

PART 3

The first stirrings of Europe: seventh to mid-tenth centuries

Barbarian kingdoms, Christian empire or independent principalities? 9

We saw that by the middle of the seventh century, and with much regional variation, the Germanic and Celtic kingdoms of the sixth century had attained a state of fragile but genuine stability. This was succeeded, roughly speaking from about 650 down to the mid-eighth century, and then, after the Carolingian interlude, from 850 to 950, by a series of manifold crises. A new cycle of devastations appeared to be in train.

In reality, the consequences of the setbacks to *romanitas* and the advances registered by Germanic innovations raise fundamental questions about the earlier successes. The two forces which had collaborated in restoring order, the kings and the clerics, were unable to prevent the irremediable disappearance of Roman customs and institutions, or to contain the upsurge of a new social stratum, the nobility. This is attributable to the development of a new outlook among peoples passing from a state of extreme weakness to one of rejuvenation, for which the return of order is itself to be held responsible. These new forces were strong enough to despoil the State and the Church by virtue of the ties between man and man, to effect a radical transformation in agricultural methods, to create new means of exchange and maritime expansion. At the same time, a new culture made it possible for the Anitique heritage to be reinserted into this world turned upside down. It is no longer a question of the cards being redealt but of another game and a different civilisation. The gradual and precarious recovery of the population released from the burden of taxation won back the lost lands and launched a first assault on lands lying fallow. The privatisation of the State gave birth to a new, powerful class; the great landowners subjected the Church to secularisation and created regional principalities. In this maelstrom some fundamentally new developments made their appearance: the ties between man and man, the exploitation of the northern seas, the bipartite organisation of estates, the type of ship known as the hulk, the silver currency, and the Bible as the all-embracing cultural authority. The mixing of the two worlds, the Germanic and the Roman, was effected through a gradual displacement of the Antique heritage from the Mediterranean to the North Sea, with the result that the intellectual and artistic pre-renaissance shone most brightly in England, which was of all territories the most Germanised. Hence it is that we are aware, all through the Carolingian interlude, of that 'stirring beneath the surface', as Duby puts it, which presaged an eventual awakening.

Funerary stele from the Frankish Christian cemetery of Niederdollendorf (late seventh century): the dead warrior, his broadsword sheathed in its scabbard, is beset by snakes from hell, but affirms his belief in immortality by combing his hair, which was the symbol of vitality.

Nearly all the agricultural and technical innovations sprang from three regions – the Thames basin, the north of Gaul and Germany, and the plain of the Po – which were precisely those where the break with the past was most profound. Fields of promise under the late empire and well-suited to cereal cultivation, these plains had seen their initial development arrested by the Germanic invasions or by plague. On becoming zones where the newcomers and old-established inhabitants most readily made contact, they formed the meeting-point of the old world and the new, of the old Europe and its youthful successor. The barbarians demonstrated here their remarkable powers of adaptation, developing these territories, from the beginning of the eighth century, on the scale they would otherwise have experienced in the fifth century. The most novel solutions were devised precisely where the disturbances had been greatest, along a sort of historical fault line which was at the same time a critical path, and which ran from Italy, by way of Austrasia and Frisia, to England. Any attempt to explain these far-reaching changes and innovations must take as its starting-point the curious alliance between Germanic bellicosity and violence and the pacific Christian faith.

Indeed, after much violent agitation, the disparate ingredients of the *romanitas– christianitas–germanitas* formula emulsified into a hitherto unknown concoction. The blend proved especially advantageous to the Austrasian Franks and to the Anglo-Saxons, who were willing to absorb the lessons of their southern mentors but saw no reason to forfeit their identity on that account. Having established themselves as masters of the new economic region in the north, and as the allies and protectors of a Church revived under their auspices, they resolutely opposed a regional power of any kind, and any religious power of a heretical or alien nature, such as Byzantium or Islam. Once the royal unction had conferred on Pippin the legitimacy he was hitherto lacking, once the first Carolingians were persuaded by their monastic mentors that the Roman empire had finally fallen with the capture of Jerusalem in 638 and stood in need of restoration, the mixture became explosive. The Germanic barbarian, smitten with guilt at having pillaged pagan Rome in 410, was about to repair his fault by becoming the saviour of Christian Rome. This enabled him, with the co-operation of the papacy, to make a bid for the domination of Europe.

The end of the barbarians

In the second half of the seventh century, and in the first half of the eighth, we see an upset to the equilibrium of the barbarian kingdoms following a number of internal crises. It is not too much to say that these reversed the existing positions, to the benefit of the Anglo-Saxon kingdoms, the Lombard realm and above all the Frankish kingdom. Politically speaking, these crises sprang from the rejection of Germanic monarchical institutions inherited from Rome and the rise of aristocracies. After the fragmentation of the empire came the fragmentation of kingdoms.

Destructions and disappearances

The birth of territorial principalities is in fact the most conspicuous feature of the age. In Gaul, profiting from the rivalries between Neustria and Austrasia, the Alamans, the Thuringians and the Bavarians reverted to their former independence. In the south, Burgundy disintegrated into a number of city–territories controlled by local princes. After 702 Provence did the same, under the overlordship of the patrician Antenor, while Aquitaine was taken in hand by a new dynasty founded by Eudo (before 700–35). In the north-west, the Bretons were becoming increasingly autonomous, while in the north-east, led by Radbod (before 689–719), the Frisians extended their area of political and economic influence along the coasts of the North Sea. The neighbouring kingdoms exhibited similar traits. In Spain, Septimania and Tarragona made constant efforts to set up an eastern Visigothic kingdom independent of Toledo, while in Italy the Lombard dukes of Benevento, Spoleto and Friuli refused to take their orders from Pavia.

These multiple seizures of power were the work of the Germanic nobility. In Neustria, a high functionary, the mayor of the palace Ebroin (653–87), spilled much blood in crushing aristocratic revolts and made so many enemies that he fell victim to the Austrasian nobility under the leadership of the Arnulfing family, which succeeded in making the mayoralty of the palace hereditary in its own line. At Tertry, in 687, Pippin II (erroneously known as Pippin 'of Herstal') finally made certain of the supremacy of Austrasia over Neustria, completing what Pippin I and Grimoald, his grand-father and uncle, had begun. In fact a new dynasty was in preparation. The cradle of its power was no longer poised between the Seine and the Scheldt but on the Meuse. Well-endowed with lands and financial resources, Pippin, mayor of the palace of Austrasia from 679 and master of Neustria from 687, now

383

styled himself *princeps Francorum* and tried to restore to the kingdom the territories which had broken away. In practice he could do no more than repel the most dangerous of his foes, the Frisians, through the reoccupation of Utrecht. Elsewhere, south of the Loire and in Burgundy in particular, his authority was non-existent. His death in 714 even inspired a Neustrian revolt, quickly crushed at the bloody battle of Vinchy in 717 by his masterful bastard son, Charles. The latter owed his nickname 'Martel' ('hammer') to the 'hammering' he administered first to this revolt, and afterwards to the independence of the Frisians, Alamans, Burgundians and Provençals.

Like the Merovingians, the Visigothic kings were powerless to withstand the rise of the aristocracy. The latter rejected the idea of hereditary succession and sought constantly to elect their own candidate. The Church made a vain attempt to make the king sacrosanct by the rite of royal unction, which had already been inaugurated before 672, the time of Wamba's election. But the revolts continued. When the Arabs began to threaten Spain, the country was divided between King Roderick and the sons of one of his predecessors, Witiza. Under the Islamic attack, as has been seen, it collapsed like a house of cards. By 718, the invaders had occupied Narbonne and Septimania, the base from which the Berbers launched their first raids on Gaul. In 721, however, they met with a serious setback when confronted by Eudo, prince of Aquitaine, before Toulouse. They made off to the Rhône valley and pillaged Autun in 725. In 732, having ravaged Aquitaine, they met Charles Martel north of Poitiers and suffered their second defeat. But it needed a serious internal crisis in Muslim Spain to enable Pippin III to reoccupy Narbonne between 752 and 759, while the emir of Cordoba, Abd ar-Rahman, was engaged in the difficult process of establishing a new regime.

Meanwhile, in fact as early as 718, profiting from the victory at Toulouse, some Hispano-Visigoths, led by Pelayo (or Pelagius?), had crushed a Muslim army near Covadonga (another date, 722, has also been proposed by Sanchez-Albornoz). The event marked the beginnings of the Christian kingdom of the Asturias. The irruption of Islam into southern Europe reduced Byzantium's control over Mediterranean waters to the Adriatic and sub-Tyrrhenian sectors, while the Frankish kingdom, the only one to put up any resistance, gained substantially in prestige. From then on the Iberian peninsula was at the mercy of the Muslims, and the tiny Asturian kingdom of Alfonso I (739–57) looked quite incapable of reconquering the former Visigothic kingdom on its own.

The European repercussions of the Battle of Poitiers were felt as far away as Britain, whose place in Christendom we shall come to later. While the Picts continued to hold sway in Scotland, the political focus of the island shifted to the Anglo-Saxon kingdom of Wessex under the rule of Ine (688–726), whose power extended from the Pas de Calais to the Bristol Channel. Admittedly there was no abatement in the rivalries between the various king-doms, but Britain's orientation was increasingly towards the North Sea and the Channel, that is to say towards the Franks. In Italy, too, attraction into the Frankish orbit increased as the fragmentation of the peninsula became more pronounced. The Italo-Byzantine territories had less and less connection with the empire. The exarchate of Ravenna showed signs of becoming an autonomous entity, the Romagna. The duchy of Rome submitted to the authority of the pope. The duchies of Naples, Calabria and Sicily were alone in

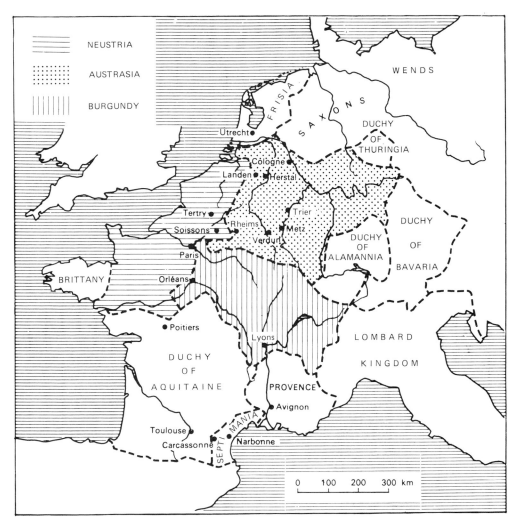

11 Gaul in the first half of the eighth century

remaining loyal. In addition, the adoption of the iconoclast heresy at Constantinople widened the rift between the papacy and the Byzantines. So when Liutprand, king of the Lombards (712–44), resumed his policy of expansion and unification, the papacy found itself completely isolated. In 739, its appeal for help to Charles Martel went unheeded. And when Aistulf, king of the Lombards, was able to threaten Rome itself, the situation was clearly critical.

Entry of the Austrasians on the scene

Since 741, the son of Charles Martel, Pippin III ('the Short'), had been ruling the Frankish kingdom without titular authority. Faced by the still powerful autonomous regions, he **385** submitted to Pope Zacharias his famous question, 'Who should be king in Francia, he who possesses power or he who does not?' The pope having obviously replied that it should be the former so that proper order could be maintained, Pippin had himself acclaimed king by the magnates at Soissons and had himself anointed. In 754, Pope Stephen II, on a visit to Gaul to request Pippin's help against the Lombards, anointed him a second time, at Saint-Denis, together with his two sons and his wife. A new dynasty was being shaped, leaving the last of the Merovingians, Childeric III, to be tonsured and shut in a monastery. The race of kings which was made holy by blood was being superseded by the race consecrated by unction. The pagan charisma was fading, giving way to the charisma of divine grace. The seeds of a new kind of legitimacy were being sown with this new dynasty which would soon be styled 'Carolingian'.

A second innovation, as great as the first and flowing from it, followed almost immediately. Wishing to repay the pope for his assistance, Pippin III, influenced perhaps by the famous 'forged donation' of Constantine which it is thought was shown to him at this time (it claimed that the emperor, before departing for the East, had granted the whole of Italy to Pope Sylvester), ended by launching two campaigns, in 754 and 756, against the Lombards. He forced them to 'restore' to the pope twenty-eight towns, formerly Byzantine, in central Italy. This marked the beginnings of the 'patrimony of St Peter', intended, as it seemed to the pope, to consolidate and guarantee his universal power over Christendom. A new balance of forces was being established.

Thus by the middle of the eighth century the crisis of the barbarian kingdoms was resolved. Out of the eight political conglomerations formed in the fifth and sixth centuries, only three remained intact, the Anglo-Saxons and the Lombards, with the Franks in the middle. Only the latter stood out as retaining their potency and drive, because they had made a real start on suppressing regional autonomy and because they aspired to the reconstruction of a political unity which was no longer merely Nordic and Frankish but European, just as it was already multi-national. The Franks were in close economic and cultural contact with the Anglo-Saxons and the Lombards, and even with the Asturians in north-western Spain. They were, therefore, at the gravitational centre of a Europe waiting to be built from scratch. Emerging victorious from the crises and changes of the seventh century, masters of a northern economic space undreamed of in the fifth century, allies and protectors of the Church, antagonists of all regional principalities and of all religious authority deemed, like Byzantium's, to be heretical, or, like Islam's, to be pagan, the Franks could not fail to be urged towards hegemony by the papacy. Having pillaged Rome in 410, three centuries later Germanic barbarians sought to restore it and to guarantee the supremacy of Roman Christianity. But once he had inaugurated the patrimony of St Peter, kernel of the future Papal State, which lasted until 1870, Pippin III left the pope to fend for himself against the continual attacks of the Lombards and preferred to concentrate on restoring order inside his kingdom where the regional principalities were again rearing their heads. For in spite of an initial subjugation of Frisia in 752–4, and ceaseless campaigning in the east, only Burgundy and Provence were securely in his grasp.

386   After his two Italian expeditions, Pippin therefore made careful preparations for his

campaigns against Waifar, prince of Aquitaine. He first outflanked his enemy by capturing Muslim Septimania and allowing the Hispano-Visigoths, who took Narbonne after a long siege (752–9), to keep their own law and to remain virtually autonomous. Next, from 760 to 768, the new king of the Franks campaigned almost annually in Aquitaine. Town by town, county by county, he conquered the whole principality as far as the Garonne. Having wrought the destruction of 35 monasteries and arrested the development of the last remaining preserve of southern civilisation for two generations, he died on returning from the last campaign and was buried at St Denis. From that time, the triumph of the Germans over the old Roman civilisation of the south could be said to be complete. By contrast, nothing but failure resulted from his repeated campaigns against the Alamans, the Saxons and the Bavarians.

Charlemagne

Following the Merovingian fashion, Pippin III had divided his kingdom between his two sons, Carloman and Charles. The partition was of brief duration: Carloman died in 771 and his brother found himself at the head of the whole territory. At the outset, he pursued the same policy as his father: 'extension of the kingdom', or more precisely recuperation of territories formerly subject to the Merovingians, even if circumstances and Charles's own temperament were later to decree otherwise.

'Dilatatio regni'

King at the age of twenty-one, this reputedly seven-foot giant (according to Einhard), with his high-pitched voice and bushy moustache, was primarily a soldier inured to war by the campaigns in Aquitaine and an inveterate huntsman, so consumed by his passion that the year before his death, at the age of about 70, he was still hunting boar in the Ardennes. A shrewd strategist, but also a pragmatist, he conducted his campaigns with foresight, broke them off in the event of defeat and brought them to a prudent conclusion. In order to clinch the possession of Frisia, he began by attempting to annex Saxony, from the Rhine to the Elbe. In 772, he destroyed the Irminsul, the main sanctuary of the Saxons' pagan cult, and started on a piecemeal conquest by winning over a section of the Saxon nobility. But in response to a call from Pope Hadrian, under threat from Desiderius, king of the Lombards, Charles crossed the Alps and laid prolonged siege to the Lombard capital, Pavia, which surrendered in 774. The king of the Franks then took on himself the crown of the Lombards, confirmed the patrimony of St Peter and received the title 'Patrician' of the Romans, which could not fail to involve him in further interventions. Returning to the conquest of Saxony, he was deflected from it by an appeal received from rebellious Muslims and Christians in Spain. In 778, he effected a crossing at each end of the Pyrenees, but, unable to see his way clearly through the Hispano-Muslim entanglement over Saragossa, he could achieve nothing positive. On the return march through the pass of Roncevaux, his rearguard, commanded by Roland, marquess of Brittany, was massacred on 15 August by

387

a combined force of Basques and Muslims. On hearing the news the whole of Saxony rose in revolt.

Charles tried to surmount this first great crisis, in the years 778–9, by a series of timely measures intended on the one hand to allay internal discontent and on the other to bring his recalcitrant external enemies to heel. In 781, he presented his sons Louis and Pippin to the Aquitanians and the Lombards respectively as their kings. Next, in 785, he issued a harsh 'capitulary' against the Saxons and devoted himself to seven years of repeated campaigning. After a serious reverse at Mt Suntal, he did not flinch from beheading 4,500 Saxon nobles in order to destroy the religious prestige attached to these warrior–priests. Elsewhere, he received oaths of fidelity from the citizens of Gerona and so gained a foothold on the southern flank of the Pyrenees. In 787, he obtained the submission in theory of the Lombard duke of Benevento, who paid him a tribute, but for the same reason began to alarm the Byzantine empire, which had territories close by. In 788, he achieved the condemnation and deposition of Tassilo III, duke of Bavaria, on the grounds of the latter's repeated refusals to abide by his submission. This done, Charles appointed his own brother-in-law, Gerold, to take charge of the region so as to suppress the Bavarians' leanings toward independence.

The adequacy of these measures has to be doubted, since the years 791–5 witnessed another crisis compounded of a Muslim raid on Septimania, a revolt by the duke of Benevento, bad harvests leading to famine, and lastly an attempt on Charles's life by his (illegitimate) son Pippin the Hunchback. His retrieval of the situation was once again due to a mixture of pliancy and force. As a means of circumventing conspiracies, Charles made all his subjects swear an oath of fidelity. To complete the conquest of Saxony, he dispensed with the special regime instituted under the preceding capitulary and replaced it with a policy of treating Franks and Saxons as equals. In the years 791–5 he organised several expeditions against the nomadic Avars, who were threatening parts of Italy and Bavaria, and in 796 he captured their ring, a circular fortification between the Danube and the Tisza. The booty it yielded enabled him to bestow lavish rewards on his faithful followers. His repeated victories were thus the chief source of his authority and of the deference he received. Charlemagne cannot be understood without taking account of his defeats, which aroused feelings of solidarity, and of his triumphs, which brought him prestige and greatness.

Christmas 800

The road to the empire was now open. In ecclesiastical circles a movement of political ideas had begun which reflected the new culture. The prince, by summoning to his court its foremost representatives – the Anglo-Saxon Alcuin in 782, the Lombard Paul the Deacon in 782, the Hispano-Visigoth Theodulf, and so on – was able to harness it in support of his power. The kingship and the papacy had successively been restored, the first through the anointings of 751 and 754, the second through the donations and confirmations of Pippin and Charles which endorsed its mastery of Rome. The biblical parallel with David and

Samuel therefore came the more readily to the pen of the Carolingian authors, in particular Alcuin, who called Charles a priestly king. Pope Hadrian I had not shrunk from coupling the sovereign's name with the imperial Roman epithet *Magnus* (great), which has been attached to it ever since. Besides this, on a mosaic in St John Lateran he was compared with the archetypal Roman and Christian emperor, Constantine. This depicts him receiving the standard which symbolised imperial power from the hands of St Peter, on the model of Constantine. In this way two ideological movements had emerged, one centred on Charles and the other on the papacy. The tendency of each – and how far the aim was conscious is hard to tell – was to impel the king of the Franks and Lombards in the direction of a government which Alcuin describes, in 798, as a 'Christian empire'. However, if the papacy envisaged restoration of the empire as the means of recovering its authority over the patriarch of Constantinople and the Eastern Church, the circle around Charlemagne seems to have adopted a more secular standpoint. Theodulf unhesitatingly rejected the idea of the pope's legal supremacy over the whole Church, supposedly vested in him by St Peter. Charlemagne himself, through the pen of Alcuin, made it clear that the pope's office was to aid Charles with prayers for his victory, while it was for the king of the Franks alone to 'defend the Church of Christ in all places from the incursions of pagans and the ravages of infidels, and to secure inward recognition of the Catholic faith'. The entourage of the Frankish king looked on the pope as the ruler's spiritual servant. The pontifical clerics held that the two powers, papacy and empire, came from St Peter and that the spiritual was therefore superior to the temporal.

While the drift of these political currents still remained unclear, the 'imperial plan' was abruptly translated into reality. At Byzantium, the Empress Irene had blinded her son, Constantine VI, and seized power in his stead. The Franks may well have taken this to mean that the empire was without an emperor. On 25 April 799, Pope Leo III, who had been held prisoner by a faction of the Roman nobles, escaped and managed to take refuge with Charles, then at Paderborn. The moment for serious negotiations had arrived. Of the three powers, the empire, the papacy and the kingship, only the last, embodied in the king of the Franks, was still intact. It was therefore the duty of that monarch to reinstate the second and to assume the first, now vacant. Accordingly, on 25 December 800, at Rome, in St Peter's basilica, the pope placed the imperial crown on Charles's head, after which the throng of Franks in arms acclaimed the new emperor: 'To Charles Augustus, crowned by God, great and pacific emperor of the Romans, life and victory!' In conclusion, the pope prostrated himself before the new emperor. From this ceremony the king of the Franks, according to his biographer Einhard, made an angry departure.

It seems undeniable that the pope had gone about the ceremony in a way that reversed the traditional order. At Byzantium, where Roman protocol was still observed, the acclamations by the crowd and military preceded coronation by the patriarch; this was to signify that imperial power came from the people and the army. Leo III, by crowning Charles at the start before the acclamations had rung out, proclaimed in this fashion that all power came from God by way of his intermediary. The lay conception of the empire held by Charlemagne was thus undermined, which explains his anger, because the emperor's

A dual investiture. St Peter confers the pallium on Pope Leo III and the Roman standard on Charlemagne, king of the Franks. Detail of the mosaic which the pope ordered to be made for his triclinium shortly before 800 (Rome, Lateran Palace).

independence was so heavily compromised. This quarrel is crucial to our understanding of the whole thrust of the medieval political programme. It lies at the root of the problematic relations between the empire and the papacy, eventually to be resolved in 1804 in brusque fashion by Napoleon when he took the imperial crown in his own hands and set it on his head.

In the remaining fourteen years of his reign Charlemagne sought to clarify the idea of empire and make his personal conception of it triumph. In keeping with his view of the empire as Frankish, he never relinquished his titles of king of the Franks and king of the Lombards. In 806, he made provision for his kingdom to be partitioned after his death between his three sons, Louis, Pippin and Charles, in the Merovingian tradition. The death of Pippin and Charles nullified the plan, but it shows how far he was influenced by Frankish ideas. Furthermore, his conception of the empire embraced all Christian people, and hence the Church. His behaviour at the Council of Frankfurt in 794, when he had insisted on condemning adoptionism, a Spanish heresy, and Byzantine iconoclasm, without heed to the pope's advice, shows that he looked on the pope merely as the premier bishop. In this respect he fitted perfectly into the Constantinian tradition. Again, through his revision and emendation of the Germanic laws he returned to the Roman idea of the emperor as law-giver. But his relations with Constantinople, where the coronation of 800 was regarded as the usurpation by a barbarian of a unique title in its own keeping, were more problematic. A first round of negotiations collapsed in 802. But after Pippin of Italy had invaded the Byzantine territories of Venice and Istria in 810, another embassy, in 812, obtained in return for the restoration of these conquests Byzantine recognition of Charles as 'emperor and basileus', although this stopped short of the right to style himself 'emperor of the Romans'. From now on, therefore, there were two emperors. When it became evident that Charles would have only one son to succeed him, the problem of the imperial investiture was clarified. Assembling the magnates in the chapel at Aachen in 813, Charlemagne had them acclaim the imperial title in favour of his son and placed the crown on his head. He had finally set the seal on his conception of empire, in which Rome and the Romans, the Church and the pope no longer had any voice. The new Romans were the Franks and Rome from now on was at Aachen.

Shadows and constraints

The end of Charlemagne's reign was thus essentially taken up with pressing problems of government. In consequence, between 800 and 814, the pace of conquests finally slowed down. From 794, indeed, Charles was in the habit of spending all the winter at Aachen, where the building works in the palace and chapel demanded his attention. His armies nevertheless made marked progress in Spain, where King Louis took part in the capture of Barcelona in 801 and of Tarragona in 808. But he failed to keep hold of Pamplona, captured in 811, and the Basques' country (including the territories they occupied in Navarre and Gascony) was subjected only in name. Only the Spanish March, later to be known as Catalonia, remained securely in Frankish hands. In Italy the Byzantines still held Venice, Istria, Apulia, Calabria, Sicily and Sardinia. The Lombard duke of Benevento remained to all intents and purposes independent. In Saxony, on the other hand, Charles made constant efforts to consolidate the frontier with the Slavs. In 804, he deported the Nordalbingians and brought Franks to colonise both banks of the Elbe estuary, where he founded Hamburg. He initiated campaigns against the Sorbs in 806, against the Czechs in 805–6, against the Wilzi in 809–12, and against the Linones in 808–11. In so doing, he came up against the Danes. Their king, Godofrid, presented a distinct threat in the years between 804 and 811. It may have been he who barred the isthmus of the Jutland peninsula with an earthwork crowned by a palisade, the Danevirk. Moreover, the empire's coastal regions were already being affected by the pirate raids of his compatriots, the Vikings.

When the emperor died, on 28 January 814, and was buried in the chapel at Aachen, he had thus reassembled, in a reign lasting 46 years, by far the greater part of the Germanic and Latin world. But this unification, whether it was due to the luck of favourable circumstances or to his own sheer doggedness (33 years spent in the conquest of Saxony!) did not lead to the disappearance, in Aquitaine, in Lombardy, or in Bavaria, of their

391

Bulgar necklace in gold, enamel and pearls, ninth or tenth century (Archaeological Museum, Preslav).

First-century Roman chalice of polished semi-precious stone set in a tenth-century Byzantine gold mount with enamel inlay (Venice, St Mark's Treasury).

Gospel cover with enamel inlay depicting St Michael, tenth century (Venice, St Mark's Treasury).

From unity to plurality

Despite the reduced scale of the external wars, which were the real driving-force behind Carolingian supremacy, the empire continued on a more or less even keel, benefiting from the initial impetus given to it by Charlemagne. Under Louis the Pious (814–40), its internal problems abruptly came to the fore, and from 840 the aristocratic factions renewed their bid for power. With foreign invasions posing a sudden threat and civil wars multiplying in 843, the empire divided into three kingdoms at the partition of Verdun, and eventually disappeared amid the general disorder.

A lay or a clerical empire?

As we have seen, the fund of authority amassed by Charlemagne contributed to the accession of his son. Louis, then aged 36, was promoted after a long spell as king of Aquitaine. Although his mother-tongue was Germanic, he had received a religious upbringing at the hands of a Hispano-Visigoth from Septimania, Benedict of Aniane, who exerted great influence on him. On arriving at Aachen, he appointed his Aquitanian advisers to key positions, for example making Helisachar chancellor, and surrounded himself with clerics such as Agobard, a Spaniard, subsequently archbishop of Lyons, whose Romanising political ideas formed a coherent whole. The empire, so their argument ran, was indivisible, and its political institutions must accurately reflect the fact that it was Christian, since the Church, which was superior to the empire, was the sole repository of true justice. The return to favour, after the death of Benedict of Aniane in 821, of two former counsellors of Charlemagne, Adalhard, abbot of Corbie, his brother Wala, previously governor of Saxony, both of whom were Charlemagne's cousins, brought little alteration to this programme based on imperial unity. They, too, were the advocates of institutional rationalisation in the interests of greater efficiency. Most of all they wanted to see the Church and papacy brought fully under the emperor's control. The emperor, who in physique did not have the commanding presence of his father – he was short of stature, with disproportionately long hands and large feet – was nevertheless not found lacking in willpower by those who sought to influence him. Not blessed with his father's political acumen, he sincerely believed his programme was feasible, unmindful of the fact that chance had made him the sole survivor of his brothers, thus eliminating any possibility of a partition in the Germanic fashion. Meanwhile, however, the border offensives, and with them the flow of booty, indispensable components of authority and wealth, continued down to 825, with campaigns against the Obodrites on the Elbe in 818–19, the Croatians in 820, 821 and 822, the Bretons in 818, 822, 824 and 825, and lastly against the Muslims in Spain in 822 and 824. The sporadic pillaging raids by the Vikings on coastal regions did not seem dangerous.

Prior attention could therefore be given to the shaping of imperial and religious policy. Louis the Pious, in contrast with his father – who for political reasons had refused to undertake the evangelisation of the Danes – took advantage of the baptism of King Harald, a refugee at his court, to send Anskar as a missionary to Denmark, and later to Birka in

12 The Carolingian Empire in 814

Louis the Pious in a mixture of German and Byzantine attire. Manuscript of the poem *De Laudibus Sanctae Crucis* by Rabanus Maurus, abbot of Fulda, later archbishop of Mainz, written at Fulda *c.* 840 (Vatican Library).

Sweden. Despite the creation of an impressively large archbishopric based on Hamburg, the results were meagre in the extreme. To set against this, under the guidance of Benedict of Aniane, the emperor convened at Aachen a whole series of councils, in 816, 817, 818 and 819 with the express purpose of reforming the Church. These were characterised, furthermore, by a determined effort to impose the monastic ideal on the secular clergy. The eschewal by Louis the Pious of the opportunity to convert the Church's landed possessions into *precariae*, even when they exceeded the minimum required to sustain each bishopric and abbey, had important political repercussions. With this risk removed, Church property once again began to accumulate. Furthermore, at a meeting with Pope Stephen IV at Rheims in 816, he acknowledged the existence of the patrimony of St Peter. In the act of reforming itself, the Church was thus escaping from lay control, in noticeable contradiction to the ideas of Charlemagne, who had set great store on keeping the clergy under his supervision. The Church, thanks to this assertion of independence, had the potential to become a power external to the empire.

Louis the Pious was much too preoccupied with the need to defend and exalt the Church to perceive any danger in his reforming policy, which in his eyes had purely moral objectives. He even abandoned his father's conception of a lay empire set above the Church. 395

From the moment of his accession, he renounced the titles 'king of the Franks and king of the Lombards', to which Charlemagne had clung, and styled himself 'by divine providence, august emperor'. The Christian basis of the unitary principle at last received affirmation at Rheims in 816, where the pope proceeded to crown Louis anew and anoint him, making it seem that the lay ceremony of 813 was valueless and that Louis was created emperor solely through the pope's intervention. Lastly there was the *Ordinatio Imperii*, drawn up by Louis the Pious in 817 with the aim of making his programme a reality and regulating the succession to retain imperial unity. Since he could not fly openly in the face of the Germanic custom of partition, he left the three existing sub-kingdoms intact: Italy, previously entrusted by Charlemagne to Bernard, Pippin's son; Bavaria, created a kingdom in 814 and given to the emperor's son and namesake Louis; and Aquitaine, assigned in that same year to his son Pippin. But he made these three kings strictly subordinate to his eldest son Lothar, whom he had proclaimed emperor and sole heir to the empire. What was more, he crowned Lothar himself, just as Charlemagne had crowned him in 813. In a word, the indivisible empire was higher than the three kingdoms. But the aristocracy, disquieted by the emperor's favours to the Church, objected that the claims of Bernard had been passed over in silence in the *Ordinatio Imperii* in order to encourage the king of Italy to rebel. Louis the Pious crushed the revolt and had Bernard blinded because of his attempted usurpation. But the emperor's nephew died as a result and Louis's ecclesiastical advisers imposed on him a public penance which he performed in 822 at the palace of Attigny. Not content with this first humiliation of the imperial power, Adalhard, Wala, Agobard and Hilduin, the arch-chaplain and abbot of St Denis, went on cutting the ground from under their own feet. They insisted on Lothar's being sent to Italy as king and had him crowned and anointed emperor at Rome by Pope Paschal I in 823, as if to imply that the coronation of 817 had been of no effect. Through these manoeuvres, the ecclesiastics managed to link the imperial title with anointing and coronation, and to give them the appearance of an exclusively religious prerogative vested in the pope and the see of St Peter. But as a counter-move, Louis and Lothar, in 824, made Rome and the pope acknowledge their authority.

The covetous clans

Lothar was backed by a second pressure group now beginning to form, led by his father-in-law, Hugh, head of an important Alsatian family and count of Tours, and Matfrid, count of Orleans. Their interests, purely material, obliged them to uphold the unity of the empire, over which their properties were widely dispersed. A third group clustered round the second wife of Louis the Pious, Judith, of the Bavarian Welf clan, whom he married in 819. In 823 she bore him a son, the future Charles the Bald. This birth made the *Ordinatio Imperii* of 817 obsolete. Judith was insistent that the system of division should be applied equally to her son. The prize would go to whomever could bend the imperial will, while the two brothers, Pippin and Louis, backed up by their clienteles, sought to profit from these jealousies.

A first crisis-point was reached in 829–30 and resulted in a triumph for the principle of division: Charles obtained the promise of a block of territory consisting of Alamannia, Rhaetia, Alsace and part of Burgundy. Lothar was relegated to Italy. A second crisis, in 833–4, saw the brothers reinstating Lothar as co-emperor, followed by enlargement of their respective kingdoms. The extent of this new triumph for the principle of division was underlined when Louis the Pious dispossessed Pippin of Aquitaine of his kingdom, for the benefit of Charles. Lothar thereupon crossed the Alps, accompanied by Pope Gregory IV, and when the leading nobles deserted the emperor, Louis the Pious was obliged to do penance, abandon his wife and enter a monastery, leaving Lothar sole emperor. But not for long: in February 834 Louis the Pious was ceremonially reinthroned by the bishops in the cathedral at Metz. The crisis thus drew attention, through the incapacity of Lothar and the lay magnates to consolidate the unity of the empire, to the gradual loss of the imperial function into the hands of the clergy.

The last years of Louis the Pious revolved around an obsession: the creation of a kingdom for Charles the Bald. While Aquitaine reverted to its old independence and Bavaria, under Louis the German, did the same, Louis the Pious was busy dividing the empire into two lots: Lothar took the share lying to the east of a dividing line formed by the Rhône, the Saône and the Meuse, while Charles was given everything to the west. When Louis the Pious died, on 20 June 840, the empire lay in ruins.

Expansion had come to a standstill. The royal fisc had seen its stock of landed properties considerably diminished, the loyalty of nobles and vassals had been sorely tried by reiterated demands for oaths of fidelity to an ever-changing procession of kings. They had found the idea of empire too abstract to defend. The clergy, while adopting the idea, altered its thrust towards control of the temporal by the spiritual. Now they were implicated in the failure of an enterprise they had aspired to direct. Nothing daunted, they stuck to the imperial theme, having naturally become its proprietors, and made constant efforts to deepen its meaning in a way that would restore its credibility as a political solution.

Verdun, 843, and its aftermath

The quarrels resulted in a conclusive division of the empire into three kingdoms, followed by the disappearance of the empire itself. In addition, there were new invasions which contributed to this fragmentation.

No sooner was their father dead than Charles the Bald and Louis the German joined forces against the eldest, Lothar, who wanted to reunite the entire imperial inheritance under his control, without granting them autonomous kingdoms. They defeated him at the battle of Fontenoy-en-Puisaye, 25 June 841, and then promised each other, with all their vassals, mutual aid against their brother. They did this at Strasbourg, on 14 February 842, through the exchange of three oaths. The texts were noted down and preserved for posterity by the historian Nithard. Each party swore his oath in the language of the other; this is the earliest text of Old French to survive. The Old High German of the other text is represented in many examples dating from the end of the eighth century onwards. This divergence into two languages is already a portent of the division that was to ensue. After a year spent in laborious negotiations, and in accordance with the expert advice of 120 arbitrators, the three brothers reached a considered agreement, the first, on the partition of the empire. It was ratified at Verdun, in August 843.

This partition, which has left its mark on Europe down to the present, was, it is thought, governed by four considerations: the ties of kinship between clans with a view to preserving inheritances, equality between the three shares, the territorial compactness of each share and respect for the integrity of the three preceding sub-kingdoms, Aquitaine, Italy and Bavaria. Clearly, this was a delicate compromise between the nobles and the monarchs. Furthermore, exceptions were needed to suit particular cases. Lothar's share had to include the Low Countries, where the magnates had rallied to his support in 840. Similarly, the county of Chalons-sur-Saône was earmarked for Charles the Bald, its count having remained loyal to him throughout. But the most difficult problem was to make sure each king had an equal number of royal fiscs. Situated principally in northern Europe, those in Neustria were allotted to Charles the Bald, those between the Meuse and the Rhine to Lothar, and those on the middle Rhine, strung out on the left bank between Mainz and Speyer, to Louis the German: hence the meandering line, which took no account of linguistic boundaries, traced by the frontiers. Generally speaking, and allowing for the exceptions already mentioned, the countries east of the Rhine were allocated to Louis. Charles the Bald received the lands to the west of Scheldt, the Meuse, the Saône and the Rhône, but here again there were exceptions, such as the areas round Lyons, Vienne, Viviers and Uzès, which went to Lothar.

The latter remained master of Frisia, the countries between the Meuse and the Rhine, Burgundy, Provence and Frankish Italy. Ensconced in the two capitals of the empire, Aachen and Rome, he could not fail to be regarded as the emperor pre-eminent over the two other kingdoms. Theoretically, as contemporaries saw it, there was an empire which contained three kingdoms. Very soon, however, it became customary to refer to the kingdom of Louis as that of the Eastern Franks and that of Charles as the kingdom of the Western Franks, or as others put it, as Eastern and Western Francia. Ethnicity played no part in the designation of the intervening kingdom, which took its name from Lothar and his son and namesake. The country of the 'Lotharingians', the followers of Lothar, which we have turned into Lorraine, therefore originated as an artificial entity bound up with an individual. In this way, the very name of Lotharingia carried within it the seed of its ultimate dissolution. The kingdom even lacked territorial continuity, bisected as it was by the formidable obstacle of the Alps.

As we see, the empire was gradually becoming drained of its content and vitality. To begin with, the three brothers made an attempt at peaceful co-existence under the aegis of the clergy, who propounded a regime of so-called 'fraternity' and concord. The shaky compromise lasted, despite various setbacks and shifting alliances, until the death of Lothar in 855. But when the emperor died, leaving his kingdom divided between his three sons, Louis, Charles and Lothar, the title and office of emperor suffered a further degradation. Louis, it is true, became 'emperor' (Louis II) but had to be content with Italy. Charles got Provence. Lothar II became master of the territories extending from the southern peaks of the Vosges to Frisia, the real 'Lotharingia'. It was not long before the uncles were casting covetous eyes on their nephews' inheritance. In 863, the prize was the kingdom of Charles of Provence, who had died without leaving an heir. His two brothers divided it in accordance with the wishes of the aristocracies. Next, having no heir from his wife Theutberga, Lothar II sought to divorce her in order to marry his mistress Waldrada, who had already given him a son. The crisis over the divorce of Lothar II (861–9) witnessed renewed intervention by the clergy, with Hincmar, archbishop of Rheims (845–83), and above all Pope Nicholas I (858–67) remaining implacably opposed to this attack on the indissolubility of marriage, regardless of the possible consequences. Hence, because Lothar II likewise died without leaving a legitimate heir, his two paternal uncles, Charles the Bald and Louis the German, eventually agreed to partition Lotharingia between them in the treaty of Meersen, 8 August 870, though this satisfied no one. Lorraine remained an apple of discord until the end of the First World War.

Charles the Bald, having ejected Gerard of Vienne from Provence, to replace him with his own brother-in-law, Boso, was awaiting the death of the Emperor Louis II of Italy, who was also without an heir. When it occurred, the clerical intelligentsia judged that only Charles the Bald was capable of restoring unity to the empire. The papacy, which had grown accustomed to seeing Louis II successfully defending Italy against the Arabs, needed a strong man to take his place. John VIII crowned Charles emperor in St Peter's on 25 December 875, the anniversary of his grand-father's coronation three-quarters of a century before. But the new emperor could do nothing: he met with a bloody defeat before Andernach in October 876 for having attempted to wrest eastern Lorraine from his nephew, Louis the Younger (son of Louis the German). Going against the advice of Hincmar, who was urging him to combat the Scandinavians in Francia, the emperor set off to subdue the rebellious Italian magnates and died on his return journey through the Maurienne valley, on 8 October 877.

The disillusionment was so great that from 877 to 881 the empire remained vacant. Out of the three sons of Louis the German, only one, Charles the Fat, survived to reunify the East Frankish kingdom, and then to be recognised as king of Western Francia by the magnates. Again at the instigation of the pope, he was crowned emperor at Rome in February 881, on the grounds that he had restored the territorial unity of the empire. However, not knowing which way to turn in the face of appeals from populations harassed by Scandinavian or Muslim invaders and revolts by the magnates, Charles the Fat abdicated in 887 and died in January 888, amid general anarchy. The title of emperor was now no more than a plaything. The Italian magnates tossed it first, in 891, to Guy of Spoleto, who was crowned by Pope Formosus, and then to Arnulf of Germany in 896. Louis the Blind, king of Provence, grabbed it 901 but held it only for a year, followed by Berengar, king of Italy, in 915. But when the latter died in 924 no one bothered to pick it up.

All in all, the decline of the empire had kept pace with an increasingly clerical coloration of the political ideal it represented. The lay conception of Charlemagne had imperceptibly vanished. As we saw, clerical influence was already at work to ensure that Lothar I was crowned emperor at Rome in 823 by Pope Paschal I, in pointed contrast with his father, who

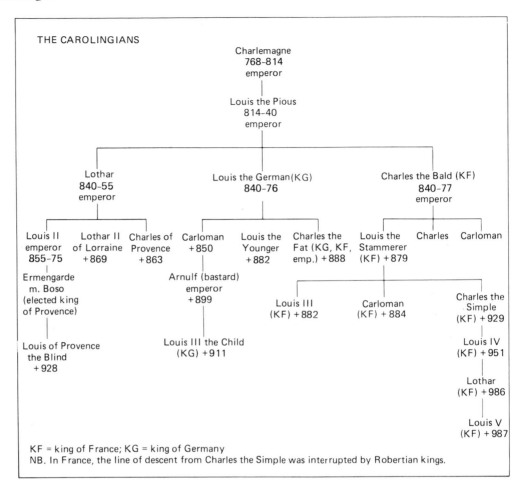

THE CAROLINGIANS

Charlemagne
768-814
emperor

Louis the Pious
814-40
emperor

| Lothar 840-55 emperor | Louis the German (KG) 840-76 | Charles the Bald (KF) 840-77 emperor |

Louis II emperor 855-75 — Lothar II of Lorraine +869 — Charles of Provence +863 — Carloman +850 — Louis the Younger +882 — Charles the Fat (KG, KF, emp.) +888 — Louis the Stammerer (KF) +879 — Charles — Carloman

Ermengarde m. Boso (elected king of Provence)

Arnulf (bastard) emperor +899

Louis III (KF) +882   Carloman (KF) +884   Charles the Simple (KF) +929

Louis of Provence the Blind +928

Louis III the Child (KG) +911

Louis IV (KF) +951

Lothar (KF) +986

Louis V (KF) +987

KF = king of France; KG = king of Germany
NB. In France, the line of descent from Charles the Simple was interrupted by Robertian kings.

had been crowned at Aachen. After 843, the trend gathered momentum: the rituals of anointing and coronation became increasingly intertwined, with Italy and the pope tending from now on to be the accepted location and author. In 850, Louis II was anointed and crowned by Leo IV, without acclamation by the magnates or the army. In 875, John VIII anointed Charles the Bald, crowned him and administered the oath binding him to defend the Church: the magnates accepted this proclamation of an emperor but took no part in it. It was the same with Charles the Fat. The papacy had thus succeeded in imposing its conception of a Roman and no longer Frankish empire, conferred on the recipient in the eternal city by the vicar of St Peter. The imperial idea had become a prerogative of the popes, in consequence of the laymen's incapacity to grasp it. It was the function of the popes to preserve the moral unity of Christendom, to inspire and direct kings, and to define the essence of the Roman empire in contrast with the empire of the East, which was relegated to the rank of an empire of the Greeks. Louis II, although no more than an Italo-Roman emperor, did not hesitate, in 871, to tell Basil: 'We are the successors of the former emperors by the grace of God and the pope.' In thus rejecting the Byzantine empire, the papacy was made more aware of the new political realities represented by Rome and the West. The failure of the Carolingians meant that their inheritance passed into the hands of the Church. By the same token, the higher clergy became emancipated from imperial tutelage. When Nicholas I could declare the Church of Rome to be the head of all the Churches and mother of all emperors, the argument used at a later date by the Gregorian reformers had already been forged. So the Carolingian empire was not just a grandiose memory; on the contrary, it had become a powerful concept, a solidly-constructed programme. An unfettered Church, a unique empire to do its bidding – such were the corner-stones of a theocratic ideal which owed its birth to the failure of the Carolingian empire, and which was destined to succeed precisely because of the lessons learned from that defeat.

Marginalisation of the king's powers

Identical conclusions are to be drawn from the internal evolution of the kingdoms issuing from the partition of Verdun in 843. Almost at once, at the assembly of Coulaines held in that same year, Charles the Bald was obliged to give his promise to the magnates and vassals not to withdraw in arbitrary fashion the lands they had received in benefice. By so doing he acquiesced in a monarchical regime that was becoming contractual rather than absolute. Next, coming up against the energetic Breton chieftains Nominoë, Erispoë and Salomon, he was forced to give way, to accept the loss of Vannes, Nantes and Rennes and even, in 867, to tolerate the advancement of the Breton frontier to the Mayenne and the Dives. In Gascony he lacked any vestige of authority over the duke, despite the latter's Frankish origin. In Aquitaine, the situation was still worse. In order to exclude Pippin II, who was supported by the magnates, in 848 Charles had himself crowned king of the Aquitanians at Orleans. Having failed to win over the nobles, he next had his second son, Charles the Child, crowned sub-king of the Aquitanians at Limoges in 855. He was clearly hoping to repeat the cure found by Charlemagne with Louis the Pious. All he achieved was a general revolt, accompanied by an appeal from the nobility to Louis the German, who invaded Western Francia in 858. Charles the Bald was only rescued from his predicament by the active intervention of the clergy, led by Hincmar, who appealed for loyalty to the legitimate king. But this was of no help in subduing Aquitaine. From about 860, Charles preferred to concentrate on setting up extensive military commands, in the nature of internal marches, which he entrusted to men of proven loyalty. He granted a group of counties between the Loire and the Seine to Robert the Strong, as a counter-measure against the Scandinavian invaders. He created another march of this kind in the neighbourhood of Autun, and divorced the Spanish and Gothic marches from the kingdom of Aquitaine. But the briefest absence or the slightest weakness might oblige him, for example, to acknowledge that the sons of counts could expect to succeed their fathers, as in the capitulary of Quierzy-sur-Oise in 877, or to allow the magnates a voice in the appointment of the *missi dominici*, his roving commissioners. His son, Louis the Stammerer (877–9), and his grandsons, Louis III (879–82) and Carloman (879–84), many a time owed their survival to the interventions of Hincmar archbishop of Rheims. Significantly, it was after the latter's death that the youngest son of Louis the Stammerer was excluded from the throne by the election of a non-Carolingian, Odo, who was the choice of the nobility.

In Lotharingia and in Italy, where all the great Frankish clans had settled, as in Western Francia, there were identical aristocratic revolts. Once the all-powerful Gerard, count of Vienne, had been ejected, Boso profited from the situation to have himself acclaimed king in Burgundy and Provence by the magnates, at Mantaille in 879. The motive for the usurpation is for once clearly indicated in our sources: Boso's wife, daughter of the Italian emperor Louis II, would not be content with less than royal status. In Italy, two Frankish families, the clan of Guy of Spoleto and the clan of Berengar, marquess of Friuli, battled it out for the crown. But revolts by aspirants to royalty were so common in these regions that it would be tedious to continue.

The clergy sought to stem the tide of anarchy by enhancing the concept of kingship. It was unction alone, the bishops declared, that made a man king, not election by the magnates. As a result of the lead given by Hincmar in particular, following the anointing of Charles the Bald in 848 it was held that any revolt against the king counted as sacrilege. At the anointing of Charles the Bald as king of Lotharingia at Metz in 869, Hincmar referred to unction as the sure sign of divine election. At his coronation in Rheims in 877 Louis the Stammerer received the sceptre, symbol of the kingdom he was charged to guide to its ultimate destiny in the hands of God. Thus, by the end of the ninth century, all the ceremonial of the West Frankish consecration rite at Rheims was set in place, to be enveloped, with the dissemination of the legend of the Holy Ampoule, in an aura of Christian magic. At the very moment when the idea of elective monarchy was reborn, the Church produced a doctrinal basis for the legitimate transmission of kingly power in Western Francia. As in the case of the imperial ideal, this theory became the prerogative of the clergy and was to lie at the root of Capetian royal power. The leading idea of the Carolingian era thus contributed to the founding of the classic medieval monarchies, despite the momentary setback they experienced in the closing years of the ninth century.

In Eastern Francia, no ecclesiastical theory of kingship was needed. Under constant threat from the Danes and the Slavs, the kingdom depended for survival on its ethnically Frankish element. The exigencies of warfare and the policy of choosing brides of exalted lineage for the royal princes ensured that the division of the kingdom between the three sons of Louis the German did not lead to further fragmentation. For all practical purposes, the monarchy was still in a commanding position on the death of the last effective Carolingian, Arnulf, in 899; and it is essential to bear this in mind.

The final catastrophe

The collapse of unity was not solely due to the blunders of the clergy or the incompetence of kings. Much more important and damaging was the combination of dangers from within and without. Furthermore, the invasions of the Scandinavians, the Muslims and the Hungarians had the side-effect of dividing communities and stimulating the revival of local

Sixth-century Viking boat depicted on the Sanda funerary stele. Note the steering-oars at the slender prow and stern, and amidships the cabin or tent on which the crew have hung their round shields (Gotlands Fornsal, Väsby, Sweden).

defence forces. The reappearance of territorial principalities is not to be explained merely by the ambitions of the nobility; military necessities clearly played their part.

The 'terror of the Northmen'

The exact causes of the raids by Danish, Swedish and Norwegian seafarers which began around 800 are not easy to explain, hidden as they are in the internal history of Scandinavia. The raids have successively been connected with demographic pressure, with the first royal attempts at unification, leading to the enforced exile of defeated clan-chieftains (*jarlar*); and even with mercantile demand – stimulated by the trade in slaves and corn opening up between the Baltic and Islam. Whatever the cause, every part of the peninsula was affected, as can be told from the miscellany of objects and coins, originating in places as far away as Ireland, Poland or Arabia, found in the graves of warriors who returned to be buried in places ranging from Norway and Jutland to the heart of the Baltic, Gotland and Finland. The Vikings (if this is indeed the correct etymology), the 'men of the Ports', were fishermen in coastal and sometimes deep-sea waters, doughty lumberjacks, and like their putative ancestors, the Goths, later skilled on horseback. They had mastered the art of voyaging for days at a time on the open sea, steering their course by the winds, the currents or the fishing grounds; the very shallow draft of the *snekkja* or longship also permitted the navigation of rivers far inland and made for rapid manoeuvring. From the military point of view, there is reason to think that their equipment was modest and became complete only through the capture of Frankish helmets and swords; but with little desire to be encumbered with prisoners, on the lookout above all for valuables and victuals, the Northmen burned and killed as they went. They added to the terror by making

403

Anglo-Saxon view of the Viking raids, from an English tenth-century manuscript; the rich monasteries of Northumbria, where it originated, were raided from 865 onwards. The monstrous head on the prow would have struck terror into coastal populations (London, British Library).

lightning raids, intended to mask the smallness of their numbers, and plundered coastal populations more or less at will, at any rate until resistance gradually began to take shape in the hinterland; after that, bands of Northmen surprised in open country were almost always overwhelmed. It should be borne in mind, however, that ecclesiastics, our only witnesses to the ravages of which they were the first victims, may well have exaggerated on this point.

The first waves of the Viking attack, beginning in 788 and gathering momentum after 840, encountered no serious opposition until about 880, and continued until the first phase of expansion ended around 930. It is generally true to say that the Norwegians' main aim was to find land to colonise, while the Danes were more interested in plunder. Monasteries, because of the precious metals in their liturgical ornaments and the wine-casks in their cellars, were a particular target. The Swedes, who also went by the name of Varangians, appear by nature to have been traders rather than plunderers. The Norwegians concentrated their voyages on the seas around Britain and its islands, while the Danes infested the North Sea and the English Channel; the route *via* the Baltic and the Russian waterways was the preserve of the Swedes. From this it follows that many regions never caught sight of a single invader: but news of a raid, however distant, seems to have resulted in panic-stricken flight and exodus to the safety of town walls, and in general to have had a very disruptive effect on society.

13 The British Isles in the eighth and ninth centuries

The brunt of the first raids was borne by Ireland and the north of England, while the Varangians, by sailing up and down the Russian rivers, and with the aid of numerous portages, succeeded in reaching the Black Sea as early as 839, and the Caspian soon after. From 840, however, the Danes directed their attacks at the richest parts of the Carolingian empire. Dorestad was pillaged for the first time, and in 842 Quentovic was left temporarily in ruins. In 843, Nantes was captured, pillaged and burnt. Bordeaux twice suffered the same fate, in 844 and 847–8. Hamburg was totally destroyed in 845. But it would take too long to enumerate the towns and monasteries that were captured, pillaged or burnt. Each time, the Danes would sail upstream to the navigable limit, transfer to stolen mounts and take by surprise the monks or townsmen who had trusted too blindly in the safety of their higher ground. There were even occasions when they would find allies among the Bretons, who were only too willing to play them off against the Franks.

From about 850, the pillaging of the various regions was put on a more systematic footing. Winter bases were set up at the mouths of the great rivers: on the Scheldt at Walcheren, on the Seine at Jeufosse, on the Loire at Noirmoutier. When summer came, the Danes would move inland to pillage regions which had so far escaped. Following each success, they were now in the habit of demanding a tribute payable in coin, the 'danegeld' ('Dane money'), which populations had to hand over to make them go away. Having milked Francia dry, the Danes would cross the Channel to demand further tributes. However, although Robert the Strong was killed in a battle against the Vikings at Brissarthe as late as 866, the tide of victory eventually turned. The first attempts by Charles the Bald to fortify bridges, or to build castles for the defence of local populations, which began about 860, are pointers in that direction. The victory won by King Louis III of France at Saucourt in the Vimeu in 881, and the obdurate defence of Paris against the besieging Danes by Count Odo, son of Robert the Strong, in 885, were the prelude to a slow but steady recovery. In 891, Arnulf of Carinthia took the Viking camp at Louvain by storm.

Meanwhile the Vikings kept up their pillaging attacks on other coastal regions. They penetrated the rivers of Muslim and Christian Spain, and in 844 sacked Seville. Next they invaded the Mediterranean between 855 and 860, sailed up the Rhône as far as Arles, and pillaged the Italian port of Luni. It seems that only the East Frankish kingdom was left more or less untouched. In the North Sea, on the other hand, Norwegian and Danish activity led for the first time to colonisation and occupation. Some Norwegian sailors installed themselves in the Shetlands and Faroes, and embarked around 870 on the systematic colonisation of Iceland, at that time completely deserted. After capturing the Isle of Man, they eventually founded four small kingdoms on the coast of Ireland which were perpetually at war with the petty Irish kings. In England, the Danes posed an even greater danger. Beginning in 866, their occupancy spread from York to Northumbria and Mercia, and in 878 to East Anglia. But after a succession of defeats, the king of Wessex, Alfred, managed to organise effective resistance. His victory at 'Ethanburh' (Edington) in 878 and the recapture of London enabled him to sign a peace treaty with the Danish leader, Guthrum, which conceded to the invaders all the territory to the north of the Thames and to the east of the River Lea and the Roman road from London to Chester (Watling Street). Alfred was left

Ninth-century Viking wagon discovered inside the Oseberg ship in Norway. Concealed in a tumulus, the ship served as a burial chamber and contained a large quantity of grave furniture (Oslo, Viking Ship Museum).

with Wessex, a small part of Mercia, Sussex and Kent, which roughly represented one-third of England. The Danish territory came to be known as the Danelaw.

In 911, a Danish army, under the command of Rollo, become so menacing that the king of West Francia, Charles the Simple, chose to concede to it possession of the lands on either side of the Seine, in the vicinity of Rouen and Évreux (treaty of Saint-Clair-sur-Epte). The Normans' occupation of Bayeux, Sées, Avranches and Coutances followed swiftly, indeed almost before their conversion and installation was complete, and led quickly to the establishment, after a period of temporary crisis, of a duchy of 'Normandy' with its own distinctive institutions, under the rule of Duke Richard I (942–56). While their settlement in that region became permanent, it failed to take root in Brittany, from which the Normans were expelled in 937. In Ireland, the Norwegian chieftains were gradually converted and made contact with Celtic society. From 979, their territories become more and more like enclaves, progressively isolated from the island as a whole. In England, by contrast, the Danish kingdom of York was the target of a determined effort at reconquest by the kings of Wessex and Mercia. Between them, Alfred's successor, Edward the Elder (899–924), and his son Athelstan (924–39) succeeded in recovering all the lost territories, and forced the Danish colonists into submission. After his victory over the Scots, Athelstan

407

could justly proclaim himself 'ruler of all Britain'. Even if the Vikings were to return in force around the year 1000, the merging of the Danish protectorate with the Anglo-Saxon kingdom was already a foregone conclusion. Stabilisation and the birth of unity went hand in hand.

The Saracen expansion and the Hungarian nightmare

An identical phenomenon is to be seen in the Mediterranean. The emergence in Ifriqiya of a new emirate, that of the Aghlabids, served to reinforce the Muslim piracy which was already a feature of Spain's eastern seaboard. In 817, as we saw, the Saracens launched an attack on Byzantine Italy, which they proceeded to conquer town by town, Taormina being the last to fall, in 902. From Sicily, they were even better poised to pillage the coastal towns of Italy: Rome in 845, Comacchio in 875–6. Despite the resistance offered by Louis II, which had its victorious moments, they captured Bari and Taranto. It took a powerful Byzantine counter-attack to eject them from Calabria. In retaliation, after 882 they set up a base at the mouth of the Garigliano. In 882–3, they sacked the abbey of Montecassino. Muslims from Spain, having pillaged Marseilles and Arles and the whole seaboard, ended up seeking a base in the Camargue. But the place they eventually fixed on, in 888, was La Garde-Freinet, where they established themselves at the foot of the cliff which may have acquired their name: Les Maures. From these fortified camps they could set out without fear of reprisal to plunder the monasteries and towns of the interior and to round up the merchandise of the slave trade at their leisure. Faced with the Saracens, the outlook seemed even darker than in the face of the Vikings, because no one had found an effective means of holding them in check, and the seaways of the western Mediterranean were apparently doomed to a state of perpetual insecurity: any attempt to patrol the coasts was useless. To make matters worse, even if the Saracens gave the appearance of being more interested in settlement than pillage, they were in the habit of taking large numbers of prisoners to be sold as slaves in the Maghrib; many of their conquests were made easier by the flight of populations fearing this fate.

The containment of the Saracens was only very gradually achieved, and even so they were left in possession of the Balearic Islands, captured in 903, and the whole of Sicily, which meant that the western Mediterranean was cut off from Egypt. In 906, their base on the Garigliano was wiped out, but this did not enable the Byzantine empire to reassert any real authority over the region. As for La Garde-Freinet, that hornets' nest from which raids of unusual audacity were launched as far afield as Sicily, the combined forces of the counts of Provence and Turin, acting on orders from the emperor, were needed to extirpate it, an operation finally accomplished in 972–3. In Spain, relations with Islam were of such a different order that we cannot expect to find the same rhythm being repeated: here it was a question of establishing a *modus vivendi* between a Cordoban caliphate at the height of its power and the tiny Christian principalities in the mountainous regions of Galicia and Cantabria. The Asturian kingdom, under Ordoño I (850–66) and Alfonso III, 'the Great' (866–910), with the aid in some instances of understandings with the Mozarabs or rebellious Muslims, succeeded in advancing to the banks of the Minho and the Douro. In 884, a truce was concluded which relieved Spanish Christians of immediate danger, and at the beginning of the eleventh century Garcia I was able to fix his capital at Leon, in the midst of reconquered territories.

Of all the new invasions, those of the Hungarians (Magyars) were the hardest to endure. These nomadic horsemen, of Turko-Mongolian origin, discovered from a reconnoitring raid that Pannonia had been left untenanted since Charlemagne's defeat of the Avars, the neighbouring Slavs having refrained from occupying this steppe-land which seemed of no value for cereal cultivation. Crossing the Carpathians at three different points, the eight Hungarian tribes installed themselves between the Danube and the Tisza. From 899, their plundering raids became a regular occurrence in Germany, Italy and even West Francia, where in 924 they penetrated to places as far distant as Mende and Nîmes. They sacked monasteries, steered clear of fortified towns, laid waste the countryside, tortured and massacred the menfolk, cut the throats of children, carried the young women off as slaves to cultivate their lands, and stole the cattle. In 937, the Magyars made a wide sweep through Germany, Champagne, Burgundy and Italy as far as the Abruzzi, returning *via* Emilia and the Venetia. As well as suffering from the panic induced by so much irreparable damage, resistance to the 'Ogres' was paralysed by the feeling of impotence once felt in the presence of the Huns; the small forts hastily constructed in the time of the Saxon Henry I (*Heinrichsburgern*) proved unequal to the problem. Another great onslaught at last produced a united response. On 10 August 955, the German king Otto I scored an overwhelming victory over the Hungarians on the banks of the Lech close to Augsburg. As a result, Hungarian expansion was brought to a full stop. In addition, their more sedentary way of life and progressive Christianisation helped to dissipate by degrees the sense of insecurity they had created, and kept them safely in Pannonia, which from then on became Hungary.

The break-up

The state of impunity so long enjoyed by the Vikings, Saracens and Hungarians was due in large part to the clashes between the kings and the leading nobles in their role of former officials or heads of clans. Having acquired the habit of selling their loyalty to the emperor or even to kings, they tried to lay hands on kingship itself, either by having themselves proclaimed sovereign, like Boso, or by engineering the election of one of their number as king. The year 888 was especially significant in this regard. In Germany, it saw the election of Arnulf. In Western Francia the magnates elected Odo, famed for his resistance to the Danes, to the exclusion of the legitimate Carolingian heir, Charles the Simple, who finally recovered his throne only in 898. In Burgundy, duke Rudolf had himself acclaimed king. In Provence, Louis, son of Boso, managed to preserve a remnant of royal power over the country. These two kingdoms, Burgundy and Provence, were eventually to be combined in 933 as the 'kingdom of Arles'. In practice, however, these kings were not obeyed. The magnates either paid them lip-service, or entered into conspiracies and rebellions against them. For real political cohesion in the tenth century we must look to the territorial principality, defined by Jan Dhondt as 'territory in which the king no longer intervenes save through the intermediary of the ruler'. Frequently the ruler in question was a former Carolingian official who had contrived to concentrate his personal estates and those attached to his office in a particular region, where he acquired the practice of government and exercised the rights of the king for his own benefit. By taking advantage of certain traditional and localised forms of particularism such as language, dialect, culture or subsisting tribalism, a dynasty was created. At once anarchical and decentralising, the thrust of the movement was towards creating order at the level of entities more homogeneous and more defensible than the kingdom. At bottom, the territorial principalities represented a resurgence of the principalities born towards the end of the Merovingian epoch, that is to say after 673.

The oldest of these, as we saw, was Aquitaine. Following numerous revolts and the disappearance of its title as a kingdom in 877, Aquitaine split into two. William the Pious, lord of the Auvergne and the Limousin, proclaimed himself duke of the Aquitanians in 909. His domain extended to the counties of Mâcon and Lyons, but his descendants allowed themselves to be robbed of territories and the title by the count of Poitou, William III, 'Towhead', who styled himself duke of 'all Aquitaine'. To the south, however, he found himself blocked by the family of Raymond, founder of the county of Toulouse. The rivalry between Poitou and Aquitaine continued throughout the tenth century. On the left bank of the Garonne, a comital family, the Sanchez, came to the fore, and a century later, in 977, it appropriated the title duke of Gascony. In the Catalonian counties, the Frankish march slowly disintegrated, initially into two principalities: Gothia, the former Septimania, and Hispania. Furthermore, between 878 and 897, Wilfrid the Hairy, the last count of Barcelona to be appointed by the king of Western Francia, took steps to build up his local power, usurped the rights of the fisc and made the title of count hereditary in his family. Although he swore a nominal oath of allegiance to the legitimate sovereign, he was virtually independent.

In the north of Burgundy, Richard, count of Autun, Mâcon and Chalon, who since 890 had been adding to his possessions, obtained the grant of a ducal title from the king. Away to the north, rather earlier, a Flemish count, Baldwin, had seized his chance, amid the troubles of Charles the Bald's reign to abduct the daughter of Charles the Bald, Judith, and so establish his family. In 891, his son Baldwin II annexed Artois and advanced his territory to the line of the Canche. In Brittany, once more independent, the local counts quarrelled over the ducal title. Lastly it should be mentioned that the family of Odo, elevated in 888 to the kingship, was directly descended from Robert the Strong, the marquess installed by Charles the Bald in the Touraine, Anjou and the Blésois. To these possessions the family now added the county of Paris and a number of abbacies.

The existence of all these territorial principalities was thus fully recognised in Francia: they were within the public domain, because the king was usually a consenting party. The development of principalities on similar lines can also be observed in Spain and England. It is instructive, for example, to watch Castille, country of castles as its name implies, coming to birth under the hand of a Count Fernan Gonzales (923–70), who detached it from the

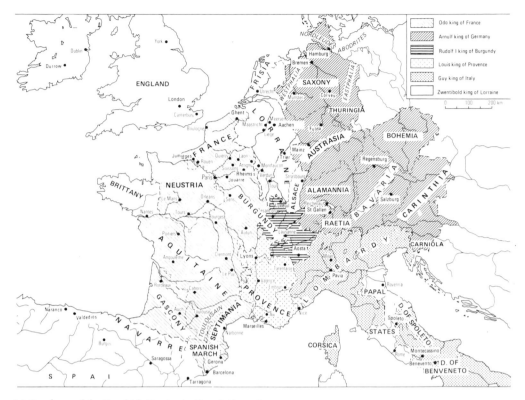

14 Break-up of the Frankish Empire in the ninth century

kingdom of the Asturias and became founder of a dynasty. To the east, Navarre raised itself to a kingdom in 905, and in 925 it temporarily annexed the small Christian county of Aragon. Such fragmentation is also to be found in England. Like Charles the Bald, Edward the Elder and Athelstan set up large military commands by grouping several counties together under the authority of an *ealdorman*. Two such commands are known to have been created for Wessex, one for Mercia, and others besides. They in fact were more or less coterminous with the kingdoms which existed prior to unification. However, these *ealdormen* did not yet possess the independence enjoyed by their continental counterparts: this came later, after a more gradual evolution which was not completed until the eleventh century, but even then the parallels are not exact. This survey of the birth of territorial principalities in Western Francia, Spain and England is very revealing in another respect, namely the presence in each case of the military expedient, the castle, which made this independence possible. The stone-built towers and fortified complexes of Catalonia (Castlania, the country of castellans) and Castille have their counterparts in the *burhs* of King Alfred's Wessex. A whole network of royal strongholds was constructed south of the Humber. But in Western Francia, the prerogative of erecting fortifications slipped from the king's grasp: to be sure, the edict of Pîtres, 864, forbade the construction of *firmitates* and

411

haias, fortified mounds surrounded by posts and impenetrable walls made of interwoven branches; but in practice the magnates were very quick to usurp this prerogative, on the pretext of protecting local populations against the Vikings or Saracens. There can have been few who omitted to contrive something of this kind. In Provence the first private castle made its appearance around 950, while in Latium the oldest known example dates from 945–6. In the north, the example we can date to these years with most certainty seems to be the motte at Douai. The picture is thus one of a mosaic of local powers criss-crossing the countryside and completely transforming the landscape. Can it be that this period of the mid-tenth century marks the beginning of a new epoch?

Resuscitation of the empire?

The fragmentation of territorial principalities into numerous castellanies did not extend to Italy, Eastern Francia or eastern Europe in general. This enfeeblement or disappearance of central or regional political authorities stopped short of the territories conquered by Charlemagne. There, it was rather a case of authority starting to gravitate around towns, as in peninsular Italy, or being reborn from Carolingian structures, as in the case of the German empire.

In the plain of the Po, following the failure of the last Italian emperors, the kingdom of Italy fell into the hands of Hugh of Arles (926–47), who was quite incapable of asserting his authority, all the more so when his grandiose schemes for domination over Rome and union with Burgundy came to nothing. He could do nothing to prevent the formation by lay rulers of great marches, such as the marquisates of Friuli, Ivrea (embracing the counties of Turin and Asti) and Tuscany. But in regions where towns were more numerous, the bishops displaced the counts and assumed responsibility for the protection of their city. In consequence, important ecclesiastical principalities were built up at Parma, Modena, Piacenza, Cremona and Bergamo. There it was the bishop who exercised regalian rights, and the bishop who built the castles. The rest of the peninsula remained a patchwork of petty principalities – Spoleto, Benevento, Salerno, Capua – which had previously been Lombard territories. More disquieting is the fate of the duchy of Rome, which fell first into the hands of an aristocratic family, the Theophylacts (904–32), and then, after the colourful interlude of Theodora and Marozia, two women who made and unmade popes, into those of Alberic, marquess of Spoleto from 954. In consequence, the papacy suffered considerable degradation.

When we turn to Germany we find an entirely different situation developing. The former regional, ethnic, or sometimes even tribal particularisms did, it is true, lead to the reappearance of territorial units which had once, in pre-Carolingian times, been headed by independent dukes, Thuringia, Swabia and Bavaria being examples. In fact, however, the old-style national dukedoms had been abolished by Charlemagne or converted in some cases into border-dukedoms. The former *Stämme*, entities bound together by a single and now territorial law, and by a single military organisation, had to be redeployed to resist the Hungarians. In Bavaria, the clan of the Liutpoldings played a crucial part in repelling the invaders. In Swabia (the former Alamannia), the clan of the former dukes, the Ahaholfings, dispossessed in 746, made a comeback, only to succumb to the Hunfrids. In Franconia, the Babenbergs, heroes of the struggle against the Scandinavians, were eventually eliminated in 902 by the Conradin clan. On the death of the last Carolingian king of Eastern Francia, Louis the Child (899–911), the head of the clan, Conrad I, was actually elected king. He could not prevent a series of territories from continuing to govern themselves like independent kingdoms: Lotharingia, Frisia, with its highly distinctive regime, Thuringia, the eastern marches of Bohemia, and Carinthia. The fact remains, however, that the five great dukes (Bavaria, Franconia, Saxony, Lorraine and Swabia) never succeeded, in contrast with their counterparts in Western Francia, in making their titles hereditary. In the eyes of the king they had no legal existence.

The failure of the German principalities was due above all to Saxony. The region still closest to its tribal origins, Saxony was also the one to bear the strongest imprint of the Carolingian system, which had sedulously destroyed the preceding structures. It was the archetypal virgin territory in which Carolingian order had been implanted in its purest form. The Saxon count Liudolf met his death fighting the Danes in 880. His brother Otto took his place and won such resounding victories over the Scandinavians, the Slavs and the Hungarians that he ended by dominating the entire region, which became completely independent. He had become so powerful that King Conrad suggested, shortly before his death, that Otto's son, Henry the Fowler, should become king. Elected in 918, Henry I carried out systematic fortification of all the great centres, and was astute enough to temporise with the Hungarians, in order to get the better of the dukes. His victories over the Wilzi, Slavs on the right bank of the Elbe, and the Czechs brought him such prestige that on his death, in 936, the five dukes agreed to elect his son Otto.

From the moment of his accession, this descendant of the Saxon rebel chieftain, Widukind, gave proof of his intention and fitness to follow in the footsteps of Charlemagne. He had himself crowned and anointed king at Aachen. Twice confronted by rebel dukes, whom he crushed in turn, he replaced them with members of his family, whom he then dismissed at will. Sometimes, as for example in the case of Franconia, annexed to Saxony, the duchy was even suppressed. Having subdued the lay aristocracy, and in the process arrested the fragmentation of the kingdom for the next two centuries, he made the clergy the mainstay of his government and resumed the programme of expansion at the expense of the Slavs which was initiated by the early Carolingians. He made the duke of Bohemia his vassal. He created two marches on the Elbe and the Saale, entrusting the one to Hermann Billung, the other to Gero, facing the Poles. While the margraves pushed ahead and reached the Oder with their repeated offensives, Otto planned to make Magdeburg the centre of a metropolitan archbishopric, with an eye to keeping control of all the Slav converts to come. Lastly, his resounding victory at the Lechfeld over the Hungarians turned Otto into the saviour of the West. Widukind, his kinsman, monk of Corvey in Saxony, paid tribute in his *Res gestae* to the glory won by the Saxon warrior people as final vanquishers of the hordes from the east. The king was from henceforth Otto 'the Great', the one who gave the impetus for the German expansion to the east, the *Drang nach Osten*. And

413

The famous gold crown of the Holy Empire, probably made in the abbey of Reichenau for the coronation of Otto I at Rome (2 February 962). It would have been worn over a mitre, to symbolise the *rex et sacerdos*. The octagonal, gem-encrusted crown pre-figures the Heavenly Jerusalem (Vienna, Kunsthistorisches Museum).

let us not forget the incorporation of Lotharingia, wrested from the feeble Frankish king in 942 to be ruled by Otto's brother Bruno, archbishop of Cologne, or, to round off the picture, the state of vassalage to which the king of Burgundy was permanently reduced. Otto, 'guardian and overseer of the West', was already more than a king.

From then on, his path to the empire was clearly staked out. Benefiting from the anarchical state of Italy in 951, Otto first invested himself with the crown of Italy and married the kingdom's last lawful queen, Adelaide. In 961, at the invitation of the pope, whose aim was to free himself from the Roman lords, he marched into Rome and had himself crowned emperor on 2 February 962. He at once demonstrated who was master by issuing an edict which brought papal elections under his control: in future, no one was to be consecrated pope without first having sworn allegiance to the emperor. He thus aligned the aspirations of Charlemagne with the practice of Louis and Lothar in 824. Into the bargain, he assumed the same title as the empire's illustrious founder: 'august emperor'. No contemporary commentator remarked on the reduction of the empire to its Germanic and Italian components. Furthermore, the falseness of the comparison is proved by the revolts of the Italian rulers and of the popes. Nevertheless, after more campaigns to subdue Italy, Otto had his son Otto II anointed, and seized Apulia and Calabria so as to obtain in exchange from Byzantium the hand of Princess Theophano for his heir, in 972. When he died in 973, he was the mightiest sovereign in Europe, but could not claim to have recreated the Frankish empire of Charlemagne. He had done no more than found a Germanic Roman empire.

All the same, the one important kingdom to evade him, Western Francia, came half-way to being under his protection. On being restored to the throne, the Carolingian kings, Charles the Simple (898–922) and Louis IV (936–54) in particular, tried to assert themselves in Lotharingia, where they hoped to retrieve a solid political and property base. By so doing, however, they fell into the domain of the kings of Germany, who could not permit such aggrandisement. In 954, the under-age son of Louis IV, Lothar, was placed under the guardianship of Bruno, archbishop of Cologne. Like his father and grandfather Lothar persisted in the policy of conquest, hopeless though it was. But there was justification for it in the steady advances being made by the Robertian clan. It is true that after Odo's brother, Robert, had briefly gained the throne in 922–3, the latter's son, Hugh the Great, warned by his failures, progressed more slowly: he was clearly waiting for the moment when Lothar would be in dire straits. Appointed duke of the Franks (from the Loire to Flanders), and nominally duke of Aquitaine and Burgundy, Hugh vastly outstripped the king, who was reduced to the royal fiscs of Attigny, Compiègne and Laon. Yet at the same time, Hugh was merely one ruler among the rest. In the mid-tenth century, it is perhaps obvious, with the wisdom of hindsight, that his family was about to usurp the throne, since the royal line, although prevented from disappearing by its German patronage, was by the same token kept in a weakened condition which offered no hope of recovery.

By the beginning of the eleventh century, the political face of Europe had thus been transformed. While the tendency towards fragmentation prevailed in the West, the themes of consolidation and expansion were dominant in the East. Around the empire's periphery we see new kingdoms being born. Denmark, with the baptism of Harald Bluetooth in 966, was placed on a firmer footing. Christianity, just starting to penetrate Norway and Sweden, shaped the beginnings of two more new entities there. Poland, with the baptism of Miesko in 966, and soon afterwards Hungary, likewise showed their desire to join the concert of Europe. In short, notwithstanding the might of the 'German Holy Roman Empire', Europe was no longer one but diverse. To the north–south divide of the barbarian era was now added the east–west contrast born of the Ottonian epoch. The age of great upheavals was at an end. The barbarians had all been incorporated into Christian kingdoms which look towards Rome. But the empire is no longer synonymous with Christendom. The Antique Rome, captured briefly in 410, was well and truly dead. The Frankish Rome of the year 800 had failed to produce unity. On the other hand, the political and religious programmes worked out in the ninth century stood ready and waiting. Their implementation in the eleventh century proved that the Carolingian failure was no more than a momentary setback due to the invasions and the ambitions of the aristocracy. The Carolingian and Ottonian empires were an indispensable stage in the reconstitution of the State. Indeed, the rise of principalities and the triumph of feudal institutions can hardly be understood apart from the intervention of Charlemagne and his successors. Thus we must examine why it was that contemporaries had the impression that the era of the emperor with the flowery beard was a golden age, succeeded by one of iron.

10 The Carolingian 'renewal'

People of the first two generations of the Carolingian era, the era of Pippin III and Charlemagne, were clearly convinced that civilisation had taken a leap forward, in as much as their previously barbarian and pagan world was becoming civilised and Christian. They found a precise word to express this sense of the unfolding and baptism of a new world: '*renovatio*', 'renewal'. This term, born of an intellectual renaissance struggling to take shape in the late seventh century, gained currency in particular through its use in the formula '*Renovatio regni Francorum*', 'renewal of the kingdom of the Franks'. The clerics in the entourage of the first Carolingians formed their mental image of the new political order not on memories of ancient Rome but on Christ's reply to Nicodemus (John iii 3): 'Except a man be born again, he cannot see the kingdom of God', signifying that birth according to nature has to be followed by a second birth in the waters of baptism, the *re-novatio* from which a new creature once again emerges. By extension, the Carolingian renaissance is to be construed as the baptism of a formerly barbarian society, or as the Christianisation of a pagan and sinful world. The monks and clerics of St Martin of Tours and St Denis, of Rheims, Corbie, Corvey or Fulda deemed it essential for this new society to be born within the framework of a new State and a new Church. The reform of the political order therefore consisted in something more than rediscovery of the empire and reconstitution of the kingship – it entailed the complete transformation of political and social structures. It further manifested itself in an undeniable blossoming of the arts and of intellectual life. But by far the greater part of it was inspired by lessons and innovations from the late Merovingian era.

Re-creation of the State?

It is of more than passing interest to learn from the historian Gregory of Tours that the term *res publica*, meaning the State, is always to be understood as applying to the Roman empire of the East. To his way of thinking, the kingdom founded by the Franks did not amount to a State. We saw that Roman society was constant in its efforts to elude the grip of the State, and that it eventually succeeded. We saw, too, that the codes of Germanic law knew no

School textbooks produced during the French Third Republic played their part in fostering the legend of the *rois fainéants* (from E. Lavisse and A. Colin, *Année préparatoire d'Histoire de France*, 1876).

distinction between public and private law. The conjunction of these two phenomena resulted, perverse as it may seem, in the privatisation of the State.

The barbarian kingdoms feel their way (sixth and seventh centuries)

The Germanic kingdoms were founded on the elective principle, whereby the warriors chose the king with respect to his battle-winning qualities. There were thus certain difficulties to be overcome before the idea of dynastic inheritance, guarantor of political continuity, could take root. In Spain, after the extinction of the Balt clan in 531, the electoral process fell into the hands of palace officials at Toledo and the bishops. While the former were constantly rebelling against their own appointee, the latter did everything they could to bolster up the kingship. From 633 onwards, councils were summoned whenever there was a major crisis at Toledo, whose functions were to advise the king, to debate all the political and religious issues of the moment, to vote on laws put before them or which they themselves proposed, to judge cases of high treason, and so on. In order to emphasise the legitimate status of kingship, the episcopal body, citing the example of the prophet Samuel, practised the rite of royal unction, which may have been used more than once in the early seventh century. By the time of King Wamba (672) it was already regarded as normal. But this consecratory reinforcement to royal legitimacy had very little effect. The nobles of Visigothic descent thrust their way on to the councils with a resulting increase of laymen at the expense of the bishops of Roman descent. This reversal of an established trend culminated in a violent clash in 711 between the sons of King Witiza and the newly-elected Roderick, which spelled the death of the Visogothic monarchy.

The elective principle also triumphed among the Lombards, after 584, when the monarchy was restored. But a form of heredity crept in when it became possible for royal wives or daughters to transmit their rights to the crown. This first happened with Queen Theodelinda and continued into the early eighth century. The Lombard people, who in the

417

seventh century were closer to their origins than the Visigoths, still observed the practice of summoning all free men to the assembly. This mass-meeting of the people in arms accompanied the promulgation of the Edict of Rothari as late as 643. Subsequently, instead of the free men meeting in assembly there were smaller assemblies composed of dukes or *gastalds* (overseers of royal estates), bishops and abbots. These would ratify treaties and take part in the drafting of laws, exercising by this means real control over the king. As for the tribal Anglo-Saxon kingships, these were cast in a still more Germanic, not to say Scandinavian, mould. The word *cyning* or *cyng* (later to become 'king') signifies 'son of', or 'kinsman', proof that kingship involved possession of a pedigree: a pedigree traced back in most cases to the time of the god Woden. So there existed a pagan charisma of kingship. Here too, however, the exigencies of warfare prevented hereditary kingship from becoming automatic. At the end of the seventh century, for example, the election of a war-leader appears to have been standard practice, although the choice, exercised by the magnates, was usually limited to the sons of the deceased king. Out of the dozen or so Anglo-Saxon kingdoms extant around 600, it is possible to point to the co-existence of three or even four 'kings' within Sussex or Essex alone. Notwithstanding the title *bretwalda* ('ruler of the British') assumed by certain kings, there was none who attained to a really dominant position. To advise him, moreover, each king had a council of wise men (*witanagemot*), who joined with him in promulgating the law of the kingdom. This was certainly the procedure when the laws of Kent were established under Aethelberht, and at the time of their revision by Wihtred. The group around King Ine of Wessex, at this same period, was made up of bishops and heads of noble families charged with important official functions. Plainly this assembly was the successor to the pagan priests and free warriors who originally sur-rounded the king. In Scandinavia, nothing changed. On the contrary, the king was completely subservient to the tribal assembly composed of priests and warriors.

The Merovingian kingship may offer the one example of an attempt to break loose from the primitive conceptions of the Germanic 'State'. The successors of Clovis, exploiting to the full the pagan charisma attaching to their flowing locks and ever-victorious dynasty, fount of never-ending booty, tried to suppress the custom of partitioning the kingdom between heirs. This conception of the kingdom, which saw it as the private property of the victorious leader, goes by the name 'patrimoniality'; it led to the civil wars we saw taking place in the second half of the sixth century. Chlothar II and Dagobert successfully put a stop to it by a series of cold-blooded murders. But as soon as Dagobert was dead, the practice reappeared. The edict of Chlothar II, which conceded in 613 that all high officials should belong by birth to the territory they administered, gradually blocked the path to undivided kingship. Besides this, the partition of 638 led to the revival of the Neustria–Burgundy block in opposition to Austrasia, while Aquitaine and Provence were becoming increasingly and conclusively remote from the Merovingian capitals. After 687, it is true, there was again only one king, Theuderic III, but since the controller of the royal domains, the mayor of the palace Pippin II of Herstal had now effectively seized power, this unity was purely fictitious. Moreover, in Neustria and elsewhere the aristocratic factions were utterly independent. The assembly of free men which under Clovis and his successors was invariably summoned at the start of each campaign and which was known from the name of the month in which it met, March, as the Field of Mars, followed its regular course only in Austrasia, from which Pippin launched continual offensives against his adversaries the Frisians and other Germanic neighbours. It is at this period perhaps that the Pippinids fabricated the legend of those 'do-nothing' ('fainéant') Merovingian kings, later depicted by Einhard as trundling in ox-drawn carts from one estate to the next. The truth is that the king was reduced to this state of dependence by the war-leader, who, not daring to lay hands on him because of the bishops' respect for legitimacy, resorted to ridicule. To sum up, wherever we look at the start of the eighth century, we see kingship undermined or in an obvious crisis, literally privatised by aristocratic factions or by assemblies of magnates charged with an official function. It retained its potency only where its source, warfare, remained undiminished. Peace put an end to Germanic kingship.

The State in the hands of private interests: seventh and eighth centuries

At the same time a new phenomenon developed in the form of territorial principalities. Leaving aside the Anglo-Saxon kingdoms, which never reached the stage of internal unity, the Lombards, Visigoths and Franks all experienced fragmentation. In Spain, the revolt by Paul, who had himself anointed king at Narbonne in 672, is one symptom of this tendency. The Tarragonese and the Septimanians remained defiantly separatist. In Italy, the continuing independence of Friuli, Tuscany and the duchies of Spoleto and Benevento provide further proof of the same tendency. The fact that after the fall of the Visigothic kingdom a Murcian principality is known to have survived for a while under the aegis of a nobleman, Theodimir, demonstrates the connection between this fragmentation and the presence of powerful local leaders. One such, Pelayo, was ultimately to be responsible for Spain's rebirth. But in Gaul the phenomenon is even broader in scope. In Aquitaine, as early as 656, the social and official distinction of the patrician of Toulouse promoted the rise of a Romanising principality which, in the time of Eudo (c. 700–35), became a sub-kingdom. In parallel, Alamannia, Thuringia and Bavaria reverted to their former independence under the auspices of a local dynasty. Frisia, part of which had been conquered by Pippin II, recovered its territory around the mouth of the Rhine. Burgundy was split up into petty dukedoms and in Provence the struggle against Islam was made the excuse for installing a patrician as leader. In short, the emergence of autonomous political units which reflect in each case certain traits specific to the region – whether in terms of the inhabitants or of their culture – is everywhere apparent. In some cases it may be linked with the return to tribal origins (Thuringians, Basques), in others with nostalgia for a real or imagined Roman past (Aquitaine), or elsewhere with the ambitions of power-hungry noblemen (Spoleto) or with the development of unprecedented maritime activity (Frisia) – but all contribute to the multiplication of these local kingships. In the Germanic countries the dislocation due to the great plague had left little trace, but the immaturity of their administrative structures and the absence of any notion of the public good produced the same effects.

It was only in Byzantine Italy, in the circle around the exarch, that the Roman

419

conception of the public servant survived in its entirety. As well as wielding authority over the civil governors (*judices*) appointed on the recommendation of the bishops and notables of the province concerned, the exarch appointed and issued orders to the military officials, the dukes.

The cohesion of the Romano-Byzantine State was a source of envy to the Visigoths and Lombards, whose kings imitated the titles and ceremonies of the court at Constantinople. But with the monarchs of Pavia this did not extend very far. Because of their failure to preserve the fiscal system, each of the 30 or so dukes dispersed throughout the kingdom lived off the lands they had appropriated, as did their subordinates, the *sculdahis*. The *gastalds* could scarcely compete, especially now that the original clans, the *farae* had disappeared. The only remnants were the *arimanni* (warriors of the tribal army) who had been settled on lands belonging to the fisc. They discharged their military obligations on orders from the *gastalds* and were under their jurisdiction. Once the fisc had become enlarged through the conquests of Rothari (636–52) in Liguria and Emilia, Aistulf (749–56) seized the opportunity to make military service binding on all the subjects of his kingdom. This reinforced an embryonic central administration at Pavia, constructed around a mayor of the palace, a chamberlain, a constable and a seneschal, head of the household servants. These same domestic officers were to be found, under varying names, at all the Germanic courts. In Visigothic Spain, they went by the titles 'count of the patrimony', 'count of the treasury', whose opposite numbers were the count of the bed-chambers, the count of the stables, responsible for the supply of horses, and the count of the *spatarii*, captain of the king's bodyguard. But we should note the presence in this instance of a chancellery and count of the notaries, whose task was to record decisions in writing. In Gaul, the chancellery was under the control of the referendary. From this it can be seen that in Spain the distinction between public and private was still maintained, since the public treasury and the king's chamber were differentiated. Again, at the level of local administration we still meet the count of the old Roman *civitas*, with his staff of *vicarii*; however, and this needs to be stressed, the military counts we encounter were holders of divisional commands in the provincial armies. The distinction between the civil and the military was still possible because the collection of direct taxes continued in the Iberian peninsula down into the eighth century. By contrast, as the habit gradually died out in Gaul, not excluding Aquitaine, where the rulers farmed out tax-collection to the Jews, the count of the *civitas*, as though to keep in step with his Germanic counterpart the *grafio*, accumulated a plurality of functions, military, judicial and financial. This accounts for his tendency to usurpation. In eighth-century Merovingian Gaul, a good many counts, especially in frontier areas, can justly be described as local potentates. But even if officialdom survived in Visigothic Spain, along with the separation of civilian counts from the military, it is still surprising to come across the old tendency to desertion. The practice left King Egica so bereft of troops that he had to fill his armies with conscript clerics and slaves from the royal estates. Thus, whether through the impotence of an already privatised central administration or through an excess of zeal on the part of one which was still public, the royal power could make itself obeyed only by adding to the lands of the fisc and adopting the system of the soldier–peasant.

In England, the private character of the king's household was even more accentuated than in the case of the Merovingians. Like their Frankish counterparts, the monarchs succeeded in attracting to their households the sons of noble families, who were nurtured and educated in the hope of training a faithful and suitably grateful core of young adult retainers. In the setting of the timber-built Anglo-Saxon palaces, the offices of butler and cup--bearer appear to have carried more kudos than those of estate-steward, chamberlain and constable. Anything in the nature of a fiscal system had of course vanished, and taxes had become privatised, assimilated to the other dues owed by peasants on their holdings. As well as possessing estates of his own, the king tapped the resources of all other estates by receiving food-rents (*feorm*, from latin *firma*) in a quantity sufficient to sustain him and his household; under this system, one can perhaps envisage the villagers taking their renders of beer, corn, cattle, honey and cheese, listed in laws of King Ine (688–94) to the nearest king's *tun*. This *feorm* (from which comes the French *ferme* and English 'farm') was sometimes commuted to money. On top of all this would be the tributes received from conquered peoples. To consume these provisions, the king would progress from one of his enclosed domains to the next. The Merovingians, it may be mentioned in passing, did the same, as is borne out by the legend of the peripatetic 'fainéant' kings. Although lacking, as this shows, any central organisation worthy of the name, the Anglo-Saxon kings developed in the seventh century some rudimentary methods of local government. In the late seventh century, certain nobles (*ealdormen*) in Wessex were given a *scir* (later 'shire', county, though perhaps at this early stage it simply meant district under someone's jurisdiction). Perhaps this already signified a territorial circumscription having as its subdivision the *centena* (English 'hundred') found in the north of the Frankish kingdom, but in the absence of substantiating evidence we cannot be sure. Here we see the Germanic 'State' still at the stage of a community without a fixed geographical centre and relying exclusively on force to provide an institutional base.

The privatisation of the State extended even to the Church. We saw what efforts were made by the kings to control the appointment of bishops. It was only natural that they strove to master the one power external to their own. The bishops, furthermore, in view of their responsibilities and the covetous eyes being cast on ecclesiastical lands by the magnates, would look to the monarchs for guarantees of their property. The Frankish kings were especially lavish in granting them exemptions from taxes, rights of mintage and charters of immunity forbidding counts to carry out their official duties on the patrimonial possessions of bishoprics and then of abbeys. These functions devolved in consequence on the bishop or abbot, who was thus accountable directly to the monarch. In this way, the secular, and before long the monastic Church came to partake in the power game. The Pippinids derived much of their support from the monasteries. Charles Martel went further, being brazen enough to place laymen at the head of bishoprics or monasteries, which were thus converted into political power-bases serving his own ends. Hugh, a close kinsman, was elevated rapidly to the appropriate clerical grade and appointed to the see of Rouen and to the abbacies of Jumièges and St Wandrille. Another ally of the family, Milo, accumulated over a 40-year span, possibly even without benefit of consecration, the bishoprics of Trier and Rheims and the abbacy of Mettlach. In the south, the so-called bishops who occupied the sees led in reality a life reminiscent of war-leaders, to such an extent that later compilers of episcopal lists refused to include their names. Matters had gone far beyond the purchase of bishoprics (simony) once castigated by Gregory the Great in a letter to Queen Brunhild. For all practical purposes, the Church had become embroiled in the privatisation of the State, and might even be described as laicised, since it was the great landowners who appointed priests to their *Eigenkirchen*. Bound up with the crisis of kingship, therefore, was the fate of the episcopate and the abbatiate. Accordingly, a warrior prince who could make himself obeyed, and who could discover new sources of authority and reward, had everything to play for.

One solution: the Christian legislative State

Pippin III looked for political advice to two bishops: Boniface and Chrodegang. Charlemagne relied on Alcuin, an Anglo-Saxon deacon, and Hildebold, archbishop of Cologne, among many others. Louis the Pious summoned to his side Benedict of Aniane, a Hispano-Visigothic monk, who was followed by Adalhard, abbot of Corbie. Charles the Bald sometimes leaned on the obtrusive archbishop of Rheims, Hincmar. We saw the role they played in the reappearance of the empire and the kingship, and how they succeeded in converting these institutions into the property of the Church.

However, when they wanted to reconstitute the State, they came up against the Frankish conception of it, which, as we have just seen, envisaged the State as a kind of condominium in which the free men and the king had succeeded in bringing other tribes into submission, and where power was respected only in as far as it produced victory, booty and prosperity. Pippin and Charlemagne were at pains to preserve the prerogatives of that power, the *bannum*, the right to punish and coerce the disobedient, and its opposite, *gratia*, the royal favour which manifested itself in lavish gifts to loyal friends. In an expanding kingdom, however, it is clear that these simple ruler–warrior relationships would not suffice. On at least three occasions, in 789, 793 and 802, Charlemagne reinstituted the taking of oaths of fidelity in the Roman fashion. Every twelve-year-old male was required to swear in front of the local count that he would never do anything which could endanger the life of the king. However, since the oath took this negative form, despite clarification and amendment on each occasion, the purpose of these oath-takings was liable to be misinterpreted. Some people may have believed the sovereign insisted on them because he needed support, and may have taken it as a sign of weakness. Others, not having taken the oath, may have believed no doubt that they did not have to obey. Accordingly, Charlemagne and his counsellors resorted to a variety of measures to ensure that their decisions were understood and implemented. The first essential was to represent the ecclesiastical counsellors as the true political experts. Charlemagne's last capitulary in 813 ordered the counts, the judges and the people to co-operate with the bishop in the exercise of his judicial functions, since he alone knew the path society should take. In similar vein, the Latin term *res publica*, State, was 'renovated' under Louis the Pious by the addition of the adjective *christiana*, implying that the State could not exist if it were not Christian. To ensure that it was, the emperor, as is stated in a capitulary of 823–5, watched over the Church and maintained peace and justice, but, when it came down to it, the responsibility was spread in such a way that 'everyone, wherever he lives and in whatever social rank he is placed, is aware of his share of the burden'. 'From this it follows,' continues the emperor, that 'I must be your admonisher in all things and all of you must be my helpers.' All subjects had a part to play in the proper functioning of the State, first and foremost the clerical authors who came forward with 'Mirrors for Princes', manuals of political advice addressed to members of the royal family. To this branch of education Smaragdus, Agobard archbishop of Lyons, Jonas, Bishop of Orleans, and Hincmar, archbishop of Rheims, made significant contributions. At the synod of Tribur in 895, Arnulf, king of Eastern Francia, did not hesitate to categorise this conception as the art of 'governing in accordance with ecclesiastical law'. Primarily, therefore, the basis proposed for the Carolingian State was essentially spiritual and ecclesial.

Annexed to the law of the Church was the secular law. Hand in hand with this virtual repatriation of the State, extending from the Byzantine East to northern Europe, went an attempt to make legislation more uniform. Charlemagne reactivated the traditional annual assembly of free men, which Pippin III had transferred in 756 from 1 March to 1 May. The 'Field of May', also known as the *placitum generale* ('general assembly'), provided the occasion, before departure on campaign, for the conduct of important trials and the proclamation to the lay and ecclesiastical magnates of the royal, subsequently imperial, decrees. A series of propositions would be presented to the nobles and the clergy, who would debate them separately and certify that they conformed with the law. They would then be read aloud to the whole people in arms, and afterwards set down in writing, chapter by chapter (*capitula*). This succession of small paragraphs gave the name 'capitulary' to the whole text, of which four copies were supposed to be made, one of them for deposit in the palace archives. The oral proclamation by the sovereign, and the right of *bannum*, which entitled him to command and to punish, were all that was needed to give the decisions immediate effect.

Here, however, Charlemagne departed from tradition, with the aim of making his decisions even more effectual. He had them put into writing so as to reinforce or even replace the oral command, since hitherto only those present at the publication of the law made a show of obedience. The capitularies were in the nature much more of administrative regulations than of legislative acts. Some applied only to Italy. They were documents to be consulted, copied, disseminated, and even re-proclaimed within each county. So by putting his decisions into writing, Charlemagne extended their effectiveness. In the specifically legal domain, he kept to the traditional personal character of laws. Throughout the empire, and despite the protestations of Agobard, archbishop of Lyons, who would have liked to see one law for everyone, in the Roman fashion, the old codes continued to be applied. While the Romans preserved their laws intact, as did the Hispano-Visigoths in Septimania, the Bavarians, the Burgundians and the Lombards, Charlemagne made emendations and additions to the Frankish, Alamannic and Bavarian codes. He had the laws of the Frisians and the Saxons committed to writing. In any mixed suit pitting a

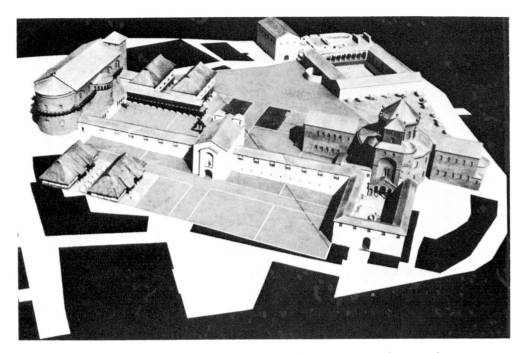

Model and (on facing page) ground-plan of the palace at Aachen. In imitation of Rome and more immediately of Byzantium, Charlemagne decided to create a permanent base for his hitherto itinerant court. Close to the excellent hunting-grounds afforded by the great forests of the Ardennes and the Eifel, and on the site of thermal baths used in Roman times, the Carolingian palace was begun in 794. The work, on a giant scale for its period, was completed in 798, and the chapel consecrated by Pope Leo III in 805. The materials used included priceless marbles plundered from Antique monuments in Italy.

member of one ethnic community against that of another, the latter, before the hearing could begin, would have to declare under which law he lived. It should be pointed out that all ecclesiastics, irrespective of their origin, came within the scope of Roman law, and also of the papal decretals, collections of which began to be formed during the ninth century. The ecclesiastics, indeed, accomplished much more in the way of legislation and standardisation than did the laity.

A superhuman attempt at overall control

The imperial government of Charlemagne and Louis the Pious thus consisted of a constant effort to advance beyond their original inheritance and to make it evolve towards greater unity with a Roman outlook. But the impetus towards centralisation stopped short of an imposed uniformity. They allowed kingdoms to subsist within the empire, most notably Aquitaine, Italy and Bavaria, the last initially as a prefecture. Each sub-kingdom, to use the term which has become conventional, possessed its own central administration and royal court and pursued its own policies, so far as the emperor of the day allowed. In any case, the

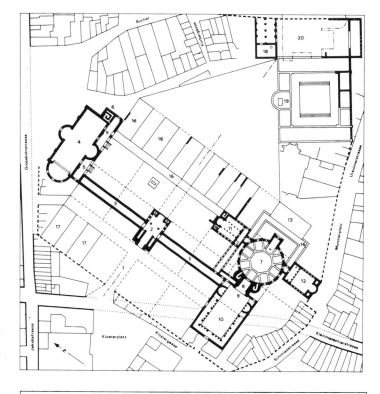

1. Main street
2. Monumental gateway
3. Connecting building
4. 'Aula palatina'
5. Colonnaded gallery
6. Staircase turret
7. Palace chapel
8. Westwork, flanked by two staircase turrets
9-10. 'atrium' with 'exedrae'
11-12. Annexes, probably the 'metatorium' (11) and 'secretarium' (12)
13. Curia ?
14. Portico
15. Wooden connecting gallery
16-17. Half-timbered or wooden buildings
18-19. Imperial baths
18. Imperial spring
19. Quirinius's spring
20. Foundations of Roman baths

——— (a) Remains of Carolingian buildings   — — — (b) Limits of the Carolingian palace

— · — · — (c) Line of the Roman streets

Layout of the palace at Aachen.

latter would need no justification for intervening directly in the internal affairs of these political entities officially subject to the Franks, amongst which, as we have seen, the Patrimony of St Peter was included. On the other hand, this relative degree of decentralisation would have underlined the necessity for a central seat of government. The perpetual removal of the court from one crown estate to the next continued to be the practice in the sub-kingdoms, but was eventually abandoned by Charlemagne. His choice fell on the fisc of Aachen, known for its thermal springs since Gallic and Roman times, eight leagues (32 km) from the busy river-port of Maastricht, at the centre of the Carolingians' patrimonial possessions. From 794 he took up residence there during the winter, and from 807 until his death he lived there all the year round. The building of a palace and a chapel

425

gave concrete expression to the new imperial ideology and to the political supremacy of the conqueror. Aachen remained ever after the symbol of a lay empire, in contradistinction to Rome, the place of consecration, the religious capital. After 840, the necessities of war sent the kings on their travels again. Charles the Bald, imbued with the same idea, tried to make Compiègne his capital, but without success, while Hincmar, archbishop of Rheims, succeeded by contrast in making Rheims the religious capital of the West Frankish kingdom.

In the palace, residence and court rolled into one, a central administration, showing ill-concealed signs of its Merovingian predecessor, was installed. The mayor of the palace, too dangerous to survive, had disappeared. But amid the classic confusion between private and public offices, the seneschal (the most senior of the household servants) was still responsible for supplying the tables with food, and in conjunction with the butler, with wine. At the same time he is overseer of the fiscal estates, through the intermediacy of the *domestici*, the day-to-day managers of the king's domains. The chamberlain still looked after the sovereign's private treasure, but with the assistance now of *sacellarii* who supervised incoming payments. The constable, with two marshals, saw to the supply of horses and provisions for the army. A newcomer, the count of the palace deputised for the sovereign in his absence to the extent of giving judgment in the increasing number of appeals addressed to the palace. Like the chamberlain, he would probably have at his disposal a rudimentary staff. Any of these great lay officials might be dispatched at a moment's notice on a diplomatic mission or to assume a military command. Lastly, it was customary for the emperor to summon a meeting of vassals or magnates (*proceres*), lay or ecclesiastical, when he needed their advice. And no doubt there was an army of door-keepers to raise or lower the curtains on each petitioner or ambassador coming to seek audience.

The clerical staff, engaged above all in furthering the renaissance of written records and correspondence, was concentrated in the chapel. This 'chaplaincy' had been set up in the first place to guard the Frankish kingdom's most celebrated relic, the cloak of St Martin of Tours, or more correctly the half which remained, the 'cope' (*cappa*). It was headed by an abbot or bishop from one of the great families, Fulrad, abbot of St Denis, under Pippin III, Angilram, bishop of Metz and then Hildebold, archbishop of Cologne under Charlemagne, who were important counsellors. The arch-chaplain had among his clergy a number of scribes who would note down in a kind of shorthand ('Tironian notes', so-called after Cicero's freedman–secretary) whatever was discussed and decided. They would then put the royal decrees and charters into official form. The head of this group, the protonotary, who was also responsible for the despatch of official correspondence and the publication of ecclesiastical canons, acquired around 808 the title of chancellor, a name perhaps, according to one suggestion, derived from the fact that his office, if it was in the chapel, may have been next to the screen of latticed stonework, called the chancel, which it is thought separated the clergy from the laity. With the widening of his responsibilities under Louis the Pious, he acquired the even grander title of arch-chancellor. He had custody of the palace archives where all documents addressed to the king were deposited along with copies of everything that was issued.

426

The orders issuing from the palace were for immediate implementation within the principal local government district, the county. According to the most recent research, it would appear that as many as 600 counties, known as *pagi*, or in Germanic regions as *gaue*, had to be reckoned with. In certain exceptional cases *pagi* and *gaue* figure as the subdivisions of counties. Clearly, these are the former Roman *civitates* now become dioceses, or the former tribal territories. In Germany the network of counties was not yet complete. Each county was headed by a count appointed by the king, and not only appointed by him but transferable on his orders and replaceable in case of misconduct. Designated an *honor*, as in the Roman empire, or alternatively a *ministerium* (office, service), the countship was remunerated in several different ways. The count enjoyed usufruct of fiscal lands, which were also designated *honores* by a process of assimilation, or otherwise known as the *res de comitatu*, which were situated within his circumscription. He received one-third of the legal fines and one-third of the tolls collected on his territory. Since the fines were generally fixed at one-third of the compensation, the count in fact received as his portion one-ninth of the sum paid over by the guilty party. Lastly, he had the right to a third of the fines imposed for breach of the royal *bannum*, thus twenty *solidi* out of the prescribed figure of 60. His revenues were therefore quite substantial. The counts' duties were numerous: carrying out the king's orders, calling up the free men each spring for service with the army or host (from Latin *hostis*, enemy), presiding over the king's court, the public *mallus*, which was held at least three times a year in each sub-division of the county for the hearing of all cases involving the major crimes of murder, adultery and treason. Not infrequently, they would be called away on special business and remain absent from their county for at least three or four months, even if it was only to conduct the troops to the place of assembly for the army.

So numerous were their duties that towards the end of Charlemagne's reign deputies were needed, the viscounts, with power to act in the count's absence; but their appearance on the scene was confined to Gaul. In any case, in Latin areas, the count was supported by *vicarii* competent to adjudicate in minor cases (disputes over joint ownership, thefts etc) and in Germanic territory by *centenarii* in charge of a small peace-keeping force. *Vicarii* and *centenarii* held a fortnightly court. Altogether, the count with his assistants would have added up to an administrative staff of about a dozen. From this it may be concluded that the Carolingian empire was served by between 8,000 and 9,000 public officials. This figure, taken on its own, is patently inferior to the number of functionaries at the disposal of the later Roman empire, of whom it is presumed there were some 15,000, 2,000 of them in Trier alone; but it has to be borne in mind that the area served by the Roman administration was larger by as much as a third. In a word, the Carolingian administration, allowing for an unknown number of officials at Aachen, must have been about equal with that of late Roman Antiquity. The political ground lost under the barbarian kingdoms had thus been made up.

Nor should the existence of certain other great functionaries be overlooked. Charlemagne adhered to the Merovingian system of dukes, or rather he created a special class of counts, the counts of the march (*Markgraf*, hence marquess), to whom he entrusted a number of counties situated in dangerous border areas. While not neglecting their own county, they also wielded civil and military authority over the others, so as to react quickly to a threat of invasion without waiting for the king or emperor to be alerted. The most important marches were those of Spain and Brittany, and the ones set up against the Danes, the Wends and the Avars. What it comes down to is that each marquess was the administrative head of the territory assigned to him, where he represented the royal authority. It is not surprising to find that in Germany, Poppo is referred to as marquess, in 891, by Arnulf, as is Liutpold of Bavaria in 898, and that they were still regarded by the king as trusted servants, at a time when in Western Francia, Robert, marquess of Neustria in 893, or Richard, marquess of Burgundy, simply did as they pleased. The count therefore shows us not only the Roman side of the imperial administration, but also, through this markedly decentralising conception of civil and military powers, its essentially Germanic character.

This encroachment of the marches into the kingdoms and of the kingdoms into the empire was consolidated by the development of the *missi dominici*. From 775, these special envoys of the sovereign, already mentioned in the Merovingian period, were utilised by Charlemagne in more systematic fashion, and with still greater regularity after 802 when their inspectorial brief was precisely defined. They would make their rounds in twos and threes, or often more, usually including at least one count and one bishop. They would check on the publication of capitularies, preside over the count's court in his stead, inquire into abuses of comital power, mete out punishments and afterwards submit their report to the emperor. Chosen invariably from members of the wealthiest families to avoid the temptations of embezzlement and bribery, as a further safeguard they carried letters of requisition to cover all their food and travelling expenses, on the model of the old Roman *cursus publicus*. Some were sent on special errands: to inspect the royal estates in a certain region, or to investigate complaints concerning a particular count. But the majority had geographically delimited *missatica* assigned to them. The territories where the *missi* were being regularly appointed year by year correspond, in 802, to Francia and northern Burgundy. In 825, they reached the Rhine, the Loire and the Rhône. As a result, this centralising institution may not have made any real or continuing impact on Aquitaine, Provence, Italy or Germany. This undoubtedly goes to show that the government of Charlemagne and his successors was truly effective only in northern Gaul, the precise basis of its economic power. Respect for the autonomy of the kingdoms was a means in the long run of integrating them, and one which was later adopted, furthermore, by the Capetians, with their system of apanages. Certainly, the *missi dominici* were so effective that under Charles the Bald the magnates insisted they should be landowners in the *missatica* to which they were assigned. Whatever may lie behind this undermining of the *missi dominici*, they did not cease their activity in the three kingdoms. In 875, a *missus* was still operating at Cambrai. They were not unknown even in the tenth century.

Trying to do justice, chasing after money

The essential business of these central and local officials, taking precedence even over financial affairs and the army, seems to have been the dispensation of justice. This was the sphere, moreover, in which Charlemagne most frequently intervened. His capitularies abound in prescriptions for the improvement of the justice delivered in the count's court. He abolished the *rachimburgii*, free men drawn from the village community who proclaimed the law, and replaced them with *scabini*, closer in character to permanent professional judges, seven for each *mallus*. They first appear around 774 in Northern Francia. To counterbalance or even replace the method of proof by oath-swearers or compurgators (the accused was acquitted if a larger number of people swore he was innocent than his accuser could produce), Charlemagne tried to win acceptance for proof by witnesses or even by written evidence. But efforts to eliminate the ordeal, pagan and probably religious in origin and still used to settle dubious cases, were fruitless. The custom continued of making the accused walk barefoot across nine white-hot ploughshares, or, for the better-off, of fighting a judicial duel through a hired champion: the one who killed the other was acquitted, since victory was always considered a proof of divine intervention. Charlemagne set up a system of appeal to the palace tribunal on complaint of a false judgment. But the count of the palace, as we saw, was very soon inundated with cases. The Carolingian judicial system, with its distinction between 'high' justice (reserved to the count) and 'low' justice (the cases dealt with by the *vicarius* or *centenarius*), remained fundamentally unchanged through the entire medieval period, notwithstanding its appropriation by its erstwhile officials. Sentence would be carried out by subordinates of the count or of the *centenarius*.

The intervention of the emperors was even greater in the financial domain. Charlemagne and Louis the Pious, not to mention their counsellors, were very insistent in their demands for information in writing about the profitability of their landed possessions. The capitulary *De villis*, ordering detailed lists to be drawn up of the tasks required of peasants on the fiscal domains, and the well-known *Brevium exempla*, models for use in surveying the resources available on the various fiscs, survive as proof of the great effort made to ascertain and quantify the empire's productive resources. The Roman tradition of recording liability to the land- or poll-tax in cadasters or census-books lived on in the ecclesiastical 'polyptychs'. Like the churchmen, the emperors and kings must have had a good idea, if not always of the number of men, at least of the quantity of fiscs and land units, the *mansi*, which they had at their disposal. The proof is, as we saw, that the experts who drew up the partition of 843 had documents to guide them in making an equal distribution of the public lands. Again, the tributes exacted in silver by Charles the Bald to buy off the Danes in 845, 860–1, 862 and 866 were levied on a sliding scale, depending on the type of *mansus*: for the 6,000 pounds of silver for the danegeld of 866 to be raised in this way, the central government would have had to know the exact number of units it could tax. The renaissance of written and arithmetical skills thus enabled the Carolingians to arrive at a certain sophistication in matters of finance.

In importance, the fiscs, public lands under cultivation or lying waste, headed the list. Besides the royal family's personal properties, they could be augmented by conquest, as for example in Saxony or Italy, by disinheritance or by confiscations, either from traitors or through judicial sentences. Heavily drawn on for the upkeep of the royal household, for the remuneration of officials, and increasingly, as we shall see, as a means of rewarding vassals

429

In 802

— Boundaries of the Carolingian empire
— — Boundaries of the kingdom of Aquitaine
— – — Boundaries of the *missatica*

In 827

— Boundaries of the Carolingian empire
— — Boundaries of the kingdom of Aquitaine
— – — Boundaries of the *missatica*

In 853

———— Boundaries of the Carolingian empire
— — — Boundaries of the West Frankish kingdom

– – – – Boundaries of the *missatica*
·········· Partition of Verdun

15 Circumscriptions of the Missi Dominici

for their services, this landed capital was under constant threat of diminution. Warfare was thus indispensable to its maintenance. Failing that, and as had already happened in the time of Charles Martel, the kings might have to fall back on distributing church lands to the nobles in order to secure their fidelity. Louis the Pious had to resign himself to this course at the first signs of revolt. His sons did the same, with the result that by the end of the ninth century the large royal estates had almost all been broken up, while those of the Church had passed into the control of laymen. It is worth remarking however that these fiscs were situated for the most part in Neustria and Austrasia. The last fiscs to remain in the dynasty's possession would be situated in precisely these regions. Charlemagne had at his disposal some 200 palaces, 600 fiscs and 200 abbeys. The remainder of his revenues came from his right to two-thirds of all legal fines (*freda*), of fines for infraction of the royal *bannum* (the remaining 40 *solidi* out of a total of 60) and fines for absence from the army (*heribannum*). Then there were the indirect taxes, the tolls, in the form (say) of a bridge-tax, a wheel-tax, a market-tax, or of a toll on crossing a mountain-pass, levied at the rate of ten per cent *ad valorem*. After deduction of the toll-keeper's pay, all the proceeds went to the royal treasury. In view of the huge amounts sometimes involved (particularly the sum of 60 *solidi*), some people must have had to discharge their obligations in kind, by surrendering weapons, horses, slaves and suchlike. The royal moneyers and the king would each have made an average profit of twelve *deniers* for every 264 pennies struck from a pound of silver. The old Roman taxes, on land and on heads, did not disappear. But, as we saw, their amount was now fixed. This 'custom' undoubtedly still existed in Aquitaine, Provence, Italy and in a few other regions, since Charlemagne ordered an exact inventory to be made

431

in places where it survived. Among 'disposable' revenues there remain the often very substantial gifts the magnates were expected to hand over at the Field of May, and the tributes received from the Bretons or from the dukes of Benevento (7,000 *solidi* per annum). And let us not forget booty: fifteen wagons were needed to transport the treasures the Avars had accumulated in their ring. In a word, warfare and the extent of the fiscs tended to camouflage the need to overhaul the old Roman tax-system which therefore continued its decline, all the more inexorable because the payment of customary tax had become a symbol of servitude.

Power rests ultimately and solely on the army

The key to the Carolingian system is therefore the army. In theory, the king's *bannum* gave him the right to summon all free men to the host in case of a general invasion. They were required to present themselves, armed at their own expense, at the Field of May, since it was still quite usual for the assembly of magnates to coincide with the assembling of the army. Mobilisation took place in three stages: first the summons would be delivered to the count, then the count would muster his contingent, and lastly he would conduct them to the general rendezvous. To speed up the process, under Louis the Pious the summons was delivered to the *missi* for direct transmission to the persons concerned, who within twelve hours would be on their way, fully equipped, to the army's point of departure. The campaigns, which almost always took place annually, would last for at least three to four months. It was necessary to make advance provision by requisitioning forage (*fodrum*) and transports, which took the form of carts covered with hides (*bastarnae*), capable of carrying food supplies for three months and enough weapons and clothing for six. When the external danger was more localised, only the vassals of the great noble families, the emperor, the abbots, the abbesses and the bishops, would be summoned. In the case of free men, it was then thought sufficient, as under the old Roman system, to requisition the services of one man for every four *mansi*. The less well-endowed would be grouped together to make up the same number of land-units so that by pooling their resources one of their number could be properly equipped. Near the frontiers, in the marches, the service demanded was more exacting. All free men would be expected to take their turn in mounting guard on towers or castles (the duty known as *wacta*). Special units, the *scarae*, composed of professional warriors, were stationed there permanently. Discipline was especially strict and desertion in the middle of a campaign (*herisliz*) punishable by death. The bulk of these armies would consist of foot-soldiers, equipped with a lance, a shield, a bow and a dozen arrows. But their contribution was minor compared with that of the horsemen who led the charge and pressed home the victory. Alongside the lightly-armed cavalry of the Bretons, Saxons, Austrasians, Gascons and Spaniards, one cannot fail to notice the increasing importance of heavy cavalry. Armed with a longsword, baldric and lance, and protected by a 'byrnie', a thick leather jerkin covered with iron plates, they would need to be the owners or tenants of at least a dozen *mansi*. Altogether their

Carolingian light cavalry. The helmets, breastplates and shields of the horsemen are clearly visible; they ride without stirrups, and their lances are used as javelins which are hurled at the enemy. The pen and ink drawings from the *Utrecht Psalter* are among the most brilliant products of Carolingian manuscript illumination. They were executed between 820 and 830 at the abbey of Hautvillers (Utrecht, Bibliotheek der Rijksuniversiteit).

armament cost between 36 and 40 *solidi*, equivalent to the very high price of twenty cows. Charlemagne and Louis the Pious were particularly adept in their deployment of these armoured horsemen. For the most part their military operations consisted in the convergence of three or four columns on a specific objective, or conversely, for pillaging operations, the dispersal of a large army, like the fingers of one hand, across the country to be brought into subjection. This novel strategy lay at the root of the Frankish successes.

Another important element in their success was the sheer number of soldiers they could command. In 811, for example, it was possible to field four armies for simultaneous operations on the Elbe, the Danube, the Ebro and on the Breton borders. Each would have comprised between 6,000 and 10,000 infantry plus from 2,500 to 3,000 cavalry, 800 of them armoured. Without recourse to a general mobilisation, the empire was capable of placing on a war footing about 52,000 men, of whom 12,000 were calvary. It is estimated that the emperors could muster in total 100,000 infantry and 35,000 cavalry. Even if these calculations may be thought to err on the side of optimism, it seems obvious that the Carolingians had in their hands a military tool especially well adapted to their purposes and certainly superior to the effective nucleus of 65,000 men at the disposal of the late Roman empire in the West. By contrast, we hear very little about naval fleets. Charlemagne restored the Roman system of coastal patrols, establishing naval bases at Ghent, Boulogne, and in the mouths of the Gironde and the Rhône in 811, to fend off attacks from the Scandinavians. Each squadron had its complement of marines, ready to embark at the first sign of danger. We are given no details of their operations, but the results cast doubt on their utility.

The Carolingian army owed its cohesion above all to another of Charlemagne's initiatives: the introduction of vassalage into the State. Clienteles, it will be remembered, played a

433

prominent part in the rise of the dynasty. Whereas the loyalties thus engendered were of a private character and the benefice bestowed by the lord on his vassal was in the nature of a completely free gift, Charlemagne proceeded to make the connection more formal, to link the benefice with the personal attachment. He exhorted all free men to become obedient to a lord through the ceremony of commendation. In return for the vassal's military service, the lord was then bound to offer him not merely, as heretofore, upkeep in his own household, but the lifelong enjoyment of one of his landed properties. The service rendered by the vassal thus became the reason for the benefice. A complete hierarchy of subordinates was created in this way. Charlemagne attached to himself royal vassals (*vassi dominici*) and 'domiciled' them on fiscal lands. Deeming ecclesiastical possessions to be his property because he protected them with the 'beneficial' grant of immunity (which meant that no public official, count or duke, was allowed to enter such lands in the exercise of their public duties), he insisted that bishops and abbots should reciprocate by entering into a personal attachment to himself by means of commendation. This explains why these great ecclesiastical personages are depicted fighting in the army surrounded by contingents of their own vassals. Through this network of intersecting loyalties leading up to himself, the emperor was hoping to rest the political edifice on men's respect for their given word, on the loyalty they swore in an oath taken on the Gospels or over relics, and above all, on the mutual obligations of lord and vassal, and on the summons warriors were bound to obey. It remains none the less evident that this crucial form of public service was in danger of being undermined and even destroyed by two inherent contradictions: the contradiction between commitment to a Christian ideal of peace and the sheer necessity to live by plunder; and the paradox whereby the monarch, in default of other means of making himself obeyed, was forced to rely on the ambitions of private persons and their clienteles.

Distorted reflections on the empire's periphery

The political entities independent of the empire had much less developed governmental structures. The Anglo-Saxon kingdom came nearest, but if anyone can claim to be the insular equivalent of Charlemagne, it was Alfred rather than Offa. Offa had provided the kingdom with a strong coinage, the new silver penny, first issued after 765, which was comparable with the new silver pennies of Pippin III. Again, to fend off attacks from the Celts of Wales, he had set the precedent of constructing a long earthwork surmounted by a palisade, Offa's Dyke. The *Tribal Hidage*, a document of the period in which the hides (equivalent of the Carolingian *mansus* or the Germanic *hufa*) in most parts of England are enumerated, proves that the Anglo-Saxon kingship was well able to assess the taxable revenues from each unit of cultivation. From the time of Ecgfrith, son of Offa, who was anointed in 787, the rite of royal unction – imitated from the Franks – added its own reinforcement to the kingship. Following on from this, the prerogative of the king in legal matters was reasserted when Alfred published a code in which, while reiterating certain laws of his predecessors, he curtailed the right of vengeance (*faida*) and emphasised the

Initiation and rites of passage. The act of commendation 'hands between hands' admitted young nobles to the following of the war-leader, who 'handed on' to them the essence of his supernatural strength; although of a later date, the illustration gives a good idea of the 'sacramental' quality of Germanic fidelity (Heidelberg, Universitätsbibliothek).

duties owed by men to their lords. The central administration of the Anglo-Saxon kings remains obscure, but we saw that at the local level counties were grouped together for military purposes under *ealdormen*. In each county (shire) there was a royal agent, the shire-reeve, later sheriff. He presided over the twice-yearly court attended by the great landowners of the district, published the royal decrees, and received the food-rents and dues owing to the king. He was the principal agent in the implementation of Alfred's military reform, which entailed, as we saw, the creation of a complete network of fortified settlements. The idea was for each to be constructed, and afterwards defended, with the help of the local inhabitants. It was left to the sheriff to determine how much individuals should pay in proportion to their means. Lastly, in virtue of the *fyrd*, analogous to the Frankish host, the king had the right to call up all Anglo-Saxons each year for military service. So as to maintain a standing army, he chose to summon only half of each contingent, twice a year, for a period of three months each time. In addition, to resist the Danes, he ordered warships to be built following neither the Frisian nor the Danish techniques. Lastly, it should not be overlooked that here, too, the free men were more or less under compulsion to enter the commendation of a lord (*thegn*), a landowner who was bound equally by the obligations of military service.

In the Danelaw, just as in Iceland, the assembly of free men, that is of warriors, remained

435

Illustration from a tenth century St Gallen manuscript of Prudentius's *Psychomachia*, executed in pen and ink on parchment; the drawing is graphically less vibrant than the sketches of the *Utrecht Psalter* (Bern, Burgerbibliothek).

the dominant factor. The Scandinavian kings functioned merely as war-leaders who carried out the will of the assemblies. In Iceland, the assembly controlled everything: the *Althing* was thus the first European 'parliament'.

As in the Irish kingdoms, government in Brittany, which retained its independence throughout most of the eighth, ninth and tenth centuries, took a highly localised form. Each parish (*plebs*) was ruled by a chieftain of ancient lineage, the *machtiern*. Like his Irish counterpart, he resided on an estate which was also the seat of his court (*lis*). Here he dispensed justice and collected the old Roman land-taxes, now in the nature of customary dues. He had no military function (unlike his island counterparts). From about 830, however, a Breton from the Vannetais, Nominoë, having won official recognition from Louis the Pious as *missus dominicus*, strove to build up a centralised government. After his crushing defeat of Charles the Bald at Ballon in 845, he made the Breton Church independent by setting up a metropolitan see at Dol. He brought in officials in the form of counts and *missi dominici*, appointing them himself. His sons, Erispoë and Salomon, styled themselves kings. In their entourage they had faithful retainers, private warriors who would serve them in the old Celtic style. But this attempt to emulate Carolingian kingship was cut short by the Scandinavian invasions, and Brittany continued to be ruled in actuality by its *machtierns*.

The picture is very different in Galicia and the Asturias, where the neo-Visigothic kingship remained faithful to the forms of government inherited from the kingdom of Toledo. Nothing changed, even the old Roman land-tax, the *tributum*, continued to be levied. All that disappeared was the coinage, while the necessities of ever-present warfare served to concentrate governmental powers in the hands of the king. From being elective,

436

the monarchy soon became hereditary. The monarch's entourage consisted of *gardingos*, bound to him by an oath of fealty. All the free men owed him military service. They received their arms from the king or may even have been granted a plot of crown land (*prestamo*) in remuneration for their services. The counts, who had under them *saions* and *merinos*, were royal appointees and remained liable to dismissal. They dispensed justice in accordance with the laws handed down in the *Forum judicium*, dating from the time of Reccesuinth. Even the Church was totally under the king's control. Between 755 and 1037, the Asturian kings founded more than 100 monasteries. They appointed bishops and even created bishoprics, all without reference to Rome. In short, as a result of their isolation and of the ever-pressing need to find fighting-men for the *fossatum*, the depopulated frontier zone forming the boundary with Islam, the Christian kings of Spain were driven to create a more highly centralised system of government, which was also much more widely obeyed. The nobility had no time to establish themselves on their estates, the meditations of the clergy played on the apocalyptical themes depicted in countless manuscripts. A classless society governed by a warrior king backed by a force of peasant–soldiers was fighting for survival.

The political regime of the Ottonian empire is again strongly reminiscent of a government on a war footing. As we saw, its programme and administrative structures did little more than imitate and re-employ those of the Carolingians. Illiterate until the age of 35, a warrior and huntsman in the mould of Charlemagne, Otto I replanted the Carolingian State in Germany, no mean achievement in a region which had experienced the Carolingian regime in its unadulterated form only in Saxony. As a prelude, Henry the Fowler had inaugurated his reign with the slogan '*Renovatio regni Francorum*', 'renewal of the kingdom of the Franks'. Like Alfred, he set about the systematic fortification of the larger monasteries and rural centres, and of towns such as Regensburg and Augsburg. Adding a new dimension to the system of calling up one warrior for every four *mansi*, he ordered that one peasant–soldier out of every nine should remain on garrison duty in a fortified centre, while billets would be provided for the others in the case of a general mobilisation. The protection afforded by these *agrarii milites*, professional soldiers provided with plots of land, would thus allow life to continue normally in places where the count's courts, councils, markets and so on were held. As well as enlisting the Saxon peasantry, Henry I drew increasingly on the *milites armati*, or armoured cavalry, to combat the Hungarian horsemen. Towards the middle of the tenth century, Otto I and Otto II could muster around 15,000 men, of whom more than 8,000 were armoured cavalry, and this was only north of the Alps. The proportion of infantry in the army had thus changed from three-quarters in Charlemagne's time to under half, while the territory affected was equivalent to only one third of Charlemagne's empire. From this it seems reasonable to suppose that the troops of the Ottonian empire were equal in number to those of Charlemagne, but that the tilting of the balance in favour of heavy cavalry portended the dawn of a new age, that of the professional warrior. It should lastly be noted that this army was attached even more firmly to the sovereign, for its members, both in his bodyguard and among the vassals, consisted of *ministeriales*, or *Dienstlehen* – that is to say former slaves with an obligation to military service – to whom he had granted a *mansus*. Here we encounter once more the dependant of servile origin familiar from primitive Germanic tradition, unswerving in his loyalty to the war-leader to whom he owed everything he had. The still-surviving military comradeship of the old days thus consolidated an essentially Carolingian institution which Charlemagne had sought to base on the ties between man and man. There can be no dispute that the military machine in western Europe had made nothing but steady progress, to the point of surpassing in quantity and quality the armies of the late Roman empire.

Making a more cohesive society?

'Charlemagne was let down by men,' as Robert Folz succinctly put it. And he might have added: 'Because there were so few who understood his intentions and those of his successors'. In fact, however, of all Charlemagne's constructions it was only the political edifice that totally collapsed. The others, in particular his innovations in the Church, in education and in the economy, in part survived. Even the charge of political failure is open to dispute, since the ablest of Charlemagne's successors, Otto I, was content to draw on him for inspiration. Investigation of the thought processes which led to the empire's internal disintegration puts that failure in its proper perspective. The fact is that misapprehensions and disagreements reared their heads not only over the question of obedience to the king and the emperor but equally in the area of the Church's religious requirements, a territory all the more perilous because men's fate in the next world was affected. The mass of disaffection is the key to our understanding of the turbulent years running from 850 to 950. The pent-up energy which had found no outlet within the imperial order was about to break out at the local level, to create the feudal order.

Obedience a matter of proximity

Charlemagne had hoped to intensify the obedience of all his subjects by means of the oath of loyalty sworn in former days by Roman citizens. The numerous revisions to the text, the valiant efforts at explanation by the *missi*, the insertion of the clause 'to be obedient as a man should be towards his lord' bear witness on the contrary to the persistent failure of this device. The cause no doubt lay in the widespread impression that the king must actually be quite weak to be reduced to exacting such a promise. The subject's oath of loyalty consequently disappeared, except in Catalonia, for example, where oaths of this type were still being sworn to the local count in the tenth century.

The situation became more serious when, as a result of marrying vassalage to the benefice, the duty of service gradually became linked no longer with a person, but with a gift of land. Under the influence of the southern notion of *stipendium* (payment for services rendered) and of the Germanic notion that every gift was outright, the idea of temporarily enjoying the fruits of an estate was not understood. To a primitive mind, accustomed to the system of gifts and counter-gifts, the initiative should come from the chieftain or other powerful personage. Whether it is a question of gifts to the king by the magnates in return for shares in the booty, or of *xenia*, gifts of eggs and poultry from peasants in return for tenure, the exchange of gifts was simply a token of mutual obligation. It signified at bottom that the gift was a duty, not a favour or an act of exceptional generosity. The social and contractual aspect of the gift robbed it of spontaneity and of any connection with charitable impulse, despite the Church's endeavour to present it in this light. In the same way the land gradually became an outright gift, in return for military service. Because of this misunderstanding, the sovereign, and the lord in his turn, became purchasers of the service and obedience of which in the normal course of events they should have been the natural beneficiaries. The Church, for all its efforts to make the emperor or king an untouchable and sacred personage, with such good effect that royal assassination became a thing of the past, acted in vain, since it was powerless to prevent the steady whittling away of his authority. More precisely, it hastened the process, by demanding, through Hincmar in particular, that bishops should no longer be subjected, on their investiture by the king with their bishopric and its possessions, to the *immixtio manuum*, that is to say the manual act of self-surrender which by Frankish custom signified the entry of an inferior into dependence on a superior. To be sure, this refusal was grounded on the Gospel maxim that no man can serve two masters, but the royal power was inevitably weakened. An outward sign of its degradation was soon manifest: to command obedience, the king had to make concessions. At Coulaines, in 843, he had to promise the Church not to despoil its possessions so as to obtain benefices, and to promise the magnates not to deprive them of their offices (*honores*) in arbitrary fashion. If he did not abide by these promises, so it was said, the subjects could consider themselves released from their oath of fealty. The causal connection between obedience and gift had undergone a total reversal. The assimilation of the contractual formula to the Roman type of contract between equals robbed the king of any coercive power, masked the rapacity of the magnates and diminished the royal power by comparison with the laws of God.

Forced to be generous, the king distributed fiscal lands with seeming abandon. After 840, indeed, not a single count was to be held in check by considerations of fidelity, even after going through the allegedly binding ceremony of commendation. The fact is that the civil wars and multiple partitions completely confused the loyalties due to the lord, king or emperor. In Burgundy, between 806 and 839, the nobles must have had to commend themselves to a new king on no less than six occasions – and this was merely to keep pace with the lawful dispositions of Louis the Pious. In such circumstances how was one to observe a promise of lifelong fidelity? Bear in mind that on the outbreak of each revolt, every vassal would be summoned to the host. Whose summons was he to obey: that of the rebel son, his immediate lord, or that of his supreme lord, the humiliated emperor? Almost without thinking, the vassal and sub-vassal would follow the lord closest to hand, the one who could immediately confiscate their benefice if they did not obey. In this way, the contractual obligation and the immediacy of power would blot out the supreme authority, interposing the lord as a screen between the king and the vassal. Therefore, to renew the vassal's fidelity a further grant of land would be necessary. Charles the Bald distributed in 37 years four times as many properties among his followers as Charlemagne had done in

46 years over the whole empire. Carloman, at the very beginning of his reign, fearing he would not be obeyed, gave away estates to all and sundry, even before there was the slightest hint of opposition. Once the capital of fiscal lands had been squandered and reduced in the tenth century to a few estates in the region of the Paris basin, the vassals deserted a king who had nothing more to give. They were even willing to receive benefices from several different lords, final proof that fidelity was a dead letter.

Local oaths

But, someone will say, these properties were only granted for a limited period or for life, and if arbitrary confiscation was no longer possible, nothing forbade their recovery in the normal course of events. In the reign of Charles the Bald, however, the count's *honores* were already becoming assimilated to his benefices. When the king wanted to transfer the count of Bourges, Gerard, in 867, to replace him with Acfrid, the latter had to force his way into the county and lost his life in the attempt. Gerard kept his county as a heritable possession. By the end of the century, no countship was revocable. Even so, the count's fiscal estates and his benefices should still have been recoverable on his death. Soon even this possibility vanished. The kindred of the deceased stepped in and tried to persuade the king or magnate that it would be prudent, for reasons well understood, to leave the heir in possession of the same lands. As early as 868, Hincmar, with reference to his own vassals on the lands of the Church of Rheims, considered it the standard practice 'to leave benefices, for the sake of military service, with sons of fathers who have served the Church well'. In 877, Charles the Bald, in the capitulary of Quierzy-sur-Oise, while endeavouring to safeguard his right of disposition over *honores* and benefices, acknowledged that in his absence, during his visit to Italy, sons should be permitted to succeed their fathers, subject to confirmation on his return or to new appointments. This seemed to concede that hereditary succession was becoming the customary practice. Imperceptibly, the right of inheritance did indeed establish itself, despite one or two setbacks, which explains why Louis IV and Lothar were so intent in the tenth century on the conquest of Lotharingia where the phenomenon had not yet appeared and where, in consequence, they might have been able to reconstitute their fisc. The personal bond disappeared. The benefice slipped from the hands of its owner into those of its holder. The gift, reward of lifelong service, had become the basis of a new political power, the rural lordship. Power followed the land down the same path. Having passed from the empire to the kingdom, it descended from the king to the territorial ruler, and at a later date to the castellan.

The tie of negative fidelity and the tie of commendation have thus sprung apart, since the former had been brought down to the level of the county and the latter had become automatic, whoever chanced to inherit. Two others remained, the bonds between equals and the ties of blood. But these, too, rebounded against the State, even though, unlike commendation, they had never implied dependence of the noble towards the sovereign. The purpose of the *convenientiae* typical of the south was to keep the peace or forge alliances between noble families, and the kings, save at Coulaines in 843, had little intention of being a party to them, because of the restrictive conditions they threatened to impose. They thus worked to the advantage of the aristocracy by reversing the roles. It was the same with the oath sworn between hands by the *trustis*, the following. This imposed, as we saw, the duty of unconditional loyalty in life or death, whatever the circumstances. If the bodyguard so created was of a private character, as would be the case for nobles who had formed a *convenientia*, and yet represented a commitment knowing no limit this side of the grave, the *trustis* could become an even greater danger to the public authorities. It was for this reason strictly forbidden by Charlemagne. Charles the Bald repeated the prohibition, probably in vain, at Dijon in 857, calling on the *missi* to take measures against the people in various localities who were engaged in pillage, house-breaking and murder, people who were forming *trustes*, sending their cattle to graze on enclosed pastures and destroying the harvests. Slaves, it appears, were forming similar associations, pressure groups in the most literal sense, laws unto themselves. This type of local association would be totally impervious to the idea of the public good. Cutting across the vertical organisation of society, it set up horizontal bonds between the free men of the same locality. On such attitudes the Carolingian State could make little impression.

It fared no better over the banning of *ghildes*, whether in 778 or 884. The reason for forbidding these sworn associations, even when they were intended as a mutual insurance against shipwreck and fire, was that the underlying principle of these 'factions' was completely antagonistic to the Christian State. The Church condemned them with especial vehemence, and it is Hincmar who tells us why these *conjurationes* were considered so dangerous. Feasts would be held at which, after over-indulgence in eating and drinking, mutual oaths promising aid and financial or physical support would be uttered, giving rise on occasion to murders or even minor civil wars. *Ghildes* appear to have been especially numerous in northern Francia. They took hold in particular in the world of overseas commerce, and ecclesiastical authors continued to denounce their avidity for profit, hardness of heart and above all the absence of any law to restrain these mercantile associations whose only guiding principle was that their group's interests must prevail, come what might. The *trustis* or the *ghilde* acknowledged only one imperative: survival at any cost. They had nothing in common with the new world the Carolingians were setting out to build and which they could not fail to reject.

More formidable still was the blood-tie. Reference has already been made to the existence, in Germanic societies, of the sacral vengeance called *faida*, handed down from one generation to another unless, which was rare, the compensation offered, the *wergild*, was sufficient to break the chain of murders without loss of honour, since the kindred could refuse it out of piety towards the dead. Under the system of personal laws still in force, with its tariff of compensations, if peace was made it would be accompanied by mutual oaths of security, the *treuwa* of the Germanic peoples, which in our language has become 'truce'. All this took place, more often than not, outside the framework of juridical institutions and lent reinforcement to the horizontal structures. If the State intervened in an effort to halt the process, it once again revealed its impotence. In England, despite the steps taken by Alfred to limit feuds, the murder of Earl Uhtred by a noble called Thurbrand set in motion a chain of murders which ended only in 1073 when the great-grandson of Uhtred, Earl Waltheof, slew the greater part of Thurbrand's descendants at Settring, not far from York. The feud might well have continued, had Waltheof not been executed by William the Conqueror in 1076. Some of the great Carolingian families were engaged in equally interminable vendettas. Charles Martel had fathered, by a concubine (Sunnihild) belonging to the ducal family of Bavaria, a son named Grifo. The latter had laid claim, in a violent and disorderly fashion, to a share of his father's inheritance. Having attempted to ally himself with the duke of Aquitaine (Waifer) and later with the Lombard king, he was eventually murdered in 753. At about the same time the Etichonid clan suffered the loss of all its ancestral possessions, having been expelled by Pippin III for the benefit of the Bernardine clan. Now the Etichonids were related to the Welfs of Bavaria, descendents of the ducal family which, in the person of Tassilo, was a thorn in Charlemagne's side until 788. When Judith married Louis the Pious, the Welf family thus re-entered the Carolingian orbit. Memories of her ancestor, Grifo, robbed of his inheritance, and of the endless battles of his half-sister Chiltrud to have him avenged by the Duke of Bavaria, may certainly have been causes of Judith's fierce determination to win a kingdom for her son Charles the Bald. But the support accorded her by the chamberlain Bernard, of Carolingian stock, was interpreted as a betrayal by the Etichonids, Hugh and Matfrid, who did all they could to destroy Judith. Might not this signify a large-scale settling of accounts between two great Austrasian clans, the Pippinids, who had managed to capture the throne, and the Etichonids, robbed of Alamannia just as the Welfs had been robbed of Bavaria? If this hypothesis could be substantiated, might not the fall of the Carolingian empire merely be regarded as the outcome of an interminable blood-feud – in which case the ties of kindred could be said to have killed off the dynasty and relegated its legitimacy to an accident of history?

The persistence of old sworn or hereditary connections explains the irreconcilable antagonism to the Aquitano-Spanish programme put forward by Louis the Pious, Benedict of Aniane, Agobard of Lyons, and other ecclesiastical counsellors. Two worlds, two attitudes, stood opposed. Whilst, on one side, two kindreds were engaged in a violent struggle to hang on to power or to avenge their murdered hopes, on the other, the archbishop of Lyons, Agobard, was haranguing the magnates in a manner which could only pour oil on the flames. With a total failure to comprehend the situation, he delivered, in a blasphemous paraphrase of the *Lamentations* of Jeremiah, a ferociously misogynistic attack on the misconduct of the empress, which the other witnesses did not corroborate. Thinking to defend the empire, he sabotaged it all the more thoroughly. He offered unexpected weapons to the enemies of Judith and of the emperor, who had been opposed in any case to the emperor's second marriage. The effect of this clerical intervention was to remove all hope of untying the knot of vipers, and the blunder left its mark on the divisions of the decade 830–40. The collision of the feuding instinct and moralising abstraction produced the same effect as sulphur in water: instantaneous combustion.

The impossible union

Other examples could be cited of rejections which sprang from psychological differences too wide to be bridged. The change in weights and measures and the introduction of new *deniers* ran again and again into categorical opposition from local populations, necessitating the threat of dire punishments for refusal to conform. The prohibition of usury, which after the capitulary of Nijmegen in 806 applied to all loans of goods returnable with interest, took its cue from biblical injunctions. Usurers were sentenced to pay a fine of 60 *solidi*. In point of fact, the very people who invoked Deuteronomy to condemn lending at interest had turned money-lenders themselves. The abbots, in particular, advanced substantial sums, thus falling within the scope of the prohibition. If the latter was of some benefit to the peasants, in the sense that it saved them, if not from ruin, at least from the debtors' prison, it was a considerable embarrassment to trade and perhaps still more to merchants who bothered about the eternal repose of their souls. It also explains why many bishops handed over the management of their capital to Jewish agents. The programme thus ran into obstacles by which, if it was not totally defeated – as happened over the weights and measures, which came to differ according to the region – it was either deflected, as in the case of usury, or at best slowed down, as with the reform of the monetary system, enduring though this was.

There remains one last cause of political failure which was conducive to fragmentation into territorial principalities: the antagonisms between peoples, which Jan Dhondt has termed the 'ethnic solvent'. For my part, in view of the absence in many cases of racial unity, I would prefer to call it 'regional particularism'. Many an example could be quoted of the stereotyped mental images which men of the ninth and tenth centuries held of their neighbours. When Louis the Pious becomes distrustful of the Franks in the West, he chose to rely instead on the Germans, that is the Saxons, reputedly valiant, true and faithful. Notker of St Gall made the same distinction between this dependable core and the 'Gauls (the Western Franks), the Aquitanians, the Burgundians, the Spaniards, the Alamans and the Bavarians' who, in the days of Charlemagne, gloried not a little in the title 'slaves of the Franks'. But those times were over and unity held no appeal, despite the exhortations of Agobard, a Spaniard to unite in an empire wherein, in line with the ideal held up by St Paul, there would be 'neither Aquitanians nor Lombards nor Bavarians, but one in all and all in Christ'. The contrast was made between the 'iron will' of the Franks and the waywardness of the 'Welch', the volatility and continuing propensity to treason of the Romans. The history of relations with Aquitaine is instructive in this regard. Charlemagne was often afraid that the young Louis the Pious would be infected by the arrogant attitudes of his subjects. These fears were fully justified, since Louis returned to Aachen in 814 accompanied by Aquitanian counsellors who persuaded him to implement a programme too ambitious for the times and too far in advance of contemporary mentalities. Conversely, the Frankish families implanted by Charlemagne in Aquitaine very quickly became southernised, seduced by the more opulent and more refined life-style of the surrounding 'Romans'. Once the Franks transplanted to Lombardy and Aquitaine adopted Mediterranean names and customs, and in so doing declared their allegiance to the old Europe rather than the new, the Carolingian army and the conception of a Frankish empire was doomed. Again, but in the opposite sense, as soon as the Aquitanian–Spanish conception of an evenly-balanced and uniform empire, as entertained by Louis the Pious, was put forward, it reactivated Germanic prejudices and hostility towards the southern traitors. 'The Romans are stupid, the Bavarians are wise', to quote the Kassel Glosses. The Basques were stereotyped as untameable, the Bretons as dull-witted: 'Total strangers to civilisation, easily provoked, they are gross in their habits and babble away in an incomprehensible patois,' says Ralph Glaber early in the eleventh century. The cultural divide between these differing peoples is among the causes of the break-up of the empire. In proof of this assertion one can point to the simple fact that after about 936 the king of Western Francia ceased to intervene south of the Loire. When in 987 the count of Barcelona appealed for help, in the name of the ancient solidarity against Islam, to his overlord, the new king Hugh Capet, the latter remained completely unmoved.

But it might be objected that fragmentation also took its toll of the original kernel of the Frankish empire, Neustria, Austrasia and northern Burgundy, where the trend towards centralisation, helped on by the regularly-appointed *missi*, had been especially pronounced. Here, surely, where the former Gallo-Roman inhabitants were proud to be called 'Franks', unity should have survived. But this was far from being the case, since the aristocracy still only accorded respect to the king in proportion to his victories. At this point the Germanic conception of the State shifted to the east, to Saxony, where the charisma of violence found re-embodiment in the lineage of Widukind, the only Saxon chieftain able to stand up to Charlemagne, represented by Henry and Otto. In parallel, the Roman idea of the State passed into the hands of Aquitanians, Gerard of Vienne, Gerald of Aurillac, Gerbert and the Cluniacs – whose first abbots, Odo included, were all southerners. In the eyes of the former the State remained a personal property, in those of the latter a public service. The breakdown in the marriage of these two dominant conceptions led to physical separation which was none the less a portent of future quarrels between papacy and empire, above all in the eleventh century.

Renewal of the church?

The prime factor in the renewal of political institutions was the clerical group of intellectuals, equivalent to 'counsellors of State' – the technocrats, so to speak, of an imperial or monarchical regime. Their influence and their desire to 'baptise' every conceivable structure is everywhere apparent. Since the early Carolingians were well aware that they could accomplish nothing without the Church, and were persuaded of their duty to defend and promote the Christian faith, it is now hard for us to tell who was sustaining whom. The truth seems to be that the ecclesiastical reforms, the missions and the intellectual and artistic endeavours stemmed from initiatives due sometimes to the Carolingians, sometimes to the Church.

Blending Church and State

It is obvious that the first series of councils, from 742 or 743 to 747, which marked the end of Charles Martel's ascendancy – for they took place only after his death – could not have been held without the authority of his successors, Carloman and Pippin III. The matter requiring most urgent attention was the status of ecclesiastical properties which had been granted to vassals. In the face of military necessities, the bishops acquiesced in these temporary alienations of ecclesiastical lands, on condition that the occupant paid a recognitory rent to the abbot or bishop as proprietor and that the property returned to the Church's patrimony after his death. This was the 'precarial' grant, made 'by the king's order'. Boniface no doubt hoped in return for a purge of the clergy and the re-establishment of archiepiscopal sees. But the monarchs and lay magnates had too large a stake in keeping the upper hand over the Church to relinquish it so soon. Chrodegang, bishop of Metz (742–66), drew up a rule for the canons, who were the priests attached to the staff of each bishop in his cathedral. Inspired by the practice of St Augustine, and owing much to the Rule of St Benedict it insisted on a communal way of life in the refectory and dormitory, while leaving the canons free to conduct cathedral services and observe the monastic hours. But this rule was not taken into general use until 816, when the council of Aachen made it obligatory on all chapters of canons. It undoubtedly bore fruit in unifying the life and spiritual culture of the higher clergy. This first generation of reformers was succeeded by a second, represented by Angilram, bishop of Metz and Theodulf, bishop of Orleans, and then by a third, amongst whom were Jonas, bishop of Orleans, and Agobard, archbishop of Lyons, whose influence was so conspicuous under Louis the Pious.

In the case of Charlemagne, relations between State and Church could hardly have been closer. And as we saw, it was his intention to be the dominant partner. As in the time of the Roman empire, no one in effect was allowed to take holy orders without his approval. He appointed all the bishops and even some of the abbots. Not infrequently, so as to obtain a larger contingent of vassals, he instituted a lay abbot alongside the regular abbot. He made the clergy enter the bonds of vassalage, and obliged the greatest of them to join the host with their vassal contingents, to sit on the tribunals at the general assemblies (*placita generalia*), to supervise counts in the capacity of *missi dominici*, or to enter the service of the royal chapel. His capitularies legislated equally for the Church and are filled with references to Christian morality. Lastly, he presided over the councils.

To the Church, this interpenetration of Church and State brought undeniable advantages. The emperor was the natural protector of the Church's lands, to which he accorded the fiscal privilege of immunity and the protection of his *bannum*. In order to shield and excuse the bishop or abbot under immunity from tasks forbidden to his clerical status (hearing criminal cases involving bloodshed, for example), Charlemagne extended the institution of the *advocatus*. This was a layman whose office was to carry out on immune properties the duties normally falling to the count. The members of the higher clergy thus had more time to devote to their spiritual function. By 814, when episcopal reorganisation was made more or less complete by the establishment of sixteen archbishoprics north of the Alps to replace the metropolitan sees that had disappeared, the multifarious duties devolving on a bishop could be performed with greater regularity: annual visitation of the rural parishes and the private churches maintained by great landowners, ordination of freedmen presented by landowners to serve as parish priests, setting up schools for cantors

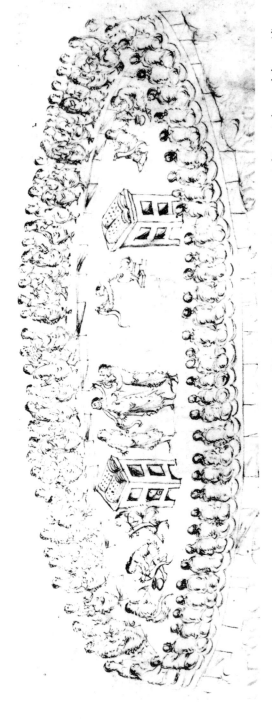

A council in the act of defining the faith and promulgating the creed of St Athanasius; the 66 participants are seated in a circle round the presiding bishop, while six scribes sit by their ink-pots and note down the text on scrolls (*Utrecht Psalter*, Utrecht, Bibliotheek der Rijksuniversiteit).

and readers, inspection of monasteries, appointment of suffragan bishops where the diocese covered a wide area, preaching and defending the faith, and lastly the upkeep, with the canons, of cathedral services. After the reform of the canons in 816, the revenues from episcopal properties were divided into two portions or *mensae*, one being earmarked for the table of the bishop (*mensa episcopalis*), the other for the table of the canons. This last was subdivided into as many 'prebends' as there were canons; the amount of each prebend was reckoned to be enough to feed and maintain a canon for the space of one year. Lastly, the bishop was the source of synodical legislation whose purpose was to regularise the position of deacons and priests.

The standard required for the latter was in fact rising, chiefly in consequence of the specification of precise educational qualifications: they had to know how to read and write, be able to recognise the symbols of the Apostles, know the Lord's Prayer, the Gregorian sacramentary, the exorcisms, the penitential, the calendar, the 'Roman' (that is to say 'Gregorian') chant, the *Pastoral* of Gregory the Great – in short, a strict minimum of acculturation was required. Through his sermons the village priest would have played a vital role in transmitting episcopal directives, and his exhortations would have helped to strengthen obedience to the king. In this respect the ecclesial structure was considerably more efficient than the State's, since through its local presence it reached all peasants, whereas the counts and their subordinates had to travel to keep in contact. Nor surprisingly, therefore, the Carolingians did as much as they could to make the priest a personage more worthy of respect and better able to support a celibate existence. Taking account of the spoliations of Church lands for *precariae*, Charlemagne agreed, in a capitulary of 779, that the clergy deserved to be compensated. He made universally binding a type of voluntary contribution which had been proposed at the council of Mâcon in 585, the tithe. On all lands, those of the king included, a tenth of the product was to be set aside for the upkeep of rural churches. A quarter of this would go to the bishopric. Finally, in 827, Louis the Pious made it obligatory to provide each rural church with a *mansus* and two slaves to work it and attend to the priest's material needs. In this way priests could be forbidden to engage in any activity not connected with their spiritual calling.

If Charlemagne's close alliance with the clergy allowed the bishop to play a conspicuous role, it had still more important consequences for the monastic world which in the mid-eighth century had displayed any number of variations. The emperor perceived in the monastery an ideal instrument of domination, exactly what was needed to outflank recalcitrant bishops, such as those in Aquitaine, or to assist in spreading the faith, above all in Germany. He bestowed his patronage on monasteries which were fulfilling a politico-religious purpose, such as St Denis and Fulda, or which could enhance his authority in certain areas, such as Aniane, founded in 782, Charroux in Aquitaine, Lorsch and Hersfeld on the banks of the Rhine and the Fulda. He converted them into royal abbeys, which in combination with their possession of immunity added to their stability, even allowing for the services and dues they owed to the king. Conversely, he looked with disfavour on monasteries in which free men congregated, because of the threat to his military potential. He was no friend to free abbatial election, preferring the system of the lay abbacy which in

447

return for the lay abbot's freedom to dispose of the abbatial lands furnished the king with a larger contingent of vassals for the host. But by demanding services on this scale from the 600 and more monasteries of the empire, 200 of which were under his direct control, Charlemagne had difficulty in making them a cohesive force, having involved them so closely in the world.

It took all the determination of Benedict of Aniane and of his imperial protector, Louis the Pious, to bring about a general reform of the monastic order. The capitularies of 23 August 816 and 10 July 817 reiterated the compulsion binding on all communities of monks and nuns to observe the Rule of St Benedict, thus making it clear that the liturgy and prayer took distinct precedence over political, missionary or cultural activity. This measure was accompanied by a rigorous condemnation of eremitical practices, considered to be a source of anarchy. As a result, this current of individualist piety dried up almost completely until the tenth century. Manual work once again became compulsory, access to the monastic school was restricted to oblates, the enclosure of nuns was strictly observed. The reform took effect only gradually and met with resistance, in particular on the score of free abbatial election, to which the magnates objected. Here, too, Louis the Pious can be seen to have laid the foundations for the Gregorian programme.

This can be seen from the fact that Otto accentuated all the drawbacks of a Church becoming increasingly subject to rulers and laymen, in spite of the good material he recruited, and the same goes for his successors. In the habit of appointing bishops and even abbots, like Charlemagne, Otto eventually found it an advantage to hand over to such exemplary servants the exercise of comital powers within their episcopal city: Speyer, Magdeburg, Mainz, Chur and Cologne are cases in point. Later he enlarged the jurisdiction of the bishop's court over ecclesiastical land enjoying immunity. He next granted the bishops the right to collect tolls and mint coinage, to forestall usurpation by the lay rulers. Lastly, he extended the bishop's comital rights to the county as a whole. These count–bishops struck the German kings as the ideal type of functionary. Graced with the privilege of immunity, they were scrupulous in their exercise of regalian rights. They punctually produced their quota of soldiers for the king: 1,822 cavalrymen from the bishoprics, 1,200 from the royal monasteries, or a quarter of the total! Lastly, on their death, since they had no heirs, the bishopric and county returned automatically to the king. Such was the end-product of the Carolingian system: a clericalised government incorporating the Church into the State and essential to the State's survival – the *Kirchensystem*.

Cluny

On the other hand, in those regions where the break-up of the empire left laymen loyal to the reform movement without a leader, things took a different course. After a period of uncertainty in which monasteries and bishoprics fell under lay domination, southern noblemen influenced by the ideals of Benedict of Aniane started to found monasteries in which the election of the abbot was left completely open. Gerard of Roussillon set up, in

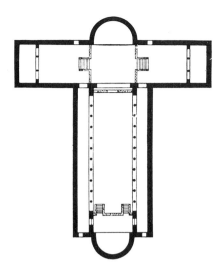

Ground-plan of the abbey church at Fulda. At Fulda, founded by Boniface, the abbatial church was rebuilt between 791 and 819. The nave, with side (traversed?) aisles and semi-circular apse, was completed at the west end by an extensive projecting transept which opened on to a second semi-circular apse.

858–9, the monastery of Vézélay which he placed under the direct authority of St Peter's in Rome. Again, Gerald of Aurillac inaugurated around 871 the monastery of St Clement of Aurillac, which later took his name, with the same regime. Lastly, on 11 September 910, the duke of Aquitaine, William the Pious, founded the monastery of Cluny, making it an express condition that its lands should be in the exclusive ownership of St Peter's of Rome. Shielded in this way from all possibility of lay interference, Berno, the first abbot, secured for the monks free abbatial election and exemption from the jurisdiction of the local bishop (Mâcon). Cluny had the satisfaction of seeing these privileges of exemption confirmed by Pope John XI. But in allowing nearly all its monks to proceed to the priesthood, Cluny departed from the Antique tradition of the layman dedicated to prayer. Later, in 951, the abbot of Cluny received permission to place under his authority all the monasteries he was setting out to reform. Abbots Odo (926–42) and Maiol (954?–94) exerted great influence over their contemporaries, the latter in particular, on account of his closeness to Otto the Great. Otto never espoused the Cluniac solution, however, which threatened to undermine his military and administrative resources. The initiatives of Gerard of Brogne, abbot of the monastery of the same name, whose freedom he ensured by founding it on his own allod, and of John of Vandières, restorer of Gorze in 933, were confined to Lotharingia. The incompatibility between the two visions of the Church, the one entertained by Charle-magne, and the other by Louis the Pious, thus stood revealed. The former saw the Church as free to enjoy its liberty under the watchful eye of a superior State; the latter saw the Church as partially independent, deferred to by the State. The inheritors of these two conceptions were to clash head on in the eleventh century.

449

Exaltation of the Church militant

There was a comparable divergence of views between Charlemagne and Louis the Pious on the matter of evangelisation. To the mind of the former, the Ciceronian adage, 'No State without justice', with its Augustinian gloss, 'No State without God', the sole teacher of righteousness, signified that a pagan State was a contradiction in terms. Therefore, by imposing his rule on the Saxons, Charlemagne brought them the combined blessings of an authentic form of government and the true God. Everything hung together. It was in all good faith, therefore, and with a sincere belief in the efficacy of the sacrament, even where the parties had not consented, that he followed the plan of enforced baptism, administered to whole groups at a time. Moreover, the famous capitulary of 785 would propose the stark choice of baptism or death, and it was only when Alcuin protested that Charlemagne eventually allowed 40 days' grace for elementary instruction. Baptism remained collective, but was no longer compulsory. Despite the issue of a more conciliatory capitulary in 797, the strict insistence on payment of tithes continued to provoke revolts. It took 33 years to bring the Saxons finally to heel. Noticeable resurgences of paganism occurred as long afterwards as 830 and 842.

At the same time, a new ecclesiastical hierarchy was being founded: Willehad, between 785 and 787, inaugurated the bishopric of Bremen, Liudger, in about 802–5, that of Münster, a Saxon, Hathumar, founded Paderborn, and so on. Under the reign of Louis the Pious, five more bishoprics were added. A new metropolitan see, Hamburg, created in 834, aspired to primacy over them, but this was a failure, because Cologne and Mainz, the two rival archbishoprics, were opposed to it. The monasteries also played an important role in the conversion, most especially the new Corbie, Corvey, founded by monks from the older establishment in 815.

Another pagan people, the Avars, was brought into the fold. The response to an attack by these nomads in 788 assumed all the trappings of a holy war. The day following the capture of their ring was observed by the whole army as a fast-day, and for three days the military followed in procession behind the clergy. The Avar mission was entrusted to Arn, archbishop of Salzburg, who employed the methods prescribed and carefully defined by a council anxious to avoid the excesses perpetrated in Saxony. As a result, the operation went smoothly, but on the other hand, Charlemagne formally forbade the Frisian Liudger to go as a missionary to Denmark, with which he was at war. This affirmed the primitive conception of mission as the instrument of imperial expansion.

With Louis the Pious the urge to achieve political ascendancy was suppressed in favour of conversion within the framework of the local culture. But this would obviously take time to show results. Furthermore, for a long time the missionaries were paralysed by fear of the Vikings. Ignorance of the code they lived by led to some resounding defeats, the more so since the Vikings saw no reason to adopt the faith of a vanquished people or to follow a God who let Himself be crucified without putting up a fight. Around 826–8, Louis the Pious had arranged for Anskar to accompany a Danish king, Harald, back to his own country, the latter having accepted baptism to win the emperor's political support. But Harald was

Corvey: reconstruction of the exterior and (right) cross-section of the monumental westwork. The ground floor was occupied by a room with a low, vaulted ceiling. The tall upper room, with open galleries on three sides, communicated with the nave on the east side by means of arcades and a transitional bay. The horizontality of the Antique basilica was replaced here by an entirely novel verticality.

defeated in battle by his compatriots. Later, when Swedish envoys came requesting priests, Anskar was sent to the Swedes (829). However, while Louis the Pious had believed the Swedes were ripe for baptism, all they wanted in reality was to establish trading relations. The missionary was kindly received at Birka, but made only a handful of converts. Returning, he had scarcely been appointed archbishop of a new metropolitan see, Hamburg, dedicated to the creation of a Scandinavian Church, when Hamburg was burned by the Vikings in 845. Retreating to Bremen, he tried without success to maintain his links with Birka but died with nothing accomplished. The whole project was abandoned.

The most crying need, in fact, was the conversion of the Danes settled in England from 876, and in Normandy from 911. All too often, the Danes would agree to baptism to obtain trading privileges, and so might be baptised several times over. The inconsistency of these converts was therefore the greatest obstacle. Christianity took proper root only when Heriveus, archbishop of Rheims, adopted the wise and enlightened methods of Gregory the Great. Among the Scandinavians, the decisive factor was the attitude of the kings. Once Gorm, the king of Denmark, had made up his mind in 949 to the conversion of his people, he allowed the bishop of Hamburg, Adalgag, to set up three bishoprics, Schleswig, Ribe and Aarhus. Harald Bluetooth, his successor, had himself baptised in company with his entire bodyguard. In Norway and Sweden, on the other hand, the process was more gradual and by the end of the first millennium was still far from being complete – even in Iceland, where in the year 1000 Christianity was accepted by the Althing as the official religion.

Clashes between the East Frankish kingdom and the pagan Slavs were taking place from

451

an early date on the Elbe, along the length of the Bohemian mountain chain, and on the Leitha. Although the history of these encounters belongs to another chapter, it should be pointed out that we see here a revival of Charlemagne's conception of mission. In about 874, the archbishop of Mainz began to convey his missionaries across the Saale in order to evangelise the Sorbs. But the resistance offered by the Slavs transformed these tentative sorties into military expeditions, with the result that Germanisation and Christianisation advanced hand in hand. The Obodrites, Liutizi, Sorbs and Lusatians were quick to put up ferocious resistance to the forward campaigns of Otto's marcher lords. In 937, Otto founded a monastery at Magdeburg, transforming it in 955 into a bishopric and later, in 968, into an archbishopric. This new metropolitan see was supposed to take under its wing three further bishoprics, founded in 947; but these did not last. There was also a scheme to make Magdeburg the metropolitan church for all the Slavs, the Poles included. But after the baptism of Prince Miesko in 966, the archbishop came up against the new church's desire to be independent. Salzburg experienced the same difficulties with the Hungarian prince, Vajk (Stephen), baptised in 995. As can be seen, the Carolingian conception of an imperial and imperialistic mission resulted in warfare, the reinforcement of paganism, and in its subsequent suppression by force and the subordination of the Church to the State. By contrast, the methods of Louis the Pious and his emulators, more southern and Roman in inspiration, bore a slowly ripening fruit in the form of local churches belonging to a pluralist Christendom.

This enlargement of Christendom had already been noticed by near contemporaries of Charlemagne. In comparison with the Roman Mediterranean zone, a new geographical entity had appeared: Europe. But it took on a political and religious meaning which did not completely fit the notion of empire. An Irish cleric, Cathulf, describes Charlemagne as 'head of the kingdom of Europe'. Nithard, grandson of the great emperor, could maintain around 840 that 'Charles, called by all the nations the great emperor, left the whole of Europe running over with his good deeds.' This concept of Europe therefore involved all Christian peoples, Latins and Romans, for according to Theodulf, speaking here as a Hispano-Goth strongly imbued with the Roman faith, 'It is the Church of Rome which decrees the Roman faith.' By definition, therefore, every European was a Roman in the religious though no longer in the political sense of the term, while the non-European betrayed himself by speaking not Latin but Greek. The wrangling of Pope Nicholas I with the patriarch Photios, during a schism which lasted from 863 to 867, pinpoints this first rejection of the Christian East in favour of a Christian Europe. Not many years afterwards, furthermore, Pope John VIII went so far as to assume the title at one time attributed to Charlemagne, 'ruler of Europe'. Revealed here is the underlying character of a new civilisation whose bond of unity was to be religious rather than political.

Obviously there were limits

Did the renewal, that is to say the baptism of pagan populations, produce the desired results? Here once again the populations of the Carolingian empire and the neighbouring kingdoms seem to have behaved like the stiff-necked Israelites, even while the Franks vaunted themselves as the new chosen people. It would be impossible to count the many pagan practices which masqueraded as Christian. Let us take another look, for example, at the *ghildes* and sworn associations. The banquets which served to initiate members of the group were in fact pagan festivals. They took place on 26 December, the feast of St Stephen, but in reality were timed to coincide with a twelve-day period, Yule, which began on that date and hence overlapped with the turn and change of the year. At this season of endings and beginnings, the dead and living made contact and sat together at the festive board. On such occasions, historic time was in abeyance, while the communion between the two worlds was realised through sharing in enormous feasts, intended to stimulate the fertility of the partakers, and in gargantuan drinking-bouts producing a divine intoxication in which the individual lost all sense of his own identity and entered at the deepest level into communion with his fellows. How, after that, could anyone refuse to honour the oaths sworn under such auspices? Hence it was from fear of displeasing the dead and their ghosts that members of the sworn fellowship performed deeds which made no sense to the clergy. It was fruitless for the latter to attempt to Christianise these gatherings by allowing them to be held in the vicinity of churches and at a later date inside them. Indeed, this only made matters worse, since the parish churches then became the scene of regular bacchanalia in the pagan and modern sense of that term. Ralph (or Rodulf), archbishop of Bourges, felt obliged to outlaw them from his diocese and to retaliate by trying to reclaim this ecclesial space for sacred uses of another kind.

It now becomes easier to understand how these pagan customs could permeate the most everyday actions and why it was necessary for the Church to insist on the observance of well over 100 days in the year as fast-days, so as to counteract the over-indulgence in food and drink which made men torpid, sottish and at the same time prone to acts of violence induced by the general alcoholic haze. Whatever the occurrence, the pagan sub-stratum was always just below the surface. Why, for example, did Lothar I, in 834, order the drowning of Gerberga, daughter of the epic hero Count William, in a barrel, 'as is the custom for women who cast spells'? Perhaps it had to do with an ordeal: had she come out alive, she would have been considered innocent. However that may be, the incident at any rate proves that the emperor, on whom the party of unity pinned its hopes, believed in the existence of witches and in their ability to cast a spell on someone (Bernard?) by means of love potions. Indeed, the whole business of ordeals is so much a part of the contemporary mentality that while Archbishop Agobard tried in vain to denounce them another bishop, Hincmar, as cultivated as Agobard but of Germanic descent, sprang a few years later to their defence. He took the line that God, having judged the Israelites in an ordeal by water represented by the crossing of the Red Sea, and punished Sodom and Gomorrah in an ordeal by fire, would not permit Himself to be deceived by any cheating of the ordeal through trickery. A fundamentalist interpretation of the Bible was thus invoked in support of a pagan mentality whose Christianisation applied only to certain zones of the religious subconscious.

The imperfect penetration of men's minds by the new teachings of Christianity had much

453

Moone, Co. Kildare, Ireland: Apostles, detail from the ninth-century cross. In this striking symbolic treatment of the human form, the square shape of the torso suggests matter, the things of the Earth, while the circularity of the heads evokes things of the spirit, the Heavenly.

to do with errors on the part of evangelists. The most obvious relates to the pagan notion of the sacred. Among all peoples of Indo-European descent, sacredness outside the individual demonstrates its ambivalence in two ways. In Latin, the word *sacer* signifies 'consecrated to the gods and bearing an indelible stain, awe-inspiring and accursed'. It thus comes very close to the notion of tabu. On the other hand, *sanctus* tends to designate someone protected from all harm by divine intervention. This doublet also existed in Old High German in the form of the two words heils and weihs. The former did not have the dangerous connotation of its Latin counterpart. It signified 'favoured by a god with good fortune, health and so on'. Now, when the Anglo-Saxon missionaries needed to translate *sanctus*, they chose *heils* and not *weihs*. This confusion between consecration and hallowing perpetuated the cult of the war-leader, priest of his tribe, proprietor of all that was sacred. The Christian signifier continued to be used and interpreted as a pagan significate by Germanic Christians. The acculturation of the new Christian meaning could not make headway against this persistence of the primitive vocabulary. The war-leader or the saint were destined to remain personages inhabited by a divine force which it was advisable to attract to oneself, by means of acclamations (*heil* = life, health, victory), sacrifices, ceremonies and prayers. In view of all this it is no surprise that the consecration of the war-leader should have survived for so long in Germany and played a part in resuscitating the empire in the sacred lineage of the Saxon Ottonians.

Whenever an objective sacred presence was detected, or an individual felt himself 'possessed' by something out of the ordinary, it had to be exorcised, if it was evil, or made use of, if it was good. Hence there was a continuing need for magical and astrological practices. The council of Leptines in 743 or 744 roundly condemned them, giving details which are highly revealing. But they lingered for a long while yet, as in the method used to charm away an eclipse of the moon, thought to be especially harmful to female fertility. One evening, while Rabanus Maurus (*c.* 780–856) was preparing a sermon in his abbey of

Fulda, he heard a sudden uproar: 'The din was produced by horns being blown as though war had broken out and the grunting of pigs, people could be seen shooting arrows and darts at the moon, others were throwing torches to the sky in all directions . . . They were convinced that a monster of some description was threatening the moon and that without their aid she would be devoured. For the same reason, other people were smashing their pots.' Now this abbey had been in existence for a century and more: it should at least have got its message across to its nearest neighbours! Under a veneer of Christianisation, the two mentalities, the old and the new, occupied watertight compartments. The forbidden nature of this magical ceremony seems to have been totally ignored.

Again, the Carolingian councils protested in vain against the use of penitentials. Charlemagne had decreed that every rural priest should have a penitential as part of his basic library. In fact, a great many were in circulation and the prescribed penances varied from one to another. The relative importance attached to the various sins reveals the prevalence of perjury and pagan practices, but the fashion for converting corporal penances – fasting on dry bread and water for example – into a certain number of masses or into money shows the extent to which the Antique conception of striking a bargain with the deity (*do ut des*: I give you a penance so that you will give me a pardon) was still operative. The totally gratuitous nature of forgiveness for sins was not understood. The ecclesiastics of the time of Louis the Pious were quite aware of this fact. The council of Chalon, 813, called for the suppression of penitentials; that of Paris, in 829, decided to burn them. They ordered a return to the old form of penitence. In the event the penitentials, better suited to a religious sensibility still at the level of retribution ('an eye for an eye . . .'), continued to proliferate. The only tangible result was the co-existence of two forms of penance: for a grave fault publicly admitted, penance would be performed in public, for a grave fault confessed in private, penance would be graded according to the tariff laid down in the penitentials. The effect of this compromise was once again to discriminate between two attitudes, characterised in the one case by awareness of a personal but terrifying God, in the other by a belief in the possibility of propitiating the sacred power by ritual practices.

The Church, proprietor of the sacred

Resistance on this scale must have convinced certain members of the clergy that accultura-tion with too great an intellectual emphasis was bound to fail and that evangelisation would do better to exploit the prevailing belief in this sacred power, to base itself on fear rather than on hope and obedience to the letter of the law. For most of his episcopal career, no one was more of a legalist than Hincmar, archbishop of Rheims. But he had to admit at the end of his life that the Roman notions of contract, of judgment before the law, and of juridical principles with permanent and universal validity had failed to make any impact and were still not understood. Shortly before his death in 882, he composed his *Life* of St Remigius, a 'testament of irrationality'. For the foreseeable future men would receive their education at the hands not of the learned ecclesiastic but of the saint, protector of the weak, of the faithful free and the poor who would listen, but equally the avenger, who put down

Irish manuscript: from the *Gospels of St Willibrord*, *c.* 690 (Paris, Bibliothèque Nationale).

Initial of the Incarnation, from the *Lindisfarne Gospels*, *c.* 698 (British Library).

Carolingian manuscript, *Bible of S. Paolo fuori le Mura, c. 870.*

times of the Third World, such as malaria and trachoma, took their toll. The disinherited, who haunted the pavements of the basilicas, were in reality men and women who, by doing penance, placed all their hopes in the power of the saints. In this way, thanks to an initially ambiguous effort at Christianisation, the Church succeeded in transferring the pagan sphere of a beneficent or maleficent sacredness into the orbit of God's – or the saints' – eternity. The Church became proprietor of the sacred, at the cost of having to purge it at a later date, but by this route reached a suffering people, persuading them to exchange fears of evil spirits for trust in the protective power of the saints. The advent around 946 of the first reliquary statues, such as the Black Madonnas, is a sign, however close the resemblance of such effigies may be to idols in the eyes of intellectuals, that the benign motherhood of Mary would henceforth introduce the idea of God incarnate.

Towards a more rigid family unit?

The unfruitfulness of the formalist, Carolingian style of evangelisation thus drew attention to the devious paths that had to be followed in order to cross the gulf between clergy and people. In another domain, the indissolubility of a monogamous marriage, the clergy was not prepared to beat about the bush in imposing its ideal. It should be explained that the social habits of pagan times, based on the extended family and consanguinity, still prevailed. Within the family circle a girl of marriageable age was regarded as an object to be exchanged with another family, which militated against freedom of consent. What was more, in the villages as much as among the aristocracy, it was very common for marriages to be endogamous. Lastly, polygamy in the ancient Germanic fashion still survived, with a free woman coming first in order, followed by free women who ranked as concubines (*friedlehe*), and last of all concubine slaves. In addition, repudiation of the wife by the husband on grounds of sterility was considered normal in a society which prized fertility as a mark of divine favour. The emperor Charlemagne provides the supreme example of polygamy as it was practised, since he is known to have had four successive wives of which the first was put away, and six concubines, apparently also in succession, who bore him a total of eighteen known children. He was no less zealous on that account in promoting the Church's policy, which was to prohibit consanguineous marriage within the seventh degree, and to campaign against abduction. The first of these prohibitions had the effect of breaking up kindred and dynastic groupings, leading eventually to the fragmentation of inheritances. It therefore encountered fierce opposition and in many cases was not heeded before the middle of the eleventh century. The purpose of abduction, as contemporaries saw it, was to thwart opposition from the kindred and make the marriage irrevocable through consummation of the union. The practice certainly went against the equality of the sexes and the freedom of consent proclaimed in all the conciliar texts. Here too, the wish of the kinsmen remained in practice a fundamental element in constituting the marriage. Lastly, as regards indissolubility, the affair which left its mark most indelibly on the Carolingian epoch was the divorce of Lothar II, who made a vain attempt to legalise his separation from his wife Theutberga, who was barren, in order to marry his concubine

Waldrada, by whom he already had a male heir. Dragging on from 860 to 868, the political aspect of the case was made all the more important by the fact that the fate of Lotharingia was at stake. Hincmar and Pope Nicholas I flatly forbade the divorce, with the result, as we saw earlier, that the kingdom was left without a legal heir and partitioned. In the event, nothing was achieved by this ecclesiastical master-stroke: many princes and magnates continued to evade the prohibition. In 887, Charles the Fat wanted to divorce his wife Richegarda and accused her of adultery. She offered to prove her innocence not merely through a judicial duel or by submitting to the ordeal of white-hot iron, but also by producing proof of her continuing virginity. The emperor then made out that he had been smitten with impotence and shut her up in a convent, disregarding the laws of religion. Clearly, then, the world of Carolingian society was in a state of flux, a prey to major transformations and to brutal negative reactions. The law of the Church interfered with time-honoured traditions, destroyed natural affinities and sparked off quarrels with catastrophic results.

The baptism of Carolingian society by the Church thus fell short of total immersion. Just as the Roman idea of the public good did not fully eradicate the conception of a State as the property of its conquerors, neither was the Church able to make populations commit themselves completely to the communion of a baptised people. The point is proved by Hincmar, who was the first to define the Church as the people of God, but in desperation rallied to the conception of the Church as the proprietor of the sacred through the indirect medium of the cult of the saints. Christianity was obliged to play a dual role as both the accomplice and the foe of paganism. To sum up, we have seen men of the time rejecting vertical bonds, such as the oath of fidelity and the relationship of superior to inferior, in favour of *trustes* and *ghildes*: we have seen them resisting suppression of the blood-feud and persisting in their contempt for neighbouring peoples, persisting also in their pagan fears and pagan practices, and standing out against the indissolubility of a sterile marriage. These accumulated blockages, these partial successes, these conflicts, were part and parcel of a society which the clergy was attempting to renovate. For such a task, the intellectual input of three generations of educated Carolingians could hardly suffice. It is remarkable that the enterprise was even attempted, astonishing that its programme failed only at certain political and spiritual levels, and revealing that it was able to pass from the universal to the local order, so that we meet it again and intact after 950, already being implemented by the Ottonians, the Cluniacs and the early Capetians, as the answer to violence and feudal disorder.

A 'renaissance'

If there is one area where the historians of this period seem to be agreed it is in the matter of a systematic renewal of the learned culture, a reorganisation 'from above' of the intellectual sector. The fact that it involved imitation of the Antique, with resonances that were sometimes purely local, and that it was chiefly an affair of the clergy no doubt accounts for the faintness of its echo among the people; it remains for all that one of the most remarkable

Intellectual renaissance. Music, Arithmetic, Geometry and Astrology. The sobriety of the composition, characteristic of Tours, draws its inspiration from the classicism of Antiquity (manuscript of Boethius's *Arithmetic*, school of Tours, *c.* 850, Bamberg, Staatliche Bibliothek).

of ninth-century endeavours. Nevertheless, to appreciate its originality and partial success, we must look back to a much earlier period to discover its premisses.

The quest for a new culture

The crises of Classical education in the sixth century and of the Church in the eighth century met with solutions dictated as much by the rupture with Rome as by the continuity of the intellectual heritage chosen for transmission.

The Germans, in fact, were not the only ones responsible for the disappearance of the Antique schools. Theodoric, indeed, did all he could to preserve them and took writers under his wing. Justinian restored the schools and they finally disappeared only in the last third of the sixth century, in Africa later still. In Spain and Gaul, they barely managed to survive into the sixth century, but private tuition long remained the rule in senatorial families. In consequence, the Iberian peninsula and southern Gaul continued to be centres of Classical Roman culture, in which law and the practical arts of surveying, architecture,

459

medicine and so on were included. But this Classical culture, still seen to be intact in Visigothic Spain, for example in the time of Julian of Toledo (died 690), remained the privilege of a select few, who were interested only in stylistic perfection and worldly knowledge. It had merely served to exasperate the monks whose thoughts were directed towards spiritual cultivation and the bishops whose chief preoccupation was teaching the basic catechism. The vehemence of monastic attacks on the paganism of Classical literature and the positive proposals for a new Christian culture emanating from St Augustine led to the gradual replacement of the *sermo scholasticus* (the refined language of the schools) by the *sermo rusticus* (plain language), and of Virgil by the Bible as the texts to be studied.

Men such as Caesarius of Arles (470–542) and Benedict of Nursia (*c.* 480–556) thus deliberately turned away from Classical education to devote themselves to a spiritual culture. In reality, study of the Bible would require a certain basic literary background if the reader was to interpret some of the difficulties in the text, and to this limited extent Classical authors were pressed into the service of Christianity. The child–oblates brought to the father–abbot by their parents began their apprenticeship under the first monks by learning the psalter by heart. The Rule of St Benedict made it obligatory to set aside some twenty hours in the week for the reading of devotional literature. It was thought that knowledge of the Desert Fathers and of the Bible should more than suffice. And Caesarius of Arles went even further, in that he tried to make the priests of his diocese conform to monastic discipline on the models of Augustine and Lérins.

Fundamentally speaking, the birth of the monastic and episcopal schools antedated their official appearance. In 527, the council of Toledo, and in 529, the council of Vaison-la-Romaine ruled that the boy-lectors in each episcopal household should be taught in such a manner that if, on reaching their majority, they chose to become priests, they could in their turn instruct the people. There is even some evidence pointing to the extension of these schools to rural parishes, but this must have been rare. The only schools to function in the proper sense were those in episcopal towns, and, since the bishops tended to be former senators, who were now turning their hand to the education of their young clergy, the Classical imprint was much stronger than in the case of the monastic schools. For all that, the need for clergy was so great that by degrees the educational qualifications required became less and less exacting. In the seventh century, when the imperatives of evangelisation had used up the supply of southerners well-versed in the Scriptures, a cultural nadir appears to have been reached. Boniface denounced the ignorance, extending in some cases to illiteracy, of certain priests in Bavaria, or their inability to pronounce the stock formulas correctly in Latin. Again, although lay members of great Germanic families would have indirectly picked up literacy through making their wills and had for utilitarian purposes acquired a minimum of culture, made up of scraps of legal knowledge and moral precepts, at the beginning of the eighth century a significant number of nobles could no longer sign their own names.

The seeds of renewal were sown by the great pioneers of Christian culture, and propagated by Celtic and Anglo-Saxon monks. Foreseeing the irredeemable decline of

Greek, Boethius, scion of one of Italy's more influential senatorial families, translated into Latin the key texts of Aristotle, the geometry of Euclid and the astronomy of Ptolemy. If his work as a translator later played an indispensable part in the resuscitation of logic, his *Consolation of Philosophy*, written in prison and imbued with Stoic wisdom, continued to be valued for its own sake. Notwithstanding the author's Christian profession, it remains the quintessence of pagan moral culture, lacking any reference to Christ, and far removed from the culture aimed at by the monks. Another of Theodoric's officials, Cassiodorus (*c.* 485–*c.* 580), experienced a belated conversion to the monastic life. In his monastery, Vivarium, he tried to realise his plan for a Christian university, but it failed. His work lived on in the *Institutions*, in effect a textbook of the seven liberal arts (grammar, rhetoric, dialectic, arithmetic, geometry, astronomy and music) in which these secular subjects find a place within the framework of a religious culture. Another senator, one of the last to have passed through the Antique school, Gregory the Great, was converted to the monastic life around 574. He too was man of considerable learning for all his protestations of ignorance. Excelling as a teacher, he made his influence felt above all through his *Dialogues*, which included a life of St Benedict, and his *Pastoral*, the blueprint, so to speak, of the perfect bishop or exemplary priest. Whatever he might have said, he did not discount the 'extraneous sciences' but regarded them as useful adjuncts in the understanding of God's word and of spiritual matters. Similarly, Isidore of Seville (*c.* 560–636) had a monastic education, but to his qualifications as an exegete, moralist and theologian he added his talents as a poet, letter-writer, grammarian and musician. He compiled a vast encyclopedia, the *Etymologiae*, which encapsulates in twenty books the learned discoveries of Antiquity, adapting them to the requirements of Christian scholarship. In so doing, Isidore of Seville laid the foundations of all medieval culture. Everywhere, his treatises became the standard works of reference and the *Etymologiae* were constantly consulted. The ground for the new culture, which was revealed to be ascetic, biblical, humanist and Latin, had thus been prepared.

Monks, propagators of spiritual culture

All the same, and although the times were critical, it had to be disseminated, a task which in the nature of things fell within the province of the clerics, and more especially of the monks. One effect of the conversion of Ireland had been to turn the Celts into expert Latinists, all the more so from having had to learn the language as a foreign tongue. They received from Aquitaine and Spain all the elements of the new culture and distinguished themselves in the arts of exegesis and even by their mastery of the florid literary style. In a word, before long their monasteries were active propagators of the culture, and we have already seen the extent to which Irish missionaries pervaded the continent. In Gaul and northern Italy, the Colombanian foundations became in their turn new cultural centres where the monastic school and the *scriptorium*, engaged in the copying of manuscripts, were the hub of an active spiritual and intellectual life. At Bobbio, Luxeuil, Corbie (founded

461

between 657 and 661) and Chelles, it gradually became evident that the purely ascetic impulse supplied by the Irish was juxtaposed with a more refined religious culture inspired by the Benedictine rule.

Similarly, the conversion of England led eventually – thanks to the combined influences of the Irish monks from Iona who founded Lindisfarne and Whitby and of the Roman monks who went out from Canterbury to found cathedral and monastic schools – to the flowering of numerous cultural centres. Not surprisingly, Anglo-Saxons such as Wilfrid (around 653), Benedict Biscop and others adopted the habit of making journeys to Rome in order to bring back numerous manuscripts, which perhaps included some of those of Cassiodorus produced at Vivarium, not to mention the liturgical practices and mode of Roman chant known later as Gregorian. In 669, a Greek monk and an African monk, Theodore and Abbot Hadrian, were sent to England by the pope; the former made the cathedral school at Canterbury his special concern, while the latter devoted himself to the monastic school of St Peter and St Paul. To Wearmouth and Jarrow in Northumbria, Benedict Biscop brought the arch-cantor of the Lateran and masons 'skilled in building in the Roman style'. These Northumbrian monastic schools at the confluence of Irish and Roman currents formed the setting in which the greatest scholar of the early Middle Ages, the Venerable Bede (c. 673–735), passed his life. Entering Wearmouth in about 680 at the age of seven, he settled permanently at Jarrow where he taught without interruption for 40 years. The author of books on scientific, historical and exegetical subjects, he wrote in a clear, flowing style, very different from the convoluted literary style which was affected by the Irish and which left its mark on Willibrord, who had studied in Ireland, as well as on Boniface. But Bede's fame was all the greater, precisely because of his simplicity. Under Bede's guidance, the ensuing generation of insular scholars proceeded to devise a curriculum which clearly involved grammar, poetry and all kinds of natural phenomena, that is to say a nucleus of the natural or astronomical sciences. About the time Bede died, his disciple Egbert admitted as an oblate the young Alcuin, around 735, and passed on to him in full this new programme which had promoted England to a position of unrivalled intellectual superiority. And Alcuin, as we shall see, was to be 'the schoolmaster' of Carolingian Europe.

Learning on the continent was admittedly at a particularly low ebb at the beginning of the eighth century, most of all because of the policy of secularisation followed by Pippin (II) and Charles Martel. Only a small elite of monks managed to maintain a certain standard. Monasteries such as Luxueil, Corbie, St Denis and above all Fleury-sur-Loire were turning to Italy, where at Pavia, Milan, Cividale, Lucca and Benevento a modest cultural revival was taking place under the auspices of King Liutprand. The future King Pippin III was sent to the court of Pavia by his father Charles Martel. Around 670–2, some monks conveyed to Fleury-sur-Loire the purported relics of St Benedict which they had stolen from Montecassino, but also a number of Italian manuscripts. In the first half of the eighth century, the Gallic monasteries, situated north of the Loire, can clearly be seen rebuilding their libraries. However, the monks of northern Gaul seem to have been less well-educated than their counterparts in the new monasteries established by the missionaries in Thurin-

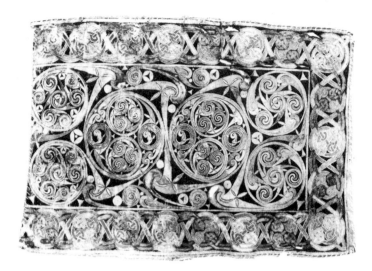

Carpet-page from the *Book of Durrow*, oldest of the fully illuminated Gospel Books: Northumbrian, *c.* 680. The six medallions of the central panel are filled with Celtic scroll-work. The 'carpet-page' was already to be found in Eastern manuscripts; Hiberno-Saxon artists clearly revelled in the free hand it gave them for experiment.

gia, Alamannia and Bavaria. The Anglo-Saxons and their emulators would have been careful to set men of sound learning at the head of their new foundations, Murbach, Weissenburg, Reichenau, Nieder-Altaich, Kremsmünster, Mondsee and most of all Fulda in 744. Moreover, in each case the Irish and Anglo-Saxon outlooks competed or intermingled in the new schools.

The exposure of Frankish Gaul and Germany to external influences paved the way for an important intellectual and artistic renovation. One is already aware of a tendency for the animal, plant or abstract motifs which characterise the Germanic art of the belt-buckle or fibula to retreat in the face of the reappearance of carving in the round, whether one thinks of the tempietto at Cividale or indeed of the crypt at Jouarre. The carpet-pages of the Northumbrian illustrated manuscripts aspired in vain to produce a purely abstract effect through their device of asymmetrical decentring, and dazzling as they are with colour, they none the less betray their susceptibility to Italian influences through the introduction of human faces and draped forms. Again, the illustrations in manuscripts produced at Corbie, Luxeuil and St Denis continued to exhibit stylised motifs devoid of plasticity, and yet to be thoroughly imbued with a new expressionism. This mingling of Germanic and Antique or Byzantine conceptions can be perceived still more clearly in goldsmiths' work, the art *par excellence* of the barbarian kingdoms. The votive crowns donated by Reccesuinth and Suinthila to the cathedral of Toledo, the jewels of Monza or the cross of St Eligius at St Denis prove that the Roman taste for symmetry and the Germanic predilection for brilliant colours could be happily combined.

It is evident that the monks, by their timely intervention, made it possible to salvage

463

Antique learning and to effect a synthesis between the Roman, Gothic and Celtic modes of artistic expression. Europe therefore owes an enormous debt of gratitude to the handful of men who, before the East began to make its contribution in the eleventh century, preserved the ancient heritage. But it must also be remarked that in setting their sights on the conversion of peoples within and without the orbit of *romanitas*, the Anglo-Saxon, Italian or Neustrian scribes systematically discarded the forms of Antique culture they deemed to be 'irrelevant'; lyric poetry, drama and the urban architecture of buildings for recreation. They saved the day, but did no more than lay rough and ready foundations.

The Carolingian reconstruction

The fundamentally Christian plan of the Carolingian renewal meant that it rested on the Bible and on a humanist culture which aimed to be universal. Charlemagne had recognised the merits of monks as educators and teachers. Having reached the age of discretion (in Einhard's words),

he cultivated the liberal arts and, filled with admiration for the men who taught them, loaded them with honours. In order to learn grammar he took lessons from Peter of Pisa, by then an old man. In the other subjects his master was Alcuin . . . the most learned man of the time. Under him he devoted much time and effort to the study of rhetoric, logic and above all astronomy. He learnt mathematics and applied himself, with accuracy and intelligence, to tracing the movements of the heavenly bodies. He tried also to master the art of writing and it was his custom to keep writing-tablets and scraps of parchment under his pillow, so that he could practise tracing the letters in his leisure moments: but he took this up too late in life and made little progress.

It is obvious how strongly the emperor was convinced of the need for educational reform since he took a hand in it himself. This was one domain in which he thought it proper to revive all the Merovingian initiatives. In the celebrated capitulary of 789, known as the *Admonitio generalis*, he ordered that 'arrangements are to be made in every diocese and monastery for teaching the Psalms, musical notation [or this may refer to shorthand or Tironian notes], singing, computation and grammar, and for the books to be carefully emended'. In the last two decades of the eighth century, a great deal was accomplished. After reforming the clergy, the most urgent need was to recast the liturgy. Charlemagne sent a request to the pope, in 774, for a complete set of conciliar texts and pontifical decrees so that he could check ecclesiastical legislation against an authoritative text.

In this way he boosted the development of a whole body of law peculiar to the Church, which received reinforcement in the mid-ninth century from the collection known as the 'False Decretals'. In about 784, he obtained from Pope Hadrian I a Gregorian sacramentary which enabled him to introduce the Roman liturgy and to expunge from the empire the Gallican, Visigothic or Irish liturgies previously in use. This gave rise in turn to a far-reaching revolution in music linked with the invention of polyphony. The latter resulted from the simultaneous employment, as a new discovery, of the neume, the notational sign used to mark the pitch of a sound, and of the trope, placed beneath a neume to represent one syllable of text. From now on, a piece of music could be committed to writing. The foundations were thus laid for the melodic counterpoint which held sway until Rameau produced his *Traité de l'harmonie* in 1750.

The emendation of manuscripts in the monastic *scriptoria* went hand in hand with other advances. Certain scribes at Corbie, in about 771–80, evolved from Merovingian half-uncial and Merovingian cursive a rounded minuscule script which we now call 'Caroline' minuscule. Because of its legibility, it remains even today, following its readoption by the printing press in the fifteenth century, the basis of all modern typographies, the so-called 'Roman' fount. Large numbers of manuscripts were copied with the aid of this clearly legible and more elegant calligraphy. The pressure on monasteries and cathedrals to set up schools was maintained throughout the ninth century. The council of Mainz of 813 ordered schools to be set up in rural areas for the training of young priests. Little by little, and above all in northern Europe, a network of schools emerged. There was a need therefore for Bibles in ever-increasing numbers. Alcuin set to work on a standard text, while Theodulf produced a critical edition based on all the variants to be found in extant manuscripts. Nor were pagan authors ignored. The monastic libraries of England and the empire began to bulge with Classical Latin or patristic texts. Around 850 authors were netted in this way and many of the modern editions of Antique works rest ultimately on Carolingian manuscripts of the ninth century. By contrast, in spite of the migration to the continent after 840 of Irish scholars put to flight by the Vikings, very few Greek works were copied or translated.

Triumph of the intellect

Most surprising of all, this rediscovery of Classical Latin was taking place just at the time when the language was ceasing to be spoken. The council of Tours, in 813, directed priests to preach in future in the 'everyday Romance or Germanic tongue'. Old French and Old High German must therefore have been widely current at this period. Simultaneously with the appearance of the first texts written down in the Germanic tongue, Catalan began to diverge from the future Castilian. In Gaul itself, a linguistic distinction developed between the dialects to the north of the Loire, which were later designated '*langues d'oïl*' (to be pronounced '*oui*', the French affirmative), and those, closer to Latin, which were soon to be called '*occitans*' or '*langues d'oc*'. The European languages can thus be seen to be clearly developed by the time that Latin embarked on its career as a dead but universal language, which corresponds well to the birth of a Europe made up of several kingdoms but unified by a single Christian culture. In all the new languages there was born at the same time a separate cultural tradition, mainly centred on the warrior. It is noteworthy that Charlemagne himself ordered the epic poems of the Germans to be committed to writing, and regrettable that no trace of this enterprise has survived. Epics in the Romance tongue, such as the celebrated *Chanson de Roland*, were already in circulation, passed on orally from generation to generation. The unlettered no doubt had a coherent popular culture of their own, but here again nothing of it has come down to us.

The world of culture and letters was thus the quasi-monopoly of the clergy. They learned quinticispluisextimoke

·etrenrumaudientirinterrozo

adashuisaslongit etpqursqururtamfortaumysols

pcasst agusasnt cadque utuncam·tconeffcacci
asst· quamquamego inusramuisparasn·pca
moueast· Recae neconsacüsßgron Tushimlas
bsrasß uasumnehocquoul praccepasfpost

&·boreassivurlmassirdaeslipsd
&scheasst tursfisvvrainenaststas:

Siquisque confsruncaur &
elesias uoluasyt foysr ecelssia

erat regnütesus·. Etabstulit filiamsuam &de
dit eam demasirio· Etabaltenauit ßtabaleyan
dro· &mantfestte facte sunt inimiciaac eius·,

&sociosiudgeos· siergoiterü adiem

(a) Uncial script, fourth to fifth century.
(b) Half-uncial script.
(c) 'Luxeuil' script, seventh to eighth century.
(d) 'Az-type' script of Laon, eighth century.
(e) Merovingian official script.
(f) Italian pre-Caroline script.
(g) Caroline minuscule.
(h) Caroline script of the *Amiens Bible*.

to read the Psalter, to write grammatically and to follow the basic rules of composition. There was little or no formal instruction in the various subjects of the *trivium* (grammar, rhetoric, logic) and *quadrivium* (arithmetic, geometry, astronomy, music); but there was enough to ensure that the standard of authorship improved from one generation to the next, even if the pen was still wielded almost exclusively by churchmen. Alcuin's pedagogical treatises, Paul the Deacon's *History of the Lombards*, Theodulf's poems, and the Annals compiled in monasteries, were all the work of clerics. We owe to one of the few lay authors, of his generation, Einhard, a classic biography of Charlemagne, saturated, it is true, with turns of phrase borrowed from Suetonius, but of great historical value. In the second generation, under Louis the Pious, the fruits of this intellectual renaissance became less derivative. The political musings of Jonas of Orleans, Agobard, or Adalhard, the religious poetry of Walafrid Strabo or Sedulius Scottus, and the elegantly-expressed letters of Lupus, abbot of Ferrières, reveal a greater maturity and a good grasp of Antique humanism. The *History of the Sons of Louis the Pious*, composed by Nithard, is the historical contribution of a layman writing with a concern for authenticity and accuracy. He made it his business, for example, to reproduce in his text a contemporary document of the first importance, the Strasbourg oaths of 842. The advances made were so considerable that the progress of this renaissance was not to be halted by the destructions of libraries by the Vikings.

The third generation of Carolingian scholars after 840 represents the apogee of this renaissance and far surpassed its predecessors. After three centuries of silence, theological speculation was reborn with the polemical exchanges between Rabanus Maurus, abbot of Fulda, then archbishop of Mainz, and the monk Gottschalk, who was accused of holding that only a few believers, and not all, were predestined for salvation; this remote precursor of Jansenism was condemned in 848 and again in 849. An Irishman, John Scottus Eriguena, translated the writings of Pseudo-Dionysius the Areopagite out of the original Greek. He paved the way for Christian philosophical reflection with the *De divisione naturae*, a wide-ranging synthesis of Neoplatonist inclination, completed in about 866, which seems to have been beyond the comprehension of his contemporaries. Political thinking became more concrete with the contribution made by Hincmar, archbishop of Rheims from 845 to 882, through his letters and his *De ordine palatii*. Man of action, pastor and jurist, Hincmar provided a solid base on which to rest the definition of the Church as a people of God, with in this instance not the slightest foreshadowing of Gregorianism. He made Rheims, whose library and school he developed, a centre of intellectual and historical activity, in particular through his authorship of the third section of the *Annals of St Bertin*. In fostering the development of a political and literary trend in favour of the kingship, Rheims resembles Fulda. Looking ahead, Rheims was to be made illustrious in the tenth century by the annalist Flodoard, by the historian Richer, keen admirer of Sallust, and above all by Gerbert, the monk from Aurillac who, after studying in Catalonia, taught in the schools at Rheims from 972 to 980 and again from 983 to 997. Gerbert was in fact the first to go beyond the limits of the Carolingian intellectual heritage and therefore inaugurate a new epoch.

Let us not lose sight, however, of the penetration of the Carolingian reforms to Germany. Many ancient manuscripts were copied at Lorsch, Würzburg, Reichenau and St Gall. Except at Fulda, intellectual drive was lacking in the ninth century, when acculturation was still at an early stage. At St Gall, however, Notker the Stammerer (died 913), the author of a fanciful life of Charlemagne, and Notker Labes (died 1022), who can claim the unique distinction of having translated Boethius, Cato, Virgil, Terence and Aristotle into Old High German, won renown as inspiring teachers. At Corvey, Widukind (925–c. 1004) produced the *Res gestae saxonicae*, a historical work composed in remarkably good Latin, which describes the great deeds of the Ottonian dynasty. It is interesting to see this renaissance manifesting itself initially through the medium of the vernacular, and turning to Latin at a later date, after the reign of Otto I. The same phenomenon had occurred in England, where King Alfred ordered Anglo-Saxon translations to be made of Gregory the Great's *Dialogues*, sundry writings of the Fathers, for example the *Historia adversus paganos* of Orosius, and still more to the point, Bede's *Ecclesiastical History*. He himself also translated some works: Gregory the Great's *Pastoral Care*, Boethius's *Consolation of Philosophy*, St Augustine's *Soliloquies* and the first 50 psalms of the Psalter. In the eleventh century, the pedagogical discourses of Aelfric (*c.* 955–1020), which include a Latin grammar and his *Colloquy*, in the form of a dialogue between master and pupil, and the well-known *Enchiridion* of Byrhtferth, may be taken as proof that English schoolboys often had more Latin than their continental counterparts. On the other hand, the *Legatio* of Bishop Liutprand of Cremona (died c. 972), a spirited account of his embassy to Constantinople, reveals to us the importance and quality of the educated laymen to be found in Lombard Italy. In that country the problem of the vernacular did not arise since Latin had not yet turned into Italian. But in Catalonia and the Asturias, the perpetual wars meant that culture remained confined to the cloister, so that no individual literary voice was to be heard. To sum up, the Carolingian cultural renaissance never lost its momentum. Continuing on its way, it widened in scope to the point of enabling a new leap forward to be made at the end of the tenth century.

Early premonitions of a European art disguised in Antique dress

The Carolingian cultural renaissance made its most remarkable contribution in the artistic domain, notably in architecture. We have only to think of the sheer number of religious and secular buildings put up in the 46 years of Charlemagne's reign: 232 monasteries, seven cathedrals and 65 palaces! The cult of relics and the adoption of the Roman liturgy called for new types of churches and monasteries. The solutions were found either in Merovingian churches, in the Constantinian basilica of St Peter's in Rome, or indeed by browsing through the treatise on Classical architecture by Vitruvius. Among the new formulae arrived at, we should pay particular attention to the introduction of crypts, semi-underground vaulted chambers intended to accommodate the relics of a saint, and to the east–west orientation of churches. Mausoleums were added to the chevet, and tribune–sanctuaries, for the celebration of Easter, were fashioned in the first storey of the towers on

Carolingian manuscript art: a monastic workshop and the opening of *St John's Gospel*: the words *In principio erat verbum* can be made out. Gospel Book from the second half of the ninth century (Cologne, Rheinisches Bildarchiv).

the facade. The result was double-apsed churches such as St Gall, whose famous ground plan was constantly imitated, St Denis, Cologne and Fulda; or better still, churches were preceded by a colossal western structure (the westwork, a kind of transept surmounted by a tower and two turrets), as at St Riquier, Corvey, Lorsch, Rheims and elsewhere. The masterpiece is, of course, the chapel at Aachen, erected between 792 and 805, designed by the architect, Odo of Metz, on an octagonal plan. He invented, three centuries ahead of his time, the interior flying buttress to support the tambour carrying the cupola. Through its layout and symbolism, the chapel brings to mind the Byzantine palaces, the Church of the Holy Sepulchre at Jerusalem, the baptistery of St John Lateran or the church of St Vitalis at Ravenna.

This Carolingian art which claims to be Antique achieves its effects with bands of coloured marble and white stone cut into cubes alternating with courses of brick stretchers, as on the triumphal gateway at Lorsch. It was transmitted without delay to Germany, thanks to the astonishing second abbatial church at Corvey, with its famous westwork (873–85). The early Ottonian churches developed in conformity with their prototypes,

469

Carolingian ivory work. Relief, *c.* 870: David the Psalmist entering the house of the Lord. Carved by artists at the court of Charles the Bald, the piece was made as a cover for the emperor's Prayer Book (Zurich, Schweizerisches Landesmuseum).

diversifying them in the process: Minden comes to mind (1064), not to mention Cluny II in Western Francia (955–81). If around 960–70 we find new churches being built, they are neither precisely Carolingian nor precisely romanesque, but both at once. Here again, nothing was lost.

The other arts had doubtless followed this lead. The interior of churches would be decorated with mosaics on a gold ground, like the one which has survived at Germigny-des-Prés, or with frescoes covering the entire walls, as at St Germain d'Auxerre or in the church of Müstair. Sculpture makes its reappearance, in low relief on the chancels, then in the round for statues. The crafts of working in ivory and precious metals, applied to chalices, reliquaries and caskets, create sumptuous objects intended to give the impression of a more than ordinary power. But where this art excels is in the decoration of books. The Antique and more precisely the Hellenistic influence can be seen at work in the reappearance of three-dimensional effects in the ceremonial manuscripts, inscribed in letters of gold or silver on a purple ground, which emanate from the workshop at Aachen. The subsequent dispersal of the artists, after 814, to centres such as St Denis, Tours, Rheims and Metz allowed freer expression to some exceptional talents. The incisive pen-strokes of the author of the Utrecht Psalter or the swirling atmosphere, born of intense emotion, created by the miniaturist of the Ebbo Gospels serve notice that figurative art has established its claim from now on to a place in the first rank, far in advance of the manuscripts from St Bertin or St Amand which perpetuate the abstract insular tradition. And once again, the Ottonian manuscripts painted at Reichenau, Trier, Echternach or Cologne, for all their imitation of a Byzantine formality, in fact reflect Carolingian innovations. The foundations of Western art – its feeling for line and depth, for the interplay of colour, its rejection of art for art's sake, its affirmation of divine and human greatness – have been laid.

So in this summary of the Carolingian renewal, the threads – political and religious, Roman and Christian – are inextricably entangled. Prompted by three generations of ecclesiastics, the Carolingian, and for that matter the Ottonian, dynasts strove to base their political, religious, intellectual and artistic constructs on the secular and religious laws. They rediscovered the Roman conception of the State by tempering the Germanic right of *bannum* to the requirements of Christian morality. They built up the empire by adding to their fiscal lands and through the conduct of unremitting warfare. They incorporated vassalage into the State. Charlemagne's empiricism prepared the ground for the more radical measures of Louis the Pious, more sympathetic towards the Church than his father had been. The Church, an essential agent in the Renewal, represented in fact the one institution which conferred on the empire, as on the other European kingdoms, a common identity and a common form of organisation, with the capacity to reach populations much less accessible to the local agents of the royal power. For this reason, Charlemagne and Otto did all they could to keep control over the Church, while Louis the Pious thought it more reasonable to allow it a certain freedom. The extension of missionary activity to regions outside the empire endorsed the nature of this distinction between the State and the Church, and enabled the concept of Europe to emerge. Unity then ceased to be a matter of

Carolingian marble. Tenth century bas-relief,
Aversa cathedral (Campagna).

political uniformity and had to be based on a common culture. The ubiquity of monastic and cathedral schools, the adoption of a culture reposing on the Bible and on Antique humanism completed the transformation and clinched the admission of Germania into the European community. Lastly, the artistic renaissance, in its many manifestations – not excluding those peculiar to Asturian Spain and Anglo-Saxon England – shows that Antique models gave rise to genuine innovations, produced to satisfy modern liturgical requirements. The programme of rebirth through baptism was thus translated into sober reality. Charlemagne and his successor Louis the Pious each slanted it in a different direction. But in both cases they were merely systematising and co-ordinating solutions already discovered in the course of the Merovingian crisis. The continuation and amplification of innovations dating from the late seventh century are the hallmarks, equally, of the social and economic evolution undergone by the generations who made the Carolingian and Ottonian renaissances.

11

Europe accumulates its first gains: sixth to ninth centuries

Carolingian men of letters attempted on several occasions to produce a rationale for their society. Having defined their programme and their aim, they concluded, falling back on an old formula of St Augustine's, that the whole of humanity on its march to God fitted into three groups: priests, monks and laymen. The clergy led the way, the monks offered their prayers, the laymen, by definition married, laboured in keeping with the biblical typology of Noah, Daniel and Job. We come across these distinctions in the writings of Theodulf, adviser to Charlemagne, and of Rabanus Maurus, mentor to Charles the Bald. We also find them enunciated by two laymen, the emperor Louis the Pious and the poet Ermoldus Nigellus. How far does this formula, which springs so readily to the minds of contemporaries, fit the reality of their times? Before attempting an answer, we must first try to determine, however approximately, the number of men we are dealing with and the way they were evolving. In the course of our investigation we shall come across rifts between priests and monks, between the powerful and the poor, between free men and slaves – in short a whole world in the grip of change, fluid and difficult to pin down. At the same time, it is a world penetrated by the beginnings of an improvement in agricultural production and in the methods of cultivation, by an urban renewal and new commercial contacts, and by the expansion of the monetary economy. These factors give us reason to reconsider the causes of the collapse of the Carolingian empire in the light of recent discoveries and to make comparisons with the failures and successes of the barbarian kingships.

The men

Despite the absence of exact figures and documentation, there is no difficulty in discerning certain general trends in the demographic evolution of the early medieval centuries. The fifth-century wars and invasions must have made a serious impact on towns and country-sides, whether as a result of massacres, as for example in North Africa and Britain, or through reductions to slavery, especially in Gaul and Italy, or lastly and most importantly because of the almost ubiquitous famines, which several chroniclers refer to as occurring in Gaul, Spain and Italy in 409 and 411. In Italy, the famine of 450 is described as 'unusually vicious': parents sold their children into slavery to procure food for themselves.

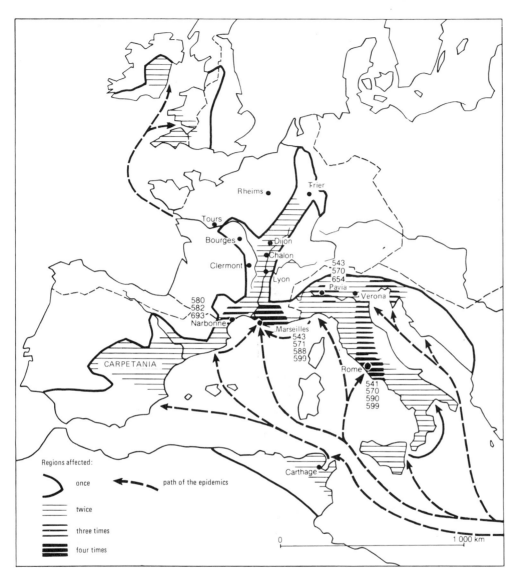

16 Epidemics of plague in the West, sixth to eighth centuries

We saw, furthermore, that the relatively small number of invaders could not have sufficed to fill the gaps. Brittany was perhaps exceptional since it profited from a continuous emigration of insular Britons and saw an increase of population, perhaps to around 300,000. But elsewhere, malnutrition left populations defenceless against a calamity imported from the East, the inguinal plague, which made its appearance in Italy, Gaul and Spain as early as 442. This first alarum made little impression, but what with the bad harvests at the end of Theodoric's reign and the regular convoys of Byzantine troops

475

arriving from Constantinople, Alexandria and Carthage, the scourge from the East unleashed itself with brutal effect in 542.

A severe demographic setback: the sixth-century plague

This first great outbreak of the plague in medieval history followed the same maritime routes as its successor would take in 1348. It struck simultaneously in Illyria and Africa and then in the whole of eastern and southern Spain. In 543, by way of Rome, it infected Tuscany and the plain of the Po; by way of Marseilles, it travelled up the Rhône and the Saône, afterwards descending the left bank of the Rhine to come to a halt at the gates of Rheims and Trier. In 544 the infection reached the coasts of Ireland and Wales. A second outbreak started in 559 in Istria and Ravenna, flaring up again in 570 at Ostia and Genoa, and in 571 in Marseilles, from which it spread this time to the Auvergne, the Berry and Burgundy. A third wave of the epidemic struck in 580–2 and 588–91. Eastern Spain was ravaged up to and including Toledo, and so later were Catalonia, the Narbonnaise, the Albigeois, Marseilles yet again, and the Rhône valley, with the exception of Lyons. Brought back from Antioch to Ravenna and Istria, this third outbreak infected central Italy as far as Rome. At the same time dysentery was raging in the Paris basin. A fourth wave of the plague in 599–600 hit the same central Italian territories as before, Marseilles, and Africa. Later the bacillus seems to have lost some of its virulence. In 654, Provence, Latium and Pavia were the only places to be infected. In 664, an Anglo-Saxon source spread the plague through southern England and as far as Northumbria, Wales and Ireland. There was a recurrence in 682–3. In 694, the Narbonnaise experienced yet another return of the epidemic in full strength. Finally, in 746 and 767, Sicily and southern Italy were infected for one last time.

Generally speaking, when compared with its counterpart of 1348, the 'Justinianic' plague probably caused fewer deaths because of its very limited penetration to inland regions. The map shows it keeping closely to the busiest long-distance trade-routes, the rivers in particular, and pinpoints its failure to progress beyond the points where cargoes were transferred. Ports and towns must have paid a heavy toll to the scourge, but it visibly faltered in the rural areas, except in peninsular Italy, where the void had already been created by famine: according to Procopius, between 538 and 542 50,000 people died of starvation in the Picenum. When it is realised that out of 200 bishoprics in the peninsula, 60 disappeared for good, it becomes evident that here, at least, the plague finished what the famine had begun. Again, precious little can have remained when, around 590–1, swarms of locusts descended on Carpetania (the Spanish Mancha), the Auvergne and Italy. In short, with the exception of Aquitaine and the Atlantic seaboard of Spain, every part of the old, urbanised Roman world was ravaged by the plague. The reduction of population resulting from the interruption to the demographic pattern worked to the benefit of the Berbers, the Basques and Bretons, who began to spread down from their hill country into the empty plains, or to emerge from their territory to make inroads on the Visigothic and Frankish kingdoms. The retreat of Roman civilisation was thereby hastened, to the advantage of indigenous barbarians. In the British Isles, the demographic rupture affected the Celts much more than the Anglo-Saxons and enabled the latter to resume their advance. Furthermore, since the Germanised or Germanic countries virtually escaped, this gave an advantage to peoples such as the Lombards, who when they invaded the Po plain as early as 568 found it largely depopulated and were able to infiltrate the peninsula with ease. In the course of the seventh century, tribal contingents of Slavs, under the aegis of the Avars, took up residence along the waterways of the western Adriatic and in the duchy of Benevento, 'on lands which were hitherto deserted', while Bulgars settled in the Pentapolis. In short, while the Italian peninsula remained at a low ebb throughout the seventh century and was more or less cut off from the rest of Europe by the Lombard invasions, elsewhere, in Galicia, Aquitaine, Bavaria and England, but above all north of the Loire, there was nothing to prevent the redress of demographic losses by natural means. In the region between the Rhine and the Moselle, the cemetery at Rübenach-Krefeld, not far from Coblenz, shows a doubling of the local population between the sixth century and the seventh. Demographically speaking, the centre of gravity therefore shifted from Mediterranean Europe to the north of the continent, which was unaffected by the great plague.

While this discrepancy in favour of the Germans was quick to show itself on the Meuse and the Lower Rhine, regional differences also became accentuated. To the west of the Scheldt, for instance, populations were still thin on the ground. The rural territories of the *civitas* of Thérouanne were still empty when two Irishmen, Lugle and Luglian, traversed them at the end of the seventh century. Again, it was not until after 700 that the inhabitants of the Po plain saw their numbers beginning to increase. One of the few southerly regions to experience an access of population was the Pyrenean chain, the Narbonnaise and Aquitaine. The first reason for this was the persecution of the Jews by the Visigothic kings, which caused a spate of migrations to the plains of lower Languedoc. The second cause was the Muslim occupation of Spain and the taxes that were imposed in consequence. The Christian Hispano-Visigoths sought refuge in the Cantabrian mountains and later, following the great famine of 749–50, on the northern slopes of the Pyrenees, spreading out as far as the southern faces of the Cévennes and sometimes beyond. This movement was not halted, in fact, until after the time of Charlemagne. Again, the desertion of the Roman towns on Spain's eastern seaboard and the lightness of the subsequent Berber occupation provide a logical explanation for the under-exploitation of the countryside and for the mounting of piratical operations from the small harbours up and down the coast, given the lack of other resources. In the Basque country north of the Pyrenees, stretching from the Adour to the Garonne, the urban network likewise vanished, probably because of a lack of indigenous population or of replenishments from outside. The plight of the coastal regions of central Italy must have been identical. It is quite possible that the flatlands of Latium ceased to be irrigated at this period, giving rise to the Pontine Marshes.

The first upsurge of population in the seventh century

This said, in the places where the latest research confirms that the demographic curve was righting itself, the human implications of this recovery need to be taken into account if its nature is to be properly appreciated. On this point, the Gallo-Roman and later Merovingian cemetery of Frénouville (Calvados), where the burials range in date from the third to the seventh centuries, is especially revealing. Whereas the inhabitants of the Gallo-Roman village numbered around 250, over the three Merovingian centuries the number fluctuated between 1,100 and 1,400 – which even on the lower figure represents a fivefold increase! As it is hard to discern a substantial Anglo-Saxon presence and warrior burials are few in number, it can be taken as certain that these villagers, left in peace, saw their population increasing in the course of the seventh century. But it should also be noted that this occurred in conditions very close to those of today's Third World. Life-expectancy at birth was low: 30 years at the outside. Infant mortality was high: 45 per cent. The average life-span in the Merovingian period was between 40 and 50 for men, but for women only between 30 and 40. Birth- and death-rates must have been very high: an average of 45 per 1,000 in both cases, but subject to constant fluctuations. Everything points to a precarious demographic recovery, with no one remaining unwed and with marriage taking place at puberty. In addition, this hazardous situation must have been exacerbated by inbreeding, of which there is proof in the evolution of cranial measurements and an above-average incidence of certain physical defects. Everything gained by this demographic recovery, which becomes noticeable in the seventh century but is much more pronounced in the eighth, would thus have been perpetually at risk from the most trifling of military skirmishes, or the first pillaging raid.

This gradual recuperation after the shock of the Justinianic plague had its effects, as we saw, on the pattern of settlement on the land. The great tracts of forest which had spread over the abandoned lands became interspersed with a few clearances. This can be seen happening in the sector between the Rhine, the Moselle and the Eifel, as well as in the low-lying plain of the Po. While in some places, on the Burgundian plateaux for example, the woods continued their advance, in the valleys of the Auxerrois the situation was reversed. Once 30 or so parishes were established on the ruins of Gallo-Roman *villae*, others were created along the line of the Loire valley from the seventh century onwards, a new departure, and sometimes an attack was even made on the wooded plateau. In general, however, once the lost ground had been recovered, progress was slight. The results of pollen analyses carried out on sites in central Belgium and in the Ardennes point to the same conclusions. From the beginning of the fifth century, trees, bracken and scrub advanced at the expense of meadow and arable lands. The latter reappeared in the sixth and seventh centuries, but there was an upsurge of beech and alder around the year 700. After that the pollens of cultivated plants again became more numerous. Here the late Merovingian period would probably represent a temporary retreat of cultivated lands until such time as the Pippinids, masters to all intents and purposes of these regions, where 90 large agricultural estates lying along the Meuse have been identified as in their possession, permanently transformed the countryside after their victory at Tertry in 687.

England, after the initial phases of partial reclamation of lands cultivated in Roman times and the freeze following the conquest, also saw the beginnings of clearances in the eighth century. These offshoots of the Anglo-Saxon colonisation begun by earlier immigrants should be recognisable, according to certain English historians, from the occasional place-

In 1858, a ploughman unearthed at Guarrazar the treasure of the Visigothic kings, including this votive crown of King Reccesuinth (mid-seventh century), intended to be hung above an altar (Madrid, Museo Archeologico Nacional).

479

As Anglo-Saxon colonisation progressed,
Christianity continued to gain ground. Chased silver
brooch with Anglo-Saxon and Christian motifs,
ninth century (London, British Museum).

names ending in -*inga* to be found in the Weald, Cambridgeshire and East Anglia. However, pollen analysis has not so far yielded the same results as on the continent. On the other hand, archaeological investigation of the Frisian terps indicates that Groningen and Frisia, despite encroachments by the sea, saw their population steadily increasing and turning, for want of space in which to grow crops or graze livestock, to seaborne trade. The situation was thus the direct opposite of the one on the coasts of eastern Spain and it highlights the tilting of the balance in the direction of northern Europe. To sum up, this first increase in population and land clearance is clearly noticeable in England, northern Gaul and the plain of the Po.

The demographic crisis of the fifth to sixth centuries therefore produced in the first place a rupture particularly damaging to the urbanised countries of the Mediterranean, and then a slow recovery which started in the seventh century, gathering speed in the eighth century in the Germanic and Germanised regions of Europe. But this revival was still too precarious, all other things being equal, to account for the pre-eminence of the Austrasians or Anglo-Saxons.

Carolingian inequalities

When we come to the ninth century, the parallel with the Merovingian epoch makes certain demographic trends easy to perceive. One difference strikes us immediately: the absence of epidemic illness. Plague had long since disappeared. Famines now occurred only as the result of floods or drought. From being rare occurrences before 840 (we know of only three between 751 and that date), the incidence of famine increased with the invasions and civil wars, eight being recorded in the space of 50 years. In Italy famines recurred in 859, 872 and 940, while in 873 Germany suffered a plague of locusts. Often, however, the annalists exaggerate by describing as famines what were clearly no more than temporary dearths. In 779, Benedict of Aniane dealt with a so-called famine by distributing meat.

There seems therefore no reason to doubt that the increase of population continued down to the middle of the ninth century.

A relevant factor in certain zones is the influx of immigrants. Disillusioned by the Saragossan fiasco of 778, crushed after their fruitless revolts at Cordoba in 850–9 and at Bobastro (850–928), the Mozarabs – that is to say the Spanish Christians – tended to migrate to the Asturian kingdom, to Catalonia or to the south of the Aquitanian kingdom. The warmth of their welcome there is shown by instructions issued by Charlemagne in 802, repeated by Charles the Bald in 844, which allowed them to settle on deserted lands in Septimania; this emigration continued down to the end of the ninth century. In England, the construction of massive earthworks cutting across valleys and hillsides, of which Offa's Dyke is the prime example, proves that there was sufficient manpower to effect forest clearances over long stretches of country. The continuing abandonment by the Frisians of their terps must surely be an indication that they were outgrowing their territory. On the other side of the North Sea, imitation of Frisian techniques by the Anglo-Saxons and Danes enabled the marshes around the Wash and the East Anglian fenland to be brought into cultivation. Lastly, Viking movements resulting in colonisation undoubtedly augmented the local populations of the Danelaw and Normandy. On Iceland, about 20,000 people, ranging from Norwegian chieftains to Irish slaves, were involved in the movement to colonise the hitherto deserted island in the late ninth century. To these proofs of local population increases can be added data with a bearing on the densities of rural population.

Using the polyptych of St Germain-des-Prés, Ferdinand Lot estimated that the average density on these estates ranged in the Paris basin from 26 to 29 inhabitants to the square km. Other historians, using the polyptych of St Bertin (844–59), have arrived at densities per square km of 34 inhabitants between the Yser and the slopes of Artois, twenty further north, from nine to twelve around Lille, and four in the Moselle valley. It has again been calculated that the zone containing the Frisian terps could support, around the year 800, twenty inhabitants to the square km on the marine clays, reducing to four on the sandy soils in south Drenthe. Work done on the polyptych of St Remigius of Rheims (compiled between 845 and 882) points to similar conclusions. A large village such as Viel-Saint-Rémi accommodated 50 inhabitants to the square km, estates such as Viller-le-Tourneur, 24, Sault-Saint-Rémi, 45, and Courtisols fifteen. When one adds to these cultivated lands all the appurtenances, which tended for the most part to be situated in the middle of wasteland, the densities fall respectively to 37, thirteen, 25 and fifteen. To sum up, for the dry country of Champagne, in the mid-ninth century, it seems safe to propose the figure of about 30 inhabitants to the square km as the average on cultivated lands, and of about twelve on uncultivated lands. These estimates, calculated from the working documents of estate management, are unlikely to be far wrong, since it is probable that the polyptychs err more on the side of omission than excess in their enumeration of peasants, always supposing of course that our assumptions in regard to the areas covered are correct. The figures prove that undeniable progress was achieved by comparison with late Antiquity in the size of the workforce on these same well-documented estates, originally the family patrimony of St Remigius, since the fifth-century figure of eight agricultural workers to the

481

square km was exceeded, and the ideal ratio of sixteen labourers proposed by the agronomist Columella was doubled! They lastly reveal that the population density of the *ager* was three times that of the *saltus*. The population of the Carolingian era was therefore concentrated in a scattering of densely-peopled hamlets surrounded by vast stretches of more or less uncultivated areas.

Clearly, it was the more cultivated zones which were attracting population. At the beginning of the tenth century, the Catalonian side of the Pyrenean range was decidedly over-populated, with densities, at a height of over 1,000 m, of up to eighteen inhabitants to the square km. Similarly, upper Lombardy and Piedmont appear to have had more occupants than the Apennines and lower Po valley. At the end of the ninth century, the open country of the Limagne was at saturation point. Taking into account these wide geographical variations in the demographic expansion, which appears at its most conspicuous in the Paris basin, Picardy, Flanders, on the axis of the Meuse and around Cologne, it is possible to venture some hypotheses about the empire's global population. Assuming a grand total of 1,200,000 square kms, a population of about fifteen million inhabitants has been proposed. Ferdinand Lot suggested between fourteen and fifteen million, but this was for the area of present-day France. Jan Dhondt, on the other hand, would not go above three million for the same territory, and gave Germany and England about 700,000 apiece. However, we should not overlook the 19,000 functionaries and 52,000 soldiers Charlemagne had at his disposal. The best solution may be to regard fifteen million as a definite minimum and perhaps allow for a total of eighteen million on the basis of ten inhabitants to the square km in respect of uncultivated lands (75 per cent of the whole) and 30 for the 25 per cent of cultivated lands. The population of the Carolingian empire would thus be slightly larger, taking into account the smaller area involved, than that of the late Roman empire, believed to total 26 million.

All this, it should once again be stressed, is only an approximation, on a par with the ascription of ten million inhabitants by some English demographers to the tenth-century Ottonian empire. The one certainty, however, is the halting of this demographic expansion after 840, probably until 950. Studies of deserted villages show that the halt in agricultural colonisation in the Eifel came around the middle of the ninth century. Saracen raids undoubtedly emptied eastern Provence of its population down to 972. In 867, we hear of 9,000 Christians from Benevento being loaded on to six Muslim ships to be sold as slaves in African Tripoli and Alexandria. The slaves carried off in Viking raids ended their days in Iceland, Norway or Denmark. Processions of naked women, tied by the hair to the wagons of their Hungarian captors, went to populate the plains of the Danube. At this same period, slaves and other agricultural labourers were taking to their heels on the approach of the Vikings, to escape falling into their clutches; a capitulary of Charles the Bald suggests they would do better to hide in the neighbouring woods. In 853, there was a sudden exodus from Neustria because of ravages by the Bretons and Danes. Nor should we forget the carnage due to the civil wars. In 841, at Fontenoy-en-Puisaye, several thousand soldiers are said to have died. In 923, Rudolf of Burgundy and Berengar of Friuli came to blows somewhere in the plain of the Po: we are told that 1,500 heavy cavalry, members of top-ranking families, were left for dead on the battlefield. Whenever there was a Viking attack, Flodoard is careful to tell us the exact number of casualties: 1,200 Northmen killed at the siege of Clermont-Ferrand in 923, 1,300 near Étampes in 925, 1,100 at Fauquembergue in 926. Losses of this magnitude could not fail to put a brake on population growth, just as the intense disturbance to the agricultural workforce could not fail to affect levels of production.

A wealthy and divided clergy

In a world as various as that of the Christian Europe of the eighth and ninth centuries, and so obviously permeated by the effects of this demographic revival, what hope was there that society could be made to fit the categories devised for it by a spiritually-orientated anthropology, with its hard and fast distinctions between priests, monks and laymen? So far as the priests and monks were concerned there was some truth in the categorisation, in so far as they represented distinct and mutually opposed categories; but it is hard to see the laymen as homogeneous, in view of the violence which might erupt at any time to divide them into two groups, composed on the one hand of laymen with an assured material or political position, that is to say, the slaves and the nobles, and on the other of laymen without influence or protectors, the free men and all those in minority groups. Similarly, the categorisation of society current in Saxony or among the Danes and Swedes, with its firm distinctions between the nobles (*edhelingi*) whose duty was to govern, and the free men (*frilingi*) and slaves (*lazzi*), whose duty was to obey, did not fully correspond with reality, since it appears that changes of social status could come about with great rapidity: if a man wanted to change his original status, or was degraded from it, there was no sure way of preventing this.

Allusion has already been made to the formidable strength of the clergy. The council of Aachen in 816 related the wealth of churches to the number of *mansi* at their disposal. Churches considered to be in the top category possessed between 3,000 and 8,000 *mansi*, those in the second category between 1,000 and 2,000, while lumped together in the third category were the smaller establishments of between 200 and 300 manses. The cathedral of Augsburg had just over 1,500 *mansi*, that of Regensburg 1,100. By contrast, monasteries such as Weissenburg, Lorsch and St Gall each had about 4,000 *mansi*, and Fulda nearly 15,000! The monks of Fontenelle (St Wandrille) who claimed to have been stripped of their possessions by the Carolingians were officially in command of 4,000 and more *mansi*. But the possessions of even a 'small' monastery like St Bertin, with its 254 *mansi* for the upkeep of the monks alone, would cover an area in excess of 10,000 hectares. Alcuin was abbot simultaneously of Ferrières, St Loup of Sens, St Josse, Flavigny, Cormery and St Martin of Tours. He thereby incurred the reproach of being master to 20,000 and more slaves. The impression of a disproportion between cathedral and monastic properties becomes stronger when the burdens carried by the former are taken into consideration. Apart from maintaining the hospice for travellers, the gate-house for the poor and the school for oblates, the monks were less encumbered with charitable duties than were the cathedral canons. All the services set up in the late Antique and Merovingian epochs –   **483**

An important Carolingian abbey: St Gallen. The former hermitage which St Gall established near Lake Constance became in 747 a monastery following the Benedictine Rule; a new phase of enlargement and rebuilding began in 830 (model shown at the *Karl der Grosse* exhibition held at Aachen in 1965).

xenodochia, assistance to the registered poor (*matricularii*), the right of asylum, the bishop's court – continued to fall on the canons, at a time when the size of their landed properties was in inverse proportion to their needs, especially by comparison with the monks. One sees why, in these circumstances, the Carolingian bishops should have gone through so many legal contortions to gain control over the monasteries. The famous case of the Le Mans forgeries, in which the bishop tried in vain to get St Calais under his thumb, is indicative of the bitterness of these disputes from which the king and magnates would often reap a material advantage. Notwithstanding the fact that episcopal possessions might be barely enough for subsistence, which is why Hincmar's correspondence is so much taken up with acrimonious efforts to recover his lands, there was clearly no feeling of solidarity between seculars and regulars. We saw moreover that Charlemagne's policy in Aquitaine was to play off the monasteries against the episcopate. The privilege of exemption, obtained in 910 by Cluny, was in part a result of this struggle to win independence from the diocesan bishop.

Emergence of the warrior aristocracy in the seventh century

A phenomenon unknown among the conquerors, but a powerful force among the conquered, aristocracies were everywhere in the saddle at the beginning of the eighth century. Where had they come from? There is no point in enlarging on the continuation and survival of the great senatorial families which, by monopolising the southern bishop-

484

rics, found their numbers diminishing through an insufficiency of heirs, but held on to their wealth, which they even augmented through fruitful alliances with the kingly families. Among the Germans, the gradual replacement of the assemblies of free men by the *officium palatinum* of the king's council, or assembly of magnates, proves that families recognised as noble had now appeared. In the case of the Lombards and the Anglo-Saxons, whose customs were the most archaic, this nobility was a true aristocracy of blood. Members of such families, the *aethelings* in Kent, or the *ealdormen* in the other kingdoms, could still lay claim to the kingship. In Lombardy, the dukes were able to suppress the monarchy altogether for ten years and afterwards to keep it constantly in check. If in Visigothic Spain and Merovingian Gaul the blood nobility was less important, this was because of the rapid rise, thanks to the 'training' they received in the royal courts, of a nobility of service, no longer equal but inferior to the king. Well-rewarded in lands by their masters, these nobles, in common with the warriors and the subjects at large, were required to swear to him an oath of loyalty on the lines of the oath taken in former days by the Roman legionaries. But their hunger for lands and power was too great to be restrained by so slight a barrier. It was no solution for Chindaswind and Ebroin to chop off the heads of the leading members of the new dynasties. More particularly in Gaul, the conjunction of three nobilities, the Gallo-Roman and the Burgundian in the south and the Frankish in the north, led to the formation of a pressure group which bartered its fidelity, as early as 614, against the edict of Chlothar II which restricted the exercise of public functions in a locality to residents of the county concerned.

It was necessary to repay the services of these 'companions' of the king now that they were charged with important official duties. In Gaul, the Merovingian king was the biggest landowner in the whole of Neustria, northern Burgundy and western Austrasia. Whereas in Hispanic territory or in southern Gaul the distinction between ownership and possession was still clearcut, this was not so among the Franks who treated anything in the nature of a stipend as a gift in perpetuity, and office in any form as a personal possession. They resembled the Anglo-Saxons and the Lombards in managing to retain the fiscal lands they had received along with the material gifts or booty. The Lombard king was unique in arresting the disappearance of his fisc in mid-course, by enlarging the fisc through his eighth-century conquests. This enabled him to form his own clientele, but he could not eliminate the clienteles which had formed around the dukes. In Merovingian Gaul, as fast as the fiscal lands fell into their hands the magnates began to acquire the privilege of immunity that went with them. These properties, which were protected against interference from public officials, apart from the overseers of the royal estates (*domestici* on the staff of the mayor of the palace), and which owed nothing to the State, did not forfeit these advantages when they were granted to new owners. The latter, in their turn, seized the opportunity to bring the slaves and *coloni* into closer subjection to themselves and thus to ensure that substantial parts of the rural population were beyond the king's reach.

There came a point when the royal fisc was inadequate to meet all the demands. Around the year 600, King Reccared came up with a solution. Arguing from the fact that ecclesiastical lands had had to be carved out of public lands and that the king was protector of the Church, he detached a portion of the landed holdings of a monastery and assigned it, in the guise of recompense for military services, to a duke. Dagobert, in 630, was quick to follow this example and absorbed a number of monastic or episcopal properties into his fisc, in order to grant them out in usufruct to his warriors. With the emergence of the principalities, the practice became widespread, and the Pippinids, in order to conserve their own estates, acted in the same fashion. Through this 'precarial' contract, the Church's possession was handed over on the 'prayer' (*precaria*) of the prince to an important layman. Charles Martel made such free use of the device that he was able to amass a sizeable army. But by undermining the ecclesial structures so completely he drew down on himself the thunderbolts of the clergy. As always at this period, crisis in the State was inseparable from crisis in the Church, the point being that since the time of Clovis the large ecclesiastical estates were subject to the same regime as the royal fiscs, which helps to explain how laymen came to be set at the head of bishoprics or abbeys.

Meanwhile, factors such as the lack of sound government, the prevalence of private violence, the feuding between clans and the rapaciousness of sundry officials were making men keener than ever to find protectors among the powerful. In the southern countries, bonds between man and man proliferated, based as ever on the promise of mutual fidelity, the revocable contract of equal with equal, and on the patron's promise of maintenance. The importance of the Visigothic *gardingi* and the Lombard *gasindi* has already been stressed. In Spain, King Ervig (680–7) admitted the *gardingi* to the *officium palatinum*, the royal council. In Italy, the *gasindi* became gastalds. All these retainers were remunerated with land deducted from the royal fisc. In Merovingian Gaul, where the relationship of superior to inferior which obtained between the lord and his vassals, or between the king and his antrustions, was more constraining, a comparable rise in the social scale is none the less evident. In spite of their lowly origin, vassals and antrustions mingled with the higher aristocracy. Similarly, the Anglo-Saxon *gesiths* rose from their position as body-guards to the ranks of a middle-ranking nobility, the *thegns*. In this way, the kings and the magnates generated around them concentric networks of subordination. In return for the performance of a domestic or personal service, or of military service on an annual or permanent basis, kings, war-leaders and potentates, under the generic name of *optimates* or *proceres*, gratuitously rewarded their 'followers' with *beneficia* (whence later the term 'benefice'), gifts which took many different forms – upkeep in the lord's household, weapons, stipends derived from the usufruct of a property, gifts of land in full or precarial ownership, and so on.

The Carolingian 'leap forward'

For all their efforts to reconstruct the State, the Carolingians could not check this tendency: or rather, they believed it possible, as has been said, to count on individual commendations to reinforce the social pyramid and to extend their authority from one link in the chain to the next, right down to the base. Their one precaution was to bestow their favours more or less exclusively on the members of clans that were related, or likely to be related, to their own line. And indeed, one never ceases to be amazed at the paucity of the great noble families and their propensity to enter into marriage alliances with the Carolingian family, in line, it is true, with the wishes of the emperors, whose aim was naturally to keep the upper hand.

The Carolingian dynasty was itself produced by the marriage of two patrimonies, that of Begga for the Austrasian part and that of Ansegisel for the region of Metz, where Arnulf, his father and later Chlodulf his brother were bishops. Again, the great abbacies were reserved for kinsmen of the ruler, such as Adalhard, followed by Wala, at Corbie, or for his friends: Einhard, for example, Charlemagne's biographer, was lay abbot of Seligenstadt, St John the Baptist in Pavia, St Servitius at Maastricht, St Peter and St Bavo at Ghent. At times the emperor favoured the old noble families of Austrasia, at others the new ones emerging in Saxony, Lombardy, Bavaria, Visigothic Spain or Frisia. For example, a single family of Frisian descent produced around 804 the bishop of Châlons, Hildegrin, the abbot, later the first bishop of Münster, St Liudger, and the latter's uncle or cousin – it is not clear which – and successor, Gerfrid. We can cite as another example the Alaman family of the Etichonids, which held sway in Alsace at the end of the Merovingian period. Between 709 and 746, Eticho's grandson, Liutfrid, conquered, on behalf of Charles Martel, the countries east of the Rhine. Under Charlemagne and Louis the Pious, Hugh was count of Tours. One of his daughters married the Emperor Lothar I, his other daughter married Count Conrad of the Welf clan, brother to the Empress Judith. His son Gerard became count of Paris and then of Vienne, and lastly regent of the kingdom of Provence. Matfrid, also descended from Eticho, was count of Orleans and, in alliance with Hugh, one of the chief opponents of Louis the Pious. His descendants monopolised the countship of the Eifel, and his daughter married Boso, who, as we saw, proclaimed himself king. This clan, through its marriage alliances, was drawn with the Unrochids into a running dispute with another great Austrasian clan, the 'Williams'. The first William was appointed by Charlemagne in 790 to the county of Toulouse. Epic hero and vanquisher of the Muslims, he retired in 804 to a monastery of his own founding. But a little later we meet his son Bernard in the roles of marquess of Septimania and later of chamberlain to Louis the Pious, denounced by Hugh and Matfrid as the Empress Judith's paramour. An inveterate and unscrupulous conspirator, Bernard was eventually convicted of treason by Charles the Bald and executed in 844. His elder son, William, another traitor, was executed at Barcelona in 850. Bernard's younger son, Bernard Hairy-Feet, was just as bad, but he found his way back into the sovereign's favour and became marquess of Septimania and count of the Auvergne. Lastly, Bernard's grandson, William the Pious, set the seal on the independence of Aquitaine and in 909 founded the monastery of Cluny. The landed possessions of this Germanic family, an 'import' into the Midi, therefore extended from Austrasia to the Toulousain, taking in the Autunois, the Mâconnais and the Auvergne on the way. Similarly, the possessions of the Guidones and the Lamberts stretched from Brittany to Italy.

All these clans were allied to the Carolingians, yet once outside Francia they intermixed with the old senatorial families and took root with surprising rapidity in the areas where they held office as count or marquis. The 'southernisation' of the Williams and Bernards is

487

especially obvious. In any case, these great families would have had to act in concert for their interests to triumph. They did nothing of the kind, but instead quarrelled amongst themselves. The originally Saxon clan of Robert the Strong, allied to the Carolingians, was introduced into the counties of Tours and Angers not just to counteract the Vikings, but also to eliminate the Guy–Lambert connection. Inter-family quarrels also developed between Ramiro II, king of the Asturias, and Fernan Gonzales (923–70), who twice revolted and was twice captured. And yet these wealthy aristocrats were men of cultivation, as can be seen from the will of the Unrochid Eberhard, marquess of Friuli, drawn up in 865, which distributes a quantity of books amongst his children. Paradoxically, while they knew from their reading of the *Mirrors for Princes* what path society should follow, they took the opposite course. Nothing could be more poignant than to read the counsels of fidelity to the king addressed by Dhuoda, out of maternal concern, to her son William in 841, when we know that in 850 he will be beheaded for treason. Instances of fidelity to the king can nevertheless be found. The Visigothic counts of Catalonia remained loyal down to 888, when the election of Odo, in their eyes an illegitimate because non-Carolingian king, put an end to their fidelity. And the Saxon nobility never wavered in their faithfulness to Louis the Pious and Louis the German.

Birth of vassalage

Their landed base therefore conferred on the nobles prestige, power and high-ranking official positions, though it does not explain their headstrong behaviour and lack of solidarity. Their tendency towards aggression and self-enrichment was countered in practice by the network of vassalic ties intended to hold society together. In 757, Pippin III sought to render indissoluble the personal bond between himself and a magnate by attaching to Germanic commendation the Roman conception of loyalty. The exact terms of fealty sworn on that occasion by Tassilo, duke of Bavaria, are revealing:

He commended himself into vassalage by his hands. He swore many and innumerable oaths while placing his hands on the relics of the saints, and promised fealty to king Pippin and to his aforementioned sons Charles and Carloman, to be their vassal with right mind and steadfast devotion, according to the law, as a vassal should be to his lord.

Obviously, this amalgam of private and public law, this mingling of the two traditions, was intended to make the contract unbreakable, until the death of one of the partners. The price of perjury was confiscation of the lands granted in usufruct (precisely what happened in the case of Bavaria), and quite possibly damnation and eternal death, because the oath was sworn before God. The personal nature of the bond, the adoptive kinship it established and the emotional charge it would carry in keeping with the Germanic tradition were calculated to restrain any vassal on the verge of disaffection, and may indeed explain why, in many cases, the contract was kept. This was an idea which the Church, unremitting in its efforts to reinstate the contracts of Roman or canon law, was only too anxious to instil in Carolingian society. Further, the nobility saw that it was in their own interests to enter into

Charles the Bald, in Byzantine dress, surrounded by lay and ecclesiastical counsellors, receiving the Bible (*Bible of Charles the Bald*, ms lat. 1, fol 423, Paris, Bibliothèque nationale).

489

commendation. A benefice obtained in exchange for military service would represent an addition to landed capital. The king or emperor would gain thereby in authority or in power. So from now on, as the practice became general, a count's landed possessions would be of three kinds. He would first have his personal or family estates, acquired by purchase, received in dowry or devised by will in full ownership, and called for that reason 'allods'. Next there would be his *honores*, fiscal lands he received in usufruct as remuneration for his office: his possession of these lands going with the *comitatus* was limited of course to his tenure of the office, and his removal to another county would automatically imply a change of incumbent. The count would lastly have at his disposal lands in a third category: the benefices he received, in this instance with a temporary title, as a consequence of entering into vassalage. To be precise, after the ceremony of placing hands (the vassal's) between hands (the king's or the lord's) and the oath of fealty would come the ceremony of investiture with the benefice, performed with the aid of a symbol: a clod of earth or a leafy branch that was taken to represent the enjoyment (and not outright ownership, it should again be stressed) of the land thus handed over. Charlemagne encouraged the nobles to come to the same arrangement with the free men, which would provide him with a host of sub-vassals, apart from the royal vassals who would answer his summons directly. In this way, through the forging of a whole series of links binding one man to another, society would be held together from the base right up to the summit, bishops and abbots not excluded. In addition, the emperor made it plain that the contracts concluded in this form were indissoluble, except where the lord was found guilty of a crime or an act of injustice against the vassal. The system of uniting benefice with vassalage came in this way to be adopted in all the countries between the Rhine and the Loire.

The emperors and kings made efforts to popularise these institutions elsewhere, in northern Italy and Aquitaine. In 844, Charles the Bald urged the Hispano-Visigothic free men to 'enter into the vassalage of our count'. But this invitation appears to have fallen on deaf ears. Outside the circle of Frankish families implanted south of the Loire and in the Po plain, oaths of loyalty in the traditional negative form continued to be the rule. Public offices in Spain and in the south of Western Francia were always rewarded by a *stipendium*, that is to say a remuneration consisting of the enjoyment of a portion of public land. In the tenth century, it so happened that the term *feo* or *fevum* gained currency to describe this mode of payment. But although this word akin to 'fief' thus makes its first appearance in the south, it is not yet to be taken as signifying the appearance there of the so-called feudal society, in contrast to events in the north. There was no link between fealty and the *feo*. The contracts of equal with equal between nobles, the *convenientiae*, became increasingly common in the tenth century in Languedoc, in Catalonia and in Lombardy. This adherence to the old Roman traditions corresponds to the limit of northern influence and to an entirely different attitude among the higher nobility.

In England and Germany, countries still close to their origins, the Carolingian experiment of linking fidelity with commendation between hands, or vassalage with benefice, was again fraught with difficulties. English landowners of noble rank were bound to the king solely by their oath of loyalty. In Saxony and Eastern Francia, the ancient custom of the oath of commendation, which allowed slaves to commend themselves to a lord 'hands between hands', was still current. Accordingly, many of the magnates in high-born noble families, unlike their counterparts in Western Francia, refused to submit to a custom and ceremony which they considered degrading. On the other hand, the warrior-bands composed of free men, the *trustes*, in which the individual commended himself to the leader by touching his hand, and not by surrendering himself with both hands, which was a mark of inferiority, must still have had its attractions. In England, the *thegns* who had been allocated lands on a royal manor, or indeed held a manor themselves, would be required to render all the various services attached to it in money. Their horizontal communities formed naturally, as extended families grouped around the lord, whether this was the king or before long the *ealdorman*. They owed the lord military service only because they had sworn him fidelity. In Spain, the *behtria* ('benefit') existed to reward the faithful warrior, but was not a right. In Italy, commendation was still separate from the grant of a benefice. In Frisia, lastly, village communities remained at an even more primitive stage and effectively prevented the appearance of any lord or master. So it now becomes clear why the relation of inferior to superior should end up making headway only between the Rhine and the Loire, the region where Carolingian power was most effective.

Four different kinds of vassal now emerged. At the apex, the royal vassals (*vassi dominici*), composed of aristocrats and great landowners; next the vassals with from four to 30 *mansi* at their disposal, dependants of the great lay or ecclesiastical magnates; and below them vassals without their own establishment, '*non casati*', who provided the bodyguards of the powerful. Among the Scandinavians, this group of warriors, analogous to the *trustis*, was called the *hird*. Lastly, the fourth group, something of a hybrid, midway between the ordinary and the undomiciled vassals, consisted of the *ministeriales*, former slaves singled out by their master for a particular duty – for example the *caballarii* of St Bertin, with holdings of about 40 ha, who accompanied their lord on horseback. They were chiefly to be found in Germanised countries, such as Flanders, Lotharingia or Germany. Only vassals of the first type formed part of the higher aristocracy. The second, the ordinary vassals, made up a middle-ranking nobility of which we still know too little. The third group came just above the slaves and the last were still regarded as essentially servile in status. Elsewhere there were only faithful followers or *thegns* – free men, it goes without saying.

Persistence of slavery in an ameliorated form

Almost without realising it, we have arrived by way of the tie of man to man in the world of the free and the unfree. From the power-hungry aristocrats we may as well pass directly to those who – in time of peace at any rate – enjoyed a material security of another kind, the slaves. As in late Antiquity, slaves can fairly be said to have possessed considerable advantages since, as we saw, they were all domiciled – like the vassals in fact, to whom the resemblance is not fortuitous. The slave trade had taken on a new lease of life thanks to the conquests of Charlemagne, only to decline again following the ban imposed on Jewish merchants, forbidding the possession of Christian slaves. True, a free man could still sell

491

himself into slavery, either permanently or until he had paid his debts by instalments. Nor was it unknown for the powerful to use the language of the imperial formularies, to reduce the poor to slavery. At the same time, however, the council of Meaux, in 845, forbade the sale of pagan slaves not only to Jews but equally to pagans. Conciliar legislation became so scrupulous, indeed, that it catered for situations we might regard as far-fetched: a slave who unwittingly married a noblewoman should be enfranchised; a slave who took his own slave as a concubine could abandon her and unite with another, in which case the marriage was legal. So by slow degrees, essentially at the dictates of the sacraments of marriage and ordination, slaves began to acquire a legal personality.

True, enfranchisements were not common and on the lands of the Church they were even prohibited. But they were unquestionably on the increase. A new mode appeared: the enfranchisement *in albis* (in swaddling-clothes), to meet the case of the infant born in the master's house to a free man and a slave woman, whose freedom was automatic. In a word, except in Germanised countries such as Flanders, Saxony and Bavaria, the stock of slaves was steadily growing smaller. On certain estates of St Germain-des-Prés, they represented no more than ten per cent of the labour-force. In Champagne, on three *villae* of St Remigius of Rheims, they formed as little as eight, seven and four per cent of the total. We have travelled quite a distance from the proportion of twelve per cent typical of estates under the late Roman empire. No doubt about it, the category was in decline. Carolingian slaves possessed an economic status and for certain purposes a legal personality. We have seen them in the guise of *ministeriales*, traders, and bodyguards. We know of some who became bishops, for example, Ebbo, archbishop of Rheims, and Arn, archbishop of Salzburg, and of others who became counts, to the great fury incidentally of their contemporaries.

But once again the trend varied with the zones of civilisation. In the new Europe, the original freedmen sought royal or ecclesiastical protection. As usual, the quest for a protector was more urgent than total independence. Why bother about a few dues, symbolic or otherwise? For much of the time, as we shall see, they were no longer related to individuals, but rather to the land. Furthermore, as can be gleaned from reading the polyptychs, it was the peasants themselves, 'free men and *coloni*', who swore before the agents of the great landowner that they had paid in full everything they owed. The power of the master could not be too overbearing, otherwise they would have fled. Now this is not the case in northern Europe, during the Carolingian period. At that time, former freedmen, *coloni* and other peasants of ill-defined status entered into a state of dependence more or less advantageous according to the region, which would later correspond to the condition known as serfdom. In 941 at Cambrai, the distinction between slaves and dependent tenants was still being made. This evolution was much less rapid in Romanised Europe. In the southern cartularies, slaves of the Antique type continued to figure down to the middle of the eleventh century. There was an obvious tendency still to regard the *coloni* and other tenant-farmers as *mancipia*, slaves of all work. In 899, Gerald of Aurillac was content to abide by the rule dating from the reign of Augustus, incorporated into the Code of Justinian, of enfranchising no more than 100 slaves although he certainly possessed many more. As before, the enfranchisements were made *cum obsequio*, which meant that the former master

A peasant. Illustration to November, Scorpio, in a St Gallen manuscript of the *Martyrology of St Wandalbert* (Vatican Library).

retained all his patronal authority over the former slave. In addition, the rigidity of the Roman law was stiffened by the presence of Muslim slaves taken captive in war. In certain regions such as Catalonia and Latium, the final disappearance of slaves was delayed until the mid-tenth century, when with the land clearances the last of them become swallowed up in the free peasantry: there would no longer be any advantage in sticking close to their master. Elsewhere, in southern Italy or in Aquitaine, the slave of the Roman type, that is to say neither Slav, Muslim, nor foreigner, took even longer to disappear because of the legal conservatism characteristic of those countries.

Is it possible to be both free and poor?

Situated midway between the powerful noble patrons and the slaves with their sheltered existence were the freeholders in each county, the *pagenses* from whom we have derived the word peasant, and the *coloni*. In this society on the brink of expansion but which quickly succumbed, after 840, to the effects of violence, they had a choice between two solutions. They could make capital out of the conquests, enter into vassalage and rise a few points in the social scale. Or they could become a source of social disturbance, a class ready to sell its armed services to the highest bidder. On the other hand, if they fell into the hands of the powerful, they would do better to become tenants and lose the status of free men, or to seek the protection of an abbey. Perpetually ascending and descending like the Cartesian toy, the free man was doomed to experience all the vicissitudes of a society in the grip of countervailing pressures.

Despite the paucity of the documentation relating to this sector of the population, which must have constituted the greater part of rural society, it seems clear enough that the *coloni*, although officially free, were regarded as not much superior in status to slaves. It is true that the fiscal burdens affecting them and the remaining free peasants were on the decline, becoming customary, disappearing, or being swallowed up in other dues. Before long, liability to pay the land-tax would be the equivalent of servitude, all the more so since the Germanic elements were totally exempt. This explains why the word 'Frank' has given us the adjective *franc*, which means 'free'. From the Loire to the Rhine, all through the seventh and eighth centuries, these peasants can be found occupying small farms called *mansi*. This word, when it came into use around 620, could designate either an allod, a peasant's freehold property, or a tenement occupied by a domiciled slave (*casatus*) or by a *colonus* belonging to a large estate. Elsewhere, in the Midi, the word for this was *colonica* and the peasant was tied to it. It is true that in 802 the capitulary addressed to the *missi* indicates that certain *coloni* on fiscal or ecclesiastical estates were holding benefices or offices (*ministeria*) and formed part of their master's retinue. The economic situation of the *coloni* was therefore quite variable.

At all events, they would all be tenants of a *mansus* or a *colonica*, or of a *hufe* in Germanic country, or in England of a hide. This tenement was often defined as 'the land of a single family'. Its size was therefore reckoned sufficient, in theory, to the needs of a peasant household. In Italy, it was defined as the amount of land that a team of two oxen could plough in the course of a year. Its actual extent varied considerably according to the region and the properties of the soil. The difference was sometimes of the order of between twelve and 45 ha, in England of between sixteen and 48. On each stood the hut, usually thatched, which housed the peasant's family. These *coloni* were summoned annually to the royal host and to the count's court or *mallus*. We saw that if they occupied fewer than four *mansi*, they had to combine with others to make up that figure, so that one of them could depart. A few managed to keep a small allod on the side or even to obtain a precarial holding from an abbot or bishop. In the Ottonian empire, the *Leibeigne* were peasants possessing a certain freedom of movement, though it appears that they belonged in full ownership to the ecclesiastical landlord. From these dependants the lord recruited his craftsmen and commercial agents. In England, the *gesith* could be equated with the *colonus*, since he was tied to the estate and had no right to bequeath the land he occupied. With the *ceorl*, however, we broach the category of men living in complete freedom and who might just as well be patrons as craftsmen, goldsmiths, blacksmiths or merchants. They were not exempt from military service or from certain contributions, and when accused they could purge themselves in court through an oath supported by three co-jurors drawn from their own social group. Their *wergild* was conspicuously high: 200 shillings, the equivalent of 33 oxen. They were clearly in a position to add to their wealth and even to aspire to the nobility. In the Carolingian empire, their counterparts were the *franci*, the free men, or rather the *pagenses*. Generally speaking, they were the owners of allods equivalent to at least four *mansi* and a maximum of twelve. The threshold of wealth and nobility seems to have been crossed at something over 100 ha, since a capitulary of 805 ruled that anyone above this mark must come to the host with the equipment of an armoured horseman.

But alongside these middle-ranking proprietors, masters of some 50 ha, we find several other varieties of free men. A type unknown hitherto, the *hospitia*, appeared on uncultivated lands in the neighbourhood of existing cultivations. In Lombard Italy, free peasants concluded with great landowners a contract going by the name of *libellum*, which granted them a 29-year lease with the possibility of renewal, or even of extension over two or three generations. The term of 29 years was set to avoid the land passing into automatic ownership at the end of 30 years in accordance with the Roman law of prescription: even so, the advantages of these leases to petty proprietors were obvious. Again, the co-planting contract, which applied chiefly to vines, provided an excellent means of increasing the number of petty proprietors, because at the end of five years the new plot brought into cultivation was divided into two. Lastly, a large number of small cultivators eked out their income by hiring out their labour. At Corbie they tended the monks' garden in return for their food. At Prüm and at St Bertin, they were called prebendaries because they took their pay as daily rations. With these we come down to the level of the poorest of the free, the day-labourer rewarded in kind.

Symptoms of an impending upheaval

Peasants of every category enjoyed in addition the benefit of living in a village community or in an extended family. This did something to tone down the differences in relative wealth. The need for communal management of the pastures and wastelands made for solidarity; these peasant communities settled differences amongst themselves. There are clear traces of such communities in Leon, in Catalonia, where they survived intact into the eleventh century, in Provence and in Languedoc, in Burgundy and in Lombard Italy, where their assemblies were held at the door of the parish church. In the North, the strength of peasant communities in Frisia was such that they refused to pay danegeld to the Danes, having already handed over their share to King Louis the German, and yet managed to dislodge the enemy. In Saxony, the old communities remained intact while in the Ottonian empire the free men known as *Königsfreie*, former *coloni* attached to the soil, who answered to the jurisdiction of the *Vogt* (the Carolingian judge presiding in the court of the hundred), continued to be liable for land- and capitation-taxes, and before long, when mounted soldiers begin to eclipse the infantry, for a tax in commutation of military service. In this instance, the king's protection acted to preserve the status of peasant communities; elsewhere we see communities defending themselves, pleading their rights before the abbot of St Gall or even refusing, in 864, the tasks of carting marl or threshing that were demanded of them.

We therefore have to picture this world of free men as being in a state of utter confusion. In some places, especially in Spain, it aspired to a position near the top of the social scale, while in others its situation was deteriorating, either as the result of abuses of comital power (prolongation of military service beyond the due date, summons to courts held at too frequent intervals), or because of attempts by the great landowners to subdue the free men to their authority. It is therefore striking that the capitularies so often speak of the free men as 'poor'. It is clear that any free man who failed to obey the summons to the host was automatically condemned to a fine of 60 *solidi*. In consequence he was irretrievably ruined. The methods used by the great landowners of late Antiquity to convert a free peasant into a *colonus* were still being applied, as is proved by the many Carolingian capitularies and conciliar decrees which fulminate against the spoliation of small freeholders by the powerful. As in the Merovingian epoch, to be poor meant being free without having a protector in high places. After 840, the Church, on whose shoulders rested the material care of these newly-impoverished individuals, made increasing demands for the restitution of its own properties in order to have the wherewithal to feed them. Although a determined effort to maintain the system for the relief of the poor and infirm seems to have been made north of the Loire before 840, with the invasions the situation can only have got worse. Hopeless indebtedness after a bad harvest, the rapacity of judges and counts, the dangerous situation created by pillaging raids and men's fear of being carried off by pirates or Hungarians into slavery all served to precipitate numerous free peasants into the arms of the powerful or to drive them quite literally to take to the roads. Every day 4,000 poor would come to the abbey of St Riquier to be fed. At Corbie, everyone in need received a loaf and a half of bread (equivalent to 2.5 kg) intended as food for the day and for his journey. Burdens on this scale must have been impossible to sustain in the second half of the ninth century and the alms wrung from the powerful by excommunication or the fear of hell came nowhere near meeting the need. Included in the poor, therefore, were oppressed people of every type. To the impoverished and cheated peasantry must be added the young, the aged, the sick, the infirm, pilgrims far from home, foreigners such as the Irish driven from their country, indeed anyone in flight from the Vikings. It is not hard to see that the threat of being reduced to slavery made it more urgent than ever to seek a protector and to acquire if possible a privileged status. The conditions were therefore ripe for the development of the seigneurial regime. Freedom, which had been an undeniable social advantage during the period of Carolingian expansion, was becoming a drawback: hence the slide into serfdom during the eleventh century.

Once again we find those contradictions which are typical of a society in the throes of demographic revival and on the brink of expansion, which is then suddenly frozen by internal and external disorders. The fact that the period of peace was followed by a period of continuing violence accounts for the conflicts we saw developing between secular and regular clergy and between the great aristocratic families, and for the tendency toward upward social mobility, or its opposite, proletarisation, observable in the world of free men. The gradual disappearance of slaves is another astonishing feature of this era, which, in spite of regional differences, demands an examination of the agrarian economy in an effort to discover whether the violent social contrasts of the period were the result of a fundamentally penurious regime or of a genuine superfluity.

The land

The land still stood alone as the fundamental source of wealth. Now it seems from numerous indications that agricultural production increased at this period, possibly through a better use of wastelands, or because of the spread of the bipartite system of working large estates, or lastly as the result of technical improvements. It should be borne in mind, however, that the mass of data accessible to us from a handful of aristocratic sources relates to an infinitesimal fraction of the land (from two to at most ten per cent) and virtually ignores the rest, about which we need to know most.

Advances in husbandry

The rural landscape had altered hardly at all and the woods, the marshes, and the heathlands remained just as before. Equally conspicuous were the vast tracts of beech and oak forest which covered the Germanic regions added to the empire by Charlemagne. But it is noticeable that more efficient methods were being used to exploit their resources. The emperors paid close attention to the upkeep of their copses, 'forests' and fishponds. The capitulary *De villis* gives copious advice on the art of preserving game while keeping wild animals at bay. In May, the wolf-catchers were to dig pits or lay poisoned bait in order to trap the cubs. In autumn, military activity came almost to a standstill for the hunting season, in which everyone took part with such zest that accidents seem to have been unavoidable: thus in 884 king Carloman was mortally wounded in the course of a boar hunt. With the increase in the number of fast-days in the year (from 120 to 130), there is a greater consumption of fish, of which the most popular kinds seem to have been eels and trout. The monks of Bobbio received from their peasants a render of 500 eels each year, the monks of St Germain-des-Prés and of Corbie an annual quota of 200. The fishing of coastal and river waters produced in addition a plentiful supply of lamprey, sturgeon and salmon. The exploitation of animal resources appears to have been over-intensive, since the aurochs disappeared around this time, and soon afterwards the beaver, which is not mentioned after the ninth century.

The polyptychs will often be found to distinguish the *silva grossa* from the *silva minuta*. From this latter type of plantation, the coppice, would come the forest-products used in farming operations, wood for fence-posts and vine-stakes, leaf-litter for the animals and so on. Forests of sweet chestnuts, increasingly cultivated in Italy, began to be found outside the Mediterranean zone. The willows growing naturally along the river banks were carefully tended for the sake of the osiers needed to make baskets for winnowing and other purposes. Groves of beech and oak were often spared in preference to resinous trees which continued to be felled in order to extract pitch. There was in fact more to be gained by allowing the spread of leaf-bearing trees, providers of beechnuts and acorns for the rearing of pigs. Salt pork was still the main meat of the peasants. Rural communities were equally dependent on the *saltus* for their grazing lands, and in the absence of clear boundaries this

497

Reaping with the sickle in August. *Astronomical Notes* compiled at Salzburg between 809 and 818 (Vienna, Österreichische Nationalbibliothek).

involved them in frequent legal disputes with neighbouring great landowners. Everyone had need of grazing for sheep, reared for the sake of their wool, cheese, tallow and parchment. Cattle were reared chiefly as plough animals and were not often found roaming the pastures. The great importance of these silvo-pastoral products in complementing the food-supply and the correspondingly intense exploitation of the wilderness made it necessary, paradoxically enough, to protect it. After all, in southern Europe, these wastelands were still within the public domain! But even where their appropriation to private use had been condoned, Charlemagne, in his capitulary *De villis*, utters a word of warning: 'If there are places to be cleared, let them be cleared, but not so as to allow the fields to encroach on the woodland; and where woods should exist, they are not to be cut back immoderately or suffer damage.' This fear of seeing the balance between the *saltus* and the *ager*, between the wasteland and the tillage, upset in favour of the arable may appear curious. We learn from it, first, that the resources of the woodland were too important to be neglected, and second, that there was a constant tendency to encroach on them with land clearances.

The existence of the latter tendency in Carolingian Europe seems undeniable. The peasants of the abbey of Montier-en-Der were encouraged to use the technique of hedging off clearings in the forest. In Germany, the custom of *bifang* continued to be practised, and in some cases the alternatives were even spelled out in advance. A charter of Lothar II granted ownership of an uncultivated area in 867: the future owner had the choice of dividing it up into a hundred *mansi* or leaving it as grazing for 1,000 pigs. In Italy, the *gualdi publici*, the equivalent of the Carolingian *forestes*, were also under attack from free peasants or former *coloni*. But the trend was most obvious in Languedoc, southern Aquitaine, Catalonia and the Asturias. The Spanish emigrants received authority from the Carolingian kings to reclaim deserted public lands with entitlement to full ownership after 30 years of continuous occupation. These *aprisio* tenures eventually gave birth to a class of small rural freeholders, living in complete isolation on their allods. This is an instance of people descending by slow degrees from their over-populated mountain fastnesses to live in the plains. As an example of the reverse process we can point to the Auvergne, where from the late ninth century the excess of population in the all-too-fertile plain of the Limagne led to clearances on the *eremi*, deserted lands on the slopes above Sauxillanges and Brioude; admittedly, this was a region remote from the contemporary conflicts. In another over-populated region, the Cantabrian mountains, we find the same phenomenon and the same form of contract, here called the *presura* (the word is essentially the same), which guaranteed ownership in return for settlement on a vacant plot in order to reclaim it from the 'untamed wilderness' (*eremus squalidus*). In Galicia and northern Portugal, more than 1,400 neo-Visigothic place-names bear witness to this inflow of population, halted only temporarily by the Douro, in which men of all social conditions were merged. In general, however, it is clear that these initiatives belonged to particular regions. In other places they appear to have been insignificant. Land-hunger, even in the Carolingian era, was not intense; but neither was it negligible.

The results of our enquiry so far

Are we therefore to conclude that the overlapping *saltus* and *ager* produced a sufficiency of resources? At this point mention should be made of the existence of cultivated meadows, on which the hay was reaped in regular fashion, as in the picture for July to be seen in the Carolingian calendar now in Vienna. These seem to have been particularly extensive in the north of Western Francia, in Frisia and in England, regions where the rearing of cattle, sheep and horses was evidently most fully developed. In Frisia, it was usual at this period to describe farms as capable of supporting sixteen ewes, fifteen cows, twelve oxen, 40 sheep, whatever the case might be. Alcuin, when he wanted to flatter the bishop of Utrecht, coined the bizarre word 'vaccipotens', 'strong in cows'. On the imperial stud-farms, the overseers were exhorted to bring the colts indoors before 11 November. The *Mulomedicus*, a veterinary treatise dealing with beasts of burden and their ailments, figured in many a monastic library.

In essence, however, cultivated lands were reserved for the growing of cereals. In the Mediterranean countries, wheat and barley stood out as staple crops. In Western Europe, with its damper climate, the combination of rye and wheat was more common. In England, barley was more popular, together with oats, especially when it came to the making of ale. But cereals of the poorer sort continued to be grown in considerable quantities: millet and sorgho in the plain of the Po and Gascony, spelt in Francia. Lastly, the various pulses, beans, chickpeas, and lentils, formed an important class of their own, because they kept so well.

Cultivation would be still more intensive in three carefully protected areas: gardens, orchards and vineyards. The texts frequently refer to garden plots of various kinds, kitchen gardens or cottage gardens, or *setici* occupying less than a hectare. Kept in good condition by regular hoeing and manuring, they produced cabbages, turnips, leeks, parsnips, garlic, shallots and other types of vegetable. On the plan of the abbey of St Gall, whose layout was frequently imitated, the garden plots are labelled with the different varieties of green vegetable and culinary herbs recommended for planting. But horticulture was also practised for medicinal purposes, many of the plants grown by monks or by peasants on the

499

imperial domains being valued for their healing properties. Out of the 72 species recommended in the capitulary *De villis* for planting on the imperial domains, only one third are of culinary interest. Orchards are less well documented and may have been quite small. At St Gall the orchard was located in the cemetery. The fruit-trees mentioned – apple, pear, plum, medlar, bay, chestnut, fig, quince, peach, hazel, almond, mulberry and walnut – could not all have been present in quantity and there may have been only one of each species; here again, allowance has to be made for climatic conditions. Cultivation of one type of tree on its own appears not to have been contemplated. The one exception to this rule is the olive, unknown in Catalonia, but starting to progress up the Rhône as far as the Donzère. Cultivation of the vine, on the other hand, whether in the arborescent or low-growing variety, was becoming ever more widely diffused. Everyone, from the bishop and the aristocratic landowner to the free peasant, joined in the competition to cultivate the vine as far north as possible, in order to produce an appreciable quantity of wine for consumption. In the group of farms dependent on the royal fisc of Annapes there was one, *Treola*, engaged in the production of wine: 'Treola' is on the site of modern Lille (which preserves a trace of its old name at Notre-Dame de la Treille), where today one would be hard put to it to make vines germinate. Vineyards were so important that in the partition of Verdun in 843 those on the left bank of the Rhine were assigned to Louis the German, because there were none in Eastern Francia: hence the otherwise inexplicable line followed by the frontier. Since wine was the only real stimulant available at the period, everyone made prodigious efforts to procure it. The vineyards of the monks of Redon stretched as far as the Vilaine. The transfer of the bishopric of Tongres to Liège was due in large part to the vines growing on the slopes above the Meuse. The solution adopted by other Flemish and Austrasian abbeys was to purchase vine-bearing plots at Laon in Champagne, or even on the shores of the Italian lakes. Article eight of the capitulary *De villis* is entirely concerned with the care of wine-presses, casks and other wine-making equipment on the imperial domains. To sum up, the estates of the wealthy could be made to produce everything that was needed and the ideal of autarchy subscribed to in the Carolingian sources was not beyond the bounds of possibility. But was it realisable in practice?

Whatever the mode of interaction between its two parts, the great estate could not in fact pursue its proclaimed ideal of an autarchic existence, because it was obliged to support what we would nowadays call the service sector. Strictly speaking, moreover, it was not self-sufficient when it came to salt and iron, which had to be purchased from outside. The great estate was therefore compelled to exceed the norms of subsistence agriculture by means of technical innovations and by adding to its productivity. At Corbie, we come across six smelters and six blacksmiths engaged in the manufacture of iron ingots, while at Celle-des-Bordes 32 slaves are required to produce a ton of iron each year, enough to make upward of 1,000 hoes. True, much of the iron produced would be consumed in the manufacture of weapons, but this itself suggests that Charlemagne's ban on the export of swords was inspired by considerations that were as much internal as strategic. Among the buildings on the fisc of Annapes were five mills and four breweries. Dotted about the estates of St Germain-des-Prés were 83, perhaps 84, watermills. At Corbie, there were watermills

Farming calendar: pruning fruit-trees in April, ploughing in June of the fallow to be sown in September (note the wheelless plough), grape-harvesting in October (provenance as for preceding illustration).

driven by three or anything up to six wheels. Irminon boasts of having installed seven watermills and renovated four. Unfortunately, this does not mean that the man-powered mill has disappeared, but merely that efforts were being made to economise on manpower in places where the people in charge, aware of what was needed and attentive readers of the Classical agronomists, were intent on running the large estate to the best advantage.

The heavy plough, equipped with a mould-board and drawn by a team of six or eight oxen, is attested in the Ile-de-France. In Frisia, archaeological researches have revealed the presence of asymmetrical and symmetrical furrows, proof that two types of ploughing implement were employed: the light Antique *aratrum*, and another implement either of Slav (compare the Moravian ploughshares of the eighth century) or of Germanic origin (cited in the Lombard Edict of Rothari, in 683, and in the Alamannic code, in 725, under the name *plum*, the German *Pflug*, or English 'plough'). Now, the more northerly the clime, the higher the proportion of hay meadows in relation to arable, which would certainly be a factor in providing fodder for the oxen needed to draw these ploughs. In addition, the heavy plough, if used in the correct way, could be expected to accentuate the economic forward-ness of the regions north of the Loire, for it would be the only implement capable of bringing into cultivation heavy soils composed of alluvial deposits or sediments of glacial clay. As if

501

by chance, as late as the nineteenth century the limitation of the heavy plough to northerly regions points precisely to the countries which profited from this innovation: Galicia, Francia, England, Germany and the lower plain of the Po. Reference should lastly be made to the appearance of the horseshoe, mentioned for the first time in 855, and to the development of the neck-collar as depicted in the Trier Apocalypse of the year 800.

Certain improvements are to be observed in the treatments given to the soil. In the month of June, according to the illustration in the Vienna calendar, the bare ground was ploughed. However, we saw the difficulties encountered by Charles the Bald when he tried to impose on the peasants as a public duty the task of carrying marl to fertilise the fields. On the other hand, carting manure was among the corvées on the estate of Viel-Saint-Rémy, and litter for the animals was demanded of tenants at Gerson. And we find Charlemagne giving order for compost to be spread on the meadows and arable. Lastly there was the triennial rotation of crops, perhaps already hinted at in a charter of St Gall in 763, and in Thuringia in 783. It appears to have been taken for granted in the capitulary *De villis* and in the polyptych of Montier-en-Der. This system seems not to have been exported in the ninth and tenth centuries anywhere outside France and Germany. Used in conjunction with leguminous crops, which keep the nitrogen in the soil and maintain its fertility, the triennial cycle could have increased yields by as much as 33 per cent: a considerable improvement, which would explain the abatement of land-hunger and the fact that land-clearances progressed so slowly, except on the pioneering frontiers of Spain and Italy, precisely those places where the light plough and the biennial crop rotation would still be in use. So it is difficult to agree with the contention of certain historians that yields were likely to have been low. The least pessimistic of them estimate the average yield at 3:1. Now, we have Columella's word for it that a yield of 4:1 would represent a very bad year. Is it conceivable that our great lay and ecclesiastical landowners, with copies of Columella and Palladius in their libraries, would have been content with, or regarded as normal, so poor a result? What needs to be stressed is that the pessimistic estimates were arrived at from the *Brevium exempla* of Annapes, from which it would appear, given the quantities of cereals mentioned, that the ratio was in the region of 1.6:1. Now, as is abundantly clear from the epithet *conlaboratus* applied to these harvests, we are dealing here with only a part of the estate's total output. The capitulary *De villis* expressly orders stewards to divide the harvests on fiscal estates into several parts, allocating one share (the *conlaboratus*) to the king, the next to the overseer of the army, another to the day-labourers, a fourth to the women's workshops, and so on. Each share is to be the subject of a separate list. This and other examples of the minuteness of the accounting on imperial and ecclesiastical estates, and of the tendency to place items under diverse headings, should warn us to regard a given set of figures not as an infallible reflection of the total output of an estate, but rather as representing a fraction of the landowner's revenues in kind. In this instance, the yields would surely have been in the region of between five or seven to one, allowing for the quantities of corn presumably accounted for in documents which have not survived. This would give us an average crop of between ten and fourteen hundredweight per hectare, at first sight a staggering figure. And even if the work on the demesne was done in a somewhat perfunctory and spasmodic fashion by peasants reluctantly fulfilling their labour obligations, we can be sure that their own tenures would have been zealously dug, turned and hoed so as to produce the maximum yield. Vineyards are a case in point. On the vineyards of St Germain-des-Prés, the monks demanded from the slaves and *coloni* with tenures containing vines a fixed amount of the product. The latter therefore had an incentive to produce more, in order to sell the surplus. The monastic demesne produced an average 30 hl to the hectare. On the tenures the average was slightly higher. Each year, after deducting what was consumed on the spot, 6,000 hectolitres of wine remained to be sold by the monks, but on top of that we have to allow for whatever was produced by the peasants, say a round total of 10,000 hl.

The Carolingian farmer was therefore able to provide for his own wants and in addition had real surpluses to dispose of. The great estate was doing the job envisaged by its promoters. This prosperity was reflected in a noticeable and no doubt welcome augmentation to the monks' daily ration. The allowance equivalent to about 330 g of bread and half a litre of wine prescribed in the *Rule* of St Benedict was increased in Carolingian times to more than one-and-a-half kilos of bread and a litre and a half of wine. To this could be added a cheese ration of 100 g, and more than 200 g of pulses served as a mash. This was not a diet only for the privileged rich, since the lay inmates of great monastic houses such as Corbie, St Germain, St Denis and Soissons received the same rations, with the addition of at least 100 g·of bacon or salt pork. This ample diet, which calls for explanation, is not to be described as near starvation or as the fate of populations in the grip of famine. The wide variety of available resources, combined with the efficacy of the great estates where the system was in operation, placed certain regions in an advantageous position. The cartage duties imposed on peasants to transport wine or cereal to river ports or urban markets prove that considerable quantities were available for sale. Some of the peasants of St Germain-des-Prés were required to journey as far as Quentovic. There can be no doubt that a sustained effort at agricultural production, rewarded with yields superior to those of late Antiquity, was finding its ultimate destiny in a market economy, at least as regards the large-scale undertakings brought to our attention by these stray shafts of light.

Development of the 'domanial system'

Hailed at one time as an original invention, later regarded as an imitation of late Antique methods of estate management, according to the first theory in the throes of expansion during the eighth century, according to the second the relic of an earlier age, the bipartite 'system' of exploiting the soil, the 'domanial' system, made an impression which lasted throughout the first half of the Middle Ages. However else we may regard it, the system was clearly the result of the problems posed to the master of the land when his servile labour-force started to disintegrate and his possessions were dispersed.

Three types of solution were applied almost at one and the same time in northern Gaul and Lombard Italy. The first consists of the parcel of cleared land called in Flemish *akker* (presumably the old Latin word *ager*) in the middle of a wilderness rich in woodland

503

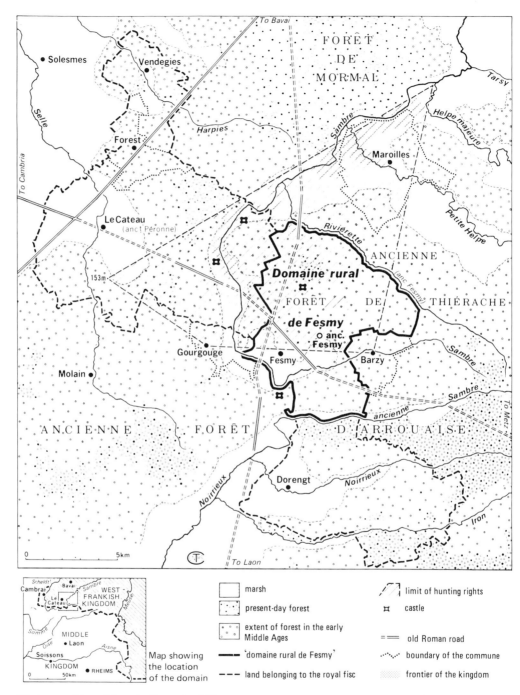

17 An uncultivated domain: Fesmy in 845

resources which went directly to the proprietor: in Italy these have been called 'pioneer homesteads'. The second solution consisted of blocks of arable fields, pieced together by sale or exchange, called in Flanders *kutter* (Latin *cultura*); the owner was also the proprietor of tenements, occupied by *coloni*, lying in the wooded or marshy zone, where communal usage formed a link between the occupants. The central portion was worked for the master's direct benefit by slaves (*mancipia*) with the aid of a few days' work each year from the tenants. This connection between the lord's part (the 'demesne') and the tenements was made still more explicit in the third solution adopted, which derived from the second. Here the peasants' holdings, the *curtes*, called *gewanne* in Flanders, lay very close to the lord's dwelling. The area he cultivated for himself, his demesne, was made up of long fields devoted to cereal crops and sometimes known as the *condamines* ('belonging to the lord'). It was tilled by slaves and by the tenement-holders, the latter being required to work there on a stipulated number of days, sometimes between one and three days each week. Wherever this last solution was adopted, it was invariably a case of heavy soils, composed of alluvial deposits or clays, which necessitated the use of the heavy plough with its iron ploughshare.

Furthermore, this new bipartite system of exploiting a large estate appears to have developed at much the same time in the south and west of England. The laws of Ine at the end of the seventh century refer explicitly to large estates whose lay lords enjoyed the fruits of lands occupied by tenement-holders, lands, it seems, which the tenants had cleared. The latter, the *gesiths*, were classed as free *coloni*. They were often confused with the *geburs*, slaves domiciled on the same type of land as that occupied by the *gesiths*, which may be referred to as *gesithland*, *gaffoland* (tax-bearing land) or even 'outland', to distinguish it from the 'inland', the lord's demesne. It is not clear whether agricultural labour on the inland was demanded from the tenants, but they would certainly have paid the dues and former taxes to their lord. There are therefore strong indications that the 'manorial system', as it was later called, was invented a little while before the proclamation of the laws of Ine, king of Wessex.

When and how was this organic link, in the form of the duty to perform so many days' service, forged between the demesne and the tenements? The second type of large estate, with the arable fields in large blocks, appears to have been inaugurated in the second century on the imperial estates of Africa, where the *coloni* with tenements owed the overseer between one and six days' work each year. On an isolated estate of the Church of Ravenna, towards the end of the sixth century, three tenants were obliged to give their services for anything between one and six days a week, but this seems to have been quite exceptional. The generalisation of the principle was probably due to Dagobert, when at some time between 623 and 635 he ratified the laws of the Alamans and the Bavarians. He asserted it as a rule that on all fiscal and ecclesiastical estates the slaves worked for three days on their master's land, the demesne, while the *coloni*, in addition to rendering their customary dues, were obliged to carry out some particular task (later called *riga*, 'furrow') in the landowner's fields, meadows or vineyards. While there was nothing unusual in setting royal slaves to work, just as they had always done, on the lord's estate, the extension of labour-dues to the *coloni* inaugurated a new method of exploiting arable lands, one which offset the shortfall in slave labour and sought to replace it with a colonate compounded of former slaves, freedmen, free men of the old style and the newly enfranchised. Thanks to their flexibility, these three potential solutions were widely adopted, in a manner which varied with the region. Although the nobles in Austrasia took advantage of the decline in royal power to apply the corvée system to their own lands, the third type of great estate was the one that made most headway, thanks to the close control which the war-leader could exercise on his *servi ministeriales*, the semi-free followers he installed as his stewards. The laws of the Alamans, written down again in 717–19, and of the Bavarians (744–8) bear witness to the spread of these large-scale properties and to the heavier burden of labour-dues being imposed on the *coloni*. In Wessex it was probably much the same. On the other hand, in the valley of the Po and in the Sabina, the second type of estate, with its looser connection between the demesne and the tenements, was more usual because the new lands won in the agrarian expansion were widely scattered. Elsewhere, in southern Gaul, in north-western Spain, in central and southern Italy, the estate of the first type, consisting of fields carved out of the *saltus*, which at bottom had little to distinguish it from the traditional estate of late Antiquity, lingered on and multiplied, as is shown by the place-names in Aquitaine and Galicia with the ending -herm or -hermas. All in all, this 'invention' of a bipartite great estate gave the best results outside the lands of the old *romanitas*, in regions where the distinction between slave and free had become blurred, and above all where the master controlled the levers of military power, as among the Lombards, the Austrasian Franks and the Anglo-Saxons.

The third type, called *villa* in our documents, was an agricultural enterprise, usually conducted by kings or churchmen, which by adding field to field aimed to create large units in which the tenements lay as near as possible to the demesne, to facilitate the exaction of labour-dues from the tenants. They covered a minimum of 100 ha, extending in several cases to several thousand. Part and parcel of the demesne, or 'lord's *mansus*' as it may be called, were large fields of arable, meadows, woods and wastes, not forgetting vineyards. The focal point was provided by the farm buildings, the *curtis*, complete with granaries, storehouses, mills and so on. The labour force of the demesne was composed of slaves living in houses adjacent to this court. Other slaves were domiciled on nearby servile *mansi* which they cultivated on their own account, but were constantly being called away by the master or his overseer to work on the demesne. Now, since their numbers were inadequate when the heavy seasonal works of ploughing, hay-making, harvesting and the vintage came round, it was necessary at such times to call on the *coloni*, who occupied so-called free *mansi* and paid rent for their land, as it were, by means of various labour services. They might be required, for example, to cultivate some specified part of the demesne, the *ansange*, or, as at St Bertin, to perform the service known as *riga*, which meant ploughing a certain number of furrows. In other instances, they owed a specified number of days or 'nights' to the demesne, to be spent in repairing fences, carting loads of wine or corn to a given destination, or in the case of women, in spinning or weaving in the women's workroom. We should mention lastly the dues in kind or coin, which were universal and not unique to this type of large estate: renders of eggs, capons, laths or shingles, sucking-pigs or hams, or a few *deniers* for the customary tax or in commutation of some formerly compulsory obligation. Our knowledge of this system is chiefly derived from the famous polyptychs of northern Francia: St Germain-des-Prés, St Bertin, St Remigius of Rheims, Montier-en-Der and Prüm, all lying in the region between the Seine and the Rhine.

But behind the apparent simplicity of the system lay a much more complex situation and the possibility of wide variations from one estate to the next. Deviations from the theoretical model were the rule rather than the exception. In the polyptych of St Germain-des-Prés, compiled early in the ninth century, the area of the servile *mansi* in terms of ploughlands ranged from 0.25 to 9.25 ha and of the free manses from 1.5 to 15 ha. If certain *mansi* were indeed occupied by a single family, others were divided between several households, while several *mansi* were occupied by a single *colonus*, and others again are recorded as vacant. In addition, some of the servile tenures were in the hands of free men, and *vice versa*. For this reason the dues gradually came to be measured by the status of the *mansus*, and had to be rendered by the occupant irrespective of his personal status. This serves to explain the levelling out of the peasant condition around the colonate and the appearance of an intermediate form of dependence which can only be described as non-freedom. These discrepancies, occurring in the heart of the region which saw the blossoming of the bipartite estate in its classic form, can only be explained by a problem which the masters encountered when it came to operating their system: the difficulty of making peasants move to less desirable *mansi* and of motivating others, who would rather remain on a *mansus* subdivided by inheritance than better themselves. The resistance of peasants to this reorganisation was at the root of the innumerable variations.

This 'system' therefore approached its 'ideal' state only in regions recently converted to arable cultivation where the tenements and demesnes could be conceived and laid out in a more generous and compact fashion right from the start, as in the north of Western Francia or in the new lands of Bavaria and Franconia. Elsewhere, it was never possible to complete the necessary realignment, and often the nomenclature applicable to the former plots of land shows through: in the Beauvaisis, for example, we come across a spacious kitchen garden (*seticus*) converted into demesne! In spite of these difficulties, this way of organising large estates, with its physical link between the demesne and the *mansi*, was imitated throughout the Carolingian realm, with some adaptation to local conditions. At St Remigius of Rheims, certain peasants described as *forenses* were callously left out of the system. In Maine, Anjou and the Touraine, plots of land resulting from past land-clearances by slaves were transformed into *mansi*. A glance through the royal charters issued by Charles the Bald suffices to show that under him the regime spread to the regions between the Seine and the Loire. But it stopped short of Brittany, and was not found south of the Loire: it left the Loire at Cosne, skirted round the Morvan, and in Burgundy progressed only as far as Mâcon, although it was typical of central and northern Lotharingia. This degree of expansion corresponds exactly to the zone covered by the *missatica*, where Carolingian authority was at its most effective. To all appearance, the diffusion of great estates of this type met with political encouragement, perhaps with a view to the co-ordination of fiscal and ecclesiastical resources – and hence the resources of the nobles in the service of the Carolingian State. The obvious economic advantages would be a natural spur to efforts at making the system general. It should not be supposed, however, that the regime applied to every inch of the land: we have ample proof that the small freeholding remained in the majority, even in the regions most affected. The simple fact is that the large estate of this type had its political uses in the machinery of government: to provide supplies for the troops, benefices for vassals, honour for the counts, food for the poor, and so on.

The system is therefore likely to have been most conspicuous wherever the political influence of the king was mediated directly. There is clear evidence of this in Anglo-Saxon England, where, following the struggles against the Danes, we find a tautening of the links between the demesne and the tenements. On a manor in Hampshire, for example, the *ceorls* who occupied hides paid the lord fourpence a year for every hide, together with renders of ale, corn and barley; they ploughed two acres on the demesne and sowed it with their own seed, cut the hay on rather less than the same amount of meadow, and were obliged to make themselves available each week (except on three occasions in each year) for compulsory agricultural services on the demesne. In the past, only the *geburs* and the *gesiths* would have been subject to these constraints. Conversely, where royal power was exercised at one remove, as in the sub-kingdoms, this Carolingian type of large estate gave way to one or other of the two types described earlier. In Aquitaine, large properties were made up of several separate areas under direct cultivation, called the seigneurial or head-*mansi*, and of a multiplicity of scattered *mansi*, often lying a considerable distance away. There is nothing to link the former with the latter. Again, in Germany, the *curtis* as a rule was merely the place where dues were collected. The co-existence of the two sectors, demesnes and tenements, is also noticeable in the parts of Italy characterised by land clearances: the lower Po valley and the Sabina. Elsewhere, while slaves cultivated the demesne, free peasants occupying tenements on contractual leases, the *libellarii*, were required to hand over a share of the harvest to the master, and sometimes owed him one to three days' agricultural service a year in addition. In Italy, arrangements for the conduct of great estates were thus considerably more flexible than in Francia. The *casa colonica*, the peasant's tenement, could never become overcrowded since as yet no move had been made towards the reconstitution or concentration of estates. The resistance of the peasants was too strong, the political power too weak.

New trade

The point has been reached when it becomes possible to observe the local economy gravitating towards the now reviving commercial economy, especially in the key areas of the Po plain, Francia, Frisia and England, and to trace the development of a rudimentary market economy, sparked off perhaps by the urban revival, or perhaps by the existence of a monetary system which, in conjunction with new international trade-routes, had become uniform throughout the known European world.

Attack on a town fortified in Roman style: the embattled people of David, illustration from the *Utrecht Psalter* (Utrecht, Bibliotheek der Rijksuniversiteit). The Psalter's illustrators, who worked under the direction of Ebbo, librarian of Louis the Pious and archbishop of Rheims, were stylistically much indebted to the Hellenistic tradition, but this does not detract from the originality of their technique.

Urban redevelopment

One of the first tasks undertaken by Pippin the Short was to prepare the way through the capitulary of 744 for the creation of rural markets in each *vicus*. Following this lead, they multiplied with great rapidity. Basic necessities would be exchanged through the medium of a single small coin, the *denier* (*per denarata*, an expression at the root of the modern French *denrée*, 'what is purchased for a denier'). These rural markets were so successful that Charles the Bald, in 864, tried to limit their number. Other markets were growing up alongside towns, in particular the wine-fairs held at Troyes, at Chappes, close to Bar-sur-Seine, and at St Denis, where the fair began each year on the saint's feast-day, 9 October. In Germany, the kings were lavish in giving authorisation for the creation of ports and markets. A wooden stake (*stäpl*) would be planted next to a circular earthwork, as in the Slav *grody*, or on the site of an old town, or even on a beach. The port of Étaples owes its name to this custom, as does the French word *étape* (stage), which originally signified 'place of exchange'. The phenomenon was so widespread that it can be taken as supplementary proof of an increase in the supply of products for trade.

All this had an explosive effect on the towns. Reference has already been made to the number of churches, abbeys and cathedrals that were built or rebuilt in the eighth and ninth centuries. After the council of Aachen, the living-quarters of the canons had to be reorganised, which meant finding space inside each cathedral city for their cloister and dwellings. As a result, the Antique towns underwent a process of remodelling. Often the opportunity was taken to demolish the encircling walls dating from the third century and

509

to incorporate their masonry into new buildings. In addition, the alteration to the liturgy entailed the abolition of the multiple wayside shrines of Merovingian times in favour of agglomerations housed under one vast roof. At Lyons, Leidrad repaired the roofs of St John and St Stephen, enlarged his episcopal palace, built the cloister for the canons, and restored two churches and three monasteries. Metz, Arras, Rheims, Le Mans and Vienne were visibly in the throes of expansion. Suburbs populated by merchants shot up outside the old ramparts. Metz had 24 churches, of which seventeen were extra-mural. Quite soon, the church-builders were seized with a passion for enlargement. Whereas Merovingian churches would rarely exceed twenty metres in length, the first church at Reichenau, already 21 m long in 724, was extended in 746 to a length of 43 m. St Just of Lyons, after its rebuilding by Agobard, reached a length of 60 m. Cologne cathedral, begun in 800, got to 94.5 m; Fulda, 39 m long in 744, had grown by 842 to a length of 98 m. St Gall, lastly, judging by its plan and the results of archaeological investigation, set the record with 102 m. Later, around 820–30, this craze for the gigantesque came to an end, starved of new financial resources. The cathedral at Hildesheim, built between 852 and 872, measures a mere 60 m. We are met with the same dichotomy as on so many previous occasions: expansion up to the middle of the ninth century, then a slowing down.

But the point to bear in mind is that the old towns were taking on a new lease of life. At Rome, between the time of Hadrian I (died 795) and Leo IV (died 852), the popes restored or rebuilt more than twenty churches. In Asturian–Leonese Spain, between the time of Ordoño I, around 860, and Ramiro II, around 940, 24 towns recaptured from the Muslims were completely repopulated with Christians from the mountains, most notably Astorga, Burgos and Avila. In England, the towns of Roman Britain had become bishoprics – Canterbury, Rochester, London, Winchester, Dorchester, Leicester and York. But they were soon overtaken by the ports, the *wics*, and above all the *burhs*, which from the reign of Alfred had the dual character of fortified towns and markets. The emergence of new towns was equally characteristic of northern France. Starting from the port at the mouth of the river Aa, a commercial settlement spread itself out at the foot of the two abbeys of St Bertin and St Omer. On the Scheldt, Ghent gradually took shape, first around the monasteries of St Peter on Mont Blandin and St Bavo, later around a castle built about 900; upstream, an imperial fisc gave birth to Valenciennes. At Regensburg, where the bishopric was founded in 739, the merchant quarter of St Emmeran became joined to the original nucleus in 917.

The Scandinavian invasions obviously put a brake on this urban revival. Townsmen who had made gaping holes in their ramparts had to make haste to repair them. In 869, Charles the Bald ordered the towns to look to their fortifications. As a first step suburbs were fenced round with palisades and wooden forts, but before long a stone wall encased abbeys such as St Vaast at Arras, St Remigius at Rheims and St Martial at Limoges. At St Omer, after 879 the two abbeys sheltered behind a single rampart. The bishop of Metz rebuilt the town's Roman walls, including one of the external churches. At Troyes, after the burning of 887, the population regrouped inside the rebuilt Gallo-Roman ramparts. In Provence, by comparison, the effects were wholly negative, with suburbs and towns such as Fréjus and Cimiez becoming deserted. The same was true of the Germanic timber-built ports of

Hamwih, Quentovic and Dorestad, where the burnings and pillagings did irremediable damage. In the end, despite temporary recoveries, all three were abandoned, chiefly because they were merely mushroom growths, without durable foundations, which had been called into existence by a primitive type of expansion. They had vanished, by the beginning of the tenth century, for the same reasons that Haithabu (Hedeby), although defended by a solidly-constructed earthwork, was gradually deserted in favour of Schleswig, seat of a bishopric and a new town in the proper sense. In general, therefore, the urban awakening had come to a standstill. But by no means everything that had been accomplished was lost and the stagnation which followed is not to be equated with a decline.

Elimination of gold

In this first, short-lived, urban upsurge, as in the revival or initiation of trade, the role of the monetary medium appears to have been crucial. After a brief recapitulation, it will require careful examination.

It should first be pointed out that the deflationist strait-jacket imposed by the monetary system of the late Roman empire was prised open as early as the seventh century by the trading initiatives of the Frisians and Anglo-Saxons. For the purchase of the bulky or trifling everyday articles which formed their stock-in-trade, the gold standard was becoming less and less appropriate. And indeed, after a period around 630–50 when the moneyers of Dorestad minted imitations of the Merovingian *trientes*, the decline of Frankish influence gave the Frisians a chance to innovate. Almost at the same time as their Anglo-Saxon rivals, between 650 and 660, they began to mint the silver coins known as *sceattas*, from the Old English *sceatt* (cf. German *Schatz*, treasure); a few carried runic inscriptions. Around 730–40, the zone in which these coins were discovered exactly matched the sphere of Frisian commercial influence: England, northern Gaul, the valleys of the Meuse and the Rhine, Frisia and Denmark. *Sceattas* also turn up as far afield as the mouths of the Loire and the Gironde, and even in Provence. Not to be outdone, and thanks to the reactivation of the silver-mines at Melle in Poitou, moneyers in the Merovingian kingdom launched their own silver coin: the *denier*. Weighing approximately 1.23 g, it finally drove out the Antique gold coinage, which in any case was being steadily debased. The last gold coins were minted at Marseilles around 690 to 700, at a time when the denier had already made its appearance, about 670. Eventually only Muslim Spain and Lombardy were left adhering to the gold standard. In the former, gold *dinars* analogous in weight and fineness to the Byzantine *numisma* were issued; in the latter, where the royal monopoly of minting remained intact, gold continued to be minted because of the region's economic links with Byzantium. And indeed, whereas Byzantine coins disappear after 670 from hoards in Gaul, they continue to be present in those found in the plain of the Po.

The advantages of the new silver currency were manifold. With a lower purchasing-power than that of the gold coinage, thanks to the ratio of 1:12 between the price of the two metals, the silver currency made it possible to buy things in smaller quantities. Whereas the

511

solidus or the *triens* had forced the peasant into selling his grain surpluses in bulk merely to pay the land-tax, with a penny he would be able to purchase a pig or the measure of corn he needed. Whereas in the sixth century the use of minted gold could produce catastrophic price-falls and equally dizzying rises by exaggerating the contingent factors in the economy, from the seventh century the silver currency permitted prices to rise or fall more slowly in sympathy with a less concentrated demand in terms of time and volume. Lastly, the lower purchasing-power of the monetary unit was largely compensated by the increase in the number of people using the new coinage. The *denier*, it is true, would be of no help in buying an egg or a loaf of bread, since no fractions of it were issued. But this was not the problem confronting society at a time when transactions took place within the framework of an extended peasant household or by barter. What mattered was the opening up of the money economy to a whole mass of producers and consumers for their direct use. In consequence, the *sceatta* and the *denier* permitted what was certainly an important increase in the volume of exchanges, in the number of customers and in the speed at which coins circulated. By the same token, their numbers can hardly have been adequate, as is proved by their continual devaluation under the early Carolingians. But this at least proves that deflation had finally given way to inflation and that the expansion had begun to take effect.

Here again, the influence of Charlemagne was to be decisive, even if he did no more than generalise the earlier solutions. Before Pippin III, the *denier* was depreciating in quality and fell to a weight of 1.10 g. The first aim of the king was to regain control over minting and to issue coins of good quality. In 751, a new *denier* of 1.23 g made its appearance. From now on, twelve deniers, not 40, make one *solidus*. Later, while the king was struggling to eliminate private mints, the weight of the *denier* was raised to 1.30 g. On becoming ruler of Italy, Charlemagne phased out its gold coinage. Finally, when issuing the capitulary of Frankfurt in 793–4, he apparently decided to imitate the heavy silver coin minted by Offa (Offa's penny) and launched a new coin weighing 1.70 g. This was paralleled by a complete recasting of the system of weights and measures. The barley-grain, the Germanic unit of weight, was abandoned in favour of the wheat-grain, the Roman unit, heavier by 0.005 g, which pushed the pound-weight up to 409 g. At the same time, a new unit of currency, the *obole*, equivalent to half a *denier*, made an appearance. Under Louis the Pious, another revaluation, around 829–35, brought the *denier* up to 1.75 g. Later, under Charles the Bald – although the monopoly of mintage had been fully recovered – as a measure against counterfeiting, the king announced, in the Edict of Pîtres of 864, his intention of restricting issues to nine mints. At the same time, the *denier* was reduced to 1.50 g. But the reform failed and under his successors the tendency of the weight to drift downwards was resumed. In the tenth century, *deniers* of the 'immobilised' type of Charles the Bald weighed around 1.30 g. Private minting started up again as early as 884–7 at Corbie, and between 900 and 910 with the coinage of the dukes of Aquitaine; the territorial rulers followed suit. On the other hand, the Ottonian empire and the Anglo-Saxon kingdom continued to keep central control of the coinage while still adhering to the Carolingian system.

Silver triumphant

This brief sketch of monetary trends calls for explanation. The triumph of the monometallic currency based on silver was no accident. Its low purchasing-power permitted the proliferation of rural markets. Furthermore, these silver *deniers* were minted in enormous numbers. As Jan Dhondt has pointed out, the 230,000 silver *dirhams* discovered in Scandinavia and Russia corresponds to the capital of some half-dozen 'Varangian' or 'Russian' merchants, while the 60,000 pounds of silver handed over in danegelds to the Vikings by Charles the Bald would represent the grand total of 14,400,000 *deniers*. The study of die-links is still more revealing. On the basis of the 5,000 known dies used by the mints of King Burgred of Mercia (852–74), it has been deduced that more than 50 million pennies were struck. The Ide hoard, found in the Netherlands and dating from 850, with its 112 pennies, points to at least ten million coins in circulation. From this it appears that we are indeed in a period of economic recovery, since the increase in coins was presumably connected with an increase of supply to the markets. But why in that case was the *denier* twice revalued? Why was there this apparent return to a deflationist monetary policy at the risk of the economic revival? Perhaps we have to see this as a consequence of the variations in price of the precious metals on the international market. The gold–silver ratio in the West was 1:12. In the Byzantine and Muslim East where gold *solidi* and gold *dinars* were being struck, and later in Spain, where from 929 the silver *dirham* was replaced by the gold *dinar*, the State caused the price of gold bullion to rise at the expense of silver. The prices of silver bullion were therefore lower in the East than in the West. The international merchants, Italian or Jewish, who regularly visited Alexandria, could therefore indulge in two types of speculation. They might buy silver at a ratio of 1:15, for example, and resell it in the West for minting as *deniers* at a rate of 1:12. In this way they made a profit on the weight of silver and in the number of *deniers*, before the reform of 794. Or they might prefer to import *dinars* and sell them at the international price against silver bullion, receiving the higher European price; their profit in that case would come from the difference in the price of silver bullion between West and East. With their horror of speculation, the Carolingian emperors would prefer in these circumstances to bring the nominal value of the *denier* into line with its intrinsic silver value and thus to revalue. This policy did not put a damper on exchanges in spite of the increase in purchasing-power, because the gold coinage was making a momentary comeback for use in very large transactions.

For there is reason to believe that gold coins called *mancusi* (not to be confused with the handful of prestige gold coins struck in 814 or 815 by Louis the Pious) were current in Italy, Francia and England. Eberhard, marquess of Friuli, in his will of 865, bequeathed 100 of them to one of his sons. Some were struck by Offa (757–96). They were imitations of the Muslim *dinar*. For what it is worth, the Arab word *manqush* means 'engraved'. This circulation of gold coins was probably confined to the wealthiest individuals in the empire, and the coins were doubtless more often hoarded than put into circulation. Judging by the texts and the distribution of finds, they seem at any rate to have been connected with the zone most active in commercial exchanges: Italy–Frisia–England. But the finds are far from numerous. Out of 36, only six relate to the period 750–850. These therefore fall within the limits of the era of prosperity which we have postulated, in which the quantity of products being exchanged would necessitate the return to gold for certain transactions. A further seven finds, ranging in date from 880 to 950 and discovered in coastal areas, are attributable to Viking raids. Therefore Muslim gold made only a very small contribution to the Carolingian economy, serving merely as an adjunct but anticipating the role it would play in the twelfth and thirteenth centuries. Furthermore, when Muslim silver ceased to reach Scandinavia, silver coins of English and Carolingian origin, rare in the ninth century (102 in Scandinavia, 115 in Poland), become predominant. We therefore need be in no doubt that a silver monetary zone was already in being, poised for the conquest of foreign markets.

Instrument of expansion, the silver *denier* was also a political tool. Charlemagne and Louis the Pious implemented in full a policy initiated by Dagobert and St Eligius, that is, the concentration of the coinage on the palace. This was supposed to eliminate the possibility of fraudulent issues. The practice of centralising the coinage was continued by all subsequent kings down to and including Odo, and may have lasted even longer. The places where coins have been found pinpoint the zones where commercial activity was at its most vigorous: Northern Francia, the Loire valley, Frisia and England. Charles the Bald, by his edict of 864, sought to concentrate the striking of coins, apart from those produced at the palace, on the mints at Quentovic, Rouen, Rheims, Sens, Paris, Orleans, Chalons-sur-Saône and Melle (where the silver-mines were). To the places singled out in this way as the major centres of the Western Frankish economy one should add the Rhenish and Mosan river-ports. Examination of the way in which Charles the Bald's coins circulated in fact reveals, taking the whole kingdom into account, that the circulation was predominantly local, except in Francia proper, that is to say the region between the Seine and the Rhine. The ports of Rouen, Quentovic and Dorestad brought in coins from Aquitaine, England and Italy. None were imported from Lotharingia, nor from Germany, which as yet had no official mints. On the other hand, coins minted in Francia were literally flooding into the Rhinelands, Neustria and Burgundy. Furthermore, twenty per cent of this circulation was made up of *oboles*, proof of numerous small transactions. All this goes to confirm the economic importance of the region in question, which came closer than any other to being the Carolingian empire's political, agricultural and commercial centre of gravity.

Lastly there were countries where no coins were minted, northern Spain, Ireland, Scotland and Scandinavia. The Vikings long remained unamenable to the monetary medium and their earliest coins date in fact from the tenth century. But that is not to say that their habit of barter remained uninfluenced by the presence of looted coins. They made use of *hacksilver*, strips of silver cut to a certain weight, or silver rings marked with a series of nicks, from which pieces could be cut as required; this no doubt explains their insistence on receiving the danegeld in silver ingots, handed over after melting-down of the coins. It therefore seems that the Scandinavian economy was set to merge with that of Northern Europe. Why, then, did the Vikings resort to plundering raids rather than commerce? The only hypothesis which might account for the increase in raids after 840 runs as follows: lacking the means of exchange to pay for their purchases of corn and wine, the Vikings were finally reduced to seizing silver wherever they could find it. Raiding served the purpose of making up for the deficiencies of a trading network which they were unable to control, in contrast with the Varangians, who succeeded in establishing their influence peacably in Russia. The Vikings obtained by force the goods which the halt to expansion prevented them from obtaining by barter. In fact, the total disappearance of gold from their shipments and the devaluation of the *denier* after 864 reflect a slowing down of trade and a reversal in the price-trend of silver bullion, which again began to rise.

The new trade-routes of the seventh and eighth centuries

The long-established Mediterranean trade was still in being in the seventh century, but it changed in character and diminished in scope. The import of luxury articles (silk, spices, incense and perfumes) continued, as did the export of basic commodities such as timber, *garum* and slaves. But olive oil had been replaced, for lighting purposes, by wax and in place of papyrus there was parchment. The sea-routes had changed course with the entry of the Lombard kingdom into Christendom and the irruption of Islam: use of the long route round the tip of Spain became intermittent. Carthage was no longer a port of call, Narbonne and Marseilles vanished as termini of the Byzantine traffic. Even if links with Alexandria were not severed, traffic in the western sector of the Mediterranean greatly diminished with the advent of Muslim piracy, to the benefit of the Tyrrhenian Sea and the Alpine crossings, which were reopened by the Lombards. After about 630–40, the route leading from Provence *via* the Rhône, the Saône, the Meuse and the Rhine was increasingly eclipsed by one which started at the Po, reaching the Rhine by way of the Alpine passes. While Anglo-Saxon merchants and pilgrims frequented this new route, Greek and Syrian merchants vanished, with Jews taking their place. It was the latter who maintained the old trading-relations with Africa through Spain, and with the East through Italy. They were also beginning to establish themselves in towns along the Meuse and the Rhine (Verdun and Mainz amongst others), where they struck bargains with Frankish traders involved in the importation of slaves and furs from the Slav countries beyond the Elbe.

Adoption of these new land-routes was matched by renewed activity at sea, especially in the Tyrrhenian. From 680 onwards, by driving the Byzantines towards the coastal fringes, the Lombards made room for internal commerce to flourish. Merchants from Comacchio travelled up the Po, bringing salt from their salt-marshes and consignments of fish to exchange for corn from the interior, but they also had pepper and oil to sell, evidence of a more far-flung trade. The townsmen who fled from the Lombards at the end of the sixth century to live with the fishermen of the lagoons had succeeded, under Byzantine aegis, in founding a number of small towns of which Venice, established on the island of the Rialto, gave signs of becoming the most important. Followed somewhat later by Ravenna, in 726–7 Venice elected its first duke, a gesture of revolt against Byzantine iconoclasm. Paul, the first doge, and his successor Orso were quick to exert their command of the sea, just as their

515

sea-captains were quick to supply the Byzantine and Muslim markets with timber and Slavonic slaves. Venice, thanks to its land connections in one direction, linking up with Pavia and the Alpine routes, and its maritime connections in the other, was set to become a power-house of economic activity at the outlet of an agricultural region, the Po valley, where the expansion which was nipped in the bud in the fifth and sixth centuries was making a fresh start. The development of Ravenna and its port, Classis, now silted up, testify to an earlier effort on the part of the Romans in late Antiquity. Located further to the north, but also closer to the Brenner pass and the Germanic countries, Venice tried again and succeeded.

Although less advanced, the situation at the other end of the continental routes was the same. With the Frankish encroachment on Frisia and the arrival of Anglo-Saxon monks and merchants, the direction of the commercial axes had changed. The old Roman road running through Boulogne, Thérouanne, Arras, Cambrai, Maastricht and Cologne fell into disuse, while along the Meuse, places like Verdun, Mouzon, Dinant, Namur and Huy developed into trading-centres which gained in importance through being the natural outlet for the products of neighbouring Carolingian estates. Lastly, in the eighth century the bishopric of the region finally came to rest at Liège. The function of the Meuse as an artery was thus becoming fundamental. Two ports developed in parallel. The Saxons of Quentovic on the Canche having turned Christian around 660, the trade of that port, like that of Rouen, was increasingly orientated towards England, whether through Hamwih or through the channel ports and London. The coasts of Ireland, England and northern Gaul as far as Poitou became busier and busier with traffic. The objects exchanged were slaves from the islands, wines from the continent, Cornish tin, lead from Melle in Poitou and salt from the mouth of the Loire. There is thus a sense in which Quentovic was the focal point on which all trade with the Anglo-Saxon world converged. It was rivalled, however, by a much superior maritime power. This was the Frisians, who succeeded in dominating the coasts and the river-mouths all the way from the Scheldt to the Elbe. Their defeat and subjugation by Charles Martel in 734 made no difference to their expansion, which continued from Dorestad, their principal emporium. Founded probably in the early seventh century between the Lek and the meandering Rhine, Dorestad quickly became the place of trans-shipment for all merchants coming from England, the Rhine or Scandinavia. With its large timber-built houses and its wharves made from logs mounted on piles, it attracted the greater part of the North Sea's maritime activity and even that of the Baltic. Archaeological excavations have confirmed the importance of its trade, which in addition to the standard products already mentioned included the export of Rhenish glassware to Sweden and the production and sale of the woollen cloth known as *pallia fresonica*, for the precise reason that it was manufactured in Frisia. The staves of wine-barrels coated with pitch point to a trade in wines resinated in the Mediterranean fashion. The enterprise of the Frisians took many forms. They journeyed up the Rhine to buy corn at Mainz and Worms, they navigated the Moselle as far as Trier, and the Seine as far as St Denis. In England, they were found in London and York. In Scandinavia, they installed themselves at Ribe, at Haithabu at the base of the Jutland peninsula, and at Birka on Lake Mälaren in Sweden. This

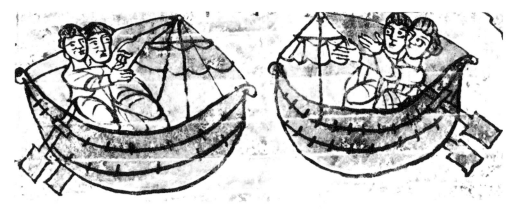

Sea-routes change direction. *Trier Apocalypse*, first half of the ninth century (Trier, Stadtbibliothek).

embyronic trading-network is proof that a new maritime region was coming into existence around the North Sea, based on the great Rhenish-Mosan river-system.

It is pertinent to enquire into the causes of this sudden expansion. The human and economic bases for it have already been indicated, but technological innovation was certainly a key factor. By the beginning of the eighth century, the use of a square sail had become customary on the Frisians' oar-powered boats, thus saving space and manpower. But more than this, in the course of the eighth century the Frisians invented a new type of ship, the 'hulk'. Rounded in shape and equipped with a mast, this craft could cope equally well with heavy seas and with the navigation of rivers. To judge from the example discovered at Utrecht, it would have been able to transport up to ten tonnes of freight; if so, this would represent the first advance on the tonnages of late Antiquity. Frisian seapower thus denoted in no uncertain fashion the advent of a new maritime trading-area in northern Europe and is a sign that civilisation was finding a new centre of gravity beyond the former limits of the Roman empire. The great axis of the European economy, the line connecting Italy with the Netherlands, is already discernible.

Early ninth century: beginnings of expansion?

The trade-routes of Carolingian and Ottonian Europe are to be imagined as revolving round the two great economic poles, Venice and Pavia in the south, Quentovic and Dorestad in the north, up to the time of their destruction. In between, the customs-posts in the Alpine defiles (in company with the two Nordic ports) were the most important in the empire, an *ad valorem* levy of ten per cent being taken on all merchandise passing through them. Europe's economic axis was thus by now well-defined. The Mediterranean sector was most lively in the Adriatic, where Venice succeeded in ousting Comacchio and took over its salt monopoly. In 883, Venice started to mint coins. It made war on the pagan Slovenes, Croats and Serbs, reducing them to slavery and selling them, in defiance of the prohibitions, to Muslims. But to the export of slaves Venice added timber for Egypt's naval dockyards and supplies of arms. Taking advantage of this connection, in 828 two Venetian merchants stole from Alexandria the relics of the apostle Mark, from now on the patron saint of the new power. The Venetians took the same products to Byzantium as to Egypt, with corn in addition, and brought away silks and spices. The towns of the Campagna did the same, while allying themselves still more openly with the neighbouring Muslims. By contrast, along a line running from the Tiber to the Ebro, the perpetual war with Islam and the pirates prevented regular commerce. The unique exception was the land-route through Languedoc and the western or eastern Pyrenees, which permitted regular trade with Muslim Spain. Slaves, eunuchs in particular, were offered for sale by Jews and Christians. At Cordoba in the time of Abd al-Rahman III, around 930, 14,000 Slavs composed the caliph's personal bodyguard; the caliph himself was the son of a Frankish captive, whose blue eyes and fair hair he inherited. In addition the Spanish Muslims bought furs, Frankish weapons and cloths, and supplied the Christians with perfumes, spices, silks and the coloured leathers of Cordoba. By contrast, and notwithstanding Offa's *dinar*, there is no proof of regular communication by sea between Spain and England.

In order to penetrate Europe from the East, it was therefore advisable to go from Venice up the Po as far as Pavia, the focal point of international trade, in order to gain access to Francia and Germany. Pavia was a halting-place, after the crossing of the Alps, for Anglo-Saxon pilgrims bound for Rome, and for merchants. While the Venetians came there to buy corn and wine, the Anglo-Saxons brought with them Frankish weapons, furs, horses, wool and linen cloths, canvas and tin. Obviously, they would depart with oriental products purchased from the Venetians. In the tenth century this commerce would continue without interruption. After the Alps, travellers had a choice of three routes, leading respectively to Rouen, Quentovic, and Dorestad and then to England. Along the whole length of the Rhine, they would encounter Frisians, who made their way upstream by hauling their boats, on foot, along the bank. They were there to buy corn from the German lowlands and wine from the Rhenish slopes: to sell they had the *pallia fresonica*, woollen cloths dyed in various colours and the forerunner of the famous Flemish cloths of the twelfth century. In passing, they would purchase pottery and lava quernstones from Mainz to sell in England and Haithabu, and glassware from Cologne for export to Sweden. The excavations at Dorestad have brought to light the many crafts carried on in the port itself: weaving, working in iron, copper, bone and amber. The number of Frankish coins discovered proves that its activity steadily increased from Pippin III to Louis the Pious. Then came the decline under Lothar I followed by total disappearance in the late ninth century.

From Dorestad, two main trading-arteries were opened up. The first, skirting the Frisian terps, gave access to the Danish isthmus and thence, by portage, to Haithabu, another focus of international trade. The Frisians evidently came there to sell silks, spices, wine and other Western products in exchange for furs, leather, amber, wax, honey and even butter transported in soapstone containers. From Haithabu it was possible, by hopping from island to island, to reach Birka in Sweden, yet another cosmopolitan centre, or even Kaupang in Norway. These were the ports from which the Scandinavians would depart for the southern shores of the Baltic and their journey into Russia. But the Vikings, as we saw,

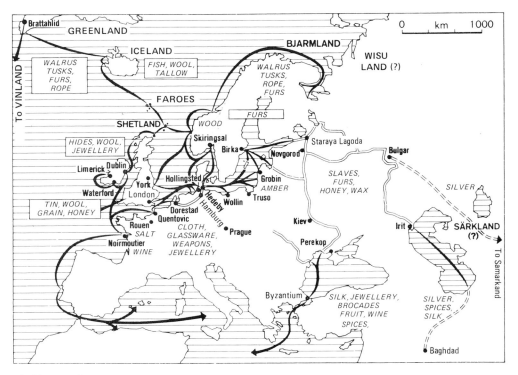

18 Viking trade-routes

caused the collapse of Frisian overseas trade around the middle of the ninth century and the archaeological evidence testifies everywhere to their domination of this stretch of sea, and even of the coasts of England and Ireland. From York and Dublin, the Danish and Norwegian colonies set in motion a new current of trade orientated towards Denmark and Iceland. Dublin would be the recipient in the tenth century of slaves and continental wines, of furs and walrus tusks from Cape North and Greenland, of silk and spices brought *via* Russia and the Baltic. Irish woollen cloth would make its way to London.

The area including the routes from Dorestad and Quentovic to London and Rouen to Hamwih was equally lively, specialising in particular in the export of wines from Paris and salt from the mouth of the Loire; in exchange, the English exported tin and cloth. We have thus seen two maritime worlds developing, in which the trade in bulk products and luxury objects was carried on simultaneously. The younger of the two, the Nordic trading-area, appears to have come to a standstill with the disappearance in the tenth century of its major ports, Quentovic, Hamwih, Dorestad, Haithabu, Birka and Kaupang. But this decline is no more than apparent since the successors to these precocious emporia were already beginning to appear in the mid-tenth century. On the other hand, with the rise of Venice, the Mediterranean area had just registered an importance advance, which would neither slow down nor be interrupted.

519

Merchants still on the fringe of society

Where there is trade there must be merchants. Greatly varying in character, they are difficult for us to track down, since merchants were of little interest to the clerical authors of our sources. The Jews, already a presence in the preceding period, still had flourishing communities in Languedoc, now paralleled by new communities in Champagne. The largest groups were to be found along the great commercial arteries, at Narbonne, Arles, Vienne, Mâcon, Verdun, Troyes and in the great Rhenish towns. Charles the Fat transferred the Jewish community of Lucca to Mainz. Another was installed at an early date at Magdeburg, departure point of the great trans-continental route which, by way of Prague and Poland, would fetch up in Kiev. At the customs-post of Raffelstetten, at the confluence of the Enns and the Danube, at the beginning of the tenth century, it was accepted as a custom of very long standing that Jews were permitted to re-enter the empire with convoys of slaves. Other Jewish merchants called Radhanites would castrate the slaves at Verdun and forward them to Spain, for sale in Saragossa or Toledo, or take them by ship to Egypt. These professional merchants, sedulously protected by the emperors and sometimes employed by them as ambassadors, must certainly have been wealthy. In 877, Charles the Bald levied a tax of a tenth on the value of their merchandise, as distinct from other merchants from whom he took an eleventh. These latter merchants were no doubt from a variety of backgrounds, but it has to be admitted that the Frisians are the most conspicuous. Their colonies were found all along the Rhine from Birten to Strasbourg, and from the tenth century alongside German rivers as at Hildesheim, Brunswick and Magdeburg. Others were planted at Hamwih, York, Haithabu and Birka in Sweden. Here, however, their stay was limited to the first half of the ninth century.

These colonies of small independent merchants set up commercial quarters inside the towns, usually next to the rivers. At Birka as at York, they already enjoyed the privilege of extra-territoriality. The only conceivable rivals to the Frisians were the Anglo-Saxons, but they were chiefly interested in trade with Francia. Attested at Rouen and at St Denis, they were also found at the mouth of the Loire. In the tenth century, they crossed the Alps to do business in Pavia. The Swedish and Danish merchants of Birka and Haithabu chiefly frequented York and Dorestad, but there were fewer of them and their trade was less specialised. And lastly, of course, there were the Italian and more particularly the Venetian merchants, 'who neither sow nor plough' and who made their entire living from trade: a thoroughly misleading assertion, incidentally, since we are informed by doge Justinian Partecipiazo in his will of 829 that his landed property provided the wherewithal to invest 1,200 pounds of silver in his maritime enterprises. In 840, Lothar I concluded with the Venetians a commercial treaty allowing free circulation inside Italy; it shows that the contracts of *commenda*, permitting the accumulation of a working capital from maritime trade, were already in existence. The Venetians in any case were not alone in the field, since they rubbed shoulders in the internal markets with merchants from Comacchio, Pavia, Cremona and elsewhere. In the south, thanks to their Byzantine contacts, the Salernitans, Amalfitans and Neapolitans launched themselves on the same overseas trade-routes. Nor

Amalfi, backed by precipitous cliffs, opens onto the Gulf of Salerno. Subject to Byzantium, Salerno was from the sixth century onwards the nodal point for trade between southern Italy and the Byzantine empire. In 839 it declared itself an independent republic and held its own against both Byzantium and the Muslims. With the prodigious expansion of its commerce with the East in the tenth century, Amalfi anticipated the rise of Venice. Its mariners perfected the magnetic compass, and the *Tabula Amalfitana* can be regarded as the first code of maritime commercial law.

521

should we overlook the clusters of more or less casual merchants, pilgrims on the scent of a good bargain, pedlars, carters, baggage-carriers travelling with caravans, *ministeriales* carrying out commissions on behalf of St Denis, St Vaast of Arras or St Germain of Auxerre. In this social world which brought together the small and great, everything hinged on the moneyer, whose services as money-changer or money-lender were usually crucial.

International trade was regulated, furthermore, by the kings and emperors. Charlemagne fixed the price of foodstuffs in 794, and forbade the export to the Slavs of mailcoats and the high-quality Frankish swords in 805. Louis the Pious, in 825, granted the merchants of the palace exemption from military service, requisitions, and tolls internal to the empire. We saw that he was at pains to check or forbid the traffic in Christian slaves. But the emperors performed an even greater service by giving sorely-needed attention to the upkeep of the Roman communications network. The *missi dominici* were instructed to see to the repair or rebuilding of bridges and inns on the public highway. In 821, they were to make the peasants rebuild the bridge over the Seine at Pont-sur-Seine, downstream from Troyes, to enable travellers to go from Meaux to Sens, from Sens to Troyes and so to the neighbouring fairs. In 853, Charles the Bald reminded the beneficiaries of fiscal lands of their obligation to repair the roads in return. This may well have been the explanation for the remarkably well-preserved state of the renowned '*chaussées Brunehaut*' in northern Francia. But in this sphere too the Danish invasions, once again, wrought havoc, since the first line of defence was to demolish bridges and submerge the highways in an effort to bar the way. Later on, when private initiative took over from the State, the Roman network was in disarray and roads of less good quality started appearing here and there. Once again, we come up against the familiar spectacle of a restraint on trade in the second half of the ninth century. But here, too, the curb was not total; despite the presence of the Moors in Provence, and their habit of blocking the Alpine crossings from time to time, Gerald of Aurillac managed on seven occasions to travel from Lyon to Rome by way of the Great St Bernard.

From now on, the economic and commercial framework of the central Middle Ages is firmly in place, subject to only minor variations and dislocations. Whatever effects the deceleration between 850 and 950 may have had on the Carolingian society and economy, the earlier demographic expansion had facilitated certain social improvements, such as the very gradual disappearance of slavery, and the introduction of more efficient methods of organising and cultivating the land. At least on the bipartite estate as it evolved in Francia, agricultural production, boosted by a political power intent on profits and backed up by an exact system of accounting, showed a healthy increase. This permitted the siphoning off of surpluses into an initial burst of trading activity, which suffered no lack of monetary means to sustain it. At the same time, war and pillage inside and outside the empire were garnering that initial 'accumulation' of primitive assets which was essential to subsequent expansion. The effects of this initial advance were felt throughout society, but they were most marked in the region where Carolingian government was at its most direct and effectual, in Francia between the Seine and the Rhine. It was here that the polyptychs of the largest known estates were compiled, that the most significant ports grew up, that the Roman roads were most diligently repaired. In short, the 'golden' age of Charlemagne and Louis the Pious was no myth. We can suppose that the decline and its attendant disorders seemed all the harsher and more painful precisely because peace and prosperity had appeared within reach. The 'age of iron' was taken for one of brass, the decline in activity for a complete standstill. Yet the energy being deployed on the Spanish or Scandinavian margins is there to prove the contrary.

Taking stock of the Carolingians

Let everyone learn from this that whoever is so foolish as to neglect the public interest, in the mad pursuit of his personal and self-seeking ambitions, offends so greatly against the Creator that he makes the very elements protest at his extravagance . . . For in the time of Charlemagne of happy memory, who died nearly 30 years ago, because the people kept undeviatingly to a single highway of God, peace and harmony everywhere prevailed; but now that everyone follows whatever path he pleases, dissensions and quarrels break out on every side. Where once there was universal abundance and joy, there is now universal poverty and sorrow.

These melancholy reflections conclude the *History of the sons of Louis the Pious* written by the historian Nithard only a few months before his death in battle in June 844. Lay-abbot of St Riquier, illegitimate offspring of the liaison between Angilbert and Bertha, a daughter of Charlemagne, Nithard, in his own person and in his bifocal view of Carolingian history, epitomises all the contradictions of an epoch which sought in vain to hold things in balance.

From 406 to 962, from the death of one empire to the birth of a third, claiming to resemble the second, which in its day had been heralded as the rebirth of the first – we may at first sight seem to have gone round in a dismal and heart-rending circle. Invasions, massacres, kingdoms, civil wars, empire, civil wars, invasions, massacres, empire . . . and so on *ad infinitum*, it is tempting to add. From 406 to 751 and from 751 to 962 two vicious circles snapped open and shut. But their repetition is illusory and misleading. If we direct our gaze at the theatre of events, we discover that the periods of upheaval lasting from 650 to 750 and from 850 to 950 are better regarded as periods when traditions and innovations were fused into a substance hitherto untried. Behind the fresh start can be discerned the thread of continuity.

One way of looking at the matter is to consider in turn the three protagonists in these dramas – the Romans, the Germans and the Church – in an effort to discover the direction in which each was evolving. Starting with the Roman order, its one aim was to keep the peace, which it sought to do by means of the public and private law, a professional army and a body of officials dedicated to the public interest. Under pressure from the necessities of war, it developed a voracious fiscal system, recruited Germans to the army, attached the *coloni* to the soil, expanded the monetary economy and turned for support to the Church. As a result, tensions were created which tore the Roman world apart and drove society into a headlong flight from the State, while at the same time new powers, generals, senators and bishops were already appearing on the scene. What remained of this Roman world in the

In an unusual blend of the sacred and the fantastic, these pediment figures adorn the manuscript known as the *Hincmar Gospels*. School of Rheims, early ninth century (Rheims, Bibliothèque municipale).

ninth century? Roman law subsisted in one part of Europe; the count, sole survivor of Roman officialdom, had usurped the public powers, most of the public lands belonging to the fisc having fallen into his hands; the Roman roads were still passable; the Jewish merchants had not vanished; and the monetary system still reposed on the pound-weight and the *solidus*. As to patronage, it had lent itself to the establishment of ties between man and man, to the bond of fidelity between equals, to the system of stipends in the form of land, and to the spread of sanctuaries which extended their protection over the peasantry of the surrounding countryside.

The Germans were to contribute the personal nature of the laws, the primacy of the war-leader, the consecration of violence, the blurring of the line between public and private, vassalage and commendation effected by placing hands between hands. They would give prominence to stock-rearing as also to the broadly fraternal nature of their community, and find it easy to give slaves their freedom. By the ninth century, they had merged with nearly all the existing populations, created fighting-forces in which heavy cavalry was increasingly predominant, preserved the laws of the tribal groupings, along with the *trustes* and the *ghildes*, and made the ties between man and man so universal that feudo-vassalic institutions were about to permeate the whole of society.

The Church, for its part, had fashioned its institutions in the mould of those of the Roman State. Nervous of monks and heresies, it installed the papacy in Rome at an early date and incurred the reproach of planting itself in a world it too greatly admired. In the ninth century, having become legatee of the Roman inheritance, the Church selected from it whatever suited its plan. Having become proprietor of the empire, the kingship and the concept of the State, it absorbed the Benedictine monks and conquered all the Celtic and

Germanic lands for the new faith. Christendom, at the last, was the one unity surviving from two attempts to resurrect the empire; from now on Rome was again the one permanent capital of the West.

In reality, these distinctions are purely intellectual, since the Roman and Germanic civilisations were united at bottom by Christianity, and as a result moreover of the concessions which Christianity made to both parties. The *rapprochement* took place in two stages, corresponding to the apogee of the barbarian kingdoms in the fifth and sixth centuries and the apogee of the Frankish kingdom in the eighth and ninth centuries. These two episodes of fusion gave rise to important new developments, especially in the crucial period when the barbarian kingdoms were in crisis. These were: the demographic revival; the privatisation of the State and of the Church through the *Eigenkirche*; the seizure of power by the new potentates; the rise of the aristocrats and their vassals; the genesis of territorial principalities; the evolution of large bipartite estates; the inauguration of the silver currency; the appearance of the Venetians and Frisians on the sea-routes; and lastly the elaboration of a new Christian culture. All the ingredients of Charlemagne's success were assembled even before his reign had begun. His genius would consist in grasping them all at once and converting them into a balanced whole.

One might be tempted to regard this period as the Gordian knot of the early Middle Ages, which strictly speaking would mean leaving out of account everything that happened between 750 and 850: for after the interruption of the empire, all the traits characteristic of the earlier era returned in full force, except that the Scandinavians had replaced the Frisians. But the sense of repetition is once again merely an illusion. The Carolingian empire was not in the nature of a wave rearing up, breaking on the shore and retiring, leaving the sands of the late Merovingians undisturbed. On the contrary, it signified a remodelling of society in depth, using as complementary tools the Roman concept of the State, the subordination of the army to the *bannum* and the ethics of Christianity.

The introduction of vassalage into the State was a master-stroke, the first lay attempt to structure society down to the lowest of the free, as the Church had succeeded in doing through its parochial organisation. But the Carolingian State could only succeed by appealing unreservedly to the Church for help in transforming men's minds, and by literally battening on the clergy. This was the solution, moreover, which Otto I imitated in due course. But Louis the Pious digressed in radical fashion from Charlemagne's programme. This supposedly 'meek' ruler (he went by the name 'Louis le Débonnaire') was bent on speeding up a policy of centralisation that no one understood and on forcing his subjects to accept political institutions appropriate to kingdoms forming part of a unitary empire. He speeded up the renewal to the point of imputing to the Church an influence it did not as yet possess. By pressing ahead with a programme too advanced for contemporary mentalities, he induced a kind of seizure in the social organism. Again, Charles the Bald, by suppressing the traditions of self-government in the kingdom of Aquitaine, blew it to pieces. Everything happened too soon and too fast. The Carolingians were obliged to leave their structure unfinished. For work to be resumed a more natural rhythm needed to be re-established. The impulse could only come from small units at the local level, entailing the abandonment of unity as the ideal. Mentally, indeed, Carolingian society continued to be torn between opposing attitudes in which the moral values of blood and lineage vied for mastery with those of an ordered State and a Church of the baptised. The total incomprehension of clans still at the vendetta stage wrecked the chances of inculcating a globalist outlook. The old pagan wisdom still had power to refute a Christian learning which as yet carried all-too-little conviction.

And yet, socially and economically speaking, the task should not have been impossible. Let us contemplate the demographic base-line of the 26 million inhabitants of the western Roman empire in the fifth century, the wastage from the great Justinianic plague, the gradual upturn in the time of 'good king Dagobert', the halt forced by the crises of the seventh century, the fresh start in the eighth century and the some fifteen to eighteen million inhabitants of Charlemagne's empire, then the next standstill lasting from 850 to 950. Let us set beside these population trends factors such as the continual depreciation of the burdens on the peasants, who in an almost literal sense melted down the amount of the Roman taxes by making them customary, the increased production on the great estates, the removal of that monetary strait-jacket, the gold currency, and the committal of tenants' obligations to writing. Might we not have here two major agrarian cycles of the Malthusian type?

Contrary to the classical theory, it seems not to have been the case that availability of foodstuffs determined the size of the population, but rather that the fragility of the demographic revival in the face of pillage and civil war slowed down the pace of economic advance. It only needed the removal of the last demands of the Carolingian State, for military service from free men and for sustenance for the army from the now privatised fiscal estates, for the great clearances to get under way. This could well be the most satisfactory explanation for these two successive take-offs, aborted almost before they left the ground. The cultural investment never having been adequate to the task of imposing the political design on contemporary society, privatisation, and therefore the abandonment of obligations relating specifically to the State, remained the sole means of releasing social energies. Productive forces equipped with the technological and financial resources necessary for real growth could now be redirected, the great estate in particular having lost its political *raison d'être*. And the peasants, in spite of continuing aristocratic oppression, could therefore take advantage of this relaxation of central authority, which had yet to find its still more peremptory successor, the coercive power of the local lord, and depart to attack virgin lands.

All that has just been said applies only to the heartlands of the former Carolingian empire. The fringes, Spain, England and Germany, held back by the struggle against Islam, the Danes and the Slavs, remained at an archaic stage where expansion was synonymous with war. The typically Germanic warrior State, in the style of Charlemagne, Alfonso III the Great, Alfred and Otto I, still had every reason to exist. The population, its ranks thinned by battle, retained its socially egalitarian character while gradually advancing its frontiers. But peace had only to become permanent for everything to change, as in Catalonia and

Scandinavian gold bracteates of the sixth century. Circular pendants worn as amulets, bracteates were decorated only on one side and hung by a loop attached to the rim.

Latium after about 950. By comparison with other parts of the continent, the heartland of the Carolingian empire was thus in the lead.

In the fifth century, of course, everything revolved round the Mediterranean. Little by little, as we saw, southern Europe paled by comparison with its northern counterpart. All the new developments were essentially to the benefit of the Po plain, Francia north of the Loire and the Thames basin. From this it is clear, however, that the rupture between the old Roman Europe and the new Germanic Europe was not total. It was precisely in those regions most disrupted by the invasions that the new syntheses, the most daring

527

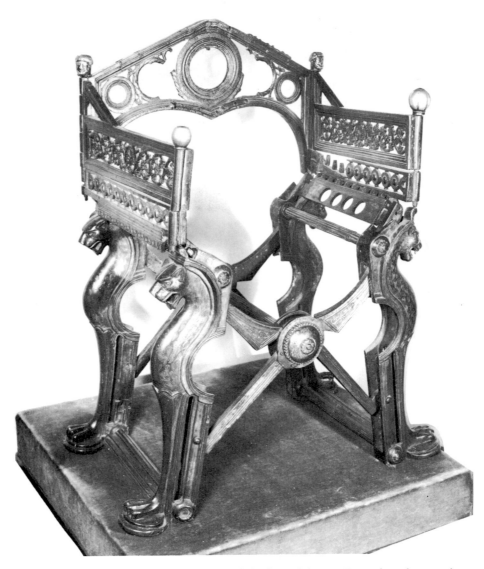

The throne of Dagobert, one of the most potent symbols of French history. Dating from the seventh century with ninth-century additions, it was rediscovered in the twelfth century by Abbot Suger; completed by him, it subsequently figured in royal coronations. Napoleon had it restored and used it himself in 1804. In bronze-gilt, only the lower part is old; its shape resembles the curule chairs of the Roman consuls (Paris, Bibliothèque nationale, Cabinet des médailles).

innovations, germinated and flourished. The fault became a source of strength. Venice, Pavia, the Alpine crossings, the Saône, the Rhine, the Meuse, the Seine, the Channel, London and York, formed a diagonal defining the new civilisation and joining the old to the new. Venice had taken the place of Ravenna, Aachen the place of Trier. Bruges would soon make good the loss of Dorestad. The centres of decision-making had migrated, significantly, to the zones with the greatest energy. At the same time, the crossing of the Rhine by Charlemagne, who succeeded where Augustus had failed, permitted the creation of a Germanic Roman empire. After the partition of Verdun, the Rhine therefore functioned both as a connecting link and as a dividing line. Western Europe, with its perpetual volatility, was to be faced by an eastern Europe anxious to cling to its archaic institutions. From south to north, from east to west, European Christendom had already acquired, in the tenth century, the aspect of a mosaic which it still wears today.

Select bibliography

Note: this list concentrates on works available in French or English. English titles marked * have been added by the translator.

THE WORLD OF THE LATE ROMAN EMPIRE

*Brown, P. R. L., *The world of Late Antiquity*, London, 1971.
Daniélou, J., Marrou, H., *The Christian centuries*, vol. 1, *The first six hundred years*, Engl. transl., London, 1964.
*Jones, A. H. M., *The decline of the Ancient World*, London, 1966.
 The Later Roman Empire 284–602, 3 vols and maps, Oxford, 1964.
Stein, E., *Histoire du Bas-Empire (284–565)*, 2 vols, Paris, 1959.
Vogt, J., *The decline of Rome*, Engl. transl., London, 1967.

THE 'BARBARIAN' WEST

GENERAL SURVEYS OF THE MEDIEVAL WEST

Balard, M., Genet, J. P., Rouche, M., *Des barbares à la Renaissance*, Paris, 1973.
Chelini, J., *Histoire religieuse de l'Occident médiéval*, Paris, 1968.
Fossier, R., *Histoire sociale de l'Occident médiéval*, Paris, 1970.
Fourquin, G., *Histoire économique de l'Occident médiéval*, Paris, 1969.

WORKS DEALING WITH THE WHOLE OR PART OF THE PERIOD 400–1000

Dhondt, J., *Le haut Moyen Age (VIIIe–XIe)*, Fr. transl., Paris, 1968.
Fournier, G., *L'Occident de la fin du Ve à la fin du IXe siècle*, Paris, 1970.
Folz, R., Guillou, A., Musset, L., Sourdel, D., *De l'antiquité au monde médiéval*, Paris, 1972.
Joris, A., *Du Ve au milieu du VIIIe siècle: à la lisière de deux mondes*, Brussels, 1978.
Lot, F., *The end of the Ancient World and the beginning of the Middle Ages*, Engl. transl., London, 1931.
 Pfister, C., Ganshof, F. L., *Les destinées de l'Empire en Occident de 395 à 888*, Paris, 1941.
Riché, P., *Grandes invasions et Empires (fin IVe–debut XIe siècle)*, Paris, 1968.
*Talbot Rice, D. (ed.), *The Dark Ages: the making of European civilisation*, London, 1965.
*Wallace-Hadrill, J. M., *The Barbarian West*, 3rd edn, London, 1967.

The invasions

Musset, L., *The Germanic invasions: the making of Europe AD 400–600*, Engl. transl., London, 1975.
   Les invasions: le second assaut contre l'Europe chrétienne, Paris, 1965.
Riché, P., *Les invasions barbares*, 4th edn, Paris, 1968.
Settimane . . . di Spoleto, *Caratteri del secolo VII in Occidente*, Spoleto, 1958.

The Carolingians

Boussard, J., *The civilisation of Charlemagne*, Engl. transl., London, 1968.
*Bullough, D. A., *The age of Charlemagne*, London, 1965.
   *'Europae Pater', in *English Historical Review*, 1970.
Fichtenau, H., *The Carolingian empire*, Engl. transl. (abridged), London, 1968.
Halphen, L., *Charlemagne and the Carolingian empire*, Engl. transl., Amsterdam, 1977.
Karl der Grosse: Lebenswerk und Nachleben, 4 vols, Düsseldorf, 1965–6.
Perroy, E., *Le monde carolingien*, Paris, 1973.
Tessier, G., *Charlemagne*, Paris, 1967.

Post-Carolingian period

*Barraclough, G., *The crucible of Europe*, London, 1976.
Boüard, M. de., *Les Vikings*, 1968.
Fasoli, G., 'Point de vue sur les incursions hongroises au Xe siècle', *Cahiers de civilisation médiévale*, 1959.
Haenens, A. d', *Les invasions normandes: une catastrophe ?*, Paris, 1970.
*Jones, Gwyn, *A history of the Vikings*, Oxford, 1968.
Mor, C. G., *L'età feudale*, Milan, 1952.
Occident et Orient au Xe s., Actes du IXe Congrès . . . Société des Historiens Médiévistes, Dijon–Paris, 1979.
Sawyer, P. H., *The age of the Vikings*, 2nd edn, London, 1971.
Steensthrupp, J., *Les invasions normandes en France*, 1969.
Zimmermann, H., *Das dunkle Jahrhundert*, Graz, 1971.

STUDIES OF PARTICULAR REGIONS

Gaul and Aquitaine

Auzias, L., *L'Aquitaine carolingienne*, Toulouse, 1937.
Fossier, R., *La terre et les hommes en Picardie jusqu'à la fin du XIIIe s*, Paris–Louvain, 1968.
Fournier, G., *Les Mérovingiens*, Paris, 1969.
   Le peuplement rural en Basse-Auvergne, Paris, 1962.·
*James, E., *The Merovingian archaeology of south-west Gaul*, British Archaeological Reports, Oxford, 1977.
   The origins of France: from Clovis to the Capetians, London, 1982.
Perrin, O., *Les Burgondes*, Neuchâtel, 1968.
Roblin, M., *Le terroir de Paris aux époques gallo-romaine et franque*, 2nd edn, Paris, 1971.
Rouche, M., *L'Aquitaine, des Wisigoths aux Arabes*, 418–781, Paris, 1979.
Salin, E., *La civilisation mérovingienne*, 4 vols, Paris, 1949–59.
Tessier, G., *Le baptême de Clovis*, Paris, 1946.
*Wallace-Hadrill, J. M., *The long-haired kings and other studies in Frankish history*, London, 1962.

Select bibliography

Germanic and Scandinavian territory

Cuvillier, J. P., *L'Allemagne médiévale: naissance d'un État*, Paris, 1979.

Faider-Feytmans, G., *La Belgique à l'époque mérovingienne*, Brussels, 1964.

*Fleckenstein, J., *Early Medieval Germany*, Engl. transl., Amsterdam, 1978.

Ganshof, F. L., *La Belgique carolingienne*, Brussels, 1958.

Holtzmann, R., *Geschichte der sächsischen Kaiserzeit*, 3rd edn, Munich, 1955.

*Leyser, K., *Rule and conflict in an early medieval society: Ottonian Saxony*, London, 1979.

Musset, L., *Les peuples scandinaves au Moyen Age*, Paris, 1951.

Perrin, C. E., *L'Allemagne et l'Italie de 843 à 962*, Paris, 1953.

British Isles

Hodgkin, R. K., *A history of the Anglo-Saxons*, 2 vols, London, 1952.

Levison, W., *England and the continent in the eighth century*, Oxford, 1956.

*Loyn, H., *Anglo-Saxon England and the Norman conquest*, London, 1962.

*Mayr-Harting, H., *The coming of Christianity to Anglo-Saxon England*, London, 1972.

*Sawyer, P. H., *From Roman Britain to Norman England*, London, 1978.

Stenton, F. M., *Anglo-Saxon England*, 3rd edn, Oxford, 1971.

Whitelock, D., *The beginnings of English society*, Harmondsworth, 1972.

Wilson, D. M., *The Anglo-Saxons*, London, 1971.

   *(ed.), *The archaeology of Anglo-Saxon England*, London, 1976.

Mediterranean peninsulas

Abadal Y de Vinyals, R. d', *Del reino de Tolosa al reino de Toledo*, Madrid, 1960.

Berolini, O., *Roma di fronte a Bizancio e ai Longobardi*, vol. 4, *Storia di Roma*, Bologna, 1941.

Cilento, N., *Italia meridionale longobardica*, Milan, 1966.

*Collins, R., *Early medieval Spain*, London, 1983.

*James, E. (ed.), *Visigothic Spain: New approaches*, Oxford, 1980.

*King, P. D., *Law and society in the Visigothic kingdom*, Cambridge, 1972.

*Llewellyn, P., *Rome in the Dark Ages*, London, 1970.

Menendez-Pidal, R., *Historia de España*, vols 3–4, Madrid, 1947–57.

Orlandis Rovira, J., *Historia social y economica de la España visigoda*, Madrid, 1975.

Perez de Urbel, J., *España cristiana 711–1038*, Madrid, 1956.

Thompson, E. A., *The Goths in Spain*, Oxford, 1969.

Garcia de Valdeavellano, L., *Historia de España*, 2nd edn, Madrid, 1968.

*Wickham, C., *Early medieval Italy*, London, 1981.

ECONOMIC AND SOCIAL ASPECTS

General surveys

Bloch, M., ' "Les invasions"; deux structures économiques', *Annales d'histoire sociale*, 1945.

Boutruche, R., *Seigneurie et féodalité: le premier âge des liens d'homme à homme*, 2nd edn, Paris, 1968.

Cambridge economic history of Europe, vol. 1, 2nd edn, 1966, vol. 2, 1952.

Daumas, M., *A history of technology and invention*, vol. 1, *The origins of technological civilisation*, Engl. transl., London, 1980.

Doehardt, R., *The early Middle Ages in the West: economy and society*, Engl. transl., Amsterdam, 1978.

Fossier, R., *Histoire sociale de l'Occident médiéval*, Paris, 1970.

Ganshof, F. L., *Feudalism*, Engl. transl., 3rd edn, London, 1964.

Latouche, R., *The birth of Western economy*, Engl. transl., 2nd edn, London, 1967.

Lelong, C., *La vie quotidienne en Gaule à l'époque mérovingienne*, Paris, 1963.

Magnou-Nortier, E., *Foi et fidélité: recherches sur l'évolution des liens personnels chez les Francs du VIIe au IXe siècle*, Toulouse, 1976.

Riché, P., *Daily life in the world of Charlemagne*, Engl. transl., Liverpool, 1978.

Singer, C. *A history of technology*, vol. 2, Oxford, 1956.

Tellenbach, G., *Vom karolingischen Reichsadel zum deutschen Reichsfürstenstand*, Berlin, 1943.

Verlinden, C., *L'esclavage dans l'Europe médiévale*, vol. 1, *Péninsule ibérique – France*, Bruges, 1955.

The Land

Chapelot, J., Fossier, R., *The village and house in the Middle Ages*, Engl. transl., London, 1985.

Duby, G., *Rural economy and country life in the medieval West*, Engl. transl., London, 1968.

Ganshof, F. L., 'Manorial organisation in the Low Countries in the 7th, 8th and 9th centuries', in *Transactions of the Royal Historical Society*, 1949.

Lesne, E., *Histoire de la propriété ecclésiastique en France*, 8 vols, Lille, 1910–43.

Rouche, M., 'La faim à l'époque carolingienne: essai sur quelques types de rations alimentaires', *Revue historique*, 1973.

Sawyer, P. H. (ed.), *Medieval settlement: continuity and change*, London, 1976.

Settimane . . . di Spoleto, Agricoltura e mundo rurale in Occidente . . ., Spoleto, 1966.

Towns and Trade

Ennen, E., *The medieval town*, Engl. transl., Amsterdam, 1973.

Ganshof, F. L., *Etude sur le développment des villes entre Loire et Rhin*, Paris, 1943.

Grierson, P., 'Carolingian Europe and the Arabs: the myth of the Mancus', in Grierson, *Dark Age Numismatics*, Variorum Reprints, 1979.

*Hodge, R., *Dark Age economics: the origins of towns and trade 600–1000*, London, 1982.

Lewis, A. R., *Naval power and trade in the Mediterranean AD 500–1100*, Princeton, 1951.

Lewis, A. R. *The Northern Seas: Shipping and Commerce in Northern Europe AD 300–1100*, Princeton, 1958.

Lombard, M., 'L'or musulman du VII au XIe siècle', *Annales d'histoire sociale*, 1947.

Lopez, R. S., 'East and West in the early Middle Ages: economic relations', *Relazioni del X Congresso Internazionale di Scienze Storiche*, vol. 3, *Storia del Medioevo*, Rome, 1955.

Pirenne, H., *Mahomet and Charlemagne*, Engl. transl, London, 1939.

Settimane . . . di Spoleto, Città nell'alto medioevo, Spoleto, 1959.

Settimane . . . di Spoleto, Moneta e scambi nell'alto medioevo, Spoleto, 1961.

THE CULTURE OF THE WEST

Political

Bonnard-Delamare, R., *L'idée de paix à l'époque carolingienne*, Paris, 1939.

Dhondt, H., *Étude sur la nàissance des principautés territoriales en France*, Bruges, 1948.

Ewig, E., 'Résidence et capitale pendant le haut Moyen Age', *Revue historique*, 1963.

Folz, R., *La naissance du Saint-Empire*, Paris, 1967.

Select bibliography

Folz, R., *The coronation of Charlemagne*, Engl. transl., London, 1974.

    The concept of empire in Western Europe from the fifth to the fourteenth century, Engl. transl., London, 1969.

Ganshof, F. L., *Recherches sur les capitulaires*, Paris, 1958.

    The Carolingians and the Frankish monarchy, London, 1971.

    The Frankish institutions under Charlemagne, Providence, 1968.

*Gibson, M., Nelson, J. (eds.), *Charles the Bald: court and kingdom*, Oxford, 1981.

Halphen, L., 'L'idée d'Etat sous les Carolingiens', *Revue historique*, 1939.

Mitteis, H., *The State in the Middle Ages*, Engl. transl., Amsterdam, 1975.

*Nelson, J., 'Symbols in context: rulers' inauguration rituals in Byzantium and the West in the early Middle Ages', in *Studies in Church History*, 1976.

*Sawyer, P. H., Wood, I. N. (eds.), *Early medieval kingship*, Leeds, 1977.

Tellenbach, G., *Die Entstehung des deutschen Reiches*, 3rd edn, Munich, 1946.

Ullmann, W., *The Carolingian Renaissance and the idea of kingship*, London, 1969.

Wallace-Hadrill, J. M., *Early Germanic kingship in England and on the continent*, Oxford, 1971.

Intellectual and artistic

Heitz, C., *L'architecture religieuse*, Paris, 1980.

Hubert, J., Porcher, J., Volbach, V., *Carolingian Art*, Engl. transl., London, 1970.

Hubert, C., *Europe in the Dark Ages*, Engl. transl., London, 1969.

Laistner, M. L. W., *Thought and letters in Western Europe AD 500–900*, 2nd edn, London, 1957.

*Marenbon, J., *From the circle of Alcuin to the School of Auxerre*, Cambridge, 1981.

*Mutherich, F., Gaehde, J. E., *Carolingian Painting*, London, 1977.

*Nordenfalk, C., *Celtic and Anglo-Saxon Painting*, London, 1977.

Riché, P., *De l'éducation antique à l'éducation chevaleresque*, Paris, 1968.

    Écoles et enseignement dans le haut Moyen Age, Paris, 1979.

Rouche, M., *L'éducation en France*, vol. 1, Paris, 1981.

Verlinden, C., *Les origines de la frontière linguistique en Belgique et la civilisation franque*, Brussels, 1955.

Wolff, P., *Les origines linguistiques de l'Europe occidentale*, Paris, 1971.

    The awakening of Europe, Harmondsworth, 1968.

Zumthor, P., *Histoire littéraire de la France médiévale (VIe–XIVe)*, Paris, 1954.

THE BYZANTINE EAST

GENERAL SURVEYS

Bréhier, L., *Le monde Byzantin*, 3 vols, 2nd edn, Paris, 1969–70. Engl. transl. of vol. 1, *The life and death of Byzantium*, Amsterdam, 1977.

The Cambridge Medieval History, vol. 4, *The Byzantine empire*, 2nd edn, 2 vols, Cambridge 1967–8.

Ducellier, A., *Le drame de Byzance: idéal et échec d'une société chrétienne*, Paris, 1976.

    Les Byzantins, 2nd edn, Paris, 1970.

    and Kaplan, M., Martin, B., *Le Proche-Orient médiéval: des barbares aux Ottomans*, Paris, 1980.

Guillou, P., *La civilisation byzantine*, Paris, 1975.

Jenkins, R. H., *Byzantium, the imperial centuries: AD 610–1071*, New York, 1969.

*Kazhdan, A., Constable, G., *People and power in Byzantium: An introduction to modern Byzantine studies*, Dumbarton Oaks, 1982.

Lemerle, P., *Histoire de Byzance*, 3rd edn, Paris, 1956.

*Mango, C. A., *Byzantium: the empire of New Rome*, London, 1980.

Ostrogorsky, G., *History of the Byzantine State*, Engl. transl., revised edn, London, 1968.

STUDIES OF SHORTER PERIODS

*Barker, J. W., *Justinian and the later Roman empire*, Madison, 1966.

Cameron, Averil M., *Continuity and change in 6th century Byzantium*, Variorum Reprints, 1981.

Rubin, B., *Das Zeitalter Justinian*, Berlin, 1960.

*Runciman, S., *The emperor Romanus Lecapenus and his reign*, Cambridge, 1929.

Stratos, A. N., *Byzantium in the seventh century, 602–634*, The Hague, 1968.

Vasiliev, A. A., *Justin the First: an introduction to the epoch of Justinian*, Cambridge, Mass., 1956.

REGIONS AND PEOPLES

The West and the Balkans

*Browning, R., *Byzantium and Bulgaria*, London, 1975.

Dvornik, F., *Les Slaves*, Paris, 1970.

Gordon, C. D., *Byzantium and the Barbarians*, London, 1972.

Guillou, A., *Régionalisme et indépendence dans l'Empire byzantin: l'example de l'exarchat et de la Pentapole d'Italie*, Rome, 1969.

Lemerle, P., 'Invasions et migrations dans les Balkans depuis la fin de l'époque romaine jusqu'au VIII siècle', in *Revue historique*, 1954.

Obolensky, D., *The Byzantine Commonwealth: eastern Europe 500–1153*, London, 1971.

Portal, R., *Les Slaves: peuples et nations (VII–XXs.)*, Paris, 1965.

Runciman, S., *A history of the First Bulgarian Empire*, London, 1930.

The East

Ahrweiler, H., 'L'Asie Mineure et les invasions arabes', in *Revue historique*, 1962.

Bratianu, G., *La mer Noire des origines à la conquête ottomane*, Munich, 1969.

Cahen, C., 'La première pénétration turque en Asie Mineure', in *Byzantion*, 1948.

Dumbarton Oaks Papers, 1970, 1972 (relations with Persia).

Honigmann, E., *Die Ostgrenze des Byzantinisches Reiches von 363 bis 1071*, Brussels, 1971.

Pigoulevskaya, N., *Byzance et l'Iran entre le VIe et le VIIe siècle*, Moscow, 1946 (in Russian).

EMPEROR AND CHURCH

The basileus and his powers

Ahrweiler, H., *Études sur les structures administratives et sociales de Byzance*, Variorum Reprints, 1981.
   L'idéologie de l'Empire byzantin, Paris, 1976.
   'Recherches sur l'administration de l'Empire byzantin aux IXe et Xe siècles', in *Bulletin de correspondence hellénique*, 1960.

Cameron, Alan, *Circus factions: Blues and Greens at Rome and Byzantium*, Oxford, 1976.

Grabar, A., *L'empereur dans l'art byzantin*, 2nd edn, Paris, 1971.

Oikonomidès, N., *Les listes de préséance byzantines des IXe et Xe siècles*, Paris, 1972.

Svoronos, N., *Études sur l'organisation intérieure, la société et l'économie de l'Empire byzantin*, Variorum Reprints, 1971.

Select bibliography

Religious questions

Alexander, P. J., *The patriarch Nicephorus of Constantinople: ecclesiastical policy and image worship in the Byzantine empire*, Oxford, 1958.

Barnard, L. W., *The Graeco-Roman and Oriental background of the iconoclastic controversy*, Leiden, 1974.

Brown, Peter R. L., 'The rise and function of the Holy Man in Late Antiquity', in *Journal of Roman Studies*, 1972.

Bryer, A., Herrin, J. (eds.), *Iconoclasm*, Birmingham, 1977.

Dagron, G., 'Les moines et la ville: le monachisme à Constantinople jusqu'au concile de Chalcédoine (451)', *Centre de recherches d'histoire et de civilisation byzantines*, Paris, 1970.

Dvornik, F., *The idea of apostolicity in Byzantium and the legend of the apostle Andrew*, Harvard, 1958.
The Photian schism: history and legend, Cambridge, 1948.

Grabar, A., *L'iconoclasme: dossier archéologique*, Paris, 1957.

Honigmann, E., *Le convent de Barsauma et le patriarcat jacobite d'Antioche et de Syrie*, Louvain, 1954.

Karlin-Hayter, P., 'Le synode à Constantinople de 886 à 912 et le rôle de Nicolas le Mystique', in *Jahrbuch der Österreichischen Byzantinistik*, 1970.

Lemerle, P., 'L'histoire des Pauliciens d'Asie Mineure d'après les sources grecques', *Centre de recherches d'histoire et civilisation byzantines*, Paris, 1973.

Maspero, G., *Histoire des patriarches d'Alexandrie depuis la mort de l'empereur Anastase jusqu'à la réconciliation des églises jacobites (518–616)*, Paris, 1923.

ECONOMIC AND SOCIAL ASPECTS

Demographic and social problems

Charanis, P., *Studies on the demography of the Byzantine empire*, Variorum Reprints, 1972.

Le féodalisme à Byzance: Problèmes du mode de production dans l'Empire Byzantin. Recherches internationales à la lumière du marxisme, Paris, 1974.

Jacoby, D., *Société et démographie à Byzance et en Romanie latine*, Variorum Reprints, 1975.

Morris, R., 'The powerful and the poor in tenth-century Byzantium: law and reality', in *Past and Present*, 1976.

Ostrogorsky, G., 'Observations on the aristocracy in Byzantium', in *Dumbarton Oaks Papers*, 1971.

Patlagean, E., *Pauvreté économique et pauvreté sociale à Byzance, IVe–VIIe siècles*, Paris, 1977.
Structure sociales, famille, chrétienté à Byzance, IVe–XIe siècles, Variorum Reprints, 1981.

Starr, J., *The Jews in the Byzantine empire (641–1204)*, Athens, 1939.

Town and country

Ahrweiler, H., *Byzance et la mer . . . aux VIIe–XVe siècle*, Paris, 1966.
Byzance: les pays et les territoires, Variorum Reprints, 1976.

Antonianis-Bibicou, H., *Recherches sur les douanes à Byzance*, Paris, 1963.

Beck, H. G., *Ideen und Realitäten im Byzanz*, Bonn, 1972.
Studien zur Frühgeschichte Konstantinopels, Munich, 1973.

Boulnois, L., *La route de la soie*, Paris, 1963.

Dagron, G., *Naissance d'une capitale: Constantinople et ses institutions de 330 à 451*, Paris, 1974.

Eickhoff, E., *Seekrieg und Seepolitik zwischen Islam und Abendland*, 2nd edn, Berlin, 1966.

Grierson, P., 'Coinage and money in the Byzantine empire, 498–1090', in *Settimane . . . di Spoleto*, 1961.

Janih, R., *Constantinople byzantine*, 2nd edn, Paris, 1964.

Kirstep, E., 'Die byzantinische Stadt', *Berichten zum XI internationalen Byzantischinen Kongress*, 1958.

Lemerle, P., 'Esquisse pour une histoire agraire de Byzance', in *Revue historique*, 1958.

Lewis, A. R. *Naval power and trade in the Mediterranean AD 500–1100*, Princeton, 1951.

*Liebeschutz, J. H. W. G., *Antioch: city and imperial administration in the later Roman empire*, Oxford, 1972.

Lopez, R. S., *Byzantium and the world around it: economic and institutional relations*, Variorum Reprints, 1978.

Morrisson, C., 'La dévaluation de la monnaie byzantine au XIe siècle: une réinterprétation', *Centre de recherches d'histoire et civilisation byzantines*, Paris, 1976.

Svoronos, N., 'Sur quelques formes de la vie rurale à Byzance', in *Annales, economies, sociétés, civilisations*, 1956.

Tchalenko, G., *Les villages antiques de Syrie du nord: le massif du Bélus à l'epoque romaine*, 3 vols, Paris, 1953–8.

Teall, J. L., 'The grain supply of the Byzantine Empire, 330–1052', in *Dumbarton Oaks Papers*, 1939.

THE CULTURE OF BYZANTIUM

*Beckwith, J., *The art of Constantinople*, 2nd edn, London, 1968.

'Byzantine Books and Bookmen', *Dumbarton Oaks Papers*, 1975.

*Cormack, R., *Writing in gold: Byzantine society and its icons*, London, 1985.

Dagron, G., 'Aux origines de la civilisation byzantine: langue de culture et langue d'État', in *Revue Historique*, 1969.

Delvoye, G., *L'art byzantin*, Paris, 1967.

Grabar, A., *L'âge d'or de Justinien*, 2 vols, Paris, 1966.
  Byzantine painting, Engl. transl., London, 1979.

*Kitzinger, E., *Byzantine art in the making*, London, 1977.

Lemerle, P., *Le style byzantin*, Paris, 1943.

*Mango, C. A., *Byzantine architecture*, New York, 1976.

Peeter, P., *Le tréfonds oriental de l'hagiographie byzantine*, Brussels, 1950.

THE MUSLIM WORLD

GENERAL SURVEYS OF MEDIEVAL ISLAM

Cahen, C., *L'Islam des origines à l'empire ottoman*, Paris, 1970.
  Les peuples musulmans dans l'histoire médiévale, Damascus, 1977.

Cambridge History of Islam, vols 1 and 2, Cambridge, 1970.

Ducellier, A., Kaplan, M., Martin, B., *Le Proche-Orient médiéval*, Paris, 1980.

Elisseeff, N., *L'Orient musulman au Moyen Age*, Paris, 1977.

The Encyclopedia of Islam, new edn, London, 1971–.

Encyclopédie de l'Islam, 2nd edn, Paris, 1960–.

Grunebaum, G. E. von, *Medieval Islam*, 2nd edn, Chicago, 1970.

Hitti, P. K., *History of the Arabs*, 6th edn, London, 1956.

Hodgson, M. G. S., *The venture of Islam: conscience and history in a world civilisation*, 3 vols, Chicago, 1974.

Select bibliography

Lewis, B., *The Arabs in history*, London, 1950.

Miquel, A., *L'Islam et sa civilisation*, Paris, 1968.

*Saunders, J. J., *A history of medieval Islam*, London, 1965.

Sauvaget, J., Cahen, C., *Introduction à l'histoire de l'Orient musulman*, 2nd edn, 1961.

*Schacht, J., Bosworth, C. E. (eds.), *The legacy of Islam*, Oxford, 1974.

Sourdel, D., *Histoire des Arabes*, Paris, 1976.

  and Sourdel, J., *La civilisation de l'Islam classique*, Paris, 1968.

STUDIES OF SHORTER PERIODS

Cahen, C., 'Points de vue sur le révolution abbasside', in *Revue historique*, 1963.

*Kennedy, H., *The early Abbasid caliphate*, London, 1981.

Lombard, M., *The golden age of Islam*, Engl. transl., Amsterdam, 1975.

Mantran, R., *L'expansion musulmane, VIIe–IXe siècle*, Paris 1969.

Shaban, M. A., *Islamic history AD 600–750: a new interpretation*, vol. 1, Cambridge, 1971; vol. 2, *750–1055*, Cambridge, 1976.

  The Abbasid revolution, Cambridge, 1970.

Wellhausen, J., *Das Arabische Reich und seine Sturz*, 2nd edn, Berlin 1960; Engl. transl. of 1st edn, Calcutta, 1927.

REGIONAL PROBLEMS AND ADMINISTRATION

The East

Cambridge History of Iran, vols 3 and 4, Cambridge, 1975–6.

Canard, M., *Byzance et les musulmans du Proche–Orient*, Variorum Reprints, 1973.

Christensen, A., *L'Iran sous le Sassanides*, Copenhagen, 1936.

Gibb, H. A. R., 'The evolution of government in early Islam', in *Studia Islamica*, 1955.

Grousset, R., *L'empire des steppes*, 2nd edn, 1969.

Sourdel, D., *Le vizirat à l'époque abbasside*, 2 vols, Damascus, 1950–60.

  'La politique religieuse du calife abbasside al-Mamoun', in *Revue des études islamiques*, 1962.

Werner, E., Markow, W., *Geschichte der Türken von den Anfängen bis zur Gegenwart*, Berlin, 1978.

The West

Brignon, J., Amine, A., Boutaleb, B., *Histoire du Maroc*, Casablanca, 1967.

Djait, H., Dachraoui, Talbi, M., *Histoire de la Tunisie*, vol. 2, Tunis, n.d.

Julien, C. A., *Histoire de l'Afrique du Nord*, 2nd edn, Paris, 1968.

Levi-Provençal, E., *Histoire de l'Espagne musulmane*, 3 vols, 1960–7.

Marçais, G., *La Berbérie musulmane et l'Orient*, Paris, 1948.

Talbi, M., *L'émirat aghlabide, 800–909*, Paris, 1966.

THE FAITH

Blachère, R., *Le Coran*, Paris, 1967.

Corbin, H., *Histoire de la philosophie islamique*, vol. 1, Paris, 1964.

Ducellier, A., *Le miroir de l'Islam; musulmans et chrétiens d'Orient au Moyen Age, VIIe–XIe siècles*, (Documents), Paris, 1971.

Fattal, A., *Le statut légal des non-musulmans en pays d'Islam*, Beirut, 1958.

Gaudefroy-Demombynes, M., *Mahomet*, 2nd edn, Paris, 1968.

Glick, T. F., *Islamic and Christian Spain in the early Middle Ages*, Princeton, 1979.

Goldziher, I., *Le dogme et la loi de l'Islam*, Fr. transl., Paris, 1920.

Laoust, H., *Les schismes de l'Islam: introduction à l'étude de la religion musulmane*, Paris, 1965.

Mones, H., 'Le rôle des hommes de religion dans l'histoire de l'Espagne musulmane jusqu'à la fin du califat', in *Studia Islamica*, 1964.

Rodinson, M., *Mohammed*, Engl. transl., London, 1971.

Watt, H. Montgomery, *Muhammad, prophet and statesman*, Oxford, 1961.

ECONOMIC, SOCIAL AND CULTURAL ASPECTS

ECONOMIC AND SOCIAL LIFE IN GENERAL

*Ashtor, E., *A social and economic history of the Near East in the Middle Ages*, London, 1976.

Cahen, C., 'Fiscalité, propriété et antagonismes sociaux aux temps des premiers Abassides', in *Arabica*, 1954.

  'L'histoire économique et sociale de l'Orient musulmane médiéval', in *Studia Islamica*, 1955.

  'L'évolution sociale du monde musulman face à celle du monde chrétien jusqu'au XIIe siècle', in *Cahiers de civilisation médiévale*, 1958, 1959.

Chalmeta, P., 'Concessions territoriales en al-Andalus . . .', in *Cuadernos de Historia Economica de Cateluna*, 1975

  El Señor del Zoce en Espana, Madrid, 1973.

Guichard, P., *Structures sociales 'orientales' et 'occidentales' dans l'Espagne musulmane*, Paris, 1977.

Rosenberg, B., 'L'histoire économique du Maghreb', in *Geschichte der islamischen Länder*, 1977.

Tyan, L., *Institutions de droit public musulman*, 2 vols, Paris, 1954–6.

Vanacker, C., 'Géographie économique de l'Afrique du nord selon les auteurs arabes (IXe–XIIe s.)', in *Annales, économies, sociétés, cultures*, 1973.

Urban life and trade

Balaguer-Prunes, A. M., *Las emisiones transicionales arabe–musulmanas de Hispania*, Barcelona, 1976.

Barcelo, M., 'El hiato en las acunaciones de ore en al-Andalus', in *Moneda y credito*, 1975.

Cahen, C., 'Mouvements populaires et autonomies urbaines dans l'Asie musulmane du Moyen Age', in *Arabica*, 1969.

Dennett, D. C., *Conversion and the poll-tax in early Islam*, Cambridge, 1950.

Devisse, J., 'Routes de commerce et échanges en Afrique occidentale en relations avec la Méditerranée', in *Revue d'histoire économique et sociale*, 1972.

Gardet, L., *La cité musulmane: vie sociale et politique*, 2nd edn, Paris, 1961.

Grierson, P., 'The monetary reform of Abd al-Malik', in Grierson, *Dark Age Numismatics*, Variorum Reprints, 1979.

Heyd, W., *Histoire du commerce du Levant au Moyen Age*, 2nd edn, Paris, 1967.

Hourani, A., Stern, S. M., *The Islamic city*, Oxford, 1970.

Teres, E., 'Le développement de la civilisation arabe à Tolede', in *Cahiers de Tunisie*, 1970.

Art and Architecture

Cresswell, K. A. C., *Early Muslim Architecture*, 2nd edn, Oxford, 1969.

*Grabar, O., *The formation of Islamic art*, New Haven and London, 1973.

Ottodorn, K., *L'art de l'Islam*, Paris, 1967.

Index

Note: A page number in italic type indicates a text illustration, and P indicates a colour plate.

Aachen, 333, 391, 398, 400, 413, 425–6, 471, 529
  chapel and palace, *424, 425,* 469
Aachen, Councils of, 395, 445, 448, 483
Abbas, uncle of Muhammad (*see also* Abbasids), 193, 194, 223
Abbasids (*see also* Islamic Empire), 183, 196, 197, 202, 205, 221–2, 223–9, 241–7, 252, 265, 279–80, *table,* 227
abbots (*see also hegoumenos,* 101, 421–2, 432, 434, 444, 447, 448–9
Abd al-Malik, Umayyad Caliph, 203, *204,* 209–10
Abraham (Ibrahim), 185, 189, 220
Abu Bakr, 193, 196
Abu Hashim, 195, 221
Abu Muslim, 217, 220, 222
Abuʾ l-Abbas, Abbasid Caliph, 222, 223, 225
Adalhard, 393, 396, 422, 467, 487
Adrianople, battle of (378), 7, 53, 111
Adriatic, 106, 172, 326, 328, 368, 373, 377, 384, 477, 517
Aegean, 201, 287, 299, 326, 327, 376, 377
Aetius, Roman general, 54, 55
Afghanistan, Afghans, 197, 204, 221, 253
Africa
  Black, 14, 275–6
  Byzantine, 60, 63, 64, 67, 70, 73, 155, 158, 172, 200, 286, 290, 294
  Islamic, *see* Ifriqiya, Maghrib
  Roman, 19, 24–7 *passim,* 37, 38, 40–3 *passim,* 47, 50, 106, 505
  Vandal, 53, 57, 59, 66, 77, 90, 474
Agilulf, King of the Lombards, 61, 90, P
Agobard, Achbishop of Lyons, 393, 396, 423, 442, 443, 445, 467, 510
Ahaholfing clan (Alamannia), 413
Ahimaʾaz of Oria, 350
Ahmad ibn Hanbal, 228, 246, 262
Aistulf, King of the Lombards, 385, 420
Alamannia (*see also* Swabia), 94, 397, 413, 419, 442, 463

Alamans, 53, 56, 57, 59, 77, 78, 83, 383, 384, 443
  laws, 65, 423, 505–6
Alans, 53, 55, 83, 148–9
Alaric, Visigothic chieftain, 7, 14, 53, 111
Alaric II, King of the Visigoths, 63, 89
  Breviarium Alarici, 63
Alcuin, 388, 389, 422, 450, 462, 464, 467, 483, 499
  biblical revision, 465
Alexandria, 75, 108, 116, 137, 142, 144, 145, 146, 164, 185, 284, 482, 513, 515, 518
  decline, 249
Alexandria, Church and Patriarchate, 111, 126, 128, 129, 140, 150, 165, 171
Alfonso I, King of the Asturias, 384
Alfonso II, King of the Asturias, 392
Alfonso III, 'the Great', King of the Asturias, 408, 526
Ali, nephew of Muhammad, 186, 190, 193–4, 195, 196, 197, 220
Alids, 195, 202, 220–3, 226–7, 243, 279 (*see also* Shiʾa)
Alps, 50, 57, 78, 159, 387, 397, 520, 522
  Alpine crossings, 75, 515–18 *passim,* 522, 529
Amalfi, Amalfitans, 275, 328, 329, *521*
Ambrose, Bishop of Milan, 19, 41, 46
Amr, Arab general, 189, 197, 265
Anastasius I, Byzantine Emperor, 57, 110, 116, 123, 151, 153, 156, 161, 171, 339
al-Andalus (Muslim Spain), 67, 200–1, 209–10, 218, 228–30, *231,* 232, 235–7, 248, 260, 261, 387, 406, 408–9, 511, 513, 518, *map,* 231
Andalusia, 53, 201
Andronikos Doukas, 358, 360
Anglo-Saxon kingdom(s) (*see also* England), 61, 383, 384, 386, 392, 411, 418, 485, 512
  coinage and currency, 88, 434, 511, 512, 513
  conversion to Christianity, 94
  government, 418, 421, 434–5, 490–1, 508

540

Anglo-Saxons (*see also* Saxons)
  occupation of Britain, 55, 77, 85, 93, 477, 478
  learning and literature, 462, 468
  missionary activity, 94–5, 102, 463
  trading activity, 511, 514
animal husbandry, 30, 38, 86, 132, 498, 499, 524
annona (bread doles), 27, 66, 70, 115, 144, 164, 283
Anskar, St, 393, 450–1
Antioch, 75, 106–8 *passim*, 115, 123, 137, *138*, 141–6 *passim*, 158, 161, 164, 167, 175, 182, 185, 249, 277, 286, 298, 332, 476
Antioch, Church and Patriarchate, 126, 128, 140, 151, 169, 170, 172
Antique culture and learning (*see also* manuscripts and libraries), 47–8, 110, 139–40, 238, 248–9, 320–3 *passim*, 352, 363–4, 459–60, 461, 464, 467, 473
Antony, St, 98, 136
antrustiones, antrustions, 84, 91, 486
Aquitaine, 27, 60–1, 70, 75, 98, 418, 420, 461, 476, 477, 493, 498, 506, 508
  Visigothic occupation, 53, 56–7, 63, 77, 78, 85, 89
  eighth-century principality, 383, 384, 419
  Carolingian sub-kingdom, 388, 393, 396–8 *passim*, 401, 428, 431, 447, 481, 484, 490
  tenth-century dukes, 410, 487, 512
Aquitanians, 67, 93–4, 102, 443
Arabs (*see also* Saracens)
  pre-Islam, in Arabia, 184–5, on Syrian borders, 111, 121, 156, 158, 169, 175, 184–5
  role in warfare, 196–200 *passim*, 202, 211, 287, 293, 298, 328, 375–7
  tribes and tribalism, 184, 195, 205, 211, 214, 216–17, 229–31, 246, 279
Arcadius, East Roman emperor, 19, 104, 113, 114
Architecture
  Armenian, 366, *374*
  in Barbarian kingdoms, 73, *97*
  Byzantine, 155, *157*, *159*, P
  Carolingian, *449*, *451*, 468–9
  Islamic, 190–1, 212, *213*, *215*, 242, 245, *247*, 247, 256–8, P
  Ottonian, 469, 471
Ardzuni clan (Armenia), 373
Arethas of Patras, 354–5, 358, 364
Ariadne, Byzantine Empress, 149, *149*, 150, 151, 153
Arianism, 56, 57–8, 59, 61, 68, 76, 89–90, 91, 98, 128, 144, 148–9
Aristotle, 238, 248, 319, 461, 468
Arles, 22, 23, 64, 71, 406, 408, 520
  'kingdom' of, 409
Armenia, 107, 111–12, 120, 158, 172, 175, 182, 197, 283, 284, 293, 294, 297, 331
  Arab conquest of, 286
  products of, 253, 254, 272
  ruling clans, 326, 373
Armenians, 281, 291, 297–8, 315, 331, 332, 375

Armorica (*see also* Brittany), 20, 50, 53, 55, 56, 66
arms and armour, 27, *28*, *82*, 82–3, 119, *119*, 296, *296*, 368, 403, 432, 500, 518, 522
Arnulf, East Frankish king, Emperor, 399, 402, 406, 409, 423, 428
Arnulfings, 102, 383, 487
art (*see also* architecture)
  Antique, *4*, *6*, *13*, *13*, *18*, *105*, 364, 463, 469, 471, P
  Bulgar, *289*, P
  Byzantine (*see also* icons), *72*, *112*, *131*, 155, 176, *324*, 333, 364, *365*, *366*, 463, 471, P
  Carolingian, 468, *470*, 471, *472*, *489*, P
  Germanic, *6*, *81*, *92*, 463, *479*
  Irish, P
  'Muslim', 254–6, *255*, *257*, 261–2, *264*, 321, 333
  Northumbrian, *60*, *99*, 463, *463*
  Scandinavian, *2*, *88*, 527
Artavasdos, Byzantine emperor, 292, 293, 297, 302, 304
Asia Minor, 105, 107–8, 132, 136, 166, 167, 170, 295, 298, 302, 346
  transfer of populations from, 175, 299
  warfare in, 112, 158, 199, 298, 301, 308, 309, 315
Aspar, Byzantine general, 148–9, 150
Asturias, kingdom of the, 384, 386, 392, 408, 411, 468, 481, 488, 498, 510
  government of, 436–7
Athanagild, King of the Visigoths, 58, 59, 60
Athelstan, King of England, 407, 410
Athens, 14, 106, 170, 298, 307, 326, 327, 337, 339, 376
Attalia (Antalya), 107, 295, 298, 377
Augustine, St, Bishop of Hippo, 7, 14, 48, 49, 53, 73, 91, 94, 95, 445, 460, 468, 474
Augustine, St, Archbishop of Canterbury, 73
Augustus, Roman emperor, 68, 113, 118, 492, 529
Austrasia, Austrasians, 60, 68, 102, 382, 383, 385, 418–19, 431, 432, 444, 485, 506
Avars, 59, 83, 111, 160, 171, 174, 175, 284, 285, 289, 388, 409, 428, 432, 450, 477
Azerbaijan, 107, 220, 241, 253, 373

Babenberg clan (East Frankish kingdom), 413
Baghdad (Madinat al-Salam; *see also* Sawad), 14, 258, 277
  as Abbasid capital, 226, 227, 241–3, 245, 246–50 *passim*, 320, 326, 333, 360, 373, 392
  crafts and industries, 246, 254, 261, 269
  intellectual life, 248, 352
  population, 249–50
  map, 241
Bagratuni clan (Armenia), 373
Balearic Islands, 201, 273, 408
Balkans (*see also* Bulgaria), 7, 106, 111, 120, 148, 150, 156, 158–60 *passim*, 171–2, 174–5, 283, 284–5, 287, 294, 326, 327, 329, 351, 372

Index

Balkh, 183, 204, 216, 226, 272, 277
Balt clan (Visigothic), 81, 417
Baltic, 273, 403, 404, 516, 518, 519
Barbarian ('Romano-Germanic') kingdoms
    fifth to sixth centuries, 52–8, 62–75, 80–4
    seventh to eighth centuries, 59–61, 67, 381–3,
      417–19, 420, 484–6
Barcelona, 39, 45, 71, 73, 76, 276, 391, 410, 444
Bardas, uncle of Michael III, 315, 323, 325, 358
Bardas Phokas, 361, 362, 375
Bari, 272, 275, 328, 377, 408
Barmakids, 183, 226, 228
Basil I, Byzantine emperor (*see also* Macedonian
    dynasty, Photios), 310, 312, 315, 319, 321,
    323, 332, 335, 336, 337, 339, 340, 345,
    355, 356, 367, 369, 375, 400
    seizure of power, 315–16
    campaigns of reconquest, 350–1, 373, 376–7
    codifications of the law, 351
    imperial image and, 323, 348, 351, 353, 363
Basil II, Byzantine emperor, 346, 360, 371
Basil, St, Bishop of Caesarea, 127, 140, 145
    monastic rule of, 34, 98, 146, 308, 310
Basra, 197, 204, 214, 216, 220, 221, 250
    market (Mirbad), 269
Basques, Basque country, 50, 60, 61, 67, 83, 388,
    391, 392, 419, 444, 476, 477
Bavaria, Bavarians
    pre-Caroligian, 57, 59, 77, 94–5, 383, 387, 412,
      419, 442, 460, 463, 477, 505
    Caroligian, 388, 391, 412, 423, 488
    Caroligian sub-kingdom, 396, 397, 398, 424
    Ottonian, 412–13
Bede, 462, 468
Belisarius, Byzantine general, 58–9, 67, 154, 158
Benedict of Aniane, St, 393, 395, 422, 442, 448
Benedict of Nursia, St, 100–2, 103, 460, 462
    Benedictine Rule, 101–2, 445, 448, 462
Benedict Biscop, 95, 462
benefices (*see also* commendation, vassalage), 401,
    434, 438–40, 486, 490, 508
Benevento, Lombard duchy of, 59, 275, 383, 391,
    392, 412, 419, 432, 462, 477, 482
Berbers, 159, 174, 199–200, 219, 228, 230–2,
    236, 384, 476
    in Spain, 209, 229, 232, 237, 259, 274, 384,
    477
Berengar of Friuli, 482
    clan of, 402
Bernard, King of Italy, 396
Bernard, Bernardine clan, 442, 487
Bible, 48, 381, 453, 460, 464, 465, 473
Birka, 393, 451, 516, 518, 519, 520
bishops (*see also* Church), 31–3, 93, 97–8, 102,
    121, 125–6, 137, 140, 304, 306, 421–2, 439,
    445–8, 461, 483–4
Black Sea, 106, 107, 277, 290, 294, 326, 327,
    330, 344, 368, 406
Boethius, 68, 90, 461, 468
Bogomils, 351, 372

Boniface, St, 95, 102, 422, 445, 460, 462
Boris (Boris-Michael), Bulgar Khan, 330, 334–5,
    369, 371
Boso of Provence, 399, 402, 409, 487
Boulogne, 53, 55, 86, 433, 516
Boyars, 335, 369, 371
Bretons (*see also* Brittany), 55, 56, 60, 67, 85, 383,
    393, 406, 432, 444, 476, 482
    laws, 66, 80, 83, 87
Britain, British Isles, 20, 26, 37, 38, 46, 50, 53,
    77, 79, 87, 91, 93, 272, 404, 408, 474, 476,
    map, 405
Britons, British, 55, 61, 77, 94
Brittany, 73, 77, 79, 89, 93, 392, 407, 428, 475,
    507
    ecclesiastical organisation, 96, 392, 436
    rulers, 66, 392, 401, 410, 436
Brunhild, Merovingian queen, 422, 522
Bruno, Archbishop of Cologne, 356, 414, 415 (*see
    also* Otto I)
bucellarii, 31, 67, 69, 158
Buddhism, 183, 197, 226
Bulgaria, Bulgar State, 289–90, 293–4, 309, 314,
    315, 317, 329, 329–30, 350, 358, 361, 368,
    369–72, *370*
    coinage, 278, 327
    conversion of Christianity, 333–5, 349, 371–2
    Law concerning the Accused, 334
Bulgars, 156, 158, 160, 289, 298, 299, 477
    and slave trade, 272, 273
Burgundians, 26, 54, 55, 62, 63, 66, 69, 71, 77,
    80, 85, 443
    sixth-century kingdom, 56, 57, 65, 89; *Lex
    Romana*
Burgundy, 60, 78, 383, 384, 409, 476, 495, 514
    Carolingian, 386, 397, 398, 439, 444
    tenth-century, 402, 409, 410, 414, 415
Byzantine (East Roman) Empire (*see also*
    Constantinople), 52, 53, 90, chapters 3 and 4
    passim, 199, 202, 226, 276, chapters 7 and 8
    passim, 388, 389, 400, 414
    agriculture, 131–2, *131*, 166, 299, 341–4, *343*
    armies, 118–19, *119*, 158, 171–2, 199, 294–6,
      297–8, *300*, 345–6, 368 (*see also* themes)
    coinage and currency, 47, 73–5, 88–9, 119–20,
      160, 161–2, *162*, 203, 283, *311*, 326–7,
      511
    crafts and industries, 141, 163–4, 294, 337–8,
      340–1, *340*, 364, 366
    culture and intellectual life, 312, 319–23, 352–3,
      354–5, 363–7
    emperor, status of, 113, 115, 154–5, 165, 176,
      284, 301, 304–6, 310–11, 312, 319, 320–1,
      323, 348–9, 351–3, 364, 368, 371
    empresses, 114, 144, *149*, 149–50, 151, 153–4,
      307, 308–9, 315, 357
    extent, 105–8, 148, 172, 283, 325–6, 330–1,
      369, 376, *map*, 173
    external relations, 110–12, 158, 294, 330,
      333–5, 341, 352, 370–3

government and administration, 113–30, 164–5,
  294–7, 339, 341, 354–5, *354*, (*see also*
  exarchates)
landed property, 297, 346–7
law, 113, 118, 154–5, 156, 310, 305, 334, 339,
  349, 351
naval forces, 295, 297, 339, 346, 377
population, 160–1; transfers of, 164, 175, 287,
  294, 297, 299, 326
reconquest of the West, 58–9, 156–9, 172, 285,
  290–1, 375
religious disputes, 128–30, 150–4, 167–70,
  316–17, 323, 325 (*see also* iconoclasm,
  Papacy)
social composition, 133–4, 139, 141–2, 166,
  297–300, 313–14, 343, 346–8, *347*, 355–6,
  360–3
taxation, 11–12, 115–18, 113–4, 161, 165–6,
  295–6, 299–300, 342–4
wars, 158–9, 174–5, 199, 283–5, 286–8,
  293–4, 325–6, 329, 330–3, 350, 368, 373–7

Cambrai, 56, 428, 492, 516
  map, 74
Canon Law
  Byzantine, 127, 140, 291–2, 311, 331
  Roman, 424, 464
canons, cathedral clergy, 447, 483–4, 509–10
  Rule for, 445
Canterbury, 73, 86, 88, 462, 510
Capetian dynasty, 402, 428, 458
capitularies (*see also* Carolingian Empire,
    Charlemagne, Charles the Bald), 297, 423,
    428, 429, 445, 494, 496
  Admonitio generalis (789), 464
  Frankfurt (793–4), 512
  Nijmegen (806), 443
  Quierzy (877), 401, 440
  Saxon, 388, 450
  De Villis, 429
Cappadocia, 107, 140, 283, 284, 332
  monks of, 136, *322*, P
Carloman, King of Western Francia, 401, 440, 497
Carolingian dynasty (*see also* Arnulfings, Pippinids),
    102, 311, 383, 386, 401, 413, 414, 442,
    471, 487–8
  table, 400
Carolingian Empire (*see also* Charlemagne, Louis the
    Pious), 328, 334, 368, 373, 376, 388–91,
    393, 397–401, 406, 409, 439, 474
  agriculture, 497, 498–9, *501*, 501–8
  art and learning, 464–8, *469*, *470*, 471–3, *472*
  and the Church, 393, 395–7, 401, 422–3, 439,
    442, 445–8, 450–52, 458, 471, 483–4, 525
    (*see also* Papacy)
  coinage and currency, 512–14
  economic resources, 276, 278, 429, 431–2,
    439–40, 507–9, 511, 513–14, 516, 522
  government, 423–31, 437, 438, 490, 525 (*see*
    also capitularies, counts, vassalage)

internal tensions, 396–7, 402, 438, 440–1,
  442–4, 452–3, 458
justice, 423, 426, 427, 428–9, 441
landed property, 396, 434, 438–40, 488, 490–1,
  497, 500, 503–8
military basis, 427–8, 432–4, 437, 439, 445,
  490, 495
population, 480–3, 526
social composition, 486–496
sub-kingdoms, 396–7, 424–5, 428 (*see also*
  Aquitaine, Bavaria, Italy)
taxation, 431, 346, 494, 495, 512, 526
Carthage, 33, 46, 48, 53, 75, 77, 90, 171, 199,
  515
Caspian Sea, 107, 110, 203, 277, 326, 406
Cassiodorus, 461, 462
Castille, 392, 410–11
castles, 237, 392, 406, 410, 411–12, 432
Catalonia, 410, 411, 438, 467, 468, 476, 481,
  482, 488, 490, 493, 495, 498, 526 (*see also*
  Spanish March, Septimania)
Caucasus, 106, 111, 156, 158, 197, 284, 293,
  326, 331, 333, 368, 373
Celts (*see also* Ireland, Irish), 50, 76, 77, 83–6
  passim, 89, 91, 434, 461
  and Christianity, 91, 92–4, 100
  laws, 64, 96
Chalcedon, Council of (451), 32, 108, 126,
  127, 129, 147, 149, 150, 151, 169,
  182
Chalcedonians, 144, 153, 154, 167, 172, 286
Chanson de Roland, 465
Charlemagne, King of the Franks, Emperor (*see also*
    Carolingian Empire), 1, *378*, 387–91, *390*,
    413–14, 415, 416, 428, 443, 491, 512, 523,
    525, 526, 529
  educational reforms, 464–5
  imperial coronation, 389, 391
  management of royal estates, 429, 431, 498,
    502
  political ideas and practices, 393, 395–6, 399,
    412, 425–9, 433–4, 438, 441, 450, 452, 481,
    490, 522, 523
  relations with the Church, 423, 445–8, 449,
    450, 455, 457, 464–5, 471
  warfare, 432–3
Charles the Bald, King of Western Francia, Emperor
    (*see also* Western Francia), 396–9, 401–2, 406,
    422, 429, 436, 439, 440, 441, 481, *489*,
    490, 509, 510, 514, 520, 522, 525
  imperial coronation, 400
Charles III, 'the Simple', King of Western Francia,
    407, 409, 414
Charles, King of Provence, 398–9
Charles the Fat, King of Eastern and Western
    Francia,
  Emperor, 399, 458, 520
  imperial coronation, 400
Charles Martel, Mayor of the Palace, 384, 385,
    421, 431, 442, 444, 462, 486, 516

Index

China, Chinese Empire, 45, 142, 158, 162, 197, 272, 276, 277, 326 (*see also* silk)
  influence on Islamic art, 261–2, *264*, 272
Chindaswind, King of the Visigoths, 66–7, 485
Chlothar, King of the Franks, 60, 418, 485
Çhosroes I, King of Persia, 10, 158, 170, 183
Christ, *see* Jesus Christ
Christendom, 20, 91, 94, 330, 386, 400, 415, 452, 525
Christianity (*see also* Church)
  in Late Antiquity, 4, 6, 20, 33, 36, 113
  spread of in the East, 108, 111, 120–5, 129
  spread of to Eastern Europe, 334, 415, 452
  spread of to Scandinavia, 451, 450–1
  spread of to Slav States, 334–5, 349, 371–3
Chrodegang, Bishop of Metz, 422, 445
chrysoboulloi, 354, *354*
Chrysocheir, Paulician leader, 332, 350
Chur, 448; *Lex Romana Curiensis*, 448
Church (*see also* bishops, Canon Law, marriage, Papacy),
  in Barbarian kingdoms, 52, 91, 96–8, 103, 381, 382, 421–2, 485–6
  in Bulgaria, 335, 372
  in the Byzantine Empire, 117, 120, 125–7, 291–2, 302–3, 306, 316–17, 325, 348–9, 357–8
  Carolingian, *see* Carolingian Empire
  Roman Catholic, *see* Papacy
  charitable role, 32–3, 73, 120, 126–7, 145, 164, 167, 345, 483–4, 496
church-building, 73, 98, 453, 468–9, 471, 509–10
civitas, civitates (*see also* towns), 9, 22, 31, 34, 40, 45, 50, 66, 75, 420, 427
Clovis, King of the Franks, 1, 7, 56–7, 71, 82, 89, 90, 418, 486
  conversion to Catholic Christianity, 56–7
Cluny, 449, 458, 471, 484, 487
Code of Justinian, 63, 113, 154–5, 156, 301, 492
coin hoards, 75, 273, *274*, 278, 511, 513
collegia, see guilds
Cologne, 25, 45, 75, 471, 482, 516, 518
  see of, 422, 426, 448, 450
Colombanus, St, 93, 95, 100, 102
colonus, coloni, 30–7 *passim*, 40, 47, 67–71 *passim*, 85, 134, 164, 236, 485, 492, 495–6, 503, 505–7
Columella, 42, 328, 482, 502
comes, see counts
commendation, 434, 435, 439, 440, 486, 488, 491, 524
Conrad I, King of Eastern Francia, 413
Constans II, Byzantine Emperor, 281, 284, 287, 290–1
Constantine I, the Great, Roman Emperor, 6, 7, 104, 113, 115, 116, 120, 126, 155, 158, 285, 305, 308, 310, 349, 389
  coinage and currency, 23, 119
Constantine IV, Byzantine Emperor, 287, 289

Constantine V, Byzantine Emperor, 293–4, 297–306, 316, 317
  Khazar marriage of, *293*, 294, 371
Constantine VI, Byzantine Emperor, 307–11, 315, 332, 389
Constantine VII, 'Porphyrogennetos', Byzantine Emperor, 336, 346, 451, 352–3, 355, 362, 375
  birth and minority, 357–8, 371
  relations with Lakapenoi, 360, 362
  Book of Ceremonies, 155, 321, 339, 353–4, 363, 375
  On the Administration of the Empire, 352, 371, 372, 377
  On the Thames, 352
Constantine-Cyril, St, 323, 334
Constantinople, 7, 19, 56, 75, chapters 3 and 4 *passim*, 199, chapters 7 and 8 *passim*, 333, 367, 420, 468, *map*, 117
  'New Rome', 104, *105*, 115, 349
  eighth-century decline, 298
  revival in ninth and tenth centuries, 339–41
  crafts and industries, 75, 141, 294, 340–1
  defence of, 114, *114*, 115, 144, 165, 199, 283–4, 285, 287, 293, 295
  Great Palace and its ceremonies, *112, 131*, 155, 176, 301, 319, 340–1, 348, 353–5
  Hippodrome, 115, 142–4, *143*, 164–5, 176, 304, 323, 341, 367
  population, 298, 340
  St Sophia, 144, 155, *157*, *324*, 349, 352, 358, 359, P
  School of Magnaura Palace, 323, 348
Constantinople, Church and Patriarchate, 114, 125–6, 150, 285–6, 308, 316, 325, 341, 351, 358, 369
  wealth of, 117, 284
Constantinople, Council of (381), 125, 128
convenientiae, 69, 440–1, 490
Copts (*see also* Egypt, Monophysitism), 108, 169, 182, 204, 261, 262
  Coptic monasticism, 129, 140, 146
Corbie (*see also* Adalhard), 416, 450, 463, 465, 495, 496, 497, 500, 503, 512
  foundation of, 461–2
Cordoba, 222, 248, 256, 257–8, 333
  emirate, 201, 205, 218, 228, 237, 384, 392
  caliphate (founded 929), 201, 408, 518
  Great Mosque, 257–8, P
Corinth, 174, 298, 326, 327, 337, 338, 339
Cornwall, 79, 94, 392
  tin from 39, 75
Corvey, 413, 416, 450, *451*, 468, 469
Cosmas Indicopleustes, 120, 162
Coulaines, assembly of (843), 401, 439, 440
counts
  late Roman (*comes civitatis*), 22, 64, 66, 420
  Carolingian, before, 840, 427–8, 432, 447, 490, 496
  Carolingian, after 840, 401, 412, 439, 490, 496

544

Crete, 106, 305, 327, 328, 337, 375, 376, 377
Croatia, 373, 393, 517
Ctesiphon, 12, 182, 185, 249
  royal palace, *183*
curia, curiae (municipal councils), 34, 138–9, 141, 142
curiales, curials, town councillors, 22, 34–6, 43, 66, 139, 175, 338
cursus publicus, *see* transport and communications
Cyprus, 106, 199, 202, 287, 283, 376, 377
Cyril, *see* Constantine-Cyril
Cyrillic script, 369
Czechs, 391, 413

Dagobert, King of the Franks, 10, 60, *75*, 418, 486, 514, 526, *528*
Damascus, (*see also* Syria, Umayyads), 196, *217*, 218, 253, 254, 269, 283
  Umayyad mosque, 197, 218, 294
Danelaw, 407, 435, 481
Danes (*see also* Denmark, Vikings), 391, 402, 404, 406–7, 428, 429, 435, 451, 482, 508, 526
  social groupings, 483
Danube, 25, 27, 54, 56, 57, 106, 111, 160, 174, 289, 293, 326, 370, 433
Danubian plain, 43, 59, 112, 174, 370, 482
Dar al-Islam, 181–2, 190, 191, 239, 254, 278, 279
al-Dawudi, 232, 236
decurions, *see curiales*
Demetrios, St, 121, 171, 172, *174*, 284, 339
Denmark, 415, 450–1, 482, 511, 519
'deserts', spiritual function of, 34, 135–6, 161, 166, 167, *168*, 184
dhimmis, 204, 206, 207, 209, 211, 236
Digenis Akritas, 332
disease (*see also* plague), 5, 145, 456–7
  animal epidemics, 161
donation of Constantine, 386
Dorestad, 61, 416, 511, 514, 516–20 *passim*, 529
Doukai clan, 360
Dublin, 519

East Anglia, kingdom of, 61, 94, 392
Eastern Francia (East Frankish kingdom), 398, 399, 402, 406, 412, 413, 423, 451–2, 490, 500
  (*see also* Germany)
Eberhard, Marquess of Friuli, 488, 513
Ebroin, Mayor of the Palace of Neustria, 383, 485
Edessa, 107, 151, 172, 175
  mandylion, 176, 373
education, *see* schools
Edward the Elder, King of England, 407, 411
Egica, King of the Visigoths, 67, 420
Egypt (*see also* Alexandria, Copts)
  Late Roman, 12, 24
  Byzantine, 104, 106, 109, 126, 129, 132, 134, 148, 150, 165, 169, 182, 254, 283–4
  Islamic, 197, 212, 216, 239, 240, 241, 247,

247, 249, 251, 253–4, 261–3 *passim*, 265–6, 270, 517, 520
Eigenkirchen, 97, 422, 445, 525
Einhard, 387, 389, 419, 464, 467, 487
Ekloga, 301, 305, 334, 351
Elbe, 391, 393, 413, 433, 452
Eligius, St, 93–4, 102, 514
Elijah, St, 348, 356
England (*see also* Anglo-Saxon kingdoms, Danelaw), 52, 79, 97, 381, 406–7, 441, 502, 510, 526
English Channel, 20, 88, 404, 516, 529
Epanogoge, 339, 349, 351
Ephesus, 107, 137, 337, 339
Ephesus, Council of (431), 129, 146
Ermoldus Nigellus, 474
Essex, kingdom of, 61, 94, 418
Ethiopia, 111, 156, 158, 161, 184, 187
Etichonids, Frankish clan, 442, 487
Euclid, 248, 320, 461
Eudo, *princeps* of Aquitaine, 67, 383, 384, 419
Euphrates, 184, 214, 241, 265, *269*, 277, 373
Euric, King of the Visigoths, 64, 74, 89
  Code of Euric, 80
Europe, 76, 102–3, 382–3, 386, 398, 415, 443, 452, 465, 471, 527, 529
  demographic fluctuations, 474–83
  land clearances, seventh–tenth centuries, 478, 480–1, 482, 493, 498, 502, 508, 526
Euthymios, Patriarch of Constantinople, 296, 355, 358, 366
Euthymios the Younger, 344–5, 367
exarchates, 64, 70, 172, 173, 290, 384 (*see also* Ravenna)

faida, *see* vengeance
famine, 5, 131, 161, 172, 347, 388, 474, 476, 477, 480
Fars, 196, 203, 220, 241, 254
Fatima, 226 (*see also* Alids)
Fatimids, 187, 222, 232, 263, 276
federates, 26–7, 53, 54–6, 62, 66, 67, 73, 76, 80, 128, 149, 295
feo, fevum, 490
Ferghana, 183, 197, 204, 277
Fernan Gonzales, Count of Castile, 410, 488
'feudal' tendencies, 377, 415, 438, 490
Fez, 216, 228, 229, 230, 257
Flanders, 85, 93, 410, 482, 491, 492, 505
Flodoard of Rheims, 467, 483
foodstuffs, 27, 38–9, *38*, 87, 130–1, 235, 252–3, 270, 456, 497, 499–500, 503, 522
Fontenoy-en-Puisaye, battle of (841), 397, 482
forests, (*see also saltus*), 37–8, 86–7, 478, 497–8
Francis (*see also* Frankish kingdom(s), Franks), 78, 386, 428, 508, 527
Franconia (Franken), 77, 413, 507
Frankfurt, Council of (794), 390
Frankish kingdom(s), (*see also* Austrasia, Neustria)
  Merovingien, 53, 56–7, 60–1, 65, 66, 70, 73–4,

Index

Frankish kingdom(s) (*cont.*)
    93, 418–19, 421, 485–6, 511–12; coinage,
    75, *75*
    Carolingian 334, 369, 385–7 (and *see*
    Carolingian Empire)
Franks (*see also* Frankish kingdoms)
    infiltration of Gaul, 26, 50, 53, 55, 62, 77–8
    under the Merovingians, 57, 89, 93
    under the Carolingians, 386, 525 (and *see*
    Carolingian Empire)
    customs and characteristics, 82, 83–4, 98
    laws, 80, 423
Frisia (*see also* Frisians, terps), 9, 94–5, 382, 386,
    387, 398, 413, 419, 499, 516
    over-population, 480
    village communities, 491, 495
Frisians, 55, 61, 77, 78, 86, 383, 384, 520, 525
    coinage, 88, 511
    laws, 423
    seafaring, 87–8, 480, 517, 525
    trading activity, 88, 511, 516–19 *passim,* 520
Friuli, 96, 383, 402, 412, 419
Fulda, 95, 102, 447, *449,* 455, 463, 467, 468,
    469, 483, 510
Fustat (*see also* Tulunids), 214, 216, 248, 249,
    250–1, 253, 256, 257, 263, 270
    glassware, 262

Gaiseric, King of the Vandals, 54, 55, 57
Galicia (*see also* Asturias, kingdom of the), 20, 37,
    278, 392, 436, 477, 499, 502, 506
    gold and tin mines, 39
    monasteries, 93, 102
Gallo-Romans, 56, 68, 78, 89, 444, 485
Garcia I, King of Leon, 409
Gascony, 401, 410
Gaul, 9, 10, 12, 13, 23, 54, 57, 71, 383, 420,
    461, 465, 474–6, 485; population *c.* 400 AD,
    36–7, *map,* 385
    northern Gaul, 43, 52, 53, 76, 85, 93, 98, 382,
    428, 462, 503, 511, 516
    southern Gaul, 11, 26, 47, 52, 67, 69, 459, 485,
    506 (*see also* Aquitaine, Provence)
George of Pisidia, 171, 285
Georgians, 366, 375
Gerald of Aurillac, 69, 444, 449, 492, 522
Gerard of Roussillon, 448
Gerard of Vienne, 399, 402, 444, 487
Gerbert of Aurillac, 444, 467
Germanic peoples (*see also* Barbarian 'Romano-
    Germanic' kingdoms, *federates, laeti*)
    and the Roman Empire, 17, 26–7, 76–9, 102–3
    legal system, 80, 83, 91, 427, 428–9, 436
    patterns of settlement, 84–6
    way of life, 80–9
germanitas, 382–3, 524
Germany, 9, 57, 95, 382, 409, 427, 428, 469,
    480, 491, 502, 508, 509, 514 (*see also* Eastern
    Francia)

tenth-century kingdom of, 412–15, 437–8, 448,
    454, 468, 526
Gero, Markgraf, 413
Ghassanids, 111, 158, 175, 184
Ghent, 94, 433, 510
ghildes (*see also* oaths), 441, 453, 458, 524
Gibraltar (Jebel al-Tariq), 200, 201, 278
glass-making, 45, 75, 262, 518, P
gnosticism, 129, 195, 332
Godofrid, King of the Danes, 391
Gorm, King of Denmark, 451
Gorze, 449
Goths (*see also* Ostrogoths, Visigoths), 3, 7, 9, 26,
    58, 63, 66, 81, 82, 83, 111, 403
Gottschalk, 467
Greece, 75, 287, 298, 308, 327, 328, 350, 376
Greek Fire, 287, *296,* 297
Gregorian chant, 447, 462
Gregorian reform movement, 401, 448, 467
Gregory I, the Great, Pope, 61, 66, 69, 90, 94, 95,
    156, 172, 285, 422, 447, 451, 461
    Dialogues, 101–2, 461
    Pastoral Care, 461, 468
Gregory II, Pope, 95, 301
Gregory III, Pope, 302
Gregory IV, Pope, 397
Gregory of Nazianzus, 140, 351
Gregory of Nyssa, 140
Gregory of Tours, 8, 416
Grimoald, Austrasian Mayor of the Palace, 383
Guidones, Frankish clan, 402, 487, 488
guilds
    Late Roman, 36, 73
    Byzantine, 117, 141, 162, 340
    Islamic, 252–3
Gundobad, King of the Burgundians, 57, 63
    Law of Gundobad, 80
Guy of Spoleto, Emperor, (*see also* Guidones), 399,
    402

hacksilver, 514
Hadrian I, Pope, 387, 389, 464, 510
Haithabu (Hedeby), 511, 516, 518, 519, 520
Hamburg, 391, 395, 406
    see of, 450, 451
Hamwih (Hamwic), 88, 511, 516, 519, 520
Hanbalites, *see* Ahmad ibn Hanbal
Harald, King of the Danes, 393, 450–1
Harald Bluetooth, Kind of Denmark, 415, 451
Harun al-Rashid, Abbasid Caliph, 185, 207, 211,
    224, 225, 226, 233, 249, 262, 263, 266,
    330, 392
Hassan ibn al-Nu'man, Arab general, 199, 209,
    256
Hebrew, *see* Languages
Hegira, the (*Hijra*), 187, 189, 202, 220, 279, 280
hegoumenos (*see also* abbots), 167, 306, 309, 321,
    358, 367

Helena, wife of Emperor Constantine VII, 360, 373
Hellenism, 121, 140, 167, 248, 284, 286, 312, 377
   Hellenisation, 314, 350
Henry I, 'the Fowler', King of Germany, 409, 413, 437, 444
   Heinrichsburgen, 409
Herakleios I, Byzantine Emperor, 10, 170–1, 175, 177, 182, 281, 283, 285, 286, 294, 325, 373
   Ekthesis, 286, 290
Heraklids, Heraklian dynasty, 281, *table*, 282
Hermann Billung, Markgraf, 413
Hijaz, 185, 189, 197, 265, 268
Hijra, see Hegira
Himerios, Byzantine admiral, 357, 360, 377
Himyarite kingdom, 106, 156, 158, 184, 185
Hincmar, Archbishop of Rheims, 399, 401–2, 422, 423, 439, 440, 441, 453, 458, 467, 484
   Annals of St Bertin, 467
   De ordine palatii, 467
   Life of St Remigius, 455
Hindu civilisation, 248, 249, 254
Hippocrates, 248
Hisham ibn Abd al-Malik, Umayyad Caliph, 212, 256, 301
Hispano-Visigoths, 384, 387, 423, 477, 490
'holy men', 122–3, 134, 140, 176, 306, 321–2, 345, 367
Honorius, Roman Emperor of the West, 19, 29, 104
hospitalitas, 11, 27, 63, 66
host, 427, 432, 435, 439, 445, 448, 494, 496
Hugh of Arles/Provence, 363, 412
Hugh, Count of Tours (*see also* Etichonids), 396, 442, 487
Hugh the Great, Duke of the Franks, 415
Hugh Capet, 444
Huneric, King of the Vandals, 57, 90
Hunfrid, clan, 413
Hungarians (*see also* Magyars), 412, 482
Hungary (*see also* Pannonia), 54, 111, 174, 370, 409, 415, 452
Huns, 52, 53, 54, 111–12, 158, 160, 289, 409
hunting, 38, *38*, 86, 87, 212, 245, 323, 387, 497
Husain, Alid prince, 194, 196

Iberia (Caucasian), 107, 326, 331
   Iberians, 315
Iberian Peninsula (*see also* Galicia, Portugal, Spain), 37, 60, 70, 205
   population around 400 AD, 37
Ibn Hanbal, *see* Ahmad ibn Hanbal
Ibn Hawqal, 230, 236
Ibn Khurdadhbih, 276–8
Ibrahim, Imam, 221–2
Iceland, 406, 435, 436, 451, 481, 482, 519
iconoclasm, 300–6, *302, 303*, 308, 312, 316–18, *313*, 319, 321, 323, 331, 332, 367, 385, 390, 515
icons, 176, *177*, 318, 319, 322, 348, 367

Idrisids, 211, 230, 257, 276
   coinage, 211
Ifrikiya (*see also* Africa, Libya, Maghrib, Tunisia), 199, 211, 218, 219, 228, 229–30, 232, 256–7, 258–60 *passim*, 275, 277, 408
Ignatios, Patriarch of Constantinople, 312, 316, 321, 323, 325, 348–9, 355, 358, 372
Illyricum (*see also* Balkans), 4, 12, 37, 38, 39, 53, 55, 106, 108
   Byzantine, 108, 111, 130, 151, 155, 283, 284, 302
immunity, 117, 342, 344–6, 434, 445, 448, 485
India, 45, 156, 162, 185, 216, 249, 262, 270, 272, 276, 278, 326
   Buzurg, *Marvels of India*, 272
Indo-China, 14, 276
Ine, King of Wessex, 10, 80, 86, 384, 418, 421, 505
Ionnikios, of Bithynia, 312, 321
Iona, 94, 462
Iran (*see also* Persian Empire), 45, 108, 111, 129, 142, 182, 183, 242, 284, 289, 309
   under Islam, 203, 207, 216, 219, 220, 222, 239, 249
   Iranians, 197, 246, 248
Iraq (*see also* Persian Empire), 182, *183*
   under Islam, 197, 204, 207, 211, 212, 214, 216, 220, 222, 233, 237–8, 240, 241, 266, 270, 301 (*see also* irrigation)
Ireland (*see also* Irish), 79, 85, 89, 403, 407, 476, 514
   kingdoms of, 392, 406, 436
Irene, Byzantine Empress, wife of Constantine V, 293, 371
Irene, Byzantine Empress, wife of Leo IV, 293, 298, 304, 306–8, 309–12, 314, 315, 316, 317, 330, 331, 332, 389
Irish (*see also* Celts), 55, 77, 87
   conversion to Christianity, 91, 93, 461
   monks as missionaries, 93–4, 96, 100, 102, 461–2
irrigation, 37, *210*, 212, 214, 233–4, *234*, 235, 237–8, 240, 241, 245, 477
Isauria, Isaurians, 107, 132, 148, 149, 150, 151, 156, 164, 166, 282
Isaurian dynasty (*see also* Zeno), 293, 313, *table*, 313
Ishaq ibn Hunayn, 248–9
Isidore, Bishop of Seville, 90, 461
Islam (*see also* Muhammad, Mu'tazilites, Islamic Law), 121, 129, 179, 184–5, 187, 190–5, 219, 279–80, 304–5, 330, 368, 383, 392
   attitudes to Christianity, 186, 187, 189, 194–5
Islamic Empire (*see also* Dar al-Islam, Muslim State), agriculture, 211–12, 233–5, 237–41
   caliphal regime, 202–4, 206–7, 209, 223–8, 241, 263
   coinage and currency, 203, *204*, 209–11, 257, 266, 268, 273, 327, 511, 513–14

Index

Islamic Empire (*cont.*)
   commerce, 216, 261, 265–73, 275–8, *map*, 271
   crafts and industries, 246, 250, 252–4, 255, 261–3
   growth of, 195–200, 203–4, 205, 284, *map*, 198
   landed properety, 206–8, 209, 212–14, 229–30, 235–7
   learning and culture, 218, 226, 248–9, 258
   military and naval forces, 197, 199, 202, 205–6, 209, 218, 223–4, 229, 230, 245, 259, 279
   social composition, 202, 206, 214, 237, 246, 251–2, 259–60, 267, 279–80
   taxation, 207–9, 211, 212–13, 233–5, 236
   towns, *see* towns, Islamic
Islamic law, 191, 218, 233, 236, 258
   fuqahas, 207, 259–60
   Hanifite school, 218–19, 260, 267, 268
   Malikite school, 219, 258, 260, 267–8
Isma⁶ilians, 252, 263
Italy
   Late Roman, 11, 12, 26, 47, 55
   Byzantine, 61, 64, 67, 158, 172, 275, 285, 290–1, 328–9, 350, 366, 375–7, 384, 391, 408, 414, 419–20, 475–6, 515
   Ostrogothic, *see* Ostrogothic kingdom, Theodoric
   Lombard, *see* Lombard kingdom and principalities
   Carolingian, 387, 399, 423, 428, 429, 431, 490, 491, 508, 512, 520; sub-kingdom, 388, 391, 396, 424
   tenth-century, 399, 402, 412, 414, 480

Jacob Baradaeus, Jacobites, 169, 182, 194, 204, 246, 331, 375
Jazira, the, 204, 207, 211, 212, 241, 266, 272
   products, 254, 265, 272
Jerome, St, 7, 136
Jerusalem, 107, 109, 137, 145, 146, 167, 190, 268, 392
   capture by the Persians, 171, 283
   recapture by Herakleios, 284, 285
   capture by the Arabs, 197, 284, 383
   Church of the Holy Sepulchre, 469
   Dome of the Rock, 191, 254, P
Jerusalem, Church and Patriarchate of, 126, 151, 182, 286
Jesus Christ
   Christologies, 89, 128–9, 182, 286
   images of, 176, 285, 303–5, 319, 348, 351, 358, 359, 373
   Islam and, 187, 189, 220
   source of imperial authority, 308, 351, 355
Jews, Judaism (*see also* Khazars, Radhanites),
   in the Byzantine Empire, 108–9, 121, 146, 164, 169–70, 171, 175, 283, 286, 291, 301, 350, 366–7
   in the Islamic Empire, 205, 246, 266, 278, 301, 304–5
   in Europe, 67, 278, 443, 477, 491
   mercantile activity, 46, 75, 277–8, 326, 341, 491, 513, 515, 518, 520

jihad, 191, 201, 202, 226, 236, 275
John I, Tzimiskes, Byzantine emperor, 361, 366, 372, 375
John VIII, Pope, 399, 400, 452
John Cassian, 34, 48, 136
John Chrysostom, St, Patriarch of Constantinople, 109, 115, 125, 126, 132, 140, 144, 146
John of Damascus, St, 194
   Discourses, 301
John, Bishop of Ephesus, 167, 169, 170
John Kourkouas, Byzantine general, 361, 362, 363, 373
John Morocharzianos, Patriarch, of Constantinople, 316, 317, 319, 320, 321
John Moschos, 176
John Scottus Eriguena, 467
Jonas, Bishop of Orleans, 423, 445, 467
Judith, Carolingian Empress, 396, 442, 487
Justin I, Byzantine Emperor, 148, 153, 154, 156, 160, 166, 167, 171
Justin II, Byzantine Emperor, 153, 171, 176, 283
   Cross of, P
Justinian I, Byzantine Emperor, 7, 10, 109, 123, 153–6, 158–66 *passim*, 170, 174, 177, 281, 294, 375, 459
   building by, 71, 73, 155
   legislation, 154–5 (*see also* Code of Justinian)
   recovery of the West, 58–9, 158, 159
   religious policy, 169–70, 333
Justinian II, Slitnose, Byzantine Emperor, 177, 282, 285, 287, 290, 291, 292
Justinian Partecipanzo, Doge of Venice, 520
Jutland, 55, 403, 516

Ka⁶ba, 185, 186, *188*, 189, 263
Kairouan, 199, 228, 232, 256, 258, 259, 262, 275
   Great Mosque, 256 P
Kassel Glosses, 444
Kaupung, 518, 519
Kent, kingdom of, 61, 86, 88, 418, 485
   laws, 80
Khadija, wife of Muhammad, 186, 193
Khalid, Arab general, 189, 197
Kharijites, 187, 194, 202, 214, 220, 232, 237, 276
Khazaria, Khazar kingdom, 276, 277, 293, 312, 326, 330, 334, 367, 371, 372
   Khazars, 272, 290
Khurasan, 196–7, 219, 226, 228
   Arab immigrants in, 202, 221, 224, 246
   insurrections, 219–20, 221–2
   artefacts, 254, 255, 262, 263
   cotton-growing, 254, 261
Kievan State (*see also* Russians), 330, 334, 335, 364, 368, 371, 372
   Byzantine treaties with, 339, 341, 372
   Chronicle of Times Past, 339, 372
   Conversion to Christianity, 372–3
kingship (*see also* Royal unction)

Germanic, 81–2, 417–19, 485
  Carolingian, 384, 386, 388–9, 438–9
Koran, 186, 187, 191, 193, 194, 222, 227, 236, 248
Krum, Bulgar Khan, 314, 329, 330
Kufa, 194, 195, 197, 216, 269, 270
  layout, 214
  scene of Alid revolts, 220, 222, 223
  mosque, 223–4, *224*
Kutama tribe, 231, 232, 236, 237

laeti, 26, 30, 37
La Garde-Freinet, 408
Lakapenoi clan, 360–1, 362, 363
Lakhmids, 111, 158, 184
Languages
  Anglo-Saxon, 79, 80, 468
  Arabic, 108, 204, 205, 232, 265, 277
  Aramaic, 108, 182, 241
  Berber, 232
  Catalan, 465
  Castilian, 465
  Celtic, 79, 91
  Coptic, 108, 182
  Greek, 6, 47, 48, 50, 106, 108–9, 155, 156, 176, 277, 331, 365–6, 367, 369, 377, 452, 461, 465, 467
  Hebrew, 108, 109, 334, 367, 376
  Latin, 6, 47–8, 65, 65, 67, 78–9, 80, 106, 108, 113, 151, 153, 155, 156, 366, 452, 460, 461, 465, 468
  Occitan, 79, 465
  Old French, 397, 465
  Old High German, 82, 397, 454, 465, 468
  Slavonic, 108, 334, 369
  Syriac, 108, 129, 151, 182, 248, 331
  vernacular, 109, 366, 465, 468
Languedoc (*see also* Septimania), 477, 490, 495, 498, 518, 520
Latium, 61, 73, 476, 477, 493, 527
Lechfeld, battle of (955), 409, 413
Leo I., Byzantine emperor, 114, 148–50, 156, 161
Leo III, Byzantine Emperor, 281, 292–3, 295, 301–2, 305, 317, 325, *327*, 332, 334
Leo IV, 'the Khazar', Byzantine emperor, 293, 298, 304, 306–7, 311, 314
Leo V, Byzantine emperor, 300, 314, 315, 317, *318*, 353
Leo VI, Byzantine emperor, 306, 336, 338, 347, 349, 355, *359*, 367, 370, 375, 376
  Book of the Prefect, 339
  legislation, 351–2
  marriages, 356–8, *359*
  Taktika, 350
Leo I, Pope, 55, 129
Leo III, Pope, 389, *390*
Leo IV, Pope, 400, 510
Leo the Philosopher (or Mathematician), 320, 321, 323
Leon, kingdom of, 409, 495, 510

Leovigild, King of the Visigoths, 60, 74, 89
Lérins, 98, 460
Libanius, Rhetor of Antioch, 109, 110, 144
Libya, 140, 187, 199
limes, 4, 8, 37, 67, 106, 107
  limitanei, 25, 26, 118, 297
Limoges, 73, 401, 510
Lindisfarne, 94, 102, 462
  Lindisfarne Gospels, 99, P
Liudger, St, Bishop of Münster, 450, 487
Liutpolding clan (Bavaria), 412, 428
Liutprand, Bishop of Cremona, 468
Liutprand, King of the Lombards, 385, 462
Loire, 78–9, 384, 406, 444, 477, 490, 491, 494, 507, 520
  salt trade, 516, 519
Lombard kingdom and principalities (*see also* Benevento, Friuli, Spoleto), 61, 75, 81, 84, 86, 309, 383, 385–6, 387, 417–18, 420, 468, 485
  coinage, 74
  conversion to Catholic Christianity, 90
  laws, 80, 418
  tenth-century principalities, 377, 412
Lombards, 56, 59, 77, 78, 83, 89, 272, 423, 443, 467, 477, 506, 515
London, 86, 88, 94, 406, 510, 516, 519, 529
Lorraine (*see also* Lotharingia), 398, 399, 413
Lorsch, 447, 468, 469, 483
Lothar I, Emperor, 396–8, 399, 414, 453, 487
Lothar II, King of Lotharingia, 398–9, 457, 498
Lothar, King of Western Francia, 415, 440
Lotharingia (*see also* Lorraine), 398, 399, 402, 413, 414, 440, 449, 458, 491, 507, 514
Louis I, the Pious, Emperor (*see also* Carolingian Empire), 278, 318, 391, 393–7, 395, 422, 424, 429, 431, 432, 433, 474, 522, 525
  in Aquitaine, 388, 390, 391, 443
  religious policy, 447, 448, 449, 450–2, 471–2
Louis II, Emperor (and King of Italy), 377, 398–9, 400, 402, 408
Louis the Child, King of Eastern Francia, 413
Louis the German, King of Eastern Francia, 396, 397–9, 401, 402, 488, 495, 500
Louis, II, 'the Stammerer', King of Western Francia, 401, 402
Lous, III, King of Western Francia, 401, 406
Louis IV, King of Western Francia, 414–15
Louis the Blind, King of Provence, 399, 409
Lucca, 462, 520
Luke the Stylite, 345
Lupus of Ferrières, 467
Luxeuil, 93, 100, 461, 462
Lyons, (*see also* Agobard), 23, 55, 278, 398, 476, 510

Macedonia, 158, 283, 287, 294, 308, 350, 369
Macedonian dynasty, 312, 336, 348–63
  historiography, 352, 353, 363
  table, 356

Magdeburg, 520
  see of, 413, 448, 452
Maghrib, 200, 201, 214, 220, 228, 230, 231–2,
    235–7, 250, 257, 274, 275, 276, 408
Magyars (see also Hungarians), 111, 330, 370, 409
mahdi, 195, 226, 227
Mahdi, Abbasid Caliph, 187, 225, 226–7, 233,
    243, 248
Mainz, 46, 278, 515, 516, 518, 520
  see of, 95, 448, 450, 452
Malaysia, 272, 276
Maleinoi clan, 346, 361
Ma'mun, Abbasid Caliph, 224, 225, 227, 243,
    246–9 passim, 262, 263, 315, 330, 333
Mani, Manichaeans, 170, 183
al-Mansur, Abbasid Caliph, 225, 226, 241, 243,
    245, 266 (see also Baghdad)
manuscripts and libraries (see also written records),
    99, 248, 341, 350, 355, 363–4, 462, 465,
    467, 468
  handwriting, 319–20, 363, 465, 466
  manuscript art, 49, 99, 366, 463, 463, 469, 471
  scriptoria, 319, 461, 465
  writing materials, 48, 109, 261
Marcian, Byzantine Emperor, 114, 148
Mardaits, 287, 297
manus, mansi, 429, 432, 434, 437, 438, 494–5,
    506–7
Marjorian, Roman Emperor, 7, 8, 22, 34
markets, 43, 45, 73, 131–2, 175, 216, 218–9,
    252–3, 268–70, 280, 344, 503, 509, 510
Marozia of Rome, 412
marriage, 36, 68, 77, 123, 125, 169, 291, 292,
    309, 311, 335, 357–8, 399, 457, 492
Marseilles, 46, 48, 73, 75, 76, 408, 474, 511, 515
Martin, St, Bishop of Tours, 33, 95
  cappa, 426
Martinakios clan, 356
martyrs
  Christian, 44, 123, 124, 176, 304, 305, 333
  Islamic, 194, 220–1, 228, 246
Matfrid, Count of Orleans, 396, 442, 487
Mauretania (Morocco), 20, 29, 37, 39
Mauri ('Moors'), 68, 172, 274
Maurice, Byzantine Emperor, 10, 64, 171–2,
    174–5, 176
mawali, 197, 200, 206, 211, 220–2, 259, 263
Maximos 'the Confessor', 290
Mayors of the Palace, 383, 418, 420, 426, 485
Mazdak, Mazdaism, 183, 203
Mecca, Meccans, 184–6, 188, 189–90, 191–2,
    195, 197, 231, 252, 269
Medina (Yathrib), 184, 187, 189–92, 196, 269
  mosque, 190, 192
Mediterranean (see also trade, long-distance), 10,
    14, 57, 59, 102, 181, 298, 328, 375–6, 381,
    408, 527
  eastern, 199, 201–2, 217
  western, 54, 65, 201, 273–5, 406, 408
Melissenoi clan, 316, 317

Melitene (Malatya), 107, 172, 293, 294, 299, 373
  emirate, 326, 331–3, 350, 375
Melkites, 169, 182, 246
merchants, (see also Frisians, Jews, Venetians), 46,
    142, 216, 260, 266–8, 270, 272, 326, 341,
    441, 513, 518, 520–1
Mercia, kingdom of, 61, 392, 411, 434, 513, 518
Merovingian dynasty (see also Clovis, Frankish
    kingdom(s)), 10, 59, 60–1, 81, 86, 384, 386,
    417, 418, 421, table, 62
Merv, 216–17, 246
  focus of insurrection, 219, 221–2
Mesopotamia, 111, 129, 156, 158, 165, 167, 172,
    182, 197, 211, 253, 284, 368, 373, 375
  art, 254, 255
Methodios, Patriarch of Constantinople, 316, 319,
    323
Methodios, St, 334, 369
Metz, 54, 78, 102, 397, 402, 426, 445, 471, 487,
    510
  Austrasian capital, 60, 71, 73
  bishops of, 426, 445
Meuse, 383, 397, 398, 477, 478, 482, 511, 516,
    529
Michael I Rangabe, Byzantine emperor, 314, 316,
    317, 331, 332
Michael II, 'the Stammerer', Byzantine emperor,
    314–15, 316, 317–19, 322, 327, 330, 331
Michael III, Byzantine emperor, 315–16, 321, 323,
    325, 333, 335, 348, 356, 357, 371
Michael Lachanodrakon, 304, 306
Miesko, Polish prince, 415, 452
Milan, 14, 22, 43, 44, 46, 71, 74, 115, 462
mines, mining, 39, 253
  gold, 39, 74–5, 106, 120, 162
  silver, 39, 511, 514
ministeriales (Dienstlehen), 437, 491, 492, 506, 522
mints, minting, 23, 74–5, 141, 210–11, 216, 218,
    257, 431, 511–12, 514
missi dominici, missatica, 401, 428, 430–1, 432,
    436, 438, 441, 444, 445, 494, 507, 522
monasticism
  Byzantine, 127, 135, 136, 145–7, 166–7, 168,
    304, 306, 309–11, 316, 321–2, 322, 323,
    367–8 (see also 'holy men')
  Egyptian, 34, 48, 93, 128–9, 135–6, 150, 174,
    204, 288
  in the West, 33–4, 93–4, 98–103, 395, 404,
    421, 437, 447–9, 450, 460–4, 483–4, 503
monophysitism, monophysites, 129, 150–4 passim,
    167, 169, 175, 182, 204, 286, 290, 293, 305
monothelitism, 182, 286, 290
Montecassino, 100, 101, 102, 408, 462
Moravia, 334, 369, 370
Moses, 189, 220, 222, 301, 305
Mt Athos, 328, 342, 344–5, 367
Mozarabs, 237, 276, 408, 481
Mu'awiya, Governor of Syria, 194, 197
Muhammad, Prophet, 184–93 passim, 196, 203,
    206, 220, 221

Muhammad ben Abdallah *see* Mahdi
Mukhtar, Alid rebel, 220, 222
music, 447, 462, 464–5
Muslim State, 187, 190–2 (*see also* Islamic Empire)
Muslims, *see* al-Andalus, Arabs, Islam
Muʿtasim, Abbasid Caliph, 227, 243, 245
Mutawakkil, Abbasid Caliph, 224, 228, 245, 246
Muʿtazilites, 194, 222, 228, 246, 248

Naples, 59, 73, 172, 201, 275, 328–9, 384, 392
Napolean I, Emperor, 390
Narses, Byzantine general, 71, 83
Navarre, 391, 392, 411
navicularii, 25, 45
Neoplatonism, 6, 121, 140, 170, 226
Nestorius, Nestorianism, 128–9, 151, 182, 205, 246, 251, 305
Neustria, 60–1, 66, 383, 398, 418, 428, 431, 444, 482, 485, 514
Nicaea, Council of (325), 6, 31, 128
Nicaea, Council of (787), 300, 304, 308
Nicholas I, Pope, 325, 335, 399, 401, 452, 458
Nicholas I, 'Mystikos', Patriarch of Constantinople, 357–8, 362, 364, 371
Nikephoros I, Byzantine emperor, 296, 312, 314, 328, 329, 330, 331
Nikephoros II, Byzantine emperor, 361, 368, 375
Nikephoros I, Patriarch of Constantinople, 303, 316, 317, 318, *318*, 319, 332
Nikephoros Caesar, uncle of Constantine VI, 298, 307, 309, 311
Nikephoros Phokas, Byzantine general, 361, 377
Nikephoros, son of Artavasdus, 302
Nile, 17, 106, 169, 212, 239, 363, 265
Nishapur, 216, 251, 253, 270, 273
   pottery, 262
Nithard, 397, 452, 467, 523
Normans, Normandy, 407, 451, 480
North Sea (*see also* Frisians), 20, 91, 381, 384, 404, 406, 517
Northumbria, kingdom of, 61, 94, 392
Norway, Norwegians (*see also* Vikings), 2, 403–4, 407, 451, 481, 482, 518
Notker of St Gall, 'the Stammerer', 443, 468
Notker Labeo, 468
Nubia, 158, 197

Oaths (*see also* commendation, *convenientiae*)
   oath of fidelity, 31, 70, 388, 422, 438, 439, 458, 485, 488, 490, 491
   mutual oath, 397, 441, 453, 458
Odo, King of Western Francia, 402, 406, 410, 415, 488, 514
Odo, abbot of Cluny, 444, 449
Odo of Metz, architect, 469
Odoacer, Germanic chieftain, 6, 55, 56, 63
Offa, King of Mercia, 392, 434, 513, 518
   Offa's Dyke, 392, 434, 481
   Offa's penny, 512
Omar ibn al-Khattab, Caliph, 186, 193, 206, 207

Omar II ben Abd al-Aziz, Ummayad Caliph, 204, 221
Omurtag, Bulgar Kha, 315, 329
ordeal, 80, 429, 453, 458
Ordinatio Imperii (817), 396
Ordoño I, King of the Asturias, 408, 510
Ostrogoths, 53, 56, 57, 59, 62, 63, 77, 83, 89, 149, 150
Ostrogothic kingdom (*see also* Theodoric), 56, 57, 67, 69, 84, 90, 159
Othman, Caliph, 186, 193, 194, 197, 251
Otto I, King of Germany, Emperor, 373, 409, 413–14, 437–8, 444, 448–9, 452, 471, 525, 526
   imperial coronation, 414
Otto II, Emperor, 414, 437
Ottonian Empire, 351, 356, 368, 414, 512
   government, 437
   military organisation, 437–8

Pachomius, St, 34, 98, 310
paganism
   Antique, 20, 120–1, *122*, 126, 162, 167, 170, 172, 291
   Germanic, 78, *92*, 91–5 *passim*, 387, 450–8 *passim*, 526 (*see also* kingship)
Palestine, 104, 107, 118, 136, 151, 167, 175, 249, 253, 283–4, 286, 298, 305
   in the Islamic Empire, 249, 253, 305
Palladius, Roman agronomist, 42–3, 93, 502
Pannonia (*see also* Hungary), 19, 23, 29, 37, 38, 56, 111, 409
Papacy (Church of Rome, see of St Peter), 20, 32, 61, 90, 95, 126, 172, 292, 304, 384–90 *passim*, *390*, 396, 400–1, 412, 414, 449, 452, 524
   and the Byzantine Empire, 150, 167, 169, 286, 290–2, 301–2, 317–18, 325, 348–9, 368, 401, 452
   Patrimony of St Peter (Papal State), 174, 386, 387, 395, 425
papyrus, papyri (*see also* written records), 75, 109, 132, 202–3, 299
Paris, 44, 56, 57, 60, 71, 406, 410, 482, 514, 519
parish (*plebs*), 96–7, 436, 445, 447, 453, 460, 525
patriarchates, 125–6, 150
Patrick, St, 93
Paul the Deacon, 388, 467
Paulicians, 322, 333, 350, 372, 373, 375
Pavia, 63, 71, 73, 383, 387, 462, 517, 518, 529
Pelayo (Palagius), 384, 419
Peloponnese, 287, 298, 299, 350, 376
Persian Empire (*see also* Iran, Sassanids), 107–8, *110*, 110–11, 113, 148, 156, 158, 159, 171, 177, 182–3, *183*, 225, 283–4, 285, 286, 293, 298
   coinage and currency, 158, 162, 203, 327
Petchenegs, 352, 370, 371
Peter, Bulgarian Tsar, 362, 371, 372
Persian Gulf, 106, 110, 142, 156, 216, 261, 265

Philaretos, 308–9
Philippikos Bardanes, Byzantine Emperor, 282, 292, 293, 297
Phocas, Byzantine Emperor, 171, 172, 175
Phokai clan, 361, 362–3
Photios, Patriarch of Constantinople, 316, 320, 325, 334, 348–50, 356, 357, 358, 372, 452
   Amphilochia, 349
   Bibliotheca, 320, 349
   correspondence, 364
Pippin I, Mayor of the Palace, 383
Pippin II, 'of Herstal', Mayor of the Palace, 94, 383–4, 418–19, 462
Pippin III, Mayor of the Palace and King of the Franks, 304, 383, 384, 385–7, 388, 416, 422, 426, 434, 442, 445, 462, 488, 509, 512
Pippin I of Aquitaine, 396, 397
Pippin II of Aquitaine, 401
Pippin the Hunchback, 388
Pippin of Italy, 388, 390, 391, 396
Pippinid clan (*see also* Carolingian dynasty), 102, 419, 442, 478, 486
Pîtres, edict of (864), 411, 512, 514
plague, 160–1, 162, 164, 166, 172, 382, 419, 475–7, 480, 526, *map*, 475
Plato, founder of Sakkoudion monastery, 306, 308, 309, 310
Plato, Greek philosopher, 248, 320, 355, 363
plebs, *see* parish
Pliska, 289, 314, 329, *329*, 369, 370
Po, 46, 158, 515, 518
Po plain, 102, 412, 476, 490, 508
   cultivation, 27, 37, 43, 382, 478, 502, 506, 516
   Lombard occupation, 59, 77, 477
Poitiers, battle of (732), 384
Poland, 273, 403, 413, 415, 452, 514, 520
polyptychs, 66, 429, 492, 497, 502, 507, 522
Popes, *see* Papacy
ports, 88–9, 339, 509, 510–11, 514, 516, 522
precaria, precariae, 347, 395, 445, 447, 486, 494
Preslav, 364, 369
Procopius of Caesarea, 123, 151, 154, 155, 161, 165
   Secret History, 154, 155, 476
Provence, 55, 57, 60, 70, 73, 102, 412, 418, 476, 495, 510
   eighth-century principality of, 383, 384
   under the Carolingians, 386, 398, 399, 428, 431
   post-Carolingian rulers, 399, 402, 409
   Saracen attacks, 275, 278, 482
Psamathia monastery, 355, 366
Ptolemy, Greek mathematician, 249, 461
Pyrenees (*see also* Basques), 37, 50, 55, 75, 388, 477, 482
   passes, 76, 276, 387, 518

Qadisiya, battle of (636), 196
Qasr al-Hayr al-Sharki, 212, *213*
Qasyr Amr, *196*, 254

Quentovic, 88, 406, 503, 511, 514, 516, 517, 518, 519
Quraysh, Qurayshites, 184, 185, 186, 189–90, 194, 195, 196–7

Rabanus Maurus, 454–5, 467, 474
Radhanites, 277–8, 520
Ramiro II, King of the Asturias, 488, 510
Ravenna, 19, 20, 22, 29, 53, 55, 59, 64, 71, 74, 154, 158, 291, 516
   exarchate, 172, 285, 384, 419–20
   St Apollinare nuovo, *72*
   St Vitalis, 154, 155, 469, P
Reccared, King of the Visigoths, 10, 60, 90, 485
Reccesuinth, King of the Visigoths, 80, 437
   votive crown, 463, *479*
Red Sea, 106, 111, 142, 158, 185, 265, 278
Regensburg, 95, 437, 483, 510
Reichenau, 102, 463, 468, 471, 510
Remigius (Remi), St, Bishop of Rheims, 56, 70, 455, 481
Rheims (*see also* Hincmar, Remigius), 71, 395–6, 402, 416, 421, 467, 469, 471, 476, 510, 514
   polyptych of St Remigius, 481, 492
Rhine, 17, 25, *25*, 26, 27, 40, 53, 56–7, 60, 387, 398
   economic importance, 38, 76, 511, 514, 515, 518
   Rhine delta, 55, 61
Rhodes, 106, 150, 156, 286–7, 375
Rhône, 55, 384, 406, 433, 397, 398
   economic importance, 38, 43, 46, 515
Richard of Burgundy, 410, 428
Richard I, Duke of Normandy, 407
Robert I, King of Western Francia, 415, 428
Robert the Strong, 401, 406, 410
Robertian clan, 415, 488
Roderick, King of the Visigoths, 200, 384, 416
Roland, marquess of Brittany, 387
Rollo, Norman chieftain, 407
Roman Empire (*see also* Romania, romanitas), 1, 6–7, 17–19, 104, *map*, 21
Roman Empire in the East, 11, 19, 36, 47, 58–9, 110–11 (*see also* Byzantine (East Roman) Empire))
Roman Empire in the West, 7, 11, 17, 19, 53–4, 58, 110, 150
   agriculture, 37, 40, 42–3
   army, *13*, 21, 24–8, *25*, 31, 53, 55
   coinage and currency, 23, 46–7
   economy, 11, 29, 36–43, 45–7
   government and administration, 19–28, 50
   landed property, 23, 30–1, 39–42
   population, 26, 36–7, 71, 526
   social composition, 29–31, 34–6
   taxation, 11–12, 23, 23–31 *passim*, 34–5, 45, 46, 47, 62, 66–7, 431, 436, 526
   towns, 43–5
Roman law and legal system, 19–20, 22–3, 50, 62–4, 69–70, 113, 154, 424, 455, 459, 524

Romania, 4, 6, 7, 8, 10, 11, 17, 104
romanitas, 13, 20, 50, 52, 59, 62, 63, 76, 108,
    121, 155, 284, 285, 286, 333, 349, 381–3
Romanos I Lakapenos, Byzantine Emperor, 336,
    345, 352, 358, 360–2 363, 367, 371, 373,
    375
Romanos II, Byzantine Emperor, 336, 362, 363
Rome, city of (*see also* Papacy), 7, 20, 23, 33, 38,
    61, 64, 90, *105*, 306, 376, 385, 388–9, 398,
    414, 426, 476, 510, 525
    attacks on, 7, 53, 55, 71, 275, 408
    inhabitants, 33, 38, 66, 71, 75
Rome, duchy of, 384, 412
Romulus Augustulus, Roman emperor, 17, 55
Roncevaux, pass of, 387
Rothari, King of the Lombards, 80, 418, 420
    Edict of Rothari, 80, 418, 501
royal unction, 384, 402, 413, 417, 419, 434
Rudolf of Burgundy, 409, 482
Russia, 273, 518, 519
Russians (*see also* Kievan State, Varangians), 312,
    326, 330, 349, 352
    as mercenaries, 297, 346, 368
    trading activity, 276–7, 513

Sabas, St, 167, 286
    Mar Saba, *168*
Saif ed-Dawla, 373, 375
St Bertin, 471, 483, 491, 495, 510
    polyptych, 481
St Catherine's monastery, Mt Sinai, 136, 167, 286,
    288
St Denis, 73, 386, 387, 416, 447, 462, 471, 503,
    522
    abbots, 396, 426
    church, 469
    fair, 509
    manuscript art, 463, 471
St Gall, 93, 468, 483, 495, 500, 502
    church, 469, 510
    garden, 499–500
St Germain-des-Prés, 492, 500
    polyptych, 481, 507
St James of Compostela (Santiago), 392
St Martin of Tours, 71, 416, 483
St Riquier, 469, 496, 523
St Sophia, *see* Constantinople
saints, cult of (*see also* 'holy men', icons, Virgin
    Mary), 121, 123, 303–4, 305, 306, 454,
    455–7, 458
Sakkoudion monastery, 308, 310
Salic law, 80, 87
saltus, 11, 37–9, 40, 63, 70, 71, 85, 86, 497–8,
    506
Salvian, 12, 30
Salzburg, 95, 450, 452
Samaritans, 151, 153, 166, 172
Samarkand, 197, 216, 261
Samarra, 243–6, *244*, 247, 249–50, 263, P
    Samarran pottery, 256, 262, 273

Samo, 60, 68
Sanchez clan (Gascony), 410
Saracens
    of Syria, 126, 332
    Saracen 'pirates', 201, 273, 275, 312, 328, 375,
        408, 412, 482, 515
Saragossa, 200, 201, 258, 276, 278, 387, 520
Sardis, 109, 137, 164, 175, 337
Sassanids (*see also* Persian Empire), 196, *196*, 206,
    211, 214, 216, 261
Sawad, 206, 211, 225, 233, 241, 278
Saxons, 55, 60, 85, 387, 443
Saxony (*see also* Germany, Ottonian dynasty,
    Saxons)
    Carolingian conquest of, 387–8, 391, 413, 429,
        432, 437, 450
    importance in tenth century, 429, 444
    persistence of slavery, 490, 492
Scandinavia (*see also* Denmark, Norway, Sweden),
    86, 272, 403, 418, 513, 514, 516
Scandinavians (*see also* Vikings), 75, 87, *88*, 399,
    401, 413, 433, 451, 518
    and Kievan State, 368, 372
    as mercenaries, 162, 368
Scotland, 19, 25, 50, 55, 77, 79, 384, 407, 514
schools
    in the Antique tradition, 47–8, 109–10, 320,
        323, 459
    episcopal, 445–6, 460, 473
    monastic, 310, 316, 460, 461–2, 473
    see of St Peter, *see* Papacy
Seine, 76, 102, 383, 401, 406, 407, 507, 514,
    516, 522, 529
senate, senatorial order, 34–5, 40–2, 64, 68–9, 90
    at Constantinople, 115
Septimania (lower Languedoc), 57, 60, 383, 384,
    387, 388, 410, 419, 423, 481, 487
serfdom, 492, 496
Sergios, Patriarch of Constantinople, 284–6
Sergius, Pope, 292
Severus, Patriarch of Antioch, 151, 153, 169, 182
Shabbetai Donnolo, Jewish physician, 376
Shi'a, Shi'ites, 194–5, 220–1, 223, 226, 228,
    246–7
ships, ship-building
    Arab, 199, 275, 286
    Byzantine, 297, 377
    Northern Europe, 54, 87–8, 381, 403, *403*, *404*,
        435, 517
    Slav, 284
Siberia, 270, 273, 276
Sicily
    late Roman, 37, 55
    Byzantine, 59, 66, 70, 74, 75, 158, 172, 283,
        290, 302, 328–9, 384, 391
    Islamic, 236, 237, 239, 240, 253, 259, 261, 265,
        275, 328, 375, 377, 408
    Norman, 270
Sigismund, King of the Burgundians, 89, 99
Sijilmasa, 201, 229, 275, 276

Sijistan, 197, 220
silk (*see also* textiles), 45, 142, 158, 162, 261, 266, 270
Siraf, 250–1, 272
'Sklavenes' (*Sklaviniai*) (*see also* Slavs), 156, 160, 171, 284, 287
Skleroi clan, 361
slave trade, 68, 75, 272–3, 275–7, 326, 408, 491, 505, 515–20 *passim*, 522
slaves
   in Late Antiquity, 29–30, 33, 42
   in Barbarian kingdoms, 67, 68–9, 83–4, 91, 95, 485
   in Carolingian society, 441, 491–4, 496, 506, 508
   in the Islamic world, 197, 204, 228, 235, 243, 259, 279
Slavs
   in the Byzantine orbit, 121, 155, 156, 171, 174–5, 283, 284–5, 287, 290, 294, 297, 299, 325, 326, 328, 333–4, 342, 345, 350, 368
   in Europe, 60, 68, 373, 402, 413, 451, 517, 518, 520, 525
   Slav pirates, 287, 328, 373
Soissons, 56, 71, 386
Spain
   late Roman, 19, 25, 32, 37–9 *passim*, 42, 43, 47, 50, 52
   Byzantine, 59, 63, 64, 159, 172, 200, 285
   Muslim, *see* al-Andalus
   Visigothic, 55, 57–8, 60, 63, 64, 66–7, 68, 76, 80, 89–90, 97, 98, 102, 172, 200, 257, 383, 384, 417, 419, 420, 460, 477, 485, 486, *map*, 231
Spanish March (*see also* Catalonia), 391, 401, 428
Speyer, 398, 448
Spoleto, Lombard principality, 59, 383, 412, 419
State, ideas of in the West, 10, 64, 415, 416–24, 440–1, 444–50, 458, 471, 486, 523, 524–6
Staurakios, 308, 309, 311, 313, 315
Stephen II, Pope, 304, 386
Stephen IV, Pope, 395
Stephen the Younger, St, 304, 305
Stoudios monastery, Stoudites (*see also* Theodore), 316–17, 319, 321, 323, 341, 358
Strasbourg, oaths of (842), 397, 467
Stylianos Zaoutzes, 351, 357, 358, 370
Stylite ascetics, 123, *124*, 167
Sudan, 106, 120, 162, 169, 187, 211, 265
Sueves, 26, 53, 55, 56, 60, 73, 77, 89
Suez (Kulzum), 277
suks, see markets
Sussex, kingdom of, 61, 392, 418
Swabia (*see also* Alamannia), 412, 413
Sweden, 87, 415, 451, 516, 518
Swedes (*see also* Varangians), 516, 518
   evangelisation of, 395, 451
   in Russia, 404
Syagrius, Roman commander, 55, 56
Symeon, Bulgarian Tsar, 369–71

Synesius, Bishop of Cyrene, 140
Syria, 104, 107, 118, 121, 132–3, 148, 151, 284
   in the Islamic Empire, 197, 202, 204–5, 217–18, 249, 254, 265, 266, 270, 286, 293, 301 (*see also* Damascus, Umayyads)
Syriac Christianity (*see also* Jacob Baradaeus, monophysitism), 108, 129, 140, 151, 182, 194, 204, 331
   Acts of Thomas, 129
   Gospel Book, *163*

Tahert, emirate of, 201, 228–9, 232, 275, 276
Tahir, Tahirids, 226, 228, 246, 261, 273
Tarasios, Patriarch of Constantinople, 307, 308, 309, 316–17, 325
Tarragona, 50, 73, 200, 383, 391, 419
Tarsus, 218, 249
   emirs, 331–2, 350, 376
Tassilo III, Duke of Bavaria, 388, 442, 488
Taurus and Anti-Taurus, 107, 199, 253, 254, 284, 293, 326, 331, 351, 373
Telerig, Bulgar Khan, 294
Tephrike (Tefrik), 332, 350, 360
Tervel, Bulgar Khan, 290
terps (*terpen*), 86, 87, 480, 481, 518
territorial principalities, rise of in Europe, 381, 383, 386, 403, 410–12, 419, 440, 443, 484, 486, 512, 525
Tertry, battle of (687), 383, 478
textiles (*see also* silk), 254, 262–3
   cotton, 246, 254
   linen, 132, 253, 272
   silk, 246, 254, 266
   woollen, 254
   workshops, 27, 141, 263, 506, 516, 518
Thames basin, 27, 37, 46, 382, 527
themes, 294–7, 332
   Anatolikon, 292–3, 295, 314–15, 331
   Armeniakon, 292, 293, 295, 298, 302, 309, 314
   Charsianon, 330, 332, 346, 361, 375
   Hellas, 298, 301
   naval, 295, 314, 328, 377
   Opsikion, 293, 295, 315
   Thrakesion 293, 295, 302, 304
Theodahad, King of the Ostrogoths, 58, 90
Theodelinda, Lombard queen, 90, 417
Theodora, Empress, wife of Justinian I, 153–4, 169, P
Theodora, Empress, wife of Theophilos, 315, 316, 319, 323, 325
Theodora of Rome, 412
Theodora, St, of Salonika, 328
Theodore the Stoudite, 306, 308, 309–10, 317–19, 321, 332
   Rule, 310, 316
Theodore of Tarsus, 462
Theodoret, Bishop of Cyr, 121, 128, 134, 140
Theodoric, King of the Ostrogoths, 10, 56, 57, 58, 63, 64, 66, 67, 69, 75, 459, 461, 475

Theodoric II, King of the Visigoths, 63
Theodosian dynasty, 17, 20, *table*, 152
Theodosius I, Roman Emperor, 7, 42, 107
  Theodosian Code, 19, 63, 113
Theodosius II, Byzantine Emperor, 113–14, 149
  Theodosian ramparts, Constantinople, *114*, 115, 144, 340
Theodotos, Patriarch of Constantinople, 316, 317, *318*
Theodulf, Bishop of Orleans, 388, 389, 445, 452, 467, 474
  biblical revision, 465
Theoktistos, 315, 323, 334
Theophanes, Byzantine chronicler, 284, 285, 287, 296, 300, 304, 306, 307, 310, 311
Theophano, Empress, first wife of Leo VI, 356–7
Theophano, Empress, wife of Otto II, 414
Theophano, Empress, wife of Romanos II, 363
Theophilos, Byzantine Emperor, 315, 316, 319, 320–1, 322, 323, 327, 330, 331, 332, 333, 348, 357, 363
Theophylact Abastaktos, 360, 361
Theophylact, Patriarch of Constantinople, 361, 372
Theophylact clan (of Rome), 412
Thessalonica, 106, 285, 287, 328, 334, 345, 377, P
  commercial importance, 299, 326, 338, 344, 367, 370
  sieges, 171, 174, 283, 284, 287, 376
Theuderic I, King of the Franks, 73–4
Theuderic III, King of the Franks, 418
Thomas 'the Slav', Byzantine pretender, 314–15, 330, 331
Thrace, 106, 132, 135, 148–9, 151–3, 156, 166, 175, 283, 287, 293–4, 298, 299, 344, 370, 372
  invasions, 111, 158, 160, 317, 370
  rebellions, 151–3, 294
Thrasamund, King of the Vandals, 57, 90
Thuringia, Thuringians, 57, 61, 77, 383, 502
  Christianisation, 95, 462
  dukes, 412, 413, 419
Tiber, 43, 46, 518
Tiberios II, Byzantine emperor, 171, 174
Tiberios III, Byzantine emperor, 282, 285, 303, 304
Tigris, 107, 211, 214, 241, 243, 278
Timothy Aelurus, Patriarch of Alexandria, 150
tiraz, 202–3, 263, *265*
Toledo, 60, 63, 71, 84, 200, 201, 205, 258, 520
Toledo, Councils of, 90, 417, 460
Totila, King of the Ostrogoths, 71, 159
Toulouse, 44, 57, 71, 384, 410, 419
  county of, 410
Tournai, 56, 78, 93
towns,
  fifth–sixth centuries, 9–10, 34–5, 43–7, 71–3, *74*, 112–13, 136–45, *138*, 162–5, 175–6 (*see also* civitas)
  Byzantine, 298, 336–9

European, ninth–tenth centuries, 509–11
Islamic, 214–17, 218, 241–52, *244*, 256–60, 268–70, 275–6
town councils, town councillors, *see* curia, *curiales*
trade, long distance (*see also* markets, merchants, transport and communications)
  Far Eastern, 142, 270–2, 326, 339, 341
  Far Northern, 273, 276–7
  Mediterranean, 46, 75, 275, 515–16, 517–18
  Northern seas, 87–8, 403, 516–17, 518–19
  trans-African, 273, 275–6
trade, regional, *see* markets
Transoxiana, 197, 216, 221, 251, 253, 254, 270
transport and communications (*see also* ports, ships and ship-building), *44*, *45*, 46, 76, 86, 106–8, 117, 265–6, *266*, 275, 522
  barid, 225, 263, 273, 276
  cursus publicus, 22, 27, 46, 118, 127, 428
Trebizond, 107, 326, 338, 344
Trier, 14, 22, 23, 43, 66, 71, 76, 78, 98, 115, 471, 476, 529
  see of, 421
  Trier Apocalypse, 502, *517*
Tripoli (North Africa), 259, 272, 275, 482
Tripoli (Syria), 286
Troyes, 510, 520, 522
  wine-fairs, 509
trustis, *trustes*, 441, 458, 491, 524
Tulunids (*see also* Egypt), 247, *247*, 249
Tunis, 258, 259, 265, 275
  mosque, 257
Tunisia, 37, 40, 261, 272
Turks, Turkic peoples, 111, 156, 160, 174–5, 197, 228, 270, 272, 279, 283, 289–90, 330, 331, 352, 370
Tuscany, marquisate of, 412, 419

Ulfila, 89
Umayyads, *see also* Islamic Empire, 186, 189, 192
  caliphs, 193–9, 202–9, 210, 216, 218, 219, 221–2, 223, 254, 269, 270
  Umayyads of Cordoba, 237, 258
  Umayyad architecture, 191, 212, *213*, *215*, 294, 321, 333, *table*, 193
Unrochid clan, 487, 488
usury, 46, 208, 209, 233, 443
Utrecht, 61, 94, 384, 499, 517
  Utrecht Psalter, *433*, *446*, 471

Vajk (Stephen), Prince of Hungary, 452
Valens, Roman emperor, 111
Valentinian I, Roman emperor, 29
Valentinian III, Roman emperor, 17, 22, 55
Vandals, *4*, 53, 68
  kingdom of, 53–4, 56, 57, 64–7 *passim*, 70, 77, 161
Varangians (*see also* Russians, Scandinavians, Swedes), 414, 416, 513, 515
vassalage, 433–4, 438–40, 488–91, 493, 524, 525

vassals, 83–4, 397, 401, 429, 432, 437, 445, 448, 468, 491, 508, 525
vengeance (*faida*), 80, 434, 441–2, 526
Venice, Venetians, 59, 328, 329, 333, 373, 391, 392, 515–16, 517–18, 519
    doges, 392, 515–16, 520, 529
    merchants, 328, 517–18, 520, 525
Verdun, 75, 515, 516, 520
Verdun, partition of (843), 393, 397–8, 401, 500, 529
Vézélay, 449
vici (*see also* village communities), 11, 45, 71, 96, 509
Vikings (*see also* Scandinavians), 273, 391, 393, 403–8, 450–1, 465, 467, 481, 482, 483, 513, 514, 518
village communities (*see also* *vici*)
    Byzantine, 132–4, 165–6, 296, 299, 341–3, 346, 347
    in Islamic territory, 208–9, 212–14, 235–7
    in northern Europe, 85, 491, 495, 497, 505
Virgil, 460, 468
Virgin Mary, cult of, 123, 176, 285, 303–4, 305, 319, 341, 348, 349, 358, 457, P
Visigoths (*see also* Goths, Spain), 10, 53, 54–5, 56, 62, 63, 77, 78, 85, 89
Vitalian, Byzantine general, 153, 166
viziers (*see also* Barmakids), 218, 222, 225, 226, 261, 263
Volga, 111, 273, 277, 290, 293, 326

Waifar of Aquitaine, 387, 442
Wala, 393, 396, 487
Wales, 50, 79, 94, 434, 476
Wamba, King of the Visigoths, 384, 417
Wasit, 220, 241, 269, 270
wazir, see viziers
Weissenburg, 102, 463, 483
Welf clan, 396, 442, 481
Wessex, kingdom of, 61, 94, 384, 392, 406–7, 411, 418, 505, 506
    laws, 80, 86

Western Francia (West Frankish kingdom), 398, 399, 401–2, 406, 407, 409, 411, 413, 414, 428, 444, 489, 490, 507, 514
Whitby, 462
    Synod of, 94
Widukind, Saxon chieftain, 413, 414
Widukind of Corvey, 413, 468
Wilfrid, St, 94, 462
Wilfrid the Hairy, Count of Barcelona, 410
William the Pious, Count of the Auvergne, 410, 449, 487
William, Count of Toulouse, 453, 487
William 'Towhead', Count of Poitou, 410
'Williams' clan (Frankish), 487–8
Willibrord, St, 94, 95, 462 P
Witiza, King of the Visigoths, 384, 417
written records (*see also* manuscripts and libraries), 22–3, 65–6, 109, 118, 206, 366, 423, 426, 429, 526

xenia, 30, 439
xenodochia, 73, 484

Yarmuk, battle of (636), 197, 284
Yazid II, Umayyad Caliph, 254
Yemen (*see also* Himyarite kingdom), 45, 106, 111, 184, 185
Yemenites, 197, 211, 221, 222, 231
York, 10, 14, 94, 406, 407, 510, 516, 519, 520, 529

Zacharias, Pope, 386
Zandjs, 250, 272
Zeno, Byzantine Emperor, 7, 56, 148–51, 156, 161, 182
    Henotikon, 150, 151
Zoe Karbonopsina, fourth wife of Emperor Leo VI, 357, 358, 361, 362
Zoe Zaoutzina, second wife of Emperor Leo VI, 357
Zoroastrianism, 10, 111, 182–3, 185, 197, 204, 219, 251